"A fundamental principle in finance is the relationship between risk and reward, yet today empirical risk measurement, valuations, and deal structuring are still the norm. Business professionals, venture capitalists, and other investors will all find Johnathan Mun's latest book on conceptualizing and quantitatively measuring risk in business of considerable value and a welcome addition to their libraries."

> —Dr. Charles T. Hardy
> Principal
> Hardy & Associates

"Mun has the uncanny ability to clarify the complex, distilling risk analysis concepts into a truly readable and practical guide for decision makers. This book blazes a trail that connects abstract yet powerful theories with real-world applications and examples, leaving the reader enlightened and empowered."

> —Stephen Hoye, MBA
> President
> Hoye Consulting Group

Additional Praise for
Applied Risk Analysis

"Strategy development has fallen on hard times and is often
longer relevant in a rapidly changing world. With this boo
attacks this poor excuse head-on by presenting a clearly org
supported methodology that logically progresses from explorin
that bounds risk to the creation of options for constructing real
strategies."

—Robert Mack
Vice President, Distinguished Anal
Gartner Group

"This book is a pleasure to read. It holds a high risk of addic
Dr. Mun leads the readers through step-by-step complex mathe
cepts with unmatched ease and clarity. Well-chosen examples a
to pitfalls complement the splendidly written chapters. This bo
bestseller in risk management and is a 'must read' for all profes
—Dr. Hans Weber
Syngenta AG (Switzerland)
Product Development Project Lead

"Once again, Dr. Johnathan Mun has attained his usual standard
in making not-so-simple but very useful quantitative analytical
accessible to the interested reader who doesn't necessarily have
or scientific training. In his new book, he presents a comprehens
everyday users of spreadsheet models, particularly those intere
analysis and management, on how to move beyond simple statis
sis into the realm of amazingly powerful software products:
(Monte Carlo simulation) and the Real Options Analysis Toolk
—Dr. Roberto J. Santillan-Salgado
Director of the Master of Science Pr
EGADE-ITESM, Monterrey Campu

Applied Risk
Analysis

Applied Risk
Analysis

Moving Beyond Uncertainty
in Business

JOHNATHAN MUN

WILEY

John Wiley & Sons, Inc.

Published by John Wiley & Sons, Inc., Hoboken, New Jersey.
Published simultaneously in Canada.

For general information on our other products and services, or technical support, contact our
Customer Care Department within the United States at 800-762-2974, outside the United
States at 317-572-3993 or fax 317-572-4002.

Wiley also publishes its books in a variety of electronic formats. Some content that appears in
print may not be available in electronic books.

For more information about Wiley products, visit our web site at www.wiley.com.

Crystal Ball and Real Options Analysis are registered trademarks of Decisioneering, Inc.

Library of Congress Cataloging-in-Publication Data:

Mun, Johnathan.
    Applied risk analysis : moving beyond uncertainty in business /
Johnathan Mun.
        p.   cm.
System requirements: System requirements for accompanying CD-ROM: IBM PC
or compatible computer with Pentium II or higher processor; 64 MB RAM;
75 MB hard-disk space; CD-ROM drive; SVGA monitor with 256 color; Excel
2000, XP, or later; Windows 2000, NT, XP, or higher.
    Includes bibliographical references and index.
    ISBN 0-471-47885-7 (CLOTH/CD-ROM)
    1. Risk assessment.   2. Risk management.   3. Risk assessment—Case
studies.   4. Risk management—Case studies.   I. Title.

HD61.M794 2004
658.15'5—dc21   2003014142

Printed in the United States of America

10 9 8 7 6 5 4 3 2 1

To my wife Penny, the love of my life.
In a world where uncertainty abounds,
you are the only constant in my life.

We live in an environment fraught with risk and operate our businesses in a risky world, as higher rewards only come with risks. Ignoring the element of risk when corporate strategy is being framed and when tactical projects are being implemented would be unimaginable. In addressing the issue of risk, *Applied Risk Analysis* provides a novel view of evaluating business decisions, projects, and strategies by taking into consideration a unified strategic portfolio analytical process. This book provides a qualitative and quantitative description of risk, as well as introductions to the methods used in identifying, quantifying, applying, predicting, valuing, hedging, diversifying, and managing risk through rigorous examples of the methods' applicability in the decision-making process.

Pragmatic applications are emphasized in order to demystify the many elements inherent in risk analysis. A black box will remain a black box if no one can understand the concepts despite its power and applicability. It is only when the black box becomes transparent so that analysts can understand, apply, and convince others of its results, value-add, and applicability, that the approach will receive widespread influence. The demystification of risk analysis is achieved by presenting step-by-step applications and multiple business cases, as well as discussing real-life applications.

This book is targeted at both the uninitiated professional and those well versed in risk analysis—there is something for everyone. It is also appropriate for use at the second-year M.B.A. level or as an introductory Ph.D. textbook. A CD-ROM comes with the book, including a trial version of the Crystal Ball software and Excel models.

JOHNATHAN MUN

San Francisco, California
JohnathanMun@cs.com
November 2003

Acknowledgments

The author is greatly indebted to Robert Fourt, Professor Morton Glantz, Dr. Charles Hardy, Steve Hoye, and Professor Bill Rodney for their business case contributions. In addition, a special word of thanks goes to Bill Falloon, senior editor at John Wiley & Sons, for his support and encouragement. Finally, a wonderful word of thanks to Soo-Beng Lim for his amazing art-work contributions throughout this book.

J.M.

About the Author

Dr. Johnathan C. Mun is the author of several other well-known books, including *Real Options Analysis* (Wiley, 2002), *Real Options Analysis Course* (Wiley, 2003), *Faith Journey* (Xulon Press, 2003), and a forthcoming book, *The Quantitative MBA*. His first two books have been adopted at major universities in the United States and around the world, and are used widely at a variety of Fortune 1000 companies. Dr. Mun has taught seminars and workshops worldwide on the topics of risk analysis, simulation, forecasting, financial analysis, and real options analysis. In addition, Dr. Mun is the creator of the *Real Options Analysis Toolkit* software introduced in this book.

He is currently the vice president of analytics services at Decisioneering, Inc., the makers of Crystal Ball Real Options Analysis Toolkit and the Crystal Ball suite of products, including applications of Monte Carlo simulation, optimization, and forecasting. He heads up the development of real options analysis and financial analytics software products, analytical consulting, training, and technical support. He is also a visiting and adjunct professor and has taught courses in financial management, investments, real options, economics, and statistics at the undergraduate and the M.B.A. levels, as well as chairing several graduate Master's theses committees. He has taught at universities all over the world, from the University of Applied Sciences (Germany and Switzerland) to Golden Gate University (California) and St. Mary's College (California), and others. Prior to joining Decisioneering, he was a consulting manager and financial economist in the Valuation Services and Global Financial Services practice of KPMG Consulting and a manager with the Economic Consulting Services practice at KPMG LLP. He has extensive experience in econometric modeling, financial analysis, real options, economic analysis, econometrics, and statistics. During his tenure both at Decisioneering and at KPMG Consulting, he consulted, advised, and trained others in the areas of real options analysis, risk analysis, economic forecasting, and financial valuation for many Fortune 1000 firms. His experience prior to joining KPMG included being department head of financial planning and analysis at Viking, Inc., of Fed Ex, responsible for performing financial forecasting, economic analysis, and market research. Prior to that, he had also performed some financial planning and freelance financial consulting work.

Dr. Mun received a Ph.D. in finance and economics from Lehigh University, where his research and academic interests were in the areas of investment finance, econometric modeling, financial options, corporate finance, and microeconomic theory. He also has an M.B.A. from Nova Southeastern University and a B.S. in biology and physics from the University of Miami. He is certified in Financial Risk Management (FRM), Certified in Financial Consulting (CFC), and is currently a third-level candidate for the Chartered Financial Analyst (CFA). He is a member of American Mensa, Phi Beta Kappa Honor Society, and Golden Key Honor Society as well as several other professional organizations, including the Eastern and Southern Finance Associations, American Economic Association, and Global Association of Risk Professionals. Finally, he has written many academic articles published in the *Journal of the Advances in Quantitative Accounting and Finance, The Global Finance Journal, The International Financial Review, Journal of Applied Financial Economics, Journal of International Financial Markets, Institutions and Money, Financial Engineering News, Journal of the Society of Petroleum Engineers,* and *The Journal of Financial Analysis.*

Contents

Introduction   **1**

PART ONE

Risk Identification

CHAPTER 1
Beyond Uncertainty   **11**
A Brief History of Risk: What Exactly Is Risk?   11
Uncertainty Versus Risk   12
Why Is Risk Important in Making Decisions?   13
Dealing with Risk the Old Fashioned Way   15
The Look and Feel of Risk and Uncertainty   18
Five-Minute Industry Spotlight: ExperCorp   21
Questions   22

PART TWO

Risk Evaluation

CHAPTER 2
From Risk to Riches   **25**
Taming the Beast   25
The Basics of Risk   26
The Nature of Risk and Returns   27
The Statistics of Risk   28
The Measurements of Risk   33
Five-Minute Industry Spotlight: Farmland   35
Five-Minute Industry Spotlight: Environmental Protection Agency   36
Questions   37

CHAPTER 3
A Gentleman's Guide to Model Building   **38**
Document the Model   38
Separate Inputs, Calculations, and Results   42

Protect the Models   43
Make the Model User-Friendly: Data Validation and Alerts   44
Track the Model   46
Automate the Model with VBA   46
Model Aesthetics and Conditional Formatting   47
Appendix—A Primer on VBA Modeling and Writing Macros   48
Exercises   57

PART THREE

Risk Quantification

CHAPTER 4

On the Shores of Monaco   61

What Is Monte Carlo Simulation?   61
Why Are Simulations Important?   62
Comparing Simulation with Traditional Analyses   65
Using Crystal Ball and Excel to Perform Simulations   70
Five-Minute Industry Spotlight: Colorado School of Mines   73
Five-Minute Industry Spotlight: Hewlett-Packard   75
Appendix—Simulation   76
Questions   90

CHAPTER 5

Peering into the Crystal Ball   91

The Basics of Crystal Ball Software   91
Getting Started with Crystal Ball Software   94
The Simulation Environment   96
Creating a Simulation   97
Interpreting the Simulation Results   100
Five-Minute Industry Spotlight: TRW   103
Five-Minute Industry Spotlight: DuPont Merck   104
Questions   105

CHAPTER 6

Pandora's Tool Box   106

Tornado and Sensitivity Tools in Simulation   106
Correlating and Fitting a Distribution Plus Precision Control   112
Precision Control   117
Bootstrap Simulation   121
Two-Dimensional Simulation   122
Decision Tables   124
Five-Minute Industry Spotlight: 3M   126

Five-Minute Industry Spotlight: Deloitte & Touche Consulting   127
Appendix—Goodness-of-Fit Tests   128
Questions   132

PART FOUR

Industry Applications

CHAPTER 7
Extended Business Cases I: From Pharma to Black Gold   135
Case Study: Pharmaceutical and Biotech—High Precision
   Quantitative Deal Structuring in the Biotechnology and
   Pharmaceutical Industries™   135
Case Study: Oil and Gas Production and Exploration   156
Five-Minute Industry Spotlight: Sierra Systems   168
Five-Minute Industry Spotlight: Motorola   170

PART FIVE

Risk Prediction

CHAPTER 8
Tomorrow's Forecast Today   175
What Is Forecasting?   175
The Nature and View of Forecasting   176
Five-Minute Industry Spotlight: Hewlett-Packard   182
Five-Minute Industry Spotlight: SunTrust Bank   183
Questions   183

CHAPTER 9
Using the Past to Predict the Future   184
Time-Series Forecasting Methodology   184
No Trend and No Seasonality   185
With Trend But No Seasonality   191
No Trend But With Seasonality   195
With Seasonality and With Trend   197
Regression Analysis   201
The Pitfalls of Forecasting: Outliers, Nonlinearity,
   Multicollinearity, Heteroskedasticity, Autocorrelation,
   and Structural Breaks   215
Other Technical Issues in Regression Analysis   223
Introduction to Advanced Forecasting   225

Appendix A—Forecast Intervals   226
Appendix B—Ordinary Least Squares   227
Appendix C—Detecting and Fixing Heteroskedasticity   230
Appendix D—Detecting and Fixing Multicollinearity   231
Appendix E—Detecting and Fixing Autocorrelation   233
Questions   234
Exercise   234

PART SIX

Risk Diversification

CHAPTER 10

The Search for the Optimal Decision   **237**

What Is an Optimization Model?   237
The Traveling Financial Planner   238
The Lingo of Optimization   240
Solving Optimization Graphically and Using Excel's Solver   243
Five-Minute Industry Spotlight: ProVise Management   249
Five-Minute Industry Spotlight: Texaco   251
Questions   252

CHAPTER 11

Optimization under Uncertainty   **253**

Project Selection Model (Discrete Optimization
    under Uncertainty)   253
Portfolio Optimization Using Risk and Return
    (Continuous Stochastic Optimization)   258
Five-Minute Industry Spotlight: Minnesota Power   262
Question   263
Exercise   263

PART SEVEN

Risk Mitigation

CHAPTER 12

What Is So Real About Real Options, and Why Are They Optional?   **267**

What Is Real Options?   267
The Real Options Solution in a Nutshell   269
Issues to Consider   269
Implementing Real Options Analysis   271

Choosing the Right Real Options Analysis Tools   272
Five-Minute Industry Spotlight: Boeing   275
Questions   277

CHAPTER 13
The Black Box Made Transparent: Real Options Analysis Toolkit   **278**
Getting Started with Real Options Analysis Toolkit Software   278
The Lattice Viewer   284
The Help Environment   288
Solving Customized Options   288
Accessing the Functions, Running Simulations and Optimization 292
Appendix—Expensing of Employee Stock Options (FAS 123):
    The Death of Black–Scholes   297

PART EIGHT
More Industry Applications

CHAPTER 14
Extended Business Cases II: From Land to Money   **325**
Case Study: Understanding Risk and Optimal Timing in a
    Real Estate Development Using Real Options Analysis   325
Case Study: Using Stochastic Optimization and Valuation
    Models to Evaluate the Credit Risk of Corporate
    Restructuring   341

PART NINE
Risk Management

CHAPTER 15
The Warning Signs   **353**
The Problem of Negligent Entrustment   353
Management's Due Diligence   354
Sins of an Analyst   354
Questions   375

CHAPTER 16
Changing a Corporate Culture   **377**
How to Get Risk Analysis Accepted in an Organization   377
Change-Management Issues and Paradigm Shifts   377
Making Tomorrow's Forecast Today   381

Five-Minute Industry Spotlight: Banker's Trust   382
Five-Minute Industry Spotlight: Environment Canada   384

Notes   **387**

List of Models   **395**

Tables You Really Need   **401**
Standard Normal Distribution (partial area)   402
Standard Normal Distribution (full area)   403
Student's t-Distribution (one and two-tails)   404
Durbin–Watson Critical Values   405
Normal Random Numbers (standard normal distribution's
  random number generated ~ ($N(0,1)$))   406
Random Numbers (multiple digits)   408
Uniform Random Numbers (uniform distribution's random
  number generated between 0.0000 and 1.0000)   410
Chi-Square Critical Values   412
F-Distribution Critical Statistics (alpha-one tail 0.10)   414
F-Distribution Critical Statistics (alpha-one tail 0.05)   416
F-Distribution Critical Statistics (alpha-one tail 0.25)   418
F-Distribution Critical Statistics (alpha-one tail 0.01)   420
Real Options Analysis Value (1-year maturity at 5%
  risk-free rate)   422
Real Options Analysis Value (3-year maturity at 5%
  risk-free rate)   424
Real Options Analysis Value (5-year maturity at 5%
  risk-free rate)   426
Real Options Analysis Value (7-year maturity at 5%
  risk-free rate)   428
Real Options Analysis Value (10-year maturity at 5%
  risk-free rate)   430
Real Options Analysis Value (15-year maturity at 5%
  risk-free rate)   432
Real Options Analysis Value (30-year maturity at 5%
  risk-free rate)   434

Answers to End of Chapter Questions and Exercises   **437**

About the CD-ROM   **447**

Index   **449**

Introduction

This book is divided into nine parts starting from a discussion of what risk is and how it is quantified, to how risk can be predicted, diversified, taken advantage of, hedged, and, finally, managed. The first part deals with *risk identification* where the different aspects of business risks are identified, including a brief historical view of how risk was evaluated in the past. The second part deals with *risk evaluation* explaining why disastrous ramifications may result if risk is not considered in business decisions. Part Three pertains to *risk quantification* and details how risk can be captured quantitatively through step-by-step applications of Monte Carlo simulation. Part Four deals with *industry applications* and examples of how risk analysis is applied in practical day-to-day issues in the oil and gas and the pharmaceutical industries. Part Five pertains to *risk prediction* where the uncertain and risky future is predicted using analytical time-series methods. Part Six deals with how *risk diversification* works when multiple projects exist in a portfolio. Part Seven's *risk mitigation* discussion deals with how a firm or management can take advantage of risk and uncertainty by implementing and maintaining flexibility in projects. Part Eight provides a second installment of *business cases* where risk analysis is applied in the banking and real estate industries. Part Nine provides a capstone discussion of applying *risk management* in companies, including how to obtain senior management's buy-in and implementing a change of perspective in corporate culture as it applies to risk analysis. Following is a synopsis of the material covered in each chapter of the book.

PART ONE—RISK IDENTIFICATION

Chapter 1—Beyond Uncertainty

To the people who lived centuries ago, risk was simply the inevitability of chance occurrence beyond the realm of human control. We have been struggling with risk our entire existence, but, through trial and error and through the evolution of human knowledge and thought, have devised ways to describe and quantify risk. Risk assessment should be an important part of the decision-making process otherwise bad decisions may be made. Chapter 1 explores the different facets of risk within the realms of applied business risk analysis, providing an intuitive feel of what risk is.

PART TWO—RISK EVALUATION

Chapter 2—From Risk to Riches

The concepts of risk and return are detailed in Chapter 2, illustrating their relationships in the financial world, where a higher risk project necessitates a higher expected return. How are uncertainties estimated and risk calculated? How do you convert a measure of uncertainty into a measure of risk? These are the topics covered in this chapter, starting from the basics of statistics to applying them in risk analysis, and including a discussion of the different measures of risk.

Chapter 3—A Gentleman's Guide to Model Building

Chapter 3 addresses some of the more common errors and pitfalls analysts make when creating a new model by explaining some of the proper modeling etiquettes. The issues discussed range from file naming conventions and proper model aesthetics to complex data validation and Visual Basic for Applications (VBA) scripting. An appendix is provided on some VBA modeling basics and techniques of macros and forms creation.

PART THREE—RISK QUANTIFICATION

Chapter 4—On the Shores of Monaco

Monte Carlo simulation in its simplest form is just a random number generator useful for forecasting, estimation, and risk analysis. A simulation calculates numerous scenarios of a model by repeatedly picking values from the probability distribution for the uncertain variables and using those values for the event—events such as totals, net profit, or gross expenses. Simplistically, think of the Monte Carlo simulation approach as repeatedly picking golf balls out of a large basket. Chapter 4 illustrates why simulation is important through the flaw of averages example. Excel is used to perform rudimentary simulations, and simulation is shown as a logical next step extension to traditional approaches used in risk analysis. An appendix to this chapter deals with the technical details of choosing specific distributions used in Monte Carlo simulation.

Chapter 5—Peering into the Crystal Ball

Chapter 5 guides the user through applying the world's premier risk analysis and simulation software: *Crystal Ball Professional*. With a few simple mouse clicks, the reader will be on his or her way to running sophisticated Monte Carlo simulation analysis to capture both uncertainty and risks using the enclosed CD-ROM's Crystal Ball trial software. However, more important is the interpretation of said analysis. The best analysis in the world is only as good as the analyst's ability to understand, utilize, present, report, and convince management or clients of the results.

Chapter 6—Pandora's Tool Box

Powerful simulation-related tools such as bootstrapping, precision control, decision tables, correlated simulation, two-dimensional simulation, tornado charts, and sensitivity charts are discussed in detail in Chapter 6, complete with step-by-step illustrations. These tools are invaluable to analysts working in the realm of risk analysis. The applicability of each tool is discussed in detail. For example, the use of nonparametric bootstrapping simulation as opposed to parametric Monte Carlo simulation approaches is discussed. An appendix to this chapter deals with the technical specifics of goodness-of-fit tests.

PART FOUR—INDUSTRY APPLICATIONS

Chapter 7—Extended Business Cases I: From Pharma to Black Gold

Chapter 7 contains the first installment of actual business cases from industry applying risk analytics. Business cases were contributed by Dr. Charles Hardy in the pharmaceutical and biotech industries and by Steve Hoye in the oil and gas production and exploration industry. The former case illustrates the use of advanced risk analysis in negotiations and dealmaking, while the latter case analyzes the oil and gas environment from cradle to grave.

PART FIVE—RISK PREDICTION

Chapter 8—Tomorrow's Forecast Today

Chapter 8 focuses on time-series forecasting methods. Specifically, the issues of seasonality and trend are discussed, together with the eight time-series models most commonly used by analysts to forecast future events given historical data. The applications and calculations of each method are discussed in detail, complete with their associated measures of forecast errors and potential pitfalls.

Chapter 9–Using the Past to Predict the Future

The main thrust of Chapter 9 is time-series and regression analysis made easy. Starting with some basic time-series models, including exponential smoothing and moving averages, and more complex models, such as the Holt–Winters' additive and multiplicative models, the reader will manage to navigate through the maze of time-series analysis. The basics of regression analysis are also discussed, complete with pragmatic discussions of statistical validity tests as well as the pitfalls of regression analysis, including how to identify and fix heteroskedasticity, multicollinearity, and autocorrelation. The five appendixes that accompany this chapter deal with the technical specifics of interval estimations in regression analysis, ordinary least squares, and some pitfalls in running regressions, including detecting and fixing heteroskedasticity, autocorrelation, and multicollinearity.

PART SIX–RISK DIVERSIFICATION

Chapter 10–The Search for the Optimal Decision

In most business or analytical models, there are variables over which you have control, such as how much to charge for a product or how much to invest in a project. These controlled variables are called *decision variables*. Finding the optimal values for decision variables can make the difference between reaching an important goal and missing that goal. Chapter 10 details the optimization process at a high level, with illustrations on solving deterministic optimization problems manually, using graphs, and applying Excel's Solver add-in. (Chapter 11 illustrates the solution to optimization problems under uncertainty, mirroring more closely real-life business conditions.)

Chapter 11–Optimization under Uncertainty

Chapter 11 illustrates two optimization models with step-by-step details. The first model is a discrete portfolio optimization of projects under uncertainty. Given a set of 12 potential projects, the model evaluates all possible discrete combinations of projects on a "go" or "no-go" basis such that a budget constraint is satisfied, while simultaneously providing the best level of returns subject to uncertainty. The best 5 projects will then be chosen based on these criteria. The second model evaluates a financial portfolio's continuous allocation of 4 distinct asset classes with different levels of risks and returns. The objective of this model is to find the optimal allocation of assets subject to a 100 percent allocation constraint that still maximizes the Sharpe ratio, or the portfolio's return-to-risk ratio. This ratio will maximize the portfolio's return subject to the minimum risks possible while accounting for the cross-correlation diversification effects of the asset classes in a portfolio.

PART SEVEN—RISK MITIGATION

Chapter 12—What's So Real about Real Options, and Why Are They Optional?

Chapter 12 describes what real option analysis is, who has used the approach, how companies are using it, and what some of the characteristics of real options are. The chapter describes real options in a nutshell, providing the reader with a solid introduction to its concepts without the need for its theoretical underpinnings. Real options are applicable if the following requirements are met: traditional financial analysis can be performed and models can be built; uncertainty exists; the same uncertainty drives value; management or the project has strategic options or flexibility to either take advantage of these uncertainties or to hedge them; and management must be credible to execute the relevant strategic options when they become optimal to do so.

Chapter 13—The Black Box Made Transparent: Real Options Analysis Toolkit

Chapter 13 introduces the readers to the world's first true real options software applicable across all industries. The chapter illustrates how a user can get started with the software in a few short moments after it has been installed. The reader is provided with hands-on experience with the *Real Options Analysis Toolkit* to obtain immediate results—a true test when the rubber meets the road. An appendix to this chapter deals with real-life applications of options theory based on a revised accounting standard by the Financial Accounting Standards Board.

PART EIGHT—MORE INDUSTRY APPLICATIONS

Chapter 14—Extended Business Cases: From Land to Money

Chapter 14 contains the second installment of actual business cases from industry applying risk analytics. Business cases were contributed by Robert

Fourt and Prof. Bill Rodney on real estate analysis applying real options and by Morton Glantz on financial risk analysis in the banking industry.

PART NINE—RISK MANAGEMENT

Chapter 15—The Warning Signs

The risk analysis software applications illustrated in this book are extremely powerful tools and could prove detrimental in the hands of untrained and unlearned novices. Management, the end user of the results from said tools, must be able to discern if quality analysis has been performed. Chapter 15 delves into the thirty-some problematic issues most commonly encountered by analysts applying risk analysis techniques, and how management can spot these mistakes. While it might be the job of the analyst to create the models and use the fancy analytics, it is senior management's job to challenge the assumptions and results obtained from the analysis. Model errors, assumption and input errors, analytical errors, user errors, and interpretation errors are some of the issues discussed in this chapter. Some of the issues and concerns raised for management's consideration in performing due diligence include challenging distributional assumptions, critical success factors, impact drivers, truncation, forecast validity, endpoints, extreme values, structural breaks, values at risk, a priori expectations, back-casting, statistical validity, specification errors, out of range forecasts, heteroskedasticity, multicollinearity, omitted variables, spurious relationships, causality and correlation, autoregressive processes, seasonality, random walks, and stochastic processes.

Chapter 16—Changing a Corporate Culture

Advanced analytics is hard to explain to management. So, how do you get risk analysis accepted as the norm into a corporation, especially if your industry is highly conservative? It is a guarantee in companies like these that an analyst showing senior management a series of fancy and mathematically sophisticated models will be thrown out of the office together with his or her results, and have the door slammed shut. Change management is the topic of discussion in Chapter 16. Explaining the results and convincing management appropriately go hand in hand with the characteristics of the analytical tools, which, if they satisfy certain change management requisites, can make acceptance easier. The approach that guarantees acceptance has to be three pronged: top, middle, and junior levels must all get in on the action. Change management specialists underscore that change comes more easily if the methodologies to be accepted are applicable to the problems at hand, are accurate and consistent, provide value-added propositions, are easy to explain, have comparative advantage over traditional approaches, are compatible with the old, have modeling flexibility, are backed by executive sponsorship, and are influenced and championed by external parties including competitors, customers, counterparties, and vendors.

ADDITIONAL MATERIAL

The book concludes with the ten mathematical tables used in the analyses throughout the book, a list of Excel models that are included on the CD-ROM, and the answers to the questions and exercises at the end of each chapter.

Risk Identification

CHAPTER 1

Beyond Uncertainty

A BRIEF HISTORY OF RISK: WHAT EXACTLY IS RISK?

Since the beginning of recorded history, games of chance have been a popular pastime. Even in Biblical accounts, Roman soldiers cast lots for Christ's robes. In earlier times, chance was something that occurred in nature, and humans were simply subjected to it as a ship is to the capricious tosses of the waves in an ocean. Even up to the time of the Renaissance, the future was thought to be simply a chance occurrence of completely random events and beyond the control of humans. However, with the advent of games of chance, human greed has propelled the study of risk and chance to evermore closely mirror real-life events. Although these games initially were played with great enthusiasm, no one actually sat down and figured out the odds. Of course, the individual who understood and mastered the concept of chance was bound to be in a better position to profit from such games of chance. It was not until the mid-1600s that the concept of chance was properly studied, and the first such serious endeavor can be credited to Blaise Pascal, one of the fathers of modern choice, chance, and probability.[1] Fortunately for us, after many centuries of mathematical and statistical innovations from pioneers such as Pascal, Bernoulli, Bayes, Gauss, LaPlace, and Fermat, our modern world of uncertainty can be explained with much more elegance through methodological applications of risk and uncertainty.

To the people who lived centuries ago, risk was simply the inevitability of chance occurrence beyond the realm of human control. Nonetheless, many phony soothsayers profited from their ability to convincingly profess their clairvoyance by simply stating the obvious or reading the victims' body language and telling them what they wanted to hear. We modern-day humans, ignoring for the moment the occasional seers among us, with our fancy technological achievements, are still susceptible to risk and uncertainty. We may be able to predict the orbital paths of planets in our solar system with astounding accuracy or the escape velocity required to shoot a man from Earth to the Moon, but when it comes to predicting a firm's revenues the following year, we are at a loss. Humans have been struggling with risk our entire existence but, through trial and error, and through the evolution of human knowledge and thought, have devised ways to describe, quantify, hedge, and take advantage of risk.

Clearly the entire realm of risk analysis is great and would most probably be intractable within the few chapters of a book. Therefore, this book is concerned with only a small niche of risk, namely *applied business risk analysis*. Even in the areas of applied business risk analysis, the diversity is great. For instance, business risk can be roughly divided into the areas of operational risk management and financial risk management. In financial risk, one can look at market risk, private risk, credit risk, default risk, maturity risk, liquidity risk, inflationary risk, interest rate risk, country risk, and so forth. This book focuses on the application of risk analysis in the sense of how to adequately apply the tools to identify, understand, quantify, and diversify risk such that it can be hedged and managed more effectively. These tools are generic enough that they can be applied across a whole spectrum of business conditions, industries, and needs.

UNCERTAINTY VERSUS RISK

Risk and uncertainty are very different-looking animals but they are of the same species; however, the lines of demarcation are often blurred. A distinction is critical at this juncture before proceeding and worthy of segue. Suppose I am senseless enough to take a skydiving trip with a good friend and we board a plane headed for the Palm Springs desert. While airborne at 10,000 feet and watching our lives flash before our eyes, we realize that in our haste we forgot to pack our parachutes on board. However, there is an old, dusty, and dilapidated emergency parachute on the plane. At that point, both my friend and I have the same level of uncertainty—the uncertainty of whether the old parachute will open and if it does not, whether we will fall to our deaths. However, being the risk-adverse, nice guy I am, I decide to let my buddy take the plunge. Clearly, he is the one taking the plunge and the same person taking the risk. I bear no risk at this time while my friend bears all the risk.[2] However, we both have the same level of uncertainty as to whether the parachute will actually fail. In fact, we both have the same level of uncertainty as to the outcome of the day's trading on the New York Stock Exchange—which has absolutely no impact on whether we live or die that day. Only when he jumps and the parachute opens will the uncertainty become resolved through the passage of time, events, and action. However, even when the uncertainty is resolved with the opening of the parachute, the risk still exists as to whether he will land safely on the ground below.

Therefore, risk is something one bears and is the outcome of uncertainty. Just because there is uncertainty, there could very well be no risk. If the only thing that bothers a U.S.-based firm's CEO is the fluctuation in the foreign exchange market of the Zairian zaire, then I might suggest shorting some zaires and shifting his portfolio to U.S.-based debt. This uncertainty, if it does not affect the firm's bottom line in any way, is only uncertainty and not risk. This book is concerned with risk by performing uncertainty analysis—the same uncertainty that brings about risk by its mere existence as it impacts the value of a particular project. It is further assumed that the end user of this uncertainty analysis uses the results appropriately, whether the analysis is for identifying, adjusting, or selecting projects with respect to their risks, and so forth. Otherwise, running millions of fancy simulation trials and letting the results "marinate" will be useless. By running simulations on the foreign exchange market of the Zairian zaire, an analyst sitting in a cubicle somewhere in downtown Denver will in no way reduce the risk of the zaire in the market or the firm's exposure to the same. Only by using the results from an uncertainty simulation analysis and finding ways to hedge or mitigate the quantified fluctuation and downside risks of the firm's foreign exchange exposure through the derivatives market could the analyst be construed as having performed risk analysis and risk management.

WHY IS RISK IMPORTANT IN MAKING DECISIONS?

Risk should be an important part of the decision-making process; otherwise bad decisions may be made without an assessment of risk. For instance, suppose projects are chosen based simply on an evaluation of returns; clearly the highest-return project will be chosen over lower-return projects. In financial theory, projects with higher returns will in most cases bear higher risks.[3] Therefore, instead of relying purely on bottom-line profits, a project should be evaluated based on its returns as well as its risks. Figures 1.1 and 1.2 illustrate the errors in judgment when risks are ignored.

> The concepts of risk and uncertainty are related but yet are very different. Uncertainty involves variables that are constantly changing, whereas risk involves only the uncertain variables that affect or impact the system's output directly.

Figure 1.1 lists three *mutually exclusive* projects with their respective costs to implement, expected net returns (net of the costs to implement), and

Name of Project	Cost	Returns	Risk
Project X	$50	$50	$25
Project Y	$250	$200	$200
Project Z	$100	$100	$10

Project X for the cost- and budget-constrained manager
Project Y for the returns-driven and nonresource-constrained manager
Project Z for the risk-averse manager
Project Z for the smart manager

FIGURE 1.1   Why is risk important?

risk levels (all in present values).[4] Clearly, for the budget-constrained manager, the cheaper the project the better, resulting in the selection of Project X.[5] The returns-driven manager will choose Project Y with the highest returns, assuming that budget is not an issue. Project Z will be chosen by the risk-averse manager as it provides the least amount of risk while providing a positive net return. The upshot is that with three different projects and three different managers, three different decisions will be made. Which manager is correct and why?

Figure 1.2 shows that Project Z should be chosen. For illustration purposes, suppose all three projects are independent and mutually exclusive,[6] and that an unlimited number of projects from each category can be chosen but the budget is constrained at $1,000. Therefore, with this $1,000 budget, 20 project Xs can be chosen, yielding $1,000 in net returns and $500 risks, and so forth. It is clear from Figure 1.2 that project Z is the best project as for the same level of net returns ($1,000), the least amount of risk is under-

Looking at bang for the buck, X (2), Y (1), Z (10), Project Z should
be chosen — with a $1,000 budget, the following can be obtained:

Project X:20 Project Xs returning $1,000, with $500 risk
Project Y:4 Project Xs returning $800, with $800 risk
Project Z:10 Project Xs returning $1,000, with $100 risk

Project X:For each $1 return, $0.5 risk is taken
Project Y:For each $1 return, $1.0 risk is taken
Project Z:For each $1 return, $0.1 risk is taken

Project X:For each $1 of risk taken, $2 return is obtained
Project Y:For each $1 of risk taken, $1 return is obtained
Project Z:For each $1 of risk taken, $10 return is obtained

Conclusion: Risk is important. Ignoring risks results in making the wrong decision.

FIGURE 1.2   Adding an element of risk.

taken ($100). Another way of viewing this selection is that for each $1 of returns obtained, only $0.1 amount of risk is involved on average, or that for each $1 of risk, $10 in returns are obtained on average. This example illustrates the concept of *bang for the buck* or getting the best value with the least amount of risk. An even more blatant example is if there are several different projects with identical single-point average net returns of $10 million each. Without risk analysis, a manager should in theory be indifferent in choosing any of the projects.[7] However, with risk analysis, a better decision can be made. For instance, suppose the first project has a 10 percent chance of exceeding $10 million, the second a 15 percent chance, and the third a 55 percent chance. The third project, therefore, is the best bet.

DEALING WITH RISK THE OLD FASHIONED WAY

Businesses have been dealing with risk since the beginning of the history of commerce. In most cases, managers have looked at the risks of a particular project, acknowledged their existence, and moved on. Little quantification was performed in the past. In fact, most decision makers look only to single-point estimates of a project's profitability. Figure 1.3 shows an example of a single-point estimate. The estimated net revenue of $30 is simply that, a single point whose probability of occurrence is close to zero.[8] Even in the simple model shown in Figure 1.3, the effects of interdependencies are ignored, and in traditional modeling jargon, we have the problem of *garbage in, garbage out* (GIGO). As an example of interdependencies, the units sold are probably negatively correlated to the price of the product,[9]

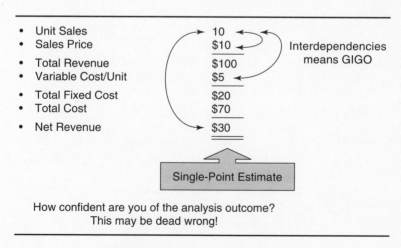

How confident are you of the analysis outcome?
This may be dead wrong!

FIGURE 1.3   Single-point estimate.

and positively correlated to the average variable cost;[10] ignoring these effects in a single-point estimate will yield grossly incorrect results. For instance, if the unit sales variable becomes 11 instead of 10, the resulting revenue may not simply be $35. The net revenue may actually decrease due to an increase in variable cost per unit while the sale price may actually be slightly lower to accommodate this increase in unit sales. Ignoring these interdependencies will reduce the accuracy of the model.

> A rational manager would choose projects based not only on returns but also on risks. The best projects tend to be those with the best bang for the buck, or the best returns subject to some specified risks.

One approach used to deal with risk and uncertainty is the application of scenario analysis, as seen in Figure 1.4. Suppose the worst-case, nominal-case, and best-case scenarios are applied to the unit sales; the resulting three scenarios' net revenues are obtained. As earlier, the problems of interdependencies are not addressed. The net revenues obtained are simply too variable, ranging from $5 to $55. Not much can be determined from this analysis.

A related approach is to perform *what-if* or *sensitivity* analysis as seen in Figure 1.5. Each variable is perturbed and varied a prespecified amount and the resulting change in net revenues is captured. This approach is great for understanding which variables drive or impact the bottom line the most.

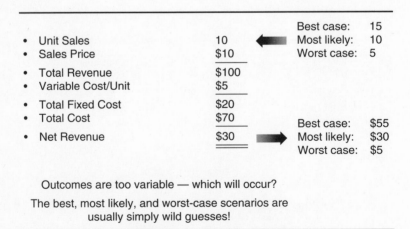

FIGURE 1.4 Scenario analysis.

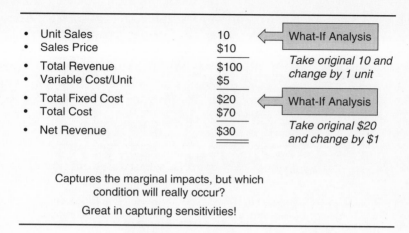

Captures the marginal impacts, but which
condition will really occur?

Great in capturing sensitivities!

FIGURE 1.5   What-if analysis.

A related approach is the use of tornado and sensitivity charts as detailed in
Chapter 6, Pandora's Tool Box, which looks at a series of simulation tools.
These approaches were usually the extent to which risk and uncertainty
analysis were traditionally performed. Clearly, a better and more robust approach is required.

This is the point where simulation comes in. Figure 1.6 shows how simulation can be viewed as simply an extension of the traditional approaches
of sensitivity and scenario testing. The critical success drivers or the variables
that affect the bottom-line net-revenue variable the most, which at the same
time are uncertain, are simulated. In simulation, the interdependencies are
accounted for using correlations. The uncertain variables are then simulated

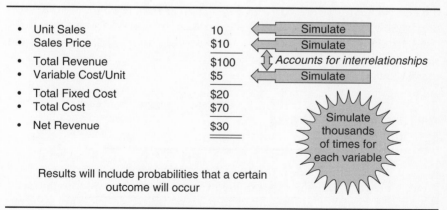

Results will include probabilities that a certain
outcome will occur

FIGURE 1.6   Simulation approach.

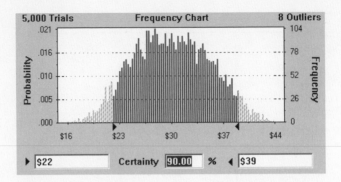

There is a 90% statistically   The complete range of
valid chance you will have   possible outcomes is from
a net revenue between $16 to $44
$22 and $39

FIGURE 1.7   Simulation results.

thousands of times to emulate all potential permutations and combinations of outcomes. The resulting net revenues from these simulated potential outcomes are tabulated and analyzed. In essence, in its most basic form, simulation is simply an enhanced version of traditional approaches such as sensitivity and scenario analysis but automatically performed for thousands of times while accounting for all the dynamic interactions between the simulated variables. The resulting net revenues from simulation, as seen in Figure 1.7, show that there is a 90 percent probability that the net revenues will fall between $22 and $39, with a 5 percent worst-case scenario of net revenues falling below $22. The complete distribution of outcomes places the net revenues between $16 and $44.[11] Rather than having only three scenarios, simulation created 5,000 scenarios, or trials, where multiple variables are simulated and changing simultaneously (unit sales, sale price, and variable cost per unit), while their respective relationships or correlations are maintained.

THE LOOK AND FEEL OF RISK AND UNCERTAINTY

In most financial risk analyses, the first step is to create a series of free cash flows, which can take the shape of an income statement or discounted cash-flow (DCF) model. The resulting deterministic free cash flows are depicted on a time line, akin to that shown in Figure 1.8. These cash-flow figures are

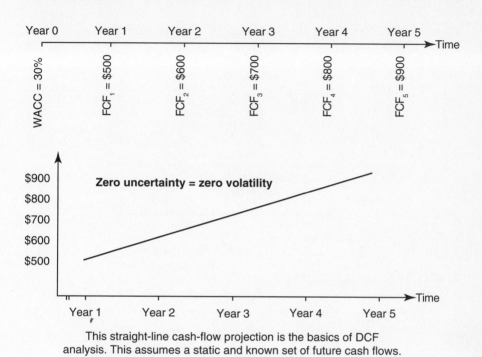

This straight-line cash-flow projection is the basics of DCF analysis. This assumes a static and known set of future cash flows.

FIGURE 1.8 The intuition of risk—deterministic analysis.

in most cases forecasts of the unknown future. In this simple example, the cash flows are assumed to follow a straight-line growth curve (of course, other shaped curves also can be constructed). Similar forecasts can be constructed using historical data and fitting these data to a time-series model or a regression analysis.[12] Whatever the method of obtaining said forecasts or the shape of the growth curve, these are point estimates of the unknown future. Performing a financial analysis on these static cash flows provides an accurate value of the project if and only if all the future cash flows are known with certainty—that is, no uncertainty exists.

However, in reality, business conditions are hard to forecast. Uncertainty exists, and the actual levels of future cash flows may look more like those in Figure 1.9. That is, at certain time periods, actual cash flows may be above, below, or at the forecast levels. For instance, at any time period, the actual cash flow may fall within a range of figures with a certain percent probability. As an example, the first year's cash flow may fall anywhere between $480 and $520. The actual values are shown to fluctuate around the forecast values at an average volatility of 20 percent.[13] (We use volatility here as a measure of uncertainty, i.e., the higher the volatility, the higher the

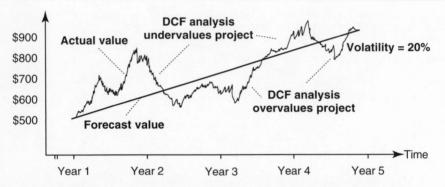

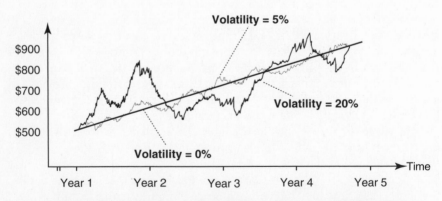

This graph shows that in reality, at different times, actual cash flows may be above, below, or at the forecast value line due to uncertainty and risk.

FIGURE 1.9   The intuition of risk—Monte Carlo simulation.

The higher the risk, the higher the volatility and the higher the fluctuation of actual cash flows around the forecast value. When volatility is zero, the values collapse to the forecast straight-line static value.

FIGURE 1.10   The intuition of risk—the face of risk.

level of uncertainty, where at zero uncertainty, the outcomes are 100 percent certain[14]). Certainly this example provides a much more accurate view of the true nature of business conditions, which are fairly difficult to predict with any amount of certainty.

Figure 1.10 shows two sample actual cash flows around the straight-line forecast value. The higher the uncertainty around the actual cash-flow levels, the higher the volatility. The darker line with 20 percent volatility fluctuates more wildly around the forecast values. These values can be quantified using Monte Carlo simulation fairly easily but cannot be properly accounted for using more simplistic traditional methods such as sensitivity or scenario analyses.

Now that the need for risk and uncertainty analysis has been established, the following chapters set the scene for the different measures of risk, how to create the models to capture those risks, and how to interpret the results obtained from said risk analysis.

FIVE-MINUTE INDUSTRY SPOTLIGHT: EXPERCORP

New Venture Planning for Recreation Markets

ExperCorp is a business-planning consulting firm located in Naperville, Illinois. The company specializes in new venture strategy and marketing research for entrepreneurs, designing entries for the fitness, recreation, and sporting goods markets. A key to small business planning is the development of good risk and reward estimates.

Following a determination of the size of the available target market, realistic assumptions were made for unit sales, realized selling price, production costs, and operating expenses in the first year of operation, ExperCorp wanted to develop a pro forma income statement. The objective was to create a profitability distribution of gross revenues and profits/losses.

An income-statement template was developed incorporating Monte Carlo simulation to create appropriate distributions for unit sales (triangular distribution), production costs (uniform distribution), operating expenses (triangular distribution), and profits/losses (normal distribution).

The most critical and difficult aspect of venture planning is developing estimates of cash flow. Developing realistic statements for the first and subsequent years of operation along with a determination of cash reserves is a task that all diligent planners must face. Today, this job has been simplified with cash-flow templates that are affixed into spreadsheets. The objective was to increase the precision of cash-flow forecasts.

Monte Carlo simulation was used to enhance cash-flow models by replacing point estimates with probability distributions of cash flows for key variables. Using the relevant data from first-year income statements, ExperCorp made assumptions about the percentage of receivables collected in 30, 60, and 90 days. Crystal Ball was able to create triangular distributions very quickly for these intervals. The total projected cash flows for each month were calculated using a triangular distribution.

Using Crystal Ball to create distributions for key financial input instead of relying on single-point estimates increased the precision of forecasting under the conditions of uncertainty that new business planners typically confront. Rather than running the standard set of sensitivity analyses, they produced robust forecasts in less time with more accuracy using Crystal Ball. It gave ExperCorp's clients and their financial sponsors a better picture of their venture landscape. They saw the probabilities of risk and reward. This is a confidence boost for them and for us—light years ahead of groping for the "right" single-point values to insert into their models.

QUESTIONS

1. Why is risk important in making decisions?
2. Describe the concept of bang for the buck.
3. Compare and contrast between risk and uncertainty.

Risk Evaluation

CHAPTER 2

From Risk to Riches

TAMING THE BEAST

Risky ventures are the norm in the daily business world. The mere mention of names such as George Soros, John Meriweather, Paul Reichmann, and Nicholas Leeson, or firms such as Long Term Capital Management, Metallgesellschaft, Barings Bank, Bankers Trust, Daiwa Bank, Sumimoto Corporation, Merrill Lynch, and Citibank brings a shrug of disbelief and fear. These names are some of the biggest in the world of business and finance. Their claim to fame is not simply being the best and brightest individuals or being the largest and most respected firms, but for bearing the stigma of being involved in highly risky ventures that turned sour almost overnight.[1]

George Soros was and still is one of the most respected names in high finance; he is known globally for his brilliance and exploits. Paul Reichmann was a reputable and brilliant real estate and property tycoon. Between the two of them, nothing was impossible, but when they ventured into investments in Mexican real estate, the wild fluctuations of the peso in the foreign exchange market was nothing short of a disaster. During late 1994 and early 1995, the peso hit an all time low and their ventures went from bad to worse, but the one thing that they did not expect was that the situation would become a lot worse before it was all over and billions would be lost as a consequence.

Long Term Capital Management was headed by Meriweather, one of the rising stars in Wall Street, with a slew of superstars on its management team, including several Nobel laureates in finance and economics (Robert Merton and Myron Scholes). The firm was backed by giant investment banks. A firm that seemed indestructible literally blew up with billions of dollars in the red, shaking the international investment community with repercussions throughout Wall Street as individual investors started to lose faith in large hedge funds and wealth-management firms, forcing the eventual massive Federal Reserve bailout.

Barings was one of the oldest banks in England. It was so respected that even Queen Elizabeth II herself held a private account with it. This multibillion dollar institution was brought down single-handedly by Nicholas Leeson, an employee halfway around the world. Leeson was a young and brilliant investment banker who headed up Barings' Singapore branch. His illegally doctored track record showed significant investment profits, which gave him more leeway and trust from the home office over time. He was able to cover his losses through fancy accounting and by taking significant amounts of risk. His speculations in the Japanese yen went south and he took Barings down with him, and the top echelon in London never knew what hit them.

Had any of the managers in the boardroom at their respective headquarters bothered to look at the risk profile of their investments, they would surely have made a very different decision much earlier on, preventing what became major embarrassments in the global investment community. If the projected returns are adjusted for risks, that is, finding what levels of risks are required to attain such seemingly extravagant returns, it would be sensible not to proceed.

Risks occur in everyday life that do not require investments in the multimillions. For instance, when would one purchase a house in a fluctuating housing market? When would it be more profitable to lock in a fixed-rate mortgage rather than keep a floating variable rate? What are the chances that there will be insufficient funds at retirement? What about the potential personal property losses when a hurricane hits? How much accident insurance is considered sufficient? How much is a lottery ticket actually worth?

Risk permeates all aspects of life and one can never avoid taking or facing risks. What we can do is understand risks better through a systematic assessment of their impacts and repercussions. This assessment framework must also be capable of measuring, monitoring, and managing risks, otherwise, simply noting that risks exist and moving on is not optimal. This book provides the tools and framework necessary to tackle risks head-on. Only with the added insights gained through a rigorous assessment of risk can one actively manage and monitor risk.

> Risks permeate every aspect of business but we do not have to be passive participants. What we can do is develop a framework to better understand risks through a systematic assessment of their impacts and repercussions. This framework also must be capable of measuring, monitoring, and managing risks.

THE BASICS OF RISK

Risk can be defined simply as any uncertainty that affects a system in an unknown fashion whereby the ramifications are also unknown but bears with it great fluctuation in value and outcome. In every instance, for risk to be evident, the following generalities must exist:

- Uncertainties and risks have a time horizon.
- Uncertainties exist in the future and will evolve over time.
- Uncertainties become risks if they affect the outcomes and scenarios of the system.
- These changing scenarios' effects on the system can be measured.
- The measurement has to be set against a benchmark.

Risk is never instantaneous. It has a time horizon. For instance, a firm engaged in a risky research and development venture will face significant amounts of risk but only until the product is fully developed or has proven itself in the market. These risks are caused by uncertainties in the technology of the product under research, uncertainties about the potential market, uncertainties about the level of competitive threats and substitutes, and so forth. These uncertainties will change over the course of the company's research and marketing activities—some uncertainties will increase while others will most likely decrease through the passage of time. However, only the uncertainties that affect the product directly will have any bearing on the risks of the product being successful. That is, only uncertainties that change the possible scenario outcomes will make the product risky (e.g., market and economic conditions). Finally, risk exists if it can be measured and compared against a benchmark. If no benchmark exists, then perhaps the conditions just described are the norm for research and development activities, and thus the negative results are to be expected. These benchmarks have to be measurable and tangible, for example, gross profits, success rates, market share, time to implementation, and so forth.

> Risk is any uncertainty that affects a system in an unknown fashion and its ramifications are unknown but it brings great fluctuation in value and outcome. Risk has a time horizon, meaning that uncertainty evolves over time, which affects measurable future outcomes and scenarios with respect to a benchmark.

THE NATURE OF RISK AND RETURNS

Nobel Laureate Harry Markowitz's groundbreaking research into the nature of risks and returns has revolutionized the world of finance. His seminal work, which is now known all over the world as the *Markowitz Efficient Frontier*, looks at the nature of risk and return. Markowitz did not look at risk as the enemy but as a condition that should be embraced and balanced out through its expected returns. The concept of risk and return was then refined through later works by William Sharpe and others, who stated that a heightened risk necessitates a higher return, as elegantly expressed through the *capital asset pricing model (CAPM)*, where the required rate of return on a marketable risky equity is equivalent to the return on an equivalent riskless asset plus a beta systematic and undiversifiable risk measure multiplied by the market risk's return premium. In essence, a higher risk asset requires a higher return. In Markowitz's model, one could strike a balance between risk and return. Depending on the risk appetite of an investor, the optimal or best-case returns can be obtained through the efficient frontier. Should the investor require a higher level of returns, he or she would have to face a higher level of risk. Markowitz's work carried over to finding combinations of individual projects or assets in a portfolio that would provide the best *bang for the buck*, striking an elegant balance between risk and return. In order to better understand this balance, also known as *risk adjustment* in modern risk analysis language, risks must first be measured and understood. The following section illustrates how risk can be measured.

THE STATISTICS OF RISK

The study of statistics refers to the collection, presentation, analysis, and utilization of numerical data to infer and make decisions in the face of uncertainty, where the actual population data is unknown. There are two branches in the study of statistics: descriptive statistics, where data is summarized and described, and inferential statistics, where the population is generalized through a small random sample, such that the sample becomes useful for making predictions or decisions when the population characteristics are unknown.

A sample can be defined as a subset of the population being measured, whereas the population can be defined as all possible observations of interest of a variable. For instance, if one is interested in the voting practices of all U.S. registered voters, the entire pool of a hundred million registered voters is considered the population, whereas a small survey of one thousand registered voters taken from several small towns across the nation is the sample. The calculated characteristics of the sample (e.g., mean, median, standard deviation) are termed statistics, while parameters imply that the entire population has been surveyed and the results tabulated. Thus, in decision making, the statistic is of vital importance, seeing that sometimes the entire population is yet unknown (e.g., who are all your customers, what is the total market share, etc.) or it is very difficult to obtain all relevant information on the population seeing that it would be too time- or resource-consuming.

In inferential statistics, the usual steps undertaken include:

- Designing the experiment—this phase includes designing the ways to collect all possible and relevant data.
- Collection of sample data—data is gathered and tabulated.
- Analysis of data—statistical analysis is performed.
- Estimation or prediction—inferences are made based on the statistics obtained.
- Hypothesis testing—decisions are tested against the data to see the outcomes.
- Goodness-of-fit—actual data is compared to historical data to see how accurate, valid, and reliable the inference is.
- Decision making—decisions are made based on the outcome of the inference.

Measuring the Center of the Distribution— The First Moment

The first moment of a distribution measures the expected rate of return on a particular project. It measures the location of the project's scenarios and possible outcomes on average. The common statistics for the first moment include the mean (average), median (center of a distribution), and mode (most commonly occurring value). Figure 2.1 illustrates the first moment— where, in this case, the first moment of this distribution is measured by the mean (μ) or average value.

Measuring the Spread of the Distribution— The Second Moment

The second moment measures the spread of a distribution, which is a measure of risk. The spread or width of a distribution measures the variability of a variable, that is, the potentiality that the variable can fall into different regions of the distribution—in other words, the potential scenarios of

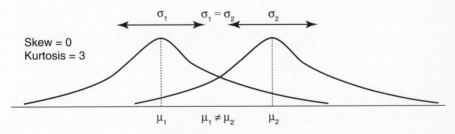

FIGURE 2.1 First moment.

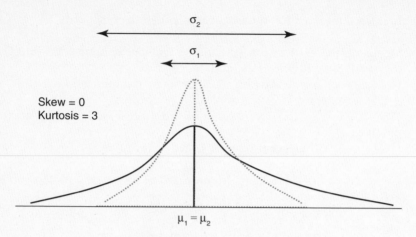

$$\sigma_2$$

$$\sigma_1$$

Skew = 0
Kurtosis = 3

$$\mu_1 = \mu_2$$

FIGURE 2.2   Second moment.

outcomes. Figure 2.2 illustrates two distributions with identical first moments (identical means) but very different second moments or risks. The visualization becomes clearer in Figure 2.3. As an example, suppose there are two stocks and the first stock's movements (illustrated by the darker line) with the smaller fluctuation is compared against the second stock's movements (illustrated by the dotted line) with a much higher price fluctuation. Clearly an investor would view the stock with the wilder fluctuation as riskier because the outcomes of the more risky stock are relatively more unknown than the less risky stock. The vertical axis in Figure 2.3 measures the stock prices, thus, the more risky stock has a wider range of potential out-

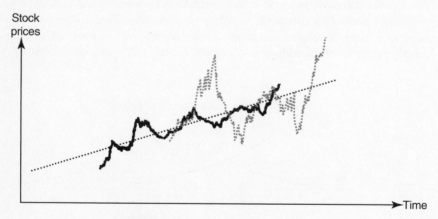

Stock
prices

Time

FIGURE 2.3   Stock price fluctuations.

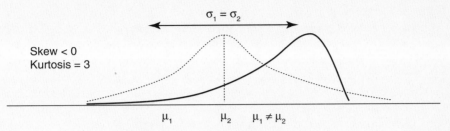

FIGURE 2.4 Third moment (left skew).

comes. This range is translated into a distribution's width (the horizontal axis) in Figure 2.2, where the wider distribution represents the riskier asset. Hence, width or spread of a distribution measures a variable's risks.

Notice that in Figure 2.2, both distributions have identical first moments or central tendencies but clearly the distributions are very different. This difference in the distributional width is measurable. Mathematically and statistically, the width or risk of a variable can be measured through several different statistics, including the range, standard deviation (σ), variance, coefficient of variation, and percentiles.

Measuring the Skew of the Distribution— The Third Moment

The third moment measures a distribution's skewness, that is, how the distribution is pulled to one side or the other. Figure 2.4 illustrates a negative or left skew (the tail of the distribution points to the left) and Figure 2.5 illustrates a positive or right skew (the tail of the distribution points to the right). The mean is always skewed toward the tail of the distribution while the median remains constant. Another way of seeing this is that the mean moves but the standard deviation, variance, or width may still remain constant. If the third moment is not considered, then looking only at the

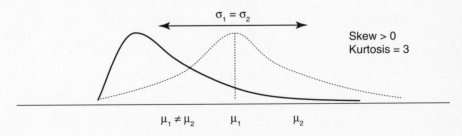

FIGURE 2.5 Third moment (right skew).

expected returns (e.g., mean or median) and risk (standard deviation), a positively skewed project might be incorrectly chosen! For example, if the horizontal axis represents the net revenues of a project, then clearly a left or negatively skewed distribution might be preferred as there is a higher probability of greater returns (Figure 2.4) as compared to a higher probability for lower level returns (Figure 2.5). Thus, in a skewed distribution, the median is a better measure of returns, as the medians for both Figures 2.4 and 2.5 are identical, risks are identical, and, hence, a project with a negatively skewed distribution of net profits is a better choice. Failure to account for a project's distributional skewness may mean that the incorrect project may be chosen (e.g., two projects may have identical first and second moments, that is, they both have identical returns and risk profiles, but their distributional skews may be very different).

Measuring the Catastrophic Tail Events in a Distribution—The Fourth Moment

The fourth moment, or kurtosis, measures the peakedness of a distribution. Figure 2.6 illustrates this effect. The background (denoted by the dotted line) is a normal distribution with a kurtosis of 3.0. The new distribution has a higher kurtosis, thus the area under the curve is thicker at the tails with less area in the central body. This condition has major impacts on risk analysis as for the two distributions in Figure 2.6, the first three moments (mean, standard deviation, and skewness) can be identical but the fourth moment (kurtosis) is different. This condition means that, although the returns and risks are identical, the probabilities of extreme and catastrophic events (potential large losses or large gains) occurring are higher for a high kurtosis

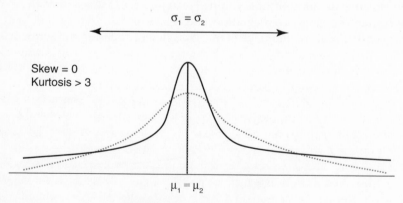

FIGURE 2.6 Fourth moment.

distribution (e.g., stock market returns are leptokurtic or have high kurtosis). Ignoring a project's return's kurtosis may be detrimental.

Most distributions can be defined up to four moments. The first moment describes the distribution's location or central tendency (expected returns), the second moment describes its width or spread (risks), the third moment its directional skew (most probable events), and the fourth moment its peakedness or thickness in the tails (catastrophic losses or gains). All four moments should be calculated and interpreted to provide a more comprehensive view of the project under analysis.

THE MEASUREMENTS OF RISK

There are multiple ways to measure risk in projects. This section summarizes some of the more common measures of risk and lists their potential benefits and pitfalls. The measures include:

- *Probability of Occurrences.* This approach is simplistic and yet effective. As an example, there is a 10 percent probability that a project will not break even (it will return a negative net present value indicating losses) within the next 5 years. Two similar projects have identical implementation costs and expected returns. Based on a single-point estimate, management should be indifferent between them. However, if risk analysis such as Monte Carlo simulation is performed, the first project might reveal a 70 percent probability of losses compared to only a 5 percent probability of losses on the second project. Clearly, the second project is better when risks are analyzed.
- *Standard Deviation and Variance.* Standard deviation is a measure of the average of each data point's deviation from the mean.[2] This is the most popular measure of risk, where a higher standard deviation implies a wider distributional width and, thus, carries a higher risk. The drawback of this measure is that both the upside and downside variations are included in the computation of the standard deviation. Some analysts define risks as the potential losses or downside; thus, standard deviation and variance will penalize upswings as well as downsides.
- *Semi-Standard Deviation.* The semi-standard deviation only measures the standard deviation of the downside risks and ignores the upside fluctuations. Modifications of the semi-standard deviation include calculating only the values below the mean, or values below a threshold

(e.g., negative profits or negative cash flows). This provides a better picture of downside risk but is more difficult to estimate.

- *Volatility.* The concept of volatility is widely used in the applications of real options and can be defined briefly as a measure of uncertainty and risks.[3] Volatility can be estimated using multiple methods, including simulation of the uncertain variables impacting a particular project and estimating the standard deviation of the resulting asset's logarithmic returns over time. This concept is more difficult to define and estimate but more powerful than most other risk measures in that this single value incorporates all sources of uncertainty rolled into one value.

- *Beta.* Beta is another common measure of risk in the investment finance arena. Beta can be defined simply as the undiversifiable, systematic risk of a financial asset. This concept is made famous through the CAPM, where a higher beta means a higher risk, which in turn requires a higher expected return on the asset.

- *Coefficient of Variation.* The coefficient of variation is simply defined as the ratio of standard deviation to the mean, which means that the risks are common-sized. For example, a distribution of a group of students' heights (measured in meters) can be compared to the distribution of the students' weights (measured in kilograms).[4] This measure of risk or dispersion is applicable when the variables' estimates, measures, magnitudes, or units differ.

- *Value at Risk.* Value at Risk (VaR) was made famous by J. P. Morgan in the mid-1990s through the introduction of its *RiskMetrics* approach, and has thus far been sanctioned by several bank governing bodies around the world. Briefly, it measures the amount of capital reserves at risk given a particular holding period at a particular probability of loss. This measurement can be modified to risk applications by stating, for example, the amount of potential losses a certain percent of the time during the period of the economic life of the project—clearly, a project with a smaller VaR is better.

- *Worst-Case Scenario and Regret.* Another simple measure is the value of the worst-case scenario given catastrophic losses. Another definition is regret. That is, if a decision is made to pursue a particular project, but if the project becomes unprofitable and suffers a loss, the level of regret is simply the difference between the actual losses compared to doing nothing at all.

- *Risk-Adjusted Return on Capital.* Risk-adjusted return on capital (RAROC) takes the ratio of the difference between the fiftieth percentile (median) return and the fifth percentile return on a project to its standard deviation. This approach is used mostly by banks to estimate returns subject to their risks by measuring only the potential downside effects and ignoring the positive upswings.

FIVE-MINUTE INDUSTRY SPOTLIGHT: FARMLAND

Farmland's Value-at-Risk Decision Making Made Less Risky

Through its use of Monte Carlo simulation, Farmland has demonstrated its desire to be on the cutting edge of companies using risk-analysis technologies.

Farmland is North America's largest farmer-owned food system and a Fortune 200 company. More than 500,000 independent family farmers and ranchers own the 1,400-plus local agricultural cooperatives which, in turn, own and control Farmland Industries. Paul Twenter is a financial project manager for Farmland. Paul has implemented Crystal Ball to aid in many areas of value-at-risk decision making. In particular, Paul uses Crystal Ball to help determine risk exposure in the various commodities markets in which Farmland has a significant presence. Some of the commodities that Farmland trades in on a regular basis are chemical fertilizers, grains, pork, beef, natural gas, crude oil, gasoline, and heating oil.

The value-at-risk analysis that Paul performs looks not only at Farmland's current exposure, but also at what it intends to purchase over the next year. Paul's goal in this analysis is to make Farmland's exposure as efficient as possible. The process that Paul uses begins with his analyzing historical commodity prices to determine volatility. He then calculates the correlation between the historical prices and, using Crystal Ball's Distribution Gallery, applies distributions to each of the commodities prices in his model. Paul then performs Monte Carlo simulation on Farmland's portfolio of commodities. The end result is a distribution of Farmland's price-risk exposure. After analyzing the results of the simulation, Farmland's management can make a determination on the appropriate exposure levels in the various commodities.

Another valuable application is in evaluating the risk of expensive decisions such as whether or not to purchase new manufacturing equipment or building versus buying a new plant. Paul has also recently begun experimenting with risk-optimizing technology to determine the most effective way to process pork in Farmland's meat-processing facilities.

Paul has demonstrated the value of risk analysis in making important decisions at Farmland. It is through these types of decisions that a company such as Farmland can feel confident that it is taking the steps necessary to make sound decisions within a risk-filled environment.

FIVE-MINUTE INDUSTRY SPOTLIGHT: ENVIRONMENTAL PROTECTION AGENCY

Environmental Impact Analysis

Evaluations of the need for cleanup of contamination at Superfund sites now require quantitative risk assessments. The Environmental Protection Agency (EPA) has produced handbooks that specify the equations and parameter values to be used for such assessments. The values are point estimates and are generally chosen conservatively (i.e., they err on the side of safety).

The EPA's methods advocate a tiered approach, beginning with point estimates of risk, and progressing to probabilistic estimates that characterize variability and uncertainty in risk using Monte Carlo analysis. In the past few years, the EPA has worked to provide technical guidance on the application of probabilistic methods to human health and ecological risk assessment, in particular for Monte Carlo methods.

"Without a quantitative assessment of uncertainty, millions of dollars may be misallocated to clean up contamination that only appears to present an unacceptable risk due to the hidden effect of compound conservatism in the EPA risk calculations." In actuality, such contamination might present a health risk that can be considered trivial.

In his risk assessments, Dr. F. Owen Hoffman, an environmental scientist previously with Oak Ridge National Laboratory and a long-time proponent of the use of uncertainty analysis, uses the EPA approach only as an initial screening calculation. Such a screening calculation is useful in identifying low-risk exposure pathways and contaminants that can be designated clearly as low priority for further investigation. For the remaining contaminants and exposure pathways, he uses risk-analysis techniques to translate his estimates of uncertainty in each of the parameters used in the risk-assessment equation into a confidence interval about the final risk estimate.

Dr. Hoffman found that risk analysis not only helped to determine the need for cleanup more appropriately but also helped in setting priorities for collection of better data.

QUESTIONS

1. What is the efficient frontier and when is it used?
2. What are inferential statistics and what steps are required in making inferences?
3. When is using standard deviation less desirable than using semi-standard deviation as a measure of risk?
4. If comparing three projects with similar first, second, and fourth moments, would you prefer a project that has no skew, a positive skew, or a negative skew?
5. If comparing three projects with similar first to third moments, would you prefer a project that is leptokurtic (high kurtosis), mesokurtic (average kurtosis), or platykurtic (low kurtosis)? Explain your reasoning with respect to a distribution's tail area. Under what conditions would your answer change?
6. What are the differences and similarities between value-at-risk and worst-case scenario as a measure of risk?

CHAPTER 3

A Gentleman's Guide to Model Building

The first step in risk analysis is the creation of a model. A model can range from a simple three-line calculation in an Excel spreadsheet (e.g., A + B = C) to a highly complicated and oftentimes convoluted series of interconnected spreadsheets. Creating a proper model takes time, patience, strategy, and practice. Evaluating or learning a complicated model passed down to you that was previously created by another analyst may be rather cumbersome. Even the person who built the model revisits it weeks or months later and tries to remember what was created can sometimes find it challenging. It is indeed difficult to understand what the model originator was thinking of when the model was first built. As most readers of this book are Excel users, this chapter lists some model building blocks that every professional model builder should at least consider implementing in his or her Excel spreadsheets.

As a rule of thumb, always remember to document the model; separate the inputs from the calculations and the results; protect the models against tampering; make the model user-friendly; track changes made in the model; automate the model whenever possible; and consider model aesthetics.

DOCUMENT THE MODEL

One of the major considerations in model building is its documentation. Although this step is often overlooked, it is crucial in order to allow continuity, survivorship, and knowledge transfer from one generation of model builders to the next. Inheriting a model that is not documented from a predecessor will only frustrate the new user. Some items to consider in model documentation include the following:

- *Strategize the Look and Feel of the Model.* Before the model is built, the overall structure of the model should be considered. This conceptualization includes how many sections the model will contain (e.g., each workbook file applies to a division; while each workbook has 10 worksheets representing each department in the division; and each worksheet has 3 sections, representing the revenues, costs, and miscellaneous items) as well as how each of these sections are related, linked, or replicated from one another.

- *Naming Conventions.* Each of these workbooks and worksheets should have a proper name. The recommended approach is simply to provide each workbook and worksheet a descriptive name. However, one should always consider brevity in the naming convention but yet provide sufficient description of the model. If multiple iterations of the model are required, especially when the model is created by several individuals over time, the date and version numbers should be part of the model's file name for proper archiving, backup, and identification purposes.

- *Executive Summary.* In the first section of the model, there should always be a welcome page with an executive summary of the model. The summary may include the file name, location on a shared drive, version of the model, developers of the model, and any other pertinent information, including instructions, assumptions, caveats, warnings, or suggestions on using the model.

- *File Properties.* Make full use of Excel's file properties (*File* | *Properties*). This simple action may make the difference between an orphaned model and a model that users will have more faith in as to how current or updated it is (Figure 3.1).

- *Document Changes and Tweaks.* If multiple developers work on the model, when the model is saved, the changes, tweaks, edits, and modifications should always be documented such that any past actions can be undone should it become necessary. This simple practice also provides a method to track the changes that have been made versus a list of bugs or development requirements.

- *Illustrate Formulas.* Consider illustrating and documenting the formulas used in the model, especially when complicated equations and calculations are required. Use Excel's Equation Editor to do this (*Insert* | *Object* | *Create New* | *Microsoft Equation*) but also remember to provide a reference for more advanced models.

- *Results Interpretation.* In the executive summary, on the reports or results summary page, include instructions on how the final analytical re-

FIGURE 3.1   Excel's file properties dialog box.

sults should be interpreted, including what assumptions are used when building the model, any theory the results pertain to, any reference material detailing the technical aspects of the model, data sources, and any conjectures made to obtain certain input parameters.

■ *Reporting Structure*. A good model should have a final report after the inputs have been entered and the analysis is performed. This report may be as simple as a printable results worksheet or as a more sophisticated macro that creates a new document (e.g., Crystal Ball has a reporting function that provides detailed analysis on the input parameters and output results).

■ *Model Navigation*. Consider how a novice user will navigate between modules, worksheets, or input cells. One consideration is to include navigational capabilities in the model. These navigational capabilities range from a simple set of naming conventions (e.g., sheets in a workbook can be named "1. Input Data," "2. Analysis," and "3. Results") where the user can quickly and easily identify the relevant worksheets by their tab names (Figure 3.2), to more sophisticated methods. More sophisticated navigational methods include using hyperlinks and Visual Basic for Applications (VBA) code.

⏮ ◀ ▶ ⏭ \ **1. Input Data** / 2. Analysis / 3. Results /

FIGURE 3.2 Worksheet tab names.

For instance, in order to create hyperlinks to other sheets from a main navigational sheet, click on *Insert | Hyperlink | Place in This Document* in Excel. Choose the relevant worksheet to link to within the workbook (Figure 3.3). Place all these links in the main navigational sheet and place only the relevant links in each sheet (e.g., only the main menu and Step 2 in the analysis are available in the Step 1 worksheet). These links can also be named as "next" or "previous," to further assist the user in navigating a large model. The second and more protracted approach is to use VBA codes to navigate the model. Refer to the appendix at the end of this chapter—A Primer on VBA Modeling and Writing Macros—for sample VBA codes used in said navigation and automation.

> Document the model by strategizing the look and feel of the model, have an adequate naming convention, have an executive summary, include model property descriptions, indicate the changes and tweaks made, illustrate difficult formulas, document how to interpret results, provide a reporting structure, and make sure the model is easy to navigate.

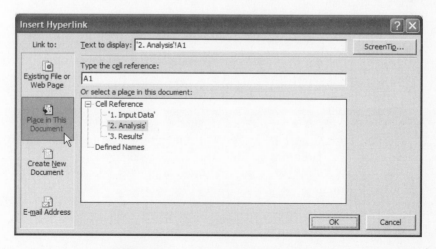

FIGURE 3.3 Insert hyperlink dialog box.

SEPARATE INPUTS, CALCULATIONS, AND RESULTS

- *Different Worksheets for Different Functions.* Consider using a different worksheet within a workbook for the model's input assumption (these assumptions should all be accumulated into a single sheet), a set of calculation worksheets, and a final set of worksheets summarizing the results. These sheets should then be appropriately named and grouped for easy identification. Sometimes, the input worksheet also has some key model results—this arrangement is very useful as a *management dashboard*, where slight tweaks and changes to the inputs can be made by management and the fluctuations in key results can be quickly viewed and captured.
- *Describe Input Variables.* In the input parameter worksheet, consider providing a summary of each input parameter, including where it is used in the model. Sometimes, this can be done through cell comments instead (*Insert | Comment*).
- *Name Input Parameter Cells.* Consider naming individual cells by selecting an input cell, typing the relevant name in the *Name Box* on the upper left corner of the spreadsheet, and hitting Enter (arrow icon in Figure 3.4). Also, consider naming ranges by selecting a range of cells and typing the relevant name in the *Name Box*. For more complicated models where multiple input parameters with similar functions exist, consider grouping these names. For instance, if the inputs "cost" and "revenues" exist in two different divisions, consider using the following hierarchical naming conventions (separated by periods in the names) for the Excel cells:

Cost.Division.A
Cost.Division.B
Revenues.Division.A
Revenues.Division.B

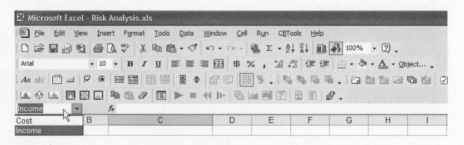

FIGURE 3.4   Name box in Excel.

- *Color Coding Inputs and Results.* Another form of identification is simply to color code the input cells one consistent color, while the results, which are usually mathematical functions based on the input assumptions and other intermediate calculations, should be color coded differently.
- *Model Growth and Modification.* A good model should always provide room for growth, enhancement, and update analysis over time. When additional divisions are added to the model, or other constraints and input assumptions are added at a later date, there should be room to maneuver. Another situation involves data updating, where, in the future, previous sales forecasts have now become a reality and the actual sales now replace the forecasts. The model should be able to accommodate this situation. Providing for data updating is where modeling strategy and experience count.
- *Report and Model Printing.* Always consider checking the overall model, results, summary, and report pages for their print layouts. Use Excel's *File | Print Preview* capability to set up the page appropriately for printing. Set up the headers and footers to reflect the dates of the analysis as well as the model version for easy comparison later. Use links, automatic fields, and formulas whenever appropriate (e.g., the Excel formula "*=Today()*" is a volatile field that updates automatically to the latest date when the spreadsheet model was last saved).

> Separate inputs, calculations, and results by creating different worksheets for different functions, describing input variables, naming input parameters, color coding inputs and results, providing room for model growth and subsequent modifications, and considering report and model printing layouts.

PROTECT THE MODELS

- *Protect Workbook and Worksheets.* Consider using spreadsheet protection (*Tools | Protection*) in your intermediate and final results summary sheet to prevent user tampering or accidental manipulation. Passwords are also recommended here for more sensitive models.[1]
- *Hiding and Protecting Formulas.* Consider setting cell properties to hide, lock, or both hide and lock cells (*Format | Cells | Protection*), then protect the worksheet (*Tools | Protection*) to prevent the user from accidentally overriding a formula (by locking a cell and protecting the

sheet), or still allow the user to see the formula without the ability to ir-
reparably break the model by deleting the contents of a cell (by locking
but not hiding the cell and protecting the sheet), or to prevent tampering with and viewing the formulas in the cell (by both locking and hiding the cell and then protecting the sheet).

Protect the models from user tampering at the workbook and worksheet
levels through password protecting workbooks, or through hiding and
protecting formulas in the individual worksheet cells.

MAKE THE MODEL USER-FRIENDLY: DATA VALIDATION AND ALERTS

- *Data Validation.* Consider preventing the user from entering bad inputs
  through spreadsheet validation. Prevent erroneous inputs through data
  validation (*Data | Validation | Settings*) where only specific inputs are al-
  lowed. Figure 3.5 illustrates data validation for a cell accepting only
  positive inputs. The *Edit | Copy* and *Edit | Paste Special* functions can
  be used to replicate the data validation if validation is chosen in the
  paste special command.
- *Error Alerts.* Provide error alerts to let the user know when an incorrect
  value is entered through data validation (*Data | Validation | Error Alert*)

FIGURE 3.5   Data validation dialog box.

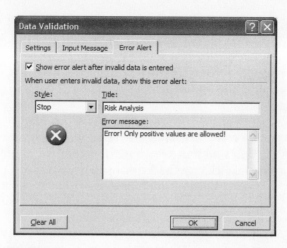

FIGURE 3.6 Error message setup for data validation.

shown in Figure 3.6. If the validation is violated, an error message box will be executed (Figure 3.7).

■ *Cell Warnings and Input Messages.* Provide warnings and input messages when a cell is selected where the inputs required are ambiguous (*Data* | *Validation* | *Input Message*). The message box can be set up to appear whenever the cell is selected, regardless of the data validation. This message box can be used to provide additional information to the user about the specific input parameter or to provide suggested input values.

■ *Define All Inputs.* Consider including a worksheet with named cells and ranges, complete with their respective definitions and where each variable is used in the model.

> Make the model user-friendly through data validation, error alerts, cell warnings, and input messages, as well as defining all the inputs required in the model.

FIGURE 3.7 Error message for data validation.

TRACK THE MODEL

- *Insert Comments.* Consider inserting comments for key variables (*Insert | Comment*) for easy recognition and for quick reference. Comments can be easily copied into different cells through the *Edit | Paste Special | Comments* procedure.
- *Track Changes.* Consider tracking changes if collaborating with other modelers (*Tools | Track Changes | Highlight Changes*). Tracking all changes is not only important but it is also a courtesy to other model developers to note the changes and tweaks that were made.
- *Avoid Hard-Coding Values.* Consider using formulas whenever possible and avoid hard-coding numbers into cells other than assumptions and inputs. In complex models, it would be extremely difficult to track down where a model breaks because a few values are hard-coded instead of linked through equations. If a value needs to be hard-coded, it is by definition an input parameter and should be listed as such.
- *Use Linking and Embedding.* Consider object linking and embedding of files and objects (*Edit | Paste Special*) rather than using a simple paste function. This way, any changes in the source files can be reflected in the linked file. If linking between spreadsheets, Excel automatically updates these linked sheets every time the target sheet is opened. However, to avoid the irritating dialog pop-ups to update links every time the model is executed, simply turn off the warnings through *Edit | Links | Startup Prompt*.

> Track the model by inserting comments, using the track changes functionality, avoiding hard-coded values, and using the linking and embedding functionality.

AUTOMATE THE MODEL WITH VBA

VBA is a powerful Excel tool that can assist in automating a significant amount of work. Although detailed VBA coding is beyond the scope of this book, an introduction to some VBA applications is provided in the appendix to this chapter—A Primer on VBA Modeling and Writing Macros—specifically addressing the following six automation issues.

1. Consider creating VBA modules for repetitive tasks (*Alt-F11* or *Tools | Macro | Visual Basic Editor*).

2. Add custom equations in place of complex and extended Excel equations.
3. Consider recording macros (*Tools | Macro | Record New Macro*) for repetitive tasks or calculations.
4. Consider placing automation forms in your model (*View | Toolbar | Forms*) and the relevant codes to support the desired actions.
5. Consider constraining users to only choosing specific inputs (*View | Toolbar | Forms*) and insert drop-list boxes and the relevant codes to support the desired actions.
6. Consider adding custom buttons and menu items on the user's model within Excel to locate and execute macros easily.

Use VBA to automate the model, including adding custom equations, macros, automation forms, and predefined buttons.

MODEL AESTHETICS AND CONDITIONAL FORMATTING

- *Units*. Consider the input assumption's units and preset them accordingly in the cell to avoid any confusion. For instance, if a discount-rate input cell is required, the inputs can either be typed in as 20 or 0.2 to represent 20 percent. By avoiding a simple input ambiguity through preformatting the cells with the relevant units, user and model errors can be easily avoided.
- *Magnitude*. Consider the input's potential magnitude, where a large input value may obfuscate the cell's view by using the cell's default width. Change the format of the cell either to automatically reduce the font size to accommodate the higher magnitude input (*Format | Cells | Alignment | Shrink to Fit*) or have the cell width sufficiently large to accommodate all possible magnitudes of the input.
- *Text Wrapping and Zooming*. Consider wrapping long text in a cell (*Format | Cells | Alignment | Wrap Text*) for better aesthetics and view. This suggestion also applies to the zoom size of the spreadsheet. Remember that zoom size is worksheet specific and not workbook specific.
- *Merging Cells*. Consider merging cells in titles (*Format | Cells | Alignment | Merge Cells*) for a better look and feel.
- *Colors and Graphics*. Colors and graphics are an integral part of a model's aesthetics as well as a functional piece to determine if a cell is an input, a calculation, or a result. A careful blend of background colors and foreground graphics goes a long way in terms of model aesthetics.
- *Grouping*. Consider grouping repetitive columns or insignificant intermediate calculations (*Data | Group and Outline | Group*).

- *Hiding Rows and Columns.* Consider hiding extra rows and columns (select the relevant rows and columns to hide by selecting their row or column headers, and then choose *Format | Rows or Columns | Hide*) that are deemed as intermediate calculations that are irrelevant.
- *Conditional Formatting.* Consider conditional formatting such that if a cell's calculated result is a particular value (e.g., positive versus negative profits) the cell or font changes to a different color (*Format | Conditional Formatting*).
- *Auto Formatting.* Consider using Excel's auto formatting for tables (*Format | Auto Format*). Auto formatting will maintain the same look and feel throughout the entire Excel model for consistency.
- *Custom Styles.* The default Excel formatting can be easily altered, or alternatively, new styles can be added (*Format | Styles | New*). Styles can facilitate the model-building process in that consistent formatting is applied throughout the entire model by default and the modeler does not have to worry about specific cell formatting (e.g., shrink to fit and font size can be applied consistently throughout the model).
- *Custom Views.* In larger models where data inputs and output results are all over the place, consider using custom views (*View | Custom Views | Add*). This custom view feature will allow the user to navigate through a large model spreadsheet with ease, especially when navigational macros are added to these views (see the appendix to this chapter—A Primer on VBA Modeling and Writing Macros—for navigating custom views using macros). In addition, different size zooms on areas of interest can be created within the same spreadsheet through custom views.

Model aesthetics are preserved by considering the input units and magnitude, text wrapping and zooming views, cell merges, colors and graphics, grouping items, hiding excess rows and columns, conditional formatting, auto formatting, custom styles, and custom views.

APPENDIX—A PRIMER ON VBA MODELING AND WRITING MACROS

The Visual Basic Environment (VBE)

In Excel, access the VBE by hitting *Alt-F11* or *Tools | Macro | Visual Basic Environment*. The VBE looks like Figure 3.8. Select the VBA project pertaining to the opened Excel file (in this case, it is the *Risk Analysis.xls* file).

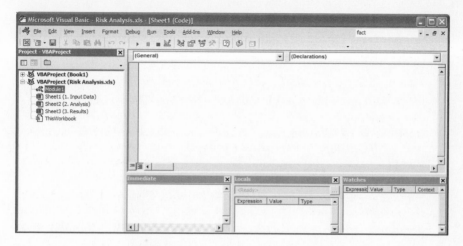

FIGURE 3.8 Visual Basic Environment.

Click on *Insert | Module* and double-click on the Module icon on the left window to open the module. You are now ready to start coding in VBA.

Custom Equations and Macros

Two Basic Equations   The following example illustrates two basic equations. They are simple combination and permutation functions. Suppose that there are three variables, A, B, and C. Further suppose that two of these variables are chosen randomly. How many pairs of outcomes are possible? In a combination, order is not important and the following three pairs of outcomes are possible: AB, AC, and BC. In a permutation, order is important and matters; thus, the following six pairs of outcomes are possible: AB, AC, BA, BC, CA, and CB. The equations are:

$$Combination = \frac{(Variable)!}{(Choose)!(Variable - Choose)!} = \frac{3!}{2!(3-2)!} = 3$$

$$Permutation = \frac{(Variable)!}{(Variable - Choose)!} = \frac{3!}{(3-2)!} = 6$$

If these two equations are widely used, then creating a VBA function will be more efficient and will avoid any unnecessary errors in larger models when Excel equations have to be created repeatedly. For instance, the manually inputted equation will have to be: *=fact(A1)/(fact(A2)*fact(A1–A2))* as compared to a custom function created in VBA where the function in Excel will now be *=combine(A1,A2)*. The mathematical expression is exaggerated if the function is more complex, as will be seen later. The VBA code to be entered into the previous module (Figure 3.8) for the two simple equations is:

> *Public Function Combine(Variable As Double, Choose As Double) As*
>   *Double*
> *Combine = Application.Fact(Variable) / (Application.Fact(Choose) ∗*
>   *Application.Fact(Variable − Choose))*
> *End Function*

> *Public Function Permute(Variable As Double, Choose As Double) As*
>   *Double*
> *Permute = Application.Fact(Variable) / Application.Fact(Variable −*
>   *Choose)*
> *End Function*

Once the code is entered, the functions can be executed in the spreadsheet.

Figure 3.9 shows the spreadsheet environment with the custom function. If multiple functions were entered, the user can also get access to those functions through the *Insert | Function* dialog wizard by choosing the user-defined category and scrolling down to the relevant functions (Figure 3.10). The functions arguments box comes up for the custom function chosen (Figure 3.11) and entering the relevant inputs or linking to input cells can be accomplished here.

Following are the VBA codes for the Black–Scholes models for estimating call and put options. The equations for the Black–Scholes are shown below and are simplified to functions in Excel named "BlackScholesCall" and "BlackScholesPut."

$$Call = S\Phi\left[\frac{\ln(S\ /\ X) + (rf + \sigma^2\ /\ 2)T}{\sigma\sqrt{T}}\right]$$

$$-\ Xe^{-rf(T)}\Phi\left[\frac{\ln(S\ /\ X) + (rf - \sigma^2\ /\ 2)T}{\sigma\sqrt{T}}\right]$$

$$Put = Xe^{-rf(T)}\Phi\left[-\frac{\ln(S\ /\ X) + (rf - \sigma^2\ /\ 2)T}{\sigma\sqrt{T}}\right]$$

$$-\ S\Phi\left[-\frac{\ln(S\ /\ X) + (rf + \sigma^2\ /\ 2)T}{\sigma\sqrt{T}}\right]$$

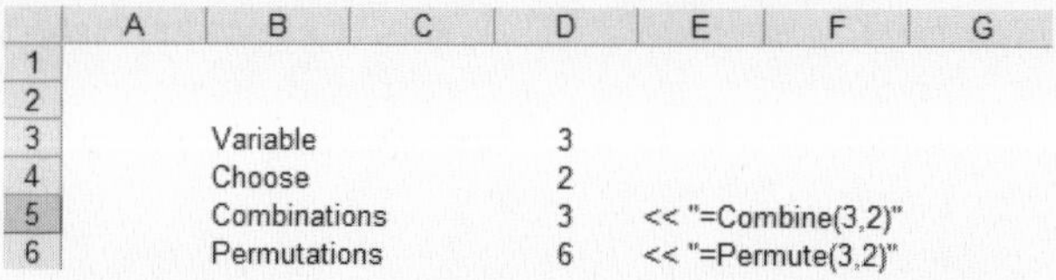

	A	B	C	D	E	F	G
1							
2							
3		Variable		3			
4		Choose		2			
5		Combinations		3	<< "=Combine(3,2)"		
6		Permutations		6	<< "=Permute(3,2)"		

FIGURE 3.9   Excel spreadsheet with custom functions.

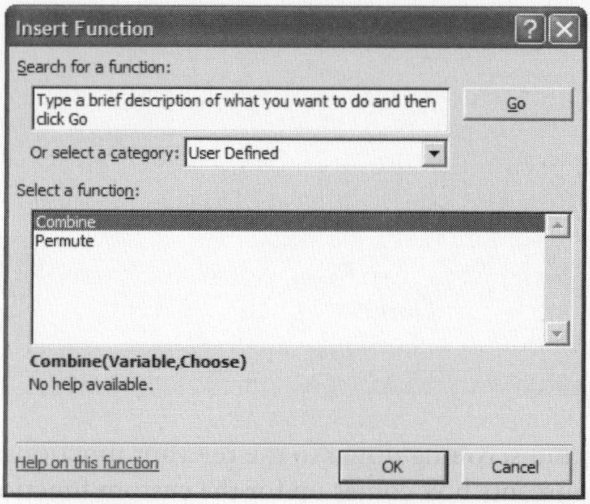

FIGURE 3.10   Insert function dialog box.

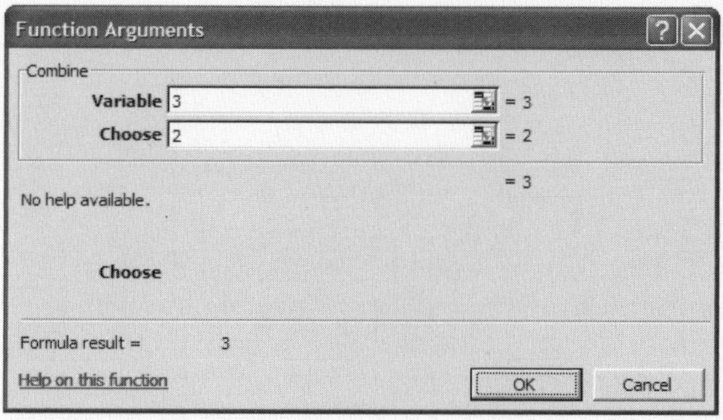

FIGURE 3.11   Function arguments box.

Public Function BlackScholesCall(Stock As Double, Strike As Double,
    Time As Double, Riskfree _
As Double, Volatility As Double) As Double
Dim D1 As Double, D2 As Double
*D1 = (Log(Stock / Strike) + (Riskfree + 0.5 * Volatility ^ 2 / 2) * Time)*
    */ (Volatility * Sqr(Time))*
*D2 = D1 – Volatility * Sqr(Time)*
*BlackScholesCall = Stock * Application.NormSDist(D1) – Strike ***
    *Exp(–Time * Riskfree) * _*
Application.NormSDist(D2)
End Function

Public Function BlackScholesPut(Stock As Double, Strike As Double,
    Time As Double, Riskfree _
As Double, Volatility As Double) As Double
Dim D1 As Double, D2 As Double
*D1 = (Log(Stock / Strike) + (Riskfree + 0.5 * Volatility ^ 2 / 2) * Time)*
    */ (Volatility * Sqr(Time))*
*D2 = D1 – Volatility * Sqr(Time)*
*BlackScholesPut = Strike * Exp(–Time * Riskfree) ***
    *Application.NormSDist(–D2) – Stock * _*
Application.NormSDist(–D1)
End Function

As an example, the function BlackScholesCall(100,100,1,5%,25%) results in 12.32 and BlackScholesPut(100,100,1,5%,25%) results in 7.44. Note that *Log* is a natural logarithm function in VBA and that *Sqr* is square root, and make sure there is a space before the underscore in the code.

Form Macros

Another type of automation is form macros. In Excel, select *View | Toolbars | Forms* and the forms toolbar will appear. Click on the insert drop-list icon as shown in Figure 3.12 and drag it into an area in the spreadsheet to insert the drop list. Then create a drop-list table as seen in Figure 3.13 (cells B10 to D17). Point at the drop list and use the right mouse click to select *Format Control | Control*. Enter the input range as cells C11 to C15, cell link at C16, and five drop-down lines (Figure 3.14).

FIGURE 3.12   Forms icon bar.

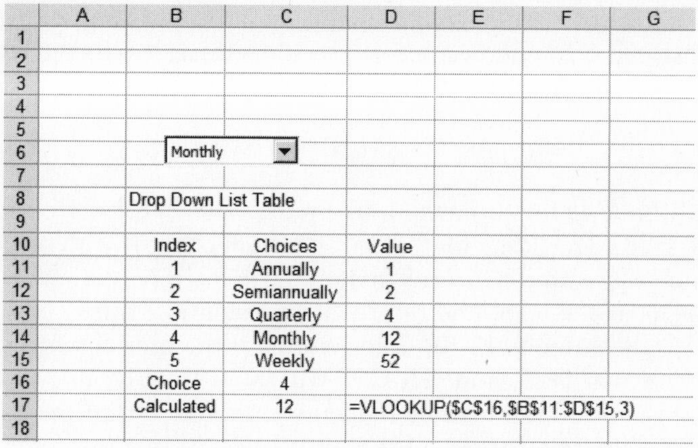

	A	B	C	D	E	F	G
1							
2							
3							
4							
5							
6		Monthly	▼				
7							
8		Drop Down List Table					
9							
10		Index	Choices	Value			
11		1	Annually	1			
12		2	Semiannually	2			
13		3	Quarterly	4			
14		4	Monthly	12			
15		5	Weekly	52			
16		Choice	4				
17		Calculated	12	=VLOOKUP($C$16,$B$11:$D$15,3)			
18							

FIGURE 3.13   Creating a drop-down box.

In Figure 3.13, the index column simply lists numbers 1 to n, where n is the total number of items in the drop-down list (in this example, n is 5). Here, the index simply converts the items (annually, semiannually, quarterly, monthly, and weekly) into corresponding indexes. The choices column in the input range is the named elements in the drop list. The value column lists the variables associated with the choice (semiannually means there are 2 periods in a year, or monthly means there are 12 periods in a year). Cell

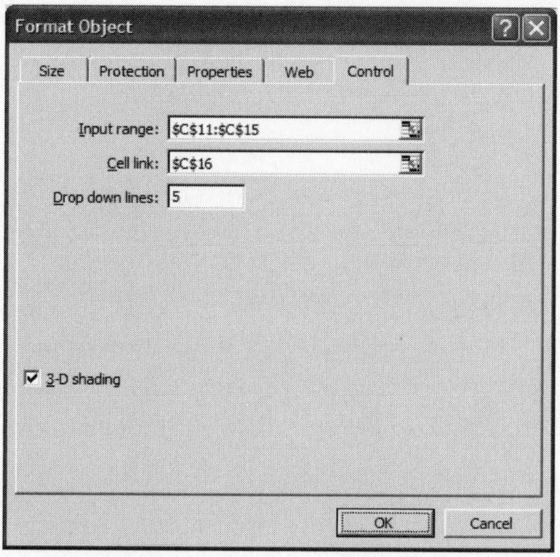

FIGURE 3.14   Format object dialog box.

C16 is the choice of the user selection, that is, if the user chooses monthly on the drop list, cell C16 will become 4, and so forth, as it is linked to the drop list in Figure 3.14. Cell C17 in Figure 3.13 is the equation

$$= Vlookup(\$C\$16, \$B\$11:\$D\$15, 3)$$

where the *VLookup* function will look up the value in cell C16 (the cell that changes in value depending on the drop-list item chosen) with respect to the first column in the area B11:D15, matches the corresponding row with the same value as in cell C16, and returns the value in the third column (3). In Figure 3.13, the value is 12. In other words, if the user chooses quarterly, then cell C16 will be 3, and cell C17 will be 4. Clearly, in proper model building, this entire table will be hidden somewhere out of the user's sight (placed in the extreme corners of the spreadsheet or in a distant corner and its font color changed to match the background, making it disappear or is placed in a hidden worksheet). Only the drop list will be shown and the models will link to cell C17 as an input parameter. This situation forces the user to choose only from a list of predefined inputs and prevents any accidental insertion of invalid inputs.

Navigational VBA Codes   A simple macro to navigate to sheet "2. Analysis" is shown here. This macro can be written in the VBA environment or recorded in the *Tools | Macros | Record New Macro*, then perform the relevant navigational actions (i.e., clicking on the "2. Analysis" sheet and hitting the stop recording button), return to the VBA environment and open up the newly recorded macro.

```
Sub MoveToSheet2()
Sheets("2. Analysis").Select
End Sub
```

However, if custom views (*View | Custom Views | Add*) are created in Excel worksheets (to facilitate finding or viewing certain parts of the model such as inputs, outputs, etc.), navigations can also be created through the following, where a custom view named "results" had been previously created.

```
Sub CustomView()
ActiveWorkbook.CustomViews("Results").Show
End Sub
```

Form buttons can then be created and these navigational codes can be attached to the buttons. For instance, click on the fourth icon in the forms icon bar (Figure 3.12) and insert a form button in the spreadsheet and assign

	A	B
1	**User:**	John
2	**Date:**	15 July, 2004
3		
4	**Sales Data**	
5	January	$ 10,000.00
6	February	$ 11,000.00
7	March	$ 12,000.00
8	April	$ 13,000.00
9	May	$ 14,000.00
10	June	$ 15,000.00
11	Sum	$ 75,000.00
12		
13	Commissions %	15.00%
14	Commissions Paid	**$ 11,250.00**
15		
16		Calculate
17		

FIGURE 3.15   Simple automated model.

the relevant macros created previously. (If the select macro dialog does not appear, right-click the form button and select *Assign Macro*).

Input Boxes   Input boxes are also recommended for their ease of use. The following illustrates some sample input boxes created in VBA, where the user is prompted to enter certain restrictive inputs in different steps or wizards. For instance, Figure 3.15 illustrates a simple sales commission calculation model, where the user inputs are the colored and boxed cells. The resulting commissions (cell B11 times cell B13) will be calculated in cell B14. The user would start using the model by clicking on the *Calculate* form button. A series of input prompts will then walk the user through inputting the relevant assumptions (Figure 3.16).

The code can also be set up to check for relevant inputs, that is, sales commissions have to be between 0.01 and 0.99. The full VBA code is shown next. The code is first written in VBA, and then the form button is placed in the worksheet that calls the VBA code.

FIGURE 3.16   Sample input box.

```
Sub UserInputs()
Dim User As Variant, Today As String, Sales As Double,
    Commissions As Double
Range("B1").Select
User = InputBox("Enter your name:")
ActiveCell.FormulaR1C1 = User
Range("B2").Select
Today = InputBox("Enter today's date:")
ActiveCell.FormulaR1C1 = Today

Range("B5").Select
Sales = InputBox("Enter the sales revenue:")
ActiveCell.FormulaR1C1 = Sales
Dim N As Double

For N = 1 To 5
  ActiveCell.Offset(1, 0).Select
  Sales = InputBox("Enter the sales revenue for the following
    period:")
  ActiveCell.FormulaR1C1 = Sales
Next N

Range("B13").Select
Commissions = 0
Do While Commissions < 0.01 Or Commissions > 0.99
  Commissions = InputBox("Enter recommended commission rate
    between 1% and 99%:")
Loop
ActiveCell.FormulaR1C1 = Commissions
Range("B1").Select
End Sub
```

Forms and Icons   Sometimes, for globally used macros and VBA scripts, a menu item or an icon can be added to the user's spreadsheet. Insert a new menu item by clicking on *Tools | Customize | Commands | New Menu* and dragging the *New Menu* item list to the Excel menu bar to a location right before the *Help* menu. Click on *Modify Selection* and rename the menu item accordingly (e.g., Risk Analysis). Also, an ampersand ("&") can be placed before a letter in the menu item name to underline the next letter such that the menu can be accessed through the keyboard by hitting the *Alternate* key and then the corresponding letter key. Next, click on *Modify Selection | Begin a Group* and then drag the *New Menu* item list again to the menu bar

FIGURE 3.17   Custom menu and icon.

but this time, right under the Risk Analysis group. Now, select this submenu item and click on *Modify Selection | Name* and rename it *Run Commissions*. Then, *Modify Selection | Assign Macro* and assign it to the User Input macro created previously.

　　Another method to access macros (other that using menu items or *Tools | Macro | Macros*, or *Alt-F8*) is to create an icon on the icon toolbar. To do this, click on *Tools | Customize | Toolbars | New*. Name the new toolbar accordingly and drag it to its new location anywhere on the icon bar. Then, select the *Commands | Macros | Custom Button*. Drag the custom button icon to the new toolbar location. Select the new icon on the toolbar and click on *Modify Selection | Assign Macro*. Assign the User Input macro created previously. The default button image can also be changed by clicking on *Modify Selection | Change Button Image* and selecting the relevant icon accordingly, or from an external image file. Figure 3.17 illustrates the new menu item (Risk Analysis) and the new icon in the shape of a calculator, where selecting either the menu item or the icon will evoke the User Input macro, which walks the user through the simple input wizard.

EXERCISES

1. Create an Excel worksheet with each of the following components activated:
    a. Cells in an Excel spreadsheet with the following data validations: no negative numbers are allowed, only positive integers are allowed, only numerical values are allowed.
    b. Create a form macro drop list (see the appendix to this chapter) with the following 12 items in the drop list: January, February, March, . . . December. Make sure the selection of any item in the drop list will change a corresponding cell's value.
2. Go through the VBA examples in the appendix to this chapter and recreate the following macros and functions for use in an Excel spreadsheet:
    a. Create a column of future sales with the following equation for future sales (Years 2 to 11): *Future sales = (1+RAND())*(Past Year Sales)* for 11 future periods starting with the current year's sales of $100

(Year 1). Then, in VBA, create a macro using the *For . . . Next* loop to simulate this calculation 1,000 times and insert a form button to activate the macro in the Excel worksheet.

b. Create the following income function in VBA for use in the Excel spreadsheet: *Income = Benefits – Cost*. Try out different benefits and cost inputs to make sure the function works properly.

Three

Risk Quantification

CHAPTER 4

On the Shores of Monaco

M onte Carlo simulation, named for the famous gambling capital of Monaco, is a very potent methodology. Statisticians and mathematicians sometimes dislike it because it solves difficult and often intractable problems with too much simplicity and ease. Instead, mathematical purists would prefer the more elegant approach: the old-fashioned way.[1] Solving a fancy stochastic mathematical model provides a sense of accomplishment and completion as opposed to the brute force method used in simulation. However, for the practitioner, simulation opens the door for solving difficult and complex but practical problems with great ease. Monte Carlo creates artificial futures by generating thousands and even millions of sample paths of outcomes and looks at their prevalent characteristics. For analysts in a company, taking graduate-level advanced math courses is just not logical or practical. A brilliant analyst would use all available tools at his or her disposal to obtain the same answer the easiest and most practical way possible. And in all cases, when modeled correctly, Monte Carlo simulation provides similar answers to the more mathematically elegant methods. So, what is Monte Carlo simulation and how does it work?

WHAT IS MONTE CARLO SIMULATION?

Monte Carlo simulation in its simplest form is a random number generator that is useful for forecasting, estimation, and risk analysis. A simulation calculates numerous scenarios of a model by repeatedly picking values from a user-predefined *probability distribution* for the uncertain variables and using those values for the model. As all those scenarios produce associated results in a model, each scenario can have a *forecast*. Forecasts are events (usually with formulas or functions) that you define as important outputs of the model. These usually are events such as totals, net profit, or gross expenses.

Simplistically, think of the Monte Carlo simulation approach as picking golf balls out of a large basket repeatedly with replacement, as seen in the example presented next. The size and shape of the basket depend on the distributional *assumptions* (e.g., a normal distribution with a mean of 100 and a standard deviation of 10, versus a uniform distribution or a triangular distribution) where some baskets are deeper or more symmetrical than others, allowing certain balls to be pulled out more frequently than others. The number of balls pulled repeatedly depends on the number of *trials* simulated. For a large model with multiple related assumptions, imagine the large model as a very large basket, where many baby baskets reside. Each baby basket has its own set of golf balls that are bouncing around. Sometimes these baby baskets are holding hands with each other (if there is a *correlation* between the variables) and the golf balls are bouncing in tandem while others are bouncing independently of one another. The balls that are picked each time from these interactions within the model (the mother of all baskets) are tabulated and recorded, providing a *forecast* result of the simulation.

WHY ARE SIMULATIONS IMPORTANT?

An example of why simulation is important can be seen in the case illustration in Figures 4.1 and 4.2, termed the Flaw of Averages.[2] The example is most certainly worthy of more detailed study. It shows how an analyst may be misled into making the wrong decisions without the use of simulation. Suppose you are the owner of a shop that sells perishable goods and you need to make a decision on the optimal inventory to have on hand. Your new-hire analyst was successful in downloading 5-years worth of monthly historical sales levels and she estimates the average to be five units. You then make the decision that the optimal inventory to have on hand is five units. You have just committed the flaw of averages. As the example shows, the obvious reason why this error occurs is that the distribution of historical demand is highly skewed while the cost structure is asymmetrical. For example, suppose you are in a meeting, and your boss asks what everyone made last year. You take a quick poll and realize that the salaries range from $60,000 to $150,000. You perform a quick calculation and find the average to be $100,000. Then, your boss tells you that he made $20 million last year! Suddenly, the average for the group becomes $1.5 million. This value of $1.5 million clearly in no way represents how much each of your peers made last year. In this case, the median may be more appropriate. Here you see that simply using the average will provide highly misleading results.[3]

Continuing with the example, Figure 4.2 shows how the right inventory level is calculated using simulation. The approach used here is called

Actual		5		Average	5.00
Inventory Held		6			

		Historical Data	(5 Yr)
Perishable Cost	$100	Month	Actual
Fed Ex Cost	$175	1	12
		2	11
Total Cost	$100	3	7
		4	0

Your company is a retailer in perishable goods and you were tasked with finding the optimal level of inventory to have on hand. If your inventory exceeds actual demand, there is a $100 perishable cost while a $175 Fed Ex cost is incurred if your inventory is insufficient to cover the actual level of demand. These costs are on a per unit basis. Your first inclination is to collect historical demand data as seen on the right, for the past 60 months. You then take a simple average, which was found to be 5 units. Hence, you select 5 units as the optimal inventory level. You have just committed a major mistake called the Flaw of Averages!

The actual demand data are shown here on the right. Rows 19 through 57 are hidden to conserve space. Being the analyst, what must you then do?

Month	Actual
5	0
6	2
7	7
8	0
9	11
10	12
11	0
12	9
13	3
14	5
15	0
16	2
17	1
18	10
58	3
59	2
60	17

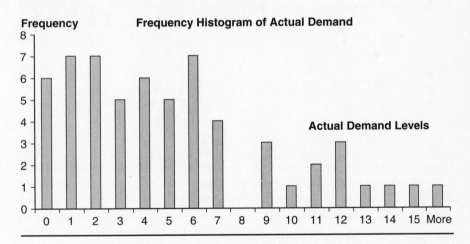

FIGURE 4.1   The flaw of averages example.

Simulated Average			
Actual Demand	8.53	Simulated Demand Range	From 7.21 and 9.85
Inventory Held	9.00	Simulated Cost Range	From 178.91 to 149

Perishable Cost	$100
Fed Ex Cost	$175
Total Cost	$46.88

The best method is to perform a nonparametric simulation where we use the actual historical demand levels as inputs to simulate the most probable level of demand going forward, which we found as 8.53 units. Given this demand, the lowest cost is obtained through a trial inventory of 9 units, a far cry from the original Flaw of Averages estimate of 5 units.

Trial Inventory	Total Cost
1.00	$1,318
2.00	$1,143
3.00	$968
4.00	$793
5.00	$618
6.00	$443
7.00	$268
8.00	$93
9.00	$47
10.00	$147
11.00	$247
12.00	$347
13.00	$447
14.00	$547
15.00	$647
16.00	$747

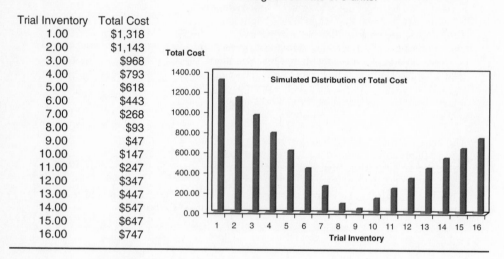

FIGURE 4.2 Fixing the flaw of averages with simulation.

nonparametric bootstrap simulation. It is nonparametric because in this simulation approach, no distributional parameters are assigned. Instead of assuming some preset distribution (normal, triangular, lognormal, or the like) and its required parameters (mean, standard deviation, and so forth) as required in a Monte Carlo *parametric* simulation, nonparametric simulation uses the data themselves to tell the story.

Imagine that you collect 5-years worth of historical demand levels and write down the demand quantity on a golf ball for each month. Throw all 60 golf balls into a large basket and mix the basket randomly. Pick a golf ball out at random and write down its value on a piece of paper, then replace the ball in the basket and mix the basket again. Do this 60 times and calculate the average. This process is a single grouped trial. Perform this entire process several thousand times, with replacement. The distribution of these thousands of averages represents the outcome of the simulation forecast. The expected value of the simulation is simply the average value of these thousands of averages. Figure 4.2 shows an example of the distribution stemming from a nonparametric simulation. As you can see, the optimal inventory rate that minimizes carrying costs is nine units, far from the average value of five units previously calculated in Figure 4.1.

Clearly, each approach has its merits and disadvantages. Nonparametric simulation, which can be easily applied using Crystal Ball's bootstrap function,[4] uses historical data to tell the story and to predict the future. The assumption is that history will repeat itself while time-dependency (time-series forecasts and seasonality, for instance) cannot be applied with ease. Parametric simulation, however, forces the simulated outcomes to follow well-behaving distributions, which is desirable in most cases. Instead of having to worry about cleaning up any messy data (e.g., outliers and nonsensical values) as is required for nonparametric simulation, parametric simulation starts fresh every time.

Monte Carlo simulation is a type of parametric simulation, where specific distributional parameters are required before a simulation can begin. The alternative approach is nonparametric simulation where the raw historical data is used to tell the story and no distributional parameters are required for the simulation to run.

COMPARING SIMULATION WITH TRADITIONAL ANALYSES

Figure 4.3 illustrates some traditional approaches used to deal with uncertainty and risk. The methods include performing sensitivity analysis, scenario analysis, and probabilistic scenarios. The next step is the application of Monte Carlo simulation, which can be seen as an extension to the next step in uncertainty and risk analysis. Figure 4.4 shows a more advanced use of Monte Carlo simulation for forecasting.[5] The examples in Figure 4.4 show how Monte Carlo simulation can be really complicated, depending on its use. The enclosed CD-ROM has several models that apply some of these more complex stochastic forecasting models, including Brownian Motion, mean-reversion, and random-walk models.

(Text continues on page 70.)

Unit Sales	10	
Unit Price	$10	
Total Revenue	$100	[10 units × $10 per unit]
Unit Variable Cost	$5	
Fixed Cost	$20	[$20 Fixed + ($5 × 10) Variable]
Total Cost	$70	
Net Income	$30	[$100 – $70]

Sensitivity Analysis

Here, we can make unit changes to the variables in our simple model to see the final effects of such a change. Looking at the simple example, we know that only Unit Sales, Unit Price and Unit Variable Cost can change. This is since Total Revenues, Total Costs and Net Income are calculated values while Fixed Cost is assumed to be fixed and unchanging, regardless of the amount of sales units or sales price. Changing these three variables by one unit shows that from the original $40, Net Income has now increased $5 for Unit Sales, increased $10 for Unit Price and decreased $10 for Unit Variable Cost.

Unit Sales	11	[Change 1 unit]
Unit Price	$10	
Total Revenue	$110	
Unit Variable Cost	$5	
Fixed Cost	$20	
Total Cost	$75	[Up $5]
Net Income	$35	

Unit Sales	10	
Unit Price	$11	[Change 1 unit]
Total Revenue	$110	
Unit Variable Cost	$5	
Fixed Cost	$20	
Total Cost	$70	
Net Income	$40	[Up $10]

Unit Sales	10	
Unit Price	$10	
Total Revenue	$100	
Unit Variable Cost	$6	[Change 1 unit]
Fixed Cost	$20	
Total Cost	$80	[Down $10]
Net Income	$20	

Hence, we know that Unit Price has the most positive impact on the Net Income bottom line and Unit Variable Cost the most negative impact. In terms of making assumptions, we know that additional care must be taken when forecasting and estimating these variables. However, we still are in the dark concerning which sensitivity set of results we should be looking at or using.

Scenario Analysis

In order to provide an added element of variability, using the simple example above, you can perform a Scenario Analysis, where you would change values of key variables by certain units given certain assumed scenarios. For instance, you may assume three economic scenarios where unit sales and unit sale prices will vary. Under a good economic condition, unit sales go up to 14 at $11 per unit. Under a nominal economic scenario, units sales will be 10 units at $10 per unit. Under a bleak economic scenario, unit sales decrease to 8 units but prices per unit stays at $10.

		[Good Economy]
Unit Sales	14	
Unit Price	$11	
Total Revenue	$154	
Unit Variable Cost	$5	
Fixed Cost	$20	
Total Cost	$90	
Net Income	$64	

		[Average Economy]
Unit Sales	10	
Unit Price	$10	
Total Revenue	$100	
Unit Variable Cost	$5	
Fixed Cost	$20	
Total Cost	$70	
Net Income	$30	

		[Bad Economy]
Unit Sales	8	
Unit Price	$10	
Total Revenue	$80	
Unit Variable Cost	$5	
Fixed Cost	$20	
Total Cost	$60	
Net Income	$20	

Looking at the Net Income results, we have $64, $30 and $20. The problem here is, the variation is too large. Which condition do I think will most likely occur and which result do I use in my budget forecast for the firm? Although Scenario Analysis is useful in ascertaining the impact of different conditions, both advantageous and adverse, the analysis provides little insight to which result to use.

Point Estimates

This is a simple example of a Point Estimate approach. The issues that arise may include the risk of how confident you are in the unit sales projections, the sales price and variable unit cost.

Since the bottom line Net Income is the key financial performance indicator here, an uncertainty in future sales volume will be impounded into the Net Income calculation. How much faith do you have on your calculation based on a simple point estimate?

Recall the Flaw of Average example where a simple point estimate could yield disastrous conclusions.

Probabilistic Scenario Analysis

We can always assign probabilities that each scenario will occur, creating a Probabilistic Scenario Analysis and simply calculate the Expected Monetary Value (EMV) of the forecasts. The results here are more robust and reliable than a simple scenario analysis since we have collapsed the entire range of potential outcomes of $64, $30 and $20 into a single expected value. This value is what you would expect to get on average.

Simulation Analysis

Looking at the original model, we know that through Sensitivity Analysis, Unit Sales, Unit Price and Unit Variable Cost are three highly uncertain variables. We can then very easily simulate these three unknowns thousands of times (based on certain distributional assumptions) to see what the final Net Income value looks like.

	Probability	Net Income
Good Economy	35%	$64.00
Average Economy	40%	$30.00
Bad Economy	25%	$20.00
EMV		$39.40

Unit Sales	10
Unit Price	$10
Total Revenue	$100

Unit Variable Cost	$5
Fixed Cost	$20
Total Cost	$70

Net Income	$30

By performing the simulation thousands of times, we essentially perform thousands of sensitivity analysis and scenario analysis given different sets of probabilities. These are all set in the original simulation assumptions (types of probability distributions, the parameters of the distributions and which variables to simulate).

The results calculated from the simulation output can then be interpreted as follows:

Discussions about types of distributional assumptions to use and the actual simulation approach will be discussed later.

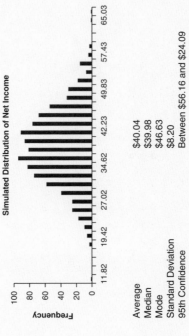

Simulated Distribution of Net Income

Average	$40.04
Median	$39.98
Mode	$46.63
Standard Deviation	$8.20
95th Confidence	Between $56.16 and $24.09

FIGURE 4.3 Point estimates, sensitivity analysis, scenario analysis, probabilistic scenarios, and simulation.

A Simple Simulation Example

We need to perform many simulations to obtain a valid distribution

Mean	15%
Sigma	30%
Timing	Daily ▶
Starting Value	100

Here we see the effects of performing a simulation of stock price paths following a Geometric Brownian Motion model for daily closing prices. Three sample paths are seen here. In reality, thousands of simulations are performed and their distributional properties are analyzed. Frequently, the average closing prices of these thousands of simulations are analyzed, based on these simulated price paths.

time days	normal deviates	value simulated
1	0.0873	100.0000
2	-0.4320	100.2259
3	-0.1389	99.4675
4	-0.4583	99.2652
5	1.7807	98.4649
6	-1.4406	101.9095
7	-0.5577	99.2212
8	0.5277	98.2357
9	-0.4844	99.2838
10	-0.2307	98.4345
11	0.8688	98.0634
12	2.1195	99.7532
13	-1.9756	83.9088
14	1.3734	100.1461
15	-0.8790	102.8517
16	-0.7610	101.2112
17	0.3168	99.8203
18	-0.0511	100.4824
19	0.0653	100.4452
20	-0.6073	100.6301
21	0.6900	99.5368
22	-0.7012	100.9091
23	1.4784	99.6353
24	-0.9195	102.5312
25	-0.3343	100.8184
26	-2.3395	100.2411
27	-1.7831	95.9465
28	-0.3247	92.8103
29	0.5053	92.2958
30	0.0386	93.2409
247	1.0418	93.3652
248	-0.7052	100.9205
249	0.1338	99.6388
250	0.0451	99.9521
		100.0978

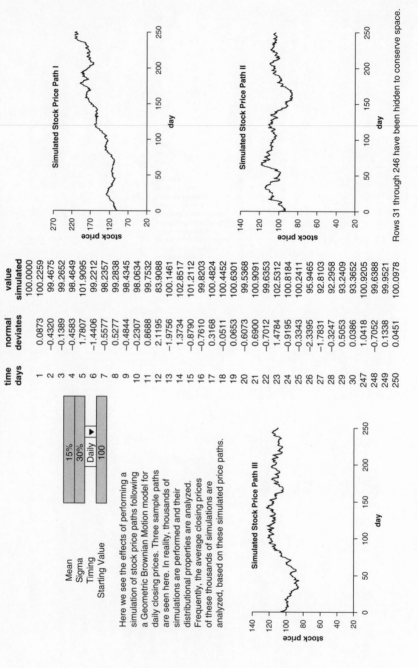

Simulated Stock Price Path I

Simulated Stock Price Path II

Simulated Stock Price Path III

Rows 31 through 246 have been hidden to conserve space.

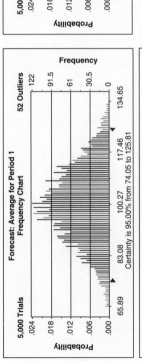

Forecast: Average for Period 20
Frequency Chart

5,000 Trials | 40 Outliers

70.54   88.38   106.23   124.08   141.92
Certainty is 90.00% from 83.53 to 127.51

Forecast: Average for Period 1
Frequency Chart

5,000 Trials | 52 Outliers

65.89   83.08   100.27   117.46   134.65
Certainty is 95.00% from 74.05 to 125.81

Forecast: Average for Period 250
Frequency Chart

5,000 Trials | 47 Outliers

75.46   93.00   110.55   128.10   145.65
Certainty is 99.02% from 77.38 to +Infinity

The thousands of simulated price paths are then tabulated into probability distributions. Here are three sample price paths at three different points in time, for periods 1, 20, and 250. There will be a total of 250 distributions for each time period, which corresponds to the number of trading days a year.

We can also analyze each of these time-specific probability distribution and calculate relevant statistically valid confidence intervals for decision-making purposes.

We can then graph out the confidence intervals together with the expected values of each forecasted time period.

Notice that as time increases, the confidence interval widens since there will be more risk and uncertainty as more time passes.

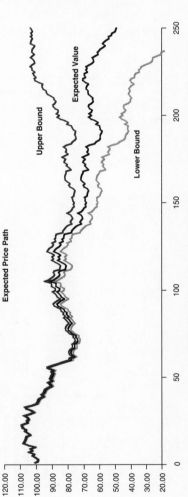

Expected Price Path

Upper Bound

Expected Value

Lower Bound

FIGURE 4.4 Conceptualizing the lognormal distribution.

USING CRYSTAL BALL AND EXCEL
TO PERFORM SIMULATIONS

Simulations can be performed using Excel. However, more advanced simulation packages such as Crystal Ball perform the task more efficiently, and have additional features preset in each simulation. We now present both Monte Carlo parametric simulation and nonparametric bootstrap simulation using Excel and Crystal Ball.

The examples in Figures 4.5 and 4.6 are created using Excel to perform a limited number of simulations on a set of probabilistic assumptions. We assume that having performed a series of scenario analyses, we obtain a set of nine resulting values, complete with their respective probabilities of oc-

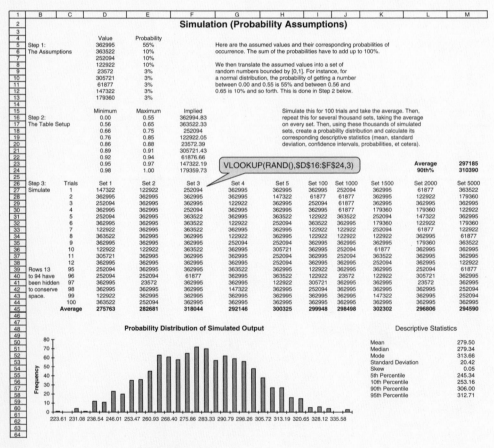

FIGURE 4.5   Simulation using Excel I.

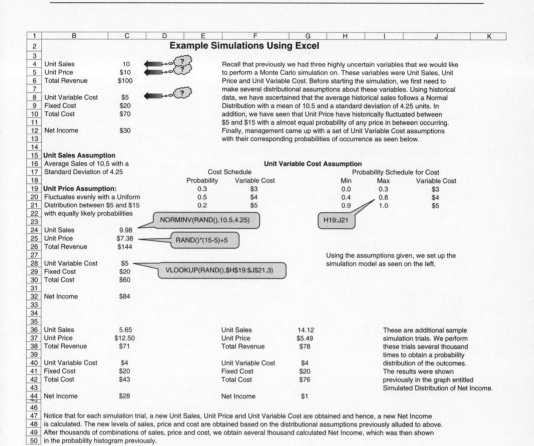

FIGURE 4.6 Simulation using Excel II.

currence. The first step in setting up a simulation in Excel for such a scenario analysis is to understand the function *"RAND( )"* within Excel. This function is simply a random number generator Excel uses to create random numbers from a uniform distribution between 0 and 1. Then translate this 0 to 1 range using the assigned probabilities in our assumption into ranges or bins. For instance, if the value $362,995 occurs with a 55 percent probability, we can create a bin with a range of 0.00 to 0.55. Similarly, we can create a bin range of 0.56 to 0.65 for the next value of $363,522 which occurs 10 percent of the time, and so forth. Based on these ranges and bins, the nonparametric simulation can now be set up.

Figure 4.5 illustrates an example with 5,000 sets of trials. Each set of trials is simulated 100 times. That is, in each simulation trial set, the original numbers are picked randomly with replacement, by using the Excel formula

VLOOKUP(RAND(), $D$16:$F$24, 3), which picks up the third column of data from the D16 to F24 area by matching the results from the *RAND()* function and data from the first column.

The average of the data sampled is then calculated for each trial set. The distribution of these 5,000 trial sets' averages is obtained and the frequency distribution is shown at the bottom of Figure 4.5. According to the Central Limit Theorem, the average of these sample averages will approach the real true mean of the population at the limit. In addition, the distribution will most likely approach normality when a sufficient set of trials are performed. Clearly, running this nonparametric simulation manually in Excel is fairly tedious. An alternative is to use Crystal Ball's Bootstrap tool, which does the same thing but in an infinitely faster and more efficient fashion. Chapter 6, Pandora's Tool Box, illustrates some of these simulation tools in more detail.

Nonparametric simulation is a very powerful tool but it is only applicable if data are available. Clearly, the more data there are, the higher the level of precision and confidence in the simulation results. However, when no data exist or when a valid systematic process underlies the data set (e.g., physics, engineering, economic relationship, etc.) parametric simulation may be more appropriate, where exact probabilistic distributions are used.

The *RAND()* function in Excel is used to generate random numbers for a uniform distribution between 0 and 1. *RAND()*(B-A)+A* is used to generate random numbers for a uniform distribution between A and B. *NORMSINV(RAND())* generates random numbers from a standard normal distribution with mean of zero and variance of one.

Using Excel to perform simulations is easy and effective for simple problems. However, when more complicated problems arise, such as the one to be presented next, the use of more specialized simulation packages is warranted. Crystal Ball is such a package. In the example shown in Figure 4.7, the cells for "Revenues," "Opex," "FCF/EBITDA Multiple," and "Revenue Growth Rates" (dark gray) are the assumption cells, where we enter our distributional input assumptions, such as the type of distribution the variable follows and what the parameters are. For instance, we can say that revenues follow a normal distribution with a mean of $1,010 and a standard deviation of $100, based on analyzing historical revenue data for the firm. The NPV cells are the forecast output cells, that is, the results of these cells are the results we ultimately wish to analyze. Refer to Chapter 5, Peering into the Crystal Ball, for details on setting up and getting started with using the Crystal Ball software.

Monte Carlo Simulation on Financial Analysis

Project A

		2001	2002	2003	2004	2005		
Revenues		$1,010	$1,111	$1,233	$1,384	$1,573	NPV	$126
Opex/Revenue Multiple		0.09	0.10	0.11	0.12	0.13	IRR	15.68%
Operating Expenses		$91	$109	$133	$165	$210	Risk Adjusted Discount Rate	12.00%
EBITDA		$919	$1,002	$1,100	$1,219	$1,363	Growth Rate	3.00%
FCF/EBITDA Multiple		0.20	0.25	0.31	0.40	0.56	Terminal Value	$8,692
Free Cash Flows	($1,200)	$187	$246	$336	$486	$760	Terminal Risk Adjustment	30.00%
Initial Investment	($1,200)						Discounted Terminal Value	$2,341
Revenue Growth Rates		10.00%	11.00%	12.21%	13.70%	15.58%	Terminal to NPV Ratio	18.52
							Payback Period	3.89
							Simulated Risk Value	$390

Project B

		2001	2002	2003	2004	2005		
Revenues		$1,200	$1,404	$1,683	$2,085	$2,700	NPV	$149
Opex/Revenue Multiple		0.09	0.10	0.11	0.12	0.13	IRR	33.74%
Operating Expenses		$108	$138	$181	$249	$361	Risk Adjusted Discount Rate	19.00%
EBITDA		$1,092	$1,266	$1,502	$1,836	$2,340	Growth Rate	3.75%
FCF/EBITDA Multiple		0.10	0.11	0.12	0.14	0.16	Terminal Value	$2,480
Free Cash Flows	($400)	$109	$139	$183	$252	$364	Terminal Risk Adjustment	30.00%
Initial Investment	($400)						Discounted Terminal Value	$668
Revenue Growth Rates		17.00%	19.89%	23.85%	29.53%	38.25%	Terminal to NPV Ratio	4.49
							Payback Period	2.83
							Simulated Risk Value	$122

Project C

		2001	2002	2003	2004	2005		
Revenues		$950	$1,069	$1,219	$1,415	$1,678	NPV	$29
Opex/Revenue Multiple		0.13	0.15	0.17	0.20	0.24	IRR	15.99%
Operating Expenses		$124	$157	$205	$278	$395	Risk Adjusted Discount Rate	15.00%
EBITDA		$827	$912	$1,014	$1,136	$1,283	Growth Rate	5.50%
FCF/EBITDA Multiple		0.20	0.25	0.31	0.40	0.56	Terminal Value	$7,935
Free Cash Flows	($1,100)	$168	$224	$309	$453	$715	Terminal Risk Adjustment	30.00%
Initial Investment	($1,100)						Discounted Terminal Value	$2,137
Revenue Growth Rates		12.50%	14.06%	16.04%	18.61%	22.08%	Terminal to NPV Ratio	74.73
							Payback Period	3.88
							Simulated Risk Value	$53

Project D

		2001	2002	2003	2004	2005		
Revenues		$1,200	$1,328	$1,485	$1,681	$1,932	NPV	$26
Opex/Revenue Multiple		0.08	0.08	0.09	0.09	0.10	IRR	21.57%
Operating Expenses		$90	$107	$129	$159	$200	Risk Adjusted Discount Rate	20.00%
EBITDA		$1,110	$1,221	$1,355	$1,522	$1,732	Growth Rate	1.50%
FCF/EBITDA Multiple		0.14	0.16	0.19	0.23	0.28	Terminal Value	$2,648
Free Cash Flows	($750)	$159	$200	$259	$346	$483	Terminal Risk Adjustment	30.00%
Initial Investment	($750)						Discounted Terminal Value	$713
Revenue Growth Rates		10.67%	11.80%	13.20%	14.94%	17.17%	Terminal to NPV Ratio	26.98
							Payback Period	3.38
							Simulated Risk Value	$56

	Implementation Cost	Sharpe Ratio	Weight	Project Cost	Project NPV	Risk Parameter	Payback Period	Technology Level	Tech Mix
Project A	$1,200	0.02	5.14%	$62	$6	29%	3.89	5	0.26
Project B	$400	0.31	25.27%	$101	$38	15%	2.83	3	0.76
Project C	$1,100	0.19	34.59%	$380	$10	21%	3.88	2	0.69
Project D	$750	0.17	35.00%	$263	$9	17%	3.38	4	1.40
Total	$3,450	0.17	100.00%	$806	$63	28%	3.49	3.5	3.11

Constraints:

	Lower Barrier	Upper Barrier	
Budget	$0	$900	(10 percentile at top 900)
Payback Mix	0.10	1.00	
Technology Mix	0.40	4.00	
Per Project Mix	5%	35%	

FIGURE 4.7   Simulation using Crystal Ball.

FIVE-MINUTE INDUSTRY SPOTLIGHT: COLORADO SCHOOL OF MINES

Crystal Ball Taught for Valuing Properties

For the past 6 years, Dr. Graham Davis has focused his research and teaching efforts on resource economics problems. As an associate professor in the Division of Economics and Business at the Colorado School of Mines, Dr. Davis's priorities include teaching graduate and undergraduate economics and business courses. Dr. Davis uses Crystal

Ball as an instructional tool in the classroom, specifically in regard to valuing mineral and oil and gas properties.

For Dr. Davis and his students, Crystal Ball provides the potential for a more accurate estimate of mine and well value. His students learn that, due to nonlinear tax effects and options to vary production levels, the valuations derived using Monte Carlo simulation technique can be more realistic than those derived from the standard spreadsheet analysis. A Crystal Ball analysis allows for the fact that certain inputs to the cash-flow analysis will vary over time, that these variations may be correlated, and that they impact tax payments and production levels in asymmetric ways.

In class, Dr. Davis shows students the difference between spreadsheet valuations based on expected values of the cash-flow parameters, and those based on a Monte Carlo simulation. In addition to having his students create their own Crystal Ball models, he discusses which distributions are more appropriate for the various uncertain parameters (e.g., capital costs, operating costs, production levels, prices, and reserves). He emphasizes that these distributions must make sense in the context of the valuation, and that a modeler may need to truncate a distribution at lower and upper engineering or financial bounds.

Aside from its utility, Crystal Ball fits easily into the classroom and curriculum. "Crystal Ball is very user-friendly and comes with good documentation and a nice online tutorial," Dr. Davis noted.

According to Dr. Davis, learning Monte Carlo simulation gives his students a competitive advantage in the job market. Learning about simulation as a tool for property analysis makes the students aware of both how to come up with expected cash-flow numbers in net present value (NPV) analysis and the weaknesses inherent in standard spreadsheet analysis. This awareness makes the students less confident and more wary of the "number" they come up with in the standard spreadsheet NPV analysis.

Dr. Davis finds that Crystal Ball's correlation, percentile analysis, and sensitivity analysis features are especially useful for valuing mineral properties. He believes that for the purposes of mining analysis, sensitivity analysis is an improvement on the standard tornado analysis because it allows for several parameters to vary at the same time.

FIVE-MINUTE INDUSTRY SPOTLIGHT: HEWLETT-PACKARD

Putting Marketing Efforts into Focus

Michael Hart works as a marketing product specialist within the market intelligence area of Hewlett-Packard. He has been using Crystal Ball for over 7 years to aid in difficult marketing decisions surrounding the forecasting of demand, new product launches, and product line extensions for Hewlett-Packard's printers. Michael also has recently begun to employ Monte Carlo simulation in an effort to further focus his market research and decision making.

When evaluating the launch of a new product or extending a current product line, significant market research and testing are conducted to obtain a general idea as to the viability of the product in question. The research explores areas such as potential market share, possible sales levels, desirable product attributes, market segmentation, and product usage patterns and is used to forecast future product performance.

Once data are obtained from this research, Michael uses Crystal Ball's distribution-fitting capabilities to fit distributions around the unknown variables in the raw data. In connection with this process, parameters are selected to define lower- and upper-end boundaries. Michael's next step is to perform a Monte Carlo simulation, which provides an associated probability level to potential areas of concern such as possible cannibalization of existing products and optimum pricing points for market entry. Additionally, Michael uses simulation to produce forecasts at a 95 percent confidence level around important financial information such as expected profit and return on investment.

Monte Carlo simulation also has provided Michael with insights he would have difficulty gathering any other way. In particular, he employs the use of tornado charts and the correlation matrix to give him a better indication of the variables that are having the greatest effect on his models. The tornado charts allow Michael to visualize as well as quantify the impact of each variable within his forecast, and the correlation matrix easily allows variables that depend on each other in any way to be correlated. Based on these tools, Michael can isolate "problem" variables and conduct additional market research to confirm the validity of the data. Or he can adjust the assumptions and variables of the model, rerun the simulation, and compare the results.

Michael also has experienced much success in using Monte Carlo simulation to help measure and plan production capacity. This information is important because, when planning production projects, Hewlett-Packard provides suppliers with estimates for the resources necessary to complete the project. Based on these estimates, the suppliers make the necessary production equipment and personnel decisions. Before the use of Monte Carlo simulation, suppliers could be left with unnecessary equipment that was purchased based on unreliable production capacity forecasts.

APPENDIX—SIMULATION

Understanding Probability Distributions

To begin to understand probability, consider this example: You want to look at the distribution of nonexempt wages within one department of a large company. First, you gather raw data—in this case, the wages of each nonexempt employee in the department. Second, you organize the data into a meaningful format and plot the data as a frequency distribution on a chart. To create a frequency distribution, you divide the wages into group intervals and list these intervals on the chart's horizontal axis. Then you list the number or frequency of employees in each interval on the chart's vertical axis. Now you can easily see the distribution of nonexempt wages within the department.

A glance at Figure 4.8 reveals that most of the employees (approximately 60 out of a total of 180) earn from $7.00 to $9.00 per hour. You can chart this data as a probability distribution. A probability distribution shows the number of employees in each interval as a fraction of the total number of employees. To create a probability distribution, you divide the number of employees in each interval by the total number of employees and list the results on the chart's vertical axis.

Figure 4.9 shows you the number of employees in each wage group as a fraction of all employees; you can estimate the likelihood or probability that an employee drawn at random from the whole group earns a wage within a given interval. For example, assuming the same conditions exist at the time

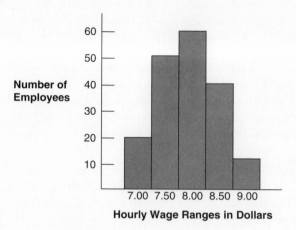

FIGURE 4.8   Frequency histogram I.

the sample was taken, the probability is 0.33 (a one in three chance) that an employee drawn at random from the whole group earns between $8.00 and $8.50 an hour.

Probability distributions are either discrete or continuous. *Discrete probability distributions* describe distinct values, usually integers, with no intermediate values and are shown as a series of vertical bars, such as in the binomial distribution in the earlier example. A discrete distribution, for ex-

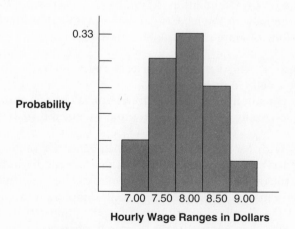

FIGURE 4.9   Frequency histogram II.

ample, might describe the number of heads in four flips of a coin as 0, 1, 2, 3, or 4. *Continuous distributions* are actually mathematical abstractions because they assume the existence of every possible intermediate value between two numbers. That is, a continuous distribution assumes there is an infinite number of values between any two points in the distribution. However, in many situations, you can effectively use a continuous distribution to approximate a discrete distribution even though the continuous model does not necessarily describe the situation exactly.

Selecting a Probability Distribution

Plotting data is one guide to selecting a probability distribution. The following steps provide another process for selecting probability distributions that best describe the uncertain variables in your spreadsheets.

- Look at the variable in question. List everything you know about the conditions surrounding this variable. You might be able to gather valuable information about the uncertain variable from historical data. If historical data are not available, use your own judgment, based on experience, listing everything you know about the uncertain variable.
- Review the descriptions of the probability distributions.
- Select the distribution that characterizes this variable. A distribution characterizes a variable when the conditions of the distribution match those of the variable.

Sampling Methods

During each trial of a simulation, Crystal Ball selects a random value for each assumption in your model. Crystal Ball selects these values based on the sampling options. The two sampling methods are:

1. Monte Carlo, which randomly selects any valid value from each assumption's defined distribution.
2. Latin Hypercube, which randomly selects values but spreads the random values evenly over each assumption's defined distribution.

Monte Carlo   With Monte Carlo, Crystal Ball generates random values for each assumption's probability distribution that are totally independent. In other words, the random value selected for one trial has no effect on the next random value generated. Using Monte Carlo sampling to approximate the true shape of the distribution requires a larger number of trials than does Latin Hypercube. Use Monte Carlo sampling when you want to simulate real-world, what-if scenarios for your spreadsheet model.

Latin Hypercube   With Latin Hypercube sampling, Crystal Ball divides each assumption's probability distribution into nonoverlapping segments, each having equal probability. Crystal Ball then selects a random assumption value for each segment according to the segment's probability distribution. The collection of values forms the Latin Hypercube sample. After Crystal Ball uses all the values from the sample, it generates a new batch of values. Latin Hypercube sampling is generally more precise than conventional Monte Carlo simulation when calculating simulation statistics, because the entire range of the distribution is sampled more evenly and consistently. Thus, with Latin Hypercube sampling, you do not need as many trials to achieve the same statistical accuracy as with Monte Carlo sampling. The added expense of this method is the extra memory required to hold the full sample for each assumption while the simulation runs. Use Latin Hypercube sampling when you are concerned primarily with the accuracy of the simulation statistics.

Confidence Intervals

Monte Carlo simulation is a technique that uses random sampling to estimate model results. Statistics computed on these results will always contain some kind of measurement error. A confidence interval (CI) is a bound calculated around a statistic that attempts to measure this error with a given level of probability. For example, a 95 percent CI around the mean statistic is defined as a 95 percent chance that the mean will be contained within the specified interval. Conversely, there is a 5 percent chance that the mean will lie outside the interval.

For most statistics, the CI is symmetric around the statistic so that $X = (CI_{max} - Mean) = (Mean - CI_{min})$. This result lets you make statements of confidence such as "the mean will equal the estimated mean plus or minus X with 95 percent probability." Confidence intervals are important for determining the accuracy of statistics and, hence, the accuracy of the simulation. Generally speaking, as more trials are calculated, the CI narrows and the statistics become more accurate.

Following is a detailed listing of the different types of probability distributions that can be used in Monte Carlo simulation. This listing is included in this appendix for the reader's reference.

Uniform Distribution

With the uniform distribution, all values fall between the minimum and maximum occur with equal likelihood.

Conditions   The three conditions underlying the uniform distribution are:

1. The minimum value is fixed.
2. The maximum value is fixed.
3. All values between the minimum and maximum occur with equal likelihood.

The mathematical constructs for the uniform distribution are as follows:

$$f(x) = \frac{1}{Max - Min} \qquad \text{for all values such that } Min < Max$$

$$\text{mean} = \frac{Min + Max}{2} \text{ and variance } = \frac{(Max - Min)^2}{12}$$

Maximum value (*Max*) and minimum value (*Min*) are the distributional parameters.

Normal Distribution

The normal distribution is the most important distribution in probability theory because it describes many natural phenomena, such as people's IQs or heights. Decision makers can use the normal distribution to describe uncertain variables such as the inflation rate or the future price of gasoline.

Conditions   The three conditions underlying the normal distribution are:

1. Some value of the uncertain variable is the most likely (the mean of the distribution).
2. The uncertain variable could as likely be above the mean as it could be below the mean (symmetrical about the mean).
3. The uncertain variable is more likely to be in the vicinity of the mean than further away.

The mathematical constructs for the normal distribution are as follows:

$$f(x) = \frac{1}{\sqrt{2\pi}\sigma} e^{-\frac{(x-\mu)^2}{2\sigma^2}} \qquad \text{for all values of } x \text{ and } \mu; \text{ while } \sigma > 0$$

$$\text{mean} = \mu \text{ and variance} = \sigma^2$$

Mean (*μ*) and standard deviation (*σ*) are the distributional parameters.

Triangular Distribution

The triangular distribution describes a situation where you know the minimum, maximum, and most-likely values to occur. For example, you could describe the number of cars sold per week when past sales show the minimum, maximum, and usual number of cars sold.

Conditions   The three conditions underlying the triangular distribution are:

1. The minimum number of items is fixed.
2. The maximum number of items is fixed.
3. The most likely number of items falls between the minimum and maximum values, forming a triangular-shaped distribution, which shows that values near the minimum and maximum are less likely to occur than those near the most-likely value.

The mathematical constructs for the triangular distribution are as follows:

$$f(x) = \begin{cases} \dfrac{2(x - Min)}{(Max - Min)(Likely - Min)} & \text{for } Min < x < Likely \\[3mm] \dfrac{2(Max - x)}{(Max - Min)(Max - Likely)} & \text{for } Likely < x < Max \end{cases}$$

Minimum value (*Min*), most-likely value (*Likely*), and maximum value (*Max*) are the distributional parameters.

Binomial Distribution

The binomial distribution describes the number of times a particular event occurs in a fixed number of trials, such as the number of heads in 10 flips of a coin or the number of defective items out of 50 items chosen.

Conditions   The three conditions underlying the binomial distribution are:

1. For each trial, only two outcomes are possible.
2. The trials are independent—what happens in the first trial does not affect the next trial.
3. The probability of an event occurring remains the same from trial to trial.

The mathematical constructs for the binomial distribution are as follows:

$$P(x) = \frac{n!}{x!\,(n-x)!}\, p^x (1-p)^{(n-x)} \quad \text{for } n > 0;\ x = 0,\ 1,\ 2,\ \ldots\ n;\ p > 0$$

$$\text{mean} = np \text{ and variance} = np(1-p)$$

Probability of success (p) and the number of total trials (n) are the distributional parameters. The number of successful trials is denoted x.

Poisson Distribution

The Poisson distribution describes the number of times an event occurs in a given interval, such as the number of telephone calls per minute or the number of errors per page in a document.

Conditions The three conditions underlying the Poisson distribution are:

1. The number of possible occurrences in any interval is unlimited.
2. The occurrences are independent. The number of occurrences in one interval does not affect the number of occurrences in other intervals.
3. The average number of occurrences must remain the same from interval to interval.

The mathematical constructs for the Poisson are as follows:

$$P(x) = \frac{e^{-\lambda} \lambda^x}{x!} \quad \text{for } x \text{ and } \lambda > 0$$

$$\text{mean and variance are both} = \lambda$$

Rate (λ) is the only distributional parameter.

Geometric Distribution

The geometric distribution describes the number of trials until the first successful occurrence, such as the number of times you need to spin a roulette wheel before you win.

Conditions The three conditions underlying the geometric distribution are:

1. The number of trials is not fixed.
2. The trials continue until the first success.
3. The probability of success is the same from trial to trial.

The mathematical constructs for the geometric distribution are as follows:

$$P(x) = p(1 - p)^{x-1} \qquad \text{for } p > 0; \ x = 1, \ 2, \ \ldots, \ n$$

$$\text{mean} = \frac{1}{p} \text{ and variance } = \frac{1-p}{p^2}$$

Probability of success (p) and the number of successful trials (x) are the distributional parameters.

Hypergeometric Distribution

The hypergeometric distribution is similar to the binomial distribution in that both describe the number of times a particular event occurs in a fixed number of trials. The difference is that binomial distribution trials are independent, whereas hypergeometric distribution trials change the probability for each subsequent trial and are called "trials without replacement." For example, suppose a box of manufactured parts is known to contain some defective parts. You choose a part from the box, find it is defective, and remove the part from the box. If you choose another part from the box, the probability that it is defective is somewhat lower than for the first part because you have removed a defective part. If you had replaced the defective part, the probabilities would have remained the same, and the process would have satisfied the conditions for a binomial distribution.

Conditions The three conditions underlying the hypergeometric distribution are:

1. The total number of items or elements (the population size) is a fixed number, a finite population. The population size must be less than or equal to 1,750.
2. The sample size (the number of trials) represents a portion of the population.
3. The known initial probability of success in the population changes after each trial.

The mathematical constructs for the hypergeometric distribution are as follows:

$$P(x) = \frac{\dfrac{(N_x)!}{x!\,(N_x - x)!} \dfrac{(N - N_x)!}{(n - x)!\,(N - N_x - n + x)!}}{\dfrac{N!}{n!\,(N - n)!}}$$

$$\text{for } x = Max(n - (N - N_x), 0), \ \ldots, \ Min(n, N_x)$$

Number of items in the population (N), trials sampled (n), and number of items in the population that have the successful trait (N_x) are the distributional parameters. The number of successful trials is denoted x.

Lognormal Distribution

The lognormal distribution is widely used in situations where values are positively skewed, for example, in financial analysis for security valuation or in real estate for property valuation.

Stock prices are usually positively skewed rather than normally (symmetrically) distributed. Stock prices exhibit this trend because they cannot fall below the lower limit of zero but might increase to any price without limit. Similarly, real estate prices illustrate positive skewness as property values cannot become negative.

Conditions   The three conditions underlying the lognormal distribution are:

1. The uncertain variable can increase without limits but cannot fall below zero.
2. The uncertain variable is positively skewed, with most of the values near the lower limit.
3. The natural logarithm of the uncertain variable yields a normal distribution.

Generally, if the coefficient of variability is greater than 30 percent, use a lognormal distribution. Otherwise, use the normal distribution.

The mathematical constructs for the lognormal distribution are as follows:

$$f(x) = \frac{1}{x\sqrt{2\pi}\,\ln(\sigma)}\, e^{-\frac{[\ln(x)-\ln(\mu)]^2}{2[\ln(\sigma)]^2}} \qquad \text{for } x > 0;\ \mu > 0 \text{ and } \sigma > 0$$

$$\text{mean } = \mu + \frac{\sigma^2}{2} \text{ and variance } = (\sigma^2 + \mu^2)(\mu^2 - 1)$$

Mean (μ) and standard deviation (σ) are the distributional parameters.

Lognormal Parameter Sets   By default, the lognormal distribution uses the arithmetic mean and standard deviation. For applications for which historical data are available, it is more appropriate to use either the logarithmic mean and standard deviation, or the geometric mean and standard deviation.

Exponential Distribution

The exponential distribution is widely used to describe events recurring at random points in time, such as the time between failures of electronic equipment or the time between arrivals at a service booth. It is related to the Poisson distribution, which describes the number of occurrences of an event in a given interval of time. An important characteristic of the exponential distribution is the "memoryless" property, which means that the future lifetime of a given object has the same distribution, regardless of the time it existed. In other words, time has no effect on future outcomes.

Condition   The condition underlying the exponential distribution is: The exponential distribution describes the amount of time between occurrences.

The mathematical constructs for the exponential distribution are as follows:

$$f(x) = \lambda e^{-\lambda x} \qquad \text{for } x \geq 0; \ \lambda > 0$$

$$\text{mean} = \lambda \text{ and variance} = \lambda^2$$

Success rate (λ) is the only distributional parameter. The number of successful trials is denoted x.

Weibull Distribution (Rayleigh Distribution)

The Weibull distribution describes data resulting from life and fatigue tests. It is commonly used to describe failure time in reliability studies as well as the breaking strengths of materials in reliability and quality control tests. Weibull distributions are also used to represent various physical quantities, such as wind speed.

The Weibull distribution is a family of distributions that can assume the properties of several other distributions. For example, depending on the shape parameter you define, the Weibull distribution can be used to model the exponential and Rayleigh distributions, among others. The Weibull distribution is very flexible. When the Weibull shape parameter is equal to 1.0, the Weibull distribution is identical to the exponential distribution. The Weibull location parameter lets you set up an exponential distribution to start at a location other than 0.0. When the shape parameter is less than 1.0, the Weibull distribution becomes a steeply declining curve. A manufacturer might find this effect useful in describing part failures during a burn-in period.

The mathematical constructs for the Weibull distribution are as follows:

$$f(x) = \frac{\beta}{\alpha}\left[\frac{x - L}{\alpha}\right]^{\beta-1} e^{-\left(\frac{x-L}{\alpha}\right)^{\beta}} \qquad \text{for } x \geq L$$

$$\text{mean} = \alpha\Gamma(1 + \beta^{-1}) \text{ and variance} = \alpha^2[\Gamma(1 + 2\beta^{-1}) - \Gamma^2(1 + \beta^{-1})]$$

Location (L), scale (α), and shape (β) are the distributional parameters, and Γ is the Gamma function.

Beta Distribution

The beta distribution is very flexible and is commonly used to represent variability over a fixed range. One of the more important applications of the beta distribution is its use as a conjugate distribution for the parameter of a Bernoulli distribution. In this application, the beta distribution is used to represent the uncertainty in the probability of occurrence of an event. It is also used to describe empirical data and predict the random behavior of percentages and fractions.

The value of the beta distribution lies in the wide variety of shapes it can assume when you vary the two parameters, alpha and beta. If the parameters are equal, the distribution is symmetrical. If either parameter is 1 and the other parameter is greater than 1, the distribution is J-shaped. If alpha is less than beta, the distribution is said to be positively skewed (most of the values are near the minimum value). If alpha is greater than beta, the distribution is negatively skewed (most of the values are near the maximum value). Because the beta distribution is very complex, the methods for determining the parameters of the distribution are beyond the scope of this appendix.

Conditions   The two conditions underlying the beta distribution are:

1. The uncertain variable is a random value between 0 and a positive value.
2. The shape of the distribution can be specified using two positive values.

The mathematical constructs for the beta distribution are as follows:

$$f(x) = \frac{\left(\dfrac{x}{s}\right)^{(\alpha-1)}\left(1-\dfrac{x}{s}\right)^{(\beta-1)}}{\left[\dfrac{\Gamma(\alpha)\Gamma(\beta)}{\Gamma(\alpha+\beta)}\right]} \qquad \text{for } \alpha > 0; \beta > 0; 0 < x < s$$

$$\text{mean} = \frac{\alpha}{\alpha+\beta} \text{ and variance} = \frac{\alpha\beta}{(\alpha+\beta)^2(1+\alpha+\beta)}$$

Alpha (α), beta (β) and scale (s) are the distributional parameters, and Γ is the Gamma function.

Gamma Distribution (Erlang and Chi-Square)

The gamma distribution applies to a wide range of physical quantities and is related to other distributions: lognormal, exponential, Pascal, Erlang, Poisson, and chi-square. It is used in meteorological processes to represent pollutant concentrations and precipitation quantities. The gamma distribution is also used to measure the time between the occurrence of events when the event process is not completely random. Other applications of the gamma distribution include inventory control, economic theory, and insurance risk theory.

Conditions The gamma distribution is most often used as the distribution of the amount of time until the rth occurrence of an event in a Poisson process. When used in this fashion, the three conditions underlying the gamma distribution are:

1. The number of possible occurrences in any unit of measurement is not limited to a fixed number.
2. The occurrences are independent. The number of occurrences in one unit of measurement does not affect the number of occurrences in other units.
3. The average number of occurrences must remain the same from unit to unit.

The mathematical constructs for the gamma distribution are as follows:

$$f(x) = \frac{\left(\dfrac{x-L}{\beta}\right)^{\alpha-1} e^{-\frac{x-L}{\beta}}}{\Gamma(\alpha)\beta} \qquad \text{for } x > L; \text{ with any value of } \alpha \text{ and } \beta$$

Alpha (α), beta (β) and location (L) are the distributional parameters, and Γ is the Gamma function.

Logistic Distribution

The logistic distribution is commonly used to describe growth, that is, the size of a population expressed as a function of a time variable. It also can be used to describe chemical reactions and the course of growth for a population or individual.

The mathematical constructs for the logistic distribution are as follows:

$$f(x) = \frac{e^{\frac{x-\mu}{\alpha}}}{\alpha \left[1 + e^{\frac{x-\mu}{\alpha}} \right]^2} \qquad \text{for any value of } \alpha \text{ and } \mu$$

$$\text{mean} = \mu \text{ and variance} = \frac{1}{3}\pi^3\alpha^2$$

Mean (μ) and scale (α) are the distributional parameters.

Calculating Parameters   There are two standard parameters for the logistic distribution: mean and scale. The mean parameter is the average value, which for this distribution is the same as the mode, because this is a symmetrical distribution. After you select the mean parameter, you can estimate the scale parameter. The scale parameter is a number greater than 0. The larger the scale parameter, the greater the variance.

Pareto Distribution

The Pareto distribution is widely used for the investigation of distributions associated with such empirical phenomena as city population sizes, the occurrence of natural resources, the size of companies, personal incomes, stock price fluctuations, and error clustering in communication circuits.

The mathematical constructs for the Pareto are as follows:

$$f(x) = \frac{\beta L^\beta}{x^{(1+\beta)}} \qquad \text{for } x > L$$

$$\text{mean} = \frac{\beta L}{\beta - 1} \text{ and variance} = \frac{\beta L^2}{(\beta - 1)^2 (\beta - 2)}$$

Location (L) and shape (β) are the distributional parameters.

Calculating Parameters   There are two standard parameters for the Pareto distribution: location and shape. The location parameter is the lower bound for the variable. After you select the location parameter, you can estimate the shape parameter. The shape parameter is a number greater than 0, usually greater than 1. The larger the shape parameter, the smaller the variance and the thicker the right tail of the distribution.

Extreme Value Distribution

The extreme value distribution (Type 1) is commonly used to describe the largest value of a response over a period of time, for example, in flood flows, rainfall, and earthquakes. Other applications include the breaking strengths of materials, construction design, and aircraft loads and tolerances. The extreme value distribution is also known as the Gumbel distribution.

The mathematical constructs for the extreme value distribution are as follows:

$$f(x) = \frac{1}{\alpha} ze^{-Z} \quad \text{where } z = e^{\frac{x-m}{\alpha}} \quad \text{for } \alpha > 0; \text{ and any value of } x \text{ and } m$$

Mode (m) and scale (α) are the distributional parameters.

Calculating Parameters   There are two standard parameters for the extreme value distribution: mode and scale. The mode parameter is the most likely value for the variable (the highest point on the probability distribution). After you select the mode parameter, you can estimate the scale parameter. The scale parameter is a number greater than 0. The larger the scale parameter, the greater the variance.

Negative Binomial Distribution

The negative binomial distribution is useful for modeling the distribution of the number of trials until the rth successful occurrence, such as the number of sales calls you need to make to close a total of 10 orders. It is essentially a *super*distribution of the geometric distribution.

Conditions   The three conditions underlying the negative binomial distribution are:

1. The number of trials is not fixed.
2. The trials continue until the rth success.
3. The probability of success is the same from trial to trial.

The mathematical constructs for the negative binomial distribution are as follows:

$$P(x) = \frac{(x-1)!}{(\beta-1)!\,(x-\beta)!} \, p^{\beta}(1-p)^{x-\beta} \qquad \text{for } x = \beta,\ \beta+1,\ \ldots; \text{ and } p > 0$$

$$\text{mean} = \frac{\beta}{p} \text{ and variance} = \frac{\beta(1-p)}{p^2}$$

Probability of success (p) and shape (β) are the distributional parameters.

QUESTIONS

1. Compare and contrast parametric and nonparametric simulation.
2. What is a stochastic process (e.g., Brownian Motion)?
3. What does the *RAND()* function do in Excel?
4. What does the *NORMSINV()* function do in Excel?
5. What happens when both functions are used together, that is, *NORM-SINV(RAND())*?
6. For modeling each of the following, determine which distribution(s) is/are most applicable and explain why. (Refer to the chapter Appendix for the different distributions).
   a. Number of phone calls a minute or number of errors in a page.
   b. Number of defective items in a batch of 100 items.
   c. Real estate prices and stock prices.
   d. Measuring earthquakes and rainfall frequency.
   e. Number of sales calls required to get to the 10th successful sale.
   f. Height, weight, and IQ of individuals.

CHAPTER 5

Peering into the Crystal Ball

T his chapter provides the novice risk analyst an introduction to the Crystal Ball software for performing Monte Carlo simulation. The chapter starts off by illustrating what Crystal Ball does and what steps are taken in a Monte Carlo simulation, as well as some of the more basic elements in a simulation, including the resulting forecast distribution charts. The chapter ends with a step-by-step example showing how to use the software for performing a forecast of magazine sales and how to interpret the results.

THE BASICS OF CRYSTAL BALL SOFTWARE

Figure 5.1 illustrates the modeling process and where Crystal Ball fits in. As with any model, there is a set of inputs, a set of calculations, and a set of results. In simulation lingo, the inputs are the *assumptions*, the calculations are the simulation *trials*, and the outputs are the *forecasts*, *charts*, and *reports*. Crystal Ball software works together with Microsoft Excel as an add-in, specifically created to perform Monte Carlo simulation, optimization, and forecasting with a few mouse clicks.

In order to use Crystal Ball, a few simple steps have to be followed (Figures 5.2 and 5.3). The first is the creation of an Excel-based model—notice that the software is an add-in for Excel; thus, simulation can only be run if there is an existing Excel model. The minimum requirements for an Excel model are some data inputs and outputs calculated with equations using these inputs. The next step is to add Monte Carlo simulation. The minimum requirements for a simulation to run are the introduction of assumptions on inputs and forecasts on outputs in the existing Excel model. Assumptions can only be defined on simple numerical cells, whereas forecasts are usually defined on cells with equations. The third step is optional, where the simulation preferences are set. These preferences include setting the number of simulation trials to run, error handling, sensitivities, precision control, and so forth. The fourth step is to run the simulation, and the last step is

Crystal Ball
 – An Excel add-in to perform Monte Carlo simulation
 – Enables use of a gallery of input distributions
 – Enables quick what-if analyses

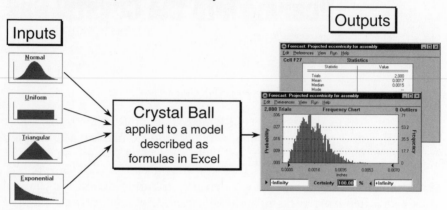

FIGURE 5.1   What is Crystal Ball?

simply to collect and interpret the results. Figure 5.3 illustrates similar steps graphically.

After running a Monte Carlo simulation, results are provided in a forecast window. Figure 5.4 illustrates the many different parts of a forecast window. In addition, the forecast window itself has multiple views, as shown in Figure 5.5. The five views are the statistics view (showing all the

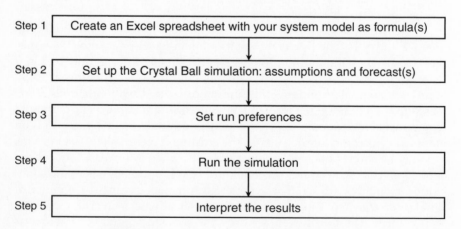

FIGURE 5.2   Steps in a Crystal Ball simulation I.

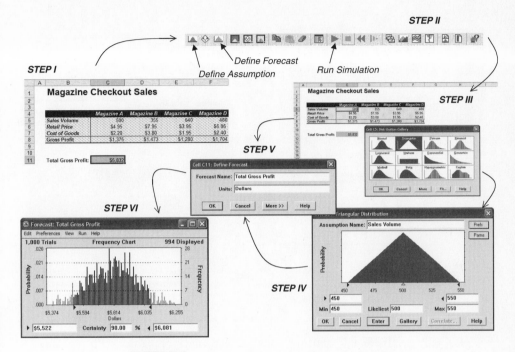

FIGURE 5.3 Steps in a Crystal Ball simulation II.

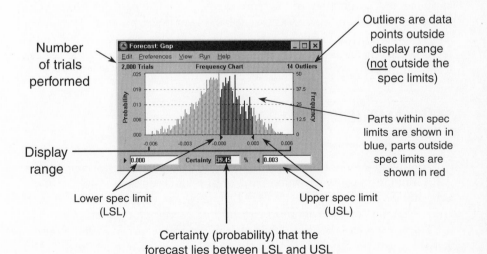

FIGURE 5.4 Forecast window in Crystal Ball.

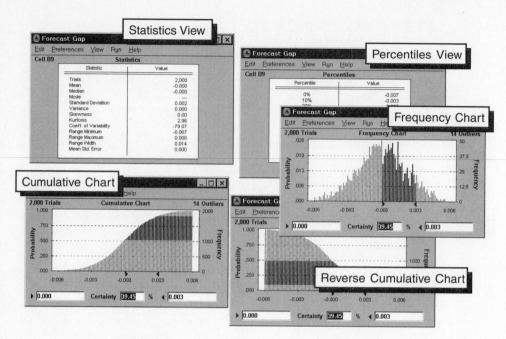

FIGURE 5.5   Forecast window views in Crystal Ball.

relevant forecast statistics of the variable of interest), percentiles view
(showing the percentiles of the forecast variable), frequency chart view
(showing the probabilities of occurrence and confidence intervals of the variable of interest), cumulative chart view (showing the cumulative probabilities of occurrence), and reverse cumulative chart view (showing the reverse
of the cumulative probabilities of occurrence).

GETTING STARTED WITH CRYSTAL BALL
SOFTWARE

The following exercise helps you get started using the Crystal Ball Monte
Carlo simulation software. Make sure Crystal Ball is already installed on the
computer from the enclosed CD-ROM. Start by opening an example spread-
sheet. Click on *Start | Programs | Crystal Ball | Examples* (Figure 5.6).

The software comes with multiple sample Excel spreadsheets. Double-
click on *Magazine Sales.xls* to start the example as shown in Figure 5.7. The
Crystal Ball splash screen in Figure 5.8 should appear momentarily.

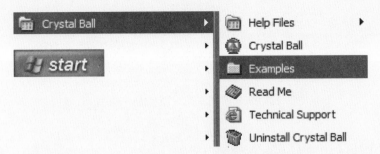

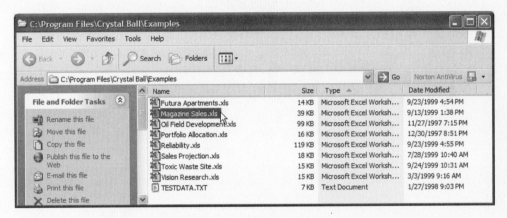

FIGURE 5.6 Location of the Crystal Ball software's example files.

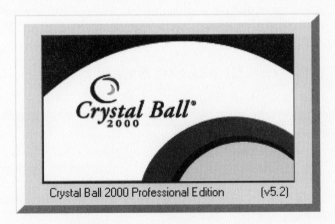

FIGURE 5.7 Contents for Crystal Ball software's example folder.

FIGURE 5.8 Crystal Ball splash screen.

Define Forecast

Define Assumption   Run Simulation

FIGURE 5.9   Crystal Ball icon bar.

THE SIMULATION ENVIRONMENT

The Crystal Ball toolbar shown in Figure 5.9 should appear in Microsoft Excel. To get started and to run a simple simulation, we are concerned with only three functions: *Define Assumption*, *Define Forecast*, and *Run Simulation* as seen in Figure 5.9. Every Monte Carlo simulation analysis requires a minimum of these three sets of commands. (If the toolbar or splash screen does not appear, click on *Tools | Add-Ins*. Then make sure the check-box beside *Crystal Ball* is selected, and click *OK*).

Defining an assumption means selecting a cell in Excel populated with a simple numerical entry and assigning a relevant distribution to it. Defining a forecast means selecting a cell with a numerical equation and requesting that Crystal Ball captures its output results. Running a simulation means the program initiates a Monte Carlo simulation of thousands of trials (depending on the prespecified number of trials to run), randomly selecting numbers from the assigned distribution, and keying these random numbers into the selected assumption cell. The resulting calculations in the forecast cell are then captured in the software.

The example opened looks at the levels of magazine checkout sales as seen in Figure 5.10. Four different magazines are listed, complete with the

	A	B	C	D	E	F
1	**Magazine Checkout Sales**					
2						
3						
4			*Magazine A*	*Magazine B*	*Magazine C*	*Magazine D*
5	*Sales Volume*		500	355	640	480
6	*Retail Price*		$4.95	$7.95	$3.95	$5.95
7	*Cost of Goods*		$2.20	$3.80	$1.95	$2.40
8	Gross Profit		$1,375	$1,473	$1,280	$1,704
9						
10						
11	Total Gross Profit:		$5,832			

FIGURE 5.10   Magazine checkout sales example Excel file.

sales volume, retail price, and cost of goods. The resulting gross profit is then calculated. The sum of the gross profits for each magazine is calculated as $5,832.

CREATING A SIMULATION

Now suppose that the projected sales volumes (the number of magazines sold) for Magazines A and B are unknown in some future period. We can perform Monte Carlo simulation on these sales volumes. First, select cell C5, which has the sales volume forecast (Figure 5.10). Click on *Define Assumption* on the Crystal Ball toolbar (Figure 5.9). A Distribution Gallery will appear, with a series of different distributions. For simplicity, assume that Magazine A's sales volume follows a triangular distribution. Select *Triangular* and click *OK* (Figure 5.11).

You will be prompted to enter the parameters in the triangular distribution (Figure 5.12). Suppose you know from historical sales that the worst-case scenario sales volume is 450 units, average and most-likely sales volume is 500 units, and a best-case scenario is 550 units. Enter the appropriate values and click *OK*. Next, select cell D5 for the sales volume forecast of Magazine B. This time, select the *Normal* distribution as seen in Figure 5.13.

You can now enter the mean and standard deviation of the normal distribution or, alternatively, you can click on the *Parms* button to locate the

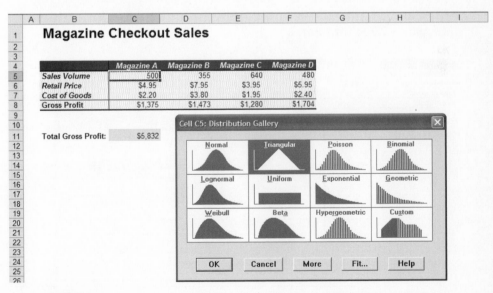

FIGURE 5.11 Magazine checkout sales with Crystal Ball's distribution gallery.

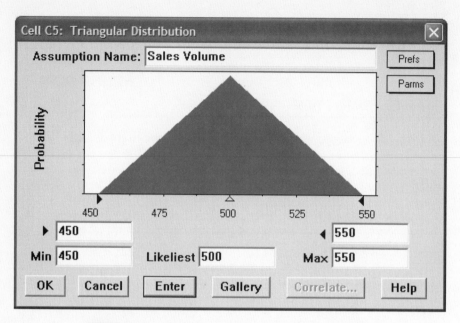

FIGURE 5.12   Triangular distribution for sales volume.

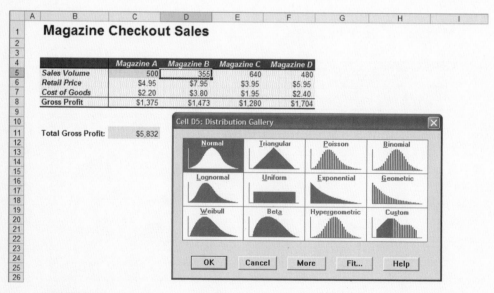

FIGURE 5.13   Magazine checkout sales with Crystal Ball assumptions defined.

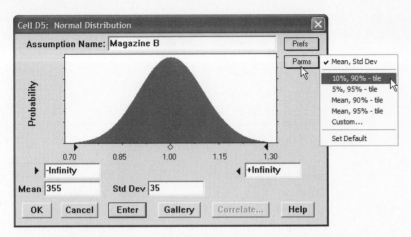

FIGURE 5.14   Crystal Ball's alternate parameters function.

gallery of alternate parameters to enter. Select the *10%, 90%-tile* to change the input parameters to the 10th and 90th percentile (Figure 5.14). That is, you can now input the relevant historical sales volumes that occurred the lowest 10 percent of the time, and the corresponding sales volume that occurred the highest 10 percent of the time. To put it another way, 80 percent of the time, your historical sales volume was between 300 and 400 units (Figure 5.15).

Now that you have assigned distributions to the unknown variables, you need to define the forecast of your analysis. Select cell C11, which has the total gross profit of the magazine sales. Then, click on *Define Forecast*

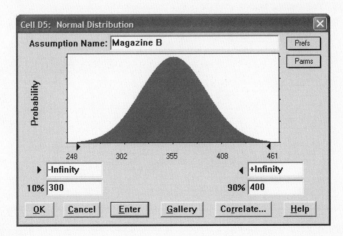

FIGURE 5.15   Crystal Ball's alternate parameters with 10th and 90th percentiles.

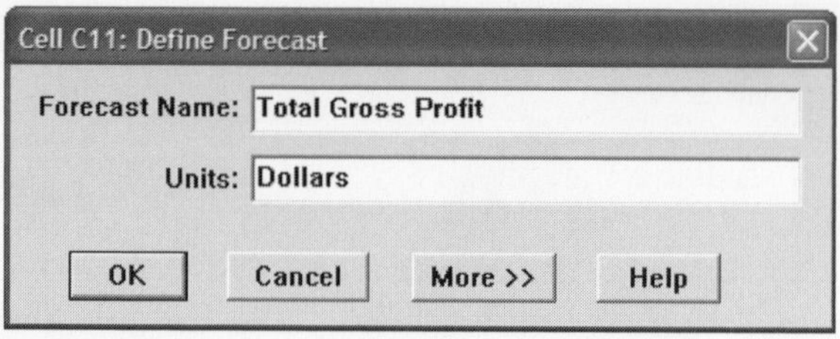

Cell C11: Define Forecast ☒

Forecast Name: Total Gross Profit

Units: Dollars

[OK]   [Cancel]   [More >>]   [Help]

FIGURE 5.16   Defining a forecast cell in Crystal Ball.

in the Crystal Ball toolbar. Enter in the relevant name and units for this forecast and click *OK* (Figure 5.16).

You are now ready to run a simulation. Click on the *Run Simulation* icon in Figure 5.9. The Excel spreadsheet should now come to life and a forecast chart will appear. If the forecast chart does not appear, simply click on *Run | Forecast Windows | Open All Forecasts*.

INTERPRETING THE SIMULATION RESULTS

Once the simulation process is complete, you can type 90 in the Certainty box of the forecast chart and hit enter on your keyboard. The 90 percent confidence interval now appears (Figure 5.17), which indicates that 90 per-

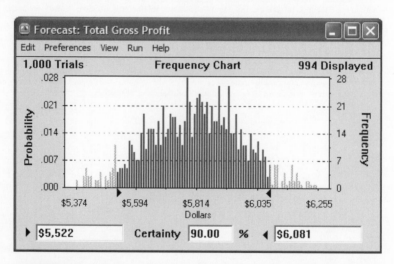

FIGURE 5.17   Forecast chart for total gross profit with a 90 percent confidence interval.

cent of the time the total gross profit of selling four magazines where the sales volume of the first two magazines is uncertain falls between $5,522 and $6,081.

In addition, you can type in a gross revenue value, say, 6,000 on the right confidence tail, hit enter, and obtain an 86.80 percent certainty level.[1] This certainty level means that there is an 86.80 percent chance that total gross revenues will be below $6,000 or a 13.20 percent chance total gross revenues will exceed $6,000 (Figure 5.18). Similarly, you can drag the certainty grabbers (black triangle straddling the horizontal axis in Figure 5.19) to obtain a particular certainty level or dollar confidence value. For instance, the Value at Risk is $5,444, such that 2 percent of the time, the worst-case scenario indicates that total gross profits will be at least this level.

Other output statistics are also available by hitting the spacebar on your keyboard or clicking on *View | Statistics*. For instance, the table in Figure 5.20 provides the basic statistics of the simulated total gross profit. Refer to Chapter 2, From Risk to Riches, for details on these statistics.

Clearly, the example illustrated here is fairly simplistic in nature but it provides a good framework and basic building blocks for more detailed simulation analysis. The following chapters explore the applications of Monte Carlo simulation in more detail through a step-by-step application of simulation, forecasting, and optimization tools. Refer to Chapter 15, The Warning Signs, for a recap of these advanced analytical tools. Chapter 15 also points out some of the potential errors an analyst may make while using these power tools and how management can spot these pitfalls and challenge the assumptions and analytics used.

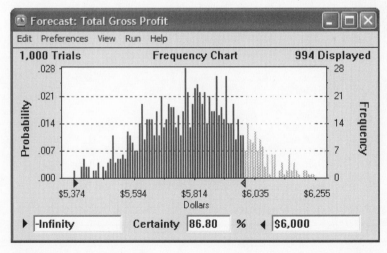

FIGURE 5.18 Forecast chart showing the probability of less than $6,000.

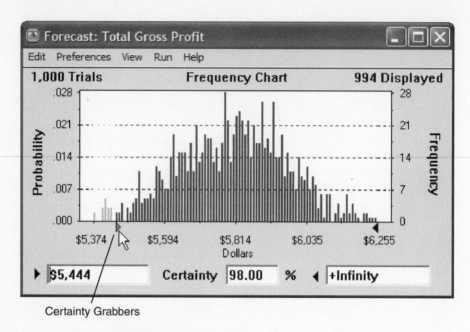

FIGURE 5.19 Forecast chart's certainty grabbers.

Forecast: Total Gross Profit

Edit Preferences View Run Help

Cell C11 — Statistics

Statistic	Value
Trials	1,000
Mean	$5,809
Median	$5,816
Mode	---
Standard Deviation	$172
Variance	$29,667
Skewness	-0.04
Kurtosis	2.93
Coeff. of Variability	0.03
Range Minimum	$5,268
Range Maximum	$6,455
Range Width	$1,187
Mean Std. Error	$5.45

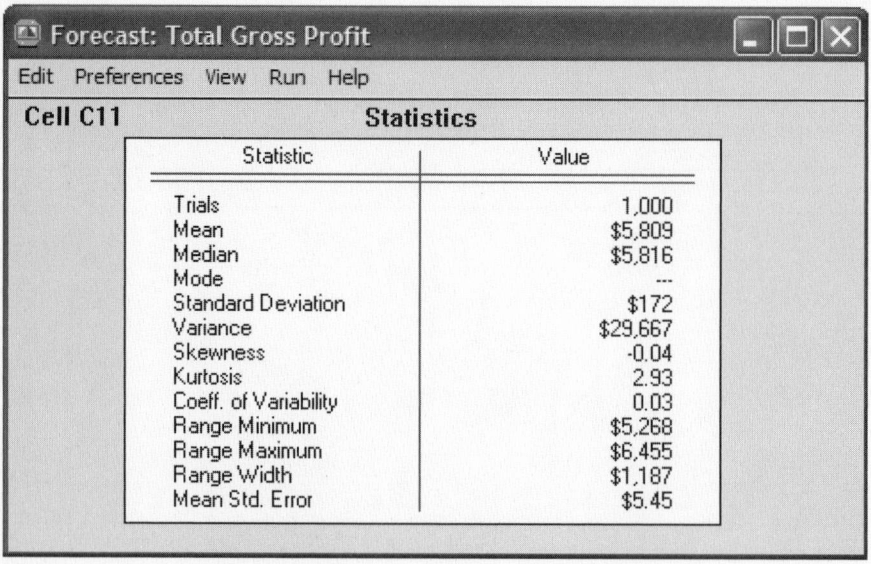

FIGURE 5.20 Forecast chart's statistics view.

FIVE-MINUTE INDUSTRY SPOTLIGHT: TRW

Increasing Flexibility and Efficiency

TRW Inc. is a global manufacturing and service company strategically focused on providing advanced technology products and services with a high technology or engineering content to the automotive, space and defense, and information technology markets. TRW is currently engaged as the major contractor in a project consisting of several consulting and high-tech firms such as SAIC, RMS, JTA, CTA, and ARNIC Corporations. This consortium of companies is charged with completing the Federal Aviation Administration's (FAA) Office of System Architecture and Investment Analysis (ASD) mission. Dennis Sawyer is the task area manager of investment analysis and operation research for TRW and has recently begun employing simulation in his day-to-day operations.

Prior to using Crystal Ball, Dennis and his talented team of financial, systems, and program analysts were forced to perform lengthy manual calculations. Specifically, Dennis and his team work with clients at the FAA to perform cost/benefit analysis on national airspace automation systems. These systems represent a portion of the improvements that have been specified in the FAA Capital Investment Plan (CIP). This plan is dedicated to advancing airspace safety, reliability, and efficiency.

One of the several tasks Dennis and his team are responsible for is to help estimate the lifecycle costs and benefits associated with the airspace automation systems. Recently, Dennis's team has used Monte Carlo simulation to assess risk in several programs and estimate 80 percent budget confidence levels. In one ongoing model, 40 different factors are varied based on historical information.

Crystal Ball is playing an integral part in this process by increasing the teams' flexibility and efficiency through reducing the time and workload necessary to perform a traditional spreadsheet analysis, and establishing higher confidence levels on the uncertain future.

Crystal Ball also has allowed the team to develop an easy method for determining the factors that will potentially influence the yearly and total cost of the program and then optimize the resulting decisions. Using the tornado chart, the analysts may view these factors based on the relative risk toward the program. This chart, along with the overlay chart, trend chart, and create report option, has the potential for reducing employee workload without compromising product quality.

FIVE-MINUTE INDUSTRY SPOTLIGHT: DUPONT MERCK

Pharmaceutical Applications

DuPont Merck is a research-focused pharmaceutical company. Pharmaceutical research has led to numerous advances in medical therapy. However, such research by its nature involves a tremendous amount of risk and uncertainty. Often 1,000 or more compounds are screened for each 1 that ultimately is nominated for development. On average, for every 10 compounds that reach development, only 1 gains Food and Drug Administration (FDA) approval.

An important aspect of pharmaceutical development is selecting the proper portfolio of compounds to develop—a portfolio that will provide the expected level of sales at the right level of cost and risk. Simulations are used to model the key risks and uncertainties for each individual project. In addition, simulations are used to estimate total portfolio value and risk—a probability distribution of potential R&D spending and sales by year.

Often, being the first or second to market can have a significant impact on total sales realized. In certain high-potential markets, there may be 10 or more competitors with compounds in development. Simulations were used to estimate the probability of being first or second to market. This information helps focus attention on the need to achieve key project milestones to ensure a reasonable level of certainty that a compound will be first to market.

QUESTIONS

1. What are the typical five steps required when running a Monte Carlo simulation model?
2. Explain what each of the following does:
   a. Defining an assumption
   b. Defining a forecast
3. What do cumulative charts and reverse cumulative charts represent?

CHAPTER 6

Pandora's Tool Box

This chapter deals with some analytical risk tools associated with Monte Carlo simulation. These analytical tools are discussed through example applications of the Crystal Ball software, complete with step-by-step illustrations. These tools are invaluable to analysts working in the realm of risk analysis. The applicability of each tool is discussed in detail in this chapter.

TORNADO AND SENSITIVITY TOOLS IN SIMULATION

One of the powerful simulation tools is the tornado chart—it captures the static impacts of each variable on the outcome of the model. That is, the tool automatically perturbs each variable in the model a preset amount, captures the fluctuation on the model's forecast or final result, and lists the resulting perturbations ranked from the most significant to the least. Figures 6.1 through 6.6 illustrate the application of a tornado chart. For instance, Figure 6.1 is a sample engineering model on the reliability model of a spring. The input assumptions in the model include the spring's wire diameter, coil diameter, and so forth. The results from the model are the materials' reliability measures.

Figures 6.2 through 6.4 show the tornado chart tool's wizard steps required to create a tornado diagram. The tornado chart tool can be obtained through the Crystal Ball menu (*CB Tools | Tornado Chart*). Figure 6.2 shows that *Material 1 Reliability* is chosen as the target result to be analyzed. Figure 6.3 shows *Material 1 Reliability*'s precedents in the model (*Add Precedents*) are chosen. Precedents are all the input and intermediate variables that affect the outcome of the model. For instance, if the model consists of A = B + C, where C = D + E, then B, D, and E are the precedents for A (C is not a precedent as it is only an intermediate calculated value). Figure 6.4 shows the testing range of each precedent variable used to estimate the target result. If the precedent variables are simple inputs, then the

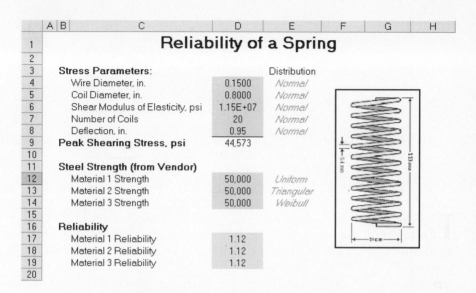

FIGURE 6.1   Reliability of a spring model.

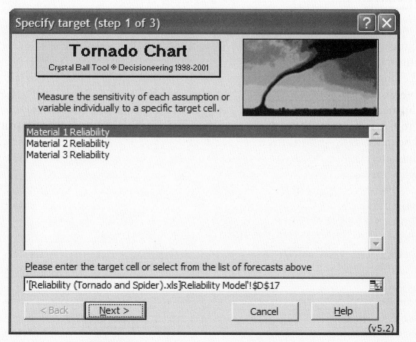

FIGURE 6.2   Step 1 of 3 for a tornado chart.

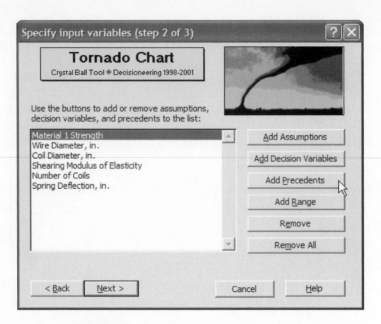

FIGURE 6.3   Step 2 of 3 for a tornado chart.

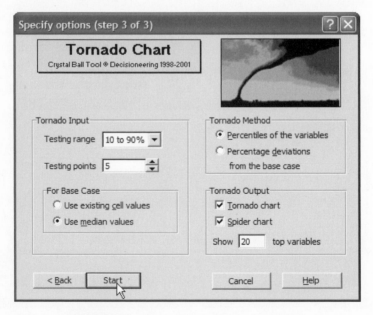

FIGURE 6.4   Step 3 of 3 for a tornado chart.

testing range will be a simple perturbation based on the range chosen (e.g., ±10%), but if the precedent variables are Crystal Ball input assumptions, then the range can be rather wide (in this example, the 10 percent to 90 percent of the distribution's range is chosen). A wider range is important as it is better able to test extreme values rather than smaller perturbations around the expected values. In certain circumstances, extreme values may have a larger, smaller, or unbalanced impact (e.g., nonlinearities may occur where increasing or decreasing economies of scale and scope creep in for larger or smaller values of a variable) and only a wider range will capture this non-linear impact.

Figure 6.5 shows the resulting tornado chart that indicates that material strength has the largest impact on material reliability, followed by coil diameter, number of coils, and so forth. The color-coded bars in Figure 6.5 illustrate each input's directional effect on the output (i.e., the sign of the correlation coefficient). Figure 6.6 provides the numerical results on the perturbation analysis.

Tornado analysis is a *static* sensitivity analysis applied on each input variable in the model—that is, each variable is perturbed individually and

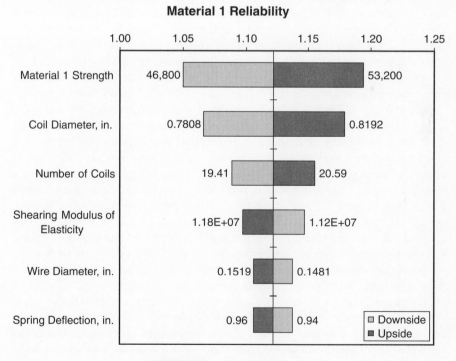

FIGURE 6.5 Tornado chart.

Variable	Material 1 Reliability			Input		
	Downside	Upside	Range	Downside	Upside	Base Case
Material 1 Strength	1.05	1.19	0.14	46,800	53,200	50,000
Coil Diameter, in.	1.07	1.18	0.11	0.7808	0.8192	0.8000
Number of Coils	1.09	1.15	0.07	19.41	20.59	20
Shearing Modulus of Elasticity	1.15	1.10	0.05	1.12E+07	1.18E+07	1.15E+07
Wire Diameter, in.	1.14	1.11	0.03	0.1481	0.1519	0.1500
Spring Deflection, in.	1.14	1.11	0.03	0.94	0.96	0.95

FIGURE 6.6   Tornado chart's table of results.

the resulting effects are tabulated. One of the very first steps in risk analysis is where the most important impact drivers in the model are captured and identified. The next step is to identify which of these important impact drivers are uncertain. These uncertain impact drivers are the critical success drivers or critical success factors of a project, where the results of the model depend on these critical success factors. These variables are the ones that should be simulated. Do not waste time simulating variables that are neither uncertain nor have little impact on the results. Tornado charts assist in identifying these critical success factors quickly and easily.

A related feature is sensitivity charts. While tornado charts are static perturbations applied before a simulation run, sensitivity charts are dynamic perturbations created after the simulation run. Tornado charts are static perturbations, meaning that each precedent or assumption variable is perturbed a preset amount and the fluctuations in the results are tabulated. In contrast, sensitivity charts are dynamic perturbations in the sense that multiple assumptions are perturbed simultaneously and their interactions are captured in the fluctuations of the results. Tornado charts therefore identify which variables drive the results the most and hence are suitable for simulation, whereas sensitivity charts identify the impact to the results when multiple interacting variables are simulated together in the model. This effect is clearly illustrated in Figures 6.7 and 6.8. Figure 6.7 shows the sensitivity charts obtained after a simulation run (select *Run | Show Sensitivity Chart | Chart Preference | Contribution to Variance* from the forecast window). Notice that the ranking of critical success factors are similar to the tornado chart. However, if correlations are added between the assumptions, Figure 6.8 shows a very different picture. Notice for instance, *wire diameter* had little impact on *material 1's reliability* but when some of the input assumptions are correlated (correlated assumptions have asterisks on the left column of the sensitivity chart in Figure 6.8), the interaction that exists between these correlated variables makes *wire diameter* have more impact. Therefore, in order to obtain a clearer picture of the interactions between assumption variables in a large and convoluted model with multiple correlations, running a sensitivity chart's contribution to variance view is vital.

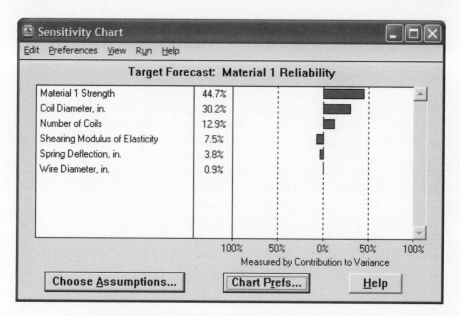

FIGURE 6.7   Sensitivity chart without correlations.

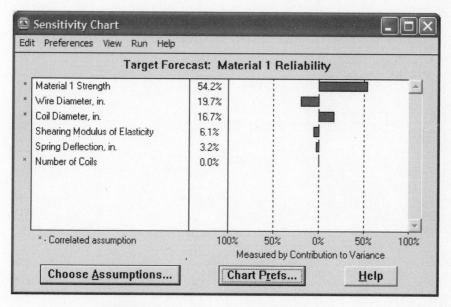

FIGURE 6.8   Sensitivity chart with correlation.

CORRELATING AND FITTING A DISTRIBUTION
PLUS PRECISION CONTROL

Another powerful tool is the application of correlated assumptions as seen briefly while comparing sensitivity charts to tornado charts. That is, certain input assumptions are correlated, thus, the simulation of these assumptions should also maintain this correlated effect. As an example, according to the law of demand in economics, the higher the price of a product, the lower its quantity demanded and vice versa, ceteris paribus. However, if in a simple revenue model where both price and quantity sold are assumed to be uncertain and simulated without a negative correlation, then the resulting revenue estimates will be flawed. That is, by virtue of Monte Carlo simulation, random occurrences are simulated, thus, high price levels can in theory occur with high quantity demanded, leading to an overexaggerated revenue forecast. Clearly, this cannot happen in reality, hence, the model's estimations are flawed. A negative correlation should be placed in the model. For example, Figure 6.9 shows a simple portfolio model with four different financial assets where the returns on each asset class is assumed to be uncertain and therefore simulated.

Obviously, some of these assets' returns are correlated. The correlation can be measured based on historical data if they exist, or based on expecta-

	A	B	C	D
1	**Portfolio Allocation Model with Correlation**			
2				
3	Fund	Historical Data	Distribution	Actual Return
4	Large Cap Stocks	H2:H251	Normal	13.00%
5	Small Cap Stocks	I2:I251	Normal	17.00%
6	Micro Cap Stocks	J2:J251	Normal	23.00%
7	Government Bonds	K2:K251	Normal	6.00%
8				
9				
10	Fund	% Invested	Min. Invested	Max. Invested
11	Large Cap Stocks	23.5%	0%	100%
12	Small Cap Stocks	13.6%	0%	100%
13	Micro Cap Stocks	6.9%	0%	100%
14	Government Bonds	56.1%	0%	100%
15				
16	*Initial Value of Portfolio*	$ 250,000		
17				
18	*Total expected return*	10.31%		
19	*Final Value of Portfolio*	$ 275,768		

FIGURE 6.9   Sample portfolio model.

tions. As a rule of thumb, even when no good measures of correlation exist whether through lack of data or exact approximations, if the a priori expectations require a correlation, one should be included. The most commonly used rule of thumb is to include a –0.75, –0.5, –0.25, 0.0, +0.25, +0.5, or +0.75 correlation for significant negative correlation, high negative correlation, mild negative correlation, no correlation, mild positive correlation, high positive correlation, and significant positive correlation variables, respectively. Inputting a –0.5 correlation coefficient, for example, will yield less incorrect estimates than not using any correlations at all when there clearly is a high negative correlation between the input variables. Figure 6.10 shows the location of the correlate function in the define assumption dialog in Crystal Ball. Figure 6.11 shows how to correlate multiple variables by selecting the list of assumptions (*small cap stocks* is currently chosen) and entering or linking the relevant correlation coefficient (cell *O2* or *0.57* is currently entered). When a large number of correlated pairs exist, the *CB Tools | Correlation Matrix* function can be used to automate entering the pairwise correlations.

Another powerful tool is distributional fitting. That is, which distribution does an analyst use for a particular input variable in a model? What are the relevant distributional parameters? If no historical data exist, then the analyst must make assumptions about the variables in question. One ap-

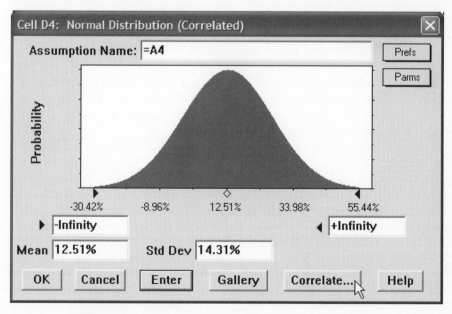

FIGURE 6.10 Sample correlated assumption in Crystal Ball.

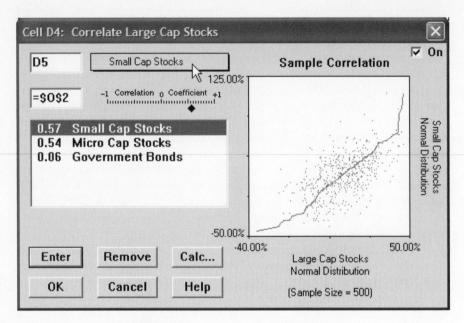

FIGURE 6.11   Correlating assumptions.

proach is to use the Delphi method where a group of experts are tasked with estimating the behavior of each variable. For instance, a group of mechanical engineers can be tasked with evaluating the extreme possibilities of a spring coil's diameter through rigorous experimentation or guesstimates. These values can be used as the variable's input parameters (e.g., uniform distribution with extreme values between 0.5 and 1.2). When testing is not possible (e.g., market share and revenue growth rate), management can still make estimates of potential outcomes and provide the best-case, most-likely case, and worst-case scenarios.

However, if reliable historical data is available, distributional fitting can be accomplished. Assuming that historical patterns hold and that history tends to repeat itself, then historical data can be used to find the best-fitting distribution with their relevant parameters to better define the variables to be simulated.[1] Figures 6.12 through 6.16 illustrate a distributional-fitting example. Figure 6.12 shows the historical returns on large cap stocks, whereas Figure 6.13 shows the distributional-fitting function located in the distribution gallery of Crystal Ball (*Cell | Define Assumption | Fit*). Multiple variables can also be fitted simultaneously through the Batch Fit tool in Crystal Ball (*CB Tools | Batch Fit*). Figures 6.14 and 6.15 illustrate the two-step wizard in distributional fitting, where all relevant distributions are chosen to test-fit the data.

H
Large Cap Stocks
30.28%
14.15%
6.94%
6.29%
1.84%
20.42%
26.43%
44.23%
28.02%
21.98%
39.85%
18.07%
3.04%
25.92%
2.06%
15.68%
19.22%
3.57%
9.10%
10.75%
11.09%
11.46%
-22.99%
-19.87%
25.81%
13.27%

FIGURE 6.12   Sample large-cap stocks' historical returns.

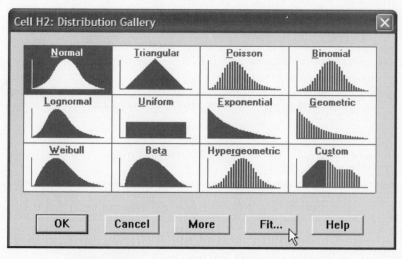

FIGURE 6.13   Distribution gallery in Crystal Ball.

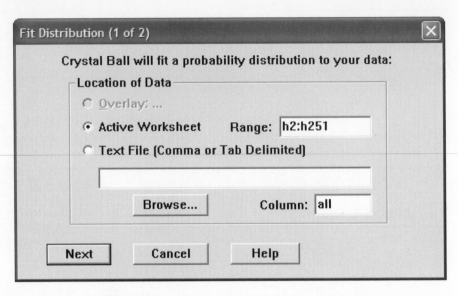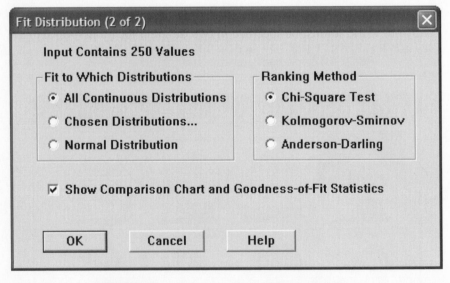

Notice that three ranking methods exist for the distributional fitting routines (Figure 6.15). They are the following three statistical goodness-of-fit statistics: chi-square test, Kolmogorov–Smirnov test, and the Anderson–Darling test. As an example, using the chi-square test, the best-fitting distribution is the normal distribution with a mean of 12.51 percent and a standard deviation of 14.31 percent (Figure 6.16). This distributional fitting tool takes the guesswork out of simulation analysis. Instead of guessing what the correct distribution should be for a variable, use the historical data to find the best-fitting distribution. See the appendix—Goodness-of-Fit Tests—at the end of this chapter for more details on these three tests.

PRECISION CONTROL

One very powerful tool in Monte Carlo simulation is that of precision control. For instance, how many trials are considered sufficient to run in a complex model? Precision control takes the guesswork out of estimating the relevant number of trials by allowing the simulation to stop if the level of prespecified precision is reached. Crystal Ball combines the individual forecast precision options found in *Cell | Define Forecast | More | Specify Precision* with the confidence level value found in the *Run | Run Preferences | Trials* dialog to calculate confidence intervals.[2] That is, in order for precision control to work, it must be specified in two different locations—once in the forecast (Figure 6.17) and once in the global-run preferences (Figure 6.18).

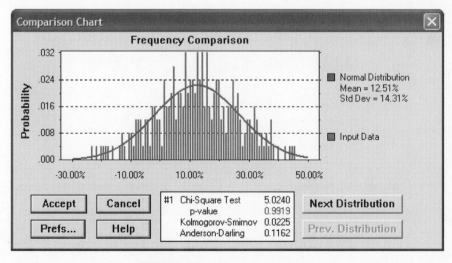

FIGURE 6.16   Comparison chart.

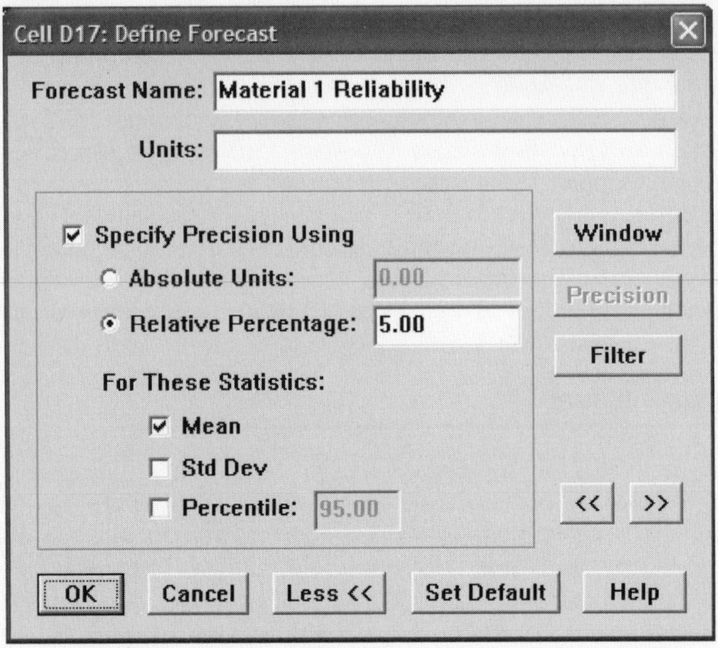

FIGURE 6.17   Define forecast dialog for precision control.

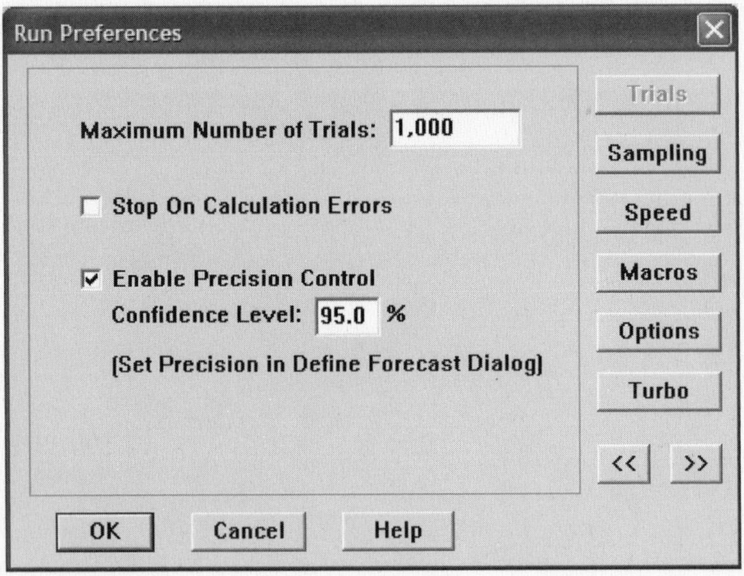

FIGURE 6.18   Run preferences dialog for precision control.

The precision control tool lets you set how precise you want one of three forecast statistics to be. Crystal Ball runs the simulation until those statistics reach the required precision as determined by calculating confidence intervals. Generally speaking, as more trials are calculated, the confidence interval narrows and the statistics become more accurate. The precision control feature in Crystal Ball uses the characteristic of confidence intervals to determine when a specified accuracy of a statistic has been reached. It compares the specified precision to the confidence interval—when the calculated confidence interval drops to less than the specified precision, the simulation stops. For each forecast, you can specify precision either in terms of absolute units of the forecast, or in relative terms as percentages. Each method has its own benefits and drawbacks.

Specifying precision in relative terms can give you greater control of the simulation when the shape and scale of the forecast distribution is largely unknown and you are interested in the accuracy only as it relates to the overall distribution itself. As an example, you might not know or care if a particular variable's distribution ranges from $25,500 to $64,000 or from $25.5 million to $64.0 million. You might require only that the simulation's estimate of the mean falls within plus or minus 5 percent of itself. However, there are drawbacks to using relative precision when the forecast statistic is close to zero in relation to the overall distribution. For instance, a forecast's distribution that straddles the break-even point of zero with a relative precision of 5 percent of the mean, or roughly $0.5 million, results in a very small confidence interval (relative to the full range width of $49.1 million) that might take an unexpectedly large number of trials to satisfy.

Specifying precision in absolute terms can give you greater control of the simulation when the shape and scale of the forecast distribution are roughly known. For a forecast that ranges from $25.5 million to $64.0 million, you can require the precision of the mean to be within plus or minus $100,000 or some other convenient measure of accuracy. However, with the same forecast range, an absolute accuracy of $1,000 might require an unreasonably large number of trials to reach. So, the drawback of using absolute precision is that it might require experimentation to determine reasonable accuracy values.

Make sure that you do not confuse three very different terms: error, precision, and confidence. Although they sound similar, the concepts are significantly different from one another. A simple illustration is in order. Suppose you are a taco shell manufacturer and are interested in finding out how many broken taco shells there are on average in a box of 100 shells. One way to do this is to collect a sample of prepackaged boxes of 100 taco shells, open them, and count how many of them are actually broken. You manufacture 1 million boxes a day (this is your *population*) but you randomly open only 10 boxes (this is your *sample* size, also known as your number of *trials* in a simulation). The number of broken shells in each box is as follows: 24, 22, 4, 15, 33, 32, 4, 1, 45, and 2. The calculated average number of broken shells is 18.2. Based on these 10 samples or trials, the average is 18.2 units, while based on the sample, the 80 percent confidence interval is between 2 and 33 units (that is, 80 percent of the time, the number of broken shells is between 2 and 33 *based on this sample size or number of trials run*). However, how sure are you that 18.2 is the correct average? Are 10 trials sufficient to establish this? The confidence interval between 2 and 33 is too wide and too variable. Suppose you require a more accurate average value where the error is ±2 taco shells 90 percent of the time—this means that if you open *all* 1 million boxes manufactured in a day, 900,000 of these boxes will have broken taco shells on average at some mean unit ±2 tacos. How many more taco shell boxes would you then need to sample (or trials run) to obtain this level of precision? Here, the 2 tacos is the error level while the 90 percent is the level of precision. If sufficient numbers of trials are run, then the 90 percent confidence interval will be identical to the 90 percent precision level, where a more precise measure of the average is obtained such that 90 percent of the time, the error and, hence, the confidence will be ±2 tacos. As an example, say the average is 20 units, then the 90 percent confidence interval will be between 18 and 22 units, where this interval is precise 90 percent of the time, where in opening all 1 million boxes, 900,000 of them will have between 18 and 22 broken tacos. The number of trials required to hit this precision is based on the sampling-error equation of

$$\bar{x} \pm Z \frac{s}{\sqrt{n}}$$

where $Z(s/\sqrt{n})$ is the error of 2 tacos, $\bar{x}$ is the sample average, Z is the standard-normal Z-score (see the tables on Standard Normal Distribution values at the end of this book) obtained from the 90 percent precision level, s is the sample standard deviation, and n is the number of trials required to hit this level of error with the specified precision. For instance, suppose the sample standard deviation of the 10 trials is 15.45 and the 90 percent precision level Z-score is 1.645 (using the Standard Normal Distribution [Partial Area] table, the area for 0.45 has a Z-score of approximately 1.645), which means that in order to obtain an error of ±2 tacos, solving

$$\pm 2 = \pm 1.645 \frac{15.45}{\sqrt{n}}$$

yields $n = 162$ minimum trials required. Figures 6.17 and 6.18 illustrate how precision control can be performed on multiple simulated forecasts in Crystal Ball, such that if precision is hit, then the simulation stops. This feature prevents the user from having to decide how many trials to run in a simulation and eliminates all possibilities of guesswork.

BOOTSTRAP SIMULATION

Bootstrap simulation is a simple technique that estimates the reliability or accuracy of forecast statistics or other sample raw data. (Figure 6.19 illustrates a sample result from bootstrap simulation). Classical methods used in the past relied on mathematical formulas to describe the accuracy of sample statistics. These methods assume that the distribution of a sample statistic approaches a normal distribution, making the calculation of the statistic's standard error or confidence interval relatively easy. However, when a statistic's sampling distribution is not normally distributed or easily found, these classical methods are difficult to use or are invalid. In contrast, bootstrapping analyzes sample statistics empirically by repeatedly sampling the data and creating distributions of the different statistics from each sampling.

Another use for bootstrap simulation is to take advantage of its nonparametric properties. That is, bootstrap simulation requires no assumptions of distributional parameters. In contrast to Monte Carlo simulation, which requires the selection of a specific probability distribution coupled with its respective parameters (e.g., mean, standard deviation, location, scale, and so forth), bootstrap simulation can be applied by letting the "data tell the story." In other words, bootstrap is a historical simulation approach where historical data is selected randomly without replacement. (See the Flaw of Averages example in Chapter 4, On The Shores of Monaco, for

	Mean	Median	Standard Deviation	Variance	Skewness	Kurtosis	Coeff. of Variability
	144562.06	143922.22	35038.02	1238661289	0.14	2.17	0.24
Correlations:							
Mean	1.000	0.849	0.162	0.162	-0.497	0.124	-0.185
Median		1.000	-0.003	-0.003	-0.664	0.137	-0.303
Standard Deviation			1.000	1.000	0.244	-0.456	0.925
Variance				1.000	0.244	-0.456	0.925
Skewness					1.000	0.146	0.425
Kurtosis						1.000	-0.480
Coeff. of Variability							1.000

FIGURE 6.19 Output from bootstrap simulation.

details of applying a nonparametric bootstrap simulation approach as well as a comparison to regular parametric Monte Carlo simulation approaches).

The term *bootstrap* comes from the saying, "to pull oneself up by one's own bootstraps," and is applicable because this method uses the distribution of statistics themselves to analyze the statistics' accuracy. To start the bootstrap simulation tool, click on *CBTools | CB Bootstrap*. Recall in Chapter 4 that nonparametric simulation is simply randomly picking golf balls from a large basket with replacement where each golf ball is based on a historical data point. Suppose there are 365 golf balls in the basket (representing 365 historical data points). Imagine if you will that the value of each golf ball picked at random is written on a large whiteboard. The results of the 365 balls picked with replacement are written in the first column of the board with 365 rows of numbers. Relevant statistics (e.g., mean, median, mode, standard deviation, and so forth) are calculated on these 365 rows. The process is then repeated, say, five thousand times. The whiteboard will now be filled with 365 rows and 5,000 columns. Hence, 5,000 sets of statistics (that is, there will be 5,000 means, 5,000 medians, 5,000 modes, 5,000 standard deviations, and so forth) are tabulated and their distributions shown. The relevant *statistics of the statistics* are listed in Figure 6.19, where from these results (select the colored cell and view the forecast's statistics) one can ascertain how confident the simulated statistics are. In other words, in a simple 10,000-trial simulation, say the resulting forecast average is found to be $5.00. How certain is the analyst of the results? Bootstrapping allows the user to ascertain the confidence interval of the calculated mean statistic, indicating the distribution of the statistics. Finally, bootstrap results are important because according to the *Law of Large Numbers* and *Central Limit Theorem* in statistics, the mean of the sample means is an unbiased estimator and approaches the true population mean when the sample size increases.

TWO-DIMENSIONAL SIMULATION

Risk analysts sometimes have to consider two sources of variation in their models—uncertainty and variability. In simulation, assumptions are defined on variables that are uncertain because of insufficient information about their true value. Examples of uncertainty include the reserve size of an oil field and the nominal Treasury rate in 12 months. You can describe an uncertainty assumption with a probability distribution. Theoretically, you can eliminate uncertainty by gathering more information. Practically, information can be missing because you have not gathered it or because it is too costly to gather.

In contrast, variability implies that the assumptions themselves can change because the assumptions describe a population with different values.

Examples of variability include individual body weights in a population or daily number of products sold over a year. You can describe a variability assumption with a frequency distribution or approximate it with a probability distribution. Variability is inherent in the system, and you cannot eliminate it by gathering more information.

For many types of risk assessments, it is important to clearly distinguish between uncertainty and variability. Separating these two concepts in a simulation lets you more accurately detect the variation in a forecast due to lack of knowledge and the variation caused by natural variability in a measurement or population. In the same way that a one-dimensional simulation is generally better than single-point estimates for showing the true probability of risk, a two-dimensional simulation is generally better than a one-dimensional simulation for characterizing risk.

The Two-Dimensional Simulation tool (*CBTools | 2D Simulation*) runs an outer loop to simulate the uncertainty values, and then freezes the uncertainty values while it runs an inner loop of the whole model to simulate the variability. This process repeats for some small number of outer simulations, providing a portrait of how the forecast distribution varies due to the uncertainty. The primary output of this process is a chart depicting a series of cumulative frequency distributions. You can interpret this chart as the range of possible risk curves associated with a population. Figure 6.20 illustrates a simple toxic waste site model where the assumptions are body weight, volume of water per day, concentration of contaminant, and cancer potency factor (CPF). Using the 2D simulation tool, body weight is defined as the input with variability. Body weight is set to vary at different values while simulation is run on the entire model repeatedly, with these updated body weight values. Figure 6.21 illustrates the results from a 2D simulation.

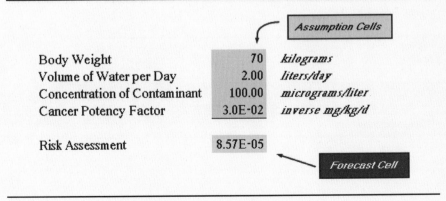

FIGURE 6.20   Toxic waste site model.

	Risk Assessment(1)	Risk Assessment(2)	Risk Assessment(3)	Risk Assessment(4)	Risk Assessment(5)	Risk Assessment(6)	Risk Assessment(7)	Risk Assessment(8)	Risk Assessment(9)	Risk Assessment(10)
Assumptions:	7.38E-06	1.21E-05	5.33E-05	5.71E-05	7.20E-05	7.78E-05	7.93E-05	1.22E-04	1.47E-04	1.54E-04
Volume of Water per Day	0.29	0.36	1.70	1.40	0.98	1.36	2.05	2.44	2.76	3.44
Concentration of Contaminant in Water	108.17	96.00	95.15	114.73	108.29	108.92	115.82	103.56	107.29	104.02
CPF	1.7E-02	2.4E-02	2.2E-02	2.4E-02	4.6E-02	3.6E-02	2.3E-02	3.3E-02	3.4E-02	2.9E-02

FIGURE 6.21 2D Simulation output.

DECISION TABLES

Decision variables are values that you can control, such as how much to charge for a product or how many wells to drill. But, in situations with uncertainty, it is not always obvious what effects changing a decision variable can have on the forecast results. The decision table tool (*CBTools | Decision Table*) runs multiple simulations to test different values for one or two decision variables. The tool tests values across the range of the decision variables and puts the results in a table that you can analyze using Crystal Ball forecast, trend, or overlay charts. The decision table tool is useful for investigating how changes in the values of a few decision variables affect the forecast results. Figure 6.22 shows the product mix model (available on the CD) where the quantities to produce for phone and computer housings are the decision variables. The idea is to use Crystal Ball's decision table tool to

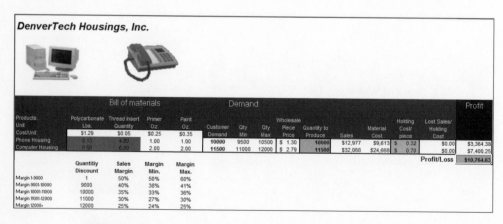

FIGURE 6.22 Using Decision tables on the product mix problem.

	Phone Housing (9500)	Phone Housing (9600)	Phone Housing (9700)	Phone Housing (9800)	Phone Housing (9900)	Phone Housing (10000)	Phone Housing (10100)	Phone Housing (10200)	Phone Housing (10300)	Phone Housing (10400)	Phone Housing (10500)
Computer Housing (11000)	$8,219.64	$8,355.06	$8,552.53	$8,695.63	$8,897.43	$9,075.48	$8,917.22	$8,762.16	$8,681.47	$8,513.70	$8,410.83
Computer Housing (11100)	$8,576.58	$8,759.40	$8,919.43	$9,049.55	$9,218.64	$9,364.63	$9,245.08	$9,116.91	$8,970.09	$8,873.46	$8,764.16
Computer Housing (11200)	$8,917.92	$9,053.30	$9,270.43	$9,429.06	$9,596.30	$9,705.81	$9,603.19	$9,501.88	$9,384.39	$9,219.22	$9,107.86
Computer Housing (11300)	$9,289.28	$9,433.35	$9,597.77	$9,819.58	$9,948.52	$10,056.25	$9,928.77	$9,829.38	$9,676.52	$9,584.86	$9,449.18
Computer Housing (11400)	$9,596.94	$9,792.42	$9,902.66	$10,044.67	$10,316.06	$10,449.79	$10,315.42	$10,195.45	$10,073.57	$9,871.58	$9,719.39
Computer Housing (11500)	$9,920.64	$10,134.45	$10,261.56	$10,441.77	$10,560.00	$10,733.54	$10,648.44	$10,516.24	$10,345.32	$10,233.55	$10,105.65
Computer Housing (11600)	$9,648.06	$9,811.68	$9,986.08	$10,153.30	$10,284.26	$10,518.14	$10,339.26	$10,200.09	$10,065.15	$9,911.97	$9,838.04
Computer Housing (11700)	$9,370.62	$9,572.04	$9,711.78	$9,833.28	$10,030.77	$10,161.08	$10,091.61	$9,921.40	$9,828.29	$9,718.79	$9,547.31
Computer Housing (11800)	$9,126.74	$9,253.16	$9,384.26	$9,561.56	$9,713.12	$9,851.39	$9,783.59	$9,674.52	$9,502.14	$9,391.98	$9,274.02
Computer Housing (11900)	$8,793.54	$8,967.90	$9,125.53	$9,306.11	$9,475.71	$9,666.11	$9,530.24	$9,360.06	$9,239.74	$9,114.62	$8,975.86
Computer Housing (12000)	$8,494.68	$8,682.28	$8,874.98	$9,037.36	$9,135.42	$9,356.08	$9,240.09	$9,102.06	$8,921.67	$8,816.22	$8,737.31

(Left-side buttons: Trend Chart, Overlay Chart, Forecast Charts)

FIGURE 6.23 Decision table results.

generate all possible combinations of quantities (at preset ranges and testing intervals) while simulating the uncertain inputs (polycarbonate weight and thread-insert quality) and observing the calculated profit and loss value. In order to use the decision table tool, decision variables have to be first assigned, complete with the test range and step-size intervals. To fully utilize the power of the decision table, assumptions and forecasts should also be assigned. The results are shown in Figure 6.23, complete with the profit and loss values based on all possible combinations of the two decision variables. The power of this tool is further illustrated in Figure 6.24 where a trend

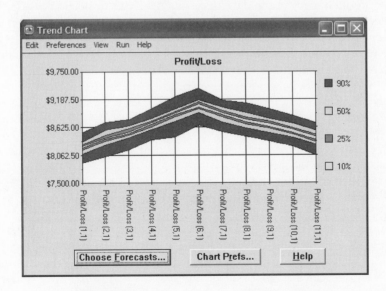

FIGURE 6.24 Trend chart from decision table.

chart is created from the first row of 11,000 units of computer housings by varying the units of phone housings. The trend chart helps locate the optimal combination of phone and computer housings that maximizes profits. In Chapter 11, Optimization under Uncertainty, stochastic optimization will be introduced. Stochastic optimization is a much more potent method used to systematically find the best combinations of decision variables in more complex models.

FIVE-MINUTE INDUSTRY SPOTLIGHT: 3M

Unit Cost Estimates

Michael Muilenburg works in the process development area at 3M Company in St. Paul, Minnesota. In this area, Michael works as an interface between the design engineers, R&D laboratory, and various manufacturing plants. The laboratory develops prototype products, the engineers design the production scale equipment, and the manufacturing plants complete the actual production. Michael has used simulation tools in the past to help identify the optimum production process steps as well as the types of equipment and raw materials to use in manufacturing processes.

Simulation played an important role in projecting unit cost figures for products early in the development stage. This projection is often a very complex and time-consuming process and includes many different variables. The unit-cost projection process began after Michael received proposals for the production of a new product. He then contacted the purchasing department to gather cost figures for the raw materials necessary to produce the product. Rather than look at only the most current raw material prices, he collected data over a 12- to 24-month period, allowing him to easily view raw material price trends and to determine the range and distribution of the prices over time. With this information Michael was able to compensate for the fluctuations in his model.

Other important variables that were part of the unit-cost calculations included production rates, material waste, changeover costs, and capital expenditures. As Michael incorporated more variables into his model, he was able to generate a clearer picture of the influence each input had on the unit-cost projection. Crystal Ball's sensitivity analysis provided a particularly helpful way to graphically display the impact of each variable. Michael was able to create different scenarios by changing production speeds, raw material costs, or other important variables. This flexibility in the planning stages provided a great opportunity to understand all of the costs and their relationships to one another. Ultimately, this information also allowed Michael to come up with a more reliable unit-cost estimate that, in turn, allowed 3M to get products through production and to market with no cost surprises.

FIVE-MINUTE INDUSTRY SPOTLIGHT: DELOITTE & TOUCHE CONSULTING

Maximizing Clients' Shareholder Value

Gary Basson is a manager of value solutions practices for Deloitte & Touche and has been a Crystal Ball user for several years. Gary works with clients to develop and implement "value-based management frameworks." These frameworks emphasize maximizing shareholder value within a company's overall business plan.

Using Crystal Ball, Gary and others within his department built a financial model that takes a company's current business assumptions and makes projections 10 or 15 years into the future to indicate which areas of the business need attention in order to maximize shareholder value. For example, the model may indicate that net present value (NPV) relative to cash flows is inadequate to maximize shareholder value. Gary can then incorporate this information into the overall framework, thereby providing his clients with a valuable tool in guiding their business decisions.

Prior to using Crystal Ball, Gary was required to use Excel to write lengthy macro codes to perform analyses that were used on a case-by-case basis by his clients. Now, Crystal Ball's Developer Kit provides Gary with the flexibility to automate these processes and integrate them into the overall framework. The Developer Kit has the dual benefit of saving Gary valuable time in programming the framework and also allows his clients to reap the benefits of Crystal Ball without becoming experts in the use of the software.

The end result of Gary's efforts is a sophisticated analysis tool, driven by Crystal Ball, that focuses a client's decisions toward maximizing shareholder value.

APPENDIX—GOODNESS-OF-FIT TESTS

Several statistical tests exist for deciding if a sample of data comes from a specific distribution. The three most commonly used are the Kolmogorov–Smirnov test, Anderson–Darling test, and the chi-square test. Each test has its advantages and disadvantages. The following sections detail the specifics of these three tests as applied in distributional fitting in Monte Carlo simulation analysis.

Kolmogorov–Smirnov Test

The Kolmogorov–Smirnov (KS) test is based on the empirical distribution function of a sample data set and belongs to a class of *nonparametric tests*. This nonparametric characteristic is the key to understanding the KS test, which simply means that the distribution of the KS test statistic does not depend on the underlying cumulative distribution function being tested. Non-parametric simply means no predefined distributional parameters are required. In other words, the KS test is applicable across a multitude of underlying distributions. Another advantage is that it is an exact test as compared to the chi-square test, which depends on an adequate sample size for the approximations to be valid. Despite these advantages, the KS test has several important limitations. It only applies to continuous distributions, and it tends to be more sensitive near the center of the distribution than at the distribution's tails. Also, the distribution must be fully specified.

Given N ordered data points Y_1, Y_2, . . . Y_N, the empirical distribution function is defined as $E_n = n(i)/N$ where $n(i)$ is the number of points less than Y_i where Y_i values are ordered from the smallest to the largest value. This is a step function that increases by $1/N$ at the value of each ordered data point.

The null hypothesis is such that the data set follows a specified distribution while the alternate hypothesis is that the data set does not follow the specified distribution. The hypothesis is tested using the KS statistic defined as

$$KS = \max_{1 \leq i \leq N} \left| F(Y_i) - \frac{i}{N} \right|$$

where F is the theoretical cumulative distribution of the continuous distribution being tested that must be fully specified (i.e., the location, scale, and shape parameters cannot be estimated from the data).

The hypothesis regarding the distributional form is rejected if the test statistic, KS, is greater than the critical value obtained from Table 6.1. *No-*

TABLE 6.1 Kolmgorov–Smirnov Test

Two-Tailed Alpha Level (%)	KS Critical
10	0.03858
5	0.04301
1	0.05155

tice that 0.03 to 0.05 are the most common levels of critical values (at the 1 percent, 5 percent, and 10 percent significance levels). Thus, any calculated KS statistic less than these critical values implies that the null hypothesis is not rejected and that the distribution is a good fit. There are several variations of these tables that use somewhat different scaling for the KS test statistic and critical regions. These alternative formulations should be equivalent, but it is necessary to ensure that the test statistic is calculated in a way that is consistent with how the critical values were tabulated. However, the rule of thumb is that a KS test statistic less than 0.03 or 0.05 indicates a good fit (see Table 6.1).

Anderson–Darling Test

The Anderson–Darling (AD) test is from the parametric family of tests and it is a modification of the KS test. The AD test gives more weight to the tails than does the KS test. The KS test is nonparametric in nature, or distribution free, in the sense that the critical values do not depend on the specific distribution being tested. The AD test, however, makes use of the specific distribution in calculating its critical values. This method has the advantage of being a more sensitive test while the disadvantage is that the critical values must be calculated for each distribution.

The null hypothesis is such that the data set follows a specified distribution while the alternate hypothesis is that the data set does not follow the specified distribution. The hypothesis is tested using the AD statistic defined as

$$AD = \sqrt{-N - \frac{1}{N} \sum_{i=1}^{N} (2i - 1)[\ln \Phi(Y_i) + \ln(1 - \Phi(Y_{N+1-i}))]}$$

where Φ is the cumulative distribution function of the specified distribution. Note that the Y_i is from the ordered data set.

TABLE 6.2   Anderson–Darling Test

One-Tailed Alpha Level (%)	Cutoff
10	0.656
5	0.787
1	1.092

The critical values for the AD test are dependent on the specific distribution that is being tested. *The test is a one-sided test* and the hypothesis that the distribution is of a specific form is rejected if the test statistic, AD, is greater than the critical value. Table 6.2 lists the critical values for a normal distribution. Critical values of other distributions vary but a *general rule of thumb is such that if the AD statistic is less than 1.5, the distribution is considered a good fit* (this is a conservative value applicable regardless of distribution).

Chi-Square Test

The chi-square (CS) goodness-of-fit test is applied to binned data (i.e., data put into classes) and an attractive feature of the CS test is that it can be applied to any univariate distribution for which you can calculate the cumulative distribution function. However, the values of the CS test statistic are dependent on how the data is binned and the test requires a sufficient sample size in order for the CS approximation to be valid. This test is sensitive to the choice of bins. The test can be applied to discrete distributions such as the binomial and the Poisson, while the KS and AD tests are restricted to continuous distributions.

The null hypothesis is such that the data set follows a specified distribution while the alternate hypothesis is that the data set does not follow the specified distribution. The hypothesis is tested using the CS statistic defined as

$$\chi^2 = \sum_{i=1}^{k} (O_i - E_i)^2 \, / \, E_i$$

where O_i is the observed frequency for bin i and E_i is the expected frequency for bin i. The expected frequency is calculated by

$$E_i = N(F(Y_U) - F(Y_L))$$

TABLE 6.3 Chi-Square Test

Alpha Level (%)	Cutoff
10	32.00690
5	35.17246
1	41.63840

Note: Chi-square goodness-of-fit test sample critical values. Degrees of freedom 23.

where F is the cumulative distribution function for the distribution being tested, Y_U is the upper limit for class i, Y_L is the lower limit for class i, and N is the sample size.

The test statistic follows a CS distribution with $(k - c)$ degrees of freedom where k is the number of nonempty cells and c = the number of estimated parameters (including location and scale parameters and shape parameters) for the distribution + 1. For example, for a three-parameter Weibull distribution, $c = 4$. Therefore, the hypothesis that the data are from a population with the specified distribution is rejected if $\chi^2 > \chi^2(\alpha, k - c)$ where $\chi^2(\alpha, k - c)$ is the CS percent point function with $k - c$ degrees of freedom and a significance level of α (see Table 6.3).

Table 6.4 provides a comparison of the three statistical tests.

TABLE 6.4 Comparison of the Three Statistical Tests

Attributes	Kolmogorov–Smirnov	Anderson–Darling	Chi-Square
Applicable to continuous distributions	yes	yes	yes
Applicable to discrete distributions	no	no	yes
Parametric statistical test	no	yes	no
Nonparametric statistical test	yes	no	no
Semiparametric statistical test	no	no	yes
Two-tailed statistical test	yes	no	yes
One-tailed statistical test	no	yes	no
Validity depends on bin size	no	no	yes
Validity sensitive to center of distribution	yes	no	no
Validity sensitive to tails of distribution	no	yes	no
Validity sensitive to data size	no	no	yes

QUESTIONS

1. Why is tornado analysis used before a simulation is run while sensitivity analysis is used after a simulation is run?
2. Explain what would happen to the results if two simulated random variables that are negatively correlated in real life are not correlated in the model?
3. What is the Delphi method?
4. Provide an example where running a two-dimensional simulation is appropriate.
5. Compare and contrast the three typical goodness-of-fit tests; that is, when is each test appropriate under different circumstances?

Industry Applications

Extended Business Cases I: From Pharma to Black Gold

T his chapter provides the first installment of two extended business cases. The first case pertains to the application of Monte Carlo simulation and risk analysis in the biotech and pharmaceutical industries. The case details the use of risk analysis for deal making and structuring, and is contributed by Dr. Charles Hardy. The second case in this chapter is contributed by Steve Hoye, a veteran of the oil and gas industry. Steve details the risks involved in oil exploration and production by illustrating a comprehensive oil exploration case from cradle to grave.

CASE STUDY: PHARMACEUTICAL AND BIOTECH—HIGH PRECISION QUANTITATIVE DEAL STRUCTURING IN THE BIOTECHNOLOGY AND PHARMACEUTICAL INDUSTRIES™

This business case is contributed by Dr. Charles Hardy, principal of BioAxia Incorporated of Foster City, California, a consulting firm specializing in valuation and quantitative deal structuring for bioscience firms. He is also chief financial officer and director of business development at Panorama Research, a biotechnology incubator in the San Francisco Bay Area. Dr. Hardy has a Ph.D. in pathobiology from the University of Washington in Seattle, Washington, and an MBA in finance and entrepreneurship from the University of Iowa in Iowa City, Iowa. He has functioned in a variety of roles for several startup companies, including being CEO of Pulmogen, an early-stage medical device company. Dr. Hardy lives and works in the San Francisco Bay Area and his personal Web site contains a large amount of information on valuation and entrepreneurship: www.charlesthardyphdmba.com.

Smaller companies in the biotechnology industry rely heavily on alliances with pharmaceutical and larger companies to finance their research and development (R&D) expenditures. Pharmaceutical and larger organizations in turn depend on these alliances to supplement their internal R&D programs. In order for smaller organizations to realize the cash flows associated with these alliances, they must have a competent and experienced business development component to negotiate and structure these crucial deals. In fact, the importance of these business collaborations to the survival of most young companies is so great that deal-making experience, polished business-development skills, and a substantial network of contacts are all frequent assets of the most successful executives of start-up and early-stage biotechnology companies.

While deal-making opportunities for biotech companies are abundant because of the pharmaceutical industry's need to keep a healthy pipeline of new products in development, in recent years deal-making opportunities have lessened. Intuitively, then, firms have to be much more careful in the way they structure and value the deals in which they do get the opportunity to participate. However, despite this importance, a large number of executives prefer to go with comparable business deal structures for these collaborations in the hope of maximizing shareholder value for their firms, or by developing deal terms using their own intuition rather then developing a quantitative methodology for deal valuation and optimization to supplement their negotiation skills and strategies. For companies doing only one deal or less a year, perhaps the risk might be lower by structuring a collaboration based on comparable deal structures; at least they will get as much as the average company, or will they?

As described in this case study, *Monte Carlo simulation, stochastic optimization*, and *real options* are ideal tools for valuing and optimizing the financial terms of collaborative biomedical business deals focused on the development of human therapeutics. A large amount of data associated with clinical trial stage lengths and completion probabilities are publicly available. By quantitatively valuing and structuring deals, companies of all sizes can gain maximum shareholder value at all stages of development, and, most importantly, future cash flows can be defined based on expected cash-flow needs and risk preference.

Deal Types

Most deals between two biotechnology companies or a biotechnology company and pharmaceutical company are strategic alliances where a cooperative agreement is made between two organizations to work together in defined ways with the goal of successfully developing or commercializing products. As the following list describes, there are several different types of strategic alliances:

- *Product Licensing.* A highly flexible and widely applicable arrangement where one party wishes to access the technology of another organization with no other close cooperation. This type of alliance carries very low risk and these types of agreements are made at nearly every stage of pharmaceutical development.
- *Product Acquisition.* A company purchases an existing product license from another company and thus obtains the right to market a fully or partially developed product.
- *Product Fostering.* A short-term exclusive license for a technology or product in a specific market that will typically include hand-back provisions.
- *Comarketing.* Two companies market the same product under different trade names.
- *Copromotion.* Two parties promote the same product under the same brand name.
- *Minority Investment Alliance.* One company buys stock in another as part of a mutually desired strategic relationship.

The historical agreement valued and optimized in this case study is an example of a product-licensing deal.

Financial Terms

Each business deal is decidedly unique, which explains why no "generic" financial model is sufficient to value and optimize every opportunity and collaboration. A biomedical collaborative agreement is the culmination of the combined goals, desires, requirements, and pressures from both sides of the bargaining table, possibly biased in favor of one party by exceptional negotiating skills, good preparation, more thorough due diligence, and accurate assumptions, and less of a need for immediate cash.

The financial terms agreed on for licensing or acquiring a new product or technology depend on a variety of factors, most of which impact the value of the deal. These include but are not limited to:

- Strength of the intellectual property position.
- Exclusivity of the rights agreed on.
- Territorial exclusivity granted.
- Uniqueness of the technology transferred.
- Competitive position of the company.

- Stage of technology developed.
- Risk of the project being licensed or sold.

Although every deal is different, most include: (1) licensing and R&D fees; (2) milestone payments; (3) product royalty payments; and (4) equity investments.

Primary Financial Models

All calculations described in this case study are based on discounted cash-flow (DCF) principals using risk-adjusted discount rates. Here, assets under uncertainty are valued using the following basic financial equation:

$$NPV = \sum_{i=0}^{n} \frac{E(CF_t)}{(1 + r_t + \pi_t)^t}$$

where NPV is the net present value, $E(CF_t)$ is the expected value of the cash flow at time t, r_t is the risk-free rate, and π_t is the risk premium appropriate for the risk of CF_t.

All subcomponents of models described here use different discount rates if they are subject to different risks. In the case of biomedical collaborative agreements, all major subcomponents (licensing fees, R&D costs and funding, clinical costs, milestone payments, and royalties) are frequently subject to many different distinct risks, and thus are all assigned their own discount rates based on a combination of factors, with the subject company's weighted average cost of capital (WACC) used as the base value. To incorporate the uncertain and dynamic nature of these risk assumptions into the model, all of these discount rates are themselves Monte Carlo variables. This discounting supplementation is critical to valuing the deal accurately, and most important for later stochastic optimization.

Historical Deal Background and Negotiated Deal Structure

The deal valued and optimized in this case study was a preclinical, exclusive product-licensing agreement between a small biotechnology company and a larger organization. The biopharmaceutical being valued had one major therapeutic indication; with an estimated market size of $1 billion at the date the deal was signed. The licensee negotiated the right to sublicense. The deal had a variety of funding provisions, with a summary of the financial terms presented in Table 7.1. The licensor estimated they were approximately 2 years away from filing an investigational new drug (IND) application that would initiate clinical trials in humans. For the purposes of the deal

TABLE 7.1   Historical Financial Terms Granted to the Licensor of the Signed
Biomedical Collaborative Deal Valued and Optimized in This Case Study

| | Deal Scenario | | | |
Component	Historical	Higher-Value, Lower-Risk	Higher-Value, Higher-Risk	Timing
Licensing Fees	$100,000	$125,000	$ 85,000	30-days from effective date
Licensing	$100,000	$125,000	$ 75,000	First anniversary
Maintenance	200,000	250,000	150,000	Second anniversary
Fees	300,000	375,000	225,000	Third anniversary
	400,000	500,000	300,000	Fourth anniversary
	500,000	500,000	300,000	Fifth anniversary
R&D Funding	$250,000	$275,000	$165,000	Per year
Milestone Payments	$500,000	$660,000	$910,000	First IND filing in United States or European equivalent.
		895,000		Successful conclusion of Phase I clinical trials in the United States or European equivalent
		1,095,000	1,400,000	Successful conclusion of Phase II clinical trials in the United States or European equivalent
	1,500,000	1,375,000	1,650,000	First PLA[a] (or NDA[b]) filing or European equivalent
	4,000,000	1,675,000	1,890,000	NDA approval in the United States or European equivalent
Royalties	2.0% Net Sales	0.5% Net Sales	5.5% Net Sales	

[a]Product License Application.
[b]New Drug Application.

valuation and optimization described here, it is assumed that no information asymmetries exist between the companies forming the collaboration (i.e., both groups feel there is an equally strong likelihood their candidate bio-pharmaceutical will be a commercial success).

Licensing fees for the historical deal consisted of an up-front fee followed by licensing maintenance fees including multipliers (Table 7.1). Licensing maintenance fees will terminate on any one of the following events: (1) first IND filing by licensor; (2) tenth anniversary of the effective date; and (3) termination of the agreement. Milestone values for the historical deal numbered only three, with a $500,000 payment awarded on IND filing, a $1,500,000 payment on new drug application (NDA) filing, and a $4,000,000 payment on NDA approval (Table 7.1). The negotiated royalties for the historical deal were a flat 2.0 percent of net sales.

As described later in this case, two additional deal scenarios were constructed and stochastically optimized from the historical structure: a higher-value, lower-risk (HVLR) scenario and a higher-value, higher-risk (HVHR) scenario (Table 7.1).

Major Assumptions   Figure 7.1 shows a time line for all three deal scenarios evaluated. Also shown are the milestone schedules for all three scenarios, along with major assumption data. The total time frame for all deal calculations was 307.9 months, where the candidate pharmaceutical gains a 20 percent maximum market share of a 1 billion dollar market, with a 20 percent standard deviation during the projected 15-year sales period of the pharmaceutical. The market is assumed to grow 1.0 percent annually starting at the effective date of the agreement and throughout the valuation period. The manufacturing and marketing costs of the potential pharmaceutical were estimated to be 58 percent, an important assumption considering that royalties are paid on net sales, not gross sales. The total market size, market growth rate, maximum market share, and manufacturing and marketing offset are all Monte Carlo variables following lognormal distributions where extreme values are unlikely. Assumptions regarding clinical trial length, completion probabilities, and major variables in the valuation model are also shown in Figure 7.1. All of these values are Monte Carlo assumptions. Throughout this case study, deal values were based on royalties from 15 years of net sales. Royalties were paid on a quarterly basis, not at the end of each sales year. Total R&D costs for the licensor were $200,000 annually, again estimated with a Monte Carlo assumption.

Inflation during the period was assumed to be 1.95 percent annually and average annual pharmaceutical price increases (APPIs) were assumed to be 5.8 percent. Thus, milestones were deflated in value, and royalties inflated by APPI less inflation. For the deal valuation described here, the licensor was assumed to be unprofitable preceding and during the clinical trial

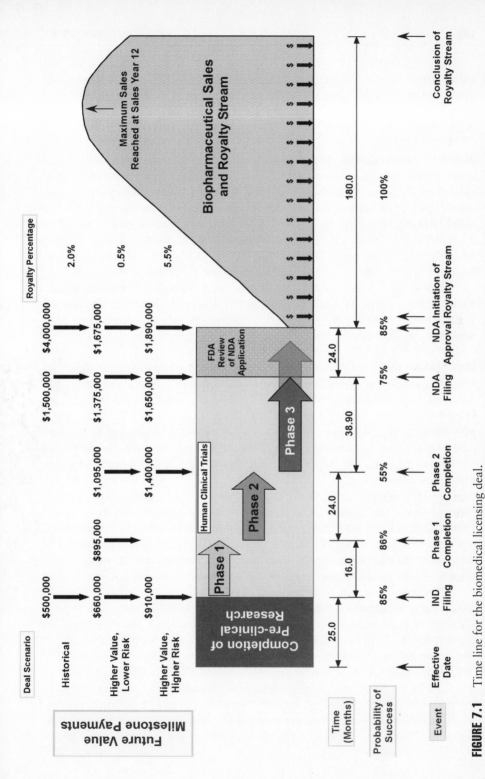

FIGURE 7.1 Time line for the biomedical licensing deal.
Milestone and royalty values for all deal scenarios evaluated are shown. R&D, licensing, and licensing maintenance fees are not shown.

process and milestone payments were not subject to taxes. However, royalties from the licensee paid to the licensor were taxed at a 33.0 percent rate.

Deal Valuations

Historical Deal Valuation   Figure 7.2 illustrates the Monte Carlo summary of the historical deal, while Figure 7.3 shows a comparative illustration of each major component of the historical scenario. Mean deal present value was $1,432,128 with a standard deviation of $134,449 (Figure 7.2). The distribution describing the mean was relatively symmetric with a skewness of 0.46. The kurtosis of the distribution, the "peakedness," was 3.47, limiting the deal range from $994,954 to $2,037,413. The coefficient of variation (CV), the primary measure of risk for the deal, was low at 9.38 percent. R&D/licensing contributed the most to total deal value with a mean present value of $722,108, while royalties contributed the least with a mean value of $131,092 (Figure 7.3). Milestones in the historical scenario also contributed greatly to the historical deal value with a mean present value of $578,927.

The riskiness of the cash flows varied greatly among individual historical deal components. R&D/licensing cash flows varied the least and had by far the lowest risk with a CV of only 7.48 percent and, proportional to the distribution's mean, had the smallest range among any deal component (data not shown). The present value of milestone cash flows was much more volatile, with a CV of 14.58 percent. Here the range was greater ($315,103 to $1,004,563) with a symmetric distribution having a skewness of only 0.40 (data not shown).

Royalty present value was by far the most volatile with a CV of 45.71 percent (data not shown). The kurtosis of royalty present value was large (5.98; data not shown), illustrating the proportionally wide distribution to the small royalty mean ($131,093; Figure 7.3). These data should not be surprising as the royalty cash flows are subject to variability of nearly all Monte Carlo assumptions in the model and are thus highly volatile.

Monte Carlo Assumption and Decision Variable Sensitivities   Figure 7.4 shows a Tornado Chart of historical deal assumptions and decision variables. The probability of IND filing had the largest influence on variation of total deal present value, as all milestones and royalties are dependent on this variable. Interestingly, next came the annual research cost for each full-time equivalent (FTE) for the licensor performing the remaining preclinical work in preparation for an IND filing, followed by the negotiated funding amount of each FTE (Figure 7.4). Thus, an area for the licensor to create shareholder value is to overestimate R&D costs in negotiating the financial terms for the

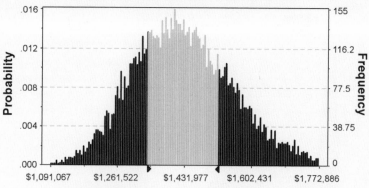

FIGURE 7.2 Historical deal scenario Monte Carlo summary.

deal, considering R&D/licensing funding contributed 50.42 percent of total deal present value (Figure 7.3). Variables impacting royalty cash flows, such as the royalty discount rate and manufacturing and marketing offset percentages, were more important than the negotiated milestone amounts, although the milestone discount rate was 10th in contribution to variance to the historical deal (Figure 7.4).

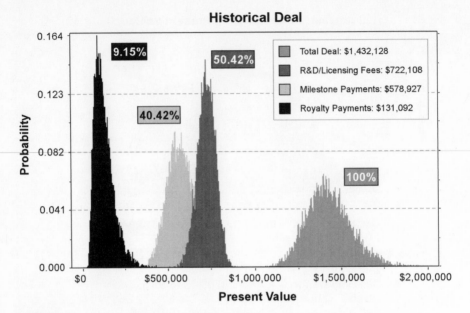

FIGURE 7.3   A comparative illustration I.
This is an illustration of the Monte Carlo distributions of the cash-flow present value of the historical deal scenario, along with the distributions of the deal's individual components. Each component has a clearly definable distribution that differs considerably from other deal components, both in value and risk characteristics. The percentage of each component to total deal present value is also shown.

Higher-Value, Lower-Risk Deal Valuation

Changes in Key Assumptions and Parameters Differing from the Historical, Signed Deal
The financial structure for the HVLR deal scenario was considerably different from the historical deal (Table 7.1). Indeed, R&D and licensing funding were significantly increased and the milestone schedule was reorganized with five payments instead of the three in the historical deal. In the HVLR scenario, the value of each individual milestone was stochastically optimized using individual restrictions for each payment. While the future value of the milestone payments was actually $300,000 less than the historical deal (Table 7.1), the present value as determined by Monte Carlo analysis was 93.6 percent higher. In devising this scenario, to compensate the licensee for increased R&D/licensing fees and milestone restructuring, the royalty value in the HVLR scenario was reduced to only a 0.5 percent flat rate (Table 7.1).

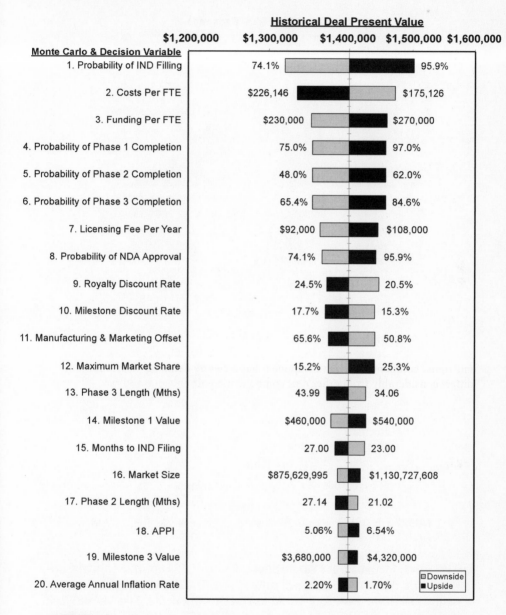

FIGURE 7.4 Historical deal Monte Carlo and decision variable tornado chart.

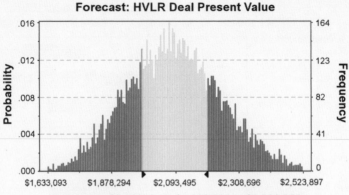

Certainty is 50.00% from $1,980,294 to $2,200,228

Summary:
Certainty Level is 50.00%
Certainty Range is from $1,980,218 to $2,199,958
Display Range is from $1,663,093 to $2,523,897
Entire Range is from $1,475,621 to $2,777,048
After 10,000 Trials, the Std. Error of the Mean is $1,643

Statistics:

Trials	10,000
Mean	$2,092,617
Median	$2,087,697
Standard Deviation	$164,274
Variance	$26,986,218,809
Skewness	0.18
Kurtosis	3.06
Coefficient of Variability	7.85%
Range Minimum	$1,475,620
Range Maximum	$2,777,047
Range Width	$1,301,427
Mean Std. Error	$1,642

FIGURE 7.5   Higher-value, lower-risk deal scenario Monte Carlo.

Deal Valuation, Statistics, and Sensitivities   Figure 7.5 shows the Monte Carlo summary of the HVLR scenario, and Figure 7.6 shows an illustration of present value of the HVLR deal and its three components. The Monte Carlo mean deal value for this scenario was $2,092,617, an increase of 46.1 percent over the historical deal, while total risk was reduced by 16.3 percent as measured by changes in the CV of cash-flow present value (Figures 7.2 and 7.5). This gain in total deal value was achieved by a 93.6 percent increase in the present value of milestone payments (Figures 7.3 and 7.6) along with a 9.6 percent reduction in milestone risk (data not shown). The present value

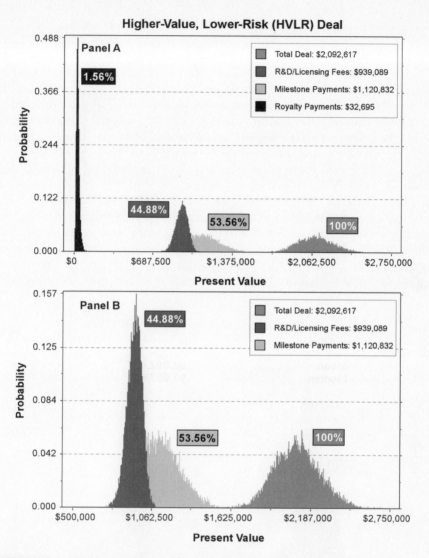

FIGURE 7.6   A comparative illustration II.

The figures illustrate the Monte Carlo distributions for cash-flow present value of the HVLR deal scenario along with the distributions of the deal's individual components. Because the royalty cash flows greatly distort the other distributions (Panel A), removing the royalties from the overlay chart allows the other distributions to be more clearly presented (Panel B). The data in Panel B are comparable to a similar representation of the historical deal (Figure 7.3). Here, proportionally, milestones contributed the most to deal value (53.56 percent), followed by R&D/licensing (44.88 percent), while royalties contributed very little (1.56 percent; Panel A).

of R&D/licensing funding also increased (30.1 percent) while there is a 22.5 percent reduction in risk. These gains came at the cost of royalty income being reduced by 75.1 percent (Figures 7.3 and 7.6).

The royalty component was so small and the mean so tightly concentrated, that the other distributions were comparatively distorted (Panel A, Figure 7.6). If the royalty component is removed, the total deal, milestone, and R&D/licensing distributions are more clearly presented (Panel B, Figure 7.6). The milestone percentage of the total HVLR scenario was much higher than the milestone component of the historical deal, while the R&D/licensing fees of the HVLR structure were less than the historical structure (Figures 7.3 and 7.7).

Cumulatively, the HVLR scenario had a 16.9 percent reduction in risk in comparison to the historical deal (Figures 7.2 and 7.5), where the R&D/licensing and milestone cash flows of HVLR structure were considerably less risky than the historical scenario (data not shown). However, not surprisingly, the risk for the royalty cash flows of the HVLR structure remained nearly identical to that of the historical deal's royalties (data not shown).

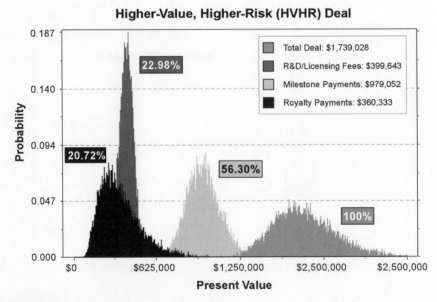

Higher-Value, Higher-Risk (HVHR) Deal

Total Deal: $1,739,028
R&D/Licensing Fees: $399,643
Milestone Payments: $979,052
Royalty Payments: $360,333

FIGURE 7.7   A comparative illustration III.
Illustrations of the Monte Carlo distributions for cash-flow present value of the HVLR deal scenario along with the distributions of the deal's individual components. Here, proportionally, milestones contributed the most to deal value (56.30 percent), followed by R&D/licensing (22.98 percent), while royalties contributed 20.72 percent to total deal value.

Monte Carlo Assumption and Decision Variable Sensitivities The tornado chart for the HVLR deal is presented in Figure 7.8. As with the historical deal, the probability of IND filing produced the largest variation in the HVLR deal. The annual research cost for each FTE for the licensor performing the

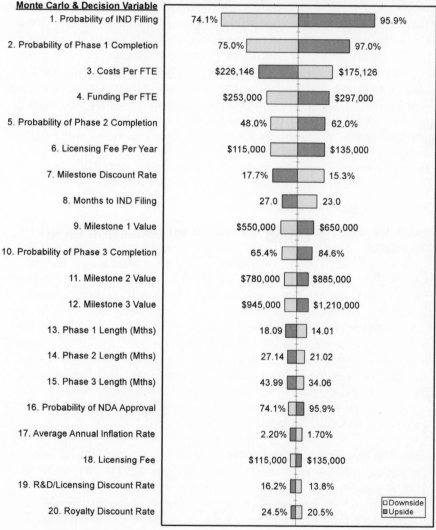

FIGURE 7.8   Higher-value, lower-risk deal scenario Monte Carlo tornado.

remaining preclinical work in preparation for IND filing was third, while the negotiated annual funding amount for each FTE was fourth. The value of each milestone was listed earlier in importance in comparison to the historical deal (Figures 7.4 and 7.8). This result should not be surprising as the present value of total milestones increased 93.6 percent over the historical structure.

The probabilities of completing various clinical trial stages were not clustered as with the historical deal (Figures 7.4 and 7.8). Indeed, the probability of completing Phase 1 was 2nd, the probability of Phase 2 completion 5th, and the probability of Phase 3 completion 10th in predicting variation in total HVLR deal value (Figures 7.8), whereas in the historical deal, these three variables were clustered and ranked 4th through 6th (Figure 7.4). This reorganization is probably because of milestone restructuring where, in the HVLR deal structure, early milestone payments are worth much more (Table 7.1 and Figure 7.1). Among the top 20 most important variables inducing variation in the HVLR deal are the lengths of Phase 1, Phase 2, and Phase 3 clinical trials (13th–15th; Figure 7.8), although their importance was considerably less than the historical deal (Figure 7.4). This is probably because of the reduced royalty component of the HVLR scenario (Table 7.1).

Higher-Value, Higher-Risk Deal Valuation

Changes in Key Assumptions and Parameters Differing from the Historical and HVLR Deal Structures
A variety of financial terms were changed for the HVHR deal structure. First, licensing and licensing maintenance fees were reduced, sometimes substantially (Table 7.1). R&D fees were reduced across the board from the historical deal and the milestone schedule was completely restructured. The historical structure had three payments and the HVLR structure five, with the HVHR deal having only four (Figure 7.1). As shown, the milestone future value for the HVHR deal was reduced to $5,850,000 from $6,000,000 in the historical deal. Like the HVLR deal, the milestone values for the HVHR scenario were stochastically optimized based on specific ranges. The sacrifices gained by lower licensing fees, R&D funding, and milestone restructuring were compensated for by a higher flat royalty rate of 5.5 percent of net sales (Table 7.1).

Deal Valuation, Statistics, and Sensitivities
Figure 7.7 shows an illustration of the total HVHR deal along with its three components. Total deal value for the HVHR scenario was $1,739,028, a 21.4 percent increase from the historical deal and 16.9 percent decrease from the HVLR structure. R&D/licensing present value decreased by 44.7 percent and 57.4 percent from the historical and HVLR deals, respectively (Figures 7.3 through 7.7).

The royalty distribution is much more pronounced and noticeably positively skewed, and illustrates the large downside potential of this deal component. Changes in the royalty percentage also significantly expanded the range maximum for the total deal ($3,462,679) with a range width of $2,402,076, a 130.4 percent increase from the historical and 84.6 percent increase over the HVLR deal widths, respectively (Table 7.2).

Milestone present value increased by 69.1 percent from the historical deal and decreased 12.6 percent from the HVLR scenario, while royalty present value increased 175 percent and 1,002 percent, respectively (Figures 7.3 through 7.7). Both the skewness and kurtosis of total deal value under the HVHR scenario were greater than the other deal structures evaluated (Figures 7.3 through 7.7). This result has to do with the greater royalty component in the HVHR scenario and its associated large cash-flow volatility.

The overall deal risk under the HVHR scenario was the greatest (14.33 percent) in comparison to the historical deal's 9.38 percent and the HVLR scenario's 7.85 percent cash-flow CV, again illustrating the strong royalty component of this deal structure with its greater volatility. With the HVHR deal, R&D/licensing cash flows had much higher risk than either the historical or HVLR deals (data not shown). This increased risk is surely because negotiated R&D funding per FTE and licensing fees were considerably less than the estimated cost per FTE, resulting in more R&D/licensing cash-flow volatility in the HVHR structure. This result again shows the importance of accurate accounting and finance in estimating R&D costs for maximizing this type of licensing deal value.

Monte Carlo Assumption and Decision Variable Sensitivities   The tornado chart for the HVHR deal scenario emphasized the importance of variables directly impacting royalty cash flows (Figure 7.9). Here, the royalty discount rate was 4th, manufacturing and marketing offset 5th, and maximum market share capture 6th in impacting total deal present value variation. Total

TABLE 7.2   Deal Scenario Summary Table as Calculated by Monte Carlo Analysis

Deal Structure	Expected Value	CV	Range Minimum	Range Maximum	Range Width
Historical	$1,432,128	9.38%	$ 994,954	$2,037,413	$1,042,459
Higher-Value, Lower-Risk	2,092,617	7.85	1,475,620	2,777,047	1,301,427
Higher-Value, Higher-Risk	1,739,028	14.33	1,060,603	3,462,679	2,402,076

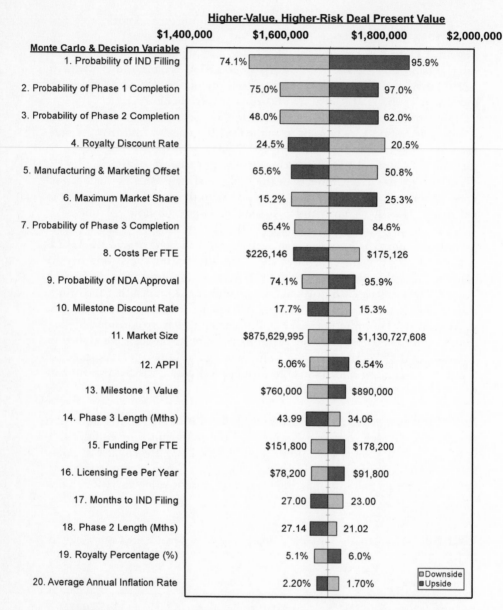

FIGURE 7.9 Higher-value, higher-risk deal scenario Monte Carlo tornado.

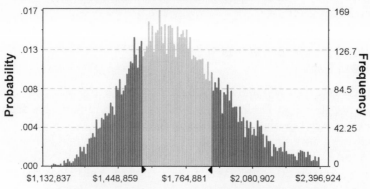

Certainty is 50.00% from $1,563,891 to $1,882,975

Summary:
Certainty Level is 50.00%
Certainty Range is from $1,563,891 to $1,882,975
Display Range is from $1,132,837 to $2,396,924
Entire Range is from $1,060,603 to $3,462,679
After 10,000 Trials, the Std. Error of the Mean is $2,493

Statistics:

Trials	10,000
Mean	$1,739,028
Median	$1,712,532
Standard Deviation	$249,257
Variance	$62,129,317,618
Skewness	0.77
Kurtosis	4.39
Coefficient of Variability	14.33%
Range Minimum	$1,060,603
Range Maximum	$3,462,679
Range Width	$2,402,076
Mean Std. Error	$2,492

FIGURE 7.10 Higher-value, higher-risk deal scenario Monte Carlo summary.

market size and the average APPI were 11th and 12th, respectively. Interestingly, the negotiated royalty percentage was only 19th in contribution to deal variance. Cost per FTE ranked 8th showing this assumption is important in all deal scenarios (Figures 7.4, 7.8, and 7.9).

The negotiated first milestone value was the only milestone listed on the sensitivity chart (13th, Figure 7.9), illustrating the importance of milestone structuring (Table 7.1 and Figure 7.1). The first milestone is impacted the least by the time value of money and the probability of completion of each clinical trial stage.

A Structural Comparison of Deal Scenario Returns and Risks

Total deal expected value and risk as measured by the CV of cash-flow present value are shown in Table 7.2. As illustrated here, higher expected value is not necessarily correlated with higher risk, which is contrary to a basic principal in finance where investments of higher risk should always yield higher returns. Thus, these data show why quantitative deal valuation and optimization is critical for *all* companies as higher deal values can be constructed with significantly less risk.

Also shown in Table 7.2 are the range minimums, maximums, and widths of the total deal value distributions as calculated by Monte Carlo analysis for each scenario evaluated. The range minimum is the smallest number and the range maximum the largest number in a distribution, while the range width is the difference between the range minimum and maximum.

Collaborative business deals in the biotechnology and pharmaceutical industries formed during strategic alliances, such as the one described here, are in fact risky asset portfolios. As such, the standard deviation of a portfolio of assets is less than the weighted average of the component asset standard deviations. To view the impact of diversification of cash-flow streams with the various deal scenarios evaluated in this case study, the weight of each deal component was determined and the weighted average CV of cash-flow present value calculated for each deal scenario (Table 7.3). The CV is used as the primary risk measure because of differences in the scale of the cash flows from individual deal components.

As expected with a portfolio of risky assets, the weighted average of the CV of individual deal components (R&D/licensing funding, milestone payments, and royalties) was always greater than the CV of the total deal present value, illustrating the impact of diversification (Table 7.3). Thus, portfolios of less than perfectly correlated assets always offer better risk–return opportunities than the individual component assets on their own. As such, companies would probably not want to completely forgo receiving milestone payments and royalties for only R&D funding and licensing fees, *if* these deal components can be valued and optimized with reasonable accuracy as described here. By combining assets whose returns are uncorrelated or partially correlated, such as cash flows from milestone payments, royalties, licensing, and R&D funding, risk is reduced (Table 7.3). Risk can be eliminated most rapidly while keeping expected returns as high as possible if a company's cumulative deal repertoire is valued, structured, and balanced from the beginning of a company's evolution and development.

TABLE 7.3 Deal Component Weights, Component CVs, Weighted Average Deal CVs, and Calculated Deal CVs

Deal Structure	Weights			Coefficient of Variation (CV)				
	$W_{R\&D}$[a]	W_{Mi}[b]	W_{Ry}[c]	R&D[d]	Milestones	Royalties	W. Avg.[e]	Calculated[f]
Historical	50.42%	40.42%	9.17%	7.47%	14.57%	45.70%	13.84%	9.38%
Higher-Value, Lower-Risk	44.88	53.56	1.56	5.79	13.18	45.95	10.38	7.85
Higher-Value, Higher-Risk	22.98	56.30	20.72	13.40	12.69	46.21	19.80	14.33

[a]Proportion of total deal present value attributable to R&D and licensing fees.

[b]Proportion of total deal present value attributable to milestone payments.

[c]Proportion of total deal present value attributable to royalty payments.

[d]CV in the present value of cash flows from R&D and licensing fees.

[e]Weighted average of the CV of total deal value.

[f]Calculated deal CV by Monte Carlo simulation.

155

Discussion and Conclusion

The historical deal evaluated in this case study was a preclinical, product-licensing deal for a biopharmaceutical with one major therapeutic indication. For collaborative deal structures containing licensing fees, R&D funding, milestone payments, and royalties, each deal component has definable expected values, variances, and widely varying risk characteristics. Alternative deal structures were developed and optimized, all of which had different expected returns and risk levels with the primary risk measure being the CV of cash-flow present values. Thus, nearly any biomedical collaborative deal with the types of financial terms described here can be quantitatively valued, structured, and optimized using financial models, Monte Carlo analysis, stochastic optimization, real options, and portfolio theory.

During this study, the author was at a considerable disadvantage because the historical deal valued and optimized here had already been signed, and he was not present during the negotiation process. Therefore, the author had to make a large number of assumptions when restructuring the financial terms of the agreement. Considering these limitations, this case is not about what is appropriate in the comparative financial terms for a biomedical licensing deal and what is not; rather, the data described here are valuable in showing the quantitative influence of different deal structures on the overall valuation of a biomedical collaborative agreement, and most importantly on the level of overall deal risk, as well as the risk of the individual deal components. The most effective approach using this technique is to work with a negotiator during the development and due diligence, and through the closing process of a collaborative agreement. During this time, data should be continually gathered and the financial models refined as negotiations and due diligence proceed.

CASE STUDY: OIL AND GAS PRODUCTION AND EXPLORATION

This case study was contributed by Steve Hoye. Steve is an independent business consultant with over 23 years of oil and gas industry experience, specializing in Monte Carlo simulation for the oil and gas industry. Starting with a bachelor of science degree from Purdue University in 1980, he served as a geophysicist with Texaco in Houston, Denver, and Midland, Texas, before earning the MBA degree from the University of Denver in 1997. Since then, Steve has held leadership roles with Texaco as the mid-continent BU technology team leader, and as asset team manager in Texaco's Permian Basin business unit, before starting his consultancy in 2002. Steve can be reached at steve@hoyeconsultinggroup.com.

The oil and gas industry is an excellent place to examine and discuss techniques for analyzing risk. The basic business model discussed involves making investments in land rights, geologic data, drilling (services and hardware), and human expertise in return for a stream of oil or gas production that can be sold at a profit. This model is beset with multiple, significant risk factors that determine the resulting project's profitability, including:

- *Dry-Hole Risk.* Investing drilling dollars with no resulting revenue from oil or gas because none is found in the penetrated geologic formation.
- *Drilling Risk.* High drilling costs can often ruin a project's profitability. While companies do their best to estimate them accurately, unforeseeable geological or mechanical difficulties can cause significant variability in actual costs.
- *Production Risk.* Even when oil or gas reservoirs are discovered by drilling, there is a high probability that point estimates of the size and recoverability of the hydrocarbon reserves over time are wrong.
- *Price Risk.* Along with the cyclical nature of the oil and gas industry, product prices can also vary unexpectedly during significant political events such as war in the Middle East, overproduction and cheating by the OPEC cartel, interruptions in supply such as large refinery fires, labor strikes or political uprisings in large producing nations (e.g., Venezuela in 2002), and changes in world demand.
- *Political Risk.* Significant amounts of the world's hydrocarbon reserves are controlled by nations with unstable governments. Companies who invest in projects in these countries take significant risks that the governments and leaders with whom they have signed contracts will no longer be in power when earned revenue streams should be shared contractually. In many well-documented cases, corporate investments in property, plants, and equipment (PPE) are simply nationalized by local governments, leaving companies without revenue or the equipment and facilities that they built to earn that revenue.

Oil and gas investments generally are very capital-intensive, often making these risks more than just of passing interest. Business units and entire companies stake their survival on their ability to properly account for these risks as they apportion their capital budgets in a manner that ensures value to their stakeholders. To underline the importance of risk management in the industry, many large oil companies commission high-level corporate panels of experts to review and endorse risk assessments done across all of their business units for large capital projects. These reviews attempt to ensure consistency of risk assessment across departments and divisions that are often under pressure to make their investment portfolios look attractive to corporate leadership as they compete for capital.

Monte Carlo simulation is a preferred approach to the evaluation of the multiple, complex risk factors in the model we discuss. Because of the inherent complexity of these risk factors and their interactions, deterministic solutions are not practical, and point forecasts are of limited use and, at worst, are misleading. In contrast, Monte Carlo simulation is ideal for economic evaluations under these circumstances. Domain experts can individually quantify and describe the project risks associated with their areas of expertise without having to define their overall effect on project economics.[1] Cash-flow models that integrate the diverse risk assumptions for each of the prospect team's experts are relatively straightforward to construct and analyze. Most importantly, the resulting predictions of performance do not result in a simple single-point estimate of the profitability of a given oil and gas prospect. Instead, they provide management with a spectrum of possible outcomes and their related probabilities. Best of all, Monte Carlo simulation provides estimates of the sensitivities of their investment outcomes to the critical assumptions in their models, allowing them to focus money and people on the critical factors that will determine whether or not they meet the financial goals defined in their business plans. Ultimately, Monte Carlo simulation becomes a project management tool that decreases risk while increasing profits.

In this case study, we explore a practical model of an oil-drilling prospect, taking into account many of the risk factors described earlier. While the model is hypothetical, the general parameters we use are consistent with those encountered drilling in a mature, oil-rich basin in the United States (e.g., Permian Basin of West Texas) in terms of the risk factors and related revenues and expenses. This model is of greater interest as a framework and approach than it is as an evaluation of any particular drilling prospect. Its value is in demonstrating the approach to quantifying important risk assumptions in an oil prospect using Monte Carlo simulation, and analyzing their effects on the profitability forecasts of the project. The techniques described herein are extensible to many other styles and types of oil and gas prospects.

Cash-Flow Model

The model was constructed using Crystal Ball from Decisioneering, which provides all of the necessary Monte Carlo simulation tools as an easy-to-use, comprehensive add-in to Microsoft Excel. The model simulates the drilling outcome as being a dry-hole or an oil discovery using dry-hole risk factors for the particular geologic formation and basin. Drilling, seismic, and land-lease costs are incurred whether the well is dry or a discovery. If the well is a discovery, a revenue stream is computed for the produced oil over time using assumptions for product price, and for the oil production rate as it declines over time from its initial value. Expenses are deducted for royalty payments to landowners, operating costs associated with producing the oil, and severance taxes levied by states on the produced oil. Finally, the resulting net cash flows are discounted at the weighted average cost of capital (WACC) for the firm and summed to a net present value (NPV) for the project. Each of these sections of the model is now discussed in more detail.

Dry-Hole Risk

Companies often have proprietary schemes for quantifying the risk associated with not finding any oil or gas in their drilled well. In general, though, there are four primary and independent conditions that must all be encountered in order for hydrocarbons to be found by the drill bit:

1. *Hydrocarbons* must be present.
2. A *reservoir* must be developed in the rock formation to hold the hydrocarbons.
3. An impermeable *seal* must be available to trap the hydrocarbons in the reservoir and prevent them from migrating somewhere else.
4. A *structure* or *closure* must be present that will cause the hydrocarbons (sealed in the reservoir) to pool in a field where the drill bit will penetrate.

Because these four factors are independent and must each be true in order for hydrocarbons to be encountered by the drill bit (and a dry hole to be avoided), the probability of a producing well is defined as:

$$P_{\text{Producing Well}} = P_{\text{Hydrocarbons}} \times P_{\text{Reservoir}} \times P_{\text{Seal}} \times P_{\text{Structure}}$$

Figure 7.11 shows the model section labeled "Dry-Hole Risk," along with the probability distributions for each factor's Monte Carlo assumption. While a project team most often describes each of these factors as a single-point estimate, other methods are sometimes used to quantify these risks. The most effective process the author has witnessed involved the presentation of the geological, geophysical, and engineering factors by the prospect team, to a group of expert peers with wide experience in the proposed area. These peer experts then rated each of the risk factors. The resulting distribution of risk factors often appeared near-normally distributed, with strong central tendencies and symmetrical tails. This approach was very amenable to Monte Carlo simulation. It highlighted those factors where there was general agreement about risk and brought the riskiest factors to the foreground where they were examined and specifically addressed.

Accordingly, the assumptions regarding dry-hole risk in this model reflect a relatively low risk profile.[2] Each of the four risk factor assumptions in Figure 7.11 (dark shaded area) are described as normally distributed vari-

Dry-Hole Risk

Risk Factor	Prob. of Success	Mean	Stdev	Min	Max
Hydrocarbons	89.7%	99.0%	5.0%	0	100%
Structure	89.7%	100.0%	0.0%	0	100%
Reservoir	89.7%	75.0%	10.0%	0	100%
Seal	89.7%	100.0%	0.0%	0	100%
Net Producing Well Prob.:	**64.8%**				

Producing Well [0=no,1=yes]   1

FIGURE 7.11   Dry-hole risk.

ables, with the mean and standard deviations for each distribution to the right of the assumption fields. The ranges of these normal distributions are confined and truncated between the *min* and *max* fields, and random samples for any simulation trial outside this range are ignored as unrealistic.

As described earlier, the *Net Producing Well Probability* field in the model corresponds to the product of the four previously described risk factors. These four risk factors are drawn as random samples from their respective normal distributions for each trial or iteration of the simulation. Finally, as each iteration of the Monte Carlo simulation is conducted, the field labeled *Producing Well* generates a random number between zero and one to determine if that simulation resulted in a discovery of oil or a dry hole. If the random number is less than the *Net Producing Well Probability*, it is a producing well and shows the number one. Conversely, if the random number is greater then the *Net Producing Well Probability*, the simulated well is a dry hole and shows zero.

Production Risk

A multiyear stream of oil can be characterized as an initial oil production rate (measured in barrels of oil per day, BOPD), followed by a decline in production rates as the natural reservoir energy and volumes are depleted over time. Reservoir engineers can characterize production declines using a wide array of mathematical models, choosing those that most closely match the geology and producing characteristics of the reservoir. Our hypothetical production stream is described with two parameters:

1. *IP*. The initial production rate tested from the drilled well.
2. *Decline Rate.* An exponentially declining production rate that describes the annual decrease in production from the beginning of the year, to the end of the same year. Production rates in BOPD for our model are calculated by:

$$\text{Rate}_{\text{Year End}} = (1 - \text{Decline Rate}) \times \text{Rate}_{\text{Year Begin}}$$

Yearly production volumes in barrels of oil are approximated as:

$$\text{Oil Volume}_{\text{Year}} = 365 \times (\text{Rate}_{\text{Year Begin}} + \text{Rate}_{\text{Year End}})/2$$

For Monte Carlo simulation, our model represents the IPs with a lognormal distribution with a mean of 441 BOPD, and a standard deviation of 165 BOPD. The decline rate was modeled with a uniform probability of occurrence between 15 percent and 28 percent. To add interest and realism to our hypothetical model, we incorporated an additional constraint in the production model that simulates a situation that might occur for a particular reservoir where higher IPs imply that the production decline rate will be higher. This constraint is implemented in Crystal Ball by imposing a correlation coefficient of 0.60 between the IP and decline rate assumptions that are drawn from their respective distributions during each trial of the simulation.

The production and operating expense sections of the model are shown in Figure 7.12. Although only the first 3 years are shown, the model accounts for up to 25 years of production. However, when production declines below the economic limit,[3] it will be zeroed for that year and every subsequent year, ending the producing life of the well. As shown, the IP is assumed to occur at the end of Year 0, with the first full year of production accounted for at the end of Year 1.

Revenue Section

Revenues from the model flow literally from the sale of the oil production computed earlier. Again there are two assumptions in our model that represent risks in our prospect:

1. *Price.* Over the past 10 years, oil prices have varied from $13.63/barrel in 1998 to nearly $30/barrel in 2000.[4] Consistent with the data, our

	Decline Rate	End of Year: 0	1	2	3
BOPD	21.5%	442	347	272	214
Net BBLS / Yr			143,866	112,924	88,636
Price / BBl			$ 20.14	$ 20.14	$ 20.14
Net Revenue Interest	77.4%		77.4%	77.4%	77.4%
Revenue			$ 2,242,311	$ 1,760,035	$ 1,381,487
Operating Costs [$/Barrel]	$ 4.80		$ (690,558)	$ (542,033)	$ (425,453)
Severance Taxes [$]	6.0%	rate	$ (134,539)	$ (105,602)	$ (82,889)
Net Sales			$ 1,417,214	$ 1,112,400	$ 873,145

FIGURE 7.12 Decline rate.

model assumes a normal price distribution with a mean of $20.14 and a standard deviation of $4.43/barrel.

2. *Net Revenue Interest.* Oil companies must purchase leases from mineral interest holders. Along with paying cash to retain the drilling and production rights to a property for a specified time period, the lessee also generally retains some percentage of the oil revenue produced in the form of a royalty. The percentage that the producing company retains after paying all royalties is the net revenue interest (NRI). Our model represents a typical West Texas scenario with an assumed NRI distributed normally with a mean of 75 percent and a standard deviation of 2 percent.

The revenue portion of the model is also shown in Figure 7.12 immediately below the production stream.

The yearly production volumes are multiplied by sampled price per barrel, and then multiplied by the assumed NRI to reflect dilution of revenues from royalty payments to lessees.

Operating Expense Section

Below the revenue portion are operating expenses, which include two assumptions:

1. *Operating Costs.* Companies must pay for manpower and hardware involved in the production process. These expenses are generally described as a dollar amount per barrel. A reasonable West Texas cost would be $4.80 per barrel with a standard deviation of $0.60 per barrel.
2. *Severance Taxes.* State taxes levied on produced oil and gas are assumed to be a constant value of 6 percent of revenue.

Operating expenses are subtracted from the gross sales to arrive at net sales, as shown in Figure 7.12.

Year 0 Expenses   Figure 7.13 shows the Year 0 expenses assumed to be incurred before oil production from the well (and revenue) is realized. These expenses are:

1. *Drilling Costs.* These costs can vary significantly as previously discussed, due to geologic, engineering, and mechanical uncertainty. It is reasonable to skew the distribution of drilling costs to account for a high-end tail consisting of a small number of wells with very large drilling costs due to mechanical failure and unforeseen geologic or serendipitous occurrences. Accordingly, our distribution is assumed to

Drilling Costs	$ 1,209,632
Completion Cost	$ 287,000
Professional Overhead	$ 160,000
Lease Costs / well	$ 469,408
Seismic Costs / well	$ 81,195

FIGURE 7.13   Year 0 expenses.

be lognormal, with a mean of $1.2 million and a standard deviation of $200,000.

2. *Completion Costs.* If it is determined that there is oil present in the reservoir (and we have not drilled a dry hole), engineers must prepare the well (mechanically/chemically) to produce oil at the optimum sustainable rates.[5] For this particular well, we hypothesize our engineers believe this cost is normally distributed with a mean of $287,000 and a standard deviation of $30,000.

3. *Professional Overhead.* This project team costs about $320,000 per year in salary and benefits, and we believe the time they have spent is best represented by a triangular distribution, with a most likely percentage of time spent as 50 percent, with a minimum of 40 percent, a maximum of 65 percent.

4. *Seismic and Lease Costs.* To develop the proposal, our team needed to purchase seismic data to choose the optimum well location, and to purchase the right to drill on much of the land in the vicinity of the well. Because this well is not the only well to be drilled on this seismic data and land, the cost of these items is distributed over the planned number of wells in the project. Uncertain assumptions are shown in Figure 7.14, and include leased acres, which were assumed to be normally distributed with a mean of 12,000 and a standard deviation of 1,000 acres. The total number of planned wells over which to distribute the costs was assumed to be uniform between 10 and 30. The number of seismic sections acquired was also assumed to be normally distributed with a mean of 50 sections and a standard deviation of 7. These costs are represented as the final two lines of Year 0 expenses in Figure 7.13.

Net Present Value Section

The final section of the model sums all revenues and expenses for each year starting at Year 0, discounted at the weighted average cost of capital (WACC—which we assume for this model is 9 percent per year), and summed across years to compute the forecast of NPV for the project. In addition, NPV/I is computed,[6] as it can be used as a threshold and ranking

Lease Expense		Comments
project lease acres	12,800	20 sections
planned wells	20.0	
acres / well	640	
acreage price	$ 733.45	$ / acre
acreage cost / well	$ 469,408	

Seismic Expense		
seismic sections acquired	50.0	
seismic sections / well	2.50	
seismic cost	$ 32,478.18	$ / section
seismic cost / well	$ 81,195	

FIGURE 7.14   Uncertain assumptions.

mechanism for portfolio decisions as the company determines how this project fits with its other investment opportunities given a limited capital budget.

Monte Carlo Simulation Results

As we assess the results of running the simulation with the assumptions defined previously, it is useful to define and contrast the point estimate of project value that is computed from our model using the mean or most likely values of the earlier assumptions. The expected value of the project is defined as:

$$E_{\text{Project}} = E_{\text{Dry Hole}} + E_{\text{Producing Well}}$$

$$= P_{\text{Dry Hole}} NPV_{\text{Dry Hole}} + P_{\text{Producing Well}} NPV_{\text{Producing Well}}$$

where $P_{\text{Producing Well}}$ = probability of a producing well and $P_{\text{Dry Hole}}$ = probability of a dry hole = $(1 - P_{\text{Producing Well}})$. Using the mean or most likely point estimate values from our model, the expected NPV of the project is $1,250,000, which might be a very attractive prospect in the firm's portfolio.

In contrast, we can now examine the spectrum of outcomes and their probability of occurrence. Our simulation was run with 8,450 trials (trial size selected by precision control) to forecast NPV, which provided a mean NPV plus or minus $50,000 with 95 percent confidence. Figure 7.15 is the frequency distribution of NPV outcomes. The distribution is obviously bimodal, with the large, sharp negative NPV peak to the left representing the outcome of a dry hole. The smaller, broader peak toward the higher NPV ranges represents the wider range of more positive NPVs associated with a producing well.

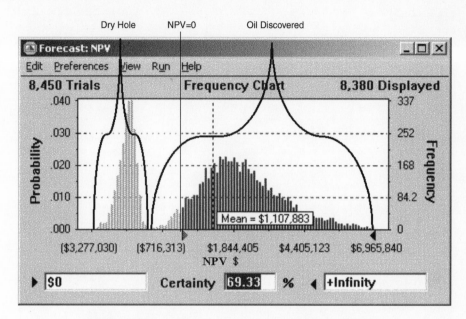

FIGURE 7.15   Frequency distribution of NPV outcomes.

All negative NPV outcomes are to the left of the *NPV = 0* line (with a lighter shade) in Figure 7.15, while positive outcome NPVs are represented by the area to the right of the *NPV = 0* line (with a darker shade), with the probability of a positive outcome (breakeven or better) shown as 69 percent. Of interest, the negative outcome possibilities include not only the dry-hole population of outcomes as shown, but also a small but significant portion of producing-well outcomes that could still lose money for the firm. From this information, we can conclude that there is a 31.67 percent chance that this project will have a negative NPV.

It is obviously not good enough for a project of this sort to avoid a negative NPV. The project must return to shareholders something higher than its cost of capital, and, further, must be competitive with other investment opportunities that the firm has. If our hypothetical firm had a hurdle rate of NPV/I greater than 25 percent for its yearly budget, we would want to test our simulated project outcomes against the probability that the project could clear that hurdle rate.

Figure 7.16 shows the forecast distribution of outcomes for NPV/I. The large peak at negative 100 percent again represents the dry-hole case, where in fact the NPV of the outcome is negative in the amount of Year 0 costs incurred, making NPV/I equal to –1. All outcomes for NPV greater than the hurdle rate of 25 percent (area with a darker shade in the figure) show that

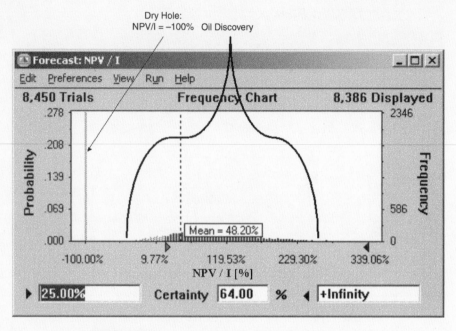

FIGURE 7.16   Forecast distribution of NPV to I ratio.

there is a 64 percent probability that the project will exceed that rate. To a risk-sensitive organization, this outcome implies a probability of greater than one in three that the project will fail to clear the firm's hurdle rate—significant risk indeed.

Finally, our simulation gives us the power to explore the sensitivity of our project outcomes to the risks and assumptions that have been made by our experts in building the model. Figure 7.17 shows a sensitivity analysis of the NPV of our project to the assumptions made in our model. This chart shows the correlation coefficient of the top 10 model assumptions to the NPV forecast in order of decreasing correlation.

At this point, the project manager is empowered to focus resources on the issues that will have an impact on the profitability of this project. Given the information from Figure 7.17, we could hypothesize the following actions to address the top risks in this project in order of importance:

■ *IP.* The initial production rate of the well has a driving influence on value of this project, and our uncertainty in predicting this rate is causing the largest swing in predicted project outcomes. Accordingly, we could have our team of reservoir and production engineers further examine known production IPs from analogous reservoirs in this area,

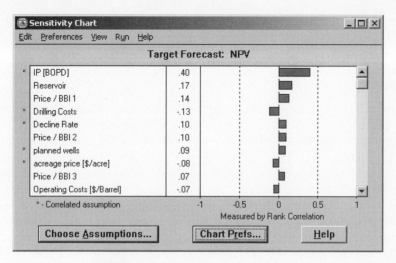

FIGURE 7.17 NPV sensitivity analysis.

and perhaps attempt to stratify the data to further refine predictions of IPs based on drilling or completion techniques, geological factors, or geophysical data.

- *Reservoir Risk.* This assumption is the driver of whether the well is a dry hole or producer, and as such it is not surprising that it is a major driving factor. Among many approaches, the project team could investigate the possibility that inadequate analysis of subsurface data is causing many companies to declare dry holes in reservoirs that have hidden producing potential.
- *Oil Price (Year 1) and Drilling Costs.* Both of these items are closely related in their power to affect NPV. Price uncertainty could best be addressed by having a standard price prediction for the firm against which all projects would be compared.[7] Drilling costs could be minimized by process improvements in the drilling team that would tighten the variation of predicted costs from actual costs. The firm could seek out companies with strong track records in their project area for reliable, low-cost drilling.
- *Decline Rate.* The observant reader will note a positive-signed correlation between decline rate and project NPV. At first glance this is unexpected, because we would normally expect that a higher decline rate would reduce the volumes of oil to be sold and hurt the revenue realized by our project. Recall, however, that we correlated higher IPs with higher decline rates in our model assumptions, which is an indirect indication of the power of the IP on the NPV of our project: Despite higher decline rates, the positive impact of higher IPs on our project

value is overriding the lost production that occurs because of the rapid reservoir decline. We should redouble our efforts to better predict IPs in our model.

Conclusion

Monte Carlo simulation can be an ideal tool for evaluating oil and gas prospects under conditions of significant and complex uncertainty in the assumptions that would render any single-point estimate of the project outcome nearly useless. The technique provides each member of multidisciplinary work teams a straightforward and effective framework for quantifying and accounting for each of the risk factors that will influence the outcome of his or her drilling project. In addition, Monte Carlo simulation provides management and team leadership something much more valuable than a single forecast of the project's NPV: It provides a probability distribution of the entire spectrum of project outcomes, allowing decision makers to explore any pertinent scenarios associated with the project value. These scenarios could include break-even probabilities as well as scenarios associated with extremely poor project results that could damage the project team's credibility and future access to capital, or outcomes that resulted in highly successful outcomes. Finally, Monte Carlo simulation of oil and gas prospects provides managers and team leaders critical information on which risk factors and assumptions are driving the projected probability of project outcomes, giving them the all-important feedback they need to focus their people and financial resources on addressing those risk assumptions that will have the greatest positive impact on their business, improving their efficiency and adding profits to their bottom line.

FIVE-MINUTE INDUSTRY SPOTLIGHT: SIERRA SYSTEMS

Cost-Effective Business Solutions

Sierra Systems Group Inc., a Western Canadian company headquartered in Vancouver, offers high-quality, cost-effective business solutions to clients in industries ranging from health care and manufacturing to mining. Established in 1966, Sierra Systems is a publicly traded company with a reputation for quality solutions and annual revenues of over $120 million. Sierra Systems applies Monte Carlo simulation to help midsize to large client organizations make near-optimal operational and policy decisions.

One of Sierra Systems recent clients is a regional power company (with over $1 billion in revenues) in transition from a regulated to a deregulated environment. With Sierra System's assistance, the power company is investigating how it can compete with market-based utilities such as electricity, gas, water, and services. Sierra Systems Group Senior Consultant Iqbal Jamal, P.Eng., who has used Crystal Ball for over 2 years, was brought in as an outside consultant to help the power company with this project.

Prior to their collaboration with Sierra Systems, the power company evaluated projects using a collection of spreadsheets of varying complexity and project requirements. The company's go/no-go decisions were based on single-value net present value (NPV) and return on equity (ROE) estimates for the life of the project and proportioned to the levels of joint venture investment. The company's deterministic spreadsheet models were detailed, but because they relied on estimates, they could not be used to assess project risk in a timely or effective manner.

Sierra Systems immediately helped the power company tackle two problems: pulling together the many different spreadsheets into one overall framework, and addressing uncertainty in a variety of financial, engineering, project, and economic variables in their models. After consolidating the worksheets, they helped the power company to apply Monte Carlo simulation to improve the accuracy of their project forecasts.

With Crystal Ball, Jamal and his colleagues replaced the single-value estimates of key uncertain variables, such as natural gas energy price, price inflation rate, power pool electricity prices, project capital costs, variable operating costs, and long-term interest rates, with probability distributions. Unlike the previously used estimated values, these distributions represented the realistic range and probability surrounding each uncertain value. They then defined the model formulas, or forecasts, that they wanted to track and analyze with Crystal Ball. These forecasts included such variables as year of payout, before and after tax return on investment, and cumulative cash flow.

Jamal and his colleagues ran 4,000 Crystal Ball simulation trials on the project model and applied the sensitivity and tornado analyses to determine which of the uncertain variables had the greatest impact on the forecasts. Early work suggests that there are five key variables that significantly impact project risk. As many of these variables are correlated over time, the power company can use Crystal Ball to generate better and tighter estimates of project ROE.

"The benefit of using Crystal Ball is that it provides a better assessment of project risk by engineers, financial analysts, senior executives, and the corporate board," said Jamal. "The software creates a clearer language around project risk and decision making and also provides a framework to evaluate 'marginal' projects. The tornado diagrams and probability distribution plots were the most useful features for our work."

Currently, Sierra System's business development section and CFO's office are considering standardizing processes and tools such as Crystal Ball for project evaluation and selection across the corporation and its subsidiaries. This standardization would provide a more consistent basis for stage-gate decision making for large multimillion dollar and multiyear projects.

FIVE-MINUTE INDUSTRY SPOTLIGHT:
MOTOROLA

Engineers Improve the Design
of Portable Products

The challenge of implementing new technologies in portable products requires a skillful application of engineering tools and sound design judgment. At Motorola Labs, one of the simulation tools that Design Reliability Team Leader Dr. William L. Olson regularly uses for engineering design is Crystal Ball.

Dr. Olson's team has developed a range of proprietary Excel-based models that describe the cost of electrical or mechanical performance of electronic assemblies used on portable consumer electronics. "Through dynamic variation of these models, we are able to better understand the relative performance and cost relationships of various competing technologies or alternative designs," noted Dr. Olson.

The design reliability team also finds that the software is useful for quickly assessing the relative impact of conflicting design requirements or design trade-offs. Such simulations can help to check the robustness of the design when particular design parameters are varied. For example, in a printed wiring board (PWB) performance simulation, they can look at the effect on line impedance as a result of variation in dielectric constant, loss tangent, or circuit design. By simulating 5,000 combinations of design model variables, a desktop computer can determine the relative robustness of a design solution in about 2 minutes. In contrast, an exact solution would require tens of hours of simulation on a far more powerful workstation.

"I call Crystal Ball my 95 percent correct solution," said Dr. Olson. "Providing that the model is appropriately structured, Crystal Ball can return an answer that is 95 percent correct in less than 5 percent of the time it would take a higher-level simulation tool to return a comparable result. In many instances, the time savings more than compensate for the increased uncertainty and result in a better, more timely decision."

Dr. Olson believes that skillful application of simulation can address a remarkable range of problems, from engineering applications involving electrical and mechanical design to projecting potential revenues from new businesses or projects.

Risk Prediction

Tomorrow's Forecast Today

WHAT IS FORECASTING?

Forecasting is the act of predicting the future whether it is based on historical data or speculation about the future when no history exists. When historical data exist, a quantitative or statistical approach is best, but if no historical data exist, then potentially a qualitative or judgmental approach is usually the only recourse. Figure 8.1 lists the most common methodologies for forecasting. This chapter illustrates the application of time-series forecasting tools using Crystal Ball Predictor, assuming that historical data exist. Chapter 9 goes into the model details and provides a glimpse behind the scenes of the eight most common time-series methods as well as regression

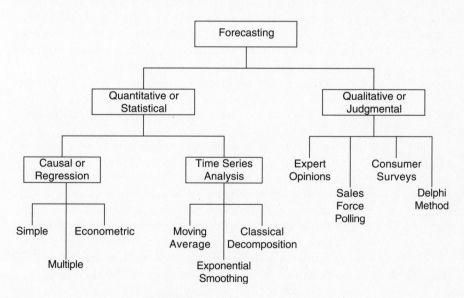

FIGURE 8.1 Forecasting methods.

analysis. In cases where historical data do not exist or are highly unreliable, then Monte Carlo simulation can be applied in conjunction with the four qualitative methods in Figure 8.1.

THE NATURE AND VIEW OF FORECASTING

To best illustrate how forecasting is performed, a simple example is in order. This example assumes that the reader is now sufficiently proficient in the use of Crystal Ball and has a good understanding of forecasting basics. This example is meant only as a guide to the reader on some of the steps taken in a comprehensive decision analysis methodology. Certain simplified assumptions are made to facilitate the computation and illustration.

> Forecasting is the art and science of predicting the future. It can be based on quantitative approaches (e.g., using historical data to predict the future through some forecasting model or making assumptions of future outcomes through simulation) and qualitative approaches (e.g., expert judgment and management assumptions).

As an example, in order to create a financial cost-benefit model on a new product development effort, one of the very first steps is to collect historical data on revenues of existing comparable products (other existing comparable products with similar characteristics, risks, and markets are used to benchmark the new product currently under development). Suppose the only available historical data on revenues are quarterly data starting from 1997 through 2002 of a highly similar product that was developed by the firm. The analyst performs time-series analysis using Crystal Ball's Predictor (*CBTools | CBPredictor*) on the historical data (Figure 8.2).

The following step (Figure 8.3) shows the selection of the historical data range using Predictor. Assuming the historical data exhibits seasonality, a quarterly seasonality correction is performed in the next step as shown in Figure 8.4. Predictor automatically chooses the best-fitting time-series model from a series of eight different approaches as shown in Figure 8.5. In addition, the user can double-click each method to obtain a short description of that method and click on *User Defined* to override the time-series parameters obtained automatically. It is suggested that these time-series parameters (e.g., alpha, beta, and gamma) be obtained automatically by the software.

Then, a forecast is created for 20 periods (Figure 8.6). For each of the 20 quarterly forecast periods, Predictor automatically creates the revenue point

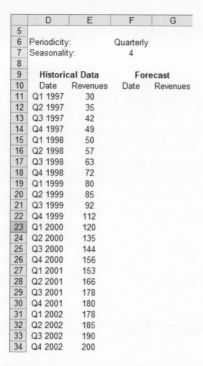

FIGURE 8.2 Sample historical data in Microsoft Excel.

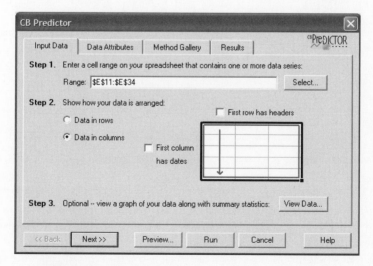

FIGURE 8.3 CB Predictor steps 1 through 3: Input data.

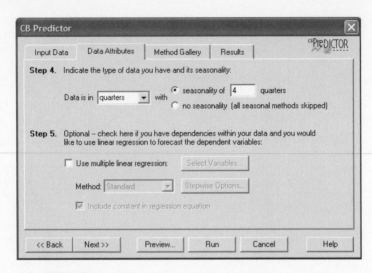

FIGURE 8.4   CB Predictor steps 4 and 5: Data attributes.

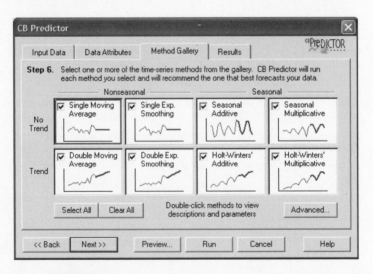

FIGURE 8.5   CB Predictor step 6: Method gallery.

forecasts with the relevant distributional assumptions (Figure 8.7). The highlighted cells (*G11* to *G30*) indicate where the resulting forecast revenues with distributional assumptions are attached.

These single-point forecasts are based on the best-fitting line in the gallery of time-series approaches. The graph shown in Figure 8.8 illustrates

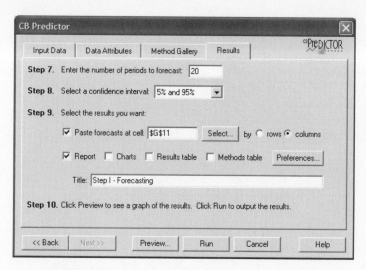

FIGURE 8.6 CB Predictor steps 7 through 10: Results.

	D	E	F	G
5				
6	Periodicity:		Quarterly	
7	Seasonality:		4	
8				
9	**Historical Data**		**Forecast**	
10	Date	Revenues	Date	Revenues
11	Q1 1997	30	Q1 2003	202.27
12	Q2 1997	35	Q2 2003	210.25
13	Q3 1997	42	Q3 2003	217.26
14	Q4 1997	49	Q4 2003	230.30
15	Q1 1998	50	Q1 2004	231.80
16	Q2 1998	57	Q2 2004	239.86
17	Q3 1998	63	Q3 2004	246.81
18	Q4 1998	72	Q4 2004	260.60
19	Q1 1999	80	Q1 2005	261.33
20	Q2 1999	85	Q2 2005	269.47
21	Q3 1999	92	Q3 2005	276.37
22	Q4 1999	112	Q4 2005	290.90
23	Q1 2000	120	Q1 2006	290.85
24	Q2 2000	135	Q2 2006	299.08
25	Q3 2000	144	Q3 2006	305.93
26	Q4 2000	156	Q4 2006	321.20
27	Q1 2001	153	Q1 2007	320.38
28	Q2 2001	166	Q2 2007	328.69
29	Q3 2001	178	Q3 2007	335.48
30	Q4 2001	180	Q4 2007	351.50
31	Q1 2002	178		
32	Q2 2002	185		
33	Q3 2002	190		
34	Q4 2002	200		

FIGURE 8.7 Forecast results with distributional assumptions in Excel.

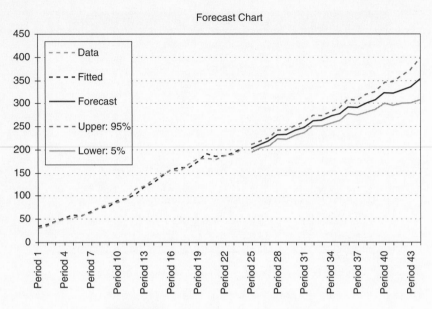

FIGURE 8.8   CB Predictor's forecast charts.

this fitting of historical data, as well as the forecast out to the future, complete with a 5th percentile and 95th percentile confidence interval. The table in Figure 8.9 lists the point forecast for each succeeding quarter, with its corresponding 5th and 95th percentiles.

Forecast

Date	Lower: 5%	Forecast	Upper: 95%
Q1 2003	194.53	202.27	210.02
Q2 2003	202.15	210.25	218.35
Q3 2003	208.78	217.26	225.74
Q4 2003	221.39	230.30	239.21
Q1 2004	222.42	231.80	241.17
Q2 2004	229.96	239.86	249.76
Q3 2004	236.34	246.81	257.29
Q4 2004	249.47	260.60	271.73
Q1 2005	249.45	261.33	273.20
Q2 2005	256.75	269.47	282.19
Q3 2005	262.67	276.37	290.07
Q4 2005	276.06	290.90	305.74
Q1 2006	274.66	290.85	307.04
Q2 2006	281.27	299.08	316.89
Q3 2006	286.13	305.93	325.72
Q4 2006	298.93	321.20	343.47
Q1 2007	294.93	320.38	345.82
Q2 2007	299.00	328.69	358.38
Q3 2007	299.86	335.48	371.11
Q4 2007	306.97	351.50	396.03

FIGURE 8.9   CB Predictor forecast results table.

Step II: DCF

Input Parameters

Discount Rate (Cash Flow)	15.00%
Discount Rate (Impl. Cost)	5.00%
Tax Rate	10.00%

Results

Present Value (Cash Flow)	$1,265.09
Present Value (Impl. Cost)	($865.90)
Net Present Value	$399.20

Year	2003	2004	2005	2006	2007
Revenue	$860.08	$979.07	$1,098.06	$1,217.06	$1,336.05
Adjustment to Revenue	$51.60	$97.91	$197.65	$316.43	$467.62
Cost of Revenue	$86.01	$97.91	$109.81	$121.71	$133.60
Royalties Paid	$43.00	$48.95	$164.71	$182.56	$200.41
Gross Profit	$679.46	$734.30	$625.90	$596.36	$534.42
Operating Expenses	$135.89	$146.86	$125.18	$119.27	$106.88
Depreciation Expense	$10.00	$10.00	$10.00	$10.00	$10.00
Interest Expense	$100.00	$100.00	$100.00	$100.00	$100.00
Income Before Taxes	$433.57	$477.44	$390.72	$367.09	$317.54
Taxes	$43.36	$47.74	$39.07	$36.71	$31.75
Income After Taxes	$390.21	$429.70	$351.65	$330.38	$285.78
Non-Cash Expenses	$4.30	$4.90	$16.47	$18.26	$20.04
Cash Flow	$394.51	$434.59	$368.12	$348.63	$305.82
Implementation Cost	($200.00)	($200.00)	($200.00)	($200.00)	($200.00)

FIGURE 8.10   Second step in the analysis: Creating a discounted cash-flow model.

As an example of applied financial risk analysis, the next step is to create a discounted cash-flow model using the forecast revenues as shown in Figure 8.10. As the revenues are based on the forecast values with distributional assumptions, the resulting net present value will have Monte Carlo simulation performed as well. In addition, other stochastic variable inputs affecting the discounted cash-flow model can also be accounted for. As an example, several adjustments to revenues such as competitive effects, cannibalization by other product substitutes, and market saturation effects are stochastic and unknown in the future. However, management can decide what the potential range of effects may be over time. These stochastic variables are linked to the discounted cash-flow model and the resulting stream of net cash flows will be stochastic, which means that the resulting variable(s) of interest (e.g., net present value) will be a forecast distribution with risk and uncertainty analysis performed on it.

> Typically, the first step in risk analysis is the prediction or forecast of future outcomes. For instance, in a financial analysis, forecasting future sales, revenue, and costs is usually the first step in building any financial model.

FIVE-MINUTE INDUSTRY SPOTLIGHT: HEWLETT-PACKARD

Bringing Printers to Market on Time

Jeff Brown is a project manager in the R&D lab of Hewlett-Packard's (HP) Work Group Color Laserjet Division. One of Jeff's main responsibilities is estimating the duration of production projects from conception to manufacturing release. An accurate production schedule provides HP the ability to effectively bring products to market on time.

In the past, Jeff used COCOMO (Constructive Cost Model) to aid in establishing production schedules. However, this method alone did not address the particular areas of variability that were causing delays in production. One of the difficult areas to accommodate in the planning process is the relative efficiency level of individual engineers because each engineer works at a different pace in various areas of expertise. Based on historical data regarding output, the engineers are grouped into "feature teams" and are responsible for the development of specific printer features. The complexity of a particular printer feature is another important variable because some features require more engineers and production time to develop. Also, Jeff must consider the levels of integration between the various feature teams, which indicates how many other teams any particular team will have to work with in order to accomplish its tasks.

Using Crystal Ball to help develop his most current production schedule, Jeff performed over 10,000 Monte Carlo simulations using just under 100 control variables to help identify those areas that posed potential risks to the production timetable. The results from these simulations gave Jeff the information necessary to most effectively allocate production resources.

When using the COCOMO method alone, the production schedules Jeff produced were often significantly incorrect, sometimes varying as much as 9 months. After employing Crystal Ball, Jeff was pleased to discover that the difference between the scheduled completion date and the actual completion date was reduced to 5 weeks. With this large difference between the two production schedules, it is easy to see why Jeff views Crystal Ball as being an integral tool in helping to bring HP's Colorjet Printers to market on time.

FIVE-MINUTE INDUSTRY SPOTLIGHT: SUNTRUST BANK

Risk Analysis Assessing the Risk of Commercial Loans

SunTrust Banks, Inc., is a premier financial services company based in the Southeastern United States. SunTrust provides a wide range of services to meet the financial needs of its growing customer base through approximately 700 full-service banking offices in Florida, Georgia, Tennessee, and Alabama. SunTrust's primary businesses include traditional deposit and credit services as well as trust and investment services. Through various subsidiaries the company provides credit cards, mortgage banking, credit-related insurance, data processing and information services, discount brokerage, and investment banking services.

A small segment of SunTrust's commercial loan department is that of lending to the construction industry. SunTrust has recently used Crystal Ball to perform Monte Carlo simulations on hotel construction loans. These simulations help quantify the risks involved in evaluating these types of loans. Formerly, bankers would do worst-case and best-case analyses on construction loans when deciding whether to provide financing. Using Crystal Ball, a method was developed to obtain a risk-adjusted return on investment. Using this finding and comparing it to the bank's cost of funds helps decision makers determine if the profitability is worth accepting the risk of approving the loan.

QUESTIONS

1. Why are confidence intervals (e.g., 5th and 95th percentiles) required in forecasting?
2. What is a time-series model and what types of data are typically used in a time-series model?
3. What are some examples of variables that exhibit seasonality versus cyclicality?
4. What are the similarities and differences between seasonality and cyclicality?

CHAPTER 9

Using the Past to Predict the Future

One of the more difficult tasks in risk analysis is forecasting, which includes forecasting of any variable's future outcomes, for example, sales, revenues, machine failure rates, demand, costs, market share, competitive threats, and so forth. Recall from Chapter 8, Tomorrow's Forecast Today, that quantitative or statistical approaches to forecasting include regression analysis and time-series analysis. Time-series analysis is applicable for variables whose data are time-dependent, whereas regression analysis is applicable for variables whose data are time-dependent, cross-sectional, or panel-based (both pooled time-dependent and cross-sectional data). This chapter explores both time-series and regression analysis in more detail through example computations. We start with time-series analysis by exploring the eight most common time-series methods or models as seen in Table 9.1. Regression analysis is then discussed, including the many pitfalls and dangers of applying regression analysis as a novice.

TIME-SERIES FORECASTING METHODOLOGY

Table 9.1 lists the eight most common time-series models, segregated by seasonality and trend. For instance, if the data variable has no trend or season-

TABLE 9.1   The Eight Most Common Time-Series Methods

	No Seasonality	With Seasonality
No Trend	Single Moving Average Single Exponential Smoothing	Seasonal Additive Seasonal Multiplicative
With Trend	Double Moving Average Double Exponential Smoothing	Holt–Winter's Additive Holt–Winter's Multiplicative

ality, then a single moving-average model or a single exponential-smoothing model would suffice. However, if seasonality exists but no discernable trend is present, either a seasonal additive or seasonal multiplicative model would be better, and so forth. The following sections explore these models in more detail through computational examples.

NO TREND AND NO SEASONALITY

Single Moving Average

The single moving average is applicable when time-series data with no trend and seasonality exist. The approach simply uses an average of the actual historical data to project future outcomes. This average is applied consistently moving forward, hence the term *moving average*.

The value of the moving average (MA) for a specific length (n) is simply the summation of actual historical data (Y) arranged and indexed in time sequence (i).

$$MA_n = \frac{\sum_{i=1}^{n} Y_i}{n}$$

An example computation of a 3-month single moving average is seen in Figure 9.1. Here we see that there are 39 months of actual historical data and a 3-month moving average is computed.[1] Additional columns of calculations also exist in the example—calculations that are required to estimate the error of measurements in using this moving-average approach. These errors are important as they can be compared across multiple moving averages (i.e., 3-month, 4-month, 5-month, and so forth) as well as other time-series models (e.g., single moving average, seasonal additive model, and so forth) to find the best fit that minimizes these errors. Figures 9.2 to 9.4 show the exact calculations used in the moving-average model. Notice that the forecast-fit value in period 4 of 198.12 is a 3-month average of the prior three periods (months 1 through 3). The forecast-fit value for period 5 would then be the 3-month average of months 2 through 4. This process is repeated moving forward until month 40 (Figure 9.3) where every month after that, the forecast is fixed at 664.97. Clearly, this approach is not suitable if there is a trend (upward or downward over time) or if there is seasonality. Thus, error estimation is important when choosing the optimal time-series forecast model. Figure 9.2 illustrates a few additional columns of calculations required for estimating the forecast errors. The values from these columns are used in Figure 9.4's error estimation.

Month	Actual	Forecast Fit	$\lvert Error \rvert$	$Error^2$	$\left\lvert \dfrac{Y_t - \hat{Y}_t}{Y_t} \right\rvert$	$\left[\dfrac{\hat{Y}_t - Y_{t-1}}{Y_{t-1}} \right]^2$	$\left[\dfrac{Y_t - Y_{t-1}}{Y_{t-1}} \right]^2$	$Error$	$\left[E_t - E_{t-1} \right]^2$
1	265.22	-	-	-	-	-	-	-	-
2	146.64	-	-	-	-	-	-	-	-
3	182.50	-	-	-	-	-	-	-	-
4	118.54	198.12	79.57	6332.12	67.13%	0.19	0.12	79.57	-
5	180.04	149.23	30.81	949.43	17.11%	0.07	0.27	-30.81	12185.39
6	167.45	160.36	7.09	50.20	4.23%	0.00	0.00	-7.09	562.99
7	231.75	155.34	76.41	5838.18	32.97%	0.21	0.15	-76.41	4805.61
8	223.71	193.08	30.63	938.22	13.69%	0.02	0.00	-30.63	2095.60
9	192.98	207.64	14.66	214.91	7.60%	0.00	0.02	14.66	2051.18
10	122.29	216.15	93.86	8808.84	76.75%	0.24	0.13	93.86	6271.97
11	336.65	179.66	157.00	24647.46	46.63%	1.65	3.07	-157.00	62925.98
12	186.50	217.31	30.81	949.17	16.52%	0.01	0.20	30.81	35270.22
13	194.27	215.15	20.88	435.92	10.75%	0.01	0.00	20.88	98.60
14	149.19	239.14	89.95	8091.27	60.29%	0.21	0.05	89.95	4771.05
15	210.06	176.65	33.41	1115.94	15.90%	0.05	0.17	-33.41	15216.99
16	272.91	184.50	88.40	7815.04	32.39%	0.18	0.09	-88.40	3024.67
17	191.93	210.72	18.79	352.98	9.79%	0.00	0.09	18.79	11489.77
18	286.94	224.96	61.97	3840.48	21.60%	0.10	0.25	-61.97	6522.06
19	226.76	250.59	23.83	567.99	10.51%	0.01	0.04	23.83	7362.34
20	303.38	235.21	68.17	4647.58	22.47%	0.09	0.11	-68.17	8465.03
21	289.72	272.36	17.36	301.32	5.99%	0.00	0.00	-17.36	2582.12
22	421.59	273.29	148.30	21993.55	35.18%	0.26	0.21	-148.30	17146.25
23	264.47	338.23	73.76	5440.32	27.89%	0.03	0.14	73.76	49310.98
24	342.30	325.26	17.04	290.41	4.98%	0.00	0.09	-17.04	8244.63
25	339.86	342.79	2.93	8.56	0.86%	0.00	0.00	2.93	398.71
26	439.90	315.54	124.35	15463.53	28.27%	0.13	0.09	-124.35	16199.87
27	315.54	374.02	58.48	3420.05	18.53%	0.02	0.08	58.48	33428.15
28	438.62	365.10	73.52	5404.80	16.76%	0.05	0.15	-73.52	17423.61
29	400.94	398.02	2.92	8.54	0.73%	0.00	0.01	-2.92	4983.77
30	437.37	385.03	52.34	2739.41	11.97%	0.02	0.01	-52.34	2442.13
31	575.77	425.64	150.13	22539.00	26.07%	0.12	0.10	-150.13	9563.01
32	407.33	471.36	64.03	4099.56	15.72%	0.01	0.09	64.03	45863.59
33	681.92	473.49	208.43	43442.59	30.57%	0.26	0.45	-208.43	74232.65
34	475.78	555.01	79.23	6277.13	16.65%	0.01	0.09	79.23	82746.68
35	581.17	521.68	59.49	3539.49	10.24%	0.02	0.05	-59.49	19243.79
36	647.82	579.62	68.20	4651.17	10.53%	0.01	0.01	-68.20	75.79
37	650.81	568.26	82.55	6814.39	12.68%	0.02	0.00	-82.55	205.92
38	677.54	626.60	50.94	2594.71	7.52%	0.01	0.00	-50.94	999.26
39	666.56	658.72	7.84	61.47	1.18%	0.00	0.00	-7.84	1857.46
Forecast 40	-	664.97	-	-	-	-	-	-	-
Forecast 41	-	664.97	-	-	-	-	-	-	-
Forecast 42	-	664.97	-	-	-	-	-	-	-

RMSE	79.00
MSE	6241.27
MAD	63.00
MAPE	20.80%
Thiel's U	0.80

$$MA_n = \frac{\sum_{i=1}^{n} Y_i}{n} \quad \forall\, i = 1, \ldots, N$$

FIGURE 9.1 Single moving average (3 months).

Error Estimation (RMSE, MSE, MAD, MAPE, Theil's U)

Several different types of errors can be calculated for time-series forecast methods, including the mean-squared error (MSE), root mean-squared error (RMSE), mean absolute deviation (MAD), and mean absolute percent error (MAPE).

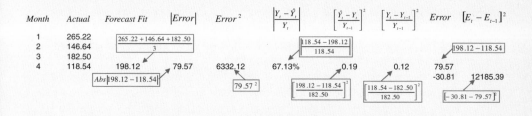

Month	Actual	Forecast Fit	$|Error|$	$Error^2$	$\left|\frac{Y_t - \hat{Y}_t}{Y_t}\right|$	$\left[\frac{\hat{Y}_t - Y_t}{Y_{t-1}}\right]^2$	$\left[\frac{Y_t - Y_{t-1}}{Y_{t-1}}\right]^2$	$Error$	$[E_t - E_{t-1}]^2$
1	265.22	$\frac{265.22 + 146.64 + 182.50}{3}$							
2	146.64				$\frac{|118.54 - 198.12|}{118.54}$				$198.12 - 118.54$
3	182.50								
4	118.54	198.12	79.57	6332.12	67.13%	0.19	0.12	79.57	
		$Abs|198.12 - 118.54|$		79.57^2	$\left[\frac{198.12 - 118.54}{182.50}\right]^2$	$\left[\frac{118.54 - 182.50}{182.50}\right]^2$		-30.81	12185.39
									$[-30.81 - 79.57]^2$

FIGURE 9.2 Calculating single moving average.

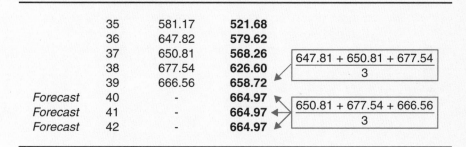

	35	581.17	**521.68**
	36	647.82	**579.62**
	37	650.81	**568.26**
	38	677.54	**626.60**
	39	666.56	**658.72**
Forecast	40	-	**664.97**
Forecast	41	-	**664.97**
Forecast	42	-	**664.97**

$$\frac{647.81 + 650.81 + 677.54}{3}$$

$$\frac{650.81 + 677.54 + 666.56}{3}$$

FIGURE 9.3 Forecasting with a single moving average.

RMSE	79.00
MSE	6241.27
MAD	63.00
MAPE	20.80%
Thiel's U	0.80

$$RMSE = \sqrt{\sum_{i=1}^{n} \frac{\left(Error^2\right)}{n}} = \sqrt{MSE}$$

$$MSE = \sum_{i=1}^{n} \frac{\left(Error^2\right)}{n} = RMSE^2$$

$$MAD = \sum_{i=1}^{n} \frac{|Error|_i}{n}$$

$$MAPE = \sum_{i=1}^{n} \frac{\left|\frac{Y_t - \hat{Y}_t}{Y_t}\right|_i}{n}$$

$$Theil's\,U = \frac{\sqrt{\sum_{i=1}^{n}\left[\frac{\hat{Y}_t - Y_t}{Y_{t-1}}\right]^2_i}}{\sqrt{\sum_{i=1}^{n}\left[\frac{Y_t - Y_{t-1}}{Y_{t-1}}\right]^2_i}}$$

FIGURE 9.4 Error estimation.

MSE is an absolute error measure that squares the errors (the difference between the actual historical data and the forecast-fitted data predicted by the model) to keep the positive and negative errors from canceling each other out. This measure also tends to exaggerate large errors by weighting the large errors more heavily than smaller errors by squaring them, which can help when comparing different time-series models. MSE is calculated by simply taking the average of the *Error*^{2} column in Figure 9.1. RMSE is the square root of MSE and is the most popular error measure, also known as the *quadratic loss function*. RMSE can be defined as the average of the absolute values of the forecast errors and is highly appropriate when the cost of the forecast errors is proportional to the absolute size of the forecast error.

MAD is an error statistic that averages the distance (absolute value of the difference between the actual historical data and the forecast-fitted data predicted by the model) between each pair of actual and fitted forecast data points. MAD is calculated by taking the average of the |*Error*| column in Figure 9.1, and is most appropriate when the cost of forecast errors is proportional to the absolute size of the forecast errors.

MAPE is a relative error statistic measured as an average percent error of the historical data points and is most appropriate when the cost of the forecast error is more closely related to the percentage error than the numerical size of the error. This error estimate is calculated by taking the average of the

$$\left| \frac{Y_t - \hat{Y}_t}{Y_t} \right|$$

column in Figure 9.1, where Y_t is the historical data at time t, while $\hat{Y}_t$ is the fitted or predicted data point at time t using this time-series method. Finally, an associated measure is the Theil's U statistic, which measures the naivety of the model's forecast. That is, if the Theil's U statistic is less than 1.0, then the forecast method used provides an estimate that is statistically better than guessing. Figure 9.4 provides the mathematical details of each error estimate.

Single Exponential Smoothing

The second approach to use when no discernable trend or seasonality exists is the single exponential-smoothing method. This method weights past data with exponentially decreasing weights going into the past; that is, the more recent the data value, the greater its weight. This weighting largely overcomes the limitations of moving averages or percentage-change models. The weight used is termed the *alpha* measure. The method is illustrated in Figures 9.5 and 9.6 and uses the following model:

$$ESF_t = \alpha Y_{t-1} + (1 - \alpha)ESF_{t-1}$$

where the exponential smoothing forecast (*ESF*) at time t is a weighted average between the actual value one period in the past (Y_{t-1}) and last period's forecast (ESF_{t-1}), weighted by the alpha parameter (α). Figure 9.6 shows an

	Alpha 0.10		RMSE 126.26

Month	Actual	Forecast Fit
1	265.22	
2	146.64	265.22
3	182.50	253.36
4	118.54	246.28
5	180.04	233.50
6	167.45	228.16
7	231.75	222.09
8	223.71	223.05
9	192.98	223.12
10	122.29	220.10
11	336.65	210.32
12	186.50	222.96
13	194.27	219.31
14	149.19	216.81
15	210.06	210.04
16	272.91	210.05
17	191.93	216.33
18	286.94	213.89
19	226.76	221.20
20	303.38	221.75
21	289.72	229.92
22	421.59	235.90
23	264.47	254.46
24	342.30	255.47
25	339.86	264.15
26	439.90	271.72
27	315.54	288.54
28	438.62	291.24
29	400.94	305.98
30	437.37	315.47
31	575.77	327.66
32	407.33	352.47
33	681.92	357.96
34	475.78	390.35
35	581.17	398.90
36	647.82	417.12
37	650.81	440.19
38	677.54	461.26
39	666.56	482.88
Forecast 40	-	501.25

$$\mathrm{ESF}_t = \alpha\, Y_{t-1} + (1 - \alpha)\, \mathrm{ESF}_{t-1}$$

FIGURE 9.5   Single exponential smoothing.

Alpha		
0.10		

Month	Actual	Forecast Fit
1	265.22	
2	146.64	265.22
3	182.50	253.36
4	118.54	246.28
5	180.04	233.50
6	167.45	228.16
7	231.75	222.09
8	223.71	223.05

$$\hat{Y}_2 = Y_1 = 265.22$$

$$0.1(146.64) + (1 - 0.1)265.22$$

$$ESF_t = \alpha \, Y_{t-1} + (1 - \alpha) \, ESF_{t-1}$$

FIGURE 9.6 Calculating single exponential smoothing.

example of the computation. Notice that the first forecast-fitted value in month $2(\hat{Y}_2)$ is always the previous month's actual value (Y_1). The mathematical equation gets used only at month 3 or starting from the second forecast-fitted period.

Optimizing Forecasting Parameters

Clearly, in the single exponential-smoothing method, the alpha parameter was not arbitrarily chosen as 0.10. In fact, the optimal alpha has to be obtained for the model to provide a good forecast. Using the model in Figure 9.5, Excel's Solver add-in package is used to find the optimal alpha parameter that minimizes the forecast errors. Figure 9.7 illustrates Excel's Solver

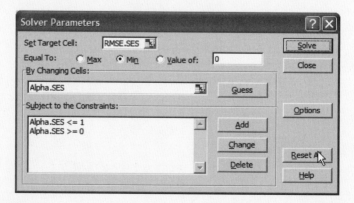

FIGURE 9.7 Optimizing parameters in single exponential smoothing.

add-in dialog box, where the target cell is set to the RMSE as the objective to be minimized by methodically changing the alpha parameter. As alpha should only be allowed to vary between 0.00 and 1.00 (this is because alpha is a weight given to the historical data and past period forecasts, and weights can never be less than zero or greater than one), additional constraints are also set up. The resulting optimal alpha value that minimizes forecast errors calculated by Solver is 0.10.

WITH TREND BUT NO SEASONALITY

For data that exhibit a trend but no seasonality, the double moving-average and double exponential-smoothing methods work rather well. The following examples assume a quarterly seasonality (i.e., there are four quarterly periods in a year).

Double Moving Average

The double moving-average method smoothes out past data by performing a moving average on a subset of data that represents a moving average of an original set of data. That is, a second moving average is performed on the first moving average. The second-moving average application captures the trending effect of the data. Figures 9.8 and 9.9 illustrate the computation involved. The example shown is a 3-month double moving average and the forecast value obtained in period 40 is calculated using the following:

$$\text{Forecast} = 2MA_{1,t} - MA_{2,t} + \frac{2}{m-1}\left[MA_{1,t} - MA_{2,t}\right]$$

where the forecast value is twice the amount of the first moving average (MA_1) at time t, less the second moving average estimate (MA_2) plus the difference between the two moving averages multiplied by a correction factor (two divided into the number of months in the moving average, m, less one).

Double Exponential Smoothing

The second approach to use when the data exhibits a trend but no seasonality is the double exponential-smoothing method. Double exponential smoothing applies single exponential smoothing twice, once to the original data and then to the resulting single exponential-smoothing data. An alpha (α) weighting parameter is used on the first or single exponential smoothing (SES) while a beta (β) weighting parameter is used on the second or double exponential smoothing (DES). This approach is useful when the historical

Period	Actual	3-month MA $_1$	3-month MA $_2$	Forecast Fit
1	265.22	-	-	-
2	146.64	-	-	-
3	182.50	-	-	-
4	118.54	198.12	-	-
5	180.04	149.23	-	-
6	167.45	160.36	169.24	142.61
7	231.75	155.34	154.98	156.08
8	223.71	193.08	169.59	240.05
9	192.98	207.64	185.35	252.20
10	122.29	216.15	205.62	237.20
11	336.65	179.66	201.15	136.68
12	186.50	217.31	204.37	243.18
13	194.27	215.15	204.04	237.37
14	149.19	239.14	223.86	269.69
15	210.06	176.65	210.31	109.33
16	272.91	184.50	200.10	153.32
17	191.93	210.72	190.62	250.90
18	286.94	224.96	206.73	261.44
19	226.76	250.59	228.76	294.26
20	303.38	235.21	236.92	231.78
21	289.72	272.36	252.72	311.64
22	421.59	273.29	260.28	299.29
23	264.47	338.23	294.62	425.44
24	342.30	325.26	312.26	351.26
25	339.86	342.79	335.42	357.51
26	439.90	315.54	327.86	290.91
27	315.54	374.02	344.12	433.82
28	438.62	365.10	351.55	392.19
29	400.94	398.02	379.04	435.96
30	437.37	385.03	382.71	389.66
31	575.77	425.64	402.90	471.13
32	407.33	471.36	427.34	559.39
33	681.92	473.49	456.83	506.81
34	475.78	555.01	499.95	665.12
35	581.17	521.68	516.72	531.58
36	647.82	579.62	552.10	634.66
37	650.81	568.26	556.52	591.73
38	677.54	626.60	591.49	696.81
39	666.56	658.72	617.86	740.45
Forecast 40	-	664.97	650.10	694.71

$$Forecast = 2MA_{1,t} - MA_{2,t} + \frac{2}{m-1}\left[MA_{1,t} - MA_{2,t}\right]$$

FIGURE 9.8   Double moving average (3 months).

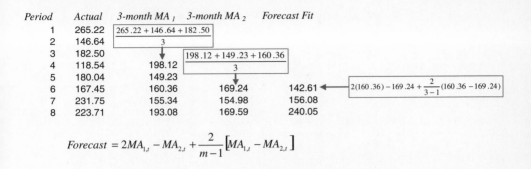

$$Forecast = 2MA_{1,t} - MA_{2,t} + \frac{2}{m-1}\left[MA_{1,t} - MA_{2,t}\right]$$

FIGURE 9.9   Calculating double moving average.

data series is not stationary. Figure 9.10 illustrates the double exponential-smoothing model, while Figure 9.11 shows Excel's Solver add-in dialog used to find the optimal alpha and beta parameters that minimizes the forecast errors. Figure 9.12 shows the computational details. The forecast is calculated using the following:

$$DES_t = \beta\left(SES_t - SES_{t-1}\right) + \left(1 - \beta\right)DES_{t-1}$$
$$SES_t = \alpha Y_t + \left(1 - \alpha\right)\left(SES_{t-1} + DES_{t-1}\right)$$

Note that the starting value (period 1 for DES in Figure 9.10) can take on different values other than the one shown. In some instances, zero is used when no prior information is available.

		Alpha 0.35	Beta 1.00	RMSE 91.95
Period	Actual	SES	DES	Forecast Fit
1	265.22	265.22	-118.58	-
2	146.64	146.64	-118.58	-
3	182.50	82.65	-63.99	28.05
4	118.54	53.97	-28.68	18.66
5	180.04	80.00	26.03	25.29
6	167.45	127.74	47.74	106.02
7	231.75	195.37	67.63	175.47
8	223.71	249.11	53.74	263.00
9	192.98	264.01	14.90	302.85
10	122.29	223.55	-40.47	278.91
11	336.65	237.37	13.82	183.08
12	186.50	228.32	-9.05	251.19
13	194.27	210.44	-17.89	219.28
14	149.19	177.22	-33.21	192.55
15	210.06	167.36	-9.87	144.01
16	272.91	198.29	30.94	157.49
17	191.93	216.04	17.75	229.23
18	286.94	252.58	36.54	233.79
19	226.76	267.07	14.49	289.12
20	303.38	289.28	22.21	281.57
21	289.72	303.79	14.51	311.48
22	421.59	354.81	51.02	318.30
23	264.47	355.86	1.05	405.84
24	342.30	351.75	-4.12	356.91
25	339.86	344.88	-6.86	347.63
26	439.90	374.03	29.15	338.02
27	315.54	372.20	-1.83	403.18
28	438.62	394.49	22.29	370.37
29	400.94	411.18	16.69	416.79
30	437.37	431.23	20.05	427.87
31	575.77	495.29	64.06	451.28
32	407.33	505.61	10.32	559.34
33	681.92	574.61	69.00	515.93
34	475.78	584.28	9.67	643.60
35	581.17	589.43	5.15	593.95
36	647.82	613.41	23.97	594.59
37	650.81	642.13	28.72	637.38
38	677.54	673.21	31.09	670.85
39	666.56	690.96	17.75	704.30
Forecast 40	-	-	-	708.70
Forecast 41	-	-	-	726.45
Forecast 42	-	-	-	744.20
Forecast 43	-	-	-	761.94

$$DES_t = \beta \, (SES_t - SES_{t-1}) + (1 - \beta) \, DES_{t-1}$$
$$SES_t = \alpha \, Y_t + (1 - \alpha)(SES_{t-1} + DES_{t-1})$$

FIGURE 9.10 Double exponential smoothing.

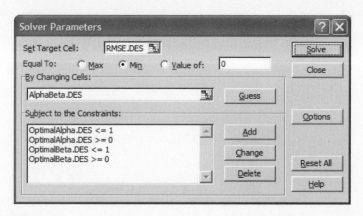

FIGURE 9.11   Optimizing parameters in double exponential smoothing.

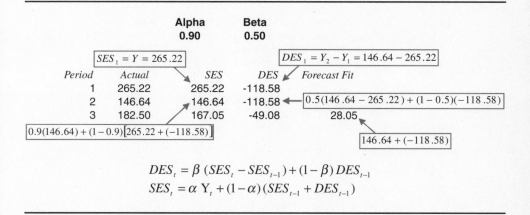

FIGURE 9.12   Calculating double exponential smoothing.

NO TREND BUT WITH SEASONALITY

Additive Seasonality

If the time-series data has no appreciable trend but exhibits seasonality, then the additive seasonality and multiplicative seasonality methods apply. The additive seasonality method is illustrated in Figures 9.13 and 9.14. The additive seasonality model breaks the historical data into a level (L) or base-case component as measured by the alpha parameter (α), and a seasonality (S) component measured by the gamma parameter (γ). The resulting forecast

	Level Alpha 0.33	Seasonal Gamma 0.40		RMSE 93.54
Period	*Actual*	*Level*	*Seasonality*	*Forecast Fit*
1	265.22	-	87.00	-
2	146.64	-	-31.59	-
3	182.50	-	4.27	-
4	118.54	178.23	-59.68	-
5	180.04	150.44	63.85	265.22
6	167.45	166.29	-18.38	118.86
7	231.75	186.25	20.90	170.56
8	223.71	217.93	-33.28	126.57
9	192.98	188.97	39.72	281.78
10	122.29	173.22	-31.51	170.58
11	336.65	219.70	59.63	194.12
12	186.50	219.73	-33.26	186.42
13	194.27	198.47	22.01	259.45
14	149.19	192.67	-36.34	166.96
15	210.06	178.90	48.15	252.31
16	272.91	220.40	1.32	145.63
17	191.93	203.94	8.29	242.41
18	286.94	242.86	-3.91	167.60
19	226.76	221.90	30.69	291.01
20	303.38	248.05	23.10	223.23
21	289.72	258.93	17.36	256.34
22	421.59	313.26	41.35	255.02
23	264.47	287.34	9.09	343.95
24	342.30	297.73	31.76	310.44
25	339.86	305.81	24.09	315.09
26	439.90	336.05	66.55	347.16
27	315.54	326.40	1.05	345.15
28	438.62	352.64	53.62	358.16
29	400.94	360.53	30.67	376.73
30	437.37	363.89	69.35	427.08
31	575.77	432.65	58.34	364.94
32	407.33	406.90	32.17	486.27
33	681.92	486.59	97.07	437.57
34	475.78	460.45	47.56	555.94
35	581.17	480.80	75.29	518.79
36	647.82	524.78	68.82	512.97
37	650.81	534.22	104.94	621.84
38	677.54	565.45	73.58	581.79
39	666.56	573.87	82.31	640.74

$$\text{Level } L_t = \alpha(Y_t - S_{t-s}) + (1-\alpha)(L_{t-1})$$
$$\text{Seasonality } S_t = \gamma(Y_t - L_t) + (1-\gamma)(S_{t-s})$$
$$\text{Forecast } F_{t+m} = L_t + S_{t+m-s}$$

FIGURE 9.13   Additive seasonality with no trend.

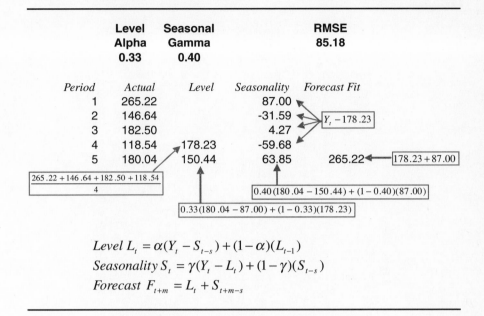

FIGURE 9.14 Calculating seasonal additive.

value is simply the addition of this base-case level to the seasonality value. (Note that calculations are rounded.)

Multiplicative Seasonality

Similarly, the multiplicative seasonality model requires the alpha and gamma parameters. The difference from additive seasonality is that the model is multiplicative, for example, the forecast value is the multiplication between the base-case level and seasonality factor. Figures 9.15 and 9.16 illustrate the computations required. (Calculations are rounded.)

WITH SEASONALITY AND WITH TREND

When both seasonality and trend exist, more advanced models are required to decompose the data into their base elements: a base-case level (L) weighted by the alpha parameter (α); a trend component (b) weighted by the beta parameter (β); and a seasonality component (S) weighted by the gamma parameter (γ). Several methods exist but the two most common are the Holt–Winters' additive seasonality and Holt–Winters' multiplicative seasonality methods.

		Level Alpha 0.22	Seasonal Gamma 0.64	RMSE 95.65
Period	*Actual*	*Level*	*Seasonality*	*Forecast Fit*
1	265.22	-	1.49	-
2	146.64	-	0.82	-
3	182.50	-	1.02	-
4	118.54	178.23	0.67	-
5	180.04	165.35	1.23	265.22
6	167.45	173.93	0.91	136.04
7	231.75	185.72	1.17	178.11
8	223.71	219.61	0.89	123.53
9	192.98	205.42	1.04	270.67
10	122.29	189.36	0.74	187.42
11	336.65	211.65	1.44	221.04
12	186.50	211.10	0.89	188.67
13	194.27	205.43	0.98	220.57
14	149.19	204.47	0.73	152.37
15	210.06	191.32	1.22	294.08
16	272.91	217.55	1.12	169.58
17	191.93	212.61	0.93	213.50
18	286.94	252.73	0.99	156.05
19	226.76	237.67	1.05	308.43
20	303.38	245.03	1.20	266.66
21	289.72	259.92	1.05	228.13
22	421.59	297.16	1.26	257.56
23	264.47	286.97	0.97	311.99
24	342.30	286.78	1.19	343.32
25	339.86	295.18	1.11	300.72
26	439.90	307.02	1.37	373.34
27	315.54	311.30	1.00	297.12
28	438.62	323.87	1.30	371.87
29	400.94	331.95	1.17	360.91
30	437.37	328.97	1.34	455.55
31	575.77	384.87	1.32	328.02
32	407.33	368.95	1.17	499.11
33	681.92	416.60	1.47	433.22
34	475.78	402.47	1.24	560.30
35	581.17	411.24	1.38	529.84
36	647.82	442.93	1.36	482.55
37	650.81	442.86	1.47	651.26
38	677.54	466.08	1.38	549.47
39	666.56	470.02	1.40	642.45

$$\text{Level } L_t = \alpha(Y_t / S_{t-s}) + (1 - \alpha)(L_{t-1})$$

$$\text{Seasonality } S_t = \gamma(Y_t / L_t) + (1 - \gamma)(S_{t-s})$$

$$\text{Forecast } F_{t+m} = L_t S_{t+m-s}$$

FIGURE 9.15 Multiplicative seasonality with no trend.

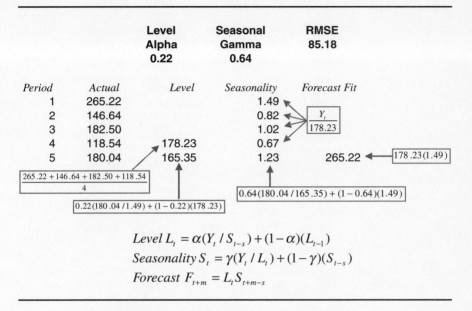

	Level		Seasonal	RMSE
	Alpha		**Gamma**	**85.18**
	0.22		**0.64**	

Period	Actual	Level	Seasonality	Forecast Fit
1	265.22		1.49	
2	146.64		0.82	Y_t
3	182.50		1.02	178.23
4	118.54	178.23	0.67	
5	180.04	165.35	1.23	265.22 ← 178.23(1.49)

$$\frac{265.22 + 146.64 + 182.50 + 118.54}{4}$$

$$0.22(180.04 / 1.49) + (1 - 0.22)(178.23)$$

$$0.64(180.04 / 165.35) + (1 - 0.64)(1.49)$$

$$Level \ L_t = \alpha(Y_t / S_{t-s}) + (1-\alpha)(L_{t-1})$$
$$Seasonality \ S_t = \gamma(Y_t / L_t) + (1-\gamma)(S_{t-s})$$
$$Forecast \ F_{t+m} = L_t S_{t+m-s}$$

FIGURE 9.16 Calculating seasonal multiplicative.

Holt–Winters' Additive Seasonality

Figures 9.17 and 9.18 illustrate the required computations for determining a Holt–Winters' additive forecast model. (Calculations are rounded.)

	Level Alpha 0.05	Trend Beta 1.00	Seasonal Gamma 0.24		RMSE 77.03
Period	Actual	Level	Trend	Seasonality	Forecast Fit
1	265.22	-	-	87.00	-
2	146.64	-	-	-31.59	-
3	182.50	-	-	4.27	-
4	118.54	178.23	0.00	-59.68	-
5	180.04	174.03	-4.20	67.96	265.22
6	167.45	171.27	-2.76	-25.06	138.25
7	231.75	171.42	0.15	17.45	172.79
8	223.71	177.07	5.65	-34.69	111.89
9	192.98	179.89	2.81	55.06	250.69
10	122.29	180.96	1.07	-32.96	157.64
11	336.65	188.78	7.83	48.11	199.48
12	186.50	197.82	9.04	-29.20	161.92
13	194.27	203.53	5.71	39.94	261.92
14	149.19	207.90	4.37	-39.01	176.27
15	210.06	209.79	1.89	36.86	260.38
16	272.91	216.14	6.35	-8.99	182.49
17	191.93	219.01	2.87	24.19	262.43
18	286.94	227.01	8.00	-15.76	182.87
19	226.76	232.79	5.78	26.78	271.87
20	303.38	242.20	9.41	7.50	229.58
21	289.72	252.30	10.10	27.30	275.80
22	421.59	271.02	18.71	23.34	246.64
23	264.47	287.17	16.15	15.15	316.51
24	342.30	304.87	17.70	14.54	310.82
25	339.86	322.08	17.21	25.06	349.87
26	439.90	343.09	21.01	40.61	362.63
27	315.54	360.97	17.88	0.91	379.26
28	438.62	381.07	20.10	24.65	393.38
29	400.94	399.93	18.86	19.41	426.24
30	437.37	417.70	17.77	35.69	459.40
31	575.77	442.34	24.64	32.06	436.38
32	407.33	462.83	20.49	5.81	491.63
33	681.92	492.14	29.31	59.45	502.72
34	475.78	517.45	25.31	17.50	557.14
35	581.17	543.06	25.62	33.48	574.81
36	647.82	572.29	29.23	22.20	574.49
37	650.81	601.02	28.73	57.18	660.98
38	677.54	631.24	30.22	24.27	647.26
39	666.56	660.07	28.82	27.14	694.95

Level $L_t = \alpha(Y_t - S_{t-s}) + (1-\alpha)(L_{t-1} + b_{t-1})$

Trend $b_t = \beta(L_t - L_{t-1}) + (1-\beta)(b_{t-1})$

Seasonalit y $S_t = \gamma(Y_t - L_t) + (1-\gamma)(S_{t-s})$

Forecast $F_{t+m} = L_t + mb_t + S_{t+m-s}$

FIGURE 9.17   Holt–Winters' additive seasonality with trend.

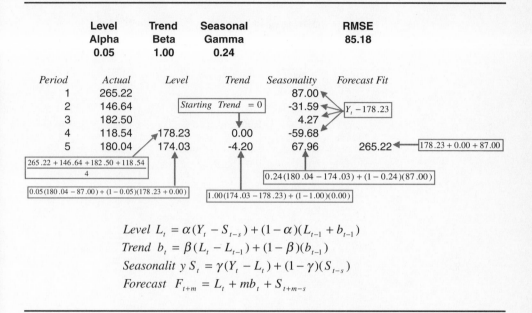

	Level	Trend	Seasonal		RMSE
	Alpha	Beta	Gamma		85.18
	0.05	1.00	0.24		

Period	Actual	Level	Trend	Seasonality	Forecast Fit
1	265.22			87.00	
2	146.64	Starting Trend = 0		-31.59	$Y_t - 178.23$
3	182.50			4.27	
4	118.54	178.23	0.00	-59.68	
5	180.04	174.03	-4.20	67.96	265.22

$$\frac{265.22 + 146.64 + 182.50 + 118.54}{4}$$

$$0.05(180.04 - 87.00) + (1 - 0.05)(178.23 + 0.00)$$

$$1.00(174.03 - 178.23) + (1 - 1.00)(0.00)$$

$$0.24(180.04 - 174.03) + (1 - 0.24)(87.00)$$

$$178.23 + 0.00 + 87.00$$

Level $L_t = \alpha(Y_t - S_{t-s}) + (1 - \alpha)(L_{t-1} + b_{t-1})$

Trend $b_t = \beta(L_t - L_{t-1}) + (1 - \beta)(b_{t-1})$

Seasonalit$y\ S_t = \gamma(Y_t - L_t) + (1 - \gamma)(S_{t-s})$

Forecast $F_{t+m} = L_t + mb_t + S_{t+m-s}$

FIGURE 9.18 Calculating Holt–Winters' additive.

Holt–Winters' Multiplicative Seasonality

Figures 9.19 and 9.20 show the required computation for determining a Holt–Winters' multiplicative forecast model when both trend and seasonality exist. (Calculations are rounded.)

REGRESSION ANALYSIS

This section deals with using regression analysis for forecasting purposes. It is assumed that the reader is sufficiently knowledgeable about the fundamentals of regression analysis. Instead of focusing on the detailed theoretical mechanics of the regression equation, we instead look at the basics of applying regression analysis and work through the various relationships that a regression analysis can capture, as well as the common pitfalls in regression, including the problems of outliers, nonlinearities, heteroskedasticity, autocorrelation, and structural breaks.

The general bivariate linear regression equation takes the form of

$$Y = \beta_0 + \beta_1 X + \varepsilon$$

	Level Alpha 0.04	Trend Beta 1.00	Seasonal Gamma 0.27		RMSE 79.15
Period	Actual	Level	Trend	Seasonality	Forecast Fit
1	265.22	-	-	1.49	-
2	146.64	-	-	0.82	-
3	182.50	-	-	1.02	-
4	118.54	178.23	0.00	0.67	-
5	180.04	176.12	-2.10	1.36	265.22
6	167.45	175.11	-1.02	0.86	143.18
7	231.75	176.01	0.90	1.10	178.26
8	223.71	182.75	6.75	0.82	117.67
9	192.98	187.75	5.00	1.27	257.93
10	122.29	190.90	3.15	0.80	165.60
11	336.65	198.12	7.22	1.27	214.19
12	186.50	206.17	8.06	0.84	167.87
13	194.27	211.98	5.81	1.17	272.12
14	149.19	216.64	4.66	0.77	174.13
15	210.06	219.27	2.63	1.18	280.20
16	272.91	225.66	6.39	0.94	186.67
17	191.93	229.53	3.88	1.08	272.38
18	286.94	238.53	9.00	0.89	179.57
19	226.76	245.48	6.95	1.11	292.61
20	303.38	254.99	9.51	1.01	237.70
21	289.72	264.63	9.63	1.09	286.13
22	421.59	281.63	17.00	1.05	243.42
23	264.47	296.40	14.77	1.05	331.98
24	342.30	312.20	15.80	1.03	314.05
25	339.86	327.45	15.25	1.07	355.98
26	439.90	345.45	18.00	1.11	361.10
27	315.54	361.12	15.67	1.00	382.29
28	438.62	378.54	17.42	1.07	389.23
29	400.94	395.15	16.61	1.06	424.62
30	437.37	411.07	15.91	1.10	458.54
31	575.77	432.37	21.30	1.09	428.40
32	407.33	451.03	18.66	1.02	484.20
33	681.92	476.14	25.11	1.16	496.30
34	475.78	498.73	22.59	1.06	551.41
35	581.17	521.70	22.97	1.10	569.70
36	647.82	547.93	26.23	1.07	556.94
37	650.81	573.70	25.77	1.15	665.46
38	677.54	600.92	27.22	1.08	635.58
39	666.56	627.35	26.43	1.09	690.07

$$\text{Level } L_t = \alpha(Y_t / S_{t-s}) + (1-\alpha)(L_{t-1} + b_{t-1})$$
$$\text{Trend } b_t = \beta(L_t - L_{t-1}) + (1-\beta)(b_{t-1})$$
$$\text{Seasonality } S_t = \gamma(Y_t / L_t) + (1-\gamma)(S_{t-s})$$
$$\text{Forecast } F_{t+m} = (L_t + mb_t)S_{t+m-s}$$

FIGURE 9.19   Holt–Winters' multiplicative seasonality with trend.

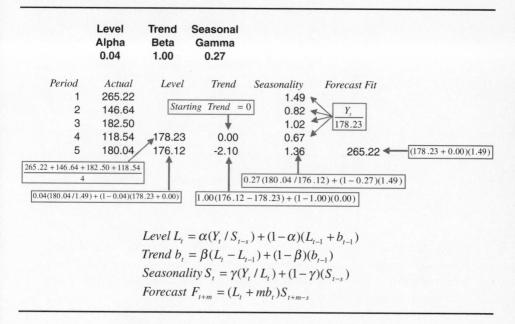

	Level Alpha 0.04	Trend Beta 1.00	Seasonal Gamma 0.27		
Period	*Actual*	*Level*	*Trend*	*Seasonality*	*Forecast Fit*
1	265.22			1.49	
2	146.64	Starting Trend = 0		0.82	Y_t
3	182.50			1.02	178.23
4	118.54	178.23	0.00	0.67	
5	180.04	176.12	-2.10	1.36	265.22

$\dfrac{265.22 + 146.64 + 182.50 + 118.54}{4}$

$0.04(180.04 / 1.49) + (1 - 0.04)(178.23 + 0.00)$

$1.00(176.12 - 178.23) + (1 - 1.00)(0.00)$

$0.27(180.04 / 176.12) + (1 - 0.27)(1.49)$

$(178.23 + 0.00)(1.49)$

$$\text{Level } L_t = \alpha(Y_t / S_{t-s}) + (1 - \alpha)(L_{t-1} + b_{t-1})$$
$$\text{Trend } b_t = \beta(L_t - L_{t-1}) + (1 - \beta)(b_{t-1})$$
$$\text{Seasonality } S_t = \gamma(Y_t / L_t) + (1 - \gamma)(S_{t-s})$$
$$\text{Forecast } F_{t+m} = (L_t + mb_t)S_{t+m-s}$$

FIGURE 9.20 Calculating Holt–Winters' multiplicative.

where β_0 is the intercept, β_1 is the slope, and ε is the error term. It is bivariate as there are only two variables, a Y or dependent variable, and an X or independent variable, where X is also known as the regressor (sometimes a bivariate regression is also known as a univariate regression as there is only a single independent variable X). The dependent variable is named as such as it *depends* on the independent variable, for example, sales revenue depends on the amount of marketing costs expended on a product's advertising and promotion, making the dependent variable sales and the independent variable marketing costs. An example of a bivariate regression is seen as simply inserting the best-fitting line through a set of data points in a two-dimensional plane as seen on the left panel in Figure 9.21. In other cases, a multivariate regression can be performed, where there are multiple or n number of independent X variables, where the general regression equation will now take the form of $Y = \beta_0 + B_1X_1 + B_2X_2 + B_3X_3 \ldots + \beta_nX_n + \varepsilon$. In this case, the best-fitting line will be within an $n + 1$ dimensional plane.

However, fitting a line through a set of data points in a scatter plot as in Figure 9.21 may result in numerous possible lines. The best-fitting line is defined as the single unique line that minimizes the total vertical errors, that is, the sum of the absolute distances between the actual data points (Y_i) and the estimated line ($\hat{Y}$) as shown on the right panel of Figure 9.21. In order

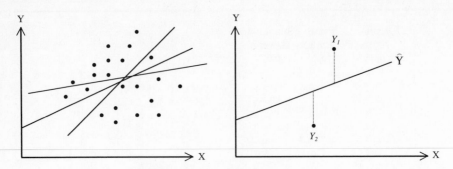

FIGURE 9.21 Bivariate regression.

to find the best-fitting line that minimizes the errors, a more sophisticated approach is required, that is, regression analysis. Regression analysis therefore finds the unique best-fitting line by requiring that the total errors be minimized, or by calculating

$$\text{Min} \sum_{i=1}^{n} (Y_i - \hat{Y}_i)^2$$

where only one unique line minimizes this sum of squared errors. The errors (vertical distance between the actual data and the predicted line) are squared to avoid the negative errors from canceling out the positive errors. Solving this minimization problem with respect to the slope and intercept requires calculating a first derivative and setting them equal to zero:

$$\frac{d}{d\beta_0} \sum_{i=1}^{n} (Y_i - \hat{Y}_i)^2 = 0 \qquad \text{and} \qquad \frac{d}{d\beta_1} \sum_{i=1}^{n} (Y_i - \hat{Y}_i)^2 = 0$$

which yields the *least squares regression equations* seen in Figure 9.22.

See Appendix B—Ordinary Least Squares, at the end of this chapter for more details on optimizing this line to find the best-fitting line.

Example Given the following sales amounts ($millions) and advertising sizes (measured as linear inches by summing up all the sides of an ad) for a local newspaper, answer the following questions.

Advertising size (inch)	12	18	24	30	36	42	48
Sales ($ millions)	5.9	5.6	5.5	7.2	8.0	7.7	8.4

$$\beta_1 = \frac{\sum_{i=1}^{n}(X_i - \bar{X})(Y_i - \bar{Y})}{\sum_{i=1}^{n}(X_i - \bar{X})^2} = \frac{\sum_{i=1}^{n}X_iY_i - \frac{\sum_{i=1}^{n}X_i \sum_{i=1}^{n}Y_i}{n}}{\sum_{i=1}^{n}X_i^2 - \frac{\left(\sum_{i=1}^{n}X_i\right)^2}{n}}$$

and $\beta_0 = \bar{Y} - \beta_1 \bar{X}$

FIGURE 9.22   Least squares regression equations.

1. Which is the dependent variable and which is the independent variable? *The independent variable is advertising size, whereas the dependent variable is sales.*

2. Manually calculate the slope (β_1) and the intercept (β_0) terms.

X	Y	XY	X²	Y²
12	5.9	70.8	144	34.81
18	5.6	100.8	324	31.36
24	5.5	132.0	576	30.25
30	7.2	216.0	900	51.84
36	8.0	288.0	1296	64.00
42	7.7	323.4	1764	59.29
48	8.4	403.2	2304	70.56
$\Sigma(X) = 210$	$\Sigma Y) = 48.3$	$\Sigma(XY) = 1534.2$	$\Sigma(X^2) = 7308$	$\Sigma(Y^2) = 342.11$

$$\beta_1 = \frac{1534.2 - \frac{210(48.3)}{7}}{7308 - \frac{210^2}{7}} = 0.0845 \quad and \quad \beta_0 = \frac{48.3}{7} - 0.0845\left[\frac{210}{7}\right] = 4.3643$$

3. What is the estimated regression equation?

$Y = 4.3643 + 0.0845X$ or   *Sales = 4.3643 + 0.0845(Size)*

4. What would the level of sales be if we purchase a 28-inch ad in the paper?

$Y = 4.3643 + 0.0845 (28) =$ *$6.73 million dollars in sales*

(Note that we only predict or forecast and cannot say for certain. This is only an expected value or on average.)

Regression Output

Using the data in the previous example, a regression analysis can be performed either using Excel's Data Analysis add-in or Crystal Ball's Predictor software.[2] Figure 9.23 shows Excel's regression analysis output. Notice that the coefficients on the intercept and X variable confirm the results we obtained in the manual calculation.

The same regression analysis can be performed using Crystal Ball Predictor.[3] The results obtained through Predictor are seen in Figure 9.24. Notice again the identical answers to the slope and intercept calculations. Clearly, there are significant amounts of additional information obtained through the Excel and Predictor analyses. Most of these additional statistical outputs pertain to goodness-of-fit measures, that is, a measure of how accurate and statistically reliable the model is.

Goodness-of-Fit

Goodness-of-fit statistics provide a glimpse into the accuracy and reliability of the estimated regression model. They usually take the form of a t-statistic, F-statistic, R-squared statistic, adjusted R-squared statistic, Durbin–Watson statistic, and their respective probabilities. (See the t-statistic, F-statistic, and critical Durbin–Watson tables at the end of this book for the corresponding critical values used later in this chapter). The following sections discuss some of the more common regression statistics and their interpretation.

SUMMARY OUTPUT

Regression Statistics	
Multiple R	0.9026
R Square	0.8146
Adjusted R Square	0.7776
Standard Error	0.5725
Observations	7

ANOVA

	df	SS	MS	F	Significance F
Regression	1	7.2014	7.2014	21.9747	0.0054
Residual	5	1.6386	0.3277		
Total	6	8.8400			

	Coefficients	Standard Error	t Stat	P-value	Lower 95%	Upper 95%	Lower 95.0%	Upper 95.0%
Intercept	4.3643	0.5826	7.4911	0.0007	2.8667	5.8619	2.8667	5.8619
X Variable 1	0.0845	0.0180	4.6877	0.0054	0.0382	0.1309	0.0382	0.1309

FIGURE 9.23   Regression output from Excel's Data Analysis add-in.

Method: Multiple Linear Regression

Statistics:
       R-squared: 0.815
       Adjusted R-squared: 0.7776
       SSE: 1.6386
       F Statistic: 21.975
       F Probability: 0.005396
       Durbin-Watson: 1.964
       No. of Values: 7
       Independent variables: 1 included out of 1 selected

Series Statistics:
       Mean: 6.90
       Std. Dev.: 1.21
       Minimum: 5.50
       Maximum: 8.40
       Ljung-Box: 6.3255

       Autocorrelations:
             Lag   Correlation   Probability
              1   0.7762   0.0695

Regression Variables:

Variable	Coefficient	t Statistic	Probability
Constant	4.3643	7.4911	6.69E-04
Advertise	0.08452	4.6877	0.005396

FIGURE 9.24   Regression output from Crystal Ball's Predictor software.

The R-squared (R^2), or coefficient of determination, is an error measurement that looks at the percent variation of the dependent variable that can be explained by the variation in the independent variable for a regression analysis. The coefficient of determination can be calculated by:

$$R^2 = 1 - \frac{\sum_{i=1}^{n}(Y_i - \hat{Y}_i)^2}{\sum_{i=1}^{n}(Y_i - \overline{Y})^2} = 1 - \frac{SSE}{TSS}$$

where the coefficient of determination is one less the ratio of the sums of squares of the errors (SSE) to the total sums of squares (TSS). In other words, the ratio of SSE to TSS is the unexplained portion of the analysis, thus, one less the ratio of *SSE* to *TSS* is the explained portion of the regression analysis.

Figure 9.25 provides a graphical explanation of the coefficient of determination. The estimated regression line is characterized by a series of predicted values ($\hat{Y}$); the average value of the dependent variable's data points is denoted $\overline{Y}$; and the individual data points are characterized by Y_i. Therefore, the total sum of squares, that is, the total variation in the data or the total variation about the average dependent value, is the total of the difference between the individual dependent values and its average (seen as the total squared distance of $Y_i - \overline{Y}$ in Figure 9.25). The explained sum of squares, the portion that is captured by the regression analysis, is the total of the difference between the regression's predicted value and the average dependent variable's data set (seen as the total squared distance of $\hat{Y} - \overline{Y}$ in Figure 9.25). The difference between the total variation (*TSS*) and the explained variation (*ESS*) is the unexplained sums of squares, also known as the sums of squares of the errors (*SSE*).

Another related statistic, the adjusted coefficient of determination, or the adjusted R-squared ($\overline{R}^2$), corrects for the number of independent variables (k) in a multivariate regression through a degrees-of-freedom correction to provide a more conservative estimate:

$$\overline{R}^2 = 1 - \frac{\displaystyle\sum_{i=1}^{n} (Y_i - \hat{Y}_i)^2 \,/\, (k - 2)}{\displaystyle\sum_{i=1}^{n} (Y_i - \overline{Y})^2 \,/\, (k - 1)} = 1 - \frac{SSE \,/\, (k - 2)}{TSS \,/\, (k - 1)}$$

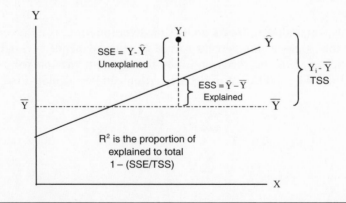

FIGURE 9.25   Explaining the coefficient of determination.

The adjusted R-squared should be used instead of the regular R-squared in multivariate regressions because every time an independent variable is added into the regression analysis, the R-squared will increase; indicating that the percent variation explained has increased. This increase occurs even when nonsensical regressors are added. The adjusted R-squared takes the added regressors into account and penalizes the regression equation accordingly, providing a much better estimate of a regression model's goodness-of-fit.

Other goodness-of-fit statistics include the t-statistic and the F-statistic. The former is used to test if *each* of the estimated slope and intercept(s) is statistically significant, that is, if it is statistically significantly different from zero (therefore making sure that the intercept and slope estimates are statistically valid). The latter applies the same concepts but simultaneously for the entire regression equation including the intercept and slope(s). Using the previous example, the following illustrates how the t-statistic and F-statistic can be used in a regression analysis. (See the t-statistic and F-statistic tables at the end of the book for their corresponding critical values). It is assumed that the reader is somewhat familiar with hypothesis testing and tests of significance in basic statistics.

Example   Given the information from Excel's regression output in Figure 9.26, interpret the following:

1. Perform a hypothesis test on the slope and the intercept to see if they are *each* significant at a two-tailed alpha (α) of 0.05.

The null hypothesis H_o is such that the slope $\beta_1 = 0$ and the alternate hypothesis H_a is such that $\beta_1 \neq 0$. The t-statistic calculated is 4.6877, which exceeds the t-critical (2.9687 obtained from the t-statistic table at the end of this book) for a two-tailed alpha of 0.05 and degrees of freedom $n - k = 7 - 1 = 6$.[4] Therefore, the null hypothesis is rejected and one can state that the slope is statistically significantly different from 0, indicating that the regression's estimate of the slope is statistically significant. This hypothesis test can also be performed by looking at the t-statistic's corresponding p-value (0.0054), which is less than the alpha of 0.05, which means the null hypothesis is rejected.[5] The hypothesis test is then applied to the intercept, where the null hypothesis H_o is such that the intercept $\beta_0 = 0$ and the alternate hypothesis H_a is such that $\beta_0 \neq 0$. The t-statistic calculated is 7.4911, which exceeds the critical t value of 2.9687 for $n - k$ (7 - 1 = 6) degrees of freedom, so, the null hypothesis is rejected indicating that the intercept is statistically significantly different from 0, meaning that the regression's estimate of the slope is statistically significant. The calculated p-value (0.0007) is also less than the alpha level, which means the null hypothesis is also rejected.

ANOVA

	df	SS	MS	F	Significance F
Regression	1	7.2014	7.2014	21.9747	0.0054
Residual	5	1.6386	0.3277		
Total	6	8.8400			

	Coefficients	Standard Error	t Stat	P-value	Lower 95%	Upper 95%	Lower 95.0%	Upper 95.0%
Intercept	4.3643	0.5826	7.4911	0.0007	2.8667	5.8619	2.8667	5.8619
X Variable 1	0.0845	0.0180	4.6877	0.0054	0.0382	0.1309	0.0382	0.1309

FIGURE 9.26   ANOVA and goodness-of-fit table.

2. Perform a hypothesis test to see if both the slope and intercept are significant as a whole, in other words, if the estimated model is statistically significant at an alpha (α) of 0.05.

The simultaneous null hypothesis H_o is such that $\beta_0 = \beta_1 = 0$ and the alternate hypothesis H_a is $\beta_0 \neq \beta_1 \neq 0$. The calculated F-value is 21.9747, which exceeds the critical F-value (5.99 obtained from the table at the end of this book) for k (1) degrees of freedom in the numerator and n – k (7 – 1 = 6) degrees of freedom for the denominator, so the null hypothesis is rejected indicating that both the slope and intercept are simultaneously significantly different from 0 and that the model as a whole is statistically significant. This result is confirmed by the p-value of 0.0054 (significance of F), which is less than the alpha value, thereby rejecting the null hypothesis and confirming that the regression as a whole is statistically significant.

3. Using Predictor's regression output in Figure 9.27, interpret the R^2 value. How is it related to the correlation coefficient?

The calculated R^2 is 0.815, meaning that 81.5 percent of the variation in the dependent variable can be explained by the variation in the independent variable. The R^2 is simply the square of the correlation coefficient, that is, the correlation coefficient between the independent and dependent variable is 0.903.

4. Determine what the Durbin–Watson statistic implies. (See the Durbin–Watson table at the end of this book for the corresponding critical values).

The Durbin–Watson statistic estimates the potential for a first-order autocorrelation, that is, if sales is correlated to itself one period prior. Many time-series data tend to be autocorrelated to their historical occurrences. There is a Durbin–Watson critical statistic table at the end of the book that provides a guide as to whether a calculated statistic implies any autocorrelation. The calculated Durbin–Watson statistic of 1.964 is fairly close to 2.0, which is the region of no autocorrelation. The critical table lists the lower

Statistics:
     R-squared: 0.815
     Adjusted R-squared: 0.7776
     SSE: 1.6386
     F Statistic: 21.975
     F Probability: 0.005396
     Durbin-Watson: 1.964
     No. of Values: 7
     Independent variables: 1 included out of 1 selected

Series Statistics:
     Mean: 6.90
     Std. Dev.: 1.21
     Minimum: 5.50
     Maximum: 8.40
     Ljung-Box: 6.3255

FIGURE 9.27   Additional regression output from Predictor.

critical bound (D_L) to be less than 1.08 for one independent variable (k) and seven observations (n).[6]

Regression Assumptions

The following six assumptions are the requirements for a regression analysis to work:

1. The relationship between the dependent and independent variables is *linear*.
2. The expected value of the errors or *residuals is zero*.
3. The errors are *independently and normally distributed*.
4. The variance of the errors is constant or *homoskedastic* and not varying over time.
5. The errors are independent and *uncorrelated* with the explanatory variables.
6. The independent variables are uncorrelated to each other meaning that no *multicollinearity* exists.

One very simple method to verify some of these assumptions is to use a scatter plot. This approach is simple to use in a bivariate regression scenario. If the assumption of the linear model is valid, the plot of the observed dependent variable values against the independent variable values should suggest a linear band across the graph with no obvious departures from linearity. Outliers may appear as anomalous points in the graph, often in the upper right-hand or lower left-hand corner of the graph. However, a point may be an outlier in either an independent or dependent variable without necessarily being far from the general trend of the data.

If the linear model is not correct, the shape of the general trend of the X–Y plot may suggest the appropriate function to fit (e.g., a polynomial, exponential, or logistic function). Alternatively, the plot may suggest a reasonable transformation to apply. For example, if the X–Y plot arcs from lower left to upper right so that data points either very low or very high in the independent variable lie below the straight line suggested by the data, while the middle data points of the independent variable lie on or above that straight line, taking square roots or logarithms of the independent variable values may promote linearity.

If the assumption of equal variances or homoskedasticity for the dependent variable is correct, the plot of the observed dependent variable values against the independent variable should suggest a band across the graph with roughly equal vertical width for all values of the independent variable. That is, the shape of the graph should suggest a tilted cigar and not a wedge or a megaphone.

A fan pattern like the profile of a megaphone, with a noticeable flare either to the right or to the left in the scatter plot, suggests that the variance in the values increases in the direction where the fan pattern widens (usually as the sample mean increases), and this in turn suggests that a transformation of the dependent variable values may be needed.

As an example, Figure 9.28 shows a scatter plot of two variables: sales revenue (dependent variable) and marketing costs (independent variable).

FIGURE 9.28   Scatter plot showing a positive relationship.

Summary:
    Number of series: 2
    Periods to forecast: 12
    Seasonality: none
    Error Measure: RMSE

Series: Sales Revenues

    Method: Multiple Linear Regression

    Statistics:
        R-squared: 0.430
        Adjusted R-squared: 0.4185
        SSE: 2732.9
        F Statistic: 36.263
        F Probability: 2.32E-7
        Durbin-Watson: 2.370
        No. of Values: 50
        Independent variables: 1 included out of 1 selected

Regression Variables:

Variable	Coefficient	t Statistic	Probability
Constant	26.897	2.215	0.03154
Marketing Expenses	0.7447	6.0219	2.32E-07

FIGURE 9.29   Bivariate regression results for positive relationship.

Clearly, there is a positive relationship between the two variables, as is evident from the regression results in Figure 9.29, where the slope of the regression equation is a positive value (0.7447). The relationship is also statistically significant at 0.05 alpha and the coefficient of determination is 0.43, indicating a somewhat weak but statistically significant relationship.

Compare that to a multiple linear regression in Figure 9.30, where another independent variable, pricing structure of the product, is added. The regression's adjusted coefficient of determination (adjusted R-squared) is now 0.62, indicating a much stronger regression model.[7] The pricing variable shows a negative relationship to the sales revenue, a very much expected result, as according to the law of demand in economics, a higher price point necessitates a lower quantity demanded, hence, lower sales revenues (this, of course, assumes an elastic demand curve). The t-statistics and corresponding probabilities (p-values) also indicate a statistically significant relationship.

In contrast, Figure 9.31 shows a scatter plot of two variables with little to no relationship, which is confirmed by the regression result in Figure 9.32, where the coefficient of determination is 0.066, close to being negligible.

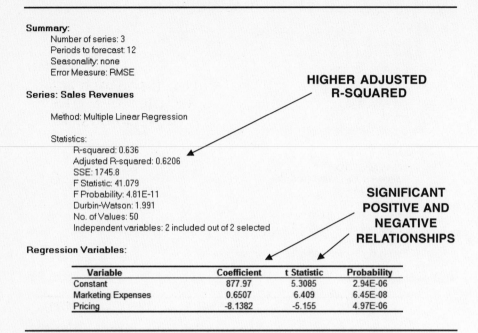

Summary:
 Number of series: 3
 Periods to forecast: 12
 Seasonality: none
 Error Measure: RMSE

Series: Sales Revenues

 Method: Multiple Linear Regression

 Statistics:

  HIGHER ADJUSTED
  R-SQUARED

  R-squared: 0.636
  Adjusted R-squared: 0.6206
  SSE: 1745.8
  F Statistic: 41.079
  F Probability: 4.81E-11
  Durbin-Watson: 1.991
  No. of Values: 50
  Independent variables: 2 included out of 2 selected

  SIGNIFICANT
  POSITIVE AND
  NEGATIVE
  RELATIONSHIPS

Regression Variables:

Variable	Coefficient	t Statistic	Probability
Constant	877.97	5.3085	2.94E-06
Marketing Expenses	0.6507	6.409	6.45E-08
Pricing	-8.1382	-5.155	4.97E-06

FIGURE 9.30 Multiple linear regression results for positive and negative relationships.

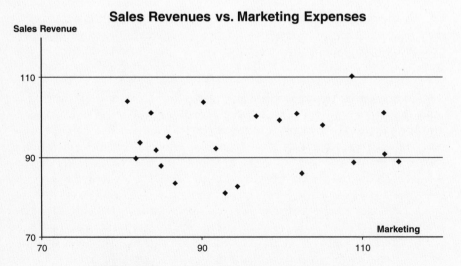

Sales Revenues vs. Marketing Expenses

FIGURE 9.31 Scatter plot showing no relationship.

Summary:
Number of series: 2
Periods to forecast: 12
Seasonality: 12 months
Error Measure: RMSE

Series: Sales Revenues

Method: Multiple Linear Regression

Statistics:
R-squared: 0.066
Adjusted R-squared: 0.04622
SSE: 13661
F Statistic: 3.3743
F Probability: 0.07242
Durbin-Watson: 2.173
No. of Values: 50
Independent variables: 1 included out of 1 selected

LOW R-SQUARED IS AN INDICATION OF LITTLE TO NO RELATIONSHIP

Regression Variables:

Variable	Coefficient	t Statistic	Probability
Constant	82.966	6.0363	2.20E-07
Marketing Expenses	0.2265	1.8369	0.07242

FIGURE 9.32 Multiple regression results showing no relationship.

In addition, the calculated t-statistic and corresponding probability indicate that the marketing-expenses variable is statistically insignificant at the 0.05 alpha level meaning that the regression equation is not significant (a fact that is also confirmed by the low F-statistic).

THE PITFALLS OF FORECASTING: OUTLIERS, NONLINEARITY, MULTICOLLINEARITY, HETEROSKEDASTICITY, AUTOCORRELATION, AND STRUCTURAL BREAKS

Other than being good modeling practice to create scatter plots prior to performing regression analysis, the scatter plot can also sometimes, on a fundamental basis, provide significant amounts of information regarding the behavior of the data series. Blatant violations of the regression assumptions can be spotted easily and effortlessly, without the need for more detailed and fancy econometric specification tests. For instance, Figure 9.33 shows the existence of outliers. Figure 9.34's regression results, which include the

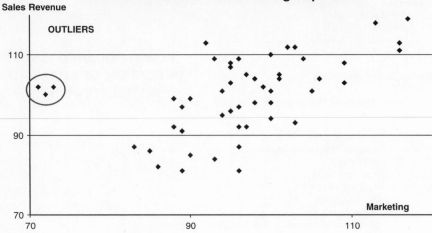

FIGURE 9.33 Scatter plot showing outliers.

Summary:
> Number of series: 2
> Periods to forecast: 12
> Seasonality: 12 months
> Error Measure: RMSE

Series: Sales Revenues

> Method: Multiple Linear Regression

> Statistics:
>> R-squared: 0.252
>> Adjusted R-squared: 0.2367
>> SSE: 3417.6
>> F Statistic: 16.198
>> F Probability: 2.01E-4
>> Durbin-Watson: 1.945
>> No. of Values: 50
>> Independent variables: 1 included out of 1 selected

Regression Variables:

Variable	Coefficient	t Statistic	Probability
Constant	53.269	4.5619	3.51E-05
Marketing Expenses	0.4857	4.0247	2.01E-04

FIGURE 9.34 Regression results with outliers.

Summary:
  Number of series: 2
  Periods to forecast: 12
  Seasonality: 12 months
  Error Measure: RMSE

**COMPARE R-SQUARED
BETWEEN REGRESSION WITH
OUTLIERS AND WITHOUT
OUTLIERS!**

Series: Sales Revenues

  Method: Multiple Linear Regression

  Statistics:
    R-squared: 0.447
    Adjusted R-squared: 0.4343
    SSE: 2524.9
    F Statistic: 36.321
    F Probability: 2.84E-7
    Durbin-Watson: 2.242
    No. of Values: 47
    Independent variables: 1 included out of 1 selected

Regression Variables:

Variable	Coefficient	t Statistic	Probability
Constant	19.447	1.4512	0.1537
Marketing Expenses	0.8229	6.0267	2.84E-07

FIGURE 9.35   Regression results with outliers deleted.

outliers, indicate that the coefficient of determination is only 0.252 as compared to 0.447 in Figure 9.35 when the outliers are removed.

Values may not be identically distributed because of the presence of outliers. Outliers are anomalous values in the data. Outliers may have a strong influence over the fitted slope and intercept, giving a poor fit to the bulk of the data points. Outliers tend to increase the estimate of residual variance, lowering the chance of rejecting the null hypothesis. They may be due to recording errors, which may be correctable, or they may be due to the dependent-variable values not all being sampled from the same population. Apparent outliers may also be due to the dependent-variable values being from the same, but nonnormal, population. Outliers may show up clearly in an X–Y scatter plot of the data, as points that do not lie near the general linear trend of the data. A point may be an unusual value in either an independent or dependent variable without necessarily being an outlier in the scatter plot.

The method of least squares involves minimizing the sum of the squared vertical distances between each data point and the fitted line. Because of this, the fitted line can be highly sensitive to outliers. In other words, least squares regression is not resistant to outliers, thus, neither is the fitted-slope esti-mate. A point vertically removed from the other points can cause the fitted line to pass close to it, instead of following the general linear trend of the rest of the data, especially if the point is relatively far horizontally from the cen-ter of the data (the point represented by the mean of the independent vari-able and the mean of the dependent variable). Such points are said to have high leverage: the center acts as a fulcrum, and the fitted line pivots toward high-leverage points, perhaps fitting the main body of the data poorly. A data point that is extreme in dependent variables but lies near the center of the data horizontally will not have much effect on the fitted slope, but by changing the estimate of the mean of the dependent variable, it may affect the fitted estimate of the intercept.

However, great care should be taken when deciding if the outliers should be removed. Although in most cases when outliers are removed, the regression results look better, a priori justification must first exist. For in-stance, if one is regressing the performance of a particular firm's stock re-turns, outliers caused by downturns in the stock market should be included; these are not truly outliers as they are inevitabilities in the business cycle. Forgoing these outliers and using the regression equation to forecast one's retirement fund based on the firm's stocks will yield incorrect results at best. In contrast, suppose the outliers are caused by a single nonrecurring business condition (e.g., merger and acquisition) and such business structural changes are not forecast to recur, then these outliers should be removed and the data cleansed prior to running a regression analysis.

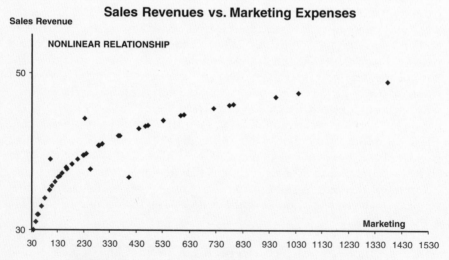

FIGURE 9.36   Scatter plot showing a nonlinear relationship.

Figure 9.36 shows a scatter plot with a nonlinear relationship between the dependent and independent variables. In a situation such as the one in Figure 9.36, a linear regression will not be optimal. A nonlinear transformation should first be applied to the data before running a regression. One simple approach is to take the natural logarithm of the independent variable (other approaches include taking the square root or raising the independent variable to the second or third power) and regress the sales revenue on this transformed marketing-cost data series. Figure 9.37 shows the regression results with a coefficient of determination at 0.938, as compared to 0.707 in Figure 9.38 when a simple linear regression is applied to the original data series without the nonlinear transformation.

If the linear model is not the correct one for the data, then the slope and intercept estimates and the fitted values from the linear regression will be biased, and the fitted slope and intercept estimates will not be meaningful. Over a restricted range of independent or dependent variables, nonlinear models may be well approximated by linear models (this is in fact the basis of linear interpolation), but for accurate prediction a model appropriate to

Summary:
> Number of series: 3
> Periods to forecast: 12
> Seasonality: none
> Error Measure: RMSE

Series: Sales Revenues

> Method: Multiple Linear Regression

> Statistics:
>> R-squared: 0.938
>> Adjusted R-squared: 0.9364
>> SSE: 101.74
>> F Statistic: 722.25
>> F Probability: 1.39E-30
>> Durbin-Watson: 1.825
>> No. of Values: 50
>> Independent variables: 1 included out of 1 selected

Regression Variables:

Variable	Coefficient	t Statistic	Probability
Constant	10.208	9.6141	9.03E-13
Nonlinear Marketing Expenses	5.3783	26.875	1.39E-30

FIGURE 9.37 Regression results using a nonlinear transformation.

Summary:
     Number of series: 3
     Periods to forecast: 12
     Seasonality: none
     Error Measure: RMSE

Series: Sales Revenues

     Method: Multiple Linear Regression

     Statistics:
          R-squared: 0.707
          Adjusted R-squared: 0.7013
          SSE: 477.72
          F Statistic: 116.04
          F Probability: 2.09E-14
          Durbin-Watson: 0.992
          No. of Values: 50
          Independent variables: 1 included out of 1 selected

Regression Variables:

Variable	Coefficient	t Statistic	Probability
Constant	33.358	52.658	4.00E-44
Linear Marketing Expenses	0.01639	10.772	2.09E-14

FIGURE 9.38   Regression results using linear data.

the data should be selected. An examination of the X–Y scatter plot may reveal whether the linear model is appropriate. If there is a great deal of variation in the dependent variable, it may be difficult to decide what the appropriate model is; in this case, the linear model may do as well as any other, and has the virtue of simplicity. Refer to Appendix C—Detecting and Fixing Heteroskedasticity—for specification tests of nonlinearity and heteroskedasticity as well as ways to fix them.

However, great care should be taken here as both the original linear data series of marketing costs should not be added with the nonlinearly transformed marketing costs in the regression analysis. Otherwise, multicollinearity occurs. That is, marketing costs are highly correlated to the natural logarithm of marketing costs, and if both are used as independent variables in a multivariate regression analysis, the assumption of no multicollinearity is violated and the regression analysis breaks down. Figure 9.39 illustrates what happens when multicollinearity strikes. Notice that the coefficient of determination (0.938) is the same as the nonlinear transformed

Summary:
    Number of series: 3
    Periods to forecast: 12
    Seasonality: none
    Error Measure: RMSE

WATCH OUT FOR MULTICOLLINEARITY!

Series: Sales Revenues

Method: Multiple Linear Regression

USE ADJUSTED R-SQUARED FOR MULTIPLE REGRESSION

Statistics:
    R-squared: 0.938
    Adjusted R-squared: 0.9358 ◄
    SSE: 100.59
    F Statistic: 357.93
    F Probability: 3.60E-29
    Durbin-Watson: 1.807
    No. of Values: 50
    Independent variables: 2 included out of 2 selected

NONLINEAR TAKES OVER LINEAR

Regression Variables:

Variable	Coefficient	t Statistic	Probability
Constant	9.0966	4.9143	1.12E-05 ▶
Linear Marketing Expenses	-0.001098	-0.7349	0.4661
Nonlinear Marketing Expenses	5.6542	13.275	1.62E-17

FIGURE 9.39   Regression results using both linear and nonlinear transformations.

regression (Figure 9.37). However, the adjusted coefficient of determination went down from 0.9364 (Figure 9.37) to 0.9358 (Figure 9.39). In addition, the previously statistically significant marketing-costs variable in Figure 9.38 now becomes insignificant (Figure 9.39) with a probability value increasing from close to zero to 0.4661. A basic symptom of multicollinearity is low t-statistics coupled with a high R-squared (Figure 9.39). See Appendix D— Detecting and Fixing Multicollinearity—for further details on detecting multicollinearity in a regression.

Another common violation is heteroskedasticity, that is, the variance of the errors increases over time. Figure 9.40 illustrates this case, where the width of the vertical data fluctuations increases or fans out over time. In this example, the data points have been changed to exaggerate the effect. However, in most time-series analysis, checking for heteroskedasticity is a much more difficult task. See Appendix C—Detecting and Fixing Heteroskedasticity—for further details. And correcting for heteroskedasticity is an even greater challenge.[8] Notice in Figure 9.41 that the coefficient of determination drops significantly when heteroskedasticity exists. As is, the current regression model is insufficient and incomplete. Refer to Appendix C for more details.

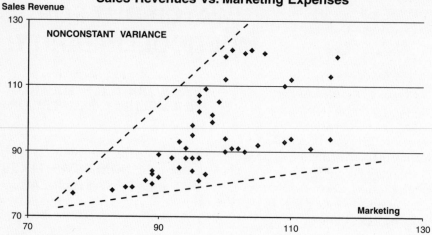

FIGURE 9.40   Scatter plot showing heteroskedasticity with nonconstant variance.

Summary:
        Number of series: 2
        Periods to forecast: 12
        Seasonality: 12 months
        Error Measure: RMSE

WATCH OUT FOR HETEROSKEDASTICITY!

Series: Sales Revenues

    Method: Multiple Linear Regression

    Statistics:
        R-squared: 0.398
        Adjusted R-squared: 0.3858
        SSE: 5190.1
        F Statistic: 31.777
        F Probability: 8.94E-7
        Durbin-Watson: 2.755
        No. of Values: 50
        Independent variables: 1 included out of 1 selected

    Regression Variables:

Variable	Coefficient	t Statistic	Probability
Constant	1.5742	0.09421	0.9253
Marketing Expenses	0.9586	5.6371	8.94E-07

FIGURE 9.41   Regression results with heteroskedasticity.

If the variance of the dependent variable is not constant, then the error's variance will not be constant. The most common form of such heteroskedasticity in the dependent variable is that the variance of the dependent variable may increase as the mean of the dependent variable increases for data with positive independent and dependent variables.

Unless the heteroskedasticity of the dependent variable is pronounced, its effect will not be severe: the least-squares estimates will still be unbiased, and the estimates of the slope and intercept will either be normally distributed if the errors are normally distributed, or at least normally distributed asymptotically (as the number of data points becomes large) if the errors are not normally distributed. The estimate for the variance of the slope and overall variance will be inaccurate, but the inaccuracy is not likely to be substantial if the independent-variable values are symmetric about their mean.

Heteroskedasticity of the dependent variable is usually detected informally by examining the X–Y scatter plot of the data before performing the regression. If both nonlinearity and unequal variances are present, employing a transformation of the dependent variable may have the effect of simultaneously improving the linearity and promoting equality of the variances. Otherwise, a weighted least-squares linear regression may be the preferred method of dealing with nonconstant variance of the dependent variable.

OTHER TECHNICAL ISSUES IN REGRESSION ANALYSIS

If the data to be analyzed by linear regression violate one or more of the linear regression assumptions, the results of the analysis may be incorrect or misleading. For example, if the assumption of independence is violated, then linear regression is not appropriate. If the assumption of normality is violated or outliers are present, then the linear regression goodness-of-fit test may not be the most powerful or informative test available, and this could mean the difference between detecting a linear fit or not. A nonparametric, robust, or resistant regression method, a transformation, a weighted least-squares linear regression, or a nonlinear model may result in a better fit. If the population variance for the dependent variable is not constant, a weighted least-squares linear regression or a transformation of the dependent variable may provide a means of fitting a regression adjusted for the inequality of the variances. Often, the impact of an assumption violation on the linear regression result depends on the extent of the violation (such as how nonconstant the variance of the dependent variable is, or how skewed the dependent variable population distribution is). Some small violations may have little practical effect on the analysis, while other violations may render the linear regression result useless and incorrect. Other potential assumption violations include:

- Lack of independence in the dependent variable.
- Independent variable is random, not fixed.
- Special problems with few data points.
- Special problems with regression through the origin.

Lack of Independence in the Dependent Variable

Whether the independent-variable values are independent of each other is generally determined by the structure of the experiment from which they arise. The dependent-variable values collected over time may be autocorrelated. For serially correlated dependent-variable values, the estimates of the slope and intercept will be unbiased, but the estimates of their variances will not be reliable and hence the validity of certain statistical goodness-of-fit tests will be flawed.

The Independent Variable Is Random, Not Fixed

The usual linear regression model assumes that the observed independent variables are fixed, not random. If the independent values are not under the control of the experimenter (i.e., are observed but not set), and if there is in fact underlying variance in the independent variable, but they have the same variance, the linear model is called an errors-in-variables model or structural model. The least-squares fit will still give the best linear predictor of the dependent variable, but the estimates of the slope and intercept will be biased (will not have expected values equal to the true slope and variance).

Special Problems with Few Data Points

If the number of data points is small (also termed *micronumerosity*), it may be difficult to detect assumption violations. With small samples, assumption violations such as nonnormality or heteroskedasticity of variances are difficult to detect even when they are present. With a small number of data points, linear regression offers less protection against violation of assumptions. With few data points, it may be hard to determine how well the fitted line matches the data, or whether a nonlinear function would be more appropriate.

Even if none of the test assumptions are violated, a linear regression on a small number of data points may not have sufficient power to detect a significant difference between the slope and zero, even if the slope is nonzero. The power depends on the residual error, the observed variation in the independent variable, the selected significance alpha level of the test, and the number of data points. Power decreases as the residual variance increases, decreases as the significance level is decreased (i.e., as the test is made more stringent), increases as the variation in observed independent variable increases, and increases as the number of data points increases. If a statistical significance test with a small number of data points produces a surprisingly nonsignificant probability value, then lack of power may be the reason. The best time to avoid such problems is in the design stage of an experiment, when appropriate minimum sample sizes can be determined, perhaps in consultation with an econometrician, before data collection begins.

Special Problems with Regression Through the Origin

The effects of nonconstant variance of the dependent variable can be particularly severe for a linear regression when the line is forced through the origin: the estimate of variance for the fitted slope may be much smaller than the actual variance, making the test for the slope nonconservative (more likely to reject the null hypothesis that the slope is zero than what the stated significance level indicates). In general, unless there is a structural or theoretical reason to assume that the intercept is zero, it is preferable to fit both the slope and intercept.

INTRODUCTION TO ADVANCED FORECASTING

One very powerful advanced times-series forecasting tool is the ARIMA or Auto Regressive Integrated Moving Average approach. ARIMA forecasting assembles three separate tools into a comprehensive model. The first tool segment is the autoregressive or "AR" term, which corresponds to the number of lagged value of the residual in the unconditional forecast model. In essence, the model captures the historical variation of actual data to a forecasting model and uses this variation or residual to create a better predicting model. The second tool segment is the integration order or the "I" term. This integration term corresponds to the number of differencing the time-series to be forecasted goes through. This element accounts for any nonlinear growth rates existing in the data. The third tool segment is the moving average or "MA" term, which is essentially the moving average of lagged forecast errors. By incorporating lagged forecast errors, the model in essence learns from its forecast errors or mistakes and corrects for them through a moving-average calculation.

In order to correctly specify an ARIMA model, many steps are necessary, including the identification of the order of autocorrelation, the predictive power of each autocorrelation and partial correlation, and so forth.

Dependent Variable: DEMAND
Method: Least Squares
Sample(adjusted): 1999:1 2002:4
Included observations: 16 after adjusting endpoints
Convergence achieved after 10 iterations
Backcast: 1998:1 1998:4

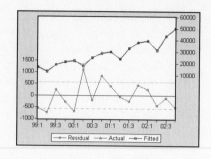

Variable	Coefficient	Std. Error	t-Statistic	Prob.
AR(4)	1.321932	0.004597	287.5724	0.0000
MA(4)	-0.898357	0.059469	-15.10629	0.0000

R-squared	0.997327	Mean dependent var	28461.44
Adjusted R-squared	0.997136	S.D. dependent var	10394.42
S.E. of regression	556.2524	Akaike info criterion	15.59679
Sum squared resid	4331835	Schwarz criterion	15.69336
Log likelihood	-122.7743	F-statistic	5223.787
Durbin-Watson stat	2.107346	Prob(F-statistic)	0.0000

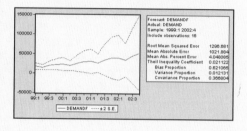

Sample: 1999:1 2002:4
Included observations: 16
Q-statistic probabilities adjusted for 2 ARMA term(s)

Autocorrelation	Partial Correlation		AC	PAC	Q-Stat	Prob
		1	-0.112	-0.112	0.2422	
		2	0.090	0.079	0.4106	
		3	0.185	0.207	1.1705	0.279
		4	-0.161	-0.132	1.7898	0.409
		5	-0.105	-0.188	2.0792	0.556
		6	-0.031	-0.075	2.1077	0.716
		7	-0.204	-0.138	3.4409	0.632
		8	-0.327	-0.371	7.2966	0.294
		9	0.113	0.032	7.8256	0.348
		10	-0.125	0.002	8.5742	0.379
		11	-0.047	-0.048	8.7025	0.465
		12	0.056	-0.158	8.9292	0.539

FIGURE 9.42　Autoregressive integrated moving average (seasonal and trend).

An example execution of an ARIMA model is presented in Figure 9.42, using the advanced econometric software called EViews.

APPENDIX A—FORECAST INTERVALS

The forecast interval estimated in a forecast (an approach also used by Crystal Ball Predictor) is illustrated in Figure 9.43. The confidence interval (*CI*) is estimated by

$$\hat{Y}_i \pm Z\left[\frac{RMSE}{N-T}\right]N$$

where $\hat{Y}_i$ is the *i*th forecast estimate; Z is the standard-normal statistic (see the standard-normal tables at the end of this book); *RMSE* is the root mean squared error previously calculated; N is the number of historical data points; and T is the forecast period. When N is a relatively small number (usually less than 30), then the same analysis can be performed using the *t*-statistic in place of the *Z*-value (see the t-statistic table at the end of this book).

Period	Raw Data	Forecast Values								
		Forecast	5%	95%						
1	265.22	710.07	586.91	833.23						
2	146.64	701.52	575.03	828.01						
3	182.50	756.04	626.04	886.04						
4	118.54	818.99	685.27	952.71						
5	180.04	794.37	656.71	932.02						
6	167.45	Estimated RMSE		72.951						
7	231.75									
8	223.71	Period	Forecast	Stdev	Z-statistic	Lower	Upper			
9	192.98		(T)							
10	122.29	40	1	74.87	1.645	586.91	833.23	RMSE		72.951
11	336.65	41	2	76.89	1.645	575.03	828.01	Data Points (N)		39
12	186.50	42	3	79.03	1.645	626.03	886.04			
13	194.27	43	4	81.29	1.645	685.27	952.71			
14	149.19	44	5	83.68	1.645	656.71	932.02			
15	210.06									
36	647.82									
37	650.81									
38	677.54									
39	666.56									

$$CI = \hat{Y} \pm Z \left[\frac{RMSE}{(N-T)} N \right]$$

FIGURE 9.43 Forecast interval estimation.

Clearly, this approach is a modification of the more common confidence interval estimate of

$$\hat{Y}_i \pm Z \frac{\sigma}{\sqrt{n}}$$

applicable within a data set. Here, it is assumed that

$$\left[\frac{RMSE}{N-T} \right] N \approx \frac{\sigma}{\sqrt{n}}$$

and the inclusion of the T variable is simply to adjust for the added degrees of freedom when forecasting outside of the original dataset.

APPENDIX B—ORDINARY LEAST SQUARES

The following illustrates the concept of the ordinary least-squares regression line. This example is based on the Excel file *Optimizing Ordinary Least Squares.xls* available on the enclosed CD-ROM. Figure 9.44 shows the data on the dependent variable (Y) and independent variable (X) as well as the results estimated using Excel's solver add-in. Arbitrary starting points of the

	A	B	C	D	E	F	G	H
1	Y	X	Slope	Intercept	Predicted	Residual	Squared Resid	
2	1000	3	91.98	2489.16	2765.09	1765.09	3115530.48	
3	3333	3	91.98	2489.16	2765.09	-567.91	322525.70	
4	2222	3	91.98	2489.16	2765.09	543.09	294942.99	
5	1111	2	91.98	2489.16	2673.11	1562.11	2440188.73	
6	5555	3	91.98	2489.16	2765.09	-2789.91	7783617.14	
7	2222	2	91.98	2489.16	2673.11	451.11	203500.54	
8	2222	3	91.98	2489.16	2765.09	543.09	294942.99	
9	5555	3	91.98	2489.16	2765.09	-2789.91	7783617.14	
10	4444	7	91.98	2489.16	3132.99	-1311.01	1718743.79	
11	3333	6	91.98	2489.16	3041.02	-291.98	85255.17	
12	2222	7	91.98	2489.16	3132.99	910.99	829905.16	
13	1111	8	91.98	2489.16	3224.97	2113.97	4468858.59	
14	5555	7	91.98	2489.16	3132.99	-2422.01	5866126.11	
15	2222	6	91.98	2489.16	3041.02	819.02	670785.76	
16	2222	7	91.98	2489.16	3132.99	910.99	829905.16	
17	5555	6	91.98	2489.16	3041.02	-2513.98	6320120.01	
18	4444	5	91.98	2489.16	2949.04	-1494.96	2234908.63	
19	1111	6	91.98	2489.16	3041.02	1930.02	3724958.34	
20	2222	4	91.98	2489.16	2857.06	635.06	403304.67	
21	3333	5	91.98	2489.16	2949.04	-383.96	147426.11	
22	2222	4	91.98	2489.16	2857.06	635.06	403304.67	
23	1111	4	91.98	2489.16	2857.06	1746.06	3048735.05	
24								

Optimization Parameter

Intercept	2489.16
Slope	91.98
Sum of Squared Residuals	52991202.91

Excel Estimated Parameter

Intercept	2489.16
Slope	91.98

FIGURE 9.44   Using optimization to estimate regression intercept and slope.

slope and intercept values are fitted back into the data points and the squared residuals are calculated. Then, the optimal slope and intercept values are calculated through minimizing the sum of the squared residuals.

To get started, make sure Excel's Solver is added in by clicking on *Tools | Add-Ins*. Verify that the check-box beside *Solver Add-In* is selected (Figure 9.45). Then, back in the Excel model, click on *Tools | Solver* and make sure the *sum of squared residuals* (cell E28) is set as the target cell to minimize through systematically changing the intercept and slope values (cells E26 and E27) as seen in Figure 9.46.

Solving yields an intercept value of 2489.16 and a slope of 91.98. These results can be verified using Excel's built-in *slope* and *intercept* functions (Figure 9.47). In other words, the ordinary least-squares regression equation approach is the unique line (as described by an intercept and slope) that minimizes all possible vertical errors (total sum of squared residuals), making it the best-fitting line through a data set.

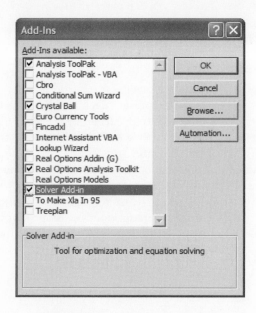

FIGURE 9.45 Excel Solver add-in.

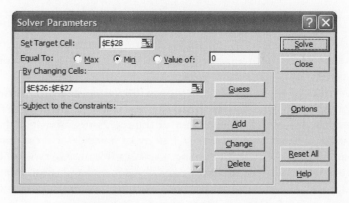

FIGURE 9.46 Excel Solver parameters.

Optimization Parameters	
Intercept	2489.16
Slope	91.98
Sum of Squared Residuals	52991202.91

Excel Estimated Parameter	
Slope	2489.16
Intercept	91.98

FIGURE 9.47 Optimized ordinary least-squares results.

APPENDIX C—DETECTING AND FIXING HETEROSKEDASTICITY

Several tests exist to test for the presence of heteroskedasticity. These tests also are applicable for testing misspecifications and nonlinearities. The simplest approach is to graphically represent each independent variable against the dependent variable as illustrated earlier in the chapter. Another approach is to apply one of the most widely used models, the White's test, where the test is based on the null hypothesis of no heteroskedasticity against an alternate hypothesis of heteroskedasticity of some unknown general form. The test statistic is computed by an auxiliary or secondary regression, where the squared residuals or errors from the first regression are regressed on all possible (and nonredundant) cross products of the regressors. For example, suppose the following regression is estimated:

$$Y = \beta_0 + \beta_1 X + \beta_2 Z + \varepsilon_t$$

The test statistic is then based on the auxiliary regression of the errors (ε):

$$\varepsilon_t^2 = \alpha_0 + \alpha_1 X + \alpha_2 Z + \alpha_3 X^2 + \alpha_4 Z^2 + \alpha_5 XZ + v_t$$

The nR^2 statistic is the White's test statistic, computed as the number of observations (n) times the centered R-squared from the test regression. White's test statistic is asymptotically distributed as a χ^2 with degrees of freedom equal to the number of independent variables (excluding the constant) in the test regression.

The White's test is also a general test for model misspecification, because the null hypothesis underlying the test assumes that the errors are both homoskedastic and independent of the regressors, and that the linear specification of the model is correct. Failure of any one of these conditions could lead to a significant test statistic. Conversely, a nonsignificant test statistic implies that none of the three conditions is violated. For instance, the resulting F-statistic is an omitted variable test for the joint significance of all cross products, excluding the constant.

One method to fix heteroskedasticity is to make it homoskedastic by using a weighted least squares (WLS) approach. For instance, suppose the following is the original regression equation:

$$Y = \beta_0 + \beta_1 X_1 + \beta_2 X_2 + \beta_3 X_3 + \varepsilon$$

Further suppose that X_2 is heteroskedastic. Then transform the data used in the regression into:

$$Y = \frac{\beta_0}{X_2} + \beta_1 \frac{X_1}{X_2} + \beta_2 + \beta_3 \frac{X_3}{X_2} + \frac{\varepsilon}{X_2}$$

The model can be redefined as the following WLS regression:

$$Y_{WLS} = \beta_0^{WLS} + \beta_1^{WLS} X_1 + \beta_2^{WLS} X_2 + \beta_3^{WLS} X_3 + v$$

Alternatively, the Park's test can be applied to test for heteroskedasticity and to fix it. The Park's test model is based on the original regression equation, uses its errors, and creates an auxiliary regression that takes the form of:

$$\ln e_i^2 = \beta_1 + \beta_2 \ln X_{k,i}$$

Suppose β_2 is found to be statistically significant based on a t-test, then heteroskedasticity is found to be present in the variable $X_{k,i}$. The remedy therefore is to use the following regression specification:

$$\frac{Y}{\sqrt{X_k^{\beta_2}}} = \frac{\beta_1}{\sqrt{X_k^{\beta_2}}} + \frac{\beta_2 X_2}{\sqrt{X_k^{\beta_2}}} + \frac{\beta_3 X_3}{\sqrt{X_k^{\beta_2}}} + \varepsilon$$

APPENDIX D—DETECTING AND FIXING MULTICOLLINEARITY

Multicollinearity exists when there is a linear relationship between the independent variables. When this occurs, the regression equation cannot be estimated at all. In near collinearity situations, the estimated regression equation will be biased and provide inaccurate results. This situation is especially true when a step-wise regression approach is used, where the statistically significant independent variables will be thrown out of the regression mix earlier than expected, resulting in a regression equation that is neither efficient nor accurate.

As an example, suppose the following multiple regression analysis exists, where

$$Y_i = \beta_1 + \beta_2 X_{2,i} + \beta_3 X_{3,i} + \varepsilon_i$$

then the estimated slopes can be calculated through

$$\hat{\beta}_2 = \frac{\sum Y_i X_{2,i} \sum X_{3,i}^2 - \sum Y_i X_{3,i} \sum X_{2,i} X_{3,i}}{\sum X_{2,i}^2 \sum X_{3,i}^2 - \left(\sum X_{2,i} X_{3,i}\right)^2}$$

$$\hat{\beta}_3 = \frac{\sum Y_i X_{3,i} \sum X_{2,i}^2 - \sum Y_i X_{2,i} \sum X_{2,i} X_{3,i}}{\sum X_{2,i}^2 \sum X_{3,i}^2 - \left(\sum X_{2,i} X_{3,i}\right)^2}$$

Now suppose that there is perfect multicollinearity, that is, there exists a perfect linear relationship between X_2 and X_3, such that $X_{3,i} = \lambda X_{2,i}$ for all positive values of λ. Substituting this linear relationship into the slope calculations for β_2, the result is indeterminate. In other words, we have

$$\hat{\beta}_2 = \frac{\sum Y_i X_{2,i} \sum \lambda^2 X_{2,i}^2 - \sum Y_i \lambda X_{2,i} \sum \lambda X_{2,i}^2}{\sum X_{2,i}^2 \sum \lambda^2 X_{2,i}^2 - \left(\sum \lambda X_{2,i}^2\right)^2} = \frac{0}{0}$$

The same calculation and results apply to β_3, which means that the multiple regression analysis breaks down and cannot be estimated given a perfect collinearity condition.

One quick test of the presence of multicollinearity in a multiple regression equation is that the R-squared value is relatively high while the t-statistics are relatively low. (See Figure 9.39 for an illustration of this effect). Another quick test is to create a correlation matrix between the independent variables. A high cross correlation indicates a potential for autocorrelation. The rule of thumb is that a correlation with an absolute value greater than 0.75 is indicative of severe multicollinearity.

Another test for multicollinearity is the use of the variance inflation factor (VIF), obtained by regressing each independent variable to all the other independent variables, obtaining the R-squared value and calculating the VIF of that variable by estimating:

$$VIF_i = \frac{1}{(1 - R_i^2)}$$

A high VIF value indicates a high R-squared near unity. As a rule of thumb, a VIF value greater than 10 is usually indicative of destructive multicollinearity.

APPENDIX E—DETECTING AND FIXING AUTOCORRELATION

One very simple approach to test for autocorrelation is to graph the time series of a regression equation's residuals. If these residuals exhibit some cyclicality, then autocorrelation exists. Another more robust approach to detect autocorrelation is the use of the Durbin–Watson statistic, which estimates the potential for a first-order autocorrelation. The Durbin–Watson test also tests for model misspecification, that is, if a particular time-series variable is correlated to itself one period prior. Many time-series data tend to be autocorrelated to their historical occurrences. This relationship can be due to multiple reasons, including the variables' spatial relationships (similar time and space), prolonged economic shocks and events, psychological inertia, smoothing, seasonal adjustments of the data, and so forth.

The Durbin–Watson statistic is estimated by the sum of the squares of the regression errors for one period prior, to the sum of the current period's errors:

$$DW = \frac{\Sigma(\varepsilon_t - \varepsilon_{t-1})^2}{\Sigma \varepsilon_t^2}$$

There is a Durbin–Watson critical statistic table at the end of the book that provides a guide as to whether a statistic implies any autocorrelation.

Another test for autocorrelation is the Breusch–Godfrey test, where for a regression function in the form of:

$$Y = f\left(X_1, X_2, \ldots, X_k\right)$$

Estimate this regression equation and obtain its errors ε_t. Then, run the secondary regression function in the form of:

$$Y = f\left(X_1, X_2, \ldots, X_k, \varepsilon_{t-1}, \varepsilon_{t-2}, \varepsilon_{t-p}\right)$$

Obtain the R-squared value and test it against a null hypothesis of no autocorrelation versus an alternate hypothesis of autocorrelation, where the test statistic follows a chi-square distribution of p degrees of freedom:

$$R^2(n - p) \sim \chi^2_{df=p}$$

Fixing autocorrelation requires more advanced econometric models including the applications of ARIMA (Auto Regressive Integrated Moving Average) or ECM (Error Correction Models). However, one simple fix is to take the lags of the dependent variable for the appropriate periods, add them into the regression function, and test for their significance, for instance:

$$Y_t = f\left(Y_{t-1}, Y_{t-2}, \ldots, Y_{t-p}, X_1, X_2, \ldots, X_k\right)$$

QUESTIONS

1. Explain what each of the following terms means:
   a. Time-series analysis
   b. Ordinary least squares
   c. Regression analysis
   d. Heteroskedasticity
   e. Autocorrelation
   f. Multicollinearity
   g. ARIMA
2. What is the difference between the R-squared versus the adjusted R-squared measure in a regression analysis? When is each applicable and why?
3. Explain why if each of the following is not detected properly or corrected for in the model, the estimated regression model will be flawed:
   a. Heteroskedasticity
   b. Autocorrelation
   c. Multicollinearity
4. Explain briefly how to fix the problem of nonlinearity in the data set.

EXERCISE

1. Based on the data in the chapter examples, recreate the following using Excel:
   a. Double-moving average model
   b. Single exponential-smoothing model
   c. Additive seasonality model
   d. Holt–Winters' multiplicative model

PART SIX

Risk Diversification

CHAPTER 10

The Search for the Optimal Decision

In most simulation models, there are variables over which you have control, such as how much to charge for a product or how much to invest in a project. These controlled variables are called decision variables. Finding the optimal values for decision variables can make the difference between reaching an important goal and missing that goal. This chapter details the optimization process at a high-level, while Chapter 11, Optimization under Uncertainty, provides two step-by-step examples on resource optimization and portfolio optimization solved using Crystal Ball's OptQuest software.

WHAT IS AN OPTIMIZATION MODEL?

In today's highly competitive global economy, companies are faced with many difficult decisions. These decisions include allocating financial resources, building or expanding facilities, managing inventories, and determining product-mix strategies. Such decisions might involve thousands or millions of potential alternatives. Considering and evaluating each of them would be impractical or even impossible. A model can provide valuable assistance in incorporating relevant variables when analyzing decisions, and finding the best solutions for making decisions. Models capture the most important features of a problem and present them in a form that is easy to interpret. Models often provide insights that intuition alone cannot. An optimization model has three major elements: decision variables, constraints, and an objective. In short, the optimization methodology finds the best combination or permutation of decision variables (e.g., which products to sell and which projects to execute) in every conceivable way such that the objective is maximized (e.g., revenues and net income) or minimized (e.g., risk and costs) while still satisfying the constraints (e.g., budget and resources).

Obtaining optimal values generally requires that you search in an iterative or ad hoc fashion. This search involves running a simulation for an initial set of values, analyzing the results, changing one or more values, re-running the simulation, and repeating the process until you find a satisfactory solution. This process can be very tedious and time consuming even for small models, and often it is not clear how to adjust the values from one simulation to the next.

A more rigorous method systematically enumerates all possible alternatives. This approach guarantees optimal solutions if the model is correctly specified. Suppose that a simulation model depends on only two decision variables. If each variable has 10 possible values, trying each combination requires 100 simulations (10^2 alternatives). If each simulation is very short (e.g., 2 seconds), then the entire process could be done in approximately three minutes of computer time.

However, instead of two decision variables, consider six, then consider that trying all combinations requires 1,000,000 simulations (10^6 alternatives). It is easily possible for complete enumeration to take weeks, months, or even years to carry out (see Figure 10.1).

THE TRAVELING FINANCIAL PLANNER

A very simple example is in order. Figure 10.2 illustrates the traveling financial planner problem. Suppose the traveling financial planner has to make three sales trips to New York, Chicago, and Seattle. Further suppose that the order of arrival at each city is irrelevant. All that is important in this simple example is to find the lowest total cost possible to cover all three cities. Figure 10.2 also lists the flight costs from these different cities.

An approach used to find the combination of inputs to achieve the best possible output subject to satisfying certain prespecified conditions
- What stocks to pick in a portfolio, as well as the weights of each stock as a percentage of total budget
- Optimal staffing needs for a production line
- Project and strategy selection and prioritization
- Inventory optimization
- Optimal pricing and royalty rates
- Utilization of employees for workforce planning
- Configuration of machines for production scheduling
- Location of facilities for distribution
- Tolerances in manufacturing design
- Treatment policies in waste management

FIGURE 10.1   What is optimization?

- You have to travel and visit clients in New York, Chicago, and Seattle
- You may start from any city and you will stay at your final city, that is, you will need to purchase three airline tickets
- Your goal is to travel as cheaply as possible given these rates:

Route	Airfare
Seattle – Chicago	$325
Chicago – Seattle	$225
New York – Seattle	$350
Seattle – New York	$375
Chicago – New York	$325
New York – Chicago	$325

- How do you solve the problem?
  - Ad Hoc approach - start trying different combinations
  - Enumeration - look at all possible alternatives

FIGURE 10.2 Traveling financial planner problem.

The problem here is cost minimization, suitable for optimization. One basic approach to solving this problem is through an ad hoc or brute force method, that is, manually list all six possible permutations as seen in Figure 10.3. Clearly the cheapest itinerary is going from the east coast to the west coast, going from New York to Chicago and finally on to Seattle.[1] Here, the problem is simple and can be calculated manually, as there are three cities and hence six possible itineraries.[2] However, add two more cities and the total number of possible itineraries jumps to 120.[3] Performing an ad hoc calculation will be fairly intimidating and time consuming. On a larger scale, suppose there are 100 cities on the salesman's list, the possible itineraries will be as many as 9.3×10^{157}. The problem will take many years to calculate manually, which is where optimization software steps in, automating the search for the optimal itinerary.

The example illustrated up to now is a deterministic optimization problem, that is, the airline ticket prices are known ahead of time and are assumed to be constant. Now suppose the ticket prices are not constant but are uncertain, following some distribution (e.g., a ticket from Chicago to Seattle averages $325, but is never cheaper than $300 and usually never exceeds $500).[4] The same uncertainty applies to tickets for the other cities. The problem now becomes an *optimization under uncertainty*. Ad hoc and brute force approaches simply do not work. Software such as Crystal Ball's Opt-Quest can take over this optimization problem and automate the entire

Seattle-Chicago-New York	$325 + $325 = **$650**
Seattle-New York-Chicago	$375 + $325 = **$700**
Chicago-Seattle-New York	$225 + $375 = **$600**
Chicago-New York-Seattle	$325 + $350 = **$675**
New York-Seattle-Chicago	$350 + $325 = **$675**
New York-Chicago-Seattle	$325 + $225 = **$550**

Additionally, say you want to visit San Antonio and Denver

For the five cities to visit (Seattle, Chicago, New York, San Antonio,
and Denver) you now have:

$5! = 5 \times 4 \times 3 \times 2 \times 1 = 120$ possible combinations

What about 100 different cities?

$100! = 100 \times 99 \times 98 \ldots \times 1 =$
93,326,215,443,944,200,000,000,000,000,000,000,000,000,
000,000,000,000,000,000,000,000,000,000,000,000,000,
000,000,000,000,000,000,000,000,000,000,000,000,000,
000,000,000,000,000,000,000,000,000,000,000,000,000

or 9.3×10^{157} different combinations

FIGURE 10.3   Multiple combinations of the traveling financial planner problem.

process seamlessly. The next section discusses the terms required in an optimization under uncertainty. Chapter 11 illustrates two business cases and
models with step-by-step instructions.

> Optimization problems can be solved using different approaches, in-
> cluding the use of simplex or graphical methods, brute force, mathe-
> matically taking calculus derivatives, or using software (e.g., Excel's
> Solver add-in and Crystal Ball's OptQuest).

THE LINGO OF OPTIMIZATION

Before embarking on solving an optimization problem, it is vital to understand the terminology of optimization—the terms used to describe certain
attributes of the optimization process. These words include decision variables, constraints, and objectives.

Decision variables are quantities over which you have control; for example, the amount of a product to make, the number of dollars to allocate

among different investments, or which projects to select from among a limited set. As an example, portfolio optimization analysis includes a go or no-go decision on particular projects. In addition, the dollar or percentage budget allocation across multiple projects also can be structured as decision variables.

Constraints describe relationships among decision variables that restrict the values of the decision variables. For example, a constraint might ensure that the total amount of money allocated among various investments cannot exceed a specified amount or at most one project from a certain group can be selected based on budget constraints, timing restrictions, minimum returns, or risk tolerance levels.

Objectives give a mathematical representation of the model's desired outcome, such as maximizing profit or minimizing cost, in terms of the decision variables. In financial analysis, for example, the objective may be to maximize returns while minimizing risks (maximizing the Sharpe ratio, or the returns-to-risk ratio).

Conceptually, an optimization model might look like Figure 10.4. The solution to an optimization model provides a set of values for the decision variables that optimizes (maximizes or minimizes) the associated objective. If the real business conditions were simple and the future was predictable, all data in an optimization model would be constant, making the model deterministic. In many cases, however, a deterministic optimization model cannot capture all the relevant intricacies of a practical decision-making environment. When a model's data are uncertain and can only be described probabilistically, the objective will have some probability distribution for any chosen set of decision variables. You can find this probability distribution by simulating the model using Crystal Ball. An optimization model under

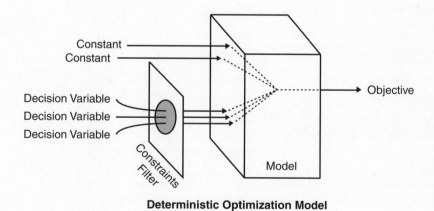

Deterministic Optimization Model

FIGURE 10.4 Visualizing a deterministic optimization.

uncertainty has several additional elements, including assumptions, forecasts, forecast statistics, and requirements.

Assumptions capture the uncertainty of model data using probability distributions, whereas forecasts are the frequency distributions of possible results for the model. Forecast statistics are summary values of a forecast distribution, such as the mean, standard deviation, and variance. The optimization process controls the optimization by maximizing, minimizing, or restricting forecast statistics. Finally, requirements are additional restrictions on forecast statistics. Upper and lower limits can be set for any statistic of a forecast distribution and a range of requirement values can be obtained by defining a variable requirement (see Figure 10.5).

Each optimization model has one objective, a forecast variable that mathematically represents the model's objective in terms of the assumption and decision variables. Optimization's job is to find the optimal value of the objective by selecting and improving different values for the decision variables. When model data are uncertain and can only be described using probability distributions, the objective itself will have some probability distribution for any set of decision variables.

Before embarking on solving an optimization problem, the analyst first has to understand the lingo of optimization: objectives, constraints, decision variables, assumptions, requirements, and forecasts.

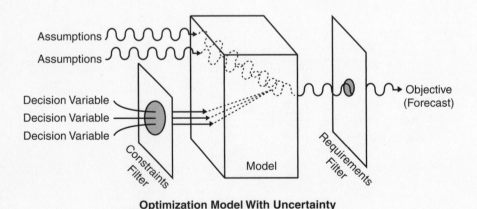

Optimization Model With Uncertainty

FIGURE 10.5 Visualizing a stochastic optimization.

SOLVING OPTIMIZATION GRAPHICALLY AND USING EXCEL'S SOLVER

Figure 10.6 illustrates a simple multiple constraint optimization problem solved using the graphical method. In this simple example of deterministic linear optimization with linear constraints, the graphical approach is easy to implement. However, great care should be taken when nonlinear constraints exist.[5] Sometimes, optimization models are specified incorrectly. For instance, Figure 10.7 shows problems arising with unbounded solutions (with a solution set at infinity), no feasible solution (where the constraints are too restrictive and impossible to satisfy), and multiple solutions (this is good news for management as it can choose from among several equally optimal solutions).

Figure 10.8 illustrates the same problem but solved using Excel's Solver add-in.[6] Solver is clearly a more powerful approach than the manual graphical method. This situation is especially true when multiple decision variables exist as a multidimensional graph would be required.[7] Figures 10.9 and 10.10 (page 248) show the use of Solver to optimize a portfolio of projects—the former assumes an integer optimization, where projects are either a go or no-go decision, whereas the latter assumes a continuous optimization, where projects can be funded anywhere from 0 percent to 100 percent.[8]

(Text continues on page 249.)

Say there are two products X and Y being manufactured. Product X provides a $20 profit and product Y a $15 profit. Product X takes 3 hours to manufacture and product Y takes 2 hours to produce. In any given week, the manufacturing equipment can make both products but has a maximum capacity of 300 hours. In addition, based on market demand, management has determined that they cannot sell more than 80 units of X and 100 units of Y in a given week and prefers not to have any inventory on hand. Therefore, management has set these demand levels as the maximum output for products X and Y respectively. The issue now becomes what is the optimal production levels of both X and Y such that profits would be maximized in any given week?

Based on the situation above, we can formulate a linear optimization routine where we have:

The Objective Function: Max 20X + 15Y

subject to Constraints: 3X + 2Y ≤ 300
                           X ≤ 80
                           Y ≤ 100

We can more easily visualize the constraints by plotting them out one at a time as follows:

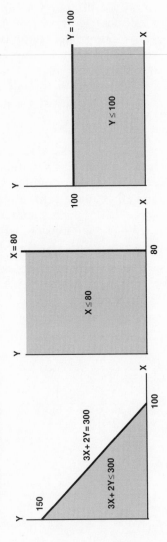

The graph below shows the combination of all three constraints. The shaded region shows the feasible area, where all constraints are simultaneously satisfied. Hence, the optimal decision should fall within this shaded region.

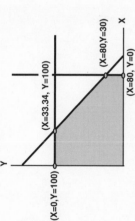

We can easily calculate the intersection points of the constraints. For example, the intersection between Y = 100 and 3X + 2Y = 300 is obtained by solving the equations simultaneously. Substituting, we get 3X + 2(100) = 300. Solving yields X = 33.34 and Y = 100.

Similarly, the intersection between X = 80 and 3X + 2Y = 300 can be obtained by solving the equations simultaneously. Substituting yields 3(80) + 2Y = 300. Solving yields Y = 30 and X = 80.

The other two edges are simply intersections between the axes. Hence, when X = 80, Y = 0 for the X = 80 line and Y = 100 and X = 0 for the Y = 100 line.

From linear programming theory, one of these four intersection edges or extreme values is the optimal solution. One method is simply to substitute each of the end points into the objective function and see which solution set provides the highest profit level.

Using the objective function where Profit = 20X + 15Y and substituting each of the extreme value sets:

When X = 0 and Y = 100:   Profit = $20 (0) + $15 (100) = $1,500
When X = 33.34 and Y = 100:   Profit = $20 (33.34) + $15 (100) = $2,167
When X = 80 and Y = 30:   Profit = $20 (80) + $15 (30) = $2,050
When X = 80 and Y = 0:   Profit = $20 (80) + $15 (0) = $1,600

Here, we see that when X = 33.34 and Y = 100, the profit function is maximized. We can also further verify this by using any combinations of X and Y within the feasible (shaded) area above. For instance, X =10 and Y =10 is a combination which is feasible but their profit outcome is only $20 (10) + $15 (10) = $350. We can calculate an infinite combinations of X and Y sets but the optimal combination is always going to be at extreme value edges.

We can easily verify which extreme value will be the optimal solution set by drawing the objective function line. If we set the objective function to be:

20X + 15Y = 0   we get X = 20, Y = 15
20X + 15Y = 1200   we get X = 60, Y = 80

If we keep shifting the profit function upwards to the right, we will keep intersecting with the extreme value edges. The edge provides the highest profit function is the optimal solution set.

In our example, point B is the optimal solution, which was verified by our calculations above, where X = 33.34 and Y = 100.

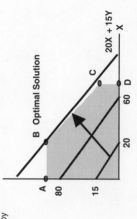

FIGURE 10.6   Solving optimization using linear programming.

245

There could be potential problems when dealing with linear programming. The three most frequently occurring problems include: Unbounded Solutions, No Feasible Solutions and Multiple Optimal Solutions.

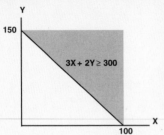

Unbounded Solutions

For instance, if the only constraint was such that $3X + 2Y \geq 300$, we have an unbounded problem. This means the machine can keep working greater than 300 hours without stop. Hence, optimally, in order to generate the most amount of profit, we would keep making products X and Y up to an infinite level. This is essentially management heaven, to produce as much as possible without any budgetary or resource constraints. Obviously, if this is the case, we should assume that the problem has not been defined correctly and perhaps an error has occurred in our mathematical models.

No Feasible Solution

Now suppose we have the following constraints:

$$3X + 2Y \leq 300$$
$$X \geq 101$$
$$Y \geq 155$$

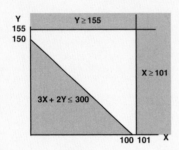

There exists no area where all constraints are binding simultaneously. In essence, any solution generated will by definition not be feasible since there will always be a constraint that is violated. Given a situation like this, it may be that the problem has been framed incorrectly or that we may have to request that management loosens some of its tight constraints since based on their expectations, the project is just not do-able. Additional resources are required (greater than 300 hours by purchasing additional machines or hiring more workers) or that the minimum required production levels (155 and 101) be reduced.

Multiple Solutions

Here, we have two extreme values (B and C) that intersect the profit objective function. Both these solution sets are optimal. This is good news for management since they have the option of choosing either combination of X and Y production levels. Other qualitative factors may be utilized on top of quantitative analytical results.

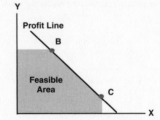

FIGURE 10.7   Potential problems of linear programming.

Using the same previous problem, where we have the following:

The Objective Function:	Max 20X + 15Y
subject to Constraints:	$3X + 2Y \leq 300$
	$X \leq 80$
	$Y \leq 100$

We can utilize Excel's Solver add-in to provide a quick analytical solution.

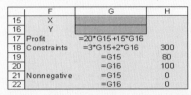

First, we need to set up the spreadsheet model. We have an X and Y variable which is to be solved. Next, we have the profit objective function in cell G17 and the constraints in cells G18 through H22. In order for Solver to perform the calculation, we needed to include two additional requirements, the nonnegative constraints, where we are setting both X and Y to be positive values only. Negative values of production are impossible. Cells H18 to H22 are the target values for the constraints. We then start Solver by clicking on Tools and Solver. (If Solver is not available, you may have to first add it in by clicking on Tools/Add-Ins and selecting Solver. Then, go back to Tools/Solver to run the program).

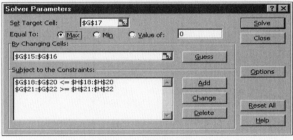

Set the profit calculation as the target cell ($G$17) and select maximization. Set the X and Y unknowns as the cells to change ($G$15:$G$16). Next, click on Add to add the constraints. The constraints could be added one at a time or in a batch group. Add $G$18:$G$20 to be less than or equal to $H$18:$H$20. Then, add in the nonnegative constraints where $G$21:$G$22 is greater than or equal to zero ($H$21:$H$22).

If we let Solver calculate the results, we would obtain the following, where the optimal solution set is when:

X	33.33	
Y	100	
Profit	$2,167	
Constraints	300	300
	33.33	80
	100	100
Nonnegative	33.33	0
	100	0

FIGURE 10.8   Using Excel's Solver in linear programming.

Integer Portfolio Optimization and Integer Linear Programming

	Cost	Return	Risk	Return-Risk Ratio	Allocation	Weighted Cost	Risk Return	Weighted Risk
Project A	$500,000	19%	32%	0.594	0%	$0	0.000	0%
Project B	$625,000	23%	39%	0.590	0%	$0	0.000	0%
Project C	$345,000	15%	22%	0.682	100%	$345,000	0.682	22%
Project D	$290,000	16%	29%	0.552	0%	$0	0.000	0%
Project E	$450,000	17%	25%	0.680	100%	$450,000	0.680	25%
					Sum	$795,000	1.362	47%

Budget Constraint $1,000,000
Each project must be between 10% and 50% allocated in funds

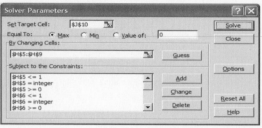

Suppose you have 5 projects you wish to allocate a fixed budget of $500,000 (this is your constraint) among, such that you will maximize the return to risk ratio (this is the objective function) subject to the requirements that each of these projects can be allocated anywhere between 10% and 50% of its total cost. You cannot allocate more than 50% of the cost of a project since you are only in the beginning stages of development while at least 10% of the project should be funded since all five projects have been previously found to be financially feasible. Using Excel's Solver add-in (use Tools/Add-Ins/Solver and then Tools/Solver) we calculate the optimal weights that will maximize the return to risk ratio.

Target cell is the objective function, which in this case is the total return to risk ratio weighted by each project, which is to be maximized. Next, add additional constraints including the budget constraint where the total cost allocated in the portfolio is ≤ the budget constraint. In addition, for each project weight, set them to be ≥ 0 and ≤ 1 as well as weight as integers. This is essentially the difference between the prior linear programming and optimization routine which allows fractional projects to be executed while in integer linear programming, projects are either chosen (1.0) or not (0.0) and nothing in between is allowed (integer constraint).

FIGURE 10.9   Excel Solver on integer linear programming.

Portfolio Optimization and Linear Programming

	Cost	Return	Risk	Return-Risk Ratio	Allocation	Weighted Cost	Total Risk-Return	Weighted Risk
Project A	$500,000	19%	32%	0.594	10%	$50,000	0.059	3%
Project B	$625,000	23%	39%	0.590	10%	$62,500	0.059	4%
Project C	$345,000	15%	22%	0.682	50%	$172,500	0.341	11%
Project D	$290,000	16%	29%	0.552	50%	$145,000	0.276	15%
Project E	$450,000	17%	25%	0.680	16%	$70,000	0.106	4%
					Sum	$500,000	0.841	36%

Budget Constraint $500,000
Each project must be between 10% and 50% allocated in funds

Suppose you have 5 projects you wish to allocate a fixed budget of $500,000 (this is your constraint) among, such that you will maximize the return to risk ratio (this is the objective function) subject to the requirements that each of these projects can be allocated anywhere between 10% and 50% of its total cost. You cannot allocate more than 50% of the cost of a project since you are only in the beginning stages of development while at least 10% of the project should be funded since all five projects have been previously found to be financially feasible. Using Excel's Solver add-in (use Tools/Add-Ins/Solver and then Tools/Solver) we calculate the optimal weights that will maximize the return to risk ratio.

Target cell is the objective function, which in this case is the total return to risk ratio weighted by each project, which is to be maximized. Next, add additional constraints including the budget constraint where the total cost allocated in the portfolio is ≤ the budget constraint. In addition, for each project weight, set them to be ≥ 0.1 and ≤ 0.5.

FIGURE 10.10   Excel Solver on continuous linear programming.

FIVE-MINUTE INDUSTRY SPOTLIGHT: PROVISE MANAGEMENT

Optimizing Portfolio Profit

During the peak of the dot-com era, many investors have come to believe that the market only goes in one direction: up. The danger of this assumption is that it fails to acknowledge that all portfolios contain risk, and that virtually all portfolios are capable of losing value. Pro-Vise Management Group, an SEC-registered investment advisor who specializes in asset management and financial planning, understands that proper portfolio management requires a rigorous analysis of risk.

William L. Raddatz, CFP, is the vice president of financial planning and senior plan writer for ProVise. According to Raddatz, portfolio design is both a science and an art. When ProVise begins to construct a client's portfolio, the two critical elements that must be thoroughly identified are the client's risk tolerance and a corresponding asset allocation. ProVise establishes the client's risk tolerance through extensive interviews and a risk tolerance questionnaire program developed by the American College at Bryn Mawr, Pennsylvania.

Once ProVise is satisfied that they understand the types and amount of risk a client can accept, they perform an optimization analysis of the client's current portfolio. In an Excel spreadsheet, they examine the potential of each asset. Key asset characteristics include its category (aggressive growth, global/foreign, high-yield bond, etc.), its dollar value, the percentage of the total portfolio that it represents, its measure of risk, its target return (using historical asset class returns) and weighted target return, and its 3- or 5-year historical average annualized return. Crystal Ball assumptions include each asset's weighted target return and weighted beta.

After the portfolio simulation is complete, ProVise helps the client understand the current risk level by showing him or her the certainty level for the overall portfolio's target return. Very often, the client will see that his or her portfolio has a substantial potential for negative returns, sometimes 30 percent or more. "Seldom do we find that a client's portfolio's risk is commensurate with the client's risk tolerance," notes Raddatz. "Often, the portfolio has considerably more risk than is apparent, which is where Crystal Ball comes in."

ProVise then constructs a new portfolio spreadsheet that contains a combination of current and new assets. They import the assets' monthly returns from one of several available services, such as Morningstar, and use Excel's data analysis (under the Tools menu) to correlate the data. The correlated data are then entered into the Crystal Ball Correlation Matrix. Uncertainty within the model is reflected in the measure of risk (beta) and target return for each asset. ProVise defines these variables as Crystal Ball assumption cells, either as a normal distribution, using an asset's historical mean return and standard deviation, or as a uniform or lognormal distribution in the case of T-bills and money market assets. ProVise typically runs 8,000 trials using Latin Hypercube sampling.

The proposed portfolio is then optimized for the client's risk tolerance and target return. In the new model, the value of each asset selected for the new portfolio is defined as a decision cell. A constraint is applied for each asset class, such as aggressive growth, where the asset class's value will equal a particular value. The OptQuest program then optimizes the portfolio by maximizing Target Return, while Risk (beta or standard deviation) is set to a selected maximum limit. Then a final Crystal Ball simulation is run on the optimized portfolio to demonstrate the portfolio's reduced risk or the enhanced return to the client.

ProVise also uses Crystal Ball's optimization tool to determine the client's probable cash flow or asset accumulation values during his or her retirement. As before, ProVise first creates a cash-flow spreadsheet, defining "inflation" and "target return" as assumption cells. This information is graphically presented using a color trend chart with confidence bands of 50 percent, 75 percent, and 90 percent.

ProVise has found this method of optimization to be superior to other optimization products in flexibility, reliability, and ease of use. The recommended portfolios are optimized efficiently, accurately, and quickly. "This has been a great time and money saver," said Raddatz. "Although the portfolio selection and management processes are dynamic, the client receives an optimized portfolio that fits like a handmade suit, which from time to time may need slight adjustments."

FIVE-MINUTE INDUSTRY SPOTLIGHT: TEXACO

Texaco Evaluates Inventory and Optimizes Production Levels

Rick Ruthrauff is an evaluation engineer in Texaco's Deep Water Exploration Group and uses Crystal Ball Professional (CB Pro) for several different applications. Rick's primary use of CB Pro is to evaluate Texaco's inventory as well as the inventory of its competition. Rick analyzes the different prospects within Texaco's portfolio in an effort to determine the size, economics, and success ranges for each area. In his Crystal Ball simulation, Rick was able to vary the numbers of prospects drilled and the chance of success, and alter the reserve and value distributions selected from the distribution gallery.

The leases held by Texaco's competitors are public record, so Rick is able to estimate the size, value, and success probability of both their drilled and undrilled inventory. There are less data and more uncertainty with these simulations, but they still provide a valuable tool in measuring the success of the competition.

Another valuable tool Rick uses is Crystal Ball's sensitivity charts. These charts allow Rick to better understand the parts of his models that are contributing the most to the results. Rick can then manipulate his model inputs to lessen the dramatic impact on results.

Rick also has employed CB Pro's OptQuest technology to help determine the optimum number of wells needed to achieve a specific objective. For example, if Texaco is interested in obtaining a certain number of barrels of oil with a particular expenditure level, OptQuest will point to the optimum combination of wells to achieve the desired production level.

Rick recalls a specific instance in which the use of CB Pro influenced Texaco's decision not to purchase a company with deep-water exploration acreage. Through conducting Crystal Ball analyses, it was determined that the money needed to purchase the company would derive more value if it were invested elsewhere.

Risk and uncertainty are an inherent part of the petroleum industry. Texaco has recognized the importance of using tools such as Crystal Ball to help mitigate the unknown factors found in difficult decisions.

QUESTIONS

1. What is the difference between deterministic optimization and optimization under uncertainty?
2. Define then compare and contrast each of the following:
   a. Objective
   b. Constraint
   c. Decision variable
   d. Requirement
3. Explain what some of the problems are in a graphical linear programming approach and if they can be easily solved.
4. What are some of the approaches to solve an optimization problem? List each approach as well as its corresponding pros and cons.

CHAPTER 11

Optimization under Uncertainty

This chapter looks at two optimization models in more detail. The first is the application of *discrete* optimization under uncertainty for a simple project selection model, where a firm is faced with 12 competing and non-mutually exclusive project choices, each with a different return and cost profile. The job of the analyst is to find the best combination of projects that will satisfy the firm's budget constraints while maximizing the portfolio's total value. The second model is an application of *continuous* optimization under uncertainty, where an investor is faced with allocating her personal resources into a portfolio of stocks. The need here is to allocate her portfolio of assets such that it will maximize expected returns while minimizing risks using the Sharpe ratio.

PROJECT SELECTION MODEL (DISCRETE OPTIMIZATION UNDER UNCERTAINTY)

The following example refers to the *Project Pro (Optimization).xls* model on the enclosed CD-ROM. Figure 11.1 shows the main worksheet of the model, complete with 12 projects and their respective estimated capital investment costs and expected returns in the form of a net present value (NPV). Notice in Figure 11.2 that these costs and returns are obtained through a detailed set of analyses with Monte Carlo simulation in the file's other worksheets and only the main summary page of the results from these detailed analyses is shown. In addition, notice that in column B in the main worksheet, there exists a series of decision variables (with default values of 1). These decision variables are the variables to be optimized. In other words, based on the estimated costs and returns of each project, what is the optimal set of projects that should be selected that will maximize the total portfolio's NPV subject to the budget constraint of $260 million?

	A	B	C	D
1		**Project Optimization Selection**		
2				
3	**Project No.**	**Selected Project (1=yes, 0=No)**	**NPV**	**Estimated Capital Investment**
4	Project 1	1	$ 27.95	$ 37.00
5	Project 2	1	$ 30.65	$ 42.00
6	Project 3	1	$ 27.28	$ 36.00
7	Project 4	1	$ 43.85	$ 57.50
8	Project 5	1	$ 28.61	$ 45.00
9	Project 6	1	$ 8.67	$ 38.00
10	Project 7	1	$ 21.07	$ 35.00
11	Project 8	1	$ 21.14	$ 38.00
12	Project 9	1	$ 37.26	$ 50.00
13	Project 10	1	$ 29.94	$ 46.00
14	Project 11	1	$ 21.52	$ 35.00
15	Project 12	1	$ 58.71	$ 42.00
16				
17		Total Project NPV	$ 356.65	
18				
19		Budget	$ 260.00	
20		Amount Invested	$ 501.50	
21		Surplus / (Shortfall)	$ (241.50)	
22				

FIGURE 11.1   Project optimization problem.

	A	B	C	D	E	F	G	H	I	J
1	Note: $MM									
2	Assumptions:							Sales Year 1		
3	Prj. 1 Sales Year 1	$110		Prj. 1 Capital Inv.	$37			Mean	Std. Dev	
4	Prj. 1 Sales Growth Rate	12%		Prj. 1 Discount Rate	10%			$110	$45	
5	Prj. 1 COGS Growth Rate	10%		Prj. 1 Tax Rate	40%			Sales Growth Rate		
6	Prj. 1 OPEX/Sales %	16%						Min	M-L	Max
7								0%	12%	12%
8			Year 1	Year 2	Year 3	Year 4				
9										
10	Sales		$110	$123	$138	$155				
11	COGS		$65	$72	$79	$87				
12	Net Sales		$45	$52	$59	$68				
13										
14	Total OPEX		$18	$20	$22	$25				
15										
16	EBITDA		$27	$32	$37	$43				
17	Taxes		$11	$13	$15	$17				
18	Capital Investment	($37)								
19	Free Cash Flow	($37)	$16	$19	$22	$26				
20										
21		NPV Project 1	$27.95							
22		IRR Project 1	38.70%							
23										

FIGURE 11.2   Project optimization worksheets.

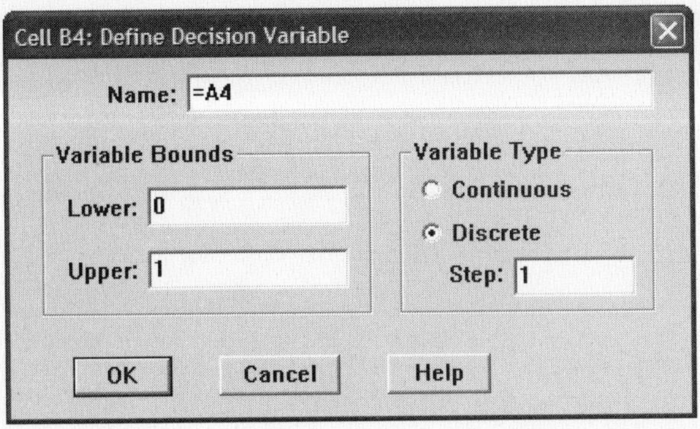

FIGURE 11.3   Discrete versus continuous decision variables.

The project analysis can be assumed to be either discrete or continuous as seen in Figure 11.3. Discrete decision variables mean that each project is either a go or no-go decision. That is, the optimal portfolio project selection that maximizes returns and minimizes risks subject to the constraints can be A only; B only; C only; D only; A and B; A and C; A and D; B and C; A, B, and C only, and so forth. The lower bound of 0 and upper bound of 1 with a discrete step size of 1 means that the decision variable can only be 0 or 1, indicative of a go or no-go decision. For this example, assume a discrete decision variable.[1]

Starting Crystal Ball's OptQuest (select *CBTools | OptQuest* in Excel) and selecting the *New* project icon will yield the decision variable selection screen in Figure 11.4. The decision variables are automatically captured by the software. Here, any modifications to the lower and upper bounds can be changed if necessary. Clicking on *OK* will take the user to the

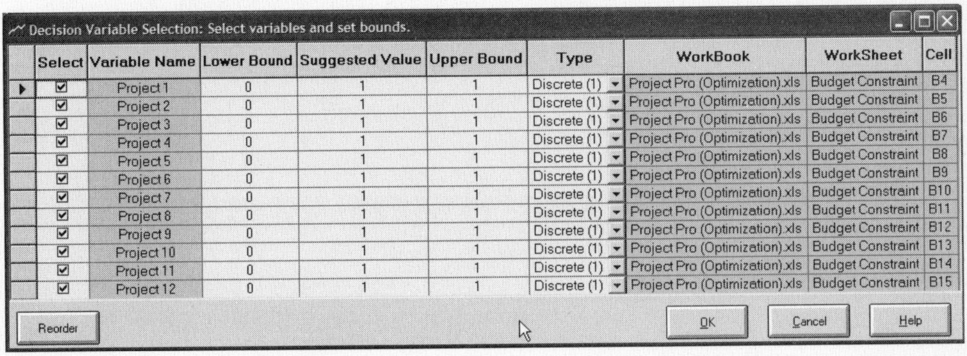

FIGURE 11.4   Decision variable selection.

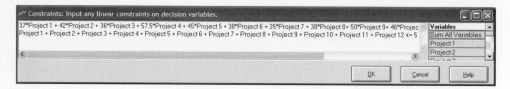

FIGURE 11.5   Constraints input.

constraints-input dialog as seen in Figure 11.5. The constraints are the budget constraint and an optional constraint on the number of projects to choose. The budget constraint is such that the cost of the entire portfolio cannot exceed the budgeted $260 million.

The budget constraint is:[2]

$$37*Project\ 1 + 42*Project\ 2 + 36*Project\ 3 + 57.5*Project\ 4 + 45*$$
$$Project\ 5 + 38*Project\ 6 + 35*Project\ 7 + 38*Project\ 8 + 50*$$
$$Project\ 9 + 46*Project\ 10 + 35*Project\ 11 + 42*Project\ 12 <= 260$$

The additional optional constraint is the number of projects to select, such that the total number of projects cannot exceed five. The project constraint is:[3]

$$Project\ 1 + Project\ 2 + Project\ 3 + Project\ 4 + Project\ 5 + Project\ 6 +$$
$$Project\ 7 + Project\ 8 + Project\ 9 + Project\ 10 + Project\ 11 +$$
$$Project\ 12 <= 5$$

The objective-selection screen is next. The objective to maximize is the mean of the total project portfolio's NPV (Figure 11.6). The optimization is then set to run for 10 minutes (Figure 11.7) to illustrate the results.[4] The optimization results are shown in Figures 11.8 and 11.9. The performance graph shows the optimization process, where a better combination of projects is progressively chosen. The best results are shown in Figure 11.9, where the best combination of projects that should be chosen subject to budget

	Select	Name	Forecast Statistic	Lower Bound	Upper Bound	Units	WorkBook	WorkSheet	Cell
▶	Maximize Objective ▾	Total Project NPV	Mean ▾				Project Pro (Optimization).xls	Budget Constraint	C17
	No ▾	Surplus / Shortfall	Mean ▾				Project Pro (Optimization).xls	Budget Constraint	C21

FIGURE 11.6   Objective selection.

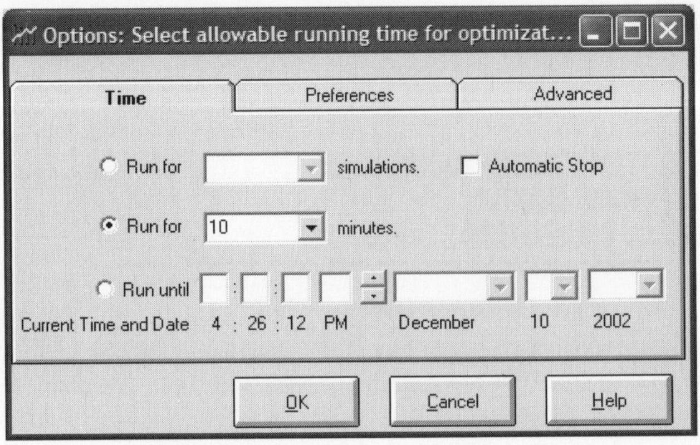

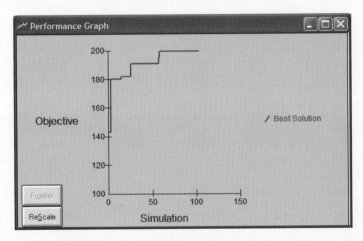

FIGURE 11.7 Optimization run time.

FIGURE 11.8 Optimization performance graph.

Simulation	Maximize Objective Total	Project 1	Project 2	Project 3	Project 4	Project 5	Project 6	Project 7	Project 8	Project 9	Project 10	Project 11	Project 12
1	142.970	1	1	1	1	1	0	0	0	0	0	0	0
3	179.819	1	0	1	0	0	0	0	0	1	0	1	1
15	181.666	0	1	0	1	0	1	0	0	0	1	0	1
26	190.823	0	1	1	1	0	0	0	0	1	1	0	0
Best: 58	199.570	0	1	0	1	0	0	0	1	1	0	0	1

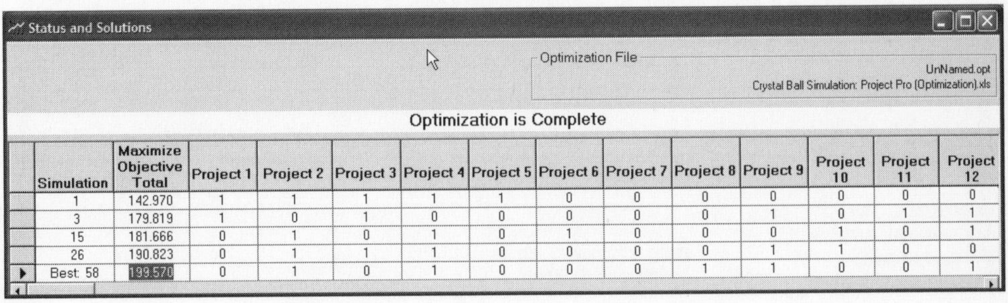

FIGURE 11.9 Project optimization results.

constraints that maximizes the portfolio's expected returns subject to uncertainties in each project, is to execute projects 2, 4, 8, 9, and 12.

PORTFOLIO OPTIMIZATION USING RISK AND RETURN (CONTINUOUS STOCHASTIC OPTIMIZATION)

Figure 11.10 illustrates another sample model of a financial asset portfolio optimization under uncertainty. The file is available on the CD-ROM and is named *Sharpe Portfolio (Optimization).xls*. The total portfolio's expected level of returns (14.75 percent) is calculated using a weighted average level of individual asset returns on the portfolio of

$$R_P = \omega_A R_A + \omega_B R_B + \omega_C R_C + \omega_D R_D$$

where R_P is the return on the portfolio, $R_{A,B,C,D}$ are the individual returns on the projects, and $\omega_{A,B,C,D}$ are the respective weights or capital allocation across each project. In addition, the value of 14.57 percent is the portfolio-level risks coefficient (σ_P), where we define the portfolio risk coefficient as

	A	B	C	D	E
1	**Sharpe Portfolio Allocation Model**				
2					
3	**Fund**	**Historical Data**	**Distribution**	**Returns**	**Risks**
4	**Large Cap Stocks**	H2:H251	Normal	13.00%	13.31%
5	**Small Cap Stocks**	I2:I251	Normal	17.00%	23.04%
6	**Micro Cap Stocks**	J2:J251	Normal	23.00%	29.45%
7	**Government Bonds**	K2:K251	Normal	6.00%	3.72%
8					
9					
10	**Fund**	**% Invested**	**Min. Invested**	**Max. Invested**	
11	**Large Cap Stocks**	25.0%	10%	50%	
12	**Small Cap Stocks**	25.0%	10%	50%	
13	**Micro Cap Stocks**	25.0%	10%	50%	
14	**Government Bonds**	25.0%	10%	50%	
15					
16	Correlation Matrix	Large Cap Stocks	Small Cap Stocks	Micro Cap Stocks	Government Bonds
17	Large Cap Stocks	1.000	0.569	0.541	0.057
18	Small Cap Stocks		1.000	0.744	0.062
19	Micro Cap Stocks			1.000	0.034
20	Government Bonds				1.000
21					
22					
23	*Portfolio Risks*	14.57%			
24	*Portfolio Returns*	14.75%			
25	*Sharpe Ratio*	1.0122			
26					

FIGURE 11.10 Sharpe portfolio allocation model.

$$\sigma_P = \sqrt{\sum_{i=1}^{i} \omega_i^2 \sigma_i^2 + \sum_{i=1}^{n} \sum_{j=1}^{m} 2\omega_i \omega_j \rho_{i,j} \sigma_i \sigma_j}$$

Here, $\rho_{i,j}$ are the respective cross correlations. Hence, if the cross correlations are negative, there are risk diversification effects, and the portfolio risk decreases. The sample model has the relevant simulation assumptions predefined for cells D4:D7 as well as a sample cross-correlation matrix.

Before optimization can be performed, decision variables have to be assigned. The weights assigned to each project are the decision variables as seen in cells B11:B14 in Figure 11.10. Notice that this optimization process assumes a continuous allocation, which means that given the budget constraint, the proportion of budget can be allocated as a percentage of the whole budget, with a minimum investment in each asset set at 10 percent and the maximum that can be allocated to each asset is set at 50 percent of the entire portfolio (cells C11:D14). The define decision variable dialog box is illustrated in Figure 11.11.

Crystal Ball OptQuest is then started and the dialog box for defining the decision variables appears (Figure 11.12). The upper and lower bounds may now be changed if necessary. Click on *Next* to continue. On the next screen, click on *Sum All Variables*, and set it equal to one before continuing. This action forces the budget weight allocations to sum to 100 percent (Figure 11.13).

In the following step, select *Maximize Objective* with respect to the *Final Value* and apply it to the Sharpe Ratio (Figure 11.14). The Sharpe Ratio is simply the ratio of the levels of portfolio returns to portfolio risks, and the

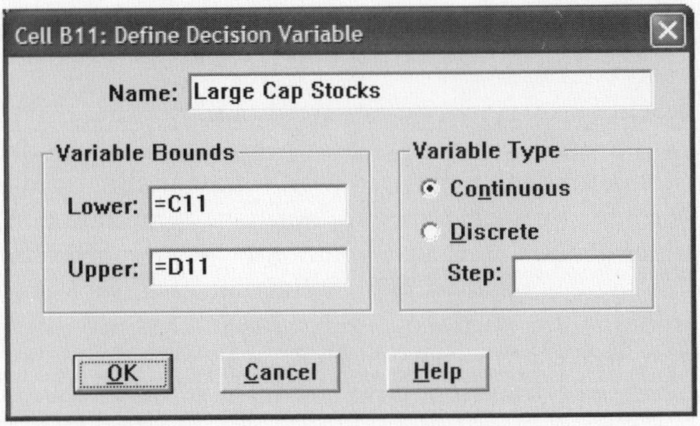

FIGURE 11.11 Continuous decision variable.

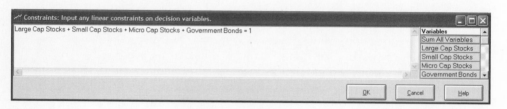

FIGURE 11.12   OptQuest's decision variable selection.

Constraints: Input any linear constraints on decision variables.

Large Cap Stocks + Small Cap Stocks + Micro Cap Stocks + Government Bonds = 1

Variables
Sum All Variables
Large Cap Stocks
Small Cap Stocks
Micro Cap Stocks
Government Bonds

FIGURE 11.13   Constraints.

Forecast Selection: Select an objective and any requirements (reqs. must have a bound).

	Select	Name	Forecast Statistic	Lower Bound	Upper Bound	Units	WorkBook	WorkSheet	Cell
▶	Maximize Objective ▾	Sharpe Ratio	Final_Value ▾				Sharpe Portfolio (Optimization).xls	Sharpe Portfolio	B25
	No ▾	Large Cap Stocks	Mean ▾				Sharpe Portfolio (Optimization).xls	Sharpe Portfolio	D4
	No ▾	Small Cap Stocks	Mean ▾				Sharpe Portfolio (Optimization).xls	Sharpe Portfolio	D5
	No ▾	Micro Cap Stocks	Mean ▾				Sharpe Portfolio (Optimization).xls	Sharpe Portfolio	D6
	No ▾	Government Bonds	Mean ▾				Sharpe Portfolio (Optimization).xls	Sharpe Portfolio	D7

FIGURE 11.14   Objective—Sharpe Ratio final value selection.

portfolio's level of risk cannot be estimated until the entire simulation has
been run, thus the analysis should be based on the final value.[5] Because projects should not be chosen on the basis of maximum return or minimum risk
alone, the Sharpe Ratio is often used for portfolio optimization to obtain the
efficient frontier of asset portfolio allocation, where the maximum return is
obtained with the combination of the minimum risk, subject to any constraints. In addition, the portfolio level returns and risks are used. The portfolio risk also accounts for any diversification effects among individual
projects selected based on their cross correlations. After the optimization
process is complete, the results look like those in Figures 11.15 and 11.16.
These are the same charts seen in the previous example.

Simulation	Maximize Objective Sharpe Ratio Final_Value	Large Cap Stocks	Small Cap Stocks	Micro Cap Stocks	Government Bonds
1	1.01210	0.250000	0.250000	0.250000	0.250000
4	1.07383	0.278992	0.302121	0.100000	0.318887
7	1.08004	0.249677	0.100000	0.285263	0.365060
20	1.13105	0.281417	0.100000	0.289965	0.328618
21	1.19209	0.313157	0.100000	0.294667	0.292176
46	1.31642	0.300000	0.100000	0.100000	0.500000
49	1.32588	0.296254	0.101873	0.101873	0.500000
109	1.40656	0.299884	0.101249	0.101249	0.497619
130	1.42590	0.301405	0.100105	0.100105	0.498385
Best 163	1.46559	0.309264	0.100000	0.100000	0.490736

Optimization File
UnNamed.opt
Crystal Ball Simulation: Sharpe Portfolio (Optimization).xls

Optimization is Complete

Status and Solutions

FIGURE 11.15 Optimization status and solutions.

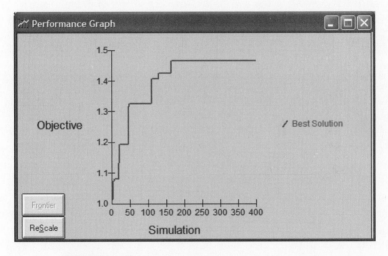

FIGURE 11.16 Optimization performance graph.

The optimal result after running thousands of simulations is such that based on the optimization assumptions the total budget should be allocated as follows: 31 percent to large-cap stocks, 10 percent to small-cap stocks, 10 percent to micro-cap stocks, and 49 percent to government bonds. This capital allocation ensures that the maximum return is obtained, with the minimum amount of risk, subject to the risk and return uncertainties in each asset class as well as the relevant constraints.

FIVE-MINUTE INDUSTRY SPOTLIGHT: MINNESOTA POWER

Financial Simulation Aids Risk Management

Part of the multiservices company ALLETE, Minnesota Power is a low-cost electric utility engaged in the generation, transmission, and distribution of electricity in Minnesota and Wisconsin, and serving some of the largest industrial customers in the United States. One of the primary tasks of Minnesota Power's risk group is the estimation, assessment, and communication of financial risk—defined as the variability of financial outcomes.

Paul Dietz, a quantitative analyst with the Risk Management Department, has used Crystal Ball for almost 3 years. "I am responsible for providing quantitative analysis support to the risk management group," he explained. "This includes developing and implementing quantitative models for valuing complex wholesale and retail contracts, tolling agreements, and generation projects. I use Crystal Ball for analyzing pro forma cash-flow and income statements and for developing probabilistic models involving derivatives. Recently, I've used the program to value real options such as power plant projects, emission credits, and nontraded embedded options."

Dietz and his colleagues are strong proponents of spreadsheet models and Monte Carlo simulation. Because analytical models approximate the real world, the risk group uses them to experiment with the natural variability within a system. For example, Dietz explained, the equation Profit = Revenue – Expenses is a very simple analytical model used by most businesses. In the real world, however, revenue and expenses are subject to variability, and so simulation is needed to examine the effects of this variability on profit. The Minnesota Power risk management group builds and simulates these types of models to help the company decide whether to buy an asset, how to allocate scarce capital, and whether to develop a new product offering.

Most of the financial models Dietz builds are intended to evaluate measures of performance or the behavior of financial systems given a specific set of inputs. He finds that the most time-consuming aspect of model building is determining the variability around the uncertain inputs, or assumptions, of the model. To ensure that the model is realistic, the risk management group first consults with the company's internal experts and takes the time necessary to research the problem. In one recent project, the risk group developed a financial model that required advice from more than 15 experts to help define assumptions that ranged from power plant reliability to environmental concerns.

Dietz sees many advantages to simulation modeling. First, the discipline of building a quantitative model forces him to better understand the data and relationships within the model. Model building also yields insights into real world problems and helps to reduce the probability and costs of poor implementation. Finally, and most importantly, modeling provides management with the valuable information they need to make less risky and more effective business decisions. "With our Monte Carlo models, we are able to assess the variability associated with investing in real options such as combustion turbines and tolling agreements," said Dietz. "This knowledge provides our management team with a new tool for ascertaining the risk-adjusted returns associated with a particular project."

QUESTION

1. Compare and contrast between a discrete versus continuous decision variable when used in an optimization under uncertainty.

EXERCISE

1. Create an Excel model for a continuous optimization problem with the following parameters:
   a. A stock portfolio consisting of four individual stocks, each with its own return and risk profile—each return and risk value has its own distributional assumption that is correlated to one another.
   b. The optimization problem is to efficiently allocate your resources to these four individual stocks such that the best bang for the buck is achieved—use a Sharpe Ratio (portfolio returns to risk ratio).
   c. Optimize this portfolio of stocks through the Sharpe ratio and progressively create and show the Markowitz efficient frontier of stock allocations.

Risk Mitigation

CHAPTER 12

What Is So Real About Real Options, and Why Are They Optional?

WHAT IS REAL OPTIONS?

In the past, corporate investment decisions were cut and dried. Buy a new machine that is more efficient, make more products costing a certain amount, and if the benefits outweigh the costs, execute the investment. Hire a larger pool of sales associates, expand the current geographical area, and if the marginal increase in forecast sales revenues exceeds the additional salary and implementation costs, start hiring. Need a new manufacturing plant? Show that the construction costs can be recouped quickly and easily by the increase in revenues the plant will generate through new and improved products, and the initiative is approved.

However, real-life business conditions are a lot more complicated. Your firm decides to go with an e-commerce strategy, but multiple strategic paths exist. Which path do you choose? What are the options you have? If you choose the wrong path, how do you get back on the right track? How do you value and prioritize the paths that exist? You are a venture capitalist firm with multiple business plans to consider. How do you value a start-up firm with no proven track record? How do you structure a mutually beneficial investment deal? What is the optimal timing to a second or third round of financing?

Real options are useful not only in valuing a firm through its strategic business options, but also as a strategic business tool in capital investment decisions. For instance, should a firm invest millions in a new e-commerce initiative? How does a firm choose among several seemingly cashless, costly, and unprofitable information-technology infrastructure projects? Should a firm indulge its billions in a risky research and development initiative? The consequences of a wrong decision can be disastrous or even terminal for certain firms. In a traditional discounted cash-flow model, these questions cannot be answered with any certainty. In fact, some of the answers generated through the use of the traditional discounted cash-flow model are flawed because the model assumes a static, one-time decision-making process while the real options approach takes into consideration the strategic managerial options certain projects create under uncertainty and management's flexibility in exercising or abandoning these options at different points in time, when the level of uncertainty has decreased or has become known over time.

Business conditions are fraught with uncertainty and risks. These uncertainties hold with them valuable information. When uncertainty becomes resolved through the passage of time, managers can make the appropriate midcourse corrections through a change in business decisions and strategies. Real options incorporate this learning model, akin to having a strategic road map, while traditional analyses that neglect this managerial flexibility will grossly undervalue certain projects and strategies.

The real options approach incorporates a learning model, such that management makes better and more informed strategic decisions when some levels of uncertainty are resolved through the passage of time. The discounted cash-flow analysis assumes a static investment decision, and assumes that strategic decisions are made initially with no recourse to choose other pathways or options in the future. To create a good analogy of real options, visualize it as a strategic road map of long and winding roads with multiple perilous turns and branches along the way. Imagine the intrinsic and extrinsic value of having such a road map when navigating through unfamiliar territory, as well as having road signs at every turn to guide you in making the best and most informed driving decisions. Such a strategic map is the essence of real options.

The answer to evaluating such projects lies in real options analysis, which can be used in a variety of settings, including pharmaceutical drug development, oil and gas exploration and production, manufacturing, start-up valuation, venture capital investment, information technology infrastructure, research and development, mergers and acquisitions, e-commerce and e-business, intellectual capital development, technology development, facility expansion, business project prioritization, enterprise-wide risk management, business unit capital budgeting, licenses, contracts, intangible asset valuation, and the like. The following section illustrates some business cases and how real options can assist in identifying and capturing additional strategic value for a firm.

THE REAL OPTIONS SOLUTION IN A NUTSHELL

Simply defined, real options is a systematic approach and integrated solution using financial theory, economic analysis, management science, decision sciences, statistics, and econometric modeling in applying options theory in valuing real physical assets, as opposed to financial assets, in a dynamic and uncertain business environment where business decisions are flexible in the context of strategic capital investment decision making, valuing investment opportunities, and project capital expenditures.

Real options are crucial in:

- Identifying different corporate investment decision pathways or projects that management can navigate given highly uncertain business conditions.
- Valuing each of the strategic decision pathways and what it represents in terms of financial viability and feasibility.
- Prioritizing these pathways or projects based on a series of qualitative and quantitative metrics.
- Optimizing the value of strategic investment decisions by evaluating different decision paths under certain conditions or using a different sequence of pathways that can lead to the optimal strategy.
- Timing the effective execution of investments and finding the optimal trigger values and cost or revenue drivers.
- Managing existing or developing new optionalities and strategic decision pathways for future opportunities.

ISSUES TO CONSIDER

Strategic options do have significant intrinsic value, but this value is only realized when management decides to execute the strategies. Real options theory assumes that management is logical and competent and that management acts in the best interests of the company and its shareholders through the maximization of wealth and minimization of risk of losses. For example, suppose a firm owns the rights to a piece of land that fluctuates dramatically in price. An analyst calculates the volatility of prices and recommends that management retain ownership for a specified time period, where within this period there is a good chance that the price of real estate will triple. Therefore, management owns a call option, an *option to wait* and defer sale for a particular time period. The value of the real estate is therefore higher than the value that is based on today's sale price. The difference is simply this option to wait. However, the value of the real estate will not command the higher value if prices do triple but management decides not to execute the option to sell. In that case, the price of real estate goes back to its original levels after the specified period and then management finally relinquishes its rights.

> Strategic optionality value can only be obtained if the option is executed; otherwise, all the options in the world are worthless.

Was the analyst right or wrong? What was the true value of the piece of land? Should it have been valued at its explicit value on a deterministic case where you know what the price of land is right now, and therefore this is its value; or should it include some types of optionality where there is a good probability that the price of land could triple in value, hence, the piece of land is truly worth more than it is now and should therefore be valued accordingly? The latter is the real options view. The additional strategic optionality value can only be obtained if the option is executed; otherwise, all the options in the world are worthless. This idea of *explicit* versus *implicit* value becomes highly significant when management's compensation is tied directly to the actual performance of particular projects or strategies.

To further illustrate this point, suppose the price of the land in the market is currently $10 million. Further, suppose that the market is highly liquid and volatile, and that the firm can easily sell off the land at a moment's notice within the next 5 years, the same amount of time the firm owns the rights to the land. If there is a 50 percent chance the price will increase to $15 million and a 50 percent chance it will decrease to $5 million within this time period, is the property worth an expected value of $10 million? If prices rise to $15 million, management should be competent and rational enough to execute the option and sell that piece of land immediately to capture the additional $5 million premium. However, if management acts inappropriately or decides to hold off selling in the hopes that prices will rise even further, the property value may eventually drop back down to $5 million. Now, how much is this property really worth? What if there happens to be an *abandonment option*? Suppose there is a perfect counterparty to this transaction who decides to enter into a contractual agreement whereby, for a contractual fee, the counterparty agrees to purchase the property for $10 million within the next 5 years, regardless of the market price and executable at the whim of the firm that owns the property. Effectively, a safety net has been created whereby the minimum floor value of the property has been set at $10 million (less the fee paid). That is, there is a limited downside but an unlimited upside, as the firm can always sell the property at market price if it exceeds the floor value. Hence, this strategic *abandonment option* has increased the value of the property significantly. Logically, with this abandonment option in place, the value of the land with the option is definitely worth more than $10 million. The real options approach seeks to value this additional inherent flexibility.

IMPLEMENTING REAL OPTIONS ANALYSIS

First of all, it is vital to understand that real options analysis is *not* a simple set of equations or models. It is an *entire decision-making process* that enhances the traditional decision analysis approaches. It takes what has been tried and true financial analytics and evolves it to the next step by pushing the envelope of analytical techniques. In addition, it is vital to understand that 50 percent of the value in real options analysis is simply thinking about it. Another 25 percent of the value comes from the number crunching activities, while the final 25 percent comes from the results interpretation and explanation to management. Several issues should be considered when attempting to implement real options analysis:

■ *Tools.* The correct tools are important. These tools must be more comprehensive than initially required because analysts will grow into them over time. Do not be restrictive in choosing the relevant tools. Always provide room for expansion. Advanced tools will relieve the analyst of detailed model building and let him or her focus instead on 75 percent of the value—thinking about the problem and interpreting the results. The next section provides details on an analytical comparison of approaches, indicating their respective benefits and pitfalls.

■ *Resources.* The best tools in the world are useless without the relevant human resources to back them up. Tools do not eliminate the analyst, but enhance the analyst's ability to effectively and efficiently execute the analysis. The right people with the right tools will go a long way. Because there are only a few true real options experts in the world who truly understand the theoretical underpinnings of the models as well the practical applications, care should be taken in choosing the correct team. A team of real options experts is vital in the success of the initiative. A company should consider building a team of in-house experts to implement real options analysis and to maintain the ability for continuity, training, and knowledge transfer over time. Knowledge and experience in the theories, implementation, training, and consulting are the core requirements of this team of individuals.

■ *Senior Management Buy-in.* The analysis buy-in has to be top-down where senior management drives the real options analysis initiative. A bottom-up approach where a few inexperienced junior analysts try to impress the powers that be will fail miserably.

CHOOSING THE RIGHT REAL OPTIONS
ANALYSIS TOOLS

In real options analysis, there are multiple methodologies and approaches used to calculate an option's value, including the following:

- Binomial lattices.
- Multinomial lattices.
- Closed-form models.
- Monte Carlo path simulation.
- Partial-differential equations.
- Dynamic optimization, variance reduction, and other numerical techniques.

The most widely used mainstream methods are the closed-form models and the binomial lattices. Binomial lattices are used to solve the most common types of options (expansion, sequential compound, contraction, abandonment, and so forth) using a binomial tree. Closed-form models are equations such as the Black–Scholes model and its modifications, where a fancy mathematical model exists. Monte Carlo path-dependent simulation methods involve simulating all possible paths of an asset and estimating its option value. Multinomial lattices (trinomial, quadranomial, pentanomial, and multinomial trees) are simply extensions of the binomial lattices but with more branches at each node, and are useful for solving more detailed and highly complex problems (e.g., jump-diffusion and mean-reverting options). Dynamic optimization, variance reduction, and other numerical techniques are more mathematically complex methods used to solve exotic options, but by themselves have limited applicability.

Criteria for Selection

Following are the most important criteria for selecting the relevant models and approaches to use in a real options analysis and each method is discussed in more detail, complete with a ranking from 1 (worst) to 10 (best) on each selection criteria.

- *Ease of Use.* The method must be easy to calculate and use. A black box is useless as you cannot understand the methods and steps used in the calculations. There will be little confidence in the results.
- *Expositional Ease.* Can the approach be explained easily to management?
- *Replicability.* The approach must provide identical answers every time if identical assumptions and inputs are used.
- *Modeling Flexibility.* Can the model or approach be flexible enough to include different tweaks and changes to more correctly mirror actual

business cases? Can this be done very easily by the user without the help of someone with an advanced degree in finance and mathematics?

- *Ease of View.* For instance, results from a binomial lattice are easier to view than a complex combinatoric mathematics chart, a dynamic programming and optimization chart, or a fancy partial-differential equation model.
- *Integration.* Can the model or approach be easily linked into an existing Excel model or will the results from an Excel sheet need to be exported and imported into the model?
- *Analytical Process.* Can the model or approach be linked to other analyses that may be required such as Monte Carlo simulation, forecasting, and portfolio optimization?

Binomial Lattices and Multinomial Lattices

Binomial lattices are easy to implement and easy to explain. They are also highly flexible, but require significant computing power and time steps to obtain good approximations. If binomial and multinomial lattices are used, it is vital that they are implemented within a software program and not manually created. It is important to note, however, that, in the limit, results obtained through the use of binomial lattices approach those derived from closed-form models and other approaches.

- *Ease of use:* 10/10
- *Expositional ease:* 10/10
- *Replicability:* 10/10
- *Modeling flexibility:* 10/10
- *Ease of view:* 10/10
- *Integration:* 10/10
- *Analytical process:* 10/10

Closed-Form Models

Closed-form solutions are models such as Black–Scholes, where there exist equations that can be solved given a set of input assumptions. They are exact, quick, and easy to implement with the assistance of some basic programming knowledge, but are difficult to explain because they tend to apply highly technical stochastic calculus mathematics. They are also very specific in nature, with limited modeling flexibility. Closed-form solutions certainly have computational ease compared to binomial lattices. However, it is more difficult to explain the exact nature of a fancy stochastic calculus equation than it would be to explain a binomial lattice tree that branches up and down. Because both methods tend to provide the same results, in the limit anyway, for ease of exposition, the binomial lattice should be presented for management discussions. There are also other issues to contend with in terms of advantages and disadvantages of each technique. For instance, closed-form solutions are mathematically elegant but are very difficult to derive and are highly specific in nature. Tweaking a closed-form equation requires facility with sophisticated stochastic mathematics. Binomial lattices, however, although sometimes computationally stressful, are easy to build and require no more than simple algebra. Binomial lattices are also very flexible in that they can be tweaked easily to accommodate most types of real options problems.

- *Ease of use:* 5/10
- *Expositional ease:* 5/10
- *Replicability:* 10/10
- *Modeling flexibility:* 5/10
- *Ease of view:* 5/10
- *Integration:* 10/10
- *Analytical process:* 10/10

Monte Carlo Path Simulation

This approach simulates all possible future paths of an asset or cash flows of an asset using Monte Carlo simulation. This approach is more difficult to implement and has limited application because American options cannot be solved through simulation; only European options can be simulated. In addition, the results obtained are never always identical because by definition of simulation, random numbers are drawn every time, hence, the results will always differ a little.[1]

- *Ease of use:* 3/10
- *Expositional ease:* 10/10
- *Replicability:* 5/10
- *Modeling flexibility:* 3/10
- *Ease of view:* 5/10
- *Integration:* 10/10
- *Analytical process:* 10/10

Partial-Differential Equations

This approach requires facility in advanced finance and mathematics because in every instance a detailed mathematical derivation is required to implement the analysis. The analysis is also case-specific, meaning that every time minor assumptions change from business case to business case, the models have to be re-derived. Recall that the Black–Scholes is a Nobel Prize-winning model. Applying partial-differential equations in real options requires re-deriving similar models as in the Black–Scholes. This approach is neither pragmatic nor applicable in most business cases.

- *Ease of use:* 1/10
- *Expositional ease:* 1/10
- *Replicability:* 10/10
- *Modeling flexibility:* 3/10
- *Ease of view:* 3/10
- *Integration:* 10/10
- *Analytical process:* 10/10

Dynamic Optimization, Variance Reduction, and other Numerical Techniques

These techniques are exact and elegant but computationally cumbersome. Programming knowledge is required to implement these techniques. In addition, only specific cases can be solved through dynamic programming and variance reduction, and facility in advanced mathematics is also required. The results stemming from these approaches are identical at the limit to simpler approaches such as the binomial lattices or closed-form models.

- *Ease of use:* 1/10
- *Expositional ease:* 1/10
- *Replicability:* 10/10
- *Modeling flexibility:* 5/10
- *Ease of view:* 3/10
- *Integration:* 5/10
- *Analytical process:* 5/10

FIVE-MINUTE INDUSTRY SPOTLIGHT: BOEING

Real Options: Analyzing Engineering Projects Using Real Options—Intelligent Investments in the Face of Uncertainty

Boeing performs extensive financial modeling, a requirement given the technical complexity and the long life cycle of its products. One of the techniques it uses is called real options, an advanced financial modeling technique that (1) extends standard net present value (NPV) to evaluate risk-adjusted return on investment and cost-versus-risk issues and (2) optimizes R&D and strategic project portfolios. Boeing's senior management recognizes that business cases for visionary and strategic projects must go beyond NPV analyses, and require quantitative data on cost and market uncertainty, analytical insights such as risk-adjusted profits, and conclusions about where to invest to increase the probability of project success.

Real options allows a corporation to be technologically daring while maintaining fiscal discipline. In other words, Boeing can be a leader in aerospace and satisfy Wall Street at the same time. Options have their origins in the financial markets where traders attempt to place a dollar value on a stream of future "risky" (or "contingent") cash flows. An option is defined as the ability, but not the obligation, to exploit a future profitable opportunity. In engineering terms, an option is a trade space between uncertainty and costs or profits. A real option can be thought of as the value of risk-adjusted profits generated by a prospective successful project. Real options is quickly becoming another engineering tool, which can help determine the worth of investing in a prospective project that has uncertainty such as significant technical risk, or market or sales unpredictability.

Wall Street heavily rewards those corporations that have lots of "options" for future growth; that is, a portfolio of many prospective business opportunities and the discipline to exploit (exercise) those options. Inserting options into a project increases its value, provided the project manager has the flexibility to position the project to take advantage of opportunities that arise in a rapidly changing business and technical environment. Examples of project options include having several market outlets to choose, numerous technical solutions to reduce risk, or a customer contract with contingencies (embedded options). In addition, discipline implies that senior management must act quickly to terminate early potentially unsuccessful business ventures. Finally, strategic investments in critical technologies and markets are required to set up the availability of these options.

QUESTIONS

1. Create your own definition of real options analysis. That is, define real options analysis in a paragraph.
2. What are some of the possible approaches used to solve a real options analysis problem?
3. In choosing the right methodology to be used in a real options analysis, what are some of the key requirements that should be considered?
4. What are the necessary conditions that must exist before real options analysis can be applied on a project?

CHAPTER 13

The Black Box Made Transparent: Real Options Analysis Toolkit

Now that you are confident with the applicability of real options analysis, it is time to move on and use the *Real Options Analysis Toolkit* trial software. As explained in Chapter 12, applying real options is not an easy task. The use of software-based models allows the analyst to apply a consistent, well-tested, and replicable set of models. It reduces computational errors and allows the user to focus more on the process and problem at hand rather than on building potentially complex and mathematically intractable models. For information on obtaining trial versions of the software, contact the author at JohnathanMun@cs.com.

GETTING STARTED WITH REAL OPTIONS ANALYSIS TOOLKIT SOFTWARE

Assuming that the *Real Options Analysis Toolkit* trial software is installed properly, start the software by clicking on *Start | Programs | Crystal Ball | Real Options Analysis Toolkit*, and select *Toolkit* (Figure 13.1). The toolkit interface now appears as illustrated in Figure 13.2. Make sure you select *Enable Macros* if prompted. The models are aggregated into three distinct categories: *Binomial Lattices with Closed-Form Models, Closed-Form Partial-Differential Models*, and *Stochastic Differential Models*. The first category of models uses the binomial approach, in concert with closed-form models. These two approaches are used together to confirm the analytical results. The second category of models consists purely of closed-form models or binomial lattice models performed in isolation. The last category of models focuses on stochastic modeling techniques.

A simple example is now in order. Click on the *Abandonment* option button from the main welcome screen. The American Abandonment Option

FIGURE 13.1   Location of the Real Options Analysis Toolkit software.

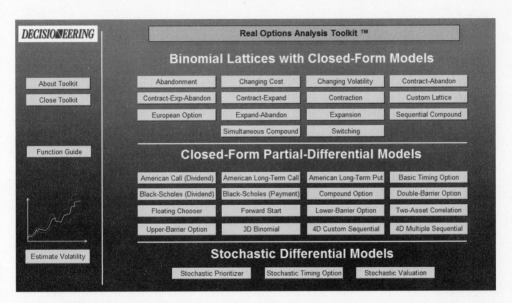

FIGURE 13.2   Real Options Analysis Toolkit software main welcome screen.

model will now appear as seen in Figure 13.3. This modeling screen is similar to most of the models in the software. That is, there is a title bar, input parameters box, intermediate calculations box, results box, Main and Help buttons, options payoff graphics, pricing and valuation lattices, and a decision lattice. Take a moment to familiarize yourself with the modeling environment. Notice that there is a Help button that will provide the user more detailed information on the model currently in use.

In this example, suppose a firm owns a piece of land in a highly liquid and volatile market. Suppose the land is currently worth $100 million (*PV Asset Value*) in the market today. If the analyst prices the land at this $100

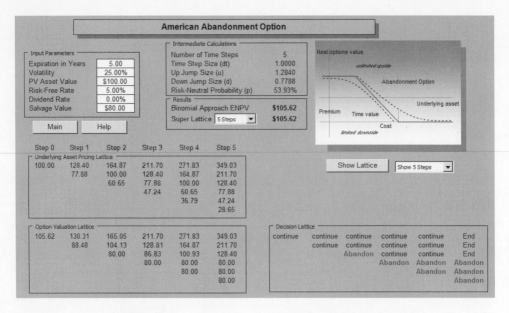

FIGURE 13.3   American Abandonment Option model.

million, it may be underpriced due to fluctuations in the market. That is, prices can be significantly higher or lower than this $100 million value (due to a *Volatility* of 25 percent), as well as there may exist options that have not been considered (building a parking structure, building a shopping mall, leaving the land undeveloped for the future, etc.) Suppose the firm decides to hedge its bets against a potential market downturn by creating an abandonment option. That is, if the firm negotiates a contract with another firm or potential buyer, whereby for a setup fee (say, $50,000) this potential buyer agrees contractually to purchase this piece of land from your firm at any time within the next 5 years (*Expiration in Years*) for a discounted price of $80 million (*Salvage Value*). Of course, the decision to sell the land is strictly at the prerogative of the firm that owns the land, while the potential buyer is obliged to purchase the land (to obtain the discount and the setup contractual fee). Effectively, your firm has created an abandonment option, a safety net or an insurance policy of sorts, where if the price in the market exceeds its current levels (say, $200 million), it can sell the land in the market and let the contract expire (capture the upside of $100 million and lose only the $50,000 fee). Otherwise, if market prices are depressed to anything lower than the contractual salvage value (say, $50 million), your firm can call up the potential buyer and execute the abandonment option, thereby reducing the risk of a downside. Hence, this insurance policy limits the minimum amount the firm will obtain selling this piece of land at $80 million.

The calculated value of the land with this option is $105.62 million (*Binomial Approach ENPV*). The additional $5.62 million is the strategic abandonment option value—the price of the $80 million insurance, or the maximum average or expected value that the firm should be willing to pay to the potential buyer in order to obtain the contract (this result also provides the firm with a great negotiation tool).

As further illustration, if the salvage value is changed to $10 million, the option value becomes $0 and the piece of land is worth $100 million, as given such a low safety net, the market will never bear a price any lower than this $10 million and the safety net is never utilized, making the option worthless. Conversely, setting the salvage value to $300 million will change the value of the land to $300 million—which means you forget about the option and sell it immediately to the potential buyer, who is currently willing to pay you three times the market value! Finally, setting the volatility to 1 percent will yield a land value of $100 million—if uncertainty is negligible (real estate prices hardly fluctuate, the option is not worth anything, and the price of land will probably stay at a constant $100 million for the foreseeable future). Thus, there is no option value if there is no uncertainty!

Let us now look at each section in detail. The first is the Input Parameters section (Figure 13.4). Here, the relevant parameters can be typed in directly or linked in from another spreadsheet. This area is characterized by its white background. A set of sample input parameters exists as a guide. Entering an incorrect input (i.e., negative values or nonnumeric values for certain inputs are not allowed) will yield a warning message as shown in Figure 13.5.

Assuming all the inputs are correct, the Intermediate Calculations section shows the time step, up jump size, down jump size, and risk-neutral probability calculations for a predetermined five-step binomial lattice (Figure 13.6). The resulting real options value calculated using the five-step binomial approach is shown in the Results section. The value shown is the Expanded Net Present Value, which is the net present value plus the value of the strategic option. The value for the Super Lattice calculation is set to

Input Parameters	
Expiration in Years	5.00
Volatility	25.00%
PV Asset Value	$100.00
Risk-Free Rate	5.00%
Dividend Rate	0.00%
Salvage Value	$80.00

FIGURE 13.4   Input parameters for the American Abandonment Option.

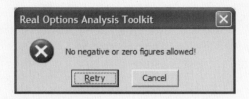

FIGURE 13.5   Sample error message dialog.

Intermediate Calculations	
Number of Time Steps	5
Time Step Size (dt)	1.0000
Up Jump Size (u)	1.2840
Down Jump Size (d)	0.7788
Risk-Neutral Probability (p)	53.93%

FIGURE 13.6   Intermediate Calculations for the American Abandonment Option.

default at five steps, indicating the same result as the binomial five-step lattice (Figure 13.7).

The drop-down box seen in Figure 13.8 beside the Super Lattice approach provides the user a choice to change the number of steps to perform using a binomial lattice. For instance, if 1,000 steps are chosen, the results indicate that the abandonment option's ENPV is $105.87. The higher the number of steps,

FIGURE 13.7   Results from the American Abandonment Option.

Results	
Binomial Approach ENPV	$105.62
Super Lattice 1000 Steps ▼	$105.87
5 Steps	
10 Steps	
50 Steps	
100 Steps	
300 Steps	
500 Steps	
1000 Steps	
5000 Steps	

FIGURE 13.8   Super Lattice drop-down box.

Underlying Asset Pricing Lattice					
100.00	128.40	164.87	211.70	271.83	349.03
	77.88	100.00	128.40	164.87	211.70
		60.65	77.88	100.00	128.40
			47.24	60.65	77.88
				36.79	47.24
					28.65

FIGURE 13.9 Underlying asset lattice for the American Abandonment Option.

the more granular the lattice and the higher the accuracy of the lattice results. (Manually creating a binomial lattice with 1,000 steps may take months to calculate, as compared to less than a few seconds using the software).

Another section of interest is the Underlying Asset Pricing Lattice (Figure 13.9). This shows the simple predetermined five-step binomial lattice of the underlying asset. The Option Valuation Lattice shows the step-by-step option valuation using a process called backward induction (Figure 13.10). Refer to the book *Real Options Analysis* (Wiley, 2002) for details on the specifics of creating and interpreting binomial lattices. There is also a section in the model for the Decision Lattice as shown in Figure 13.11, which calculates the optimal decision for when and if to execute the abandonment option.

Option Valuation Lattice					
105.62	130.31	165.05	211.70	271.83	349.03
	88.48	104.13	128.81	164.87	211.70
		80.00	86.83	100.93	128.40
			80.00	80.00	80.00
				80.00	80.00
					80.00

FIGURE 13.10 Valuation Lattice for the American Abandonment Option.

Decision Lattice					
continue	continue	continue	continue	continue	End
	continue	continue	continue	continue	End
		Abandon	continue	continue	End
			Abandon	Abandon	Abandon
				Abandon	Abandon
					Abandon

FIGURE 13.11 Decision Lattice for the American Abandonment Option.

THE LATTICE VIEWER

If a higher number of time steps is required, the user can select the relevant number of steps to show in the lattice (see Figure 13.12). Clicking on *Show Lattice* provides a view of the binomial lattice in a separate window (Figure 13.13). The underlying asset lattice is shown as the first number on the lattice and the valuation lattice as the second number. The decision lattice is also shown with different colors based on the optimal decision at each node. Notice that the preferences on the lattice viewer can be changed by clicking on the *Tree Prefs* or *Node Prefs* icon on the toolbar. For instance, click on *Node Prefs* and deselect the *Draw Border* under the Symbol section, and *Colorize Nodes by Option Type* under the Options section, and click *OK* (Figure 13.14). The lattice viewer will change to take into account the changes in the preferences as seen in Figure 13.15. Close the lattice viewer by selecting *File | Close Window* on the menu bar.

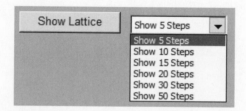

FIGURE 13.12   Show lattice drop-down list.

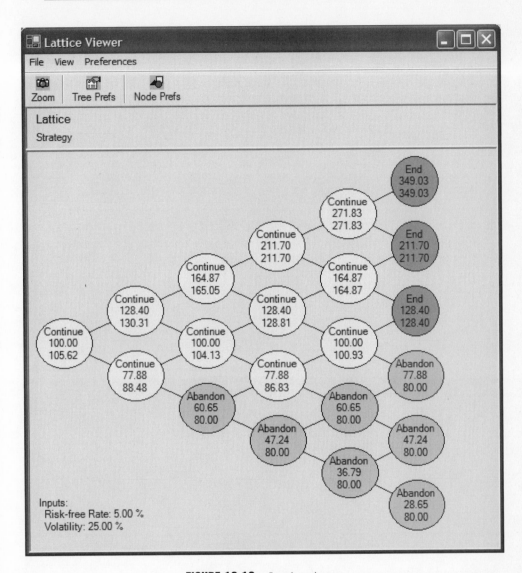

FIGURE 13.13   Lattice viewer.

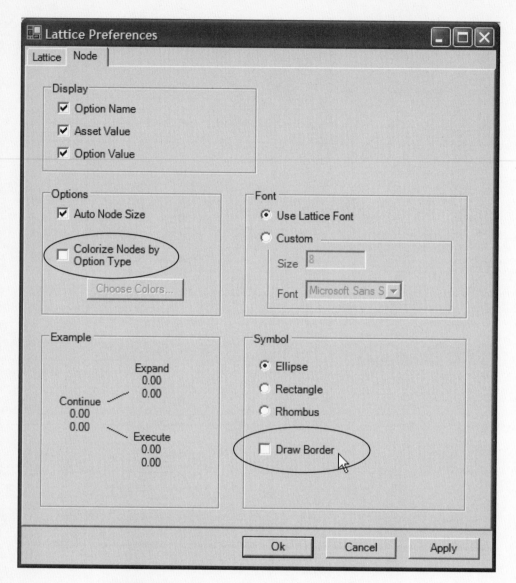

FIGURE 13.14   Lattice viewer's preferences dialog box.

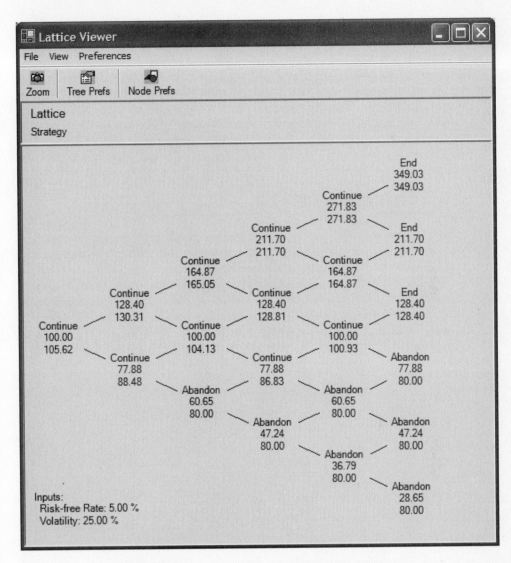

FIGURE 13.15   Lattice viewer with updated preferences.

THE HELP ENVIRONMENT

In addition, the user can click on *Help* to visit the help tips for the abandonment option model (see Figure 13.16). The scroll text provides the user a quick reference for the option model. In addition, moving the mouse over the numerical values with red triangular tags will provide the user additional information on what each numerical value represents. Return to the abandonment model by clicking *Close Help*. Return to the main welcome screen by clicking on *Main*.

SOLVING CUSTOMIZED OPTIONS

From the main welcome screen, select *Custom Lattice* to launch the customized options analysis model. Click on *Step 1: Reset Sheet* to reset the spreadsheet before creating a customized option model. This step is important because any prior input parameters will be cleared from memory. Then, click on *Step 2: Enter Starting Asset Value* and you will see the dialog box in Figure 13.17 appear. Click on *OK* and enter a starting value for the pricing lattice, which is the present value of future cash flows. Type *100* and hit enter (Figure 13.18). Then, click on *Step 3: Create Pricing Lattice* and you

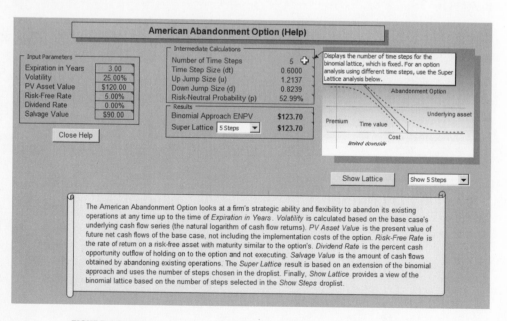

FIGURE 13.16 Help screen for the American Abandonment Option.

FIGURE 13.17   Custom Lattice's second step message box.

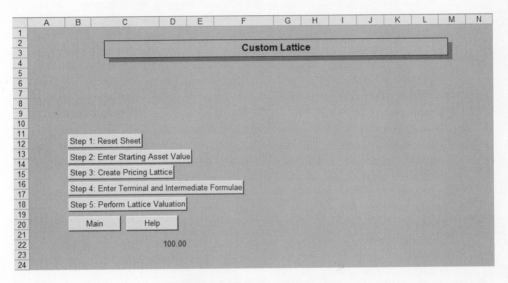

FIGURE 13.18   Custom Lattice.

will be prompted for more information as seen in Figure 13.19. Enter the cell reference (e.g., D22) that contains the *100* value previously entered. Enter the additional parameters requested, such as volatility in percent, maturity in years, risk-free rate in percent, dividends in percent, and the number of steps. Click *Create* and the pricing lattice will be created, together with a summary of the input parameters (Figure 13.20).

Then click on *Step 4: Enter Terminal and Intermediate Formulae* to continue. A dialog box provides further information as shown in Figure 13.21. Click *OK*. The next step is to enter the customized valuation lattice equations, first for the terminal nodes and then for the intermediate nodes. In cell P36, type in the terminal period formula; for example, type in the following equation:

$$= MAX(P22 - 100,0)$$

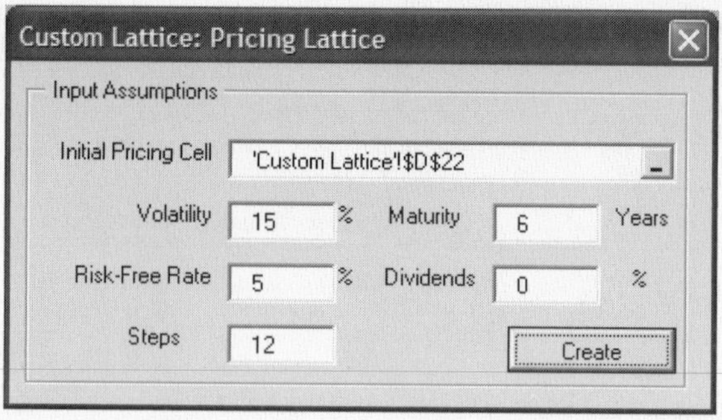

FIGURE 13.19   Custom Lattice's setup dialog for creating a pricing lattice.

where *P22* refers to the corresponding node on the pricing lattice and *100* is the cost to execute this option. Then, in cell O36, enter in the intermediate formula; for example, type in the following equation:

$$= MAX((0.5926*P36 + (1 - 0.5926)*P37)*0.9753, O22 - 100)$$

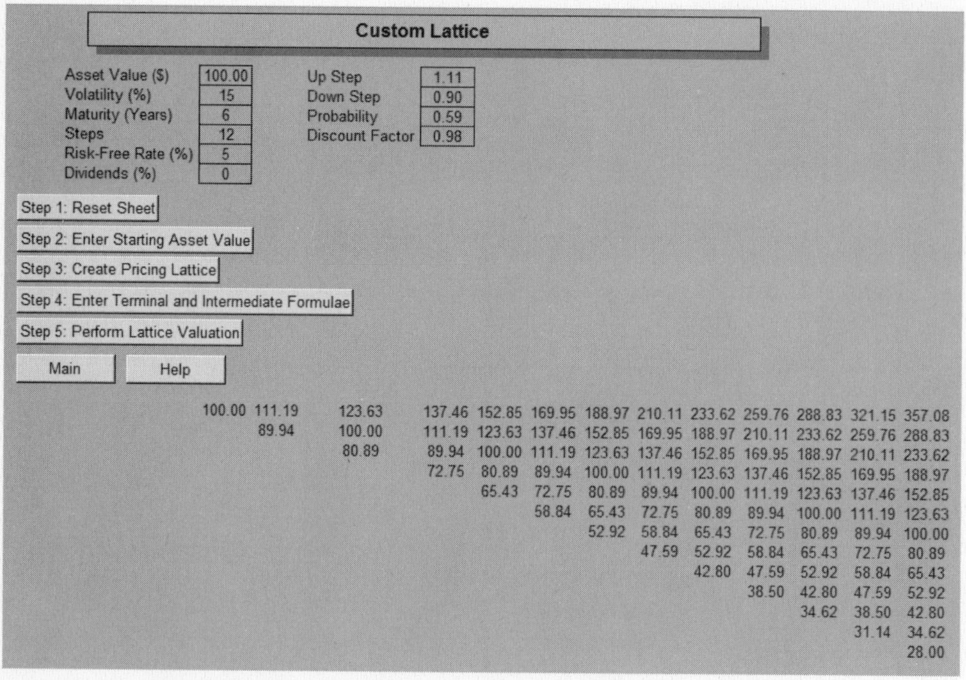

FIGURE 13.20   Custom Lattice with a calculated pricing lattice.

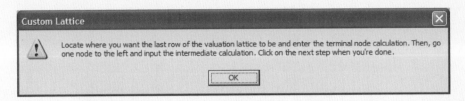

FIGURE 13.21   Custom Lattice's fourth step message box.

where *0.5926* is the risk-neutral probability based on the previous inputs and *0.9753* is the discount factor (see Figure 13.22). These values were calculated for you in Step 3 (Figure 13.20).

Then click on *Step 5: Perform Lattice Valuation* and you will be prompted with the dialog box shown in Figure 13.23. Enter or select the cell with the terminal formula (e.g., P36) and enter or select the cell with the

	C	D	E	F	G	H	I	J	K	L	M	N	O	P
21														
22		100.00	111.19	123.63	137.46	152.85	169.95	188.97	210.11	233.62	259.76	288.83	321.15	357.08
23			89.94	100.00	111.19	123.63	137.46	152.85	169.95	188.97	210.11	233.62	259.76	288.83
24				80.89	89.94	100.00	111.19	123.63	137.46	152.85	169.95	188.97	210.11	233.62
25					72.75	80.89	89.94	100.00	111.19	123.63	137.46	152.85	169.95	188.97
26						65.43	72.75	80.89	89.94	100.00	111.19	123.63	137.46	152.85
27							58.84	65.43	72.75	80.89	89.94	100.00	111.19	123.63
28								52.92	58.84	65.43	72.75	80.89	89.94	100.00
29									47.59	52.92	58.84	65.43	72.75	80.89
30										42.80	47.59	52.92	58.84	65.43
31											38.50	42.80	47.59	52.92
32												34.62	38.50	42.80
33													31.14	34.62
34														28.00
35														
36													221.15	257.08

FIGURE 13.22   Custom Lattice with sample terminal and intermediate calculations.

Custom Lattice: Valuation Lattice

Valuation Assumptions

Terminal Formula   'Custom Lattice'!$P$36

Intermediate Formula   'Custom Lattice'!$O$36

Number of Steps   12

Value!

FIGURE 13.23   Custom Lattice's setup dialog for creating a pricing lattice.

	C	D	E	F	G	H	I	J	K	L	M	N	O	P	Q
21															
22		100.00	111.19	123.63	137.46	152.85	169.95	188.97	210.11	233.62	259.76	288.83	321.15	357.08	
23			89.94	100.00	111.19	123.63	137.46	152.85	169.95	188.97	210.11	233.62	259.76	288.83	
24				80.89	89.94	100.00	111.19	123.63	137.46	152.85	169.95	188.97	210.11	233.62	
25					72.75	80.89	89.94	100.00	111.19	123.63	137.46	152.85	169.95	188.97	
26						65.43	72.75	80.89	89.94	100.00	111.19	123.63	137.46	152.85	
27							58.84	65.43	72.75	80.89	89.94	100.00	111.19	123.63	
28								52.92	58.84	65.43	72.75	80.89	89.94	100.00	
29									47.59	52.92	58.84	65.43	72.75	80.89	
30										42.80	47.59	52.92	58.84	65.43	
31											38.50	42.80	47.59	52.92	
32												34.62	38.50	42.80	
33													31.14	34.62	
34														28.00	
35															
36		29.26	37.26	46.83	58.09	71.12	86.02	102.88	121.85	143.13	166.98	193.70	223.61	257.08	
37			19.44	25.66	33.37	42.73	53.87	66.84	81.69	98.47	117.33	138.49	162.23	188.83	
38				11.61	16.03	21.82	29.19	38.35	49.40	62.36	77.17	93.84	112.58	133.62	
39					5.89	8.62	12.45	17.69	24.66	33.62	44.69	57.72	72.42	88.97	
40						2.28	3.59	5.60	8.65	13.15	19.61	28.51	39.93	52.85	
41							0.51	0.88	1.52	2.64	4.56	7.89	13.66	23.63	
42								0.00	0.00	0.00	0.00	0.00	0.00	0.00	
43									0.00	0.00	0.00	0.00	0.00	0.00	
44										0.00	0.00	0.00	0.00	0.00	
45											0.00	0.00	0.00	0.00	
46												0.00	0.00	0.00	
47													0.00	0.00	
48														0.00	

FIGURE 13.24 Custom Lattice with calculated pricing lattice and valuation lattice.

intermediate formula (e.g., O36), enter the number of steps corresponding to the number of steps entered previously when generating the pricing lattice, and click on *Value!* to create the valuation lattice. The value of this simple option is $29.26 as shown in Figure 13.24.

Using the same approach, the user can create multiple and complex custom option types easily and effectively, by merely entering the correct terminal and intermediate formulas for each successive valuation lattice.

ACCESSING THE FUNCTIONS, RUNNING SIMULATIONS AND OPTIMIZATION

If the user requires access to only the functions and results as well as to run Monte Carlo simulation or optimization, he or she should then first exit the Real Options Analysis Toolkit software by exiting Excel. Open any existing Excel spreadsheet. For instance, click on *Start | Programs | Crystal Ball | Real Options Analysis Toolkit | Examples | Simulation* (Figure 13.25). The spreadsheet shown in Figure 13.26 appears. The spreadsheet example is a

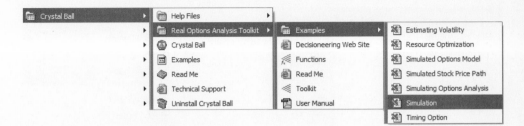

FIGURE 13.25   Location of the Real Options Analysis Toolkit software's example models.

	Simulation					
Input Parameters				**Results**		
Discount Rate (Cash Flow)	15.00%			Present Value (Cash Flow)	$328.24	
Discount Rate (Impl. Cost)	5.00%			Present Value (Impl. Cost)	$189.58	
Tax Rate	10.00%			Net Present Value	$138.67	
	2002	**2003**	**2004**	**2005**	**2006**	
Revenue	$100.00	$200.00	$300.00	$400.00	$500.00	
Cost of Revenue	$40.00	$80.00	$120.00	$160.00	$200.00	
Gross Profit	$60.00	$120.00	$180.00	$240.00	$300.00	
Operating Expenses	$22.00	$44.00	$66.00	$88.00	$110.00	
Depreciation Expense	$5.00	$5.00	$5.00	$5.00	$5.00	
Interest Expense	$3.00	$3.00	$3.00	$3.00	$3.00	
Income Before Taxes	$30.00	$68.00	$106.00	$144.00	$182.00	
Taxes	$3.00	$6.80	$10.60	$14.40	$18.20	
Income After Taxes	$27.00	$61.20	$95.40	$129.60	$163.80	
Non-Cash Expenses	$12.00	$12.00	$12.00	$12.00	$12.00	
Cash Flow	$39.00	$73.20	$107.40	$141.60	$175.80	
Implementation Cost	$25.00	$25.00	$50.00	$50.00	$75.00	

FIGURE 13.26   Sample simulation model.

simple discounted cash-flow model with the appropriate resulting net present value. Suppose this is the user's own spreadsheet that requires additional real options analysis. To perform a real options analysis on this existing model, launch the real options functions by clicking on *Start | Programs | Crystal Ball | Real Options Analysis Toolkit | Functions* (Figure 13.27). A splash screen will appear, indicating that the functions have been loaded into Excel. Select cell D49 in the spreadsheet and click on Excel's paste function icon on the taskbar (Figure 13.28). Then, select the *Financial* category and

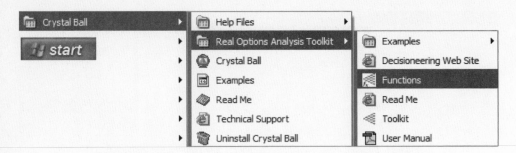

FIGURE 13.27   Location of the Real Options Analysis Toolkit software's functions.

FIGURE 13.28   Excel's paste function icon.

scroll down the functions list until you come to the section that starts with the prefix *RO* (Figure 13.29). The functions with *RO* prefixes indicate the real options analysis functions that were loaded into Excel. Selecting any function on the list also provides a brief description of the function. Select the *ROBlackScholesCall* function and click *OK*.

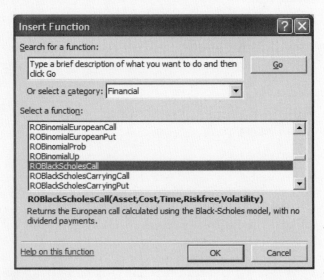

FIGURE 13.29   Microsoft Excel's Insert Function dialog box.

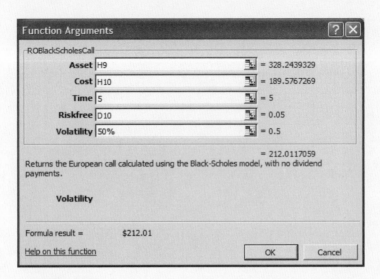

FIGURE 13.30 Microsoft Excel's Function dialog box for the Black–Scholes model.

The formula palette dialog box in Figure 13.30 appears. You can now use the real options analysis function as you would any Excel function. For instance, the user can enter in the cell reference (H9) for the asset value, link the function to a cell (H10), or simply type the value in directly. When all the inputs are entered, and assuming that each of the inputs is relevant, the results are indicated at the bottom of the dialog box. For instance, the result is $212.01. Incorrect or irrelevant inputs will not yield an answer. Click *OK* and the result will be pasted into the existing Excel spreadsheet (Figure 13.30).

Note that for the expert user, the equation can be entered in directly, that is, in cell D49, the user can type (without spaces) the following and obtain the same $212.01 result:

$$= ROBlackScholesCall(H9,H10,5,D10,0.5)$$

Because the functions loaded are completely compatible with Microsoft Excel, the user can now perform Monte Carlo simulation or optimization using Crystal Ball. The simulation spreadsheet (Figure 13.31) used previously has distributional assumptions assigned. However, the real options analysis function we pasted needs to be defined as a forecast. Select cell D49 with the options function, and click on *Define Forecast* in the Crystal Ball toolbar. Provide a relevant name and units for the forecast and click *OK*

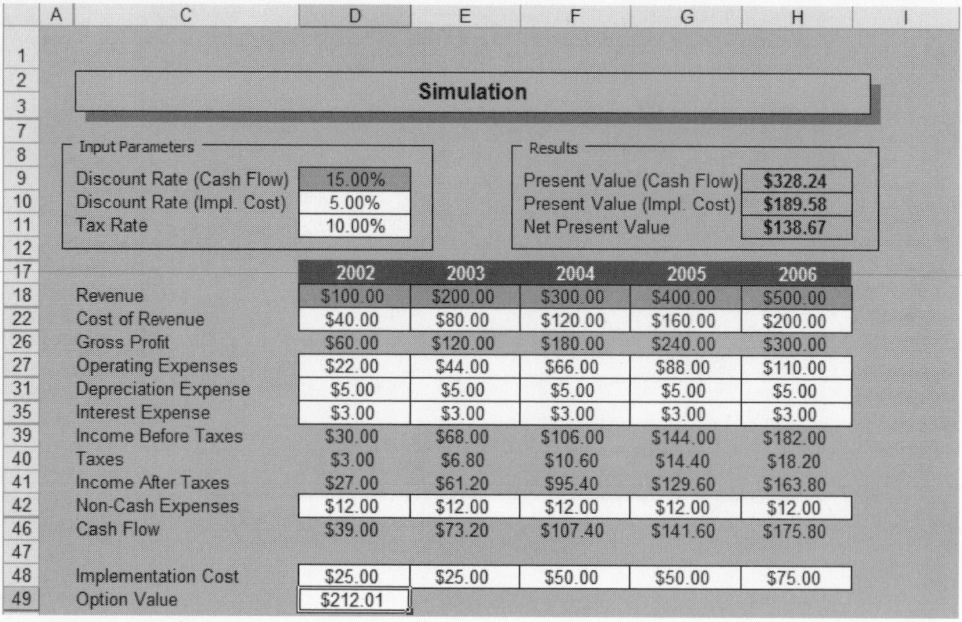

	2002	2003	2004	2005	2006
Revenue	$100.00	$200.00	$300.00	$400.00	$500.00
Cost of Revenue	$40.00	$80.00	$120.00	$160.00	$200.00
Gross Profit	$60.00	$120.00	$180.00	$240.00	$300.00
Operating Expenses	$22.00	$44.00	$66.00	$88.00	$110.00
Depreciation Expense	$5.00	$5.00	$5.00	$5.00	$5.00
Interest Expense	$3.00	$3.00	$3.00	$3.00	$3.00
Income Before Taxes	$30.00	$68.00	$106.00	$144.00	$182.00
Taxes	$3.00	$6.80	$10.60	$14.40	$18.20
Income After Taxes	$27.00	$61.20	$95.40	$129.60	$163.80
Non-Cash Expenses	$12.00	$12.00	$12.00	$12.00	$12.00
Cash Flow	$39.00	$73.20	$107.40	$141.60	$175.80
Implementation Cost	$25.00	$25.00	$50.00	$50.00	$75.00
Option Value	$212.01				

Input Parameters: Discount Rate (Cash Flow) 15.00%, Discount Rate (Impl. Cost) 5.00%, Tax Rate 10.00%

Results: Present Value (Cash Flow) $328.24, Present Value (Impl. Cost) $189.58, Net Present Value $138.67

FIGURE 13.31 Simulation example complete with assumptions and forecasts defined.

(Figure 13.32). Then, click the *RUN* icon on the Crystal Ball toolbar to initiate the simulation process. When the simulation is complete, the forecast chart in Figure 13.33 will be presented. The same interpretation applicable to any simulation result is also applicable here for real options.

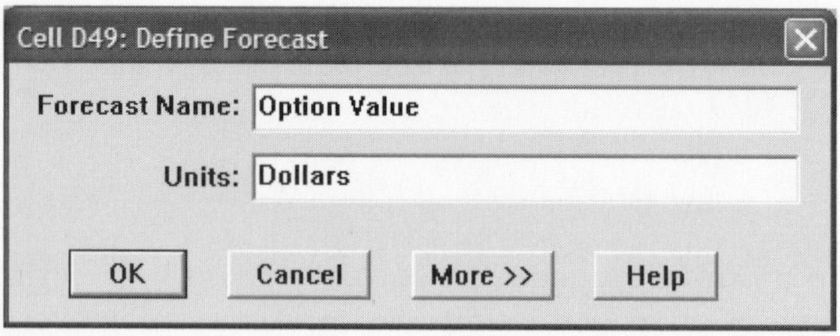

Cell D49: Define Forecast — Forecast Name: Option Value — Units: Dollars — OK / Cancel / More >> / Help

FIGURE 13.32 Defining a forecast on the calculated option value.

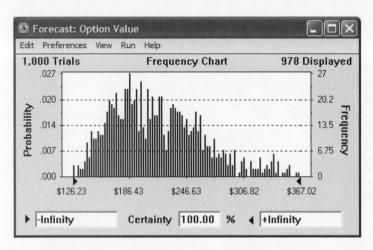

FIGURE 13.33   Forecast chart result of the option value.

APPENDIX—EXPENSING OF EMPLOYEE STOCK OPTIONS (FAS 123): THE DEATH OF BLACK–SCHOLES

The following case study illustrates real-life applications of options analysis (binomial lattices, simulation, and closed-form models as shown in the book) in the areas of financial accounting. This analytical case study was presented to the Financial Accounting Standards Board (FASB) in July 2003 for consideration when developing the new revised Financial Accounting Standard 123 (FAS 123). The author would like to thank Wendy Metcalfe of FASB for her valuable insights into the models and cases presented here. For further details on some of the models used to solve the problems throughout the case, contact the author.

Executive Summary

In the spring of 2003, the Financial Accounting Standards Board (FASB) decided that all companies are required to expense the value of their employees' stock options. This requirement is reflected in the new amendments to the existing Financial Accounting Standard 123 (FAS 123) where the value of the stock option award is determined at the date of grant.[1] At the time of writing, one of the challenges that FASB is currently facing is how the cost of employee stock options' fair value should be calculated. This case study broaches the subject of fair market value determination through an analytical assessment of the three mainstream approaches used in option pricing. The first approach is a set of closed-form models,[2] including the

Black–Scholes model (BSM) for option pricing and the American option approximation pricing models. The second approach is the use of Monte Carlo path simulation, including its applications in option pricing as well as its use in simulating the option model's uncertain and probabilistic inputs. The final approach is the use of binomial lattices. These three sets of methodologies are reviewed earlier in Chapter 12. The reviews were based on several criteria, including method applicability, underlying assumptions, robustness of analytical results, and ease of use.[3]

It can be concluded that the BSM, albeit theoretically correct and elegant, is insufficient and inappropriately applied when it comes to quantifying the fair market value of an employee stock option. This conclusion is based on the fact that the BSM is only applicable to European options without dividends, where the holder of the option can only exercise the option on its maturity date, and that the underlying stock does not pay any dividends. However, in reality, most employee stock options are American-type options with dividends, where the option holder can execute the option at any time up to (after the vesting period) and including the maturity date, while the underlying stock pays dividends. A stock's price drops by the amount of the dividend on the ex dividend date, which means that the value of an American stock option (with its ability for early exercise) is greater than that of a European-type option. However, for fairness of comparison, the Generalized Black–Scholes model (GBM) is used—the GBM allows for the inclusion of dividends, although it is only applicable for valuing European options.

In addition, under real-world conditions, employee stock options have a time to vesting before the employee can execute the option, which is also contingent on the firm or the individual employee attaining a specific performance level (e.g., profitability, growth rate, stock price hitting a minimum barrier before the options become live), and subject to forfeitures when the employee leaves the firm or is terminated prematurely before reaching the vested period. Also, certain options follow a tranching or graduated scale, where a certain percentage of the stock option grants become exercisable every year, and if the firm underperforms, it may be required to repurchase the options at a specific termination price. A change of control vesting with or without stay provisions is another potential real-life issue. Just as important, the GBM assumes that the employee executes the option optimally—that is, the model assumes that the employee is intelligent enough to execute the option whenever it becomes optimal to do so. In reality, employees tend to execute their stock options prematurely and often suboptimally. Finally, the firm may undergo some corporate restructuring (e.g., divestitures, or mergers and acquisitions that may require a stock swap that changes the volatility of the underlying stock). All these real-life scenarios make the GBM insufficient and inappropriate when used to place a fair market value on the option grant. In summary, firms can implement a variety of provisions that affect the fair value of the options where the preceding list provides only a few examples.

On the one hand, the BSM and GBM will *understate* the fair value of employee stock options that are of the American type and where the underlying stock pays dividends. On the other hand, the BSM and GBM may in fact *overstate* the fair value of employee stock options where there is suboptimal early exercise behavior coupled with vesting requirements, or when the risk-free rates and volatilities change over the life of the option. In fact, firms using the BSM and GBM to value and expense employee stock options may be significantly overstating its true expense, incurring hundreds of thousands, if not millions, of dollars in excess expenses.

This case study illustrates that, under very specific conditions (European options with and without dividends), the binomial lattice and Monte Carlo simulation approaches yield identical values to the GBM, indicating that the two former approaches are robust and exact at the limit. When American options with dividends are analyzed, the traditional BSM and GBM undervalue the options significantly, whereas binomial lattices, American options approximation models, and Monte Carlo simulation methodologies are more exact. However, when specific real-life business conditions are modeled (i.e., probability of forfeiture, probability that the firm or stock underperforms, time-vesting, tranching, suboptimal execution, and so forth), the American approximation models or Monte Carlo simulation by themselves are also insufficient to capture all of the uncertainty nuances. Only when the binomial lattice (which is highly flexible in its modeling capabilities) is used will the true fair market value of the stock option be captured—Monte Carlo simulation can be applied to further simulate the uncertain inputs that go into the binomial lattices. That is, the binomial lattice is used to calculate the American stock option with dividend, while the inputs into the binomial lattice can be simulated to capture the uncertainty and probabilistic effects of the real-life conditions mentioned. Binomial lattices are extremely easy to use and apply as compared to the other methods. Binomial lattices can even account for exotic events such as stock price barriers (a barrier option exists when the stock option becomes either in-the-money or out-of-the-money only when it hits a stock price barrier), vesting tranches (a specific percent of the options granted becomes vested or exercisable each year), changing volatilities (business conditions changing or corporate restructuring), suboptimal exercise behaviors (early execution by employees who leave the company prematurely or are risk-averse), and so forth—the same conditions where the BSM and GBM fail miserably. Monte Carlo simulation can then be applied to simulate the probabilities of forfeitures and underperformance of the firm, and use these as the inputs into the binomial lattices. *Without the use of binomial lattices, firms may be* overvaluing *employee stock options and end up overexpensing millions of dollars a year!*

Key Points and Recommendations in This Case Study

- FAS 123 requiring stock options expensing is clearly a significant step in the right direction, but the remaining question is which option valuation model to use to obtain the fair market value of the stock option.
- It has been over 30 years since Fisher Black and Myron Scholes derived their option pricing model and significant advancements have been made; therefore, do not restrict stock option pricing to one specific model while a plethora of other models and applications can be explored.
- The three mainstream approaches to valuing stock options are closed-form models (e.g., BSM, GBM, and American option approximation models), Monte Carlo simulation, and binomial lattices.
- On the one hand, the BSM and GBM will *understate* the fair value of employee stock options that are of the American type and where the underlying stock pays dividends. On the other hand, the BSM and GBM may in fact *overstate* the fair value of employee stock options where there is suboptimal early exercise behavior coupled with vesting requirements. *In fact, firms using the BSM and GBM to value and expense employee stock options may be significantly overstating its true expense.*
- The BSM requires many underlying assumptions before it works and, as such, has significant limitations, including being applicable only for European options without dividends. In addition, American option approximation models are very complex and difficult to create in a spreadsheet.[4] The BSM *cannot* account for American options, options based on stocks that pay dividends (however, the GBM model can account for dividends in a European option), forfeitures, underperformance, stock price barriers, vesting periods, changing business environments and volatilities, suboptimal early exercise, and a slew of other conditions.
- Monte Carlo simulation when used alone is another option valuation approach, but is restricted only to European options. Simulation can be used in two different ways: solving the option's fair market value through path simulations of stock prices, or used in conjunction with other approaches (e.g., binomial lattices and closed-form models) to capture multiple sources of uncertainty in the model.[5]
- Binomial lattices are flexible and easy to implement. They are capable of valuing American-type stock options with dividends, but they require significant computational power. Software applications should be used to facilitate this computation. Binomial lattices can be used to calculate American options paying dividends and can be easily adapted to solve options with stock price barriers and used in conjunction with Monte Carlo simulation to account for the uncertain input assumptions (e.g., probabilities of forfeiture, underperformance, and so forth).

■ Recommendations: The use of a model that assumes an employee stock option is European style, when, in fact, the option is American style, should not be permitted as this assumption substantially understates or overstates compensation expense. Many factors (e.g., vesting, performance-based options, forfeitures) influence the fair value of employee stock options, and a probabilistic approach to valuation that considers these factors should be required. Option valuations using BSM, GBM, or other closed-form models should not be permitted where the requirements for those models are not met. Binomial lattice valuation models combined with Monte Carlo simulation provide the fairest available valuation for determining compensation expense. Given that their implementations are now relatively straightforward (and will become more so if their use becomes standard accounting practice) due to the widespread availability of applications software, their use should be expressly permitted.

Introduction to the Analysis

Analysis indicates that the BSM used alone is insufficient to measure the true fair market value of American options with dividends,[6] and the other closed-form models are insufficient when some of the inputs are stochastic or uncertain. Option pricing has made vast strides since 1972 when Fisher Black and Myron Scholes published their path-breaking paper providing a model for valuing European options. While Black and Scholes's derivations are mathematically complex, other approaches broached in this case study, namely, using Monte Carlo and binomial lattices, provide much simpler applications while at the same time enable a similar wellspring of information.[7] In fact, applying binomial lattices has been made much easier with the use of software and spreadsheets.

This case study begins with a brief introduction of all three types of option pricing methodologies and continues with a quantitative assessment of their analytical robustness under different conditions. *For the sake of brevity, only relevant subparts of the entire report submitted to FASB are presented here.*

The Black–Scholes Model

In order to fully understand and use the BSM, you need to understand the assumptions under which the model was constructed. These are essentially the caveats that go into using the BSM option pricing model. These assumptions are violated quite often, but the model still holds up to scrutiny when applied appropriately to European options. European options are the types of options that can only be exercised on their expiration dates and not before. In contrast, most executive stock options awarded are American options, where the holder of the option is allowed to exercise at any time once the award has been fully vested.

The main assumption that goes into the BSM is that the underlying asset's price structure follows a Geometric Brownian Motion with static drift and volatility parameters, and that this motion follows a Markov–Weiner stochastic process. In other words, it assumes that the returns on the stock prices follow a lognormal distribution. The other assumptions are fairly standard, including a fair and timely efficient market with no riskless arbitrage opportunities, no transaction costs, and no taxes. Price changes are also assumed to be continuous and instantaneous. Finally, the risk-free rate and volatility are assumed to be constant throughout the life of the option, and the stock pays no dividends.[8] However, for fairness of comparison, a modification of the BSM is used—the GBM. This modification allows the incorporation of dividends in a standard European option.

Monte Carlo Path Simulation

Monte Carlo simulation can be easily adapted for use in an options valuation paradigm. There are multiple uses of Monte Carlo simulation including its use in risk analysis and forecasting. Here, the discussion focuses on two distinct applications of Monte Carlo simulation: solving a stock option valuation problem and obtaining a range of solved option values. Although these two approaches are discussed separately, they can be used together in an analysis.

Applying Monte Carlo Simulation to Obtain a Stock Options Result   Monte Carlo simulation can be applied to solve an options valuation problem, that is, to obtain a fair market stock option value. Recall that the mainstream approaches in solving options problems are the binomial approach, closed-form equations, and simulation. In the simulation approach, a series of forecast asset values are created using the Geometric Brownian Motion stochastic process, and the maximization calculation is applied to the end point of the series and discounted back to time zero, at the risk-free rate.

Note that simulation can be easily used to solve European-type options, but it is fairly difficult to apply simulation to solve American-type options.[9] In fact, certain academic texts list Monte Carlo simulation's major limitation as that it can only be used to solve European-type options.[10] If the number of simulation trials is adequately increased, coupled with an increase in the simulation steps, the results stemming from Monte Carlo simulation also approach the Black–Scholes value for a European option.

Applying Monte Carlo Simulation to Obtain a Range of Stock Option Values   Alternatively, Monte Carlo simulation can be applied to obtain a range of calculated stock option fair values. That is, any of the inputs into the stock options valuation model can be chosen for Monte Carlo simulation if they are uncertain and stochastic. Distributional assumptions are assigned to these variables, and the resulting option values using the BSM, GBM, path simulation, or binomial lattices are selected as forecast cells. These modeled uncertainties include the probability of forfeiture and the firm underperforming in the future.[11]

The results of the simulation are essentially a distribution of the stock option values. Keep in mind that the simulation application here is used to vary the inputs to an options valuation model to obtain a range of results, not to model and calculate the options themselves. However, simulation can be applied both to simulate the inputs to obtain the range of options results and also to solve the options model through path-dependent simulation.

Binomial Lattices

Binomial lattices, in contrast, are easy to implement and explain. They are also highly flexible, but require significant computing power and time-steps to obtain good approximations, as will be seen later in this case study. The results from closed-form solutions can be used in conjunction with the binomial lattice approach when presenting a complete stock options valuation solution. Binomial lattices are particularly useful in capturing the effect of early exercise as in an American option with dividends, vesting and blackout periods, suboptimal early exercise behaviors, performance-based vesting, changing volatilities and business environments, and so forth—the same real-life conditions that cannot be accounted for in the BSM, GBM, or simulation.[12] Binomial lattices can even account for exotic events such as stock price barriers (a barrier option exists when the stock option becomes either in-the-money or out-of-the-money only when it hits a stock price barrier), vesting tranches (a specific percentage of the options granted becomes vested or exercisable each year), senior management having different option grants than regular employees, and so forth. Monte Carlo simulation can then be applied to simulate the probabilities of forfeitures and underperformance of the firm, and use these as the inputs into the binomial lattices. See Johnathan Mun's *Real Options Analysis* (Wiley, 2002) for the technical details on setting up and solving binomial lattices.

Analytical Comparison

The following presents only certain relevant parts of the analyses originally presented to FASB for their consideration in writing the new and revised FAS 123. The main goal of the analysis is to show that under certain restrictive conditions, all three methodologies provide identical results, indicating that all three methods are robust and correct. However, when conditions are changed to mirror real-life scenarios, binomial lattices provide a much more accurate fair value assessment than the GBM and BSM approaches, where the latter approaches may sometimes overvalue and at other times undervalue the employee stock option.

Figure 13.34 provides a comparative analysis of the three different option valuation methodologies for a simple set of inputs. The usual inputs in the option valuation model are expiration in years, initial stock price, volatility, risk-free rate, dividend rate, and strike price. Notice that with a simple set of inputs where the stock is assumed not to pay any dividends, the binomial approach with 5,000 steps yields $39.43, identical to the BSM of $39.43. The path simulation approach also yields a value of $39.43.[13] Notice in addition, that the American closed-form model results indicate identical values when no dividend payments exist, and that all methods yield the same values in a European option. In American options when dividend exists, the values obtained from the three methodologies are vastly different, as seen in Figure 13.35.

When dividends exist, that is, when the underlying firm's stocks pay dividends, the results from a BSM or GBM are no longer robust or correct because early execution is optimal, making the stock option, an American-type option, more valuable than is estimated using the Black–Scholes model. Figure 13.35 illustrates this point. For instance, the first panel on Figure 13.35 shows the results from a BSM, and the second panel, the binomial lattice for a European option, while the third panel shows the results from an American closed-form approximation model, and the fourth panel shows the binomial approach for an American option. Notice that for all four panels, the first column results are identical when no dividends exist. These identical results indicate that all four methodologies are robust and consistent, provide identical values at the limit, under the condition of no dividends, and are valid for European-type options only. However, when dividends exist, the BSM breaks down and is no longer valid, especially when the option is of the American type.

Figure 13.36 shows the results for the GBM and binomial lattice approaches where different volatility and dividend inputs are used. The percentage differences between the two methods are significant at higher dividend and volatility rates.

Figure 13.37 and Figure 13.38 illustrate the effects of dividends and volatility when vesting requirements exist. All three figures show that the GBM approach consistently underestimates the true value of the stock option when the binomial lattice is applied.

However, an interesting twist arises when suboptimal early exercise behavior is modeled. Figure 13.39 through Figure 13.42 show that the *GBM consistently overestimates the true value of the stock option when employee*

(Text continues on page 315.)

Input Parameters

Expiration in Years	5.00
Volatility	35.00%
Initial Stock Price	$100.00
Risk-free Rate	5.00%
Dividend Rate	0.00%
Strike Cost	$100.00

Simulation Calculation

Simulate Value	0.00
Payoff Function	19.47

European Option Results

Binomial Approach	$39.43
Black-Scholes Model	$39.43
Path Dependent Simulation	$39.43
Generalized Black-Scholes	$39.43

American Option Results

Binomial Approach	$39.43
Black-Scholes Model	N/A
Path Dependent Simulation	N/A
Closed-Form Approximation Model	$39.43

Binomial Steps

Time	Simulate	Steps	Value
00	.000	.00	100.00
1-	0.59	-4.40	95.60
2-	0.85	-6.14	89.46
31	.238	.81	98.28
4-	0.62	-4.56	93.72
50	.947	.14	100.85
60	.846	.92	107.77
7-	1.17	-9.60	98.17
8-	1.02	-7.62	90.55
9-	0.09	-0.40	90.15
10	-0.66-	4.40	85.76
11	-0.99-	6.45	79.30
12	0.35	2.36	81.66
13	2.12	13.76	95.42
14	-0.27-	1.75	93.67
15	-1.49-	10.72	82.95
16	-0.57-	3.48	79.48
17	0.06	0.58	80.06
18	0.87	5.67	85.73
19	-0.34-	2.08	83.65
20	-0.14-	0.69	82.96

Binomial Steps — 5000 Steps

Time	Value (2)	Simulate	Steps	Value
21	100.00	-0.05-	0.09	82.87
22	95.60	0.24	1.78	84.65
23	89.18	-2.00-	13.05	71.61
24	99.03	-0.66-	3.49	68.11
25	94.39	1.20	6.57	74.68
26	102.01	-1.59-	9.13	65.55
27	108.87	-0.54-	2.59	62.96
28	99.96	-1.38-	6.65	56.30
29	92.20	-1.50-	6.48	49.83
30	91.76	0.20	0.89	50.71
31	86.88	0.24	1.06	51.78
32	79.36	-1.65-	6.55	45.23
33	82.33	-0.88-	2.99	42.23
34	99.18	-1.29-	4.17	38.07
35	97.35	-0.50-	1.40	36.67
36	85.91	-0.26-	0.64	36.03
37	81.72	0.65	1.92	37.95
38	82.45	0.54	1.69	39.63
39	89.53	-0.57-	1.67	37.96
40	87.10	-0.42-	1.15	36.81
41	86.27	0.68	2.06	38.88

Binomial Steps — 5000 Steps

Time	Value (2)	Simulate	Steps	Value
42	86.17	-1.30-	3.87	35.01
43	88.32	-1.27-	3.40	31.61
44	72.91	1.13	2.88	34.48
45	68.03	-0.29-	0.70	33.79
46	77.68	1.34	3.64	37.42
47	65.45	0.43	1.34	38.77
48	61.49	0.17	0.61	39.38
49	50.92	-0.69-	2.03	37.35
50	39.42	-0.78-	2.19	35.16
51	41.20	0.62	1.79	36.95
52	43.30	-1.64-	4.66	32.29
53	30.64	-0.68-	1.64	30.65
54	24.03	-1.90-	4.48	26.17
55	14.16	-0.52-	0.99	25.17
56	10.50	1.04	2.12	27.29
57	8.75	0.21	0.51	27.80
58	14.06	0.52	1.19	28.99
59	18.51	-0.78-	1.70	27.29
60	14.29	0.00	0.06	27.35
61	11.27	1.17	2.57	29.92
62	16.87	1.64	3.92	33.84

FIGURE 13.34 Comparing the three approaches.

Black-Scholes Model

	Dividend (0.00%)	Dividend (1.00%)	Dividend (2.00%)	Dividend (3.00%)	Dividend (4.00%)	Dividend (5.00%)	Dividend (6.00%)	Dividend (7.00%)	Dividend (8.00%)	Dividend (9.00%)	Dividend (10.00%)
	1	2	3	4	5	6	7	8	9	10	11
Years (1.00)	$16.13	$16.13	$16.13	$16.13	$16.13	$16.13	$16.13	$16.13	$16.13	$16.13	$16.13
Years (2.00)	$23.75	$23.75	$23.75	$23.75	$23.75	$23.75	$23.75	$23.75	$23.75	$23.75	$23.75
Years (3.00)	$29.78	$29.78	$29.78	$29.78	$29.78	$29.78	$29.78	$29.78	$29.78	$29.78	$29.78
Years (4.00)	$34.91	$34.91	$34.91	$34.91	$34.91	$34.91	$34.91	$34.91	$34.91	$34.91	$34.91
Years (5.00)	$39.43	$39.43	$39.43	$39.43	$39.43	$39.43	$39.43	$39.43	$39.43	$39.43	$39.43
Years (6.00)	$43.47	$43.47	$43.47	$43.47	$43.47	$43.47	$43.47	$43.47	$43.47	$43.47	$43.47
Years (7.00)	$47.14	$47.14	$47.14	$47.14	$47.14	$47.14	$47.14	$47.14	$47.14	$47.14	$47.14
Years (8.00)	$50.48	$50.48	$50.48	$50.48	$50.48	$50.48	$50.48	$50.48	$50.48	$50.48	$50.48
Years (9.00)	$53.55	$53.55	$53.55	$53.55	$53.55	$53.55	$53.55	$53.55	$53.55	$53.55	$53.55
Years (10.00)	$56.39	$56.39	$56.39	$56.39	$56.39	$56.39	$56.39	$56.39	$56.39	$56.39	$56.39

Binomial Approach (European)

	Dividend (0.00%)	Dividend (1.00%)	Dividend (2.00%)	Dividend (3.00%)	Dividend (4.00%)	Dividend (5.00%)	Dividend (6.00%)	Dividend (7.00%)	Dividend (8.00%)	Dividend (9.00%)	Dividend (10.00%)
	1	2	3	4	5	6	7	8	9	10	11
Years (1.00)	$16.13	$15.51	$14.91	$14.33	$13.76	$13.21	$12.68	$12.16	$11.66	$11.17	$10.70
Years (2.00)	$23.74	$22.42	$21.16	$19.95	$18.79	$17.69	$16.63	$15.62	$14.66	$13.74	$12.87
Years (3.00)	$29.78	$27.71	$25.75	$23.90	$22.15	$20.50	$18.95	$17.49	$16.12	$14.84	$13.64
Years (4.00)	$34.91	$32.06	$29.39	$26.89	$24.57	$22.40	$20.39	$18.53	$16.80	$15.21	$13.74
Years (5.00)	$39.43	$35.76	$32.37	$29.24	$26.36	$23.71	$21.27	$19.05	$17.01	$15.16	$13.48
Years (6.00)	$43.47	$38.98	$34.87	$31.11	$27.69	$24.58	$21.76	$19.22	$16.92	$14.85	$13.00
Years (7.00)	$47.13	$41.80	$36.97	$32.60	$28.66	$25.13	$21.96	$19.13	$16.62	$14.38	$12.40
Years (8.00)	$50.48	$44.29	$38.74	$33.78	$29.36	$25.43	$21.95	$18.88	$16.17	$13.80	$11.74
Years (9.00)	$53.55	$46.50	$40.25	$34.71	$29.82	$25.53	$21.77	$18.49	$15.63	$13.17	$11.04
Years (10.00)	$56.38	$48.47	$41.52	$35.42	$30.10	$25.47	$21.46	$18.01	$15.04	$12.50	$10.33

American Closed-Form Approximation

	Dividend (0.00%)	Dividend (1.00%)	Dividend (2.00%)	Dividend (3.00%)	Dividend (4.00%)	Dividend (5.00%)	Dividend (6.00%)	Dividend (7.00%)	Dividend (8.00%)	Dividend (9.00%)	Dividend (10.00%)
Years (1.00)	$16.13	$15.51	$14.91	$14.33	$13.79	$13.33	$12.88	$12.45	$12.05	$11.67	$11.31
Years (2.00)	$23.75	$22.43	$21.16	$19.99	$18.96	$18.10	$17.26	$16.49	$15.77	$15.11	$14.49
Years (3.00)	$29.78	$27.71	$25.77	$24.03	$22.58	$21.33	$20.16	$19.10	$18.12	$17.22	$16.40
Years (4.00)	$34.91	$32.06	$29.45	$27.20	$25.37	$23.76	$22.30	$20.98	$19.78	$18.68	$17.69
Years (5.00)	$39.43	$35.77	$32.51	$29.80	$27.61	$25.67	$23.95	$22.40	$21.01	$19.75	$18.61
Years (6.00)	$43.47	$39.00	$35.12	$31.99	$29.47	$27.23	$25.26	$23.52	$21.96	$20.56	$19.30
Years (7.00)	$47.14	$41.84	$37.39	$33.86	$31.03	$28.51	$26.33	$24.42	$22.71	$21.19	$19.83
Years (8.00)	$50.48	$44.37	$39.38	$35.48	$32.35	$29.58	$27.22	$25.15	$23.32	$21.69	$20.24
Years (9.00)	$53.55	$46.64	$41.14	$36.90	$33.49	$30.49	$27.96	$25.75	$23.81	$22.09	$20.56
Years (10.00)	$56.39	$48.69	$42.71	$38.15	$34.48	$31.27	$28.58	$26.25	$24.21	$22.41	$20.82
	1	2	3	4	5	6	7	8	9	10	11

Binomial Approach (American)

	Dividend (0.00%)	Dividend (1.00%)	Dividend (2.00%)	Dividend (3.00%)	Dividend (4.00%)	Dividend (5.00%)	Dividend (6.00%)	Dividend (7.00%)	Dividend (8.00%)	Dividend (9.00%)	Dividend (10.00%)
Years (1.00)	$16.13	$15.51	$14.91	$14.34	$13.83	$13.36	$12.93	$12.52	$12.14	$11.77	$11.42
Years (2.00)	$23.74	$22.42	$21.17	$20.03	$19.05	$18.16	$17.35	$16.59	$15.89	$15.23	$14.61
Years (3.00)	$29.78	$27.71	$25.79	$24.13	$22.70	$21.43	$20.27	$19.21	$18.24	$17.34	$16.51
Years (4.00)	$34.91	$32.06	$29.50	$27.35	$25.50	$23.88	$22.42	$21.10	$19.89	$18.79	$17.79
Years (5.00)	$39.43	$35.78	$32.61	$29.98	$27.76	$25.81	$24.08	$22.52	$21.12	$19.86	$18.70
Years (6.00)	$43.47	$39.02	$35.26	$32.19	$29.61	$27.37	$25.40	$23.64	$22.07	$20.66	$19.38
Years (7.00)	$47.13	$41.88	$37.56	$34.08	$31.17	$28.66	$26.47	$24.54	$22.82	$21.28	$19.90
Years (8.00)	$50.48	$44.42	$39.57	$35.71	$32.49	$29.74	$27.36	$25.26	$23.41	$21.77	$20.30
Years (9.00)	$53.55	$46.70	$41.35	$37.12	$33.63	$30.66	$28.10	$25.86	$23.90	$22.16	$20.62
Years (10.00)	$56.38	$48.76	$42.93	$38.36	$34.61	$31.44	$28.72	$26.36	$24.29	$22.48	$20.87
	1	2	3	4	5	6	7	8	9	10	11

FIGURE 13.35 Comparison results of the three approaches.

Binomial Lattice Results (1,000 Steps)	Volatility (30.00%)	Volatility (35.00%)	(Volatility (40.00%)	Volatility (45.00%)	Volatility (50.00%)	Volatility (55.00%)	Volatility (60.00%)	Volatility (65.00%)	Volatility (70.00%)	Volatility (75.00%)	
Dividends (0.00%)	$2.63	$2.82	$3.01	$3.19	$3.37	$3.53	$3.69	$3.83	$3.97	$4.09	1
Dividends (1.00%)	$2.24	$2.44	$2.63	$2.82	$3.00	$3.17	$3.34	$3.49	$3.63	$3.76	2
Dividends (2.00%)	$1.94	$2.15	$2.35	$2.54	$2.73	$2.91	$3.07	$3.23	$3.38	$3.51	3
Dividends (3.00%)	$1.71	$1.92	$2.12	$2.32	$2.51	$2.69	$2.86	$3.01	$3.16	$3.30	4
Dividends (4.00%)	$1.52	$1.73	$1.94	$2.13	$2.32	$2.50	$2.67	$2.83	$2.98	$3.12	5
Dividends (5.00%)	$1.36	$1.57	$1.77	$1.97	$2.16	$2.33	$2.50	$2.66	$2.81	$2.95	6
Dividends (6.00%)	$1.23	$1.44	$1.64	$1.83	$2.01	$2.19	$2.36	$2.52	$2.67	$2.81	7
	1	2	3	4	5	6	7	8	9	10	

Generalized Black-Scholes Model (GBM)	Volatility (30.00%)	Volatility (35.00%)	Volatility (40.00%)	Volatility (45.00%)	Volatility (50.00%)	Volatility (55.00%)	Volatility (60.00%)	Volatility (65.00%)	Volatility (70.00%)	Volatility (75.00%)	
Dividends (0.00%)	$2.63	$2.82	$3.01	$3.19	$3.37	$3.53	$3.69	$3.83	$3.97	$4.09	1
Dividends (1.00%)	$2.23	$2.42	$2.61	$2.79	$2.96	$3.12	$3.27	$3.41	$3.54	$3.66	2
Dividends (2.00%)	$1.89	$2.08	$2.26	$2.43	$2.59	$2.75	$2.89	$3.03	$3.15	$3.27	3
Dividends (3.00%)	$1.59	$1.77	$1.95	$2.11	$2.27	$2.42	$2.56	$2.69	$2.81	$2.92	4
Dividends (4.00%)	$1.33	$1.51	$1.67	$1.83	$1.98	$2.13	$2.26	$2.38	$2.50	$2.60	5
Dividends (5.00%)	$1.11	$1.27	$1.43	$1.59	$1.73	$1.87	$1.99	$2.11	$2.22	$2.32	6
Dividends (6.00%)	$0.91	$1.07	$1.23	$1.37	$1.51	$1.64	$1.76	$1.87	$1.97	$2.06	7
	1	2	3	4	5	6	7	8	9	10	

% Difference from GBM	Volatility (30.00%)	Volatility (35.00%)	Volatility (40.00%)	Volatility (45.00%)	Volatility (50.00%)	Volatility (55.00%)	Volatility (60.00%)	Volatility (65.00%)	Volatility (70.00%)	Volatility (75.00%)	
Dividends (0.00%)	0.0%	0.0%	0.0%	0.0%	0.0%	0.0%	0.0%	0.0%	0.0%	0.0%	1
Dividends (1.00%)	-0.3%	-0.6%	-0.9%	-1.2%	-1.5%	-1.8%	-2.1%	-2.3%	-2.6%	-2.8%	2
Dividends (2.00%)	-2.6%	-3.4%	-4.1%	-4.7%	-5.3%	-5.8%	-6.2%	-6.7%	-7.1%	-7.5%	3
Dividends (3.00%)	-7.3%	-8.3%	-9.1%	-9.8%	-10.5%	-11.1%	-11.6%	-12.2%	-12.7%	-13.2%	4
Dividends (4.00%)	-14.1%	-15.0%	-15.7%	-16.3%	-16.9%	-17.5%	-18.1%	-18.7%	-19.2%	-19.8%	5
Dividends (5.00%)	-23.1%	-23.4%	-23.7%	-24.1%	-24.6%	-25.1%	-25.6%	-26.2%	-26.8%	-27.4%	6
Dividends (6.00%)	-34.4%	-33.8%	-33.5%	-33.4%	-33.6%	-33.8%	-34.3%	-34.8%	-35.3%	-36.0%	7
	1	2	3	4	5	6	7	8	9	10	

FIGURE 13.36 American option (binomial lattices and GBM with different volatility and dividends).

Binomial Lattice Results (1,000 Steps) with Vesting Period	Dividends (0.00%)	Dividends (1.00%)	Dividends (2.00%)	Dividends (3.00%)	Dividends (4.00%)	Dividends (5.00%)	Dividends (6.00%)	
Vesting (2.00)	$2.63	$2.24	$1.94	$1.71	$1.52	$1.36	$1.22	1
Vesting (3.00)	$2.63	$2.24	$1.94	$1.70	$1.51	$1.35	$1.21	2
Vesting (4.00)	$2.63	$2.24	$1.94	$1.70	$1.50	$1.33	$1.18	3
Vesting (5.00)	$2.63	$2.24	$1.94	$1.69	$1.49	$1.31	$1.15	4
Vesting (6.00)	$2.63	$2.24	$1.93	$1.68	$1.46	$1.28	$1.11	5
Vesting (7.00)	$2.63	$2.24	$1.92	$1.66	$1.44	$1.24	$1.07	6
Vesting (8.00)	$2.63	$2.24	$1.92	$1.64	$1.41	$1.20	$1.02	7
	1	2	3	4	5	6	7	

Generalized Black-Scholes Model (GBM) No Vesting Period	Dividends (0.00%)	Dividends (1.00%)	Dividends (2.00%)	Dividends (3.00%)	Dividends (4.00%)	Dividends (5.00%)	Dividends (6.00%)	
Vesting (2.00)	$2.63	$2.23	$1.89	$1.59	$1.33	$1.11	$0.91	1
Vesting (3.00)	$2.63	$2.23	$1.89	$1.59	$1.33	$1.11	$0.91	2
Vesting (4.00)	$2.63	$2.23	$1.89	$1.59	$1.33	$1.11	$0.91	3
Vesting (5.00)	$2.63	$2.23	$1.89	$1.59	$1.33	$1.11	$0.91	4
Vesting (6.00)	$2.63	$2.23	$1.89	$1.59	$1.33	$1.11	$0.91	5
Vesting (7.00)	$2.63	$2.23	$1.89	$1.59	$1.33	$1.11	$0.91	6
Vesting (8.00)	$2.63	$2.23	$1.89	$1.59	$1.33	$1.11	$0.91	7
	1	2	3	4	5	6	7	

% Difference from GBM	Dividends (0.00%)	Dividends (1.00%)	Dividends (2.00%)	Dividends (3.00%)	Dividends (4.00%)	Dividends (5.00%)	Dividends (6.00%)	
Vesting (2.00)	0.0%	-0.3%	-2.6%	-7.3%	-14.1%	-22.8%	-33.7%	1
Vesting (3.00)	0.0%	-0.3%	-2.6%	-7.2%	-13.7%	-21.9%	-32.0%	2
Vesting (4.00)	0.0%	-0.3%	-2.6%	-6.9%	-12.9%	-20.4%	-29.2%	3
Vesting (5.00)	0.0%	-0.3%	-2.4%	-6.4%	-11.8%	-18.2%	-25.7%	4
Vesting (6.00)	0.0%	-0.3%	-2.2%	-5.6%	-10.2%	-15.5%	-21.5%	5
Vesting (7.00)	0.0%	-0.3%	-1.8%	-4.6%	-8.2%	-12.3%	-16.8%	6
Vesting (8.00)	0.0%	-0.2%	-1.4%	-3.3%	-5.8%	-8.6%	-11.7%	7
	1	2	3	4	5	6	7	

FIGURE 13.37 American option with vesting requirements (binomial lattices and GBM with changing dividends and vesting periods).

Binomial Lattice Results (1,000 Steps) with a 5 Year Vesting Period	Volatility (30.00%)	Volatility (35.00%)	(Volatility (40.00%)	Volatility (45.00%)	Volatility (50.00%)	Volatility (55.00%)	Volatility (60.00%)	Volatility (65.00%)	Volatility (70.00%)	Volatility (75.00%)	
Dividends (0.00%)	$2.63	$2.82	$3.01	$3.19	$3.37	$3.53	$3.69	$3.83	$3.97	$4.09	1
Dividends (1.00%)	$2.24	$2.44	$2.63	$2.82	$3.00	$3.17	$3.33	$3.48	$3.62	$3.75	2
Dividends (2.00%)	$1.94	$2.14	$2.34	$2.53	$2.71	$2.89	$3.05	$3.20	$3.34	$3.47	3
Dividends (3.00%)	$1.69	$1.90	$2.10	$2.29	$2.47	$2.64	$2.80	$2.96	$3.10	$3.23	4
Dividends (4.00%)	$1.49	$1.69	$1.89	$2.08	$2.26	$2.43	$2.58	$2.73	$2.87	$3.00	5
Dividends (5.00%)	$1.31	$1.51	$1.70	$1.89	$2.06	$2.23	$2.38	$2.53	$2.67	$2.79	6
Dividends (6.00%)	$1.15	$1.34	$1.53	$1.71	$1.88	$2.05	$2.20	$2.34	$2.48	$2.60	7
	1	2	3	4	5	6	7	8	9	10	

Generalized Black-Scholes Model (GBM)	Volatility (30.00%)	Volatility (35.00%)	Volatility (40.00%)	Volatility (45.00%)	Volatility (50.00%)	Volatility (55.00%)	Volatility (60.00%)	Volatility (65.00%)	Volatility (70.00%)	Volatility (75.00%)	
Dividends (0.00%)	$2.63	$2.82	$3.01	$3.19	$3.37	$3.53	$3.69	$3.83	$3.97	$4.09	1
Dividends (1.00%)	$2.23	$2.42	$2.61	$2.79	$2.96	$3.12	$3.27	$3.41	$3.54	$3.66	2
Dividends (2.00%)	$1.89	$2.08	$2.26	$2.43	$2.59	$2.75	$2.89	$3.03	$3.15	$3.27	3
Dividends (3.00%)	$1.59	$1.77	$1.95	$2.11	$2.27	$2.42	$2.56	$2.69	$2.81	$2.92	4
Dividends (4.00%)	$1.33	$1.51	$1.67	$1.83	$1.98	$2.13	$2.26	$2.38	$2.50	$2.60	5
Dividends (5.00%)	$1.11	$1.27	$1.43	$1.59	$1.73	$1.87	$1.99	$2.11	$2.22	$2.32	6
Dividends (6.00%)	$0.91	$1.07	$1.23	$1.37	$1.51	$1.64	$1.76	$1.87	$1.97	$2.06	7
	1	2	3	4	5	6	7	8	9	10	

% Difference from GBM	Volatility (30.00%)	Volatility (35.00%)	Volatility (40.00%)	Volatility (45.00%)	Volatility (50.00%)	Volatility (55.00%)	Volatility (60.00%)	Volatility (65.00%)	Volatility (70.00%)	Volatility (75.00%)	
Dividends (0.00%)	0.0%	0.0%	0.0%	0.0%	0.0%	0.0%	0.0%	0.0%	0.0%	0.0%	1
Dividends (1.00%)	-0.3%	-0.6%	-0.8%	-1.1%	-1.4%	-1.6%	-1.9%	-2.1%	-2.3%	-2.5%	2
Dividends (2.00%)	-2.4%	-3.1%	-3.7%	-4.2%	-4.6%	-5.0%	-5.4%	-5.7%	-6.0%	-6.3%	3
Dividends (3.00%)	-6.4%	-7.2%	-7.8%	-8.4%	-8.8%	-9.2%	-9.6%	-10.0%	-10.3%	-10.7%	4
Dividends (4.00%)	-11.8%	-12.3%	-12.8%	-13.3%	-13.7%	-14.0%	-14.4%	-14.7%	-15.1%	-15.4%	5
Dividends (5.00%)	-18.2%	-18.4%	-18.6%	-18.8%	-19.0%	-19.3%	-19.6%	-19.9%	-20.2%	-20.6%	6
Dividends (6.00%)	-25.7%	-25.3%	-25.0%	-24.9%	-25.0%	-25.1%	-25.3%	-25.5%	-25.8%	-26.1%	7
	1	2	3	4	5	6	7	8	9	10	

FIGURE 13.38 American option with vesting requirements (binomial lattices and GBM with changing volatilities and dividends).

Binomial Lattice Results (1,000 Steps) with suboptimal exercise pattern at 1.25	Asset ($5.00)	Asset ($10.00)	Asset ($15.00)	Asset ($20.00)	Asset ($25.00)	Asset ($30.00)	Asset ($35.00)	Asset ($40.00)	Asset ($45.00)	Asset ($50.00)	
Dividends (0.00%)	$0.79	$1.58	$2.37	$3.16	$3.95	$4.74	$5.53	$6.32	$7.11	$7.90	1
Dividends (1.00%)	$0.78	$1.56	$2.34	$3.12	$3.90	$4.68	$5.47	$6.25	$7.03	$7.81	2
Dividends (2.00%)	$0.77	$1.54	$2.32	$3.09	$3.86	$4.63	$5.40	$6.17	$6.95	$7.72	3
Dividends (3.00%)	$0.76	$1.52	$2.29	$3.05	$3.81	$4.57	$5.34	$6.10	$6.86	$7.62	4
Dividends (4.00%)	$0.75	$1.51	$2.26	$3.01	$3.77	$4.52	$5.27	$6.02	$6.78	$7.53	5
Dividends (5.00%)	$0.74	$1.49	$2.23	$2.97	$3.72	$4.46	$5.20	$5.95	$6.69	$7.43	6
Dividends (6.00%)	$0.73	$1.47	$2.20	$2.93	$3.67	$4.40	$5.14	$5.87	$6.60	$7.34	7
	1	2	3	4	5	6	7	8	9	10	

Generalized Black-Scholes Model (GBM) with suboptimal exercise pattern at 1.25	Asset ($5.00)	Asset ($10.00)	Asset ($15.00)	Asset ($20.00)	Asset ($25.00)	Asset ($30.00)	Asset ($35.00)	Asset ($40.00)	Asset ($45.00)	Asset ($50.00)	
Dividends (0.00%)	$2.14	$4.28	$6.43	$8.57	$10.71	$12.85	$15.00	$17.14	$19.28	$21.42	1
Dividends (1.00%)	$1.88	$3.77	$5.65	$7.53	$9.42	$11.30	$13.18	$15.07	$16.95	$18.84	2
Dividends (2.00%)	$1.65	$3.30	$4.95	$6.60	$8.25	$9.90	$11.55	$13.20	$14.85	$16.50	3
Dividends (3.00%)	$1.44	$2.88	$4.32	$5.76	$7.20	$8.64	$10.08	$11.52	$12.96	$14.40	4
Dividends (4.00%)	$1.25	$2.50	$3.76	$5.01	$6.26	$7.51	$8.76	$10.01	$11.27	$12.52	5
Dividends (5.00%)	$1.08	$2.17	$3.25	$4.33	$5.42	$6.50	$7.59	$8.67	$9.75	$10.84	6
Dividends (6.00%)	$0.93	$1.87	$2.80	$3.74	$4.67	$5.61	$6.54	$7.47	$8.41	$9.34	7
	1	2	3	4	5	6	7	8	9	10	

% Difference from GBM	Asset ($5.00)	Asset ($10.00)	Asset ($15.00)	Asset ($20.00)	Asset ($25.00)	Asset ($30.00)	Asset ($35.00)	Asset ($40.00)	Asset ($45.00)	Asset ($50.00)	
Dividends (0.00%)	63.1%	63.1%	63.1%	63.1%	63.1%	63.1%	63.1%	63.1%	63.1%	63.1%	1
Dividends (1.00%)	58.5%	58.5%	58.5%	58.5%	58.5%	58.5%	58.5%	58.5%	58.5%	58.5%	2
Dividends (2.00%)	53.2%	53.2%	53.2%	53.2%	53.2%	53.2%	53.2%	53.2%	53.2%	53.2%	3
Dividends (3.00%)	47.0%	47.0%	47.0%	47.0%	47.0%	47.0%	47.0%	47.0%	47.0%	47.0%	4
Dividends (4.00%)	39.8%	39.8%	39.8%	39.8%	39.8%	39.8%	39.8%	39.8%	39.8%	39.8%	5
Dividends (5.00%)	31.4%	31.4%	31.4%	31.4%	31.4%	31.4%	31.4%	31.4%	31.4%	31.4%	6
Dividends (6.00%)	21.5%	21.5%	21.5%	21.5%	21.5%	21.5%	21.5%	21.5%	21.5%	21.5%	7
	1	2	3	4	5	6	7	8	9	10	

FIGURE 13.39 American option with suboptimal early exercise (binomial lattices and GBM with changing assets and dividends).

Binomial Lattice Results (1,000 Steps) with suboptimal exercise pattern at 1.25	Asset ($5.00)	Asset ($10.00)	Asset ($15.00)	Asset ($20.00)	Asset ($25.00)	Asset ($30.00)	Asset ($35.00)	Asset ($40.00)	Asset ($45.00)	Asset ($50.00)	
Volatility (30.00%)	$0.60	$1.20	$1.80	$2.40	$3.00	$3.61	$4.21	$4.81	$5.41	$6.01	1
Volatility (35.00%)	$0.59	$1.17	$1.76	$2.34	$2.93	$3.52	$4.10	$4.69	$5.27	$5.86	2
Volatility (40.00%)	$0.67	$1.34	$2.01	$2.67	$3.34	$4.01	$4.68	$5.35	$6.02	$6.68	3
Volatility (45.00%)	$0.75	$1.50	$2.25	$3.00	$3.75	$4.50	$5.25	$6.00	$6.75	$7.50	4
Volatility (50.00%)	$0.65	$1.30	$1.96	$2.61	$3.26	$3.91	$4.57	$5.22	$5.87	$6.52	5
Volatility (55.00%)	$0.72	$1.43	$2.15	$2.86	$3.58	$4.29	$5.01	$5.72	$6.44	$7.16	6
Volatility (60.00%)	$0.78	$1.56	$2.33	$3.11	$3.89	$4.67	$5.45	$6.22	$7.00	$7.78	7
Volatility (65.00%)	$0.84	$1.68	$2.52	$3.36	$4.20	$5.04	$5.88	$6.72	$7.56	$8.40	8
Volatility (70.00%)	$0.63	$1.26	$1.90	$2.53	$3.16	$3.79	$4.42	$5.06	$5.69	$6.32	9
Volatility (75.00%)	$0.68	$1.35	$2.03	$2.70	$3.38	$4.05	$4.73	$5.40	$6.08	$6.75	10
	1	2	3	4	5	6	7	8	9	10	

Generalized Black-Scholes Model (GBM) with suboptimal exercise pattern at 1.25	Asset ($5.00)	Asset ($10.00)	Asset ($15.00)	Asset ($20.00)	Asset ($25.00)	Asset ($30.00)	Asset ($35.00)	Asset ($40.00)	Asset ($45.00)	Asset ($50.00)	
Volatility (30.00%)	$2.14	$4.28	$6.43	$8.57	$10.71	$12.85	$15.00	$17.14	$19.28	$21.42	1
Volatility (35.00%)	$2.33	$4.65	$6.98	$9.31	$11.64	$13.96	$16.29	$18.62	$20.95	$23.27	2
Volatility (40.00%)	$2.51	$5.02	$7.53	$10.04	$12.55	$15.06	$17.58	$20.09	$22.60	$25.11	3
Volatility (45.00%)	$2.69	$5.38	$8.07	$10.76	$13.45	$16.14	$18.83	$21.52	$24.21	$26.90	4
Volatility (50.00%)	$2.86	$5.73	$8.59	$11.46	$14.32	$17.19	$20.05	$22.92	$25.78	$28.65	5
Volatility (55.00%)	$3.03	$6.07	$9.10	$12.13	$15.17	$18.20	$21.23	$24.27	$27.30	$30.33	6
Volatility (60.00%)	$3.19	$6.39	$9.58	$12.78	$15.97	$19.17	$22.36	$25.56	$28.75	$31.95	7
Volatility (65.00%)	$3.35	$6.70	$10.05	$13.39	$16.74	$20.09	$23.44	$26.79	$30.14	$33.49	8
Volatility (70.00%)	$3.49	$6.99	$10.48	$13.98	$17.47	$20.97	$24.46	$27.96	$31.45	$34.95	9
Volatility (75.00%)	$3.63	$7.27	$10.90	$14.53	$18.16	$21.80	$25.43	$29.06	$32.69	$36.33	10
	1	2	3	4	5	6	7	8	9	10	

% Difference from GBM	Asset ($5.00)	Asset ($10.00)	Asset ($15.00)	Asset ($20.00)	Asset ($25.00)	Asset ($30.00)	Asset ($35.00)	Asset ($40.00)	Asset ($45.00)	Asset ($50.00)	
Volatility (30.00%)	71.9%	71.9%	71.9%	71.9%	71.9%	71.9%	71.9%	71.9%	71.9%	71.9%	1
Volatility (35.00%)	74.8%	74.8%	74.8%	74.8%	74.8%	74.8%	74.8%	74.8%	74.8%	74.8%	2
Volatility (40.00%)	73.4%	73.4%	73.4%	73.4%	73.4%	73.4%	73.4%	73.4%	73.4%	73.4%	3
Volatility (45.00%)	72.1%	72.1%	72.1%	72.1%	72.1%	72.1%	72.1%	72.1%	72.1%	72.1%	4
Volatility (50.00%)	77.2%	77.2%	77.2%	77.2%	77.2%	77.2%	77.2%	77.2%	77.2%	77.2%	5
Volatility (55.00%)	76.4%	76.4%	76.4%	76.4%	76.4%	76.4%	76.4%	76.4%	76.4%	76.4%	6
Volatility (60.00%)	75.6%	75.6%	75.6%	75.6%	75.6%	75.6%	75.6%	75.6%	75.6%	75.6%	7
Volatility (65.00%)	74.9%	74.9%	74.9%	74.9%	74.9%	74.9%	74.9%	74.9%	74.9%	74.9%	8
Volatility (70.00%)	81.9%	81.9%	81.9%	81.9%	81.9%	81.9%	81.9%	81.9%	81.9%	81.9%	9
Volatility (75.00%)	81.4%	81.4%	81.4%	81.4%	81.4%	81.4%	81.4%	81.4%	81.4%	81.4%	10
	1	2	3	4	5	6	7	8	9	10	

FIGURE 13.40 American option with suboptimal early exercise (binomial lattices and GBM with changing assets and volatilities).

Binomial Lattice Results (1,000 Steps) with suboptimal exercise pattern at 1.25	Volatility (30.00%)	Volatility (35.00%)	Volatility (40.00%)	Volatility (45.00%)	Volatility (50.00%)	Volatility (55.00%)	Volatility (60.00%)	Volatility (65.00%)	Volatility (70.00%)	Volatility (75.00%)	
Dividends (0.00%)	$0.68	$0.64	$0.72	$0.81	$0.69	$0.75	$0.81	$0.88	$0.65	$0.69	1
Dividends (1.00%)	$0.66	$0.63	$0.71	$0.80	$0.68	$0.75	$0.81	$0.87	$0.65	$0.69	2
Dividends (2.00%)	$0.65	$0.62	$0.71	$0.79	$0.68	$0.74	$0.80	$0.86	$0.64	$0.69	3
Dividends (3.00%)	$0.64	$0.61	$0.70	$0.78	$0.67	$0.73	$0.80	$0.86	$0.64	$0.68	4
Dividends (4.00%)	$0.63	$0.60	$0.69	$0.77	$0.66	$0.73	$0.79	$0.85	$0.64	$0.68	5
Dividends (5.00%)	$0.61	$0.60	$0.68	$0.76	$0.66	$0.72	$0.78	$0.85	$0.63	$0.68	6
Dividends (6.00%)	$0.60	$0.59	$0.67	$0.75	$0.65	$0.72	$0.78	$0.84	$0.63	$0.68	7
	1	2	3	4	5	6	7	8	9	10	

Generalized Black-Scholes Model (GBM) with suboptimal exercise pattern at 1.25	Volatility (30.00%)	Volatility (35.00%)	Volatility (40.00%)	Volatility (45.00%)	Volatility (50.00%)	Volatility (55.00%)	Volatility (60.00%)	Volatility (65.00%)	Volatility (70.00%)	Volatility (75.00%)	
Dividends (0.00%)	$2.14	$2.33	$2.51	$2.69	$2.86	$3.03	$3.19	$3.35	$3.49	$3.63	1
Dividends (1.00%)	$1.88	$2.07	$2.25	$2.43	$2.60	$2.76	$2.92	$3.07	$3.21	$3.34	2
Dividends (2.00%)	$1.65	$1.83	$2.01	$2.18	$2.35	$2.51	$2.66	$2.81	$2.95	$3.08	3
Dividends (3.00%)	$1.44	$1.62	$1.79	$1.96	$2.12	$2.28	$2.43	$2.57	$2.70	$2.83	4
Dividends (4.00%)	$1.25	$1.43	$1.60	$1.76	$1.92	$2.07	$2.21	$2.35	$2.48	$2.60	5
Dividends (5.00%)	$1.08	$1.25	$1.42	$1.58	$1.73	$1.88	$2.01	$2.15	$2.27	$2.39	6
Dividends (6.00%)	$0.93	$1.10	$1.26	$1.41	$1.56	$1.70	$1.83	$1.96	$2.08	$2.20	7
	1	2	3	4	5	6	7	8	9	10	

% Difference from GBM	Volatility (30.00%)	Volatility (35.00%)	Volatility (40.00%)	Volatility (45.00%)	Volatility (50.00%)	Volatility (55.00%)	Volatility (60.00%)	Volatility (65.00%)	Volatility (70.00%)	Volatility (75.00%)	
Dividends (0.00%)	68.5%	72.6%	71.2%	70.0%	76.0%	75.2%	74.5%	73.8%	81.4%	80.9%	1
Dividends (1.00%)	64.7%	69.5%	68.2%	67.1%	73.8%	73.0%	72.3%	71.6%	79.9%	79.4%	2
Dividends (2.00%)	60.5%	66.1%	64.9%	63.9%	71.3%	70.5%	69.9%	69.2%	78.2%	77.7%	3
Dividends (3.00%)	55.5%	62.1%	61.2%	60.3%	68.5%	67.8%	67.2%	66.6%	76.3%	75.8%	4
Dividends (4.00%)	49.9%	57.6%	56.9%	56.3%	65.4%	64.8%	64.3%	63.7%	74.3%	73.8%	5
Dividends (5.00%)	43.3%	52.5%	52.2%	51.8%	61.9%	61.5%	61.1%	60.6%	72.1%	71.6%	6
Dividends (6.00%)	35.7%	46.6%	46.8%	46.8%	58.1%	57.8%	57.5%	57.2%	69.6%	69.3%	7
	1	2	3	4	5	6	7	8	9	10	

FIGURE 13.41 American option with suboptimal early exercise (binomial lattices and GBM with changing volatilities and dividends).

Binomial Lattice Results (1,000 Steps) with suboptimal exercise pattern at 1.25	Exercise (1.25)	Exercise (1.35)	Exercise (1.45)	Exercise (1.55)	Exercise (1.65)	Exercise (1.75)	Exercise (1.85)	Exercise (1.95)	Exercise (2.05)	Exercise (2.15)	Exercise (2.25)	
Volatility (30.00%)	$0.84	$1.01	$1.09	$1.14	$1.18	$1.21	$1.22	$1.23	$1.23	$1.23	$1.23	1
Volatility (35.00%)	$0.90	$1.05	$1.17	$1.27	$1.33	$1.36	$1.40	$1.42	$1.43	$1.43	$1.44	2
Volatility (40.00%)	$0.92	$1.11	$1.27	$1.34	$1.44	$1.48	$1.55	$1.57	$1.59	$1.62	$1.63	3
Volatility (45.00%)	$0.90	$1.14	$1.34	$1.42	$1.56	$1.61	$1.66	$1.70	$1.73	$1.78	$1.80	4
Volatility (50.00%)	$0.99	$1.26	$1.38	$1.48	$1.65	$1.72	$1.78	$1.83	$1.87	$1.91	$1.94	5
Volatility (55.00%)	$1.08	$1.24	$1.38	$1.51	$1.71	$1.80	$1.87	$1.94	$1.99	$1.99	$2.04	6
Volatility (60.00%)	$0.99	$1.35	$1.50	$1.63	$1.75	$1.85	$1.94	$2.02	$2.02	$2.09	$2.15	7
Volatility (65.00%)	$1.07	$1.27	$1.45	$1.61	$1.75	$1.88	$1.99	$2.08	$2.17	$2.17	$2.24	8
Volatility (70.00%)	$1.14	$1.36	$1.55	$1.72	$1.87	$1.87	$2.00	$2.12	$2.22	$2.22	$2.31	9
Volatility (75.00%)	$0.96	$1.44	$1.44	$1.65	$1.83	$1.98	$2.12	$2.12	$2.24	$2.35	$2.35	10
	1	2	3	4	5	6	7	8	9	10	11	

Generalized Black-Scholes Model (GBM) with suboptimal exercise pattern at 1.25	Exercise (1.25)	Exercise (1.35)	Exercise (1.45)	Exercise (1.55)	Exercise (1.65)	Exercise (1.75)	Exercise (1.85)	Exercise (1.95)	Exercise (2.05)	Exercise (2.15)	Exercise (2.25)	
Volatility (30.00%)	$2.14	$2.20	$2.20	$2.20	$2.20	$2.20	$2.25	$2.25	$2.25	$2.25	$2.25	1
Volatility (35.00%)	$2.33	$2.33	$2.39	$2.39	$2.39	$2.39	$2.39	$2.39	$2.44	$2.44	$2.44	2
Volatility (40.00%)	$2.51	$2.51	$2.51	$2.58	$2.58	$2.58	$2.58	$2.58	$2.58	$2.58	$2.63	3
Volatility (45.00%)	$2.69	$2.69	$2.69	$2.69	$2.76	$2.76	$2.76	$2.76	$2.76	$2.76	$2.76	4
Volatility (50.00%)	$2.86	$2.86	$2.86	$2.86	$2.93	$2.93	$2.93	$2.93	$2.93	$2.93	$2.93	5
Volatility (55.00%)	$3.03	$3.03	$3.03	$3.03	$3.03	$3.10	$3.10	$3.10	$3.10	$3.10	$3.10	6
Volatility (60.00%)	$3.19	$3.19	$3.19	$3.19	$3.19	$3.19	$3.26	$3.26	$3.26	$3.26	$3.26	7
Volatility (65.00%)	$3.35	$3.35	$3.35	$3.35	$3.35	$3.35	$3.35	$3.42	$3.42	$3.42	$3.42	8
Volatility (70.00%)	$3.49	$3.49	$3.49	$3.49	$3.49	$3.49	$3.49	$3.49	$3.56	$3.56	$3.56	9
Volatility (75.00%)	$3.63	$3.63	$3.63	$3.63	$3.63	$3.63	$3.63	$3.63	$3.63	$3.70	$3.70	10
	1	2	3	4	5	6	7	8	9	10	11	

% Difference from GBM	Exercise (1.25)	Exercise (1.35)	Exercise (1.45)	Exercise (1.55)	Exercise (1.65)	Exercise (1.75)	Exercise (1.85)	Exercise (1.95)	Exercise (2.05)	Exercise (2.15)	Exercise (2.25)	
Volatility (30.00%)	60.8%	54.3%	50.7%	48.1%	46.3%	45.1%	45.7%	45.5%	45.5%	45.5%	45.5%	1
Volatility (35.00%)	61.5%	54.8%	50.9%	47.0%	44.2%	43.1%	41.5%	40.6%	41.5%	41.3%	41.2%	2
Volatility (40.00%)	63.5%	55.6%	49.3%	48.1%	44.0%	42.4%	39.9%	38.9%	38.2%	37.2%	38.1%	3
Volatility (45.00%)	66.7%	57.5%	50.1%	47.1%	43.5%	41.5%	39.8%	38.4%	37.2%	35.4%	34.8%	4
Volatility (50.00%)	65.4%	55.9%	51.9%	48.3%	43.7%	41.4%	39.4%	37.6%	36.2%	34.9%	33.9%	5
Volatility (55.00%)	64.2%	59.1%	54.4%	50.3%	43.5%	42.0%	39.6%	37.5%	35.7%	35.7%	34.3%	6
Volatility (60.00%)	69.1%	57.9%	53.1%	48.9%	45.2%	42.0%	40.4%	38.0%	38.0%	35.9%	34.1%	7
Volatility (65.00%)	68.2%	62.1%	56.7%	51.9%	47.7%	43.9%	40.6%	39.0%	36.5%	36.5%	34.4%	8
Volatility (70.00%)	67.3%	61.2%	55.7%	50.8%	46.5%	46.5%	42.7%	39.4%	37.7%	37.7%	35.2%	9
Volatility (75.00%)	73.5%	60.2%	60.2%	54.7%	49.7%	45.4%	41.6%	41.6%	38.2%	36.5%	36.5%	10
	1	2	3	4	5	6	7	8	9	10	11	

FIGURE 13.42 American option with suboptimal early exercise (binomial lattices and GBM with changing early exercise behavior and dividends).

Binomial Lattice Results (1,000 Steps) with suboptimal exercise pattern at 1.25	Exercise (1.25)	Exercise (1.35)	Exercise (1.45)	Exercise (1.55)	Exercise (1.65)	Exercise (1.75)	Exercise (1.85)	Exercise (1.95)	Exercise (2.05)	Exercise (2.15)	Exercise (2.25)	
Dividends (0.00%)	$1.08	$1.42	$1.58	$1.72	$1.98	$2.10	$2.21	$2.31	$2.40	$2.48	$2.56	1
Dividends (1.00%)	$1.06	$1.40	$1.54	$1.68	$1.93	$2.03	$2.13	$2.22	$2.31	$2.38	$2.45	2
Dividends (2.00%)	$1.05	$1.37	$1.51	$1.64	$1.87	$1.97	$2.06	$2.14	$2.22	$2.28	$2.34	3
Dividends (3.00%)	$1.04	$1.34	$1.48	$1.60	$1.81	$1.91	$1.99	$2.06	$2.13	$2.19	$2.24	4
Dividends (4.00%)	$1.02	$1.32	$1.45	$1.56	$1.76	$1.84	$1.92	$1.98	$2.04	$2.09	$2.14	5
Dividends (5.00%)	$1.01	$1.29	$1.41	$1.52	$1.70	$1.78	$1.85	$1.91	$1.96	$2.00	$2.03	6
Dividends (6.00%)	$0.99	$1.26	$1.38	$1.48	$1.65	$1.72	$1.78	$1.83	$1.87	$1.91	$1.94	7
	1	2	3	4	5	6	7	8	9	10	11	

Generalized Black-Scholes Model (GBM) with suboptimal exercise pattern at 1.25	Exercise (1.25)	Exercise (1.35)	Exercise (1.45)	Exercise (1.55)	Exercise (1.65)	Exercise (1.75)	Exercise (1.85)	Exercise (1.95)	Exercise (2.05)	Exercise (2.15)	Exercise (2.25)	
Dividends (0.00%)	$2.14	$2.20	$2.20	$2.20	$2.20	$2.20	$2.25	$2.25	$2.25	$2.25	$2.25	1
Dividends (1.00%)	$1.88	$1.93	$1.93	$1.93	$1.93	$1.93	$1.97	$1.97	$1.97	$1.97	$1.97	2
Dividends (2.00%)	$1.65	$1.68	$1.68	$1.68	$1.68	$1.68	$1.71	$1.71	$1.71	$1.71	$1.71	3
Dividends (3.00%)	$1.44	$1.46	$1.46	$1.46	$1.46	$1.46	$1.48	$1.48	$1.48	$1.48	$1.48	4
Dividends (4.00%)	$1.25	$1.27	$1.27	$1.27	$1.27	$1.27	$1.28	$1.28	$1.28	$1.28	$1.28	5
Dividends (5.00%)	$1.08	$1.09	$1.09	$1.09	$1.09	$1.09	$1.10	$1.10	$1.10	$1.10	$1.10	6
Dividends (6.00%)	$0.93	$0.94	$0.94	$0.94	$0.94	$0.94	$0.94	$0.94	$0.94	$0.94	$0.94	7
	1	2	3	4	5	6	7	8	9	10	11	

% Difference from GBM	Exercise (1.25)	Exercise (1.35)	Exercise (1.45)	Exercise (1.55)	Exercise (1.65)	Exercise (1.75)	Exercise (1.85)	Exercise (1.95)	Exercise (2.05)	Exercise (2.15)	Exercise (2.25)	
Dividends (0.00%)	49.7%	35.5%	28.5%	21.9%	10.1%	4.8%	2.1%	-2.3%	-6.4%	-10.2%	-13.7%	1
Dividends (1.00%)	43.5%	27.7%	20.0%	12.9%	0.2%	-5.4%	-8.4%	-13.1%	-17.3%	-21.1%	-24.7%	2
Dividends (2.00%)	36.4%	18.6%	10.2%	2.5%	-11.1%	-17.0%	-20.5%	-25.3%	-29.6%	-33.6%	-37.1%	3
Dividends (3.00%)	28.1%	8.2%	-1.1%	-9.5%	-24.0%	-30.3%	-34.3%	-39.3%	-43.7%	-47.7%	-51.2%	4
Dividends (4.00%)	18.5%	-4.1%	-14.2%	-23.3%	-39.0%	-45.6%	-50.2%	-55.4%	-59.9%	-63.9%	-67.3%	5
Dividends (5.00%)	7.2%	-18.3%	-29.5%	-39.5%	-56.3%	-63.2%	-68.6%	-73.9%	-78.5%	-82.4%	-85.7%	6
Dividends (6.00%)	-6.1%	-35.1%	-47.4%	-58.3%	-76.3%	-83.7%	-90.0%	-95.4%	-100.0%	-103.8%	-106.9%	7
	1	2	3	4	5	6	7	8	9	10	11	

FIGURE 13.43 American option with suboptimal early exercise (binomial lattices and GBM with changing early exercise behavior and dividends).

suboptimal exercise behavior is included in the analysis. This is valuable information for firms as hundreds of thousands or millions of dollars of overexpensing may ensue if a simple GBM or BSM is used, especially so when suboptimal early exercise behavior is not included.

Figure 13.43 shows an interesting set of results where the GBM at different levels of dividends and early exercise behaviors sometimes overestimates and sometimes underestimates the true fair market value of the option. In other words, when a firm blindly uses the BSM or GBM, it does not know if under- or overestimation occurs. Figure 13.44 and Figure 13.45 further illustrate this valuation confusion by incorporating both suboptimal early exercise behavior and vesting requirements under different scenarios. Figure 13.45 again shows that sometimes the GBM overestimates and sometimes it underestimates the true value of the option.

Binomial Lattice Results (1,000 Steps)	Early Exercise (1.25)	Early Exercise (1.35)	Early Exercise (1.45)	Early Exercise (1.55)	Early Exercise (1.65)	Early Exercise (1.75)	Early Exercise (1.85)	Early Exercise (1.95)	Early Exercise (2.05)	Early Exercise (2.15)	Early Exercise (2.25)	
Vesting (2.00)	$1.08	$1.17	$1.22	$1.26	$1.30	$1.32	$1.34	$1.35	$1.36	$1.36	$1.36	1
Vesting (3.00)	$1.14	$1.21	$1.25	$1.28	$1.31	$1.32	$1.34	$1.35	$1.35	$1.35	$1.35	2
Vesting (4.00)	$1.17	$1.23	$1.26	$1.28	$1.30	$1.32	$1.32	$1.33	$1.33	$1.33	$1.33	3
Vesting (5.00)	$1.19	$1.24	$1.26	$1.28	$1.29	$1.30	$1.30	$1.31	$1.31	$1.31	$1.31	4
Vesting (6.00)	$1.20	$1.23	$1.25	$1.26	$1.27	$1.27	$1.28	$1.28	$1.28	$1.28	$1.28	5
Vesting (7.00)	$1.19	$1.21	$1.22	$1.23	$1.24	$1.24	$1.24	$1.24	$1.24	$1.24	$1.24	6
Vesting (8.00)	$1.17	$1.19	$1.19	$1.20	$1.20	$1.20	$1.20	$1.20	$1.20	$1.20	$1.20	7
	1	2	3	4	5	6	7	8	9	10	11	

Generalized Black-Scholes Model (GBM)	Early Exercise (1.25)	Early Exercise (1.35)	Early Exercise (1.45)	Early Exercise (1.55)	Early Exercise (1.65)	Early Exercise (1.75)	Early Exercise (1.85)	Early Exercise (1.95)	Early Exercise (2.05)	Early Exercise (2.15)	Early Exercise (2.25)	
Vesting (2.00)	$1.10	$1.10	$1.10	$1.10	$1.10	$1.10	$1.10	$1.10	$1.10	$1.10	$1.10	1
Vesting (3.00)	$1.09	$1.09	$1.09	$1.09	$1.09	$1.09	$1.09	$1.09	$1.09	$1.09	$1.09	2
Vesting (4.00)	$1.06	$1.06	$1.06	$1.06	$1.06	$1.06	$1.06	$1.06	$1.06	$1.06	$1.06	3
Vesting (5.00)	$1.02	$1.02	$1.02	$1.02	$1.02	$1.02	$1.02	$1.02	$1.02	$1.02	$1.02	4
Vesting (6.00)	$0.97	$0.97	$0.97	$0.97	$0.97	$0.97	$0.97	$0.97	$0.97	$0.97	$0.97	5
Vesting (7.00)	$0.88	$0.88	$0.88	$0.88	$0.88	$0.88	$0.88	$0.88	$0.88	$0.88	$0.88	6
Vesting (8.00)	$0.76	$0.76	$0.76	$0.76	$0.76	$0.76	$0.76	$0.76	$0.76	$0.76	$0.76	7
	1	2	3	4	5	6	7	8	9	10	11	

% Difference from GBM	Early Exercise (1.25)	Early Exercise (1.35)	Early Exercise (1.45)	Early Exercise (1.55)	Early Exercise (1.65)	Early Exercise (1.75)	Early Exercise (1.85)	Early Exercise (1.95)	Early Exercise (2.05)	Early Exercise (2.15)	Early Exercise (2.25)	
Vesting (2.00)	2.3%	-6.3%	-11.0%	-14.8%	-17.9%	-20.2%	-21.8%	-22.8%	-23.1%	-23.3%	-23.3%	1
Vesting (3.00)	-4.5%	-11.2%	-14.9%	-17.8%	-20.1%	-21.9%	-23.0%	-23.7%	-23.9%	-24.1%	-24.1%	2
Vesting (4.00)	-10.4%	-15.8%	-18.6%	-20.9%	-22.6%	-23.9%	-24.7%	-25.2%	-25.3%	-25.4%	-25.4%	3
Vesting (5.00)	-16.5%	-20.7%	-22.9%	-24.7%	-26.0%	-26.9%	-27.5%	-27.7%	-27.8%	-27.8%	-27.8%	4
Vesting (6.00)	-23.9%	-27.3%	-29.0%	-30.3%	-31.2%	-31.8%	-32.2%	-32.3%	-32.3%	-32.3%	-32.3%	5
Vesting (7.00)	-34.9%	-37.5%	-38.8%	-39.6%	-40.2%	-40.6%	-40.7%	-40.8%	-40.8%	-40.8%	-40.8%	6
Vesting (8.00)	-54.5%	-56.4%	-57.1%	-57.6%	-57.9%	-58.1%	-58.1%	-58.1%	-58.1%	-58.1%	-58.1%	7
	1	2	3	4	5	6	7	8	9	10	11	

FIGURE 13.44 American option with vesting and suboptimal behavior including dividends (binomial lattices and GBM with changing early exercise behavior and vesting periods).

Binomial Lattice Results (1,000 Steps) with 0% Dividends	Early Exercise (1.25)	Early Exercise (1.35)	Early Exercise (1.45)	Early Exercise (1.55)	Early Exercise (1.65)	Early Exercise (1.75)	Early Exercise (1.85)	Early Exercise (1.95)	Early Exercise (2.05)	Early Exercise (2.15)	Early Exercise (2.25)	
Vesting (2.00)	$1.44	$1.59	$1.69	$1.78	$1.87	$1.95	$2.03	$2.10	$2.14	$2.20	$2.25	1
Vesting (3.00)	$1.65	$1.77	$1.85	$1.92	$1.99	$2.05	$2.11	$2.17	$2.19	$2.24	$2.29	2
Vesting (4.00)	$1.84	$1.93	$1.99	$2.05	$2.10	$2.15	$2.20	$2.24	$2.26	$2.30	$2.34	3
Vesting (5.00)	$2.01	$2.08	$2.13	$2.17	$2.21	$2.25	$2.28	$2.32	$2.33	$2.36	$2.39	4
Vesting (6.00)	$2.16	$2.22	$2.25	$2.28	$2.31	$2.34	$2.37	$2.39	$2.40	$2.42	$2.44	5
Vesting (7.00)	$2.30	$2.34	$2.37	$2.39	$2.41	$2.43	$2.45	$2.46	$2.47	$2.48	$2.50	6
Vesting (8.00)	$2.43	$2.46	$2.47	$2.48	$2.50	$2.51	$2.52	$2.53	$2.53	$2.54	$2.55	7
	1	2	3	4	5	6	7	8	9	10	11	

Generalized Black-Scholes Model (GBM)	Early Exercise (1.25)	Early Exercise (1.35)	Early Exercise (1.45)	Early Exercise (1.55)	Early Exercise (1.65)	Early Exercise (1.75)	Early Exercise (1.85)	Early Exercise (1.95)	Early Exercise (2.05)	Early Exercise (2.15)	Early Exercise (2.25)	
Vesting (2.00)	$2.34	$2.34	$2.34	$2.34	$2.34	$2.34	$2.34	$2.34	$2.34	$2.34	$2.34	1
Vesting (3.00)	$2.17	$2.17	$2.17	$2.17	$2.17	$2.17	$2.17	$2.17	$2.17	$2.17	$2.17	2
Vesting (4.00)	$1.99	$1.99	$1.99	$1.99	$1.99	$1.99	$1.99	$1.99	$1.99	$1.99	$1.99	3
Vesting (5.00)	$1.80	$1.80	$1.80	$1.80	$1.80	$1.80	$1.80	$1.80	$1.80	$1.80	$1.80	4
Vesting (6.00)	$1.58	$1.58	$1.58	$1.58	$1.58	$1.58	$1.58	$1.58	$1.58	$1.58	$1.58	5
Vesting (7.00)	$1.34	$1.34	$1.34	$1.34	$1.34	$1.34	$1.34	$1.34	$1.34	$1.34	$1.34	6
Vesting (8.00)	$1.06	$1.06	$1.06	$1.06	$1.06	$1.06	$1.06	$1.06	$1.06	$1.06	$1.06	7
	1	2	3	4	5	6	7	8	9	10	11	

% Difference from GBM	Early Exercise (1.25)	Early Exercise (1.35)	Early Exercise (1.45)	Early Exercise (1.55)	Early Exercise (1.65)	Early Exercise (1.75)	Early Exercise (1.85)	Early Exercise (1.95)	Early Exercise (2.05)	Early Exercise (2.15)	Early Exercise (2.25)	
Vesting (2.00)	38.2%	31.7%	27.6%	23.6%	19.8%	16.3%	13.0%	9.9%	8.5%	5.9%	3.5%	1
Vesting (3.00)	23.9%	18.5%	15.0%	11.7%	8.5%	5.5%	2.8%	0.2%	-1.0%	-3.3%	-5.4%	2
Vesting (4.00)	7.7%	3.0%	0.1%	-2.7%	-5.4%	-7.9%	-10.3%	-12.5%	-13.5%	-15.5%	-17.3%	3
Vesting (5.00)	-11.7%	-15.8%	-18.3%	-20.7%	-23.0%	-25.1%	-27.1%	-28.9%	-29.8%	-31.4%	-32.9%	4
Vesting (6.00)	-36.6%	-40.2%	-42.4%	-44.4%	-46.3%	-48.0%	-49.7%	-51.2%	-51.9%	-53.2%	-54.4%	5
Vesting (7.00)	-71.8%	-74.8%	-76.6%	-78.3%	-79.8%	-81.2%	-82.5%	-83.7%	-84.2%	-85.3%	-86.3%	6
Vesting (8.00)	-129.2%	-131.7%	-133.1%	-134.4%	-135.5%	-136.6%	-137.5%	-138.4%	-138.8%	-139.5%	-140.3%	7
	1	2	3	4	5	6	7	8	9	10	11	

FIGURE 13.45 American option with vesting and suboptimal behavior excluding dividends (binomial lattices and GBM with changing early exercise behavior and vesting periods).

Figure 13.46 through Figure 13.48 show differences in valuation when volatility and risk-free rates are allowed to change over time, to more closely reflect real-life changing business and economic environments. When volatilities are allowed to change (e.g., when legitimate business restructuring is expected to occur in the near future—merger, acquisition, divestiture, liquidation, globalization, and so forth), the stock's volatility may change to reflect the new environment—historical volatility may not be entirely representative of future stock volatilities. When volatilities are expected to decrease over time (the –5.00% volatility increment shown in Figure 13.46), when there is a volatility frown (when volatility rises initially, then decreases

Binomial Lattice Results (1,000 Steps) with all volatility changes in the first year	Volatility (30.00%)	Volatility (35.00%)	Volatility (40.00%)	Volatility (45.00%)	Volatility (50.00%)	Volatility (55.00%)	Volatility (60.00%)	Volatility (65.00%)	Volatility (70.00%)	Volatility (75.00%)	
Volatility Increment (-5.00%)	$2.01	$2.12	$2.28	$2.46	$2.65	$2.84	$3.03	$3.21	$3.39	$3.55	1
Volatility Increment (5.00%)	$3.35	$3.52	$3.67	$3.82	$3.96	$4.08	$4.20	$4.30	$4.39	$4.48	3
Volatility Increment (10.00%)	$3.95	$4.07	$4.19	$4.29	$4.39	$4.47	$4.55	$4.61	$4.67	$4.72	4
Volatility Increment (15.00%)	$4.36	$4.45	$4.52	$4.59	$4.65	$4.71	$4.75	$4.79	$4.83	$4.86	5

Higher volatility means higher option value, and higher increments at each interval means a higher option value.
Positive increments suggest a normal sloping yield curve, while negative increments suggest an inverted yield curve.

| | 1 | 2 | 3 | 4 | 5 | 6 | 7 | 8 | 9 | 10 |

Generalized Black-Scholes Model (GBM) with all volatility changes in the first year	Volatility (30.00%)	Volatility (35.00%)	Volatility (40.00%)	Volatility (45.00%)	Volatility (50.00%)	Volatility (55.00%)	Volatility (60.00%)	Volatility (65.00%)	Volatility (70.00%)	Volatility (75.00%)	
Volatility Increment (-5.00%)	$2.26	$2.44	$2.63	$2.82	$3.01	$3.19	$3.37	$3.53	$3.69	$3.83	1
Volatility Increment (5.00%)	$3.01	$3.19	$3.37	$3.53	$3.69	$3.83	$3.97	$4.09	$4.21	$4.31	3
Volatility Increment (10.00%)	$3.37	$3.53	$3.69	$3.83	$3.97	$4.09	$4.21	$4.31	$4.40	$4.49	4
Volatility Increment (15.00%)	$3.69	$3.83	$3.97	$4.09	$4.21	$4.31	$4.40	$4.49	$4.56	$4.63	5

Higher volatility means higher option value, and higher increments at each interval means a higher option value.
Positive increments suggest a normal sloping yield curve, while negative increments suggest an inverted yield curve.

| | 1 | 2 | 3 | 4 | 5 | 6 | 7 | 8 | 9 | 10 |

% Difference from GBM	Volatility (30.00%)	Volatility (35.00%)	Volatility (40.00%)	Volatility (45.00%)	Volatility (50.00%)	Volatility (55.00%)	Volatility (60.00%)	Volatility (65.00%)	Volatility (70.00%)	Volatility (75.00%)	
Volatility Increment (-5.00%)	11.1%	12.9%	13.2%	12.6%	11.8%	10.9%	10.0%	9.1%	8.2%	7.4%	1
Volatility Increment (5.00%)	-11.4%	-10.3%	-9.2%	-8.2%	-7.3%	-6.5%	-5.7%	-5.0%	-4.4%	-3.9%	3
Volatility Increment (10.00%)	-17.3%	-15.4%	-13.6%	-12.0%	-10.5%	-9.2%	-8.1%	-7.0%	-6.1%	-5.3%	4
Volatility Increment (15.00%)	-18.2%	-16.2%	-13.9%	-12.2%	-10.5%	-9.3%	-8.0%	-6.7%	-5.9%	-5.0%	5

A higher volatility means the increments is less relevant (e.g., 5% increase on 75% is less impactful than a 5% increase on 30% initial volatility. Higher increments (both positive and negative) means the median volatility used on a BSM is less precise than a binomial lattice. Suffice it to say that the binomial captures this changing volatility effect while the BSM does not. Also, this effect is more relevant at lower volatilities as the % increment is more impactful when the starting volatility is lower. As most stock returns tend to have volatilities within the 20% to 50% range, the binomial lattice should be used.

FIGURE 13.46 American changing volatility option (binomial lattices and GBM with changing initial volatilities and volatility increments).

Volatility Frown (when volatility rises initially, then decreases, i.e., 30%, 45%, 70%, 65%, then 20%	Volatility (30.00%)	Volatility (35.00%)	Volatility (40.00%)	Volatility (45.00%)	Volatility (50.00%)	Volatility (55.00%)	Volatility (60.00%)	Volatility (65.00%)	Volatility (70.00%)	Volatility (75.00%)
Binomial Lattice	$2.35	$2.52	$2.71	$2.90	$3.08	$3.26	$3.43	$3.59	$3.74	$3.88
Generalized Black-Scholes	$3.19	$3.37	$3.53	$3.69	$3.83	$3.97	$4.09	$4.21	$4.31	$4.40
Difference %	26.47%	25.02%	23.31%	21.51%	19.72%	17.97%	16.31%	14.73%	13.25%	11.87%

Notice that as for a volatility frown, where the yield curve slopes upwards and then downwards (this actually appears in real life) the difference using a 1,000 step changing volatility is significantly different from the values estimated using a median volatility on the GBM. This suggests that in order to mirror real life, the binomial lattice is vital.

Volatility Smile (when volatility decreases initially, then increases, i.e., 30%, 25%, 5%, 20%, then 65%	Volatility (30.00%)	Volatility (35.00%)	Volatility (40.00%)	Volatility (45.00%)	Volatility (50.00%)	Volatility (55.00%)	Volatility (60.00%)	Volatility (65.00%)	Volatility (70.00%)	Volatility (75.00%)
Binomial Lattice	$3.80	$3.94	$4.06	$4.18	$4.28	$4.38	$4.46	$4.54	$4.61	$4.67
Generalized Black-Scholes	$2.44	$2.63	$2.82	$3.01	$3.19	$3.37	$3.53	$3.69	$3.83	$3.97
Difference %	-55.84%	-49.82%	-44.13%	-38.94%	-34.27%	-30.09%	-26.38%	-23.08%	-20.15%	-17.55%

Notice that as for a volatility smile, where the yield curve slopes downwards and then upwards (this actually appears in real life) the difference using a 1,000 step changing volatility is significantly different from the values estimated using a median volatility on the GBM. This suggests that in order to mirror real life, the binomial lattice is vital.

FIGURE 13.47 American changing volatility option (binomial lattices and GBM with changing volatility curves).

over time), or when these changes are not smoothed over time but occur in lumps, GBM significantly overvalues the stock option value. Finally, when the risk-free rates are allowed to change over time to reflect the term structure of interest rates (reflecting the U.S. Treasury's zero yield curves), the GBM overestimates the true option value (results not shown). All these assumptions make the GBM calculations invalid and insufficient in capturing the true fair market value of the employee stock option.

Conclusion and Suggestions

FASB's concern is with choosing the correct option valuation model for its new update of FAS 123 pertaining to expensing all executive stock options. This case study is meant to shed some light on the analytics involved in stock option valuation. There are multiple approaches that exist for option valuation, including, but not limited to, closed-form models like the BSM, GBM, and American option approximation models; binomial lattices; and Monte Carlo simulation. This case study has shown that all three methodologies approach identical answers at the limit for a simple European option without dividends. However, most stock options are American options where the

Binomial Lattice Results (1,000 Steps)	RiskFree Increments (-0.10%)	RiskFree Increments (0.10%)	RiskFree Increments (0.20%)	RiskFree Increments (0.30%)	RiskFree Increments (0.40%)	RiskFree Increments (0.50%)	
Initial Riskfree (2.00%)	$2.03	$2.18	$2.25	$2.32	$2.40	$2.47	1
Initial Riskfree (3.00%)	$2.19	$2.34	$2.41	$2.49	$2.56	$2.63	2
Initial Riskfree (4.00%)	$2.36	$2.50	$2.57	$2.65	$2.72	$2.78	3
Initial Riskfree (5.00%)	$2.52	$2.66	$2.73	$2.80	$2.87	$2.94	4
Initial Riskfree (6.00%)	$2.68	$2.82	$2.89	$2.95	$3.02	$3.08	5
Initial Riskfree (7.00%)	$2.83	$2.97	$3.03	$3.10	$3.16	$3.23	6
Initial Riskfree (8.00%)	$2.98	$3.11	$3.18	$3.24	$3.30	$3.36	7
	1	2	3	4	5	6	

Generalized Black-Scholes Model (GBM)	RiskFree Increments (-0.10%)	RiskFree Increments (0.10%)	RiskFree Increments (0.20%)	RiskFree Increments (0.30%)	RiskFree Increments (0.40%)	RiskFree Increments (0.50%)	
Initial Riskfree (2.00%)	$2.07	$2.22	$2.29	$2.36	$2.44	$2.51	1
Initial Riskfree (3.00%)	$2.23	$2.38	$2.45	$2.53	$2.60	$2.67	2
Initial Riskfree (4.00%)	$2.40	$2.54	$2.61	$2.68	$2.75	$2.82	3
Initial Riskfree (5.00%)	$2.56	$2.70	$2.77	$2.84	$2.91	$2.97	4
Initial Riskfree (6.00%)	$2.71	$2.85	$2.92	$2.99	$3.06	$3.12	5
Initial Riskfree (7.00%)	$2.87	$3.00	$3.07	$3.13	$3.20	$3.26	6
Initial Riskfree (8.00%)	$3.02	$3.15	$3.21	$3.27	$3.33	$3.39	7
	1	2	3	4	5	6	

% Difference from GBM	RiskFree Increments (-0.10%)	RiskFree Increments (0.10%)	RiskFree Increments (0.20%)	RiskFree Increments (0.30%)	RiskFree Increments (0.40%)	RiskFree Increments (0.50%)	
Initial Riskfree (2.00%)	2.0%	1.8%	1.8%	1.7%	1.7%	1.6%	1
Initial Riskfree (3.00%)	1.8%	1.7%	1.6%	1.6%	1.5%	1.5%	2
Initial Riskfree (4.00%)	1.7%	1.5%	1.5%	1.4%	1.4%	1.4%	3
Initial Riskfree (5.00%)	1.5%	1.4%	1.4%	1.3%	1.3%	1.2%	4
Initial Riskfree (6.00%)	1.4%	1.3%	1.3%	1.2%	1.2%	1.1%	5
Initial Riskfree (7.00%)	1.3%	1.2%	1.1%	1.1%	1.1%	1.0%	6
Initial Riskfree (8.00%)	1.2%	1.1%	1.0%	1.0%	1.0%	0.9%	7
	1	2	3	4	5	6	

FIGURE 13.48 American changing risk-free rate option (binomial lattices and GBM with changing risk-free rates).

holder has the right to execute the option at any time of his or her choosing, after some prespecified vesting period, and the underlying stocks sometimes pay dividends. As such, a BSM is insufficient in capturing a stock option's full fair market value.

This case study has further shown that the application of binomial lattices and American option approximation models provide a robust measurement of the fair value of American-type stock options paying dividends. Coupled with Monte Carlo simulation used in simulating various uncertain inputs, the resulting option valuation is very robust. In real-life conditions, stock options are usually American-type options with dividends, where the option holder can execute the option at any time up to and including the maturity date while the underlying stock pays dividends. Employee stock options have a time to vesting before the employee can execute the option, which is also contingent on the firm or the individual employee attaining a specific performance level (e.g., profitability, growth rate, stock price hitting a minimum barrier before the options become live), and the options are subject to forfeitures when the employee leaves the firm or is terminated prematurely before reaching the vested period. In addition, certain options follow a tranching or graduated scale, where a certain percentage of the stock option grants become exercisable every year, and if the firm underperforms, it may be required to repurchase the options at a specific termination price. Finally, the firm may undergo some corporate restructuring (e.g., divestitures, mergers, and acquisitions that may require a stock swap that changes the volatility of the underlying stock). All these real-life scenarios make the BSM and GBM insufficient and inappropriate when used to place a fair market value on the option grant. The only way the fair market value can be ascertained under these conditions is the application of binomial lattices in conjunction with Monte Carlo simulation, and now these seemingly complex calculations can be performed with ease and great efficiency with the advent of options valuation and simulation software.

More Industry Applications

CHAPTER 14

Extended Business Cases II: From Land to Money

This chapter provides two additional applied case studies. The first case is contributed by Robert Fourt and Professor Bill Rodney on real estate development using real options analysis techniques. For more details on the techniques used in this case—specifically relating to optimal timing, binomial lattices, and state-pricing approaches, refer to *Real Options Analysis* by Johnathan Mun (Wiley, 2002) and *Real Options Analysis Course* also by Johnathan Mun (Wiley, 2003). The second case is contributed by Professor Morton Glantz on the application of risk analysis, simulation, and optimization under uncertainty with respect to credit risk modeling in the banking industry.

CASE STUDY: UNDERSTANDING RISK AND OPTIMAL TIMING IN A REAL ESTATE DEVELOPMENT USING REAL OPTIONS ANALYSIS

This case study is contributed by Robert Fourt (contact: Gerald Eve, 7 Vere Street, London W1G OJB, UK, +44(0)2074933338, rfourt@geraldeve.com) and Bill Rodney (contact: Cass Business School, 106 Bunhill Row, London, EC1Y8TZ, UK, +44(0)2070408600, whr@dial.pipex.com). Robert is a partner within the planning and development team of UK-based real estate consultants, Gerald Eve. He specializes in development consultancy, providing advice on a wide range of schemes to corporate and public sector clients with a particular emphasis on strategy, finance, and project management. Gerald Eve is a multidisciplinary practice employing over 300 people operating from a head office in central London and a regional network that spans the United Kingdom. The firm provides specialist advice in all real estate sectors. Bill is a senior lecturer in real estate finance at the Cass Business School, as well as undertaking research and providing advice to a number of institutions on real estate risk analysis, financing strategies, and the risk pricing of PPP/PFI projects. The Cass Business School (part of the City University) is a leading European center for finance research, investment management, and risk assessment and benefits from its location in the heart of London's financial district and involvement of leading practitioners in its teaching and research.

Consideration of risk and its management is key in most real estate investment and development opportunities. Recognition of this, particularly in recent years, has led to various financial techniques being employed, including simulation analysis and Value at Risk (VaR), to assess various proposed transactions. The UK Investment Property Forum has sought to establish a real estate sector standard for risk. This standard for risk has provided a greater insight into the risk structure and returns on investments for management to review. Notwithstanding these approaches, they have nevertheless largely relied on traditional deterministic appraisals as a basis for assessing risk and return.

An addition to understanding the risks and returns of a project is to apply a real options analysis (ROA). In commercial real estate, the application of an ROA to date has largely been academically driven. While this has provided a strong theoretical base with complex numerical and analytical techniques employed, there has been limited practical application. This lack in some respects is surprising, given that real estate contains a multiplicity of embedded real options due to its intrinsic nature and that the sector operates under conditions of uncertainty. In particular, real estate development provides flexibility in deferring, commencing, or abandoning a project, which in turn are options that convey value.

This case example, which focuses on a large site in the town center of Croydon, 20 minutes from central London in the United Kingdom, highlights the differences of an investment's risk structure and average return when comparing a static net present value (NPV) to an ROA approach. It also illustrates the apparent irrationality of why land is left undeveloped in downtown locations despite the apparent redevelopment potential, an issue that has been the subject of several seminal real option real estate papers (see Notes at the end of this case).

The ROA approach for this example initially formed the basis for advice to the Council (local authority) who were working closely with an investor developer. For this case study, the analysis is from the perspective of the investor in seeking to understand the optimal timing for development and its associated risk structure. In order to maintain confidentiality and simplify certain steps, prices and issues referred to have been adapted.

The right or flexibility to develop (i.e., construct) land is a real option and this often comes in the form of an American Call option. This case study utilizes a binomial lattice approach and methodology. The call option is combined with an American Put to sell the site either to the Council at open market value (OMV) or as a result of compulsory purchase order (CPO). Therefore, the strategic decision is whether to defer, sell (i.e., abandon), or develop. This flexibility conveys value, which is not captured by a conventional deterministic or NPV appraisal.

A five-step ROA approach was adopted and comprised:

1. **Stage I**   Mapping or framing the problem.
2. **Stage II**   Base scoping appraisal (deterministic).
3. **Stage III**   Internal and external uncertainty inputs.
4. **Stage IV**   Real options quantitative analysis.
5. **Stage V**   Explanation and strategic decisions.

Three quantitative variations using a lattice approach were considered: a binomial lattice; state pricing; and a binomial lattice with two volatility variables. The reasoning for this approach is explained later. A Monte Carlo analysis was undertaken at both the deterministic analysis (Stage II) and with the ROA (Stage IV), which further illustrates the risk profile comparison between real options and NPV.

The lattice approach allows for decisions to be taken at each node. This features provides an investor with the ability to determine the optimal timing with respect to development, or to defer, or to abandon (disposal of the property).

The basic simplified details of this case study are as follows:

- An undeveloped town center site of approximately 2.43 ha (6 acres) adjacent to a major public transport interchange.
- A comprehensive mixed-use scheme has been granted planning permission comprising: a supermarket (7,756 sq m, 83,455 sq ft); retail units (6,532 sq m, 68,348 sq ft); restaurants and bar (7,724 sq m, 83,110 sq ft); health club and swimming pool (4,494 sq m, 48,355 sq ft); night club (3,718 sq m, 40,006 sq ft); casino (2,404 sq m, 25,867 sq ft); offices (12,620 sq m, 135,791 sq ft); and a car park (500 spaces).
- A Fund acquired part of the site (in a larger portfolio acquisition) at a book (accounting) cost of £8m, reflecting the development potential. It also inherited option agreements with other adjoining landowners in order to assemble the entirety of the site, which would result in a total site acquisition cost of £12.75m, thereby enabling the implementation of a comprehensive scheme.
- The costs of holding the site and keeping the options open with the other landowners are £150,000pa. Income from a car park on the site is £50,000pa. Therefore, net outgoings are £100,000pa (totaling £500k

over 5 years, that is, this is assumed to be an intrinsic sunk cost in developing the site).

■ The Council wishes to see the site comprehensively developed for the scheme and have granted permission. They also have a long-held objective of developing a sports and entertainment arena in the center of Croydon. Under an agreement with the investor in conjunction with granting the planning permission, the Council has said it would acquire the land at OMV (i.e., equivalent to the book cost) at any time up to 5 years from grant of planning permission should the investor wish to sell and not implement the scheme. Thereafter, the Council would acquire the site using CPO powers (a statutory procedure) if comprehensive development has not been started. The case for granting a CPO is believed to be given, among other reasons, due to the fragmented ownership and that this high-profile site has lain undeveloped for many years. Compensation from the Council to the Fund in acquiring the site via a CPO based on a *no scheme* world (i.e., ignoring any development potential) has been calculated at £5m.

Stage I: Mapping the Problem

Three basic real options were identified that conveyed *flexibility* in terms of optionality in real estate development. They were the option to abandon (i.e., sell), the option to defer investment, and the option to execute (i.e., implement the development). Any of these should be exercised prior to the expiration of 5 years given that the site would be compulsorily acquired at what the Fund estimated as being at subbook value under a CPO. In addition to these options, the option to alter the planning permission subject to market circumstances could also be added. While this would often occur in practice, it is not examined in this instance. The optionality of achieving an optimal tenant mix could also be considered.

As indicated earlier, these options are American (two Calls and one Put), although the decision just prior to the expiration of 5 years or the CPO could be considered a European Put and therefore should be calculated as such.

The Croydon market was considered uncertain in terms of occupier requirements and rental levels, which were sensitive to general real estate market movements for both offices and retail. The ability to attract a supermarket operator and a major office pre-let were seen as key prerequisites prior to implementation of construction. The scheme would not be developed speculatively.

An ROA strategy matrix was prepared. Table 14.1 provides a simplified summary. It is evident from Table 14.1 that even in applying a qualitative analysis, values may evolve asymmetrically. There could be a considerable

TABLE 14.1 ROA Development Strategy Matrix

Strategy/ Approach	Type of Development	Market Factors	Planning Issues	Timing	Embedded Option Appraisal
Pessimistic	Comprehensive Development	Poor office market; uncertain retail requirements	Reduce office content; reconfigure retail	3–5 yrs	Defer or sell
Cautious		Occupiers require 50% of offices; anchor retail tenant but at low rent gain	Consider phasing offices and retail (review planning obligations)	2–4 yrs	Defer or develop/ expansion option
Optimistic		Major office pre-let; quality anchor retailers secured; demand is high for all uses in the scheme	Consider increasing office content	1–3 yrs	Develop and expansion option

upside relative to the downside. It was a characteristic of the Croydon office market, for example, that other competitor office schemes if implemented could encourage office sector activity and upward pricing of space with a high probability of occupier relocations. In this instance the investor did not have other real estate holdings in the town center. If the investor did, implementation of the scheme may also be considered a strategic (growth) option and could be analyzed as such.

Stage II: Base-Scoping Approach

A cash-flow residual development appraisal was produced, with key value drivers of the scheme being the supermarket and office components accounting for 47.15 percent of the expected capital value of the entire project.

An overall blended yield of 7.8 percent was expected, which in market terms was considered cautious. An office rent of £215 per sq m (£20 per sq ft) was applied, although this was considered to have underperformed London's (and United Kingdom) office growth as illustrated in the two graphs in Figure 14.1. Total office returns also underperformed London (and the United Kingdom), which is in line with historic patterns for Croydon.

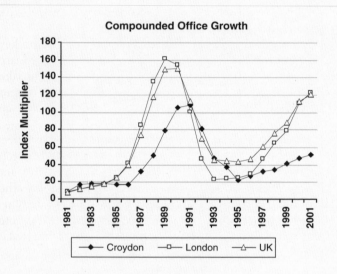

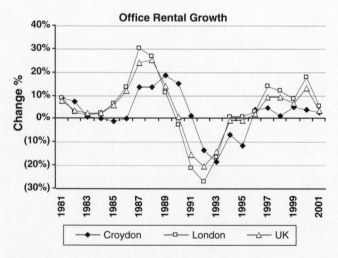

FIGURE 14.1   Croydon office rental and compounded growth. (*Source:* Data from IPD 2001)

Costs comprised land acquisition, construction, professional fees, other agents' fees and costs, and finance (rolled up interest on costs). Land and construction costs excluding profit totaled £90.48m. The gross development value (GDV) of the scheme was £105.76m. It was considered by the investor that, for a project of this scale, a developer's profit on cost of 17.5 percent would be required (although profit on land was acceptable at 10 percent). The scheme on this basis outlined previously was marginally producing a total profit of £15.28m, in other words, a deterministic (NPV) measure of development profit. The next stage was to consider the project risks in a state without strategic flexibility.

A Monte Carlo simulation analysis was undertaken based on key input variables of supermarket and office rents and yields and office construction costs (a fuller analysis with other variables was initially undertaken and then narrowed down to key variables together with preliminary sensitivity and scenario analysis). The results are shown in the frequency chart in Figure 14.2.

Figure 14.2 shows a mean total profit return of £13.7m (90 percent certainty range of £8.3m to £19.0m) against a minimum required return of £14.7m (assuming 10 percent and 17.5 percent profit on land and construction cost, respectively). These returns can be compared with the ROA and explanation that incorporate a simulation of the option values in Figure 14.7 and Table 14.3, which appear in a later section. It should be noted that the project risk testing and use of simulation analysis, as illustrated earlier, is in itself a complex area, as highlighted earlier in this book.

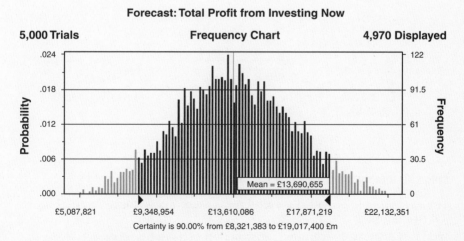

FIGURE 14.2 Base scoping Monte Carlo analysis.

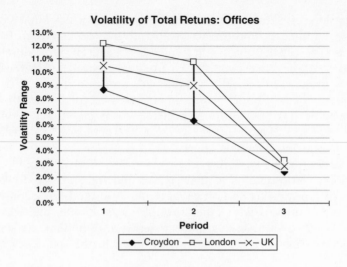

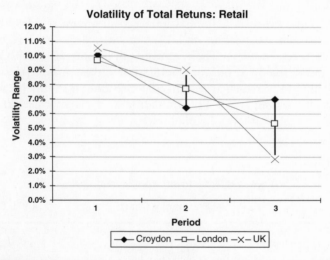

FIGURE 14.3   Croydon retail and office volatility of total returns. (*Source:* Data from IPD 2001)

Stage III: Internal and External Uncertainty Inputs

The base scoping provided a useful measure of the financial internal uncertainties and their interdependencies. In addition, it was necessary to regard specialist reports concerning construction constraints, cost variables, and programming. These also aided the simulation analysis in Stage II.

An ROA requires an assessment of volatility, a key input into the risk-neutral framework of real options pricing. In this instance state pricing was also used. An assessment of the magnitude of the upside and downside within an underlying lattice in order to capture the likely asymmetry of the Croydon market was therefore undertaken.

As volatility is key to ROA, research and subsequent analysis are critical in obtaining suitable input data and then reviewing the resultant computations in Stage V. Indexes, as outlined later, are based on professional valuations as opposed to market transactions. Academic papers have highlighted the potential for what is known as valuation "smoothing" within the indexes with the result that volatility of real estate may be understated. Various techniques and data sources have been used for backing out true, historic, implied, and expected volatility in real estate over alternative time-frames. However, this remains a significant area of research. The following approach has been simplified for practical reasons in obtaining appropriate volatility rates for this case study.

The U.K. Investment Property Databank (IPD) data on office and retail rental growth and total returns for Croydon, London, and the United Kingdom between 1981 and 2002 were analyzed. As investment performance is judged on total returns, it was these volatility figures that were used with respect to the underlying asset value. Volatility of total returns for office and retail for three periods—1981–2002(1); 1991–2002(2); and 1995–2001(3)—are shown in Figure 14.3. Both graphs show volatility decreasing over the three periods from a range of 8.6 percent to 12.1 percent (offices) and 6.4 percent to 8.7 percent (retail) to 2.4 percent to 3.3 percent (offices) and 1.15 percent to 3.4 percent (retail). These appear to be low volatility rates compared to empirical research.

Another way of considering the volatility over this period for offices and retail is on a 5-year rolling basis as shown in the two charts in Figure 14.4.

From Figure 14.4 we see that the Croydon office market showed an average volatility of 8.95 percent (range 2.2 percent to 14.7 percent), which was below both London (average 11.39 percent, range 4.1 percent to 24.1 percent) and the United Kingdom (average 10.12 percent, range 2.6 percent to 10.9 percent). For retail (except in Croydon) the volatility levels were generally lower than for offices, with the Croydon market showing an average of 10.27 percent (range 3.2 percent to 18.9 percent) compared with a London average of 9.29 percent (range 3.5 percent to 19 percent) and the United Kingdom average of 7.46 percent (range 1.5 percent to 14.3 percent).

It is necessary for the underlying asset to arrive at a single volatility, that is, combining retail and offices. Further research and analysis in practice was undertaken, including cross correlations. For the purposes here, a figure of 10 percent with an analysis range of between 5 percent and 35 percent is utilized, taking account of sector empirical studies and desmoothing of base indexes.

FIGURE 14.4　Croydon retail and office returns—5-year rolling volatility.
(*Source:* Data from IPD 2001)

So far as the price probability falls under the ROA analytical approach state pricing, this has regard to compounded growth in capturing the asymmetry of future underlying asset changes. Again, further research in practice was undertaken. Indeed, an alternative approach in option pricing would be via a jump-diffusion whereby an initial jump (i.e., upside) could be followed by a reversion to appropriate volatility levels. Nonrecombining lattices or multiple recombining lattices with changing volatilities could also achieve similar results. For state pricing, the upstate was assumed at 15 percent and downstate 5 percent. See Johnathan Mun's *Real Options Analysis Course* (Wiley, 2003) for technical details.

So far as costs were concerned, cost inflation was set at 5 percent and cost volatility at 5 percent. The latter was considered low in comparison to empirical examples and therefore was analyzed within a range of 5 percent to 25 percent. U.K.-published construction cost indexes have been criticized as not reflecting the true volatility found in the sector. This criticism has again led to other alternative measures and proxies being sought and analyzed, including traded call options of construction companies.

Stage IV: Real Options (Quantitative) Analysis

The three lattice approaches together with the inputs and assumptions outlined earlier were computed. The cost of implementation input excluded profit on cost and land in order to directly compare the option price to development profit. The value input was that derived from the deterministic appraisal. Under each approach, the lattices were as follows:

- An underlying asset pricing lattice, the price evolution.
- An underlying cost lattice, the cost growth or evolution.
- The value of exercising the development, in simple terms the NPV in each moment of time of making an investment.
- A valuation lattice, where the value would be the maximum of price less cost; the option to defer less the intrinsic sunk costs; or the offer to be acquired by the Council. The termination boundary (year 5) would be the maximum of the underlying price less costs or the offer to be acquired by the Council.
- A decision lattice, which was based on the valuation lattice in determining at each node whether to defer, sell, or develop.

Option values were calculated under each of the three approaches, which were then compared to the development profit of the deterministic approach, as shown in Table 14.2. In each case the value (profit) of the

TABLE 14.2 A Comparison of Real Option Values with NPV

NPV (£m)	ROA		
	Binomial (£m)	State Pricing (£m)	Binomial (Dual Volatility) (£m)
15.28[a]	18.13	18.09	23.77
Additional Value Created by ROA	2.85	2.81	8.49

[a]This amount represents the total profit of investing now of which £14.7m would be the minimum required return.

option to defer (i.e., now or later) is higher than the current or expected profit of investing immediately. The difference in the real option values results from the evolution of the lattice and risk-neutral pricing of each approach.

Stage V: Explanation

The option price takes into account all possible future outcomes under the three ROA approaches that were not captured by the deterministic analysis. It was, however, necessary to consider the sensitivity of the inputs, particularly with respect to volatility (price and cost) and price probabilities under state pricing as well as the impact on the decision lattice at the different nodes. The decision lattices in Figure 14.5 (with time in years in bold) are set out for comparative purposes.

Taking an overview with regard to all of the approaches, development should probably be deferred in years 1 and 2; deferral or selling were the dominant options in year 3; and development should only probably be envisaged in years 4 or 5. This scheme essentially provided an analytical underpinning for a professional judgment and decision framework. The surface graphs in Figure 14.6 illustrated the sensitivity for each approach. Figure 14.6 clearly indicated the effect and interaction of volatility on the option price (OP), which again emphasized the importance attached to establishing base volatility inputs as discussed earlier in Stage II. This analysis in practice was analyzed and reported on further. A Monte Carlo analysis of each option price was undertaken and the frequency charts are set out in Figure 14.7 together with a certainty level of 90 percent. These charts can be compared to the base-scoping frequency chart (Figure 14.2) and illustrate the narrowing (particularly with state pricing) of the risk structure and higher average return.

It was notable that the risk structure range's downside of the three approaches was relatively similar, being between £16.2m and £18.6m (see Table 14.3 on page 340). In this particular instance the downsides provided useful benchmarks to the minimum required return of £14.7m under an NPV approach, as an alternative measure to comparing average returns. Notwithstanding this NPV result, the upsides under the three approaches were significant.

The investor, as a result of an ROA, could clearly form a strategy in terms of optimal timing or whether to invest at all. The flexibility of this decision created additional value over and above a conventional valuation of the development. This additional value would perhaps be incorporated within a price, if the investor were to dispose of the opportunity to a third party at the beginning of the period.

Binomial

0	1	2	3	4	5
					Develop
			Develop		
		Develop		Develop	
	Defer			Defer	
	Defer		Defer		Sell
Defer		Defer		Sell	
	Defer		Sell		Sell
	Sell		Sell		
		Sell		Sell	
			Sell		
					Sell

State Pricing

0	1	2	3	4	5
					Develop
			Develop		
		Develop		Develop	
	Develop		Develop		
	Defer		Develop		Develop
Defer		Defer		Defer	
	Defer		Defer		Sell
	Defer		Sell		
		Sell		Sell	
			Sell		
					Sell

Price & Cost Volatility

0	1	2	3	4	5
					Develop
			Defer		
		Defer		Defer	
	Defer		Defer		Develop
	Defer		Defer		
Defer		Defer		Defer	Develop
	Defer		Defer		
	Defer		Defer		Develop
		Sell		Defer	
			Sell		Sell
					Sell

FIGURE 14.5 Binomial lattices.

(A) Binomial Lattice: Price Volatility & Time Sensitivity

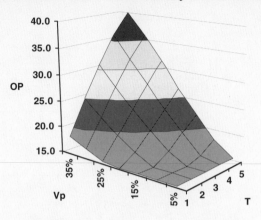

(B) State Pricing: Up & Down Sensitivity

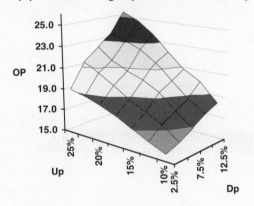

(C) Cost & Value Volatility Sensitivity

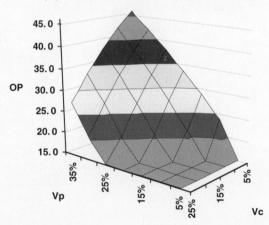

FIGURE 14.6 Croydon ROA sensitivity graphs.

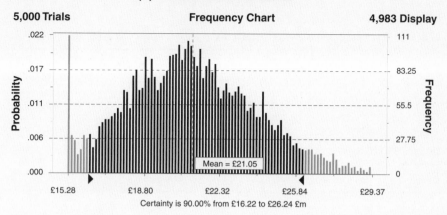

(A) Forecast: Binomial Lattice

5,000 Trials   Frequency Chart   4,983 Display

Certainty is 90.00% from £16.22 to £26.24 £m

Mean = £21.05

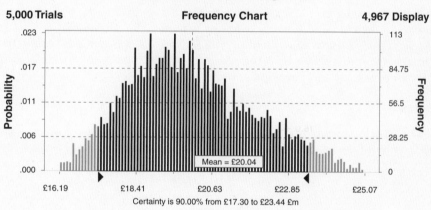

(B) Forecast: State Pricing

5,000 Trials   Frequency Chart   4,967 Display

Certainty is 90.00% from £17.30 to £23.44 £m

Mean = £20.04

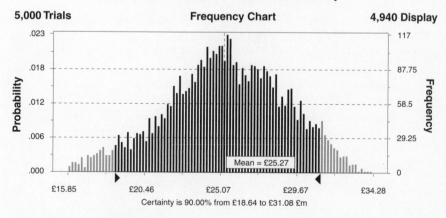

(C) Forecast: Binomial: Price & Cost Volatility

5,000 Trials   Frequency Chart   4,940 Display

Certainty is 90.00% from £18.64 to £31.08 £m

Mean = £25.27

FIGURE 14.7   ROA Monte Carlo application.

TABLE 14.3   Simulated NPV and Option Values Croydon (Average and Range)

	Average Return (£m)	Risk Structure Range 90% (£m)	Percentage Above Required Return (£m)
NPV	13.7	8.3–19.0	(6.8)
Binomial Lattice	21.1	16.2–26.2	43.5
State Pricing	20.6	17.3–23.4	40.0
Binomial (Cost/Price Volatility)	25.1	18.6–31.1	70.7

The real option paradigm when applied to real estate potentially high-lights, on one hand, the seemingly intuitive action of investors and, on the other hand, undervalued investment opportunities and suboptimal decisions. As such the ROA, as illustrated previously, therefore provides another approach and valuable layer to the risk analysis and potential returns of real estate investment and development.

Notes

The following papers provide further reading on the subjects of investment risk, volatility measures, and real options in real estate development.

Brown, G., and G. Matysiak. *Real Estate Investment, A Capital Market Approach*. London: Financial Times Prentice Hall, 2000.

Grenadier, S. "The Strategic Exercise of Options: Development Cascades and Overbuilding in Real Estate Markets." *Journal of Finance* 51, no. 5 (1996): 1653–1679.

Quigg, L. "Empirical Testing of Real Option-Pricing Models." *Journal of Finance* 68, no. 2 (1993): 621–639.

Sing T. (2001), "Optimal Timing of Real Estate Development under Uncertainty." *Journal of Property Investment & Finance*, Special Issue: Real Options, 19, no. 1 (2001): 35–52.

Titman, S. (1985) "Urban Land Prices under Uncertainty." *The American Economic Review* 75, no. 3 (1985): 505–514.

Ward C. "Arbitrage and Investment in Commercial Property." *Journal of Business & Accounting* 9, no. 1 (1982): 93–108.

Williams, J. (1991), "Real Estate Development as an Option." *Journal of Real Estate Finance and Economics* 4, no. 2 (1991): 191–208.

CASE STUDY: USING STOCHASTIC OPTIMIZATION AND VALUATION MODELS TO EVALUATE THE CREDIT RISK OF CORPORATE RESTRUCTURING

This business case is contributed by Professor Morton Glantz. The models used in this case are included on the enclosed CD-ROM. The files start with the name Credit Risk Models. Professor Glantz is on the finance faculty of Fordham Graduate Business School in New York. He is widely published in financial journals and has authored a number of books, including Optimal Trading Strategies, Managing Bank Risk, Scientific Financial Management, *and* Loan Management Risk. *He is a financial advisor to government and business, and can be reached at* mglantz1@msn.com.

Companies restructure their product mix to boost sales and profits, increase shareholder value, or to survive when the corporate structure becomes impaired. In successful restructurings, management not only actualizes lucrative new projects, but abandons existing projects when they no longer yield sufficient returns, thereby channeling resources to more value-creating uses.

At one level, restructuring can be viewed as changes in financing structures and management. At another level, restructuring may be operational—in response to production overhauls, market trends, technology, and industry or macroeconomic disturbances. It is often the essence of strategy formulation, that is, management's response to changes in the environment to creatively deploy internal resources that improves the firm's competitive position. Indeed, changing operating and financial structures in pursuit of a long-run strategy is a key corporate goal—the most direct path to shareholder value.

For banks called on to finance corporate restructurings, things are a bit different. For example, most loans provide a fixed return over fixed periods that are dependent on interest rates and the borrower's ability to pay. A good loan will be repaid on time and in full. It is hoped that the bank's cost of funds will be low, with the deal providing attractive risk-adjusted returns. If the borrower's business excels, *the bank will not participate in upside corporate values* (except for a vicarious pleasure in the firm's success). However, if a borrower ends up financially distressed, lenders share much, perhaps most, of the pain.

Two disparate goals—controlling default (credit) risk, the bank's objective, and value maximization, a traditional corporate aspiration—are often at odds, particularly if borrowers want term money to finance excessively aggressive projects. In the vast majority of cases of traditional credit analysis, where the spotlight focuses on deterministically drawn projections, hidden risks are often exceedingly difficult to uncover. Devoid of viable projections, bankers will time and again fail to bridge gaps between their agendas and client aspirations.

This case study offers ways for bankers to advance both their analytics and communication skills—senior bank officials and clients alike to "get the deal done" and ensure risk/reward agendas are set in equilibrium. Undeniably, the direct way to achieve results is to take a stochastic view of strategic plans rather than relying inappropriately on deterministic base case or conservative scenarios. Let us start with the following fundamentals:

- Stochastically driven optimization models allow bankers to more realistically represent the flow of random variables.
- In negotiating restructuring loans, borrowers (and bankers) can determine under stochastic assumptions optimal amounts to invest in or borrow to finance projects.
- McKinsey & Company, Inc.[1] suggests that business units should be defined and separated into lines of business. Business units should be broken down into the smallest components and analyzed at the base level first.
- Consolidating financials, rather than consolidated reports, should be used to perform business-unit valuations.
- Knowing the market value and volatility of the borrower's assets is crucial in determining the probability of default.
- A firm's leverage has the effect of magnifying its underlying asset volatility. As a result, industries with low-asset volatility can take on larger amounts of leverage, whereas industries with high-asset volatility tend to take on less.
- After restructuring is optimized at the unit stage, unit level valuations are linked to the borrower's consolidated worksheet to process corporate valuations.

The Business Case

Consider the data in Excel spreadsheets depicted in Figures 14.8, 14.9, and 14.10. The worksheets depict management's original restructuring plan. ABC Bank is asked to approve a $3,410,000 loan facility for the hypothetical firm RI Furniture Manufacturing LTD. Management wants to restructure four of its operating subsidiaries. In support of the facility, the firm supplied the bank with deterministic base case and conservative consolidating and consolidated projections—income statement, balance sheet, and cash flows.

The deterministic or static forecasts tendered the bank limited the variability of outcomes. From a banker's perspective it is often difficult to single out which of a series of *strategic options* the borrower should pursue if the bank fails to understand differences in the range and distribution shape of possible outcomes and the most likely result associated with each option. Indeed an overly aggressive restructuring program might reduce the firm's credit grade and increase default probabilities. We will not let this happen. Undeniably, this deal deserves stochastic analytics rather than a breadbasket consisting of passé deterministic tools.

From (deterministic) consolidating projections, bankers developed a stochastic spreadsheet depicted in Figure 14.10. This spreadsheet included maximum/minimum investment ranges supporting restructuring in each of four product lines. Using Crystal Ball's OptQuest along with the deterministic McKinsey DCF Valuation 2000 Model, the firm's bankers came up with a stochastic solution. On a unit level, they developed a probability distribution assigned to each uncertain element in the forecast, established an optimal funding array for the various business combinations, held cash-flow volatility to acceptable levels preserving the credit grade (again at the unit level). Finally, the last optimization (worksheet) was linked to the consolidating/consolidated DCF valuation worksheet(s). The firm's bankers then determined postrestructuring equity values, specific confidence levels, and probabilities that asset values fall below debt values.

Business History

RI Furniture started operations in 1986. The firm manufactures a full line of indoor and outdoor furniture. Operating subsidiaries targeted for restructuring, depicted later, represent approximately 65 percent of consolidated operations.

- *All Weather Resin Wicker Sets.* This furniture comes with a complete aluminum frame with handwoven polypropylene resin produced to resist weather. *Operating profit margin distributions and investment ranges for each subsidiary are shown in Figures 14.8 through 14.10.*
- *Commuter Mobile Office Furniture.* The commuter rolls from its storage location to any work area and sets up in minutes. It integrates computer peripherals (monitor, CPU tower, keyboard, and printer) in a compact, secure mobile unit.
- *Specialty Furniture.* After restructuring, this business segment will include production of hotel reception furniture, cafe furniture, canteen furniture, restaurant seating, and banqueting furniture.
- *Custom-Built Furniture.* Furniture will be custom built, in the firm's own workshop or sourced from a host of reputable manufacturers both at home and abroad.

	Distribution	Operating Profit Margin Range	Operating Profit Margin Most Likely
All Weather Resin Wicker Sets	Triangular	5.5% – 12.6%	11.0%
Commuter Mobile Office Furniture	Triangular	6.5% – 8.7%	7.5%
Specialty Furniture	Triangular	0.5% – 5.3%	4.7%
Custom Built Furniture	Uniform	3.3% – 6.6%	None

FIGURE 14.8   Distributional assumptions.

Product Line	Lower Bound	Upper Bound
All Weather Resin Wicker Sets	1,000,000	1,250,000
Commuter Mobile Office Furniture	600,000	1,000,000
Specialty Furniture	570,000	1,100,000
Custom Built Furniture	400,000	900,000

FIGURE 14.9   Investment boundaries.

Open the Excel worksheet *Credit Risk Model—OptimizeRIFurnOriginal* and set up Run One by placing a constraint on $3,410,000 investment— that is, the bank's facility cannot exceed $3,410,000. Later we place an additional constraint: the forecast variable's volatility. From the information in Figures 14.8 and 14.9, the bank developed the spreadsheet depicted in Figure 14.10.

Using OptQuest, a constraint on investment/loan facility was entered:

All Weather Resin Wicker Sets + Commuter Mobile Office Furniture + Specialty Furniture + Custom Built Furniture <=3410000.

Crystal Ball macros were used to copy results to the original spreadsheet with results depicted in Figure 14.11. Note that investment falls to within the constraint boundary, while expected return increased.

Simulation statistics reveal that volatility of the expected return (the forecast variable), as measured by the standard deviation, was $20,000. Again, *volatility of operating results affects the volatility of assets*. This point is important. Suppose we determine the market value of a corporation's assets as well as the volatility of that value. Moody's KMV demonstrates that volatility measures the propensity of asset values to change within a given time period. This information determines the probability of default, given

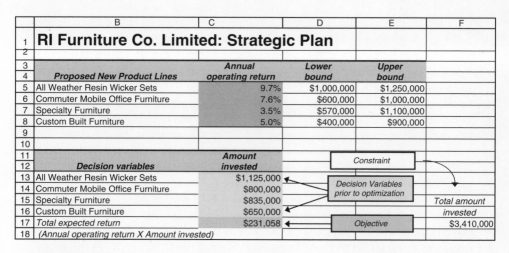

	B	C	D	E	F
1	**RI Furniture Co. Limited: Strategic Plan**				
2					
3		*Annual*	*Lower*	*Upper*	
4	*Proposed New Product Lines*	*operating return*	*bound*	*bound*	
5	All Weather Resin Wicker Sets	9.7%	$1,000,000	$1,250,000	
6	Commuter Mobile Office Furniture	7.6%	$600,000	$1,000,000	
7	Specialty Furniture	3.5%	$570,000	$1,100,000	
8	Custom Built Furniture	5.0%	$400,000	$900,000	
9					
10					
11		*Amount*		Constraint	
12	*Decision variables*	*invested*			
13	All Weather Resin Wicker Sets	$1,125,000		Decision Variables	
14	Commuter Mobile Office Furniture	$800,000		prior to optimization	
15	Specialty Furniture	$835,000			*Total amount*
16	Custom Built Furniture	$650,000			*invested*
17	*Total expected return*	$231,058		Objective	$3,410,000
18	*(Annual operating return X Amount invested)*				

FIGURE 14.10 Borrower's original strategic restructuring plan (reworked by the bank in a stochastic mode, not yet optimized).

	B	C	D	E	F
10					
11		*Amount*		Constraint	
12	*Decision variables*	*invested*			
13	All Weather Resin Wicker Sets	$1,247,100		Decision Variables prior	
14	Commuter Mobile Office Furniture	$993,671		to optimization	
15	Specialty Furniture	$570,000			*Total amount*
16	Custom Built Furniture	$598,998			*invested*
17	*Total expected return*	$245,757		Objective	$3,409,769
18	*(Annual operating return X Amount invested)*				
19					

Forecast: Total expected return

Edit Preferences View Run Help

Cell C17 **Statistics**

Statistic	Value
Trials	1,000
Mean	$248,203
Median	$249,817
Mode	---
Standard Deviation	$20,373
Variance	$415,070,724
Skewness	-0.31
Kurtosis	2.70
Coeff. of Variability	0.08
Range Minimum	$186,464
Range Maximum	$300,475
Range Width	$114,011
Mean Std. Error	$644.26

FIGURE 14.11 Run Two optimization results.

the corporation's obligations. For instance, KMV suggests that if the current asset market value is $150 million and a corporation's debt is $75 million and is due in 1 year, then default will occur if the asset value turns out to be less than $75 million in 1 year. Thus, as a prudent next step, bankers discuss the first optimization run (Figure 14.11) with management on three levels: (1) maximum expected return, (2) optimal investments/loan facility, and (3) volatility of expected return. If volatility is unacceptable, the standard deviation must be reduced to preserve credit grade integrity. We assume the bank requires project standard deviation to be equal to or below $17,800 as shown in Figure 14.12 *(Requirement total expected return Std_Dev <=17800)*.

The final simulation shown in Figure 14.13 produced an optimization that reconciled both risk/reward agendas discussed earlier. The loan facility effectively reduces to (optimized) $3,331,102, and because the firm requires less money, financial leverage improves. We note that $227,889 is the maximized expected return, lower than the $245,757 produced with no volatility constraint—lower risk reduces rewards.

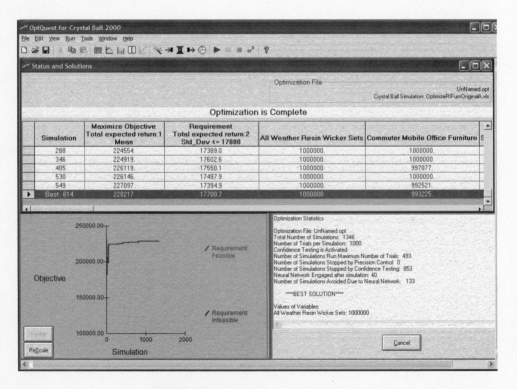

FIGURE 14.12   Optimization windows.

	B	C	D	E	F
10					
11		*Amount*		Constraint	
12	*Decision variables*	*invested*			
13	All Weather Resin Wicker Sets	$1,000,000	Decision Variables		
14	Commuter Mobile Office Furniture	$993,225	prior to optimization		
15	Specialty Furniture	$723,457			Total amount
16	Custom Built Furniture	$614,420			invested
17	Total expected return	$227,889		Objective	$3,331,102
18	(Annual operating return X Amount invested)				
19		Expected	Total		
20	Summary	Return	Investment	Standard Deviation	
21	Borrower's Original Projections	$231,058	$3,410,000	n/a	
22	Run One: Original Projections Optimized	$245,757	$3,409,769	$20,373	
23	Run Two: Project Volitility Constraint	$227,889	$3,331,102	$17,800	
24	Run Two: Project Volitility Actual			$17,701	
25	Expected Return and Loan Reduction	$17,868	$78,667		
26	(Bank Requirement: Reduce Project Risk)				
27					
28			Run One	Run Two	
29	Investment (Loan Amounts)	Original Strategy	Optimized; No	Optimized; Risk	
30		Not Optimized	Risk Constraint	Constraint	
31	All Weather Resin Wicker Sets	$1,125,000	$1,247,100	$1,000,000	
32	Commuter Mobile Office Furniture	$800,000	$993,671	$993,225	
33	Specialty Furniture	$835,000	$570,000	$723,457	
34	Custom Built Furniture	$650,000	$598,998	$614,420	
35	Total	$3,410,000	$3,409,769	$3,331,102	

FIGURE 14.13   Final optimization results.

The story does not end here; our analysis up to now was restricted to the unit level—that is, business segments involved in the restructuring. While the spreadsheet in Figure 14.13 worked its stochastic wonders, it *must now link to consolidating and consolidated discounted cash-flow (DCF) valuation worksheets.* Consolidated DCF valuations provide a *going-concern* value—the value driven by a company's future economic strength. RI Furniture value is determined by the present value of future cash flows for a specific forecast horizon (projection period) plus the present value of cash flow *beyond* the forecast horizon (residual or terminal value). In other words, the firm's value depends on cash-flow potential and the risks (threats) of those future cash flows. It is these perceived risks or threats that help define the discounting factor used to measure cash flows in present value terms. Cash flow depends on the industry and the economic outlook for the RI Furniture's products, current and future competition, sustainable competitive advantage, projected changes in demand, and this borrower's capacity to grow in light of its past financial and operating performance. Risk factors that the firm's bankers will examine carefully include their borrower's financial condition; quality, magnitude, and volatility of cash flows; financial and operating leverage; and management's capacity to sustain operations on a profitable basis. *These primary attributes cannot be ignored when bankers determine distributions associated with assumption variables.*

Sensitivity Chart

Target Forecast: Shareholder Value

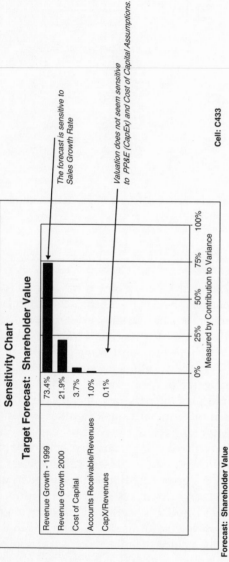

Revenue Growth - 1999	73.4%
Revenue Growth 2000	21.9%
Cost of Capital	3.7%
Accounts Receivable/Revenues	1.0%
CapX/Revenues	0.1%

Measured by Contribution to Variance

The forecast is sensitive to Sales Growth Rate

Valuation does not seem sensitive to PP&E (CapEx) and Cost of Capital Assumptions.

Forecast: Shareholder Value

Summary:

Certainty Level is 0.10%
Certainty Range is from -Infinity to 7,500.0
Display Range is from 7,500.0 to 27,500.0
Entire Range is from 6,654.6 to 26,266.6
After 1,000 Trials, the Std. Error of the Mean is 115.7

Statistics:

	Value
Trials	1,000.0
Mean Sharderholder Value	*17,211.4*
Median Shareholder Value	*17,322.8*
Mode	- - -
Standard Deviation	3,660.1
Variance	13,396,134.5
Skewness	-0.21
Kurtosis	2.49
Coeff. of Variability	0.21
Range Minimum	6,654.6
Range Maximum	26,266.6
Range Width	19,612.0
Mean Std. Error	115.74

Cell: C433

This means that there is almost a zero probability that shareholder value falls below $11 million. Thus, the EDF's or Expected Default Factor is zero. S & P would rate this company AAA

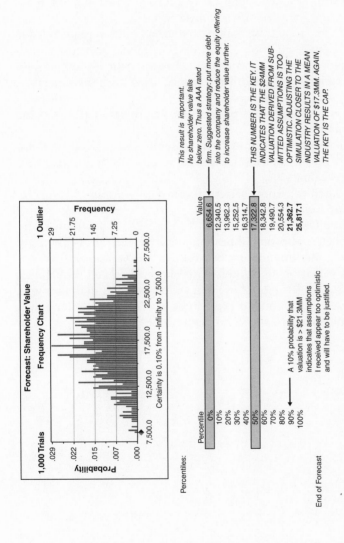

FIGURE 14.14 Crystal Ball partial report explained.

Crystal Ball (CB) embedded into powerful valuation models provides an intuitive advantage; it is a decidedly efficient and precise way to get deals analyzed, done, and sold. Summarizing, seven suggestions are offered:

1. Use consolidating financials to determine valuation building blocks intrinsic in operating segments you are analyzing. Consolidated statements alone do not provide sufficient answers.
2. Employ the McKinsey DCF Valuation 2000 Model software included in the previously mentioned book *Valuation*. The model contains preformatted financial statements and analytical reports for evaluating performance and valuing projected performance using both the Enterprise DCF and Economic Profit approaches.
3. Enter the borrower's most likely projections, adding residual period and cost of capital assumptions.
4. Start CB and determine the value drivers (assumption variables) and distributions—first on the unit level, then use results to refine consolidating/consolidated valuations.
5. On the consolidated valuation, select a forecast cell—*Equity Value, Operating Value,* or *Enterprise Value.*
6. Run a simulation. Determine the forecast variable's value within a confidence level. Then find probabilities that equity value falls below zero. The last step is quite illuminating because *within the universe or constraints* of your valuation model, this is the expected default probability.
7. Run a CB report. Finally, if borrowers or colleagues are unfamiliar with CB report statistics, take time to explain the key numbers. Enter explanations along the margins, shown in Figure 14.14.

Risk Management

CHAPTER 15

The Warning Signs

T he finding of absence is very different from an absence of findings. How does management appropriately evaluate the validity and applicability of analytical results? How should management challenge the assumptions used in the analysis? What are some of the questions that should be asked? This chapter deals with some of the more difficult questions when evaluating the results of Monte Carlo simulation, time-series forecasting, stochastic optimization, and real options analysis.

THE PROBLEM OF NEGLIGENT ENTRUSTMENT

Power tools such as Crystal Ball Professional, Predictor, OptQuest, and Real Options Analysis Toolkit took years to build and many more years to be perfected. It is extremely likely that a new user can simply pick up software products such as these and hit the ground running immediately. However, some knowledge of the theoretical underpinnings is required. In short, to create and perform sophisticated modeling, the analyst first needs to understand some of the underlying assumptions and approaches used in these analytics. Otherwise, it is akin to giving a 3-year-old child a loaded machine gun. The correct term for this situation might be "negligent entrustment." In fact, when the rubber meets the road, more often than not, even so-called *power users* are perplexed and have a difficult time using these tools with respect to their models and business cases. These software tools, despite their analytical power are just tools. They do not replace the analyst in any way. In fact, tools such as these only accouter the analyst with analytics at their fingertips and do not by themselves make the relevant decisions. Such tools only relieve the analyst from having facility with fancy mathematics in order to build sophisticated models. As stated previously, 50 percent of the challenge in decision making is simply thinking about the problem, with 25 percent being the actual modeling and analytics, and the remaining 25 percent being able to convince and explain the results to senior management, clients, colleagues, and yourself.

MANAGEMENT'S DUE DILIGENCE

It might be the job of the analyst to create the models and use the fancy analytics, but it is senior management's job to challenge the assumptions and results obtained from said analysis. For instance, Figure 15.1 lists some of the issues that may arise when running a multivariate regression analysis and time-series forecasting. Although it may not be senior management's job to understand the mathematical or theoretical implications of these issues, management must nonetheless have a good grasp of what they mean.

The following sections are written specifically for senior management who are recipients of different types of advanced analyses results. The next section starts off with a general set of warning signs and moves on to the specifics of each analytical methodology used throughout this book.

SINS OF AN ANALYST

In general, warning signs can be grouped into five categories:

1. Model errors.
2. Assumption and input errors.
3. Analytical errors.
4. User errors.
5. Interpretation errors.

- Out of Range Forecasts
- Structural Breaks
- Specification Errors
- Omitted and Redundant Variables
- Heteroskedasticity and Homoskedasticity
- Multicollinearity
- Spurious Regression and Time Dependency
- Autocorrelation and Serial Correlation
- Correlation versus Causation
- Random Walks
- Mean Reversions
- Jump Processes
- Stochastic Processes

FIGURE 15.1   Warning signs in regression analysis.

Model errors are the errors an analyst would make while creating models. For instance, a financial model created in Excel may have errors stemming from broken links, incorrect functions and equations, poor modeling practices, or a break in the knowledge transfer between the originator of the model and subsequent users as well as successors of the model. This error can be eliminated through diligence on the part of the model creator. Good model-building practices also can assist in eliminating messy models. These practices include:

- Good documentation of the approaches used in the model as well as the integration and connectivity of the subparts that exist in the model.
- Creating a starting page that is linked through hyperlinks or macros with sufficient descriptions of each subpage or worksheet.
- Differentiate assumption input sheets from the models actually performing the number crunching, and from the results or reports page.
- Allow changes to be made only on the input assumptions page and not directly in the model to prevent accidentally breaking the model.

For a detailed listing of good model-building practices and modeling etiquette, refer to Chapter 3, A Gentleman's Guide to Model Building.

Assumption and input errors are more difficult to tackle. These errors include the inputs required to make the model compute; for example, items such as levels of competitive threats, levels of technological success, revenue projections, income growth rates, market share determination, and so forth. Many of these determinant factors are almost impossible to determine. In fact, the old adage of *garbage in, garbage out* holds true here. The analyst can only do so much.

Multiple approaches exist to help clean up these so-called garbage assumptions. One way is simply to use expert knowledge and advice. For instance, the Delphi method requires the presence of a group of expert engineers in a room to discuss the levels of technological success rates. These engineers with intimate knowledge of the potential success rates are able to provide valuable insights that would otherwise be unavailable to a financial analyst sitting in front of a computer, far removed from the everyday technological challenges. Senior management, based on their many years of experience and expertise, can often provide valuable insights into what certain market outcomes may be. A double-blind experiment also can be conducted, where experts in a group are asked on anonymous questionnaires what their objective estimates of an outcome are. These quantitative outcomes are then tabulated and, on occasion, more experienced participants' comments will be weighted more heavily. The expected value is then used in the model. Here, Monte Carlo simulation can be applied on the distribution of the outcomes related to these expert testimonies. A custom distribution can be constructed using Crystal Ball, which relates back to the weights given to each outcome, or a simple nonparametric bootstrap simulation can also be applied on all possible outcomes obtained. Obviously, if there are ample historical data, then it is relatively easier to project the future, whether it is using some time-series forecast, regression analysis, or Monte Carlo simulation. That is, *when in doubt, simulate!* Instead of arguing and relying on a particular single-point input value of a particular variable, an analyst can just simulate it around the potential outcomes of that input, whether it is the worst-case scenario, nominal-case scenario, or best-case scenario using a triangular distribution or some other distribution through expert assumptions.

No matter the approach used to obtain the data, management must test and challenge these assumptions. One way is to create tornado and sensitivity charts. The variables that drive the bottom line the most (the variable of interest, e.g., net present value, net income, return on investment) that are unpredictable and subject to uncertain levels of fluctuations are the ones that management should focus on. These critical success factors are the ones that management should care about, not some random variable that has little to no effect on the bottom line no matter how attractive or important the variable may be in other instances.

The upshot being that the more expert knowledge and historical data that exist, the better the assumption estimates will be. A good test of the assumptions used is through the application of back-casting, as opposed to forecasting, which looks forward into the future. Back-casting uses historical data to test the validity of the assumptions. One approach is to take the historical data, fit them to a distribution using Crystal Ball's distributional-fitting routines, and test the assumption input. Observe where the assumption value falls within this historical distribution. If it falls outside of the distribution's normal set of parameters (e.g., 95 percent or 99 percent confidence intervals), then the analyst should be able to better describe why there will be a potential structural shift going forward (e.g., mergers and acquisition, divestiture, reallocation of resources, economic downturn, entry of formidable competition, and so forth). In forecasting, similar approaches can be used such as historical data-fitting of the forecast model and holdout approaches (i.e., some historical data are left out in the original forecast model but are used in the subsequent forecast-fitting to verify the model's accuracy).

Reading the Warning Signs in Monte Carlo Simulation

Monte Carlo simulation is a very potent methodology. Statisticians and mathematicians sometimes dislike it because it solves difficult and often intractable problems with too much simplicity and ease. Instead, mathematical purists would prefer the more elegant approach: the old fashioned way. Solving a fancy stochastic mathematical model provides a sense of accomplishment and completion as opposed to the brute force method. Monte Carlo creates artificial futures by generating thousands and even millions of sample paths of outcomes and looks at their prevalent characteristics. For analysts in a company, taking graduate-level advanced mathematics courses is neither logical nor practical. A brilliant analyst would use all available tools at his or her disposal to obtain the same answer the easiest way possible. One such tool is Monte Carlo simulation using Crystal Ball. The major benefit that Crystal Ball brings is its simplicity of use. The major downfall that Crystal Ball brings is also its simplicity of use!

Here are 14 due-diligence issues management should evaluate when an analyst presents a report with a series of advanced analytics using simulation.

1. How Are the Distributions Obtained?   One thing is certain: If an analyst provides a report showing all the fancy analyses undertaken and one of these analyses is the application of Monte Carlo simulation of a few dozen variables, where each variable has the same distribution (e.g., triangular distribution), management should be very worried indeed and with good reason. One might be able to accept the fact that a few variables are triangularly distributed, but to assume that this holds true for several dozen other variables is ludicrous. One way to test the validity of distributional assumptions is to apply historical data to the distribution and see how far off one is.

Another approach is to take the distribution and test its alternate parameters. For instance, if a normal distribution is used on simulating market share, and the mean is set at 55 percent with a standard deviation of 35 percent, one should be extremely worried. Using Crystal Ball's alternate-parameter function, the 5th and 95th percentiles indicate a value of –2.57 percent and 112.57 percent. Clearly these values cannot exist under actual conditions. How can a product have –2.57 or 112.57 percent of the market share? The alternate-parameters function is a very powerful tool to use in conditions such as these. Almost always, the first thing that should be done is the use of alternate parameters to ascertain the logical upper and lower values of an input parameter.

2. How Sensitive Are the Distributional Assumptions?   Obviously, not all variables under the sun should be simulated. For instance, a U.S.-based firm doing business within the 48 contiguous states should not have to worry about what happens to the foreign exchange market of the Zairian zaire. Risk is something one bears and is the outcome of uncertainty. Just because there is uncertainty, there could very well be no risk. If the only thing that bothers a U.S.-based firm's CEO is the fluctuation of the Zairian zaire, then

I might suggest shorting some zaires and shifting his or her portfolio to U.S.-based bonds.

In short, simulate when in doubt, but simulate the variables that actually have an impact on what you are trying to estimate. Two very powerful tools to decide which variables to analyze are tornado and sensitivity charts. Make sure the simulated variables are the critical success factors—variables that have a significant impact on the bottom line being estimated while at the same time being highly uncertain and beyond the control of management.

3. What Are the Critical Success Factors? Critical success factors are related to how sensitive the resulting bottom line is to the input variables and assumptions. The first step that should be performed before using Monte Carlo simulation is the application of tornado charts. Tornado charts help identify which variables are the most critical to analyze. Coupled with management's and the analyst's expertise, the relevant critical success factors—the variables that drive the bottom line the most while being highly uncertain and beyond the control of management—can be determined and simulated. Obviously the most sensitive variables should receive the most amount of attention.

4. Are the Assumptions Related, and Have Their Relationships Been Considered? Simply defining assumptions on variables that have significant impact without regard to their interrelationships is also a major error most analysts make. For instance, when an analyst simulates revenues, he or she could conceivably break the revenue figures into price and quantity, where the resulting revenue figure is simply the product of price and quantity. The problem is if both price and quantity are considered as independent variables occurring in isolation, a major error arises. Clearly, for most products, the law of demand in economics takes over, where the higher the price of a product, ceteris paribus, or holding everything else constant, the quantity demanded of the same product decreases. Ignoring this simple economic truth, where both price and quantity are assumed to occur independently of one another, means that the possibility of a high price and a high quantity demanded may occur simultaneously, or vice versa. Clearly this condition will never occur in real life, thus, the simulation results will most certainly be flawed. The revenue or price estimates can also be further disaggregated into several product categories, where each category is correlated to the rest of the group (competitive products, product life cycle, product substitutes, complements, and cannibalization). Other examples include the possibility of economies of scale (where a higher production level forces cost to decrease over time), product life cycles (sales tend to decrease over time and plateau at a saturation rate), average total costs (the average of fully allocated cost decreases initially and increases after it hits some levels of diminishing returns). Therefore, relationships, correlations, and causalities have to be modeled appropriately. If data are available, a simple correlation matrix can be generated through Excel to capture these relationships.

5. Considered Truncation?   Truncation is a major error Crystal Ball users commit, especially when using the infamous triangular distribution. The triangular distribution is very simple and intuitive. As a matter of fact, it is probably the most widely used distribution in Crystal Ball, apart from the normal and uniform distributions. Simplistically, the triangular distribution looks at the minimum value, the most probable value, and the maximum value. These three inputs are often confused with the worst-case, nominal-case, and best-case scenarios. This assumption is indeed incorrect.

In fact, a worst-case scenario can be translated as a highly unlikely condition that *will* still occur given a percentage of the time. For instance, one can model the economy as high, average, and low, analogous to the worst-case, nominal-case, and best-case scenarios. Thus, logic would dictate that the worst-case scenario might have, say, a 15 percent chance of occurrence, the nominal-case a 50 percent chance of occurrence, and a 35 percent chance that a best-case scenario will occur. This approach is what is meant by using a best-, nominal-, and worst-case scenario analysis. However, compare that to the triangular distribution, where the minimum and maximum cases will almost never occur, with a probability of occurrence set at zero!

For instance, see Figure 15.2, where the worst-, nominal-, and best-case scenarios are set as 5, 10, and 15, respectively. Note that at the extreme

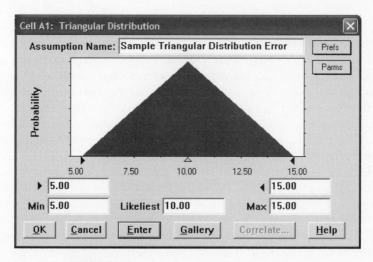

FIGURE 15.2   Sample triangular distribution.

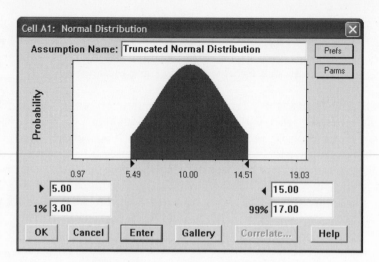

FIGURE 15.3   Truncating a distribution.

values, the probability of 5 or 15 occurring is virtually zero, as the areas under the curve (the measure of probability) of these extreme points are zero. In other words, 5 and 15 will almost *never* occur. Compare that to the economic scenario where these extreme values have either a 15 percent or 35 percent chance of occurrence. Instead, distributional truncation should be considered here. The same applies to any other distribution. Figure 15.3 illustrates a truncated normal distribution where the extreme values do not extend to both positive and negative infinities, but are truncated at 5 and 15.

6. How Wide Are the Forecast Results?   I have seen models that are as large as 30MB with over 1,000 distributional assumptions. When you have a model that big with so many assumptions, there is a huge problem! For one, it takes an unnecessarily long time to run in Excel, and for another, the results generated are totally bogus. One thing is certain: The final forecast distribution of the results will most certainly be too large to make any definitive decision with. Besides, what is the use of generating results that are close to a range between negative and positive infinity?

The results that you obtain should fall within decent parameters and intervals. One good check is to simply look at the single-point estimates. In theory, the single-point estimate is based on all precedent variables at their respective expected values. Thus, if one perturbs these expected values by instituting distributions about their single-point estimates, then the resulting single-point bottom line estimate should also fall within this forecast interval.

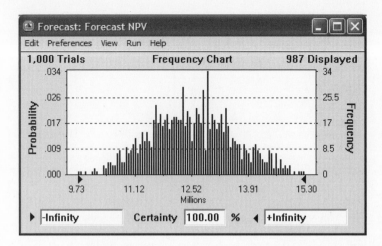

FIGURE 15.4   Truncated extreme values.

7. What Are the End Points and Extreme Values?   Mistaking end points is both an error of interpretation and a user error. For instance, Figure 15.4 illustrates the results obtained from a financial analysis with extreme values between $9.73 million and $15.30 million. By making the leap that the worst possible outcome is $9.73 million and the best possible outcome is $15.30 million, the analyst has made a major error. Notice that the upper righthand corner of the chart states that only 987 values are displayed. Clicking on the *Preferences* menu and selecting *Display Range*, one can clearly see that the default display range of 2.60 standard deviations is chosen (Figure 15.5).

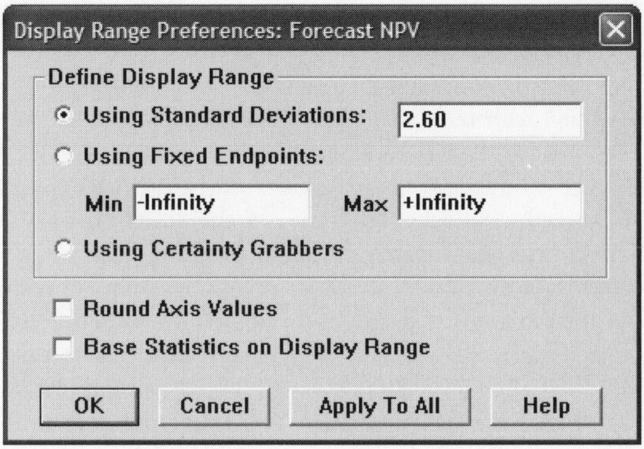

FIGURE 15.5   Display range preferences.

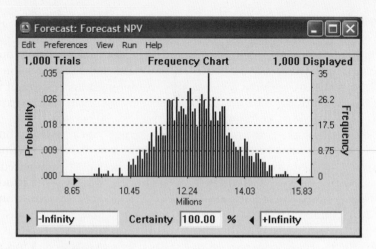

FIGURE 15.6   Display range using fixed end points.

Clearly, if the *Using Fixed Endpoints* option is chosen, the graph looks somewhat different, indicating the actual worst and best cases (Figure 15.6). Of course, the interpretation would be quite different here than with the 2.60 standard deviations option chosen.

8. Are There Breaks Given Business Logic and Business Conditions?   Assumptions used in the simulation may be based on valid historical data, which means that the distributional outcomes would be valid if the firm indeed existed in the past. However, going forward, historical data may not be the best predictor of the future. In fact, past performance is no indicator of future ability to perform, especially when structural breaks in business conditions are predicted to occur. Structural breaks include situations where firms decide to go global, acquire other firms, divest part of their assets, enter into new markets, and so forth. The resulting distributional forecasts need to be revalidated based on these conditions. The results based on past performance could be deemed as the base-case scenario, with additional adjustments and add-ons as required. This situation is especially true in the research and development arena, where by definition of research and development, things that are yet to be developed are new and novel in nature; thus by definition, there exist no historical data to base the future forecasts on. In situations such as these, it is best to rely on experience and expert opinions of future outcomes. Other approaches where historical data do not exist include using market proxies and project comparables—where current or historical projects and firms with similar functions, markets, and risks are used as benchmarks.

9. Do the Results Fall Within Expected Economic Conditions?   One of the most dangerous traps analysts fall into is the trap of data mining. Rather than relying on solid theoretical frameworks, analysts let the data sort things out by themselves. For instance, analysts who blindly use stepwise regression and distributional fitting fall directly into this data-mining trap. Instead of relying on theory a priori, or before the fact, analysts use the results to explain the way things look, a posteriori, or after the fact.

A simple example is the prediction of the stock market. Using tons of available historical data on the returns of the Standards & Poor's 500 index, an analyst runs a multivariate stepwise regression using over a hundred different variables ranging from economic growth, gross domestic product, and inflation rates, to the fluctuations of the Zairian zaire, to who won the Super Bowl and the frequency of sunspots on particular days. Because the stock market by itself is unpredictable and random in nature, as are sunspots, there seems to be some relationship over time. Although this relationship is purely spurious and occurred out of happenstance, a stepwise regression and correlation matrix will still pick up this spurious relationship and register the relationship as statistically significant. The resulting analysis will show that sunspots do in fact explain fluctuations in the stock market. Therefore, is the analyst correct in setting up distributional assumptions based on sunspot activity in the hopes of beating the market? When one throws a computer at data, it is almost certain that a spurious connection will emerge.

The lesson learned here is to look at particular models with care when trying to find relationships that may seem on the surface to be valid, but in fact are spurious and accidental in nature, and that holding all else constant, the relationship dissipates over time. Merely correlating two randomly occurring events and seeing a relationship is nonsense and the results should not be accepted. Instead, analysis should be based on economic and financial rationale. In this case, the economic rationale is that the relationship between sunspots and the stock market are completely accidental and should thus be treated as such.

10. What Are the Values at Risk?   Remember the story about my friend and me going skydiving in the first chapter? Albeit fictitious, it illustrates the differences between risk and uncertainty. When applying Monte Carlo simulation, an analyst is looking at uncertainty; that is, distributions are applied to different variables that drive a bottom-line forecast. Figure 15.7 shows a very simple calculation, where on a deterministic basis, if revenue is $2, cost is $1, the resulting net income is simply $1 (i.e., $2 − $1). However, in the dynamic model, where revenue is "around $2," cost is "around $1," the net income is "around $1." This "around" comment signifies the uncertainty

STATIC MODEL   DYNAMIC MODEL

Revenue	$ 2.00	Revenue	$ 2.00	<<---This is an input (Assumption)
Cost	$ 1.00	Cost	$ 1.00	<<---This is an input (Assumption)
Income	$ 1.00	Income	$ 1.00	<<---This is an output (Forecast)

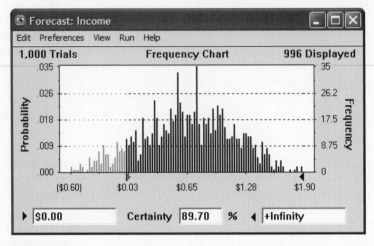

FIGURE 15.7   Illustrating the differences between risk and uncertainty.

involved in each of these variables. The resulting variable will also be an "around" number. In fact, when Crystal Ball is applied, the resulting single-point estimate also ends up being $1. The only difference being that there is a forecast distribution surrounding this $1 value. By performing Monte Carlo simulation, a level of uncertainty surrounding this single-point estimate is obtained. Risk analysis has *not yet* been done. Only uncertainty analysis has been done thus far. By running simulations, only the levels of uncertainty have been quantified if the reports are shown but the results are not used to adjust for risk.

For instance, one can in theory simulate everything under the sun, including the fluctuations of the Zairian zaire, but if the Zairian zaire has no impact on the project being analyzed, not to mention that capturing the uncertainty surrounding the currency does not mean one has managed, reduced, or analyzed the project's foreign exchange risks. It is only when the results are analyzed and used appropriately, that risk analysis has been done. For instance, if an analyst is evaluating three similar projects where each project has an expected value of $1 in net income but with different distributions, no new information is realized. However, when the results are used appropriately, where we say the first project has a $0.30 VaR at the 5th percentile, while the second and third projects have $0.20 and –$0.10 VaRs at the 5th percentile, has risk analysis been done. Holding everything else constant, the best project is clearly the first project, where in the worst-case scenario 5 percent of the time, the minimum amount to be gained is $0.30, the largest of the three. Obviously, other measures can be used, including the mean divided by the standard deviation (creating a coefficient of variability or bang-for-the-buck measure), risk-adjusted return on capital (RAROC or median less the 5th percentile divided by the volatility), and so forth, as detailed in Chapter 2, From Risk to Riches. Suffice it to say, as long as the risk adjustment is applied appropriately across all projects for comparability purposes, the measurement will be valid. The upshot being that simply noting the uncertainty levels around a value is not risk analysis. It is only when this value is adjusted according to its risk levels has risk analysis actually been performed.

11. How Do the Assumptions Compare to Historical Data and Knowledge?　Suspect distributional assumptions should be tested through the use of back-casting, which uses these historical data to test the validity of the assumptions. One approach is to take the historical data, fit them to a distribution using Crystal Ball's distributional-fitting routines, and test the assumption inputs. See if the distributional-assumption values fall within this historical distribution. If they fall outside of the distribution's normal set of parameters (e.g., 95 percent or 99 percent confidence intervals), then the analyst should better be able to describe and explain this apparent discontinuity, which can very well be because of changing business conditions and so forth.

12. How Do the Results Compare Against Traditional Analysis?　A very simple test of the analysis results is through its single-point estimates. For instance, remember the $1 net income example? If the single-point estimate shows $1 as the expected value of net income, then, in theory, the uncertainty surrounding this $1 should have the initial single-point estimate somewhere within its forecast distribution. If $1 is not within the resulting forecast distribution, something is amiss here. Either the model used to calculate the original $1 single-point estimate is flawed or the simulation assumptions are flawed. To recap, how can "around $2" minus "around $1" not be "around $1"?

13. Do the Statistics Confirm the Results?　Crystal Ball provides a wealth of statistics after performing a simulation. Figure 15.8 shows a sample listing of these statistics, which can be obtained through the *View | Statistics* menu in Crystal Ball. Some of these statistics when used in combination provide a solid foundation of the validity of the results. When in doubt as to what the *normal*-looking statistics should be, simply run a simple simulation in Crystal Ball and set the distribution to normal with a mean of 0.00 and a standard deviation of 1.00. This condition would create a standard-normal

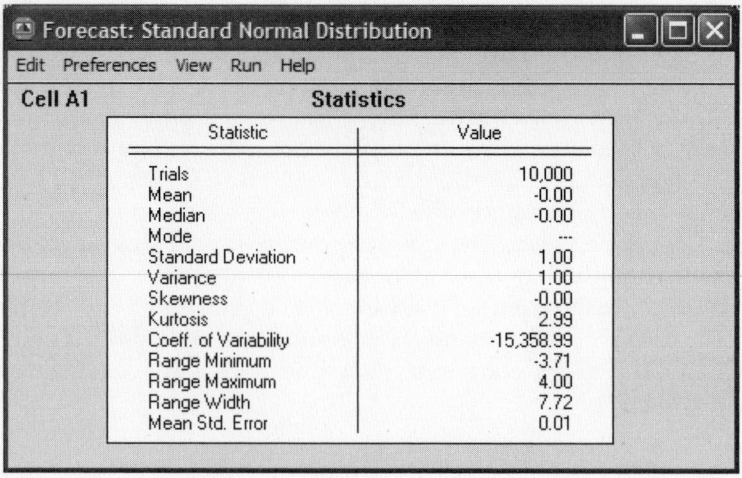

FIGURE 15.8   Standard-normal distribution statistics.

distribution, one of the most basic statistical distributions. The resulting set of statistics is shown in Figure 15.8. See Chapter 2, From Risk to Riches, for more details on some basic statistics and interpreting distributional moments.

Clearly, after running 10,000 trials, the resulting mean is 0.00 with a standard deviation of 1.00, as specified in the assumption. Of particular interest are the skewness and kurtosis values. For a normally distributed result, the skewness is close to 0.00, and the kurtosis is close to 3.00. If the results from your analysis fall within these parameters, it is clear that the forecast values are symmetrically distributed with no excess areas in the tail. A highly positive or negative skew would indicate that something might be going on in terms of some distributional assumptions that are skewing the results either to the left or to the right. This skew may be intentional or something is amiss in terms of setting up the relevant distributions. Also, a significantly higher kurtosis value would indicate that there is a higher probability of occurrence in the tails of the distribution, which means extreme values or catastrophic events are prone to occur more frequently than predicted in most normal circumstances. This result may be expected or not. If not, then the distributional assumptions in the model should be revisited with greater care, especially the extreme values of the inputs.

14. Are the Correct Methodologies Applied?   The problem of whether the correct methodology is applied is where user error comes in. The analyst should be able to clearly justify why a lognormal distribution is used instead of a uniform distribution, and so forth, and why distributional fitting is used instead of bootstrap simulation, or why a tornado chart is used instead of a sensitivity chart. All of these methodologies and approaches require some basic levels of understanding and questions such as these are most certainly required as part of management's due diligence when evaluating an analyst's results.

Warning signs to watch out for in Monte Carlo simulation and questions to ask include how the distributions are obtained, how sensitive are the distributional assumptions, how to identify the critical success factors, how the distributional assumptions are related, if the distributions are truncated, how wide are the forecast values, what are the end points and extreme values, are there breaks in business logic and conditions, do the results follow economic rationale, what are the values-at-risk, how do the results compare with historical data and knowledge, how do the results compare with traditional analyses, do the statistics confirm expectations, and are the correct methodologies applied.

Reading the Warning Signs in Time-Series Forecasting and Regression

Another frequently used decision-analysis tool is forecasting. One thing is certain: You can never predict the future with perfect accuracy. The best that you can hope for is to get as close as possible. In addition, it is actually okay to be wrong on occasion. As a matter of fact, it is sometimes good to be wrong, as valuable lessons can be learned along the way. It is better to be wrong consistently than to be wrong on occasion because if you are wrong consistently in one direction, you can correct or reduce your expectations, or increase your expectations when you are consistently overoptimistic or underoptimistic. The problem arises when you are occasionally right and occasionally wrong, and you have no idea when or why. Some of the issues that should be addressed when evaluating a time-series or any other forecasting results include the following.

1. Out of Range Forecasts Not all variables can be forecast using historical data. For instance, did you know that you can predict, rather reliably, the ambient temperature given the frequency of cricket chirps? Collect a bunch of crickets and change the ambient temperature, collect the data, and run a bivariate regression, and you would get a high level of confidence as seen in the coefficient of determination or R-squared value. Given this model, you could reasonably predict ambient temperature whenever crickets chirp, correct? Well, if you answered yes, you have just fallen into the trap of forecasting out of range.

Suppose your model holds up to statistical scrutiny, which it may very well do, assuming you do a good job with the experiment and data collection. Using the model, one finds that crickets chirp more frequently the higher the ambient temperature, and less frequently the colder it gets. What do you presume would happen if one were to toss a poor cricket in the oven and turn it up to 550 degrees? What happens when the cricket is thrown into the freezer instead? What would occur if a Malaysian cricket were used instead of the Arizona reticulated cricket? The quick answer is you can toss your fancy statistical regression model out the window if any of these things happened. As for the cricket in the oven, you would most probably hear the poor thing give out a very loud chirp and then complete silence. Regression and prediction models out of sample, that is, modeling events that are out of place and out of the range of the data collected in ordinary circumstances, on occasion will fail to work, as is clearly evident from the poor cricket.

2. Structural Breaks   Structural breaks in business conditions occur all the time. Some example instances include going public, going private, merger, acquisition, geographical expansion, adding new distribution channels, existence of new competitive threats, union strikes, change of senior management, change of company vision and long-term strategy, economic downturn, and so forth. Suppose you are an analyst at FedEx performing volume, revenue, and profitability metric forecasting of multiple break-bulk stations. These stations are located all around the United States and each station has its own seasonality factors complete with detailed historical data. Some advanced econometric models are applied, ranging from ARIMA (autoregressive integrated moving average) and ECM (error correction models) to GARCH (generalized autoregressive conditional heteroskedasticity) models; these time-series forecasting models usually provide relatively robust forecasts. However, within a single year, management reorganization, union strikes, pilot strikes, competitive threats (UPS, your main competitor, decided to enter a new submarket), revised accounting rules, and a plethora of other *coincidences* simply made all the forecasts invalid. The analyst must decide if these coincidences are just that, coincidences, or a fundamental structural change in the way global freight businesses are run. Obviously, certain incidences are planned or expected, whereas others are unplanned and unexpected. The planned incidences should thus be considered when performing forecasting.

3. Specification Errors   Sometimes, models are incorrectly specified. A nonlinear relationship can be very easily masked through the estimation of a linear model. In the forecasting chapter, running a linear regression model on a clearly nonlinear data set still resulted in statistically valid models and provided decent estimates. Another specification error that is fairly common has to do with autocorrelated and seasonal data sets. Estimating the demand of flowers in a floral chain without accounting for the holidays (Valentine's Day, Mother's Day, and so forth) is a blatant specification error. Failure to clearly use the correct model specification or first sanitizing the data may result in highly erroneous results.

4. Omitted and Redundant Variables   This type of model error in multivariate regression exists when regression is used to forecast the future. Suppose an analyst uses multivariate regression to obtain a statistical relationship between a dependent variable (e.g., sales, prices, revenues) and other regressors or independent variables (e.g., economic conditions, advertising levels, market competition) and he or she hopes to use this relationship to forecast the future. Unfortunately, the analyst may not have all the available information at his or her fingertips. If important information is unavailable, an important variable may be omitted (e.g., market saturation effects, price elasticity of demand, threats of emerging technology), or if too much data is available, redundant variables may be included in the analysis (e.g., inflation rate, interest rate, economic growth). It may be counterintuitive but the problem of redundant variables is more serious than omitted variables.[1] In a situation where redundant variables exist,[2] and if these redundant variables are perfectly correlated or collinear with each other, the regression equation does not exist and cannot be solved. In the case where slightly less severe collinearity exists, the estimated regression equation will be less accurate than without this collinearity. For instance, suppose both interest rates and inflation rates are used as explanatory variables in the regression analysis, where if there is a significant negative correlation between these variables with a time lag, then using both variables to explain sales revenues in the future is redundant. Only one variable is sufficient to explain the relationship with sales. If the analyst uses both variables, the errors in the regression analysis will increase. The prediction errors of an additional variable increase the errors of the entire regression.

5. Heteroskedasticity   If the variance of the errors in a regression analysis increases over time, the regression equation is said to be flawed and suffers from heteroskedasticity. Although this may seem to be a technical matter, many regression practitioners fall into this heteroskedastic trap without even realizing it. See Chapter 9, Using the Past to Predict the Future, for details on heteroskedasticity, testing for its existence, and methods to fix the error.

6. Multicollinearity   One of the assumptions required for a regression to run is that the independent variables are noncorrelated or noncollinear. These independent variables are exactly collinear when a variable is an exact linear combination of the other variables. This error is most frequently encountered when dummy variables are used.[3] A quick check of multicollinearity is to run a correlation matrix of the independent variables.[4] In most instances, the multicollinearity problem will prevent the regression results from being computed. See Chapter 9's Appendix D—Detecting and Fixing Multicollinearity—for more details.

7. Spurious Regression, Data Mining, Time Dependency, and Survivorship Bias

Spurious regression is another danger that analysts often run into. This mistake is made through certain uses of data-mining activities. Data mining refers to using approaches such as a step-wise regression analysis, where analysts do not have some prior knowledge of the economic effects of what independent variables drive the dependent variable, and use all available data at their disposal. The analyst then runs a step-wise regression, where the methodology ranks the highest correlated variable to the least correlated variable.[5] Then the methodology automatically adds each successive independent variable in accordance with its correlation until some specified stopping statistical criteria. The resulting regression equation is then taken as the final and best result. The problem with this approach is that some independent variables may simply be randomly moving about while the dependent variable may also be randomly moving about, and their movements depend on time.[6] Suppose this randomness in motion is somehow related at certain points in time but the actual economic fundamentals or financial relationships do not exist. Data-mining activities will pick up the coincidental randomness and not the actual relationship, and the result is a spurious regression. That is, the relationship estimated is bogus and is purely a chance happenstance. Multicollinearity effects may also unnecessarily eliminate highly significant variables from the step-wise regression.

Finally, survivorship bias and self-selection bias are important, as only the best-performing realization will always show up and have the most amount of visibility. For instance, looking to the market to obtain proxy data can be dangerous for only successful firms will be around and have the data. Firms that have failed will most probably leave no trails of their existence, let alone credible market data for an analyst to collect. Self-selection occurs when the data that exist are biased and selective. For instance, pharmacology research on a new cancer treatment will attract cancer patients of all types, but the researchers will clearly only select those patients in the earlier stages of cancer, making the results look more promising than they actually are.

8. Autoregressive Processes, Lags, Seasonality, and Serial Correlation   In time-series data, certain variables are autoregressive in nature. That is, future values of variables such as price, demand, interest rates, inflation rates, and

so forth depend on values that occurred in the past, or are autoregressive.[7] This reversion to the past occurs because of many reasons, including seasonality and cyclicality.[8] Because of these cyclical or seasonal and autoregressive effects, regression analysis using seasonal or cyclical independent variables as is will yield inexact results. In fact, some of these autoregressive, cyclical, or seasonal variables will affect the dependent variable differently over time. There may be a time lag between effects. For example, an increase in interest rates may take 1 to 3 months before the mortgage market feels any effect of this decline. Ignoring this time lag will downplay the relationships of highly significant variables.

9. Correlation and Causality   Regression analysis looks at correlation effects, not causality.[9] To say that there is a cause in X (independent variable) that drives the outcome of Y (dependent variable) through the use of regression analysis is flawed. For instance, there is a high correlation between the number of shark attacks and lunch hour around the world. Clearly, sharks cannot tell that it is time to have lunch. However, because lunchtime is the warmest time of the day, this is also the hour that beaches around the world are most densely populated. With a higher population of swimmers, the chances of heightened shark attacks are almost predictable. Lunchtime does not *cause* sharks to go hungry and prompt them to search for food. Just because there is a correlation does not mean that there is causality. Making this leap will provide analysts and management an incorrect interpretation of the results.

10. Random Walks   Certain financial data (e.g., stock prices, interest rates, inflation rates) follow something called a random walk. Random walks can take on different characteristics, including random walks with certain jumps, random walks with a drift rate, or a random walk that centers or reverts to some long-term average value. Even the models used to estimate random walks are varied, from geometric to exponential, among other things. A simple regression equation will yield no appreciable relationship when random walks exist.[10]

11. Jump Processes   Jump processes are more difficult to grasp but are nonetheless important for management to understand and challenge the assumptions of an analyst's results. For instance, the price of oil in the global market may sometimes follow a jump process. When the United States goes to war with another country, or when OPEC decides to cut the production of oil by several billion barrels a year, oil prices will see a sudden jump. Forecasting revenues based on these oil prices over time using historical data may not be the best approach. These sudden probabilistic jumps should most certainly be accounted for in the analysis. In this case, a jump-diffusion stochastic model is more appropriate than simple time-series or regression analyses.

12. Stochastic Processes   Other stochastic processes are also important when analyzing and forecasting the future. Interest rates and inflation rates may follow a mean-reversion stochastic process. That is, interest rates and inflation rates cannot increase or decrease so violently that they fall beyond all economic rationale. In fact, economic factors and pressures will drive these rates to their long-run averages over time. Failure to account for these effects over the long run may yield statistically incorrect estimates, resulting in erroneous forecasts.

> Warning signs to watch out for in time-series forecasting and regression as well as questions to ask include whether the forecasts are out of range, are there structural and business breaks anticipated in the forecast period, are there any misspecifications in the model, are there any possibilities of omitted and redundant variables, are there heteroskedasticity effects, are there any spurious relationships and biases, are there autoregressive lags, are correlations confused with causality, and are there variables that follow a random walk, jump processes, or other stochastic processes.

Reading the Warning Signs in Real Options Analysis

Risk analysis is never complete without the analysis of real options. What are uncertainty and risk analyses good for if one cannot make use of them? Real options analysis looks at the flexibility of a project or management's ability to make midcourse corrections when uncertainty becomes resolved over time. At the outset, real options analysis looks like a very powerful analytical tool, but care should be taken when real options analysis is applied. For instance, consider the following.

1. Do Not Let Real Options Simply Overinflate the Value of a Project   One of the most significant criticisms of real options approaches is that of overinflating the value of a project. This criticism of course is false. Real options are applicable if and only if the following requirements are met: traditional financial analysis can be performed and models can be built; uncertainty exists; the same uncertainty drives value; management or the project has strategic options or flexibility to either take advantage of these uncertainties or to hedge them; and management must be credible in executing the relevant strategic options when it becomes optimal to do so, otherwise all the options in the world would be useless. Thus, an analyst should not simply apply real options analysis to every project that comes across his or her desk, only those that are appropriate and ripe for analysis.

An option will always bear a value greater than or equal to zero. Hence, critics argue that by applying real options analysis, a project's value will be artificially inflated. In reality, real options may sometimes appear without cost, but in most cases firms need to pay to acquire these options (e.g., spending money to retrofit a refinery to obtain a switching option to choose between input fuels) and although the value of an option may be positive, its value can be clouded by the cost to obtain the option, making the entire strategy unprofitable and reduce the value of a project. So, although the value of an option is positive, the entire strategy's value may be negative. The lesson here is well learned—do not apply real options analysis on everything in sight, just to those projects that actually do have strategic options. Without doing so may mean leaving money on the table.

2. How Is Volatility Obtained and How Do You Reconcile Its Value? Fifty percent of the value of a real options analysis is simply thinking about it and realizing that management has the flexibility to make midcourse corrections when uncertainty becomes resolved over time. Twenty-five percent is crunching the numbers and the remaining 25 percent of the value in applying real options comes from being able to convince and explain the results to management. One of the toughest things to explain is the concept of where and how volatility is obtained. Volatility should be obtained from a project based on a project's level of uncertainty going forward. One major error is to use external market proxies for volatility. Using a firm's stock price to estimate volatility of a single project in a company with hundreds or even thousands of projects is not only incorrect, it is ludicrous. An analyst should hence be able to defend the choice of volatility estimates. See Johnathan Mun's *Real Options Analysis* (Wiley, 2002) for details on converting volatility to probability, and explaining volatility to management in an easy to understand manner.

3. What About Competing Options or Options That Have Not Even Been Considered? If a project has 10 strategic options, do you analyze all 10 options? What about projects in the distant future, where the options are not yet known for certain, that may be highly valuable? For a project with many options, the analyst has to determine which of these options are independent and which are interacting type options. If the options are interacting, dominant strategies will always dominate over less valuable options and the value of the project's total set of options will revert to these dominant options.[11] Thus, do not evaluate all the options in the world if only a few options capture a significant portion of the value. Focus instead on valuing those important or dominant options.

4. The Error of Interpretation of Option Results   Sometimes options come without a cost, while sometimes they do have a cost. On other occasions, option value is tangible or explicit, and sometimes option value is implicit or intangible. As an example, the land seller illustration used in Chapter 13, The Black Box Made Transparent: Real Options Analysis Toolkit, looks at the value of having an abandonment option, where if the counterparty signs the contractual agreement, the maximum expected cost of the contract is the option value.[12] However, in the case of some of the illustrations in Chapter 12, What's So Real About Real Options, and Why Is It Optional? where a research and development outfit performing stage-gate development has the option to abandon at every stage, valuing these options does not automatically mean the IRS or a counterparty will show up at the door and give the company a check in that amount. In this situation, the option value is an intangible or implicit value, useful as a measure against other projects and alternate strategies with or without such a flexibility option value.[13]

> Warning signs to watch out for in real options analysis and questions to ask include whether the real options analysis is applied inappropriately when there are no options such that the value of a project is inappropriately overinflated, how the volatility measure is obtained, are competing or omitted options appropriately considered, and are the results interpreted correctly.

Reading the Warning Signs in Optimization under Uncertainty

Finally, uncertainty and risk analyses are irrelevant if these quantified risks cannot be diversified away. Optimization looks at the ability to diversify away risks to find the best combination of projects subject to some prespecified constraints.

1. Why Are the Decision Variables the Decision Variables?   Decision variables are the variables that management has control over (e.g., which projects to execute, which products to manufacture, which vendor to purchase from, which wells to drill). However, sometimes things that are seemingly decision variables on the outset may not exactly be decision variables. For instance, the CEO's pet project is definitely a "go" decision no matter what the analytical results. The internal politics involved in decision making is something that cannot be taken lightly. Decision variables in an optimization analysis should most certainly be decision variables, not decisions that have already been made with the façade that their existence still has to be justified. Finally, certain decision variables are related to other decision variables and this interaction must be considered. For instance, Project A is a precursor to Projects B, C, and D; however, Project C cannot be executed if project B is executed, and Project C is a precursor to Project D.[14]

2. How Certain Are the Optimization Results?   Has the analyst looked at enough combinations to obtain the optimal results? In static optimization without simulation, whether it is using Crystal Ball OptQuest, Excel's goal seek, or Excel's Solver add-in, the optimal solution will be found, if there is one, rather quickly, as the computer can calculate all possible combinations and permutations of inputs to yield the optimal results. However, in optimization under uncertainty,[15] the process will take much longer and the results may not achieve optimality quickly. Even if the results do seem to be optimal, it is hard to tell, thus, it is safer to run the optimization much longer than required. An impatient analyst may fall into the trap of not running sufficient simulation trials and running the optimization insufficiently long to obtain robust results.

3. What Is the Analyst's Level of Training?   Little knowledge of probability will lead to more dangerous conclusions than no knowledge at all. Knowledge and experience together will prove to be an impressive combination, especially when dealing with advanced analytics. Almost always, the first step in getting more advanced analytics accepted and rolled out corporate-wide is to have a group of in-house experts trained in both the art and science of advanced analytics. Without a solid foundation, plans on rolling out these analytics will fail miserably.

> Warning signs to watch out for in an optimization under uncertainty and questions to ask include whether the decision variables are indeed decisions to be made, what are the levels of certainty of the results, and what is the level of training of the analyst.

QUESTIONS

1. Define what is meant by negligent entrustment.
2. What are some of the general types of errors encountered by an analyst when creating a model?

3. Why is truncation in a model's assumption important? What would happen to the results if truncation is not applied when it should be?
4. What is a critical success factor?
5. What are some of the normal-looking statistics?
6. What are structural breaks and specification errors, and why are they important?

CHAPTER 16

Changing a Corporate Culture

HOW TO GET RISK ANALYSIS ACCEPTED IN AN ORGANIZATION

Advanced analytics is hard to explain to management.[1] So, how do you get risk analysis accepted as the norm in a corporation, especially if your industry is highly conservative? It is almost a guarantee in conservative companies that an analyst showing senior management a series of fancy, mathematically complex, and computationally sophisticated models will be thrown out of the office together with his or her results and have the door slammed in his or her face. Changing management's thinking is the topic of discussion in this chapter. Explaining results and convincing management appropriately go hand in hand with the characteristics of the advanced analytical tools, which if they satisfy certain change-management requisites, the level and chances of acceptance become easier.

CHANGE-MANAGEMENT ISSUES AND PARADIGM SHIFTS

Change-management specialists have found that there are several criteria to be met before a paradigm shift in thinking is found to be acceptable in a corporation. For example, in order for senior management to accept a new and novel set of advanced analytical approaches—simulation, forecasting, real options, and portfolio optimization—the models and processes themselves must have applicability to the problem at hand, and not merely be an academic exercise.[2] Figure 16.1 lists the criteria required for change.

As we saw previously, it is certainly true that large multinationals have embraced the concept of risk analysis with significant fervor, and that risk analysis is here to stay.[3] It is not simply an academic exercise, nor is it the

"No change of paradigm comes easily"

Criteria for instituting change:

- Method applicability
  - Not just an academic exercise
- Accurate, consistent, and replicable
  - Creates a standard for decision making
- Value-added propositions
  - Competitive advantage over competitors
  - Provide valuable insights otherwise unavailable
- Exposition
  - Making the black box transparent
  - Explaining the value to senior management
- Comparative advantage
  - Better method than the old
  - It takes a good theory to kill an old one
- Compatibility with the old approach
  - Based on the old with significant improvements
- Flexibility
  - Able to be tweaked
  - Covers a multitude of problems
- External influences
  - From "Main Street" to "Wall Street"
  - Communicating to the investment community the value created internally

FIGURE 16.1 Changing a corporate culture.

latest financial analysis fad that is here today and gone tomorrow. In addition, the process and methodology have to be consistent, accurate, and replicable, that is, they pass the scientific process. Given similar assumptions, historical data, and assertions, one can replicate the results with ease and predictability. This replicability is especially true with the use of software programs and Excel models such as the ones included on the CD-ROM.

Next, the new method must provide a compelling value-added proposition. Otherwise, it is nothing but a fruitless and time-consuming exercise. The time, resources, and effort spent must be met and even surpassed by the method's added value. This added value is certainly the case in larger capital investment initiatives, where a firm's future or the future of a business unit may be at stake—incorrect and insufficient results may be obtained, and disastrous decisions made if risk analysis is not undertaken.

Other major criteria include the ability to provide the user a comparative advantage over competitors, which is certainly the case when the additional valuable insights generated through advanced risk analysis will help management identify options, value, prioritize, and select strategic and less risky alternatives that may otherwise be overlooked.

Finally, in order to accept a change in mind-set, the new methodology, analysis, process, or model must be easy to explain and understand. In addition, there has to be a link to previously accepted methods, whether the new methodology is an extension of the old or a replacement of the old due to some clear superior attributes. These last two points are the most difficult to tackle for an analyst. The sets of criteria prior to this are direct and easy to define.

The new set of risk analytics is nothing but an extension of existing methodologies.[4] For instance, Monte Carlo simulation can be explained simply as scenario analysis applied to the nth degree. Simulation is nothing but scenario analysis done thousands of times but not just on a single variable (e.g., the three common scenarios: good economy, average economy, and bad economy complete with their associated probabilities of occurrence and payoffs at each state), but on multiple variables interacting simultaneously, where multiple variables are changing independently or dependently, in a correlated or uncorrelated fashion (e.g., competition, economy, market share, technological efficacy, and so forth). In fact, the results stemming from new analytics is simply a logical extension of the traditional approaches. Figure 16.2 illustrates this logical extension.

The static model in the illustration shows a revenue value of $2, cost of $1, and the resulting income value, calculated as the difference between the two, as $1. Compare that to the dynamic model, where the same inputs are used but the revenue and cost variables have been subjected to Monte Carlo simulation. Once simulation has been completed, the dynamic model still shows the same single-point estimate of $1 as in the static model. In other words, adding in the more advanced analytics, namely, Monte Carlo simulation, the model or results have not changed. If management still wants the single-point estimate of $1 reported, then so be it. However, by logical extension, if both revenues and costs are uncertain, then by definition, the resulting income will also be uncertain. The forecast chart for the income variable shows this uncertainty of the resulting income with fluctuations around $1. In fact, additional valuable information is obtained using simulation, where the probability or certainty of breakeven or exceeding $0 in income is shown as 89.70 percent in Figure 16.2. In addition, rather than relying on the single-point estimate of $1, simulation reveals that the business only has a 26.10 percent probability of exceeding the single-point estimate of $1 in income (Figure 16.3).

STATIC MODEL

Revenue	$	2.00
Cost	$	1.00
Income	$	1.00

DYNAMIC MODEL

Revenue	$	2.00	<<---This is an input (Assumption)
Cost	$	1.00	<<---This is an input (Assumption)
Income	$	1.00	<<---This is an output (Forecast)

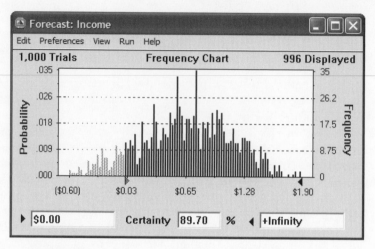

FIGURE 16.2 Monte Carlo simulation as a logical extension of traditional analysis.

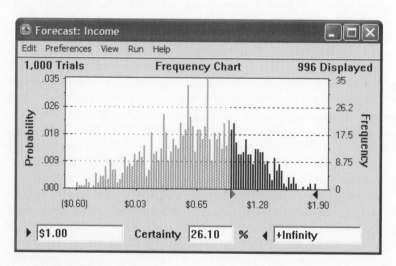

FIGURE 16.3 Probability of exceeding the original $1 income.

If simulation is not applied here, the riskiness of this project will never be clearly elucidated. Imagine if management has multiple but similar types of projects where every project has a single-point estimate of $1. In theory, management should be indifferent in choosing any of these projects. However, if the added element of risk is analyzed, each project may have different probabilities of breakeven and different probabilities of exceeding the $1 income threshold. Clearly, the project with the least amount of risk should be chosen (i.e., highest probability of breakeven and exceeding the threshold value).

MAKING TOMORROW'S FORECAST TODAY

Firms that are at first skeptical about applying advanced analytics in their decision-making activities should always consider first applying these new rules to smaller projects. Instead of biting off too much immediately, a small-scale project is always preferable. Companies new to advanced risk analytics should first learn to crawl before they start running and head straight for the wall. If management can be eased into the new analytical paradigm slowly, the transition will be more palatable.

Having a vision to change the entire organization's decision-making processes overnight is very admirable but will be very short-lived and bound for disaster. Before an organization can learn to make tomorrow's forecast today, it has to learn from the lessons of yesterday. One approach is to look at high-profile projects in the past. Instead of starting with forecasting, perform some back-casting first. Instead of waiting for years to verify if the results from the analysis were actually correct or valuable, the result from a back-casting analysis is almost immediate. If the analyst is true to himself or herself, using the actual data coupled with the assumptions used in the past (without the advantage of hindsight), the new analytical results can then be compared to the decisions that were made to see if different strategies and decisions would have been undertaken instead. However, care should be taken as corporate politics come into play because the individuals who made the decisions in the past may not take it too kindly when their decisions are negatively scrutinized.

No matter the strategy moving forward, one thing is certain: If senior management buys into the techniques, acceptance would be imminent. Otherwise, a few junior analysts in a cubicle somewhere trying to get management's attention will fail miserably. In retrospect, a midlevel manager trying to impress his or her superiors without the adequate knowledge and support from analysts will not work either.

The approach for successful implementation has to be comprehensive and three pronged. Senior management must keep an open mind to alternatives. Middle management must keep championing the approach and not let minor setbacks be permanent, while attempting to be the conduit of information between the junior analysts and senior management. However, analysts should attempt to acquire as much knowledge about the techniques and applications as possible. The worst possible outcome is where extreme expectations are set from high above and the powers that be, while the lower rungs cannot deliver the goods as required.

In order to facilitate adoption of a new set of analytical methods in an organization, several criteria must first be met. To judge the level of potential adoption, the following questions should be asked, including whether the method is applicable to the problem at hand, how accurate, consistent, and replicable are the methods, what are the value-added propositions, what is the level of expositional ease, what are the comparative advantages, how compatible is the new method to the old models, how flexible is the new method, and what are some of the external influences in using the methods.

FIVE-MINUTE INDUSTRY SPOTLIGHT: BANKER'S TRUST

Banker's Trust Develops Award-Winning Risk Management Group

Bankers Trust's (BT) Risk Management Advisory (RMA) group has been a dedicated Crystal Ball user for approximately 5 years. RMA builds on its recognized strengths in risk measurement and management to help clients reshape their perception of the risks in their businesses and elevate their competitive positions by enhancing their risk management. RMA clients span all industries and geographic sectors. In particular, RMA possesses extensive advisory experience for oil and gas companies, electric utilities, corporations, and financial institutions in the Americas, Europe, Asia, and Oceania. These resources, combined with BT's ability to execute customized risk-management solutions, allow clients the opportunity to reshape their risk-return profile to enhance shareholder value.

RMA earned Euromoney's Risk Management Advisors of the Year award for an unprecedented and unparalleled 3 years in a row: 1996, 1997, and 1998.

Crystal Ball has played an integral part in RMA's success by enabling it to build customized financial and strategic models for its clients. While each of these models is unique, most contain stochastic processes and necessitate the incorporation of Crystal Ball. Whether the RMA group is building an asset-valuation model for electric utilities, a cash-flow-at-risk model for a large corporation, or a hedging model for trading portfolios, they all involve forward projections and back testing results. With its intuitive, easy-to-use interface, Crystal Ball makes building, running, and testing intricate models such as these much easier for both the developer and the end user. In addition, many of the models created by RMA are quite large, sometimes containing up to 100,000 calculations per Excel workbook. Without the use of Crystal Ball, models of this size would require significant amounts of time to run simulations. With Crystal Ball, however, RMA is able to perform its simulations with minimal time commitments from the model developers.

Banker's Trust's RMA Group has also found significant value in the way Crystal Ball displays a simulation's results in well-organized, comprehensive, easy-to-read forecast charts. In addition, Crystal Ball's correlated assumptions feature and sensitivity chart allow RMA to perform extensive analysis on its models.

Crystal Ball provides RMA with the software necessary to create customized solutions to its customers' needs efficiently and effectively. Because of Crystal Ball's flexibility, RMA can provide its customers with transparent quantitative methodologies and approaches to risk management, as opposed to traditional black-box solutions, ensuring that a significant amount of knowledge is transferred between RMA and its clients, adding value for everyone involved, and contributing to BT's stature as a leader in the financial services industry.

FIVE-MINUTE INDUSTRY SPOTLIGHT: ENVIRONMENT CANADA

Environmental Risk Assessment and Chemical Risk Assessment

Environment Canada applied Crystal Ball in an investigation of the effects of ammonia in aquatic environments. Crystal Ball was used to generate distributions for the raw hydrological and effluent data and to combine these distributions to generate a set of hypothetical river conditions for a plume model.

Environment Canada has determined that ammonia released in large quantities under some river conditions is toxic to aquatic life. A risk-management process will be developed to discuss reduction strategies with Canadian municipalities.

Miles Constable, a senior toxic substances officer for Environment Canada in Edmonton, coordinates teams of professionals conducting ecological risk assessments of chemicals on Environment Canada's Priority Substances List. The list is developed jointly by Environment Canada and Health Canada to address chemicals suspected of being either inherently hazardous or released in such large quantities as to pose a hazard to the environment. This assessment process determines the entry, exposure, effects, and risks of chemicals to Canada's environment.

If a chemical released into the environment is determined to be toxic, Environment Canada negotiates with the industrial or municipal sector releasing the chemical to reduce quantities released. This action can have a major economic impact on that sector, as reduction strategies can vary from simple technological improvements in facilities to "virtual elimination" of the chemical from the Canadian environment—in essence a ban on the release of the chemical.

With such serious consequences, Environment Canada must conduct a balanced assessment of the hazards that a chemical poses to various Canadian ecosystems. This balanced assessment includes an open and transparent accounting of the uncertainties that exist regarding the effects of the chemical to biota. In 1997, Environment Canada established a methodology or "tool box" to help conduct probabilistic risk assessments. When Miles Constable was tasked with putting together a team to complete a risk assessment of ammonia in aquatic environments, his first decision was to hire an environmental statistics consultant to help develop the assessment. The consultant recommended Crystal Ball as a powerful statistical tool that could propagate sources of variability and incertitude through environmental exposure models.

Ammonia is a common component of sewage effluents that are typically released into waterways. Only three case studies were available for use: two had very good field-monitoring data and one had a good ammonia profile. Miles Constable decided that it would be necessary to model the sewage dispersion profile for the third case study as a typical Canadian river because of the lack of in-stream monitoring data. Crystal Ball formed a key component of this modeling effort.

The modeling case study had a good profile of ammonia concentrations through a sewage effluent plume for a single sampling. Miles Constable, his group, and the consultant developed a set of spreadsheets containing hydrological data (depth, width, flow rate, temperature, and pH), and sewage effluent data (effluent flow rates, ammonia concentrations, and temperature) from government monitoring records and the sewage treatment plant. They wanted to estimate the ammonia concentrations in the plume under a large number of hypothetical flow conditions that could be expected in the river.

Crystal Ball was used to determine the statistical distributions inherent in the hydrological and sewage effluent data. Once the distributions were established for the most important variables, Crystal Ball was used to generate 500 data sets of hypothetical flow and effluent conditions based on the distributions. They then entered the 500 data sets into a plume-modeling program (CORMIX 3) to estimate ammonia concentrations downstream of the outfall for each of the river flow conditions.

Crystal Ball proved very useful for generating distributions for the raw hydrological and effluent data and combining these distributions to generate a set of hypothetical river conditions. The group developed a series of ammonia distribution predictions for each month of a hypothetical average year and was able to use this information in predicting the toxic risk to aquatic biota exposed to the sewage effluent plume. "While it was tedious work to put together the data set," said Constable, "it was also intriguing to see if the approach would work and if we had enough data to properly generate an average monthly flow and effluent regime for the modeled location."

The Environment Canada team members then used Crystal Ball to develop larger data sets for their final risk analyses and to generate the final predictions of risk. First, they used Crystal Ball to generate cumulative density functions (CDF) of the probability of being in a specific range of concentration. They also generated a relationship between toxicity and ammonia concentration for a number of different species. Next, they combined these two CDFs to provide a relationship of probability of a toxic impact versus the percentage of species affected. This relationship was the crux of the project, to determine the risk of a toxic impact to an aquatic community from the release of sewage effluents.

For this final analysis they chose to use sets of 300 ranges for the CDFs. They then ran Crystal Ball with the number of trials set to 10,000 to develop a large enough data set to ensure a good distribution of data across the ranges. Crystal Ball was used to predict the probability of an ammonia concentration being within a given range and the percentage of species that would be affected.

The result was a set of probabilities of a toxic impact at different distances or locations from the sewage outfalls, which enabled Environment Canada to show that ammonia, under some conditions, posed an unacceptable risk to aquatic biota and was thus toxic. Following the official release of the assessment report, a risk-management process will initiate discussions with Canadian municipalities on risk-reduction strategies.

Notes

Chapter 1   Beyond Uncertainty

1. Peter L. Bernstein, *Against the Gods: The Remarkable Story of Risk.* (John Wiley & Sons, 1996).
2. Save the potentiality of a plane crash, at which I would have very much regretted not taking the parachute.
3. The concepts of high risk and high return are nothing new and are central to the development of the *capital asset pricing model (CAPM)* used to estimate the required rate of return on a project based on its *systematic risk*. In the CAPM model, the higher the risk, the higher the expected rate of return (ceteris paribus, or holding everything else constant).
4. Risk can be measured in different ways. In this example, it is measured using the standard deviation of the distribution of returns.
5. This selection is because Project X bears a positive net return (positive net present value) above its implementation cost, making it profitable. Thus, the cheapest project is selected.
6. "Independence" means that the projects themselves are noncorrelated, thus it is assumed that there are no risk-diversification effects. "Mutually exclusive" means that the manager cannot mix and match among the different projects (e.g., 2 Project Xs with 3 Project Ys).
7. This choice of course is based purely on financial analysis alone by holding everything else constant (management's taste and preferences, or other strategic values inherent in different projects).
8. On a continuous basis, the probability of hitting exactly $30 (i.e., $30.0000000000 and so forth) is very close to zero. The probability in a distribution is measured as the area under the curve, which means two values are required, for example, the probability of net revenues being between $29 and $31 is 25 percent. Thus, the area under the curve for a single-point estimate (a single line in a distribution) is close to zero.
9. The *Law of Demand* in economics requires that, in most cases, price and quantity demanded are negatively correlated, in accordance with a downward-sloping demand curve. The exception being Giffen or status goods where a higher price may yield a higher quantity demanded (e.g., Porsches are desirable and have a higher status because they are expensive, among other things).

10. A firm's average variable cost curve is U shaped, with an initial downward slope at lower quantities (economies of scale), hits a global minimum value where marginal cost equals average variable cost, and then continues to slope upward (diseconomies of scale).
11. As will be seen in later chapters, the complete range of outcomes of the distribution is greater than those values shown due to outliers. However, for now, assuming the outliers are ignored, the extreme values of $16 and $44 are assumed to be correct.
12. See Chapter 9 for details on time-series and regression models.
13. The simulated actual values depicted graphically are based on a Geometric Brownian Motion with a volatility of 20 percent calculated as the standard deviation of the simulated natural logarithms of historical returns.
14. See Chapters 2 and 3 for details of other measures of risk and uncertainty.

Chapter 2   From Risk to Riches

1. Ron Dembo and Andrew Freeman, *Seeing Tomorrow: Rewriting the Rules of Risk* (John Wiley & Sons, 1998). This book provides an interesting nonmathematical review of risk management.
2. That is, the standard deviation of the population (σ) and the standard deviation of a sample (s) are

$$\sigma = \sqrt{\frac{\sum_{i=1}^{N} (x_i - \mu)^2}{N}} \qquad s = \sqrt{\frac{\sum_{i=1}^{n} (x_i - \bar{x})^2}{n-1}}$$

where the standard deviation is the square root of the sum of the deviation of each data point (x_i) from the population mean (μ) or sample mean ($\bar{x}$) squared, and then divided into the population size (N) or sample size (n) less one. For the sample statistic, the division is into n less one to correct for the degrees of freedom in a smaller sample size. The variance is simply the square of the standard deviation.
3. Johnathan Mun, *Real Options Analysis* (John Wiley & Sons, 2002); Johnathan Mun, *Real Options Analysis Course* (John Wiley & Sons, 2003). Refer to these books for details on estimating volatility in a real options context.
4. For instance, the height distribution's mean is 10 m with a standard deviation of 1 m, which yields a coefficient variation of 0.1, versus the weight distribution's mean of 100 kg and a standard deviation of 20 kg, which yields a coefficient of variation of 0.2. Clearly, the weight distribution carries with it more variability.

Chapter 3   A Gentleman's Guide to Model Building

1. However, be aware that password busters are abundant and certain spreadsheet models can very easily be hacked by outsiders. A better approach is to convert sensitive functions and macros into ActiveX ".*dll*" files that are encrypted, providing a much higher level of security.

Chapter 4   On the Shores of Monaco

1. The old-fashioned way in this case is also known as the *pencil and paper* method.
2. This example is an adaptation from papers and lectures provided by Professor Sam Savage of Stanford University.
3. In this example, the median is a better measure of central tendency.
4. The same nonparametric simulation can also be applied using Crystal Ball's custom distribution where each occurrence has an equal chance of being selected.
5. The approach used here is the application of a Geometric Brownian Motion stochastic process for forecasting and simulating potential outcomes.

Chapter 5   Peering into the Crystal Ball

1. In order to do this, you may need to first type 100 in the certainty box, hit enter, click anywhere in the chart, and then type in the right confidence tail and hit enter.

Chapter 6   Pandora's Tool Box

1. The other approach is to use time-series methods and regression to analyze and forecast time-series and cross-sectional data.
2. Generally, it is a good idea to leave this value at 95 percent or 90 percent so that you can have a high degree of confidence that the precision requirements have been met. However, if you have a large number of forecasts defined with precision control set, you can adjust the confidence level up or down to globally change the accuracy of all forecasts simultaneously.

Chapter 7   Extended Business Cases I: From Pharma to Black Gold

1. For example, drilling engineers can review historical drilling cost data and provide a probability distribution of drilling costs in a geographic area in the proposed rock formation. They are not required to know how important this risk is to the project economics versus the risk that an oil and gas reservoir is not present after the well is drilled. This risk is better evaluated by geological/geophysical staff.

2. While "low risk" is a subjective term, the risk in our model reflects a well that might be drilled in or very close to an existing producing oil field in a mature, well-established oil basin such as the Permian Basin of West Texas.

3. The economic limit is the point at which the marginal expense of producing the well exceeds the marginal revenue associated with the oil or gas produced. It is highly dependent on the company's organization and producing infrastructure. For our model we assume 10 BOPD is the economic limit.

4. Calculated from average weekly prices of West Texas Intermediate Crude, then averaged over 52 weeks of each year, from November 1991 to March 2003

5. Note that if it is determined that the well has not encountered significant oil and gas reserves, the well is not completed and these costs are not incurred. This cost is the only one of the Year 0 costs in our model that is not incurred in the case of a dry hole.

6. NPV/I is simply the net present value of the project divided by the sum of Year 0 investments, and provides a measure of bang for the buck in a capital-rationing corporate environment.

7. In fact, most oil and gas companies do maintain proprietary price forecasts for the purpose of portfolio and investment analysis. Sensitivity of projects to these forecasts suggests that corporations (not just project teams) are well advised to model the variability in earnings and cash flow that will propagate from unavoidable errors in their proprietary price forecasts.

Chapter 9   Using the Past to Predict the Future

1. An arbitrary 3-month moving average is chosen. For modeling purposes, different n-length moving averages should be computed and the one with the least amount of errors should be chosen.

2. To start Excel's Data Analysis, first click on the *Tools* menu in Excel and select *Add-Ins*. Then make sure the check box beside *Analysis Tool Pak* is selected and hit *OK*. Then return to the *Tools* menu and select *Data Analysis*. The *Regression* functionality should now exist.

3. See Chapter 8, Making Tomorrow's Forecast Today, for specifics on using Crystal Ball Predictor.

4. The critical *t-statistic* can be found in the t-distribution table at the end of this book, by looking down the two-tailed alpha 0.025 (alpha 0.05 for two tails means that each tail has an area of 0.025) and cross-referencing it to 6 degrees of freedom. The degrees of freedom is calculated as the number of data points, n, (7) used in the regression, less the number of independent regressors, k (1).

5. As this is a two-tailed hypothesis test, the alpha should be halved, which means that as long as the p-value calculated is less than 0.025 (half of 0.05), then the null hypothesis should be rejected.

6. Although the Durbin–Watson critical table starts from $n = 15$, one can infer that the lower the number of observations (n), the lower the D_L value will be. Thus, the critical statistic should be less than 1.08.

7. The adjusted R-squared is used here as this is a multivariate regression, and the adjustment in the coefficient of determination accounts for the added independent variable.

8. The two most notable and challenging econometric models include the ARCH (Autoregressive Conditional Heteroskedasticity) and GARCH (Generalized Autoregressive Conditional Heteroskedasticity) models.

Chapter 10   The Search for the Optimal Decision

1. For a total cost of $550 for the entire trip.

2. The number of possible itineraries is the factorial of the number of cities, that is, $3! = 3 \times 2 \times 1 = 6$.

3. A total of five cities means $5! = 5 \times 4 \times 3 \times 2 \times 1 = 120$.

4. A triangular distribution can be applied here, with the minimum level set at $300, most likely value of $325, and a maximum level set at $500.

5. The straight lines in Figure 10.6 would now be nonlinear and the problem would be difficult to solve graphically.

6. To access Solver, start Excel, click on *Tools | Add-Ins*. Make sure the check box beside *Solver Add-In* is selected. Solver can then be accessed by clicking on *Tools | Solver*.

7. A two-decision variable optimization problem requires a two-dimensional graph, which means an n-decision variable problem requires the use of an n-dimensional graph, making the problem mathematically and manually intractable using the graphical method.

8. Chapter 11, Optimization under Uncertainty, illustrates a similar portfolio-optimization process but under uncertainty using Crystal Ball's OptQuest.

Chapter 11   Optimization under Uncertainty

1. The next example will use a continuous decision variable in allocating resources across a portfolio of financial assets.

2. The values 37, 42, and others are the costs associated with each project, such that the total value of the portfolio cannot exceed $260 million.

3. The variables Project 1, 2, 3, and so forth are binary values (0 or 1 to represent either a no-go or go decision) such that the total number of projects chosen cannot exceed five.

4. Obviously, the longer the optimization is run, the higher the level of precision and accuracy of the results. Ten minutes is used here only for illustration purposes.

5. If the final value is not chosen, the risk levels will be based on standard deviations of the simulated results, at every step in the simulation. That is, every trial will have a different level of standard deviation, making the results incorrect. The risk level should be the final simulated forecast distribution's standard deviation.

Chapter 12   What Is So Real about Real Options, and Why Are They Optional?

1. One method to solve this is to use a random number generator *seed*.

Chapter 13   The Black Box Made Transparent: Real Options Analysis Toolkit

1. See www.fasb.org and KPMG's "Defining Issues," April 2003 issue, No. 03-8.

2. Closed-form models simply means there exists a mathematical representation of the model, for instance, A = B + C is a closed-form model, where if one provides the values of B and C, the model yields an exact result A.

3. In order to facilitate computation and test of robustness, Crystal Ball Monte Carlo simulation software and the author's Real Options Analysis Toolkit, and Options Pricing software were used.

4. See Johnathan Mun's *Real Options Analysis* (John Wiley & Sons, 2002) for solved models of American options approximation approaches using the Real Options Analysis Toolkit software.

5. Crystal Ball Professional was used to calculate the option value in this case study.

6. American options are the options that can be executed at any time up to maturity, while European options can only be executed on the maturity dates.

7. Aswath Damodaran, *Investment Valuation* (John Wiley & Sons, 1996).

8. Don M. Chance, *An Introduction to Derivatives*, 4th ed. (Dryden Press, 1998).

9. This is due to the mathematical properties of American options, which require the knowledge of what the optimal stopping times and optimal execution barriers are. Using simulation to solve American-type options is very difficult and is beyond the scope of this case study.

10. John C. Hull, *Options, Futures, and Other Derivatives*, 3rd ed. (Prentice Hall, 1997).

11. See Chapter 5 on applying forecasts in a Monte Carlo simulation.

12. Chance, *An Introduction to Derivatives.*
13. A simulation running 100,000 trials under Latin Hypercube with a size of 1,000 at an initial seed of 1 was applied on 100 path-dependent time steps.

Chapter 14   Extended Business Cases II: From Land to Money

1. McKinsey & Company, Inc., Tom Copeland, Tim Koller, and Jack Murrin, *Valuation: Measuring and Managing the Value of Companies,* 3rd ed. (John Wiley & Sons, 2000).

Chapter 15   The Warning Signs

1. The problem of omitted variables is less vital as an analyst will simply have to work with all available data. If everything about the future is known, then why bother forecasting? If there is no uncertainty, then the future is known with certainty.
2. The problem of redundant variables is also known as multicollinearity.
3. For instance, if a dummy variable on sex is used (i.e., "0" for male and "1" for female), then a regression equation with *both* dummy variables will be perfectly collinear. In such a situation, simply drop one of the dummy variables as they are mutually exclusive of each other.
4. Make sure there are no independent variables that are perfectly or almost perfectly correlated to each other. In addition, regression analysis can be performed to test the linear relationships among the independent variables.
5. If Y is the dependent variable and X_i are the independent variables, then the correlation pairs are between all possible combinations of Y and X_i.
6. Interest rates tend to be time dependent (mean-reverting over longer periods of time) and demand for a product that is not related to interest rate movements may also be time dependent (exhibiting cyclicality and seasonality effects).
7. The term "auto" means self and "regressive" means reverting to the past. Hence, the term "autoregressive" means to revert back to one's own past history.
8. Seasonality effects are usually because of periodicities in time (12-month seasonality in a year, 4-quarter seasonality in a year, 7-day seasonality in a week, etc.) while cyclical effects are because of larger influences without regard to periodicities (e.g., business cycle movements and technological innovation cycles).
9. However, there are other approaches used to estimate causality, for example, Granger causality approaches look at statistical causalities.

10. More advanced econometric models are required to estimate random walks, including methods using differences and unit root models.

11. See *Real Options Analysis* (Wiley, 2002) and *Real Options Analysis Course* (Wiley, 2003) for details on interacting options in evaluating the chooser option.

12. In this case, the option value is explicit, or something that is tangible and the seller of the option can actually acquire this value.

13. Therefore, management's compensation should not be tied to actualizing this implicit option value.

14. This means the decision strategies are: A–B, A–C, and A–C–D.

15. Optimization under uncertainty means to run a set of simulations for a certain number of trials (e.g., 1,000 trials), pauses, estimates the forecast distributions, tests a set of combinations of decision variables, and re-runs the entire analysis again, for hundreds to thousands of times.

Chapter 16   Changing a Corporate Culture

1. Advanced analytics are all the applications discussed in this book, including simulation, time-series forecasting, regression, optimization, and real options analysis.

2. Examples of an academic exercise that has little pragmatic application for general consumption in the areas of advanced analytics include sensitivity simulation, variance reduction, closed-form partial-differential models, stochastic optimization, and so forth. These are mathematically elegant approaches, but they require analysts with advanced degrees in finance and mathematics to apply, making the methodology and results very difficult to explain to management.

3. The case is made through the many actual business cases and example 5-minute industry spotlight applications throughout this book.

4. This is particularly true for Monte Carlo simulation where simulation cannot be applied unless there already is a spreadsheet model.

List of Models

Following is a list of the Excel models that are included on the accompanying CD-ROM. These models are listed in alphabetical order of their respective file names, complete with titles and categories as well as a short description. Some models require that Crystal Ball be already installed in order to run.

File: Brownian Motion with Drift (Excel).xls

Description: This model illustrates the Brownian Motion stochastic process with a drift rate. An example application includes the simulation of a stock price path. Press the *Simulate Once* button to perform a stepwise simulation and see why it is so difficult to predict stock prices. Other applications include forecasting prices, revenues, costs, and so forth, as long as these variables follow a Brownian Motion. Enter some values into the colored input boxes (default values are $100 for starting value, 10 percent for annualized drift, 45 percent for annualized volatility, and 1 for forecast horizon).

File: Brownian Motion with Drift (Simulated).xls

Description: This model illustrates the Brownian Motion stochastic process with a drift rate. An example application includes the simulation of a stock price path. This model requires Crystal Ball to run. Click on Crystal Ball's *Single Step* button to perform a stepwise simulation and see why it is so difficult to predict stock prices. Click on *Start Simulation* to estimate the distribution of stock prices at certain time intervals. Enter some values into the colored input boxes (default values are $100 for starting value, 10 percent for annualized drift, 45 percent for annualized volatility, and 1 for forecast horizon).

File: Credit Risk Model—OptimizeRIFurnOriginalA.xls.xls
File: Credit Risk Model—OptimizeRIFurnRun1.xls
File: Credit Risk Model—OptimizeRIFurnRun2.xls

Description: These three models are contributed by Professor Morton Glantz and they follow his case study examples in Chapter 14.

File: Historical Data (Forecasting and Trend).xls

Description: This model provides a set of raw historical data of sales dating from January 2000 to December 2003. This data set is used in conjunction with Crystal Ball Predictor to forecast future cash flows using time-series analysis methods.

File: Logarithmic Random Walk with Drift (Excel).xls

Description: This model illustrates the Logarithmic Random Walk stochastic process with a drift rate. An example application includes the simulation of a stock price path. Press the *Simulate Once* button to perform a stepwise simulation and see why it is so difficult to predict stock prices. Other applications include forecasting prices, revenues, costs, and so forth, as long as these variables follow a random walk. Enter some values into the colored input boxes (default values are $100 for starting value, 10 percent for annualized drift, 45 percent for annualized volatility, and 1 for forecast horizon).

File: Logarithmic Random Walk with Drift (Simulated).xls

Description: This model illustrates the Logarithmic Random Walk stochastic process with a drift rate. An example application includes the simulation of a stock price path. This model requires Crystal Ball to run. Click on Crystal Ball's *Single Step* button to perform a stepwise simulation and see why it is so difficult to predict stock prices. Click on *Start Simulation* to estimate the distribution of stock prices at certain time intervals. Enter some values into the colored input boxes (default values are $100 for starting value, 10 percent for annualized drift, 45 percent for annualized volatility, and 1 for forecast horizon).

File: Mean Reversion with Drift (Excel).xls

Description: This model illustrates the Mean Reversion stochastic process with a drift rate. An example application includes the simulation of an interest rate or inflation rate path. Press the *Simulate Once* button to perform a stepwise simulation and see why it is so difficult to predict inflation or interest rates. Other applications include forecasting oil and utility prices, revenues, costs, and so forth, as long as these variables revert to the mean if it strays away from the long-term mean too much. Enter some values into the colored input boxes (default values are $1 for starting value, 15 percent for mean value, 20 percent for annualized volatility, 15 percent for long-term mean, and 10 for forecast horizon).

File: Mean Reversion with Drift (Simulated).xls

Description: This model illustrates the Mean Reversion stochastic process with a drift rate. An example application includes the simulation of stock prices, interest rates or inflation rate paths. This model requires Crystal Ball to run. Click on Crystal Ball's *Single Step* button to perform a stepwise simulation and see why it is so difficult to predict interest rates. Click on *Start Simulation* to estimate the distribution of stock prices at certain time intervals. Enter some values into the colored input boxes (default values are $1 for starting value, 15 percent for mean value, 20 percent for annualized volatility, 15 percent for long-term mean, and 10 for forecast horizon).

File: NPV and IRR Analysis (Simulation).xls

Description: This model provides a simple product sales analysis using Crystal Ball to run Monte Carlo simulations. The green cells (product cost, labor cost, price, price increase, selling price, and project cost) are the input assumptions, while the blue cells (net present value [NPV] and internal rate of return [IRR]) are the output forecast variables. Simply click on the *Run Simulation* icon to initiate Monte Carlo simulation.

File: Optimizing Ordinary Least Squares.xls

Description: This model illustrates how the ordinary least squares (OLS) regression model works. OLS is the unique linear line estimate that minimizes the sum of squared residuals (cell E28) by systematically changing the intercept and slope values (cells E26 and E27). These values are optimized by using Excel's Solver add-in. Compare the results with Excel's slope and intercept functions (cells H26 and H27). See the instructions in the spreadsheet to run this model.

File: Portfolio Allocation Model (Fit and Correlation).xls

Description: This model illustrates Crystal Ball's ability to perform correlated simulation and distributional fitting. For correlated assumptions, simply select any assumption input cell (D4:D7) and select *Correlation* to access the correlated simulation routine. For distributional fitting, either use the individual distributional fitting routine (click on the *Assign Assumption* icon, *Distributional Gallery* and choose fit) or use the batch-fit routine (*CBTools, Batch Fit*). In this example, simply choose cell H2 and select *Assign Assumption* (choose *Fit, range H2:H251*, choose all continuous distributions, Kolmogorov–Smirnov, show comparison charts, and so forth).

File: Product Mix Problem.xls

Description: This example provides a production profitability model. This model is particularly useful in illustrating the power of decision tables. To run the decision table using this model, click on *CBTools* and select *Decision Table.* Select *Profit/Loss* as the target cell and select both *phone* and *computer housing* as the decision variables to test.

File: Project Selection and Optimization.xls

Description: This model illustrates the application of optimization under uncertainty. That is, the decision variables (yellow cells in area B4:B15) are systematically and combinatorically chosen such that the budget constraint (37*Project 1 + 42*Project 2 + 36*Project 3 + 57.5*Project 4 + 45*Project 5 + 38*Project 6 + 35*Project 7 + 38*Project 8 + 50*Project 9 + 46*Project 10 + 35*Project 11 + 42*Project 12 <= 260) of less than $260 million is satisfied, such that the portfolio's net present value (NPV) is maximized, while considering the uncertainty and risks involved in each individual project (see Projects 1 to 12 worksheets in the model). To run this model, first start OptQuest (*CBTools* and *OptQuest*) and copy/paste the constraint into *OptQuest* and run the stochastic optimization project.

File: Reliability (Tornado and Spider).xls

Description: This example provides a simple engineering reliability model of a spring. This model is particularly useful in illustrating the power of tornado analysis. Assuming that Crystal Ball Professional is properly installed, click on *CBTools* and select *Tornado Chart.* Select *Material 1 Reliability* as the target cell and click on *Add Precedents.* The tornado chart analysis will show the critical success factors of the model., indicating which inputs impact the resulting Material 1 Reliability calculation the most.

File: Sharpe Portfolio (Optimization).xls

Description: This model illustrates the Markowitz efficient frontier and portfolio optimization allocation across four asset classes that are correlated with each other. Cells B11:B14 are the continuous decision variables having prespecified minimum and maximum values. Using Crystal Ball OptQuest, the maximum Sharpe Ratio (returns-to-risk ratio) is maximized subject to the prespecified constraints that the total portfolio must be 100 percent allocated across these four asset classes.

File: Toxic Waste Site.xls

Description: This example provides a simple model of toxic waste site risk-assessment. This model is particularly useful in illustrating the power of two-dimensional simulation. To run the two-dimensional simulation using this model, click on *CBTools* and select *2D Simulation*. Select *Risk Assessment* as the target cell and select *Body Weight* as the variability. The outer variability loop (Body Weight) will run after each successful set of simulation trials are completed.

Tables You Really Need

Standard Normal Distribution (partial area)
Standard Normal Distribution (full area)
Student's t-Distribution (one and two-tails)
Durbin–Watson Critical Values
Normal Random Numbers (standard normal distribution's random
    number generated ~ $(N(0,1))$
Random Numbers (multiple digits)
Uniform Random Numbers (uniform distribution's random number
    generated between 0.0000 and 1.0000)
Chi-Square Critical Values
F-Distribution Critical Statistics (alpha-one tail 0.10)
F-Distribution Critical Statistics (alpha-one tail 0.05)
F-Distribution Critical Statistics (alpha-one tail 0.25)
F-Distribution Critical Statistics (alpha-one tail 0.01)
Real Options Analysis Value (1-year maturity at 5% risk-free rate)
Real Options Analysis Value (3-year maturity at 5% risk-free rate)
Real Options Analysis Value (5-year maturity at 5% risk-free rate)
Real Options Analysis Value (7-year maturity at 5% risk-free rate)
Real Options Analysis Value (10-year maturity at 5% risk-free rate)
Real Options Analysis Value (15-year maturity at 5% risk-free rate)
Real Options Analysis Value (30-year maturity at 5% risk-free rate)

Standard Normal Distribution (partial area)

Z	0.00	0.01	0.02	0.03	0.04	0.05	0.06	0.07	0.08	0.09
0.0	0.0000	0.0040	0.0080	0.0120	0.0160	0.0199	0.0239	0.0279	0.0319	0.0359
0.1	0.0398	0.0438	0.0478	0.0517	0.0557	0.0596	0.0636	0.0675	0.0714	0.0753
0.2	0.0793	0.0832	0.0871	0.0910	0.0948	0.0987	0.1026	0.1064	0.1103	0.1141
0.3	0.1179	0.1217	0.1255	0.1293	0.1331	0.1368	0.1406	0.1443	0.1480	0.1517
0.4	0.1554	0.1591	0.1628	0.1664	0.1700	0.1736	0.1772	0.1808	0.1844	0.1879
0.5	0.1915	0.1950	0.1985	0.2019	0.2054	0.2088	0.2123	0.2157	0.2190	0.2224
0.6	0.2257	0.2291	0.2324	0.2357	0.2389	0.2422	0.2454	0.2486	0.2517	0.2549
0.7	0.2580	0.2611	0.2642	0.2673	0.2704	0.2734	0.2764	0.2794	0.2823	0.2852
0.8	0.2881	0.2910	0.2939	0.2967	0.2995	0.3023	0.3051	0.3078	0.3106	0.3133
0.9	0.3159	0.3186	0.3212	0.3238	0.3264	0.3289	0.3315	0.3340	0.3365	0.3389
1.0	0.3413	0.3438	0.3461	0.3485	0.3508	0.3531	0.3554	0.3577	0.3599	0.3621
1.1	0.3643	0.3665	0.3686	0.3708	0.3729	0.3749	0.3770	0.3790	0.3810	0.3830
1.2	0.3849	0.3869	0.3888	0.3907	0.3925	0.3944	0.3962	0.3980	0.3997	0.4015
1.3	0.4032	0.4049	0.4066	0.4082	0.4099	0.4115	0.4131	0.4147	0.4162	0.4177
1.4	0.4192	0.4207	0.4222	0.4236	0.4251	0.4265	0.4279	0.4292	0.4306	0.4319
1.5	0.4332	0.4345	0.4357	0.4370	0.4382	0.4394	0.4406	0.4418	0.4429	0.4441
1.6	0.4452	0.4463	0.4474	0.4484	0.4495	0.4505	0.4515	0.4525	0.4535	0.4545
1.7	0.4554	0.4564	0.4573	0.4582	0.4591	0.4599	0.4608	0.4616	0.4625	0.4633
1.8	0.4641	0.4649	0.4656	0.4664	0.4671	0.4678	0.4686	0.4693	0.4699	0.4706
1.9	0.4713	0.4719	0.4726	0.4732	0.4738	0.4744	0.4750	0.4756	0.4761	0.4767
2.0	0.4772	0.4778	0.4783	0.4788	0.4793	0.4798	0.4803	0.4808	0.4812	0.4817
2.1	0.4821	0.4826	0.4830	0.4834	0.4838	0.4842	0.4846	0.4850	0.4854	0.4857
2.2	0.4861	0.4864	0.4868	0.4871	0.4875	0.4878	0.4881	0.4884	0.4887	0.4890
2.3	0.4893	0.4896	0.4898	0.4901	0.4904	0.4906	0.4909	0.4911	0.4913	0.4916
2.4	0.4918	0.4920	0.4922	0.4925	0.4927	0.4929	0.4931	0.4932	0.4934	0.4936
2.5	0.4938	0.4940	0.4941	0.4943	0.4945	0.4946	0.4948	0.4949	0.4951	0.4952
2.6	0.4953	0.4955	0.4956	0.4957	0.4959	0.4960	0.4961	0.4962	0.4963	0.4964
2.7	0.4965	0.4966	0.4967	0.4968	0.4969	0.4970	0.4971	0.4972	0.4973	0.4974
2.8	0.4974	0.4975	0.4976	0.4977	0.4977	0.4978	0.4979	0.4979	0.4980	0.4981
2.9	0.4981	0.4982	0.4982	0.4983	0.4984	0.4984	0.4985	0.4985	0.4986	0.4986
3.0	0.4987	0.4987	0.4987	0.4988	0.4988	0.4989	0.4989	0.4989	0.4990	0.4990

Example: For a Z-value of 1.96, refer to the 1.9 row and 0.06 column for the area of 0.4750. This means there is 47.50% in the shaded region and 2.50% in the single tail. Similarly, there is 95% in the body or 5% in both tails.

Standard Normal Distribution (full area)

Z	0.00	0.01	0.02	0.03	0.04	0.05	0.06	0.07	0.08	0.09
0.0	0.5000	0.5040	0.5080	0.5120	0.5160	0.5199	0.5239	0.5279	0.5319	0.5359
0.1	0.5398	0.5438	0.5478	0.5517	0.5557	0.5596	0.5636	0.5675	0.5714	0.5753
0.2	0.5793	0.5832	0.5871	0.5910	0.5948	0.5987	0.6026	0.6064	0.6103	0.6141
0.3	0.6179	0.6217	0.6255	0.6293	0.6331	0.6368	0.6406	0.6443	0.6480	0.6517
0.4	0.6554	0.6591	0.6628	0.6664	0.6700	0.6736	0.6772	0.6808	0.6844	0.6879
0.5	0.6915	0.6950	0.6985	0.7019	0.7054	0.7088	0.7123	0.7157	0.7190	0.7224
0.6	0.7257	0.7291	0.7324	0.7357	0.7389	0.7422	0.7454	0.7486	0.7517	0.7549
0.7	0.7580	0.7611	0.7642	0.7673	0.7704	0.7734	0.7764	0.7794	0.7823	0.7852
0.8	0.7881	0.7910	0.7939	0.7967	0.7995	0.8023	0.8051	0.8078	0.8106	0.8133
0.9	0.8159	0.8186	0.8212	0.8238	0.8264	0.8289	0.8315	0.8340	0.8365	0.8389
1.0	0.8413	0.8438	0.8461	0.8485	0.8508	0.8531	0.8554	0.8577	0.8599	0.8621
1.1	0.8643	0.8665	0.8686	0.8708	0.8729	0.8749	0.8770	0.8790	0.8810	0.8830
1.2	0.8849	0.8869	0.8888	0.8907	0.8925	0.8944	0.8962	0.8980	0.8997	0.9015
1.3	0.9032	0.9049	0.9066	0.9082	0.9099	0.9115	0.9131	0.9147	0.9162	0.9177
1.4	0.9192	0.9207	0.9222	0.9236	0.9251	0.9265	0.9279	0.9292	0.9306	0.9319
1.5	0.9332	0.9345	0.9357	0.9370	0.9382	0.9394	0.9406	0.9418	0.9429	0.9441
1.6	0.9452	0.9463	0.9474	0.9484	0.9495	0.9505	0.9515	0.9525	0.9535	0.9545
1.7	0.9554	0.9564	0.9573	0.9582	0.9591	0.9599	0.9608	0.9616	0.9625	0.9633
1.8	0.9641	0.9649	0.9656	0.9664	0.9671	0.9678	0.9686	0.9693	0.9699	0.9706
1.9	0.9713	0.9719	0.9726	0.9732	0.9738	0.9744	0.9750	0.9756	0.9761	0.9767
2.0	0.9772	0.9778	0.9783	0.9788	0.9793	0.9798	0.9803	0.9808	0.9812	0.9817
2.1	0.9821	0.9826	0.9830	0.9834	0.9838	0.9842	0.9846	0.9850	0.9854	0.9857
2.2	0.9861	0.9864	0.9868	0.9871	0.9875	0.9878	0.9881	0.9884	0.9887	0.9890
2.3	0.9893	0.9896	0.9898	0.9901	0.9904	0.9906	0.9909	0.9911	0.9913	0.9916
2.4	0.9918	0.9920	0.9922	0.9925	0.9927	0.9929	0.9931	0.9932	0.9934	0.9936
2.5	0.9938	0.9940	0.9941	0.9943	0.9945	0.9946	0.9948	0.9949	0.9951	0.9952
2.6	0.9953	0.9955	0.9956	0.9957	0.9959	0.9960	0.9961	0.9962	0.9963	0.9964
2.7	0.9965	0.9966	0.9967	0.9968	0.9969	0.9970	0.9971	0.9972	0.9973	0.9974
2.8	0.9974	0.9975	0.9976	0.9977	0.9977	0.9978	0.9979	0.9979	0.9980	0.9981
2.9	0.9981	0.9982	0.9982	0.9983	0.9984	0.9984	0.9985	0.9985	0.9986	0.9986
3.0	0.9987	0.9987	0.9987	0.9988	0.9988	0.9989	0.9989	0.9989	0.9990	0.9990

Example: For a Z-value of 2.33, refer to the 2.3 row and 0.03 column for the area of 0.99. This means there is 99% in the shaded region and 1% in the one-sided left or right tail.

Student's t-Distribution
(one and two tails)

one tail

two tail

alpha	0.1	0.05	0.025	0.01	0.005	alpha	0.1	0.05	0.025	0.01	0.005
df = 1	3.0777	6.3137	12.7062	31.8210	63.6559	df = 1	6.3137	12.7062	25.4519	63.6559	127.3211
2	1.8856	2.9200	4.3027	6.9645	9.9250	2	2.9200	4.3027	6.2054	9.9250	14.0892
3	1.6377	2.3534	3.1824	4.5407	5.8408	3	2.3534	3.1824	4.1765	5.8408	7.4532
4	1.5332	2.1318	2.7765	3.7469	4.6041	4	2.1318	2.7765	3.4954	4.6041	5.5975
5	1.4759	2.0150	2.5706	3.3649	4.0321	5	2.0150	2.5706	3.1634	4.0321	4.7733
6	1.4398	1.9432	2.4469	3.1427	3.7074	6	1.9432	2.4469	2.9687	3.7074	4.3168
7	1.4149	1.8946	2.3646	2.9979	3.4995	7	1.8946	2.3646	2.8412	3.4995	4.0294
8	1.3968	1.8595	2.3060	2.8965	3.3554	8	1.8595	2.3060	2.7515	3.3554	3.8325
9	1.3830	1.8331	2.2622	2.8214	3.2498	9	1.8331	2.2622	2.6850	3.2498	3.6896
10	1.3722	1.8125	2.2281	2.7638	3.1693	10	1.8125	2.2281	2.6338	3.1693	3.5814
15	1.3406	1.7531	2.1315	2.6025	2.9467	15	1.7531	2.1315	2.4899	2.9467	3.2860
20	1.3253	1.7247	2.0860	2.5280	2.8453	20	1.7247	2.0860	2.4231	2.8453	3.1534
25	1.3163	1.7081	2.0595	2.4851	2.7874	25	1.7081	2.0595	2.3846	2.7874	3.0782
30	1.3104	1.6973	2.0423	2.4573	2.7500	30	1.6973	2.0423	2.3596	2.7500	3.0298
35	1.3062	1.6896	2.0301	2.4377	2.7238	35	1.6896	2.0301	2.3420	2.7238	2.9961
40	1.3031	1.6839	2.0211	2.4233	2.7045	40	1.6839	2.0211	2.3289	2.7045	2.9712
45	1.3007	1.6794	2.0141	2.4121	2.6896	45	1.6794	2.0141	2.3189	2.6896	2.9521
50	1.2987	1.6759	2.0086	2.4033	2.6778	50	1.6759	2.0086	2.3109	2.6778	2.9370
100	1.2901	1.6602	1.9840	2.3642	2.6259	100	1.6602	1.9840	2.2757	2.6259	2.8707
200	1.2858	1.6525	1.9719	2.3451	2.6006	200	1.6525	1.9719	2.2584	2.6006	2.8385
300	1.2844	1.6499	1.9679	2.3388	2.5923	300	1.6499	1.9679	2.2527	2.5923	2.8279
500	1.2832	1.6479	1.9647	2.3338	2.5857	500	1.6479	1.9647	2.2482	2.5857	2.8195
100000	1.2816	1.6449	1.9600	2.3264	2.5759	100000	1.6449	1.9600	2.2414	2.5759	2.8071

Example: For an alpha in the single right tail area of 2.5% with 15 degrees of freedom, the critical t value is 2.1315.

Durbin–Watson Critical Values (alpha 0.05)

n	k = 1 D_L	k = 1 D_U	k = 2 D_L	k = 2 D_U	k = 3 D_L	k = 3 D_U	k = 4 D_L	k = 4 D_U	k = 5 D_L	k = 5 D_U
15	1.08	1.36	0.95	1.54	0.82	1.75	0.69	1.97	0.56	2.21
16	1.10	1.37	0.98	1.54	0.86	1.73	0.74	1.93	0.62	2.15
17	1.13	1.38	1.02	1.54	0.90	1.71	0.78	1.90	0.67	2.10
18	1.16	1.39	1.05	1.53	0.93	1.69	0.82	1.87	0.71	2.06
19	1.18	1.40	1.08	1.53	0.97	1.68	0.86	1.85	0.75	2.02
20	1.20	1.41	1.10	1.54	1.00	1.67	0.90	1.83	0.79	1.99
21	1.22	1.42	1.13	1.54	1.03	1.66	0.93	1.81	0.83	1.96
22	1.24	1.43	1.15	1.54	1.05	1.66	0.96	1.80	0.86	1.94
23	1.26	1.44	1.17	1.54	1.08	1.66	0.99	1.79	0.90	1.92
24	1.27	1.45	1.19	1.55	1.10	1.66	1.01	1.78	0.93	1.90
25	1.29	1.45	1.21	1.55	1.12	1.65	1.04	1.77	0.95	1.89
26	1.30	1.46	1.22	1.55	1.14	1.65	1.06	1.76	0.98	1.88
27	1.32	1.47	1.24	1.56	1.16	1.65	1.08	1.76	1.01	1.86
28	1.33	1.48	1.26	1.56	1.18	1.65	1.10	1.75	1.03	1.85
29	1.34	1.48	1.27	1.56	1.20	1.65	1.12	1.74	1.05	1.84
30	1.35	1.49	1.28	1.57	1.21	1.65	1.14	1.74	1.07	1.83
31	1.36	1.50	1.30	1.57	1.23	1.65	1.16	1.74	1.09	1.83
32	1.37	1.50	1.31	1.57	1.24	1.65	1.18	1.73	1.11	1.82
33	1.38	1.51	1.32	1.58	1.26	1.65	1.19	1.73	1.13	1.81
34	1.39	1.51	1.33	1.58	1.27	1.65	1.21	1.73	1.15	1.81
35	1.40	1.52	1.34	1.58	1.28	1.65	1.22	1.73	1.16	1.80
36	1.41	1.52	1.35	1.59	1.29	1.65	1.24	1.73	1.18	1.80
37	1.42	1.53	1.36	1.59	1.31	1.66	1.25	1.72	1.19	1.80
38	1.43	1.54	1.37	1.59	1.32	1.66	1.26	1.72	1.21	1.79
39	1.43	1.54	1.38	1.60	1.33	1.66	1.27	1.72	1.22	1.79
40	1.44	1.54	1.39	1.60	1.34	1.66	1.29	1.72	1.23	1.79
45	1.48	1.57	1.43	1.62	1.38	1.67	1.34	1.72	1.29	1.78
50	1.50	1.59	1.46	1.63	1.42	1.67	1.38	1.72	1.34	1.77
55	1.53	1.60	1.49	1.64	1.45	1.68	1.41	1.72	1.38	1.77
60	1.55	1.62	1.51	1.65	1.48	1.69	1.44	1.73	1.41	1.77
65	1.57	1.63	1.54	1.66	1.50	1.70	1.47	1.73	1.44	1.77
70	1.58	1.64	1.55	1.67	1.52	1.70	1.49	1.74	1.46	1.77
75	1.60	1.65	1.57	1.68	1.54	1.71	1.51	1.74	1.49	1.77
80	1.61	1.66	1.59	1.69	1.56	1.72	1.53	1.74	1.51	1.77
85	1.62	1.67	1.60	1.70	1.57	1.72	1.55	1.75	1.52	1.77
90	1.63	1.68	1.61	1.70	1.59	1.73	1.57	1.75	1.54	1.78
95	1.64	1.69	1.62	1.71	1.60	1.73	1.58	1.75	1.56	1.78
100	1.65	1.69	1.63	1.72	1.61	1.74	1.59	1.76	1.57	1.78

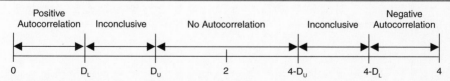

Example: For 30 observations (*n*) of a multivariate regression with three independent variables, the critical Durbin–Watson statistics are 1.21 (D_L) and 1.65 (D_U). If the calculated Durbin–Watson is 1.05, there is positive autocorrelation.

Normal Random Numbers (standard normal distribution's random number generated ~ $N(0,1)$)

	1	2	3	4	5	6	7	8	9	10
1	-1.0800	-0.5263	-0.7099	-0.3124	0.0216	-0.7768	-0.0752	0.4273	0.7708	0.1887
2	-1.1028	1.0904	-0.9228	-0.8881	-1.7909	0.6459	0.8982	-0.9736	-0.8630	0.1361
3	-0.8336	0.1454	-1.5907	1.0843	0.6271	1.1925	1.4669	0.5701	-2.7364	0.2500
4	0.2296	-0.2436	-0.0639	0.2307	-0.0560	-1.8494	0.6068	-0.2562	0.2168	-0.0261
5	1.2795	-0.6267	0.3133	0.3831	0.8894	0.9869	1.6185	0.7713	0.1421	-0.9623
6	1.2079	-0.8924	0.0491	0.0250	-0.5501	-0.8312	0.5067	-0.4316	0.7880	0.3858
7	-0.9474	-1.1758	-2.0242	-1.1567	-0.3838	0.8031	-0.5129	1.3572	-0.6772	1.0510
8	-0.7296	-0.8073	0.1137	-0.3553	-2.5826	-0.2768	0.0300	0.6233	-2.0171	-1.0818
9	0.0939	-0.1833	0.5550	0.3809	0.4096	0.0930	0.0257	-0.0603	-2.3620	-0.2656
10	-1.2110	-0.3240	0.8859	0.3776	-1.9103	2.0585	0.5215	-1.3543	-0.6975	-1.5965
11	-0.4614	-0.7827	0.8294	0.4460	-0.6563	0.4167	-0.3699	-0.0852	0.5010	0.3579
12	-0.5282	1.2526	-0.3289	1.5912	0.8460	1.2919	-0.6255	-0.2466	0.6740	1.6007
13	1.1204	0.5921	0.3115	0.1986	-0.6793	0.0694	-0.2777	0.5517	-0.5385	1.2437
14	-0.3726	0.0955	-2.3786	-1.7042	0.6656	0.0641	0.3874	1.1669	-0.6837	-0.0934
15	-0.5656	-0.0949	-0.3845	-0.6864	0.9967	0.0695	1.4614	1.0945	-1.2097	-1.4070
16	-0.2430	-2.4107	-2.5924	0.2724	-0.0967	-0.0315	-0.8218	0.2390	0.5987	-0.6879
17	-0.2820	-0.4370	0.7358	-0.3511	-0.2308	-0.7651	-0.7652	-0.4937	-1.0157	-0.1394
18	-0.3955	0.5096	0.1447	-0.4119	1.3781	-0.7365	0.4475	1.7877	0.3629	1.4260
19	0.1652	-0.4687	0.1058	-0.4183	-0.3782	-2.4017	0.9160	-1.8322	-0.6279	0.0098
20	-0.0504	-1.0931	-1.6450	-0.6165	-0.0279	-0.9539	-1.6489	-0.7252	0.3962	0.8928
21	0.1841	-0.1236	0.7653	-0.9054	0.8158	-0.8576	1.9970	-0.1568	-1.6658	-0.6698
22	-1.1091	0.5140	0.4505	-1.7429	0.0854	0.1573	-2.2687	0.4879	-0.0820	0.4840
23	0.6553	0.4692	0.9139	0.9639	-0.9046	-0.6695	-0.3393	-1.8453	1.0532	0.9795
24	0.5185	0.8624	0.6098	0.7062	0.3533	0.1695	0.1840	-0.5235	0.7202	0.0790
25	-0.6228	-0.0052	0.1012	0.9541	1.4046	-0.2620	-0.2783	0.7601	-0.0375	1.8253
26	0.5867	0.3346	-0.0588	-0.4356	0.0004	0.2037	-1.1411	-0.4674	2.2770	-0.8338

27	0.2450	1.0948	-0.8954	1.0444	-0.2184	-1.1320	1.5127	-0.9275	-0.4799	0.1281
28	-0.0279	-0.1937	-1.2914	-0.9880	1.1571	0.5578	0.4071	1.2601	1.1695	-0.2957
29	-0.4161	-0.5507	-0.4475	0.0689	0.4422	-1.1679	-0.5163	0.3915	-0.7226	0.9784
30	-0.8053	0.3502	-1.4505	-0.5941	-0.7228	-0.7034	-1.0992	0.3020	-0.1026	-1.2502
31	1.0404	0.1097	0.4544	-0.5799	-0.2926	1.2725	-0.5619	-0.0821	-0.5477	1.0231
32	0.2528	0.5059	-1.4190	0.3989	-1.3937	-1.2064	0.0228	-0.6627	1.1379	0.5220
33	-0.2739	-0.9455	-2.2941	0.0276	1.7592	-1.7925	-0.5070	-0.2650	1.5300	-0.3373
34	-0.9423	0.3491	-1.3512	0.4576	1.0860	-0.1653	0.4558	-0.6405	-1.2085	-0.7493
35	0.0883	0.2888	-0.5136	2.1450	-0.0262	2.9286	-1.7310	1.1511	-0.6439	-0.3583
36	-0.4517	0.2437	0.2776	-0.7868	0.1671	1.0155	-0.3549	0.7456	-0.3971	-1.9802
37	-1.1278	-2.3892	-0.2134	0.2925	1.2178	-0.3160	0.9686	-1.2743	-0.0707	1.5162
38	1.3791	-0.4170	-0.1155	-0.1992	-1.1890	1.2458	-1.6882	0.3428	-1.3231	-0.3701
39	0.0819	0.5604	-1.7606	-0.6743	-1.0426	-0.8501	1.1497	0.0442	0.5657	-1.2778
40	-0.4175	0.4203	1.2675	1.2768	-0.4826	-2.3268	0.0747	1.0223	0.2681	-0.3952
41	0.6801	-0.6346	-0.4628	0.1047	1.0032	-1.4099	0.3401	-0.5051	-1.2245	-0.4696
42	0.9200	-0.4411	1.9065	-0.8623	-0.8896	-1.3154	-0.2427	1.4517	0.6037	0.7206
43	-2.0794	-0.0927	1.0023	-0.2296	-0.6263	-0.7918	-0.6372	2.7211	0.3840	-0.5358
44	0.5448	0.6405	0.3647	-1.9654	-1.8430	-0.4946	-0.6691	1.3191	0.9991	1.6156
45	1.0963	1.2051	0.7243	2.3032	-0.4820	2.0831	0.6108	0.8796	0.5527	0.8128
46	-0.9386	1.2509	-2.1745	-0.4204	-0.6400	-1.0716	0.0190	-1.9153	-1.4322	0.0870
47	2.4524	1.5695	-0.6953	-2.4997	-0.0891	-0.5719	-0.9301	-0.3394	-2.6532	-0.0226
48	0.4448	-1.8947	0.7942	0.3552	-0.4288	1.0699	0.7316	-1.1951	1.4356	0.2318
49	0.1323	-0.0470	1.5664	0.1610	0.4068	-1.1848	-1.2338	0.1546	-0.3490	2.4516
50	-0.6323	1.7106	-0.6715	0.2511	0.7708	-0.6902	0.8453	1.1715	1.4897	0.0401

Random Numbers (multiple digits)

	1	2	3	4	5	6	7	8	9	10
1	2721.5177	7927.3605	5509.2000	7755.4229	8910.1600	9583.6638	9063.9590	8043.2820	9974.8278	7685.4216
2	5427.5197	6573.0674	6996.6637	9135.8127	2718.8760	8982.9624	4576.1065	5844.0620	2435.0249	2281.9131
3	1570.2192	5024.3217	6764.9039	1023.2814	6548.8675	3329.6628	4520.5547	9269.9768	6344.4565	2809.3591
4	6617.8598	5903.1769	7002.3606	2085.2144	4792.4796	6844.4960	8697.2448	6543.3337	2982.5475	6500.9816
5	1042.3463	4784.7013	2453.3249	2006.1324	2128.2118	4070.3922	7223.9221	9040.6234	3864.3067	8258.1458
6	5152.2026	2683.5095	3648.9192	7937.8332	9361.6421	6588.8570	9066.6720	7688.1069	4799.6166	4936.4821
7	8092.3323	5697.0313	7446.0071	3138.0076	3274.5303	3064.3907	9283.3996	3169.3531	5119.0202	9799.3380
8	3200.8200	8155.2797	2903.4796	3975.4799	2090.4880	2584.4027	2321.1790	9201.1671	5563.8958	4922.1343
9	2182.8695	9863.5501	3827.3677	5479.6807	5846.3606	7009.6787	1956.4793	9485.3016	6048.6349	4545.7721
10	4929.3461	1009.5500	6692.1558	6563.8505	6478.1138	1457.2554	2607.2569	1772.3479	1130.7805	9296.8716
11	9478.2765	9055.7916	8831.3015	9113.9356	3863.2465	6845.3370	7956.4931	3620.3660	6516.1395	5908.0984
12	1336.6521	6161.7270	8222.4781	5859.3163	8247.4744	8348.0894	6487.8202	6784.5221	4693.3882	5667.7078
13	7460.0083	5643.3684	2422.6688	6932.7146	2091.5401	3917.1395	5129.1433	1218.7031	8785.2712	7050.3969
14	5849.9114	5882.0649	6661.0100	6681.4560	9481.2436	2195.1850	4813.7851	9085.3021	1653.4790	3719.3843
15	6975.6430	9691.5555	6668.4537	7785.4196	6508.2217	9147.5266	9760.7188	1920.8204	1278.8593	5578.9917
16	9178.9897	3759.3978	3947.4711	6015.4509	2645.6605	9933.6472	8250.7021	4046.9983	2472.1532	6918.8681
17	1105.8190	7150.7795	1707.7886	6093.6588	5725.3097	6168.8648	6322.9949	8035.1053	1670.8308	3130.7888
18	4378.4322	8484.7097	7236.2981	4585.2984	6117.0657	1604.2704	6441.3144	9050.4318	1192.4602	3053.1196
19	6589.7603	8938.1669	5639.4775	9210.1063	3355.4245	5526.0291	2033.4076	8997.8637	6921.5642	9584.1109
20	4455.2372	6786.2862	4018.8972	5491.1575	1560.0462	4115.5836	1048.3373	9623.0486	8862.3072	7621.1737
21	4448.7636	6209.5568	9959.7063	3177.2467	1641.8797	6802.2869	8161.5705	1685.3721	1941.6971	8308.9046
22	8654.4590	9343.3206	6653.9854	9692.1930	3929.0176	4784.0031	4596.3431	6587.9375	9035.8024	1517.4567
23	8844.1890	9681.9999	2822.7265	2899.0180	5158.0016	5636.0479	2528.0603	6982.0078	9200.3319	6361.4182
24	7390.3963	5983.7082	5900.1055	3837.7891	8828.4116	7731.9270	3157.1180	1957.9680	6105.4342	4370.7669
25	5203.6897	4338.6493	4776.3189	1129.9635	1273.6261	8183.6248	2281.0786	2374.5525	2381.9855	3381.8613
26	4161.9959	6863.8237	9514.2372	2225.4123	4676.0563	6451.0761	5920.1725	2916.4971	5819.8761	7904.7086

27	8044.9759	8610.4069	8708.4209	8303.2069	6696.6600	5799.8857	9579.7723	6845.5490	1039.0858	8763.7395
28	2587.5116	5853.4249	4388.2114	5526.0319	2061.3728	4644.3832	1388.8595	5890.9486	3907.8750	4141.8542
29	7052.2487	6036.5176	2541.3818	2812.2029	7546.7513	2546.8478	2494.0563	6029.0624	1324.0261	8162.4338
30	1163.9374	1931.4068	6247.8204	7745.6642	3070.3767	5071.9130	6159.3637	3013.1682	1226.8873	8162.4898
31	1714.6545	1523.8375	8509.5616	8306.2575	9657.2873	3120.0271	6688.3472	5159.6344	3671.7474	7133.5930
32	3919.0191	5588.6388	4923.3729	5347.2862	1600.1555	2029.1451	3136.0774	2317.8933	3932.5034	3018.1371
33	5026.6414	2547.0444	4424.7295	4170.3210	7624.0027	5232.2546	5874.4753	4124.2614	5273.4984	5929.6120
34	5621.6736	5358.4125	2870.7415	6454.0855	8476.0039	2736.0572	6719.2599	2753.2847	4911.0976	1791.5700
35	9910.5203	6121.8213	3308.4460	3150.5253	9211.2410	5499.6467	3931.8208	5313.8206	5934.1154	4849.0388
36	4312.4452	8426.2265	8872.6974	1663.1930	9120.5661	5981.5407	2613.1288	5439.7424	9611.6777	5188.4457
37	7626.7677	5387.7439	2935.0787	8309.7795	8246.8356	2074.3136	5736.0131	3286.1149	8836.6044	7193.7667
38	9884.8894	6400.4452	3674.4606	6779.5470	9832.8283	8108.7365	4803.5534	7599.8840	2362.3725	8762.0338
39	3835.9843	9103.7538	2867.9787	6320.5689	2208.7881	3409.7276	7836.5953	5104.6250	3424.2561	6521.1725
40	1337.4881	5372.2827	4089.9067	9875.2185	1422.7835	6058.8479	5847.4650	8856.1609	1258.4403	3044.5864
41	3785.1585	4943.2358	2420.7229	5821.4256	5122.6017	8973.0601	6324.9297	9036.6863	1197.9443	2913.1478
42	8926.2929	6024.7767	4233.9264	2292.9495	1958.8263	5534.9091	8243.9129	9370.1993	9628.7974	2321.1484
43	8900.4838	4553.4951	8777.2026	8809.0081	6170.5223	4601.8483	6653.8133	8002.2370	2871.4168	4085.8857
44	6385.5759	1642.6064	4939.2942	8710.5348	2064.4489	7854.8362	4247.8259	3799.9352	6065.6772	9917.2978
45	9684.0981	5429.2985	6042.3134	5461.5755	8034.5336	5056.7885	1621.9722	9290.8556	4395.0623	9808.8263
46	6385.0021	5007.4273	2845.5347	1898.6996	9031.1549	9874.3671	2061.4315	5221.1304	4624.0654	8847.7553
47	8706.7893	1279.1794	8722.8166	5683.5057	9611.4135	2593.5565	2220.1057	6559.8872	3554.2664	5352.1678
48	4542.1757	5609.2758	9599.0981	7644.5129	8663.3854	7009.6717	1887.5296	7330.2408	9197.2417	3012.4571
49	3242.9899	8305.9299	6439.2860	7130.1905	6503.2924	5736.9502	3489.9470	3671.3190	2925.8024	7207.2956
50	7751.6580	7934.9861	8400.8779	2923.6741	4305.5792	3995.4573	9288.3303	6593.9721	5302.2203	9007.2129

Uniform Random Numbers (uniform distribution's random number generated between 0.0000 and 1.0000)

	1	2	3	4	5	6	7	8	9	10
1	0.8470	0.8006	0.8185	0.5479	0.6664	0.4772	0.8983	0.9434	0.0272	0.1912
2	0.8538	0.1840	0.0235	0.5733	0.5103	0.9165	0.2052	0.6861	0.4069	0.8930
3	0.4816	0.0929	0.0404	0.1688	0.4297	0.1381	0.5717	0.3440	0.3050	0.3347
4	0.1827	0.6090	0.2067	0.0201	0.1809	0.4326	0.5870	0.4826	0.8274	0.4693
5	0.6736	0.7903	0.0910	0.7829	0.9657	0.3531	0.5095	0.4019	0.9799	0.4321
6	0.9953	0.8069	0.5096	0.8088	0.5747	0.5876	0.6151	0.7627	0.3793	0.4698
7	0.7613	0.8829	0.9609	0.6287	0.0849	0.9027	0.2761	0.5469	0.5634	0.0308
8	0.1317	0.7907	0.5440	0.0469	0.7220	0.5695	0.2482	0.3742	0.1409	0.3288
9	0.5269	0.6977	0.4061	0.0950	0.2114	0.4113	0.7619	0.6854	0.1402	0.2956
10	0.9121	0.5435	0.3236	0.6256	0.7646	0.3120	0.8037	0.1198	0.8887	0.5443
11	0.5390	0.4622	0.3459	0.1427	0.7762	0.8186	0.5059	0.1905	0.8696	0.8893
12	0.9055	0.4771	0.6290	0.8068	0.5124	0.9142	0.6397	0.5279	0.2051	0.1220
13	0.6644	0.9212	0.2139	0.3678	0.8107	0.1869	0.5594	0.8278	0.2343	0.9175
14	0.7403	0.1068	0.9122	0.1193	0.5645	0.9703	0.9102	0.3528	0.6891	0.0330
15	0.8611	0.9607	0.1820	0.8349	0.4017	0.2822	0.3624	0.8583	0.1495	0.1532
16	0.4914	0.1137	0.2635	0.6062	0.1728	0.5471	0.1065	0.4250	0.7094	0.3168
17	0.7664	0.6767	0.5264	0.9354	0.9880	0.1942	0.9594	0.2610	0.9933	0.3406
18	0.0126	0.5592	0.3942	0.4020	0.7840	0.8675	0.1734	0.0476	0.3372	0.4067
19	0.5251	0.8027	0.6730	0.9985	0.4706	0.2960	0.3305	0.1006	0.1012	0.4638
20	0.7772	0.4434	0.1596	0.3856	0.0163	0.5783	0.4055	0.1490	0.7172	0.2243
21	0.8973	0.7618	0.4225	0.9524	0.7371	0.3863	0.2146	0.3799	0.8521	0.7857
22	0.1709	0.1966	0.1125	0.1454	0.0325	0.2262	0.3624	0.3600	0.6517	0.4073
23	0.1785	0.6833	0.9630	0.3603	0.8863	0.4362	0.5985	0.2979	0.6837	0.0957
24	0.5644	0.2031	0.9500	0.0418	0.9262	0.6584	0.5958	0.9879	0.4332	0.0198
25	0.3672	0.4599	0.2637	0.9380	0.8343	0.6933	0.4732	0.5802	0.2715	0.1287
26	0.8391	0.1803	0.4345	0.7670	0.5298	0.7905	0.4120	0.9688	0.8540	0.8267

27	0.7135	0.8772	0.5661	0.4345	0.8710	0.6183	0.1704	0.3377	0.1432	0.9205
28	0.9477	0.0880	0.0476	0.2050	0.5699	0.5680	0.3438	0.9242	0.1429	0.0283
29	0.2862	0.0944	0.0698	0.6541	0.5945	0.5464	0.1861	0.8030	0.8177	0.8099
30	0.9237	0.5355	0.9374	0.4701	0.8763	0.3914	0.5917	0.6042	0.0596	0.2829
31	0.5876	0.2458	0.6085	0.6830	0.5682	0.9463	0.5392	0.0854	0.7900	0.3149
32	0.0677	0.4571	0.6932	0.0656	0.3131	0.9006	0.8570	0.7966	0.4101	0.5311
33	0.9369	0.3878	0.8473	0.9510	0.9292	0.1164	0.4611	0.7247	0.7077	0.0106
34	0.1777	0.1686	0.1624	0.9553	0.2083	0.9768	0.2229	0.1562	0.6361	0.0027
35	0.4455	0.5007	0.0395	0.4937	0.9753	0.3447	0.0391	0.6322	0.3977	0.4147
36	0.4002	0.5214	0.1770	0.8398	0.2889	0.5151	0.4960	0.6892	0.4331	0.8813
37	0.4288	0.7095	0.6115	0.1138	0.7932	0.7117	0.6252	0.1275	0.6600	0.0738
38	0.3327	0.3886	0.6723	0.0747	0.7562	0.2142	0.1860	0.9814	0.0407	0.7521
39	0.5113	0.4232	0.2029	0.9034	0.0154	0.6591	0.0515	0.8867	0.5985	0.0338
40	0.2530	0.2622	0.2013	0.0351	0.1554	0.4416	0.0300	0.7017	0.4546	0.6329
41	0.3086	0.7557	0.6003	0.5604	0.6615	0.8889	0.2757	0.8436	0.1147	0.2306
42	0.7732	0.6118	0.3301	0.7272	0.4494	0.4960	0.6787	0.2748	0.4064	0.1111
43	0.6713	0.2170	0.5049	0.7975	0.6739	0.9117	0.0948	0.9233	0.6709	0.6739
44	0.9708	0.0705	0.0987	0.5948	0.1022	0.1206	0.2131	0.3548	0.0826	0.7013
45	0.4756	0.6014	0.8200	0.5208	0.3044	0.4410	0.1012	0.5467	0.7132	0.2751
46	0.6130	0.0888	0.2238	0.1298	0.5416	0.7280	0.9447	0.6551	0.0112	0.5960
47	0.2792	0.7500	0.3124	0.0277	0.3785	0.9622	0.7501	0.6412	0.1556	0.1384
48	0.5724	0.0308	0.7103	0.1949	0.9440	0.9585	0.4508	0.3737	0.7383	0.6845
49	0.2825	0.9384	0.6804	0.3165	0.1243	0.6089	0.2623	0.8008	0.2408	0.9563
50	0.3294	0.4181	0.5703	0.4162	0.8578	0.3346	0.5491	0.1812	0.7001	0.6394

Chi-Square Critical Values

df	0.10	0.09	0.08	0.07	0.06	0.05	0.04	0.03	0.02	0.01
1	2.7055	2.8744	3.0649	3.2830	3.5374	3.8415	4.2179	4.7093	5.4119	6.6349
2	4.6052	4.8159	5.0515	5.3185	5.6268	5.9915	6.4377	7.0131	7.8241	9.2104
3	6.2514	6.4915	6.7587	7.0603	7.4069	7.8147	8.3112	8.9473	9.8374	11.3449
4	7.7794	8.0434	8.3365	8.6664	9.0444	9.4877	10.0255	10.7119	11.6678	13.2767
5	9.2363	9.5211	9.8366	10.1910	10.5962	11.0705	11.6443	12.3746	13.3882	15.0863
6	10.6446	10.9479	11.2835	11.6599	12.0896	12.5916	13.1978	13.9676	15.0332	16.8119
7	12.0170	12.3372	12.6912	13.0877	13.5397	14.0671	14.7030	15.5091	16.6224	18.4753
8	13.3616	13.6975	14.0684	14.4836	14.9563	15.5073	16.1708	17.0105	18.1682	20.0902
9	14.6837	15.0342	15.4211	15.8537	16.3459	16.9190	17.6083	18.4796	19.6790	21.6660
10	15.9872	16.3516	16.7535	17.2026	17.7131	18.3070	19.0208	19.9219	21.1608	23.2093
11	17.2750	17.6526	18.0687	18.5334	19.0614	19.6752	20.4120	21.3416	22.6179	24.7250
12	18.5493	18.9395	19.3692	19.8488	20.3934	21.0261	21.7851	22.7418	24.0539	26.2170
13	19.8119	20.2140	20.6568	21.1507	21.7113	22.3620	23.1423	24.1249	25.4715	27.6882
14	21.0641	21.4778	21.9331	22.4408	23.0166	23.6848	24.4854	25.4931	26.8727	29.1412
15	22.3071	22.7319	23.1992	23.7202	24.3108	24.9958	25.8161	26.8480	28.2595	30.5780
16	23.5418	23.9774	24.4564	24.9901	25.5950	26.2962	27.1356	28.1908	29.6332	31.9999
17	24.7690	25.2150	25.7053	26.2514	26.8701	27.5871	28.4449	29.5227	30.9950	33.4087
18	25.9894	26.4455	26.9467	27.5049	28.1370	28.8693	29.7450	30.8447	32.3462	34.8052
19	27.2036	27.6695	28.1813	28.7512	29.3964	30.1435	31.0367	32.1577	33.6874	36.1908
20	28.4120	28.8874	29.4097	29.9910	30.6488	31.4104	32.3206	33.4623	35.0196	37.5663
21	29.6151	30.0998	30.6322	31.2246	31.8949	32.6706	33.5972	34.7593	36.3434	38.9322
22	30.8133	31.3071	31.8494	32.4526	33.1350	33.9245	34.8672	36.0491	37.6595	40.2894
23	32.0069	32.5096	33.0616	33.6754	34.3696	35.1725	36.1310	37.3323	38.9683	41.6383
24	33.1962	33.7077	34.2690	34.8932	35.5989	36.4150	37.3891	38.6093	40.2703	42.9798
25	34.3816	34.9015	35.4721	36.1065	36.8235	37.6525	38.6417	39.8804	41.5660	44.3140
26	35.5632	36.0914	36.6711	37.3154	38.0435	38.8851	39.8891	41.1461	42.8558	45.6416
27	36.7412	37.2777	37.8662	38.5202	39.2593	40.1133	41.1318	42.4066	44.1399	46.9628
28	37.9159	38.4604	39.0577	39.7213	40.4710	41.3372	42.3699	43.6622	45.4188	48.2782
29	39.0875	39.6398	40.2456	40.9187	41.6789	42.5569	43.6038	44.9132	46.6926	49.5878
30	40.2560	40.8161	41.4303	42.1126	42.8831	43.7730	44.8335	46.1600	47.9618	50.8922
31	41.4217	41.9895	42.6120	43.3033	44.0840	44.9853	46.0595	47.4024	49.2263	52.1914

k-c										
32	42.5847	43.1600	43.7906	44.4909	45.2815	46.1942	47.2817	48.6410	50.4867	53.4857
33	43.7452	44.3278	44.9664	45.6755	46.4759	47.3999	48.5005	49.8759	51.7429	54.7754
34	44.9032	45.4930	46.1395	46.8573	47.6674	48.6024	49.7159	51.1073	52.9953	56.0609
35	46.0588	46.6558	47.3101	48.0364	48.8560	49.8018	50.9281	52.3350	54.2439	57.3420
36	47.2122	47.8163	48.4782	49.2129	50.0420	50.9985	52.1372	53.5596	55.4889	58.6192
37	48.3634	48.9744	49.6440	50.3869	51.2253	52.1923	53.3435	54.7811	56.7304	59.8926
38	49.5126	50.1305	50.8074	51.5586	52.4060	53.3835	54.5470	55.9995	57.9689	61.1620
39	50.6598	51.2845	51.9688	52.7280	53.5845	54.5722	55.7477	57.2151	59.2040	62.4281
40	51.8050	52.4364	53.1280	53.8952	54.7606	55.7585	56.9459	58.4278	60.4361	63.6908
41	52.9485	53.5865	54.2852	55.0603	55.9345	56.9424	58.1415	59.6379	61.6654	64.9500
42	54.0902	54.7347	55.4405	56.2234	57.1062	58.1240	59.3348	60.8455	62.8918	66.2063
43	55.2302	55.8811	56.5940	57.3845	58.2759	59.3035	60.5257	62.0505	64.1156	67.4593
44	56.3685	57.0258	57.7456	58.5437	59.4436	60.4809	61.7144	63.2531	65.3367	68.7096
45	57.5053	58.1689	58.8955	59.7011	60.6094	61.6562	62.9010	64.4535	66.5552	69.9569
46	58.6405	59.3104	60.0437	60.8568	61.7734	62.8296	64.0855	65.6515	67.7714	71.2015
47	59.7743	60.4503	61.1903	62.0107	62.9355	64.0011	65.2679	66.8475	68.9852	72.4432
48	60.9066	61.5887	62.3353	63.1630	64.0959	65.1708	66.4484	68.0413	70.1967	73.6826
49	62.0375	62.7257	63.4788	64.3137	65.2547	66.3387	67.6270	69.2331	71.4060	74.9194
50	63.1671	63.8612	64.6209	65.4629	66.4117	67.5048	68.8039	70.4229	72.6132	76.1538
51	64.2954	64.9954	65.7615	66.6105	67.5673	68.6693	69.9789	71.6109	73.8183	77.3860
52	65.4224	66.1282	66.9006	67.7567	68.7212	69.8322	71.1521	72.7971	75.0215	78.6156
53	66.5482	67.2598	68.0385	68.9015	69.8737	70.9934	72.3238	73.9813	76.2225	79.8434
54	67.6728	68.3902	69.1751	70.0449	71.0248	72.1532	73.4938	75.1639	77.4217	81.0688
55	68.7962	69.5192	70.3104	71.1870	72.1744	73.3115	74.6622	76.3447	78.6191	82.2920
56	69.9185	70.6472	71.4444	72.3278	73.3227	74.4683	75.8291	77.5239	79.8148	83.5136
57	71.0397	71.7740	72.5773	73.4673	74.4697	75.6237	76.9944	78.7015	81.0085	84.7327
58	72.1598	72.8996	73.7090	74.6055	75.6153	76.7778	78.1583	79.8775	82.2007	85.9501
59	73.2789	74.0242	74.8395	75.7426	76.7597	77.9305	79.3208	81.0520	83.3911	87.1658
60	74.3970	75.1477	75.9689	76.8785	77.9029	79.0820	80.4820	82.2251	84.5799	88.3794

Example: For a degree of freedom (k-c) of 23, the critical values are 32.0069 for 10% alpha level (0.10), 35.1725 for 5% alpha level (0.05), and 41.6383 for 1% alpha level (0.01).

F-Distribution Critical Statistics (alpha-one tail 0.10)

$\alpha = 0.10$

Denominator df	Numerator (df)											
	1	2	3	4	5	6	7	8	9	10	15	20
1	39.86	49.50	53.59	55.83	57.24	58.20	58.91	59.44	59.86	60.19	61.22	61.74
2	8.53	9.00	9.16	9.24	9.29	9.33	9.35	9.37	9.38	9.39	9.42	9.44
3	5.54	5.46	5.39	5.34	5.31	5.28	5.27	5.25	5.24	5.23	5.20	5.18
4	4.54	4.32	4.19	4.11	4.05	4.01	3.98	3.95	3.94	3.92	3.87	3.84
5	4.06	3.78	3.62	3.52	3.45	3.40	3.37	3.34	3.32	3.30	3.24	3.21
6	3.78	3.46	3.29	3.18	3.11	3.05	3.01	2.98	2.96	2.94	2.87	2.84
7	3.59	3.26	3.07	2.96	2.88	2.83	2.78	2.75	2.72	2.70	2.63	2.59
8	3.46	3.11	2.92	2.81	2.73	2.67	2.62	2.59	2.56	2.54	2.46	2.42
9	3.36	3.01	2.81	2.69	2.61	2.55	2.51	2.47	2.44	2.42	2.34	2.30
10	3.29	2.92	2.73	2.61	2.52	2.46	2.41	2.38	2.35	2.32	2.24	2.20
15	3.07	2.70	2.49	2.36	2.27	2.21	2.16	2.12	2.09	2.06	1.97	1.92
20	2.97	2.59	2.38	2.25	2.16	2.09	2.04	2.00	1.96	1.94	1.84	1.79
25	2.92	2.53	2.32	2.18	2.09	2.02	1.97	1.93	1.89	1.87	1.77	1.72
30	2.88	2.49	2.28	2.14	2.05	1.98	1.93	1.88	1.85	1.82	1.72	1.67
35	2.85	2.46	2.25	2.11	2.02	1.95	1.90	1.85	1.82	1.79	1.69	1.63
40	2.84	2.44	2.23	2.09	2.00	1.93	1.87	1.83	1.79	1.76	1.66	1.61
45	2.82	2.42	2.21	2.07	1.98	1.91	1.85	1.81	1.77	1.74	1.64	1.58
50	2.81	2.41	2.20	2.06	1.97	1.90	1.84	1.80	1.76	1.73	1.63	1.57
100	2.76	2.36	2.14	2.00	1.91	1.83	1.78	1.73	1.69	1.66	1.56	1.49
200	2.73	2.33	2.11	1.97	1.88	1.80	1.75	1.70	1.66	1.63	1.52	1.46
300	2.72	2.32	2.10	1.96	1.87	1.79	1.74	1.69	1.65	1.62	1.51	1.45
500	2.72	2.31	2.09	1.96	1.86	1.79	1.73	1.68	1.64	1.61	1.50	1.44
100000	2.71	2.30	2.08	1.94	1.85	1.77	1.72	1.67	1.63	1.60	1.49	1.42

Example: For an alpha in the single right-tail area of 10% with 10 degrees of freedom in the numerator and 15 degrees of freedom in the denominator, the critical F value is 2.06.

| | Numerator (df) | | | | | | | | | | |
Denominator df	25	30	35	40	45	50	100	200	300	500	100000
1	62.05	62.26	62.42	62.53	62.62	62.69	63.01	63.17	63.22	63.26	63.33
2	9.45	9.46	9.46	9.47	9.47	9.47	9.48	9.49	9.49	9.49	9.49
3	5.17	5.17	5.16	5.16	5.16	5.15	5.14	5.14	5.14	5.14	5.13
4	3.83	3.82	3.81	3.80	3.80	3.80	3.78	3.77	3.77	3.76	3.76
5	3.19	3.17	3.16	3.16	3.15	3.15	3.13	3.12	3.11	3.11	3.11
6	2.81	2.80	2.79	2.78	2.77	2.77	2.75	2.73	2.73	2.73	2.72
7	2.57	2.56	2.54	2.54	2.53	2.52	2.50	2.48	2.48	2.48	2.47
8	2.40	2.38	2.37	2.36	2.35	2.35	2.32	2.31	2.30	2.30	2.29
9	2.27	2.25	2.24	2.23	2.22	2.22	2.19	2.17	2.17	2.17	2.16
10	2.17	2.16	2.14	2.13	2.12	2.12	2.09	2.07	2.07	2.06	2.06
15	1.89	1.87	1.86	1.85	1.84	1.83	1.79	1.77	1.77	1.76	1.76
20	1.76	1.74	1.72	1.71	1.70	1.69	1.65	1.63	1.62	1.62	1.61
25	1.68	1.66	1.64	1.63	1.62	1.61	1.56	1.54	1.53	1.53	1.52
30	1.63	1.61	1.59	1.57	1.56	1.55	1.51	1.48	1.47	1.47	1.46
35	1.60	1.57	1.55	1.53	1.52	1.51	1.47	1.44	1.43	1.42	1.41
40	1.57	1.54	1.52	1.51	1.49	1.48	1.43	1.41	1.40	1.39	1.38
45	1.55	1.52	1.50	1.48	1.47	1.46	1.41	1.38	1.37	1.36	1.35
50	1.53	1.50	1.48	1.46	1.45	1.44	1.39	1.36	1.35	1.34	1.33
100	1.45	1.42	1.40	1.38	1.37	1.35	1.29	1.26	1.24	1.23	1.21
200	1.41	1.38	1.36	1.34	1.32	1.31	1.24	1.20	1.18	1.17	1.14
300	1.40	1.37	1.34	1.32	1.31	1.29	1.22	1.18	1.16	1.14	1.12
500	1.39	1.36	1.33	1.31	1.30	1.28	1.21	1.16	1.14	1.12	1.09
1000	1.38	1.34	1.32	1.30	1.28	1.26	1.19	1.13	1.11	1.08	1.01

F-Distribution Critical Statistics (alpha-one tail 0.05) $\alpha = 0.05$

Denominator df	\multicolumn{12}{c}{Numerator (df)}
	1	2	3	4	5	6	7	8	9	10	15	20
1	161	199	216	225	230	234	237	239	241	242	246	248
2	18.51	19.00	19.16	19.25	19.30	19.33	19.35	19.37	19.38	19.40	19.43	19.45
3	10.13	9.55	9.28	9.12	9.01	8.94	8.89	8.85	8.81	8.79	8.70	8.66
4	7.71	6.94	6.59	6.39	6.26	6.16	6.09	6.04	6.00	5.96	5.86	5.80
5	6.61	5.79	5.41	5.19	5.05	4.95	4.88	4.82	4.77	4.74	4.62	4.56
6	5.99	5.14	4.76	4.53	4.39	4.28	4.21	4.15	4.10	4.06	3.94	3.87
7	5.59	4.74	4.35	4.12	3.97	3.87	3.79	3.73	3.68	3.64	3.51	3.44
8	5.32	4.46	4.07	3.84	3.69	3.58	3.50	3.44	3.39	3.35	3.22	3.15
9	5.12	4.26	3.86	3.63	3.48	3.37	3.29	3.23	3.18	3.14	3.01	2.94
10	4.96	4.10	3.71	3.48	3.33	3.22	3.14	3.07	3.02	2.98	2.85	2.77
15	4.54	3.68	3.29	3.06	2.90	2.79	2.71	2.64	2.59	2.54	2.40	2.33
20	4.35	3.49	3.10	2.87	2.71	2.60	2.51	2.45	2.39	2.35	2.20	2.12
25	4.24	3.39	2.99	2.76	2.60	2.49	2.40	2.34	2.28	2.24	2.09	2.01
30	4.17	3.32	2.92	2.69	2.53	2.42	2.33	2.27	2.21	2.16	2.01	1.93
35	4.12	3.27	2.87	2.64	2.49	2.37	2.29	2.22	2.16	2.11	1.96	1.88
40	4.08	3.23	2.84	2.61	2.45	2.34	2.25	2.18	2.12	2.08	1.92	1.84
45	4.06	3.20	2.81	2.58	2.42	2.31	2.22	2.15	2.10	2.05	1.89	1.81
50	4.03	3.18	2.79	2.56	2.40	2.29	2.20	2.13	2.07	2.03	1.87	1.78
100	3.94	3.09	2.70	2.46	2.31	2.19	2.10	2.03	1.97	1.93	1.77	1.68
200	3.89	3.04	2.65	2.42	2.26	2.14	2.06	1.98	1.93	1.88	1.72	1.62
300	3.87	3.03	2.63	2.40	2.24	2.13	2.04	1.97	1.91	1.86	1.70	1.61
500	3.86	3.01	2.62	2.39	2.23	2.12	2.03	1.96	1.90	1.85	1.69	1.59
100000	3.84	3.00	2.60	2.37	2.21	2.10	2.01	1.94	1.88	1.83	1.67	1.57

	Numerator (df)										
Denominator df	25	30	35	40	45	50	100	200	300	500	100000
1	249	250	251	251	251	252	253	254	254	254	254
2	19.46	19.46	19.47	19.47	19.47	19.48	19.49	19.49	19.49	19.49	19.50
3	8.63	8.62	8.60	8.59	8.59	8.58	8.55	8.54	8.54	8.53	8.53
4	5.77	5.75	5.73	5.72	5.71	5.70	5.66	5.65	5.64	5.64	5.63
5	4.52	4.50	4.48	4.46	4.45	4.44	4.41	4.39	4.38	4.37	4.37
6	3.83	3.81	3.79	3.77	3.76	3.75	3.71	3.69	3.68	3.68	3.67
7	3.40	3.38	3.36	3.34	3.33	3.32	3.27	3.25	3.24	3.24	3.23
8	3.11	3.08	3.06	3.04	3.03	3.02	2.97	2.95	2.94	2.94	2.93
9	2.89	2.86	2.84	2.83	2.81	2.80	2.76	2.73	2.72	2.72	2.71
10	2.73	2.70	2.68	2.66	2.65	2.64	2.59	2.56	2.55	2.55	2.54
15	2.28	2.25	2.22	2.20	2.19	2.18	2.12	2.10	2.09	2.08	2.07
20	2.07	2.04	2.01	1.99	1.98	1.97	1.91	1.88	1.86	1.86	1.84
25	1.96	1.92	1.89	1.87	1.86	1.84	1.78	1.75	1.73	1.73	1.71
30	1.88	1.84	1.81	1.79	1.77	1.76	1.70	1.66	1.65	1.64	1.62
35	1.82	1.79	1.76	1.74	1.72	1.70	1.63	1.60	1.58	1.57	1.56
40	1.78	1.74	1.72	1.69	1.67	1.66	1.59	1.55	1.54	1.53	1.51
45	1.75	1.71	1.68	1.66	1.64	1.63	1.55	1.51	1.50	1.49	1.47
50	1.73	1.69	1.66	1.63	1.61	1.60	1.52	1.48	1.47	1.46	1.44
100	1.62	1.57	1.54	1.52	1.49	1.48	1.39	1.34	1.32	1.31	1.28
200	1.56	1.52	1.48	1.46	1.43	1.41	1.32	1.26	1.24	1.22	1.19
300	1.54	1.50	1.46	1.43	1.41	1.39	1.30	1.23	1.21	1.19	1.15
500	1.53	1.48	1.45	1.42	1.40	1.38	1.28	1.21	1.18	1.16	1.11
100000	1.51	1.46	1.42	1.39	1.37	1.35	1.24	1.17	1.14	1.11	1.01

F-Distribution Critical Statistics (alpha-one tail 0.025)

$\alpha = 0.025$

Denominator df	Numerator (df)											
	1	2	3	4	5	6	7	8	9	10	15	20
1	648	799	864	900	922	937	948	957	963	969	985	993
2	38.51	39.00	39.17	39.25	39.30	39.33	39.36	39.37	39.39	39.40	39.43	39.45
3	17.44	16.04	15.44	15.10	14.88	14.73	14.62	14.54	14.47	14.42	14.25	14.17
4	12.22	10.65	9.98	9.60	9.36	9.20	9.07	8.98	8.90	8.84	8.66	8.56
5	10.01	8.43	7.76	7.39	7.15	6.98	6.85	6.76	6.68	6.62	6.43	6.33
6	8.81	7.26	6.60	6.23	5.99	5.82	5.70	5.60	5.52	5.46	5.27	5.17
7	8.07	6.54	5.89	5.52	5.29	5.12	4.99	4.90	4.82	4.76	4.57	4.47
8	7.57	6.06	5.42	5.05	4.82	4.65	4.53	4.43	4.36	4.30	4.10	4.00
9	7.21	5.71	5.08	4.72	4.48	4.32	4.20	4.10	4.03	3.96	3.77	3.67
10	6.94	5.46	4.83	4.47	4.24	4.07	3.95	3.85	3.78	3.72	3.52	3.42
15	6.20	4.77	4.15	3.80	3.58	3.41	3.29	3.20	3.12	3.06	2.86	2.76
20	5.87	4.46	3.86	3.51	3.29	3.13	3.01	2.91	2.84	2.77	2.57	2.46
25	5.69	4.29	3.69	3.35	3.13	2.97	2.85	2.75	2.68	2.61	2.41	2.30
30	5.57	4.18	3.59	3.25	3.03	2.87	2.75	2.65	2.57	2.51	2.31	2.20
35	5.48	4.11	3.52	3.18	2.96	2.80	2.68	2.58	2.50	2.44	2.23	2.12
40	5.42	4.05	3.46	3.13	2.90	2.74	2.62	2.53	2.45	2.39	2.18	2.07
45	5.38	4.01	3.42	3.09	2.86	2.70	2.58	2.49	2.41	2.35	2.14	2.03
50	5.34	3.97	3.39	3.05	2.83	2.67	2.55	2.46	2.38	2.32	2.11	1.99
100	5.18	3.83	3.25	2.92	2.70	2.54	2.42	2.32	2.24	2.18	1.97	1.85
200	5.10	3.76	3.18	2.85	2.63	2.47	2.35	2.26	2.18	2.11	1.90	1.78
300	5.07	3.73	3.16	2.83	2.61	2.45	2.33	2.23	2.16	2.09	1.88	1.75
500	5.05	3.72	3.14	2.81	2.59	2.43	2.31	2.22	2.14	2.07	1.86	1.74
100000	5.02	3.69	3.12	2.79	2.57	2.41	2.29	2.19	2.11	2.05	1.83	1.71

						Numerator (df)					
Denominator df	25	30	35	40	45	50	100	200	300	500	100000
1	998	1001	1004	1006	1007	1008	1013	1016	1017	1017	1018
2	39.46	39.46	39.47	39.47	39.48	39.48	39.49	39.49	39.49	39.50	39.50
3	14.12	14.08	14.06	14.04	14.02	14.01	13.96	13.93	13.92	13.91	13.90
4	8.50	8.46	8.43	8.41	8.39	8.38	8.32	8.29	8.28	8.27	8.26
5	6.27	6.23	6.20	6.18	6.16	6.14	6.08	6.05	6.04	6.03	6.02
6	5.11	5.07	5.04	5.01	4.99	4.98	4.92	4.88	4.87	4.86	4.85
7	4.40	4.36	4.33	4.31	4.29	4.28	4.21	4.18	4.17	4.16	4.14
8	3.94	3.89	3.86	3.84	3.82	3.81	3.74	3.70	3.69	3.68	3.67
9	3.60	3.56	3.53	3.51	3.49	3.47	3.40	3.37	3.36	3.35	3.33
10	3.35	3.31	3.28	3.26	3.24	3.22	3.15	3.12	3.10	3.09	3.08
15	2.69	2.64	2.61	2.59	2.56	2.55	2.47	2.44	2.42	2.41	2.40
20	2.40	2.35	2.31	2.29	2.27	2.25	2.17	2.13	2.11	2.10	2.09
25	2.23	2.18	2.15	2.12	2.10	2.08	2.00	1.95	1.94	1.92	1.91
30	2.12	2.07	2.04	2.01	1.99	1.97	1.88	1.84	1.82	1.81	1.79
35	2.05	2.00	1.96	1.93	1.91	1.89	1.80	1.75	1.74	1.72	1.70
40	1.99	1.94	1.90	1.88	1.85	1.83	1.74	1.69	1.67	1.66	1.64
45	1.95	1.90	1.86	1.83	1.81	1.79	1.69	1.64	1.62	1.61	1.59
50	1.92	1.87	1.83	1.80	1.77	1.75	1.66	1.60	1.58	1.57	1.55
100	1.77	1.71	1.67	1.64	1.61	1.59	1.48	1.42	1.40	1.38	1.35
200	1.70	1.64	1.60	1.56	1.53	1.51	1.39	1.32	1.29	1.27	1.23
300	1.67	1.62	1.57	1.54	1.51	1.48	1.36	1.28	1.25	1.23	1.18
500	1.65	1.60	1.55	1.52	1.49	1.46	1.34	1.25	1.22	1.19	1.14
100000	1.63	1.57	1.52	1.48	1.45	1.43	1.30	1.21	1.17	1.13	1.01

F-Distribution Critical Statistics (alpha one-tail 0.01)

$\alpha = 0.01$

	Numerator (df)											
Denominator df	1	2	3	4	5	6	7	8	9	10	15	20
1	4052	4999	5404	5624	5764	5859	5928	5981	6022	6056	6157	6209
2	98.50	99.00	99.16	99.25	99.30	99.33	99.36	99.38	99.39	99.40	99.43	99.45
3	34.12	30.82	29.46	28.71	28.24	27.91	27.67	27.49	27.34	27.23	26.87	26.69
4	21.20	18.00	16.69	15.98	15.52	15.21	14.98	14.80	14.66	14.55	14.20	14.02
5	16.26	13.27	12.06	11.39	10.97	10.67	10.46	10.29	10.16	10.05	9.72	9.55
6	13.75	10.92	9.78	9.15	8.75	8.47	8.26	8.10	7.98	7.87	7.56	7.40
7	12.25	9.55	8.45	7.85	7.46	7.19	6.99	6.84	6.72	6.62	6.31	6.16
8	11.26	8.65	7.59	7.01	6.63	6.37	6.18	6.03	5.91	5.81	5.52	5.36
9	10.56	8.02	6.99	6.42	6.06	5.80	5.61	5.47	5.35	5.26	4.96	4.81
10	10.04	7.56	6.55	5.99	5.64	5.39	5.20	5.06	4.94	4.85	4.56	4.41
15	8.68	6.36	5.42	4.89	4.56	4.32	4.14	4.00	3.89	3.80	3.52	3.37
20	8.10	5.85	4.94	4.43	4.10	3.87	3.70	3.56	3.46	3.37	3.09	2.94
25	7.77	5.57	4.68	4.18	3.85	3.63	3.46	3.32	3.22	3.13	2.85	2.70
30	7.56	5.39	4.51	4.02	3.70	3.47	3.30	3.17	3.07	2.98	2.70	2.55
35	7.42	5.27	4.40	3.91	3.59	3.37	3.20	3.07	2.96	2.88	2.60	2.44
40	7.31	5.18	4.31	3.83	3.51	3.29	3.12	2.99	2.89	2.80	2.52	2.37
45	7.23	5.11	4.25	3.77	3.45	3.23	3.07	2.94	2.83	2.74	2.46	2.31
50	7.17	5.06	4.20	3.72	3.41	3.19	3.02	2.89	2.78	2.70	2.42	2.27
100	6.90	4.82	3.98	3.51	3.21	2.99	2.82	2.69	2.59	2.50	2.22	2.07
200	6.76	4.71	3.88	3.41	3.11	2.89	2.73	2.60	2.50	2.41	2.13	1.97
300	6.72	4.68	3.85	3.38	3.08	2.86	2.70	2.57	2.47	2.38	2.10	1.94
500	6.69	4.65	3.82	3.36	3.05	2.84	2.68	2.55	2.44	2.36	2.07	1.92
100000	6.64	4.61	3.78	3.32	3.02	2.80	2.64	2.51	2.41	2.32	2.04	1.88

Denominator df	Numerator (df)										
	25	30	35	40	45	50	100	200	300	500	100000
1	6240	6260	6275	6286	6296	6302	6334	6350	6355	6360	6366
2	99.46	99.47	99.47	99.48	99.48	99.48	99.49	99.49	99.50	99.50	99.50
3	26.58	26.50	26.45	26.41	26.38	26.35	26.24	26.18	26.16	26.15	26.13
4	13.91	13.84	13.79	13.75	13.71	13.69	13.58	13.52	13.50	13.49	13.46
5	9.45	9.38	9.33	9.29	9.26	9.24	9.13	9.08	9.06	9.04	9.02
6	7.30	7.23	7.18	7.14	7.11	7.09	6.99	6.93	6.92	6.90	6.88
7	6.06	5.99	5.94	5.91	5.88	5.86	5.75	5.70	5.68	5.67	5.65
8	5.26	5.20	5.15	5.12	5.09	5.07	4.96	4.91	4.89	4.88	4.86
9	4.71	4.65	4.60	4.57	4.54	4.52	4.41	4.36	4.35	4.33	4.31
10	4.31	4.25	4.20	4.17	4.14	4.12	4.01	3.96	3.94	3.93	3.91
15	3.28	3.21	3.17	3.13	3.10	3.08	2.98	2.92	2.91	2.89	2.87
20	2.84	2.78	2.73	2.69	2.67	2.64	2.54	2.48	2.46	2.44	2.42
25	2.60	2.54	2.49	2.45	2.42	2.40	2.29	2.23	2.21	2.19	2.17
30	2.45	2.39	2.34	2.30	2.27	2.25	2.13	2.07	2.05	2.03	2.01
35	2.35	2.28	2.23	2.19	2.16	2.14	2.02	1.96	1.94	1.92	1.89
40	2.27	2.20	2.15	2.11	2.08	2.06	1.94	1.87	1.85	1.83	1.80
45	2.21	2.14	2.09	2.05	2.02	2.00	1.88	1.81	1.79	1.77	1.74
50	2.17	2.10	2.05	2.01	1.97	1.95	1.82	1.76	1.73	1.71	1.68
100	1.97	1.89	1.84	1.80	1.76	1.74	1.60	1.52	1.49	1.47	1.43
200	1.87	1.79	1.74	1.69	1.66	1.63	1.48	1.39	1.36	1.33	1.28
300	1.84	1.76	1.70	1.66	1.62	1.59	1.44	1.35	1.31	1.28	1.22
500	1.81	1.74	1.68	1.63	1.60	1.57	1.41	1.31	1.27	1.23	1.16
100000	1.77	1.70	1.64	1.59	1.55	1.52	1.36	1.25	1.20	1.15	1.01

Real Options Analysis Value (1-year maturity at 5% risk-free rate)

Volatility	-99%	-90%	-80%	-70%	-60%	-50%	-40%	-30%	-20%	-10%
				Profitability Ratio (% in-the-money)						
1%	0.00%	0.00%	0.00%	0.00%	0.00%	0.00%	0.00%	0.00%	0.00%	0.00%
3%	0.00%	0.00%	0.00%	0.00%	0.00%	0.00%	0.00%	0.00%	0.00%	0.04%
5%	0.00%	0.00%	0.00%	0.00%	0.00%	0.00%	0.00%	0.00%	0.00%	0.35%
7%	0.00%	0.00%	0.00%	0.00%	0.00%	0.00%	0.00%	0.00%	0.02%	0.88%
9%	0.00%	0.00%	0.00%	0.00%	0.00%	0.00%	0.00%	0.00%	0.10%	1.52%
11%	0.00%	0.00%	0.00%	0.00%	0.00%	0.00%	0.00%	0.01%	0.30%	2.22%
13%	0.00%	0.00%	0.00%	0.00%	0.00%	0.00%	0.00%	0.05%	0.60%	2.96%
15%	0.00%	0.00%	0.00%	0.00%	0.00%	0.00%	0.01%	0.13%	1.01%	3.72%
17%	0.00%	0.00%	0.00%	0.00%	0.00%	0.00%	0.02%	0.28%	1.49%	4.49%
19%	0.00%	0.00%	0.00%	0.00%	0.00%	0.00%	0.06%	0.50%	2.03%	5.26%
21%	0.00%	0.00%	0.00%	0.00%	0.00%	0.01%	0.13%	0.78%	2.63%	6.05%
23%	0.00%	0.00%	0.00%	0.00%	0.00%	0.02%	0.24%	1.13%	3.26%	6.84%
25%	0.00%	0.00%	0.00%	0.00%	0.00%	0.05%	0.40%	1.54%	3.93%	7.63%
27%	0.00%	0.00%	0.00%	0.00%	0.01%	0.11%	0.61%	2.00%	4.62%	8.43%
29%	0.00%	0.00%	0.00%	0.00%	0.02%	0.18%	0.86%	2.50%	5.33%	9.22%
31%	0.00%	0.00%	0.00%	0.00%	0.04%	0.29%	1.17%	3.05%	6.06%	10.02%
33%	0.00%	0.00%	0.00%	0.00%	0.07%	0.44%	1.52%	3.63%	6.80%	10.82%
35%	0.00%	0.00%	0.00%	0.01%	0.12%	0.62%	1.92%	4.24%	7.55%	11.62%
37%	0.00%	0.00%	0.00%	0.02%	0.18%	0.84%	2.35%	4.88%	8.32%	12.42%
39%	0.00%	0.00%	0.00%	0.03%	0.27%	1.10%	2.82%	5.54%	9.09%	13.21%
41%	0.00%	0.00%	0.00%	0.05%	0.39%	1.39%	3.33%	6.22%	9.86%	14.01%
43%	0.00%	0.00%	0.00%	0.08%	0.53%	1.73%	3.87%	6.91%	10.64%	14.80%
45%	0.00%	0.00%	0.01%	0.13%	0.70%	2.10%	4.44%	7.62%	11.43%	15.60%
47%	0.00%	0.00%	0.01%	0.19%	0.91%	2.50%	5.03%	8.35%	12.22%	16.39%
49%	0.00%	0.00%	0.02%	0.26%	1.14%	2.93%	5.64%	9.09%	13.01%	17.18%
51%	0.00%	0.00%	0.03%	0.36%	1.41%	3.40%	6.28%	9.83%	13.80%	17.97%
53%	0.00%	0.00%	0.05%	0.48%	1.71%	3.90%	6.94%	10.59%	14.60%	18.76%
55%	0.00%	0.00%	0.08%	0.62%	2.03%	4.42%	7.61%	11.35%	15.40%	19.55%
57%	0.00%	0.00%	0.11%	0.78%	2.39%	4.96%	8.30%	12.12%	16.20%	20.33%
59%	0.00%	0.00%	0.16%	0.97%	2.78%	5.54%	9.00%	12.90%	16.99%	21.12%
61%	0.00%	0.00%	0.21%	1.18%	3.19%	6.13%	9.72%	13.68%	17.79%	21.90%
63%	0.00%	0.01%	0.29%	1.42%	3.63%	6.74%	10.44%	14.46%	18.59%	22.68%
65%	0.00%	0.01%	0.37%	1.69%	4.10%	7.37%	11.18%	15.25%	19.39%	23.45%
67%	0.00%	0.02%	0.47%	1.98%	4.59%	8.02%	11.92%	16.04%	20.18%	24.23%
69%	0.00%	0.03%	0.59%	2.30%	5.11%	8.68%	12.68%	16.83%	20.98%	25.00%
71%	0.00%	0.04%	0.73%	2.64%	5.65%	9.36%	13.44%	17.63%	21.77%	25.77%
73%	0.00%	0.06%	0.88%	3.01%	6.21%	10.05%	14.21%	18.42%	22.56%	26.53%
75%	0.00%	0.08%	1.06%	3.40%	6.79%	10.76%	14.98%	19.22%	23.35%	27.30%
77%	0.00%	0.11%	1.26%	3.82%	7.38%	11.47%	15.76%	20.02%	24.14%	28.06%
79%	0.00%	0.15%	1.48%	4.26%	8.00%	12.20%	16.54%	20.82%	24.93%	28.82%
81%	0.00%	0.19%	1.72%	4.72%	8.63%	12.94%	17.32%	21.61%	25.71%	29.57%
83%	0.00%	0.24%	1.98%	5.21%	9.28%	13.68%	18.11%	22.41%	26.49%	30.33%
85%	0.00%	0.30%	2.26%	5.72%	9.94%	14.43%	18.90%	23.21%	27.27%	31.07%
87%	0.00%	0.38%	2.57%	6.24%	10.62%	15.19%	19.70%	24.00%	28.05%	31.82%
89%	0.00%	0.46%	2.90%	6.79%	11.30%	15.95%	20.49%	24.80%	28.83%	32.56%
91%	0.00%	0.56%	3.25%	7.35%	12.00%	16.72%	21.29%	25.59%	29.60%	33.30%
93%	0.00%	0.67%	3.62%	7.93%	12.71%	17.50%	22.09%	26.38%	30.37%	34.04%
95%	0.00%	0.79%	4.01%	8.53%	13.43%	18.28%	22.88%	27.17%	31.13%	34.77%
97%	0.00%	0.93%	4.43%	9.15%	14.16%	19.06%	23.68%	27.96%	31.90%	35.50%
99%	0.00%	1.09%	4.86%	9.78%	14.90%	19.85%	24.48%	28.75%	32.66%	36.23%
101%	0.00%	1.26%	5.32%	10.42%	15.65%	20.64%	25.28%	29.53%	33.41%	36.95%

Example: Suppose a real option exists that has a $110 million present value of free cash flows (S), $100 million in implementation costs (X), 33% volatility, 5% risk-free rate and a 1-year maturity, estimate the real options value of this simple option. The calculated profitability ratio is $110/$100 or 10% in-the-money. Using the 1-year table, the option value as a percent of asset is 20.13%, for a 10% profitability ratio and 33% volatility. This means that for the $110 asset value, the option value is 20.13% of $110 or $22.15 million. In addition, if the asset value

Profitability Ratio (% in-the-money)

Volatility	0%	10%	20%	30%	40%	50%	60%	70%	80%	90%	100%
1%	4.88%	13.52%	20.73%	26.83%	32.06%	36.58%	40.55%	44.05%	47.15%	49.94%	52.44%
3%	4.94%	13.52%	20.73%	26.83%	32.06%	36.58%	40.55%	44.05%	47.15%	49.94%	52.44%
5%	5.28%	13.53%	20.73%	26.83%	32.06%	36.58%	40.55%	44.05%	47.15%	49.94%	52.44%
7%	5.83%	13.57%	20.73%	26.83%	32.06%	36.58%	40.55%	44.05%	47.15%	49.94%	52.44%
9%	6.47%	13.71%	20.74%	26.83%	32.06%	36.58%	40.55%	44.05%	47.15%	49.94%	52.44%
11%	7.15%	13.97%	20.79%	26.83%	32.06%	36.58%	40.55%	44.05%	47.15%	49.94%	52.44%
13%	7.86%	14.32%	20.90%	26.86%	32.06%	36.59%	40.55%	44.05%	47.15%	49.94%	52.44%
15%	8.59%	14.76%	21.08%	26.92%	32.07%	36.59%	40.55%	44.05%	47.15%	49.94%	52.44%
17%	9.33%	15.24%	21.33%	27.02%	32.11%	36.60%	40.55%	44.05%	47.15%	49.94%	52.44%
19%	10.08%	15.78%	21.63%	27.17%	32.18%	36.63%	40.56%	44.05%	47.16%	49.94%	52.44%
21%	10.83%	16.34%	21.99%	27.37%	32.28%	36.67%	40.58%	44.06%	47.16%	49.94%	52.44%
23%	11.58%	16.94%	22.40%	27.62%	32.42%	36.75%	40.62%	44.08%	47.17%	49.94%	52.44%
25%	12.34%	17.55%	22.84%	27.91%	32.60%	36.85%	40.68%	44.11%	47.18%	49.95%	52.45%
27%	13.09%	18.18%	23.31%	28.23%	32.81%	36.99%	40.76%	44.16%	47.21%	49.97%	52.46%
29%	13.85%	18.82%	23.81%	28.60%	33.06%	37.16%	40.87%	44.23%	47.26%	49.99%	52.47%
31%	14.61%	19.47%	24.33%	28.99%	33.35%	37.35%	41.01%	44.32%	47.32%	50.03%	52.50%
33%	15.37%	20.13%	24.87%	29.41%	33.66%	37.58%	41.17%	44.43%	47.39%	50.09%	52.53%
35%	16.13%	20.80%	25.42%	29.85%	34.00%	37.84%	41.36%	44.57%	47.49%	50.16%	52.58%
37%	16.89%	21.47%	25.99%	30.31%	34.36%	38.12%	41.57%	44.73%	47.61%	50.24%	52.65%
39%	17.64%	22.15%	26.57%	30.79%	34.75%	38.42%	41.81%	44.91%	47.75%	50.35%	52.73%
41%	18.40%	22.83%	27.16%	31.28%	35.15%	38.75%	42.07%	45.11%	47.91%	50.47%	52.82%
43%	19.16%	23.52%	27.75%	31.79%	35.57%	39.09%	42.34%	45.34%	48.09%	50.62%	52.94%
45%	19.91%	24.20%	28.36%	32.30%	36.01%	39.46%	42.64%	45.58%	48.29%	50.78%	53.06%
47%	20.67%	24.89%	28.97%	32.83%	36.46%	39.83%	42.96%	45.84%	48.50%	50.95%	53.21%
49%	21.42%	25.58%	29.58%	33.37%	36.92%	40.23%	43.29%	46.12%	48.74%	51.15%	53.37%
51%	22.17%	26.27%	30.20%	33.91%	37.39%	40.63%	43.64%	46.42%	48.99%	51.36%	53.55%
53%	22.92%	26.96%	30.82%	34.46%	37.88%	41.05%	44.00%	46.73%	49.25%	51.58%	53.74%
55%	23.66%	27.65%	31.44%	35.02%	38.37%	41.48%	44.37%	47.05%	49.53%	51.82%	53.95%
57%	24.41%	28.34%	32.07%	35.58%	38.87%	41.92%	44.76%	47.39%	49.82%	52.08%	54.16%
59%	25.15%	29.03%	32.70%	36.15%	39.37%	42.37%	45.15%	47.73%	50.12%	52.34%	54.40%
61%	25.89%	29.72%	33.33%	36.72%	39.88%	42.82%	45.56%	48.09%	50.44%	52.62%	54.64%
63%	26.63%	30.40%	33.96%	37.29%	40.40%	43.29%	45.97%	48.46%	50.76%	52.91%	54.90%
65%	27.37%	31.09%	34.59%	37.87%	40.92%	43.75%	46.39%	48.83%	51.10%	53.21%	55.16%
67%	28.10%	31.78%	35.22%	38.44%	41.44%	44.23%	46.82%	49.22%	51.44%	53.51%	55.44%
69%	28.84%	32.46%	35.86%	39.02%	41.97%	44.71%	47.25%	49.61%	51.80%	53.83%	55.73%
71%	29.57%	33.14%	36.49%	39.61%	42.50%	45.19%	47.69%	50.01%	52.16%	54.16%	56.02%
73%	30.29%	33.83%	37.12%	40.19%	43.04%	45.68%	48.13%	50.41%	52.52%	54.49%	56.32%
75%	31.02%	34.50%	37.75%	40.77%	43.57%	46.17%	48.58%	50.82%	52.90%	54.83%	56.63%
77%	31.74%	35.18%	38.38%	41.35%	44.11%	46.66%	49.03%	51.23%	53.28%	55.18%	56.95%
79%	32.46%	35.86%	39.01%	41.94%	44.65%	47.16%	49.49%	51.65%	53.66%	55.53%	57.27%
81%	33.18%	36.53%	39.64%	42.52%	45.19%	47.66%	49.95%	52.08%	54.05%	55.89%	57.60%
83%	33.89%	37.20%	40.27%	43.11%	45.73%	48.16%	50.41%	52.50%	54.45%	56.25%	57.94%
85%	34.60%	37.87%	40.89%	43.69%	46.27%	48.66%	50.88%	52.93%	54.84%	56.62%	58.28%
87%	35.31%	38.54%	41.52%	44.27%	46.81%	49.17%	51.34%	53.37%	55.25%	56.99%	58.63%
89%	36.02%	39.20%	42.14%	44.85%	47.36%	49.67%	51.81%	53.80%	55.65%	57.37%	58.98%
91%	36.72%	39.87%	42.76%	45.43%	47.90%	50.18%	52.28%	54.24%	56.06%	57.75%	59.33%
93%	37.42%	40.53%	43.38%	46.01%	48.44%	50.68%	52.76%	54.68%	56.47%	58.13%	59.69%
95%	38.11%	41.18%	44.00%	46.59%	48.98%	51.19%	53.23%	55.12%	56.88%	58.52%	60.05%
97%	38.81%	41.84%	44.61%	47.17%	49.52%	51.69%	53.70%	55.57%	57.30%	58.91%	60.41%
99%	39.50%	42.49%	45.23%	47.74%	50.06%	52.20%	54.18%	56.01%	57.71%	59.30%	60.78%
101%	40.18%	43.13%	45.84%	48.32%	50.60%	52.70%	54.65%	56.45%	58.13%	59.69%	61.14%

were $330 million, then the option value is 20.13% of $330 million or $66.44 million as long as the 10% profitability ratio remains the same (implementation cost now becomes $300 million). The option value as a percentage of asset value does not change as long as the maturity, profitability ratio and volatility remain constant for these tables.

Real Options Analysis Value (3-year maturity at 5% risk-free rate)

Volatility	Profitability Ratio (% in-the-money)									
	-99%	-90%	-80%	-70%	-60%	-50%	-40%	-30%	-20%	-10%
1%	0.00%	0.00%	0.00%	0.00%	0.00%	0.00%	0.00%	0.00%	0.00%	4.37%
3%	0.00%	0.00%	0.00%	0.00%	0.00%	0.00%	0.00%	0.00%	0.19%	4.92%
5%	0.00%	0.00%	0.00%	0.00%	0.00%	0.00%	0.00%	0.03%	1.00%	6.00%
7%	0.00%	0.00%	0.00%	0.00%	0.00%	0.00%	0.01%	0.24%	2.11%	7.23%
9%	0.00%	0.00%	0.00%	0.00%	0.00%	0.00%	0.07%	0.74%	3.35%	8.51%
11%	0.00%	0.00%	0.00%	0.00%	0.00%	0.02%	0.26%	1.49%	4.65%	9.81%
13%	0.00%	0.00%	0.00%	0.00%	0.00%	0.08%	0.62%	2.42%	5.99%	11.12%
15%	0.00%	0.00%	0.00%	0.00%	0.02%	0.22%	1.16%	3.47%	7.35%	12.44%
17%	0.00%	0.00%	0.00%	0.00%	0.06%	0.49%	1.86%	4.62%	8.72%	13.76%
19%	0.00%	0.00%	0.00%	0.01%	0.16%	0.88%	2.70%	5.84%	10.10%	15.08%
21%	0.00%	0.00%	0.00%	0.03%	0.33%	1.40%	3.65%	7.10%	11.48%	16.40%
23%	0.00%	0.00%	0.00%	0.08%	0.60%	2.05%	4.68%	8.40%	12.86%	17.72%
25%	0.00%	0.00%	0.01%	0.18%	0.96%	2.80%	5.80%	9.72%	14.25%	19.04%
27%	0.00%	0.00%	0.02%	0.32%	1.43%	3.66%	6.97%	11.07%	15.63%	20.35%
29%	0.00%	0.00%	0.05%	0.54%	1.99%	4.60%	8.18%	12.43%	17.00%	21.65%
31%	0.00%	0.00%	0.11%	0.83%	2.65%	5.61%	9.44%	13.79%	18.37%	22.96%
33%	0.00%	0.00%	0.19%	1.20%	3.40%	6.69%	10.73%	15.17%	19.74%	24.25%
35%	0.00%	0.01%	0.32%	1.65%	4.23%	7.82%	12.04%	16.55%	21.10%	25.54%
37%	0.00%	0.02%	0.50%	2.18%	5.14%	9.01%	13.38%	17.93%	22.46%	26.83%
39%	0.00%	0.04%	0.73%	2.80%	6.11%	10.23%	14.73%	19.31%	23.81%	28.10%
41%	0.00%	0.07%	1.03%	3.49%	7.15%	11.48%	16.09%	20.69%	25.15%	29.37%
43%	0.00%	0.12%	1.38%	4.26%	8.24%	12.77%	17.46%	22.07%	26.49%	30.64%
45%	0.00%	0.19%	1.81%	5.10%	9.38%	14.08%	18.83%	23.44%	27.81%	31.89%
47%	0.00%	0.28%	2.30%	6.00%	10.56%	15.40%	20.21%	24.81%	29.13%	33.14%
49%	0.00%	0.41%	2.87%	6.96%	11.77%	16.75%	21.59%	26.18%	30.44%	34.38%
51%	0.00%	0.58%	3.50%	7.97%	13.02%	18.10%	22.98%	27.53%	31.74%	35.61%
53%	0.00%	0.79%	4.20%	9.04%	14.29%	19.47%	24.36%	28.88%	33.03%	36.82%
55%	0.00%	1.05%	4.96%	10.15%	15.59%	20.84%	25.73%	30.22%	34.31%	38.03%
57%	0.00%	1.36%	5.78%	11.31%	16.91%	22.22%	27.11%	31.55%	35.58%	39.24%
59%	0.00%	1.72%	6.66%	12.49%	18.25%	23.60%	28.47%	32.88%	36.84%	40.43%
61%	0.00%	2.13%	7.59%	13.72%	19.60%	24.98%	29.84%	34.19%	38.09%	41.61%
63%	0.00%	2.60%	8.58%	14.97%	20.96%	26.36%	31.19%	35.49%	39.33%	42.77%
65%	0.01%	3.13%	9.61%	16.25%	22.33%	27.74%	32.54%	36.78%	40.56%	43.93%
67%	0.01%	3.72%	10.69%	17.55%	23.70%	29.12%	33.87%	38.06%	41.77%	45.08%
69%	0.02%	4.36%	11.81%	18.87%	25.08%	30.49%	35.20%	39.33%	42.98%	46.21%
71%	0.03%	5.05%	12.96%	20.20%	26.46%	31.85%	36.52%	40.59%	44.17%	47.34%
73%	0.05%	5.81%	14.15%	21.55%	27.84%	33.21%	37.83%	41.83%	45.35%	48.45%
75%	0.08%	6.61%	15.37%	22.91%	29.23%	34.56%	39.12%	43.06%	46.51%	49.55%
77%	0.11%	7.47%	16.62%	24.28%	30.60%	35.90%	40.40%	44.28%	47.66%	50.64%
79%	0.16%	8.38%	17.90%	25.65%	31.98%	37.23%	41.68%	45.49%	48.80%	51.71%
81%	0.21%	9.33%	19.19%	27.03%	33.35%	38.55%	42.93%	46.68%	49.93%	52.78%
83%	0.29%	10.33%	20.50%	28.41%	34.71%	39.86%	44.18%	47.86%	51.04%	53.83%
85%	0.38%	11.37%	21.83%	29.79%	36.06%	41.16%	45.41%	49.02%	52.14%	54.86%
87%	0.49%	12.45%	23.18%	31.17%	37.41%	42.45%	46.63%	50.17%	53.22%	55.89%
89%	0.62%	13.57%	24.53%	32.55%	38.74%	43.72%	47.83%	51.31%	54.30%	56.90%
91%	0.78%	14.72%	25.90%	33.93%	40.07%	44.98%	49.02%	52.43%	55.35%	57.89%
93%	0.97%	15.91%	27.27%	35.30%	41.38%	46.22%	50.20%	53.54%	56.40%	58.88%
95%	1.19%	17.12%	28.65%	36.66%	42.69%	47.46%	51.36%	54.63%	57.42%	59.85%
97%	1.44%	18.37%	30.03%	38.01%	43.98%	48.67%	52.50%	55.70%	58.44%	60.80%
99%	1.72%	19.63%	31.41%	39.36%	45.25%	49.87%	53.63%	56.77%	59.44%	61.75%
101%	2.04%	20.92%	32.79%	40.70%	46.52%	51.06%	54.74%	57.81%	60.42%	62.67%

	Profitability Ratio (% in-the-money)										
Volatility	0%	10%	20%	30%	40%	50%	60%	70%	80%	90%	100%
1%	13.93%	21.75%	28.27%	33.79%	38.52%	42.62%	46.21%	49.37%	52.18%	54.70%	56.96%
3%	13.93%	21.75%	28.27%	33.79%	38.52%	42.62%	46.21%	49.37%	52.18%	54.70%	56.96%
5%	14.06%	21.76%	28.27%	33.79%	38.52%	42.62%	46.21%	49.37%	52.18%	54.70%	56.96%
7%	14.51%	21.84%	28.28%	33.79%	38.52%	42.62%	46.21%	49.37%	52.18%	54.70%	56.96%
9%	15.22%	22.09%	28.35%	33.81%	38.52%	42.62%	46.21%	49.37%	52.18%	54.70%	56.96%
11%	16.10%	22.54%	28.54%	33.88%	38.55%	42.63%	46.21%	49.37%	52.18%	54.70%	56.96%
13%	17.08%	23.14%	28.86%	34.03%	38.62%	42.66%	46.22%	49.38%	52.19%	54.70%	56.96%
15%	18.13%	23.87%	29.32%	34.29%	38.76%	42.73%	46.26%	49.40%	52.19%	54.71%	56.97%
17%	19.22%	24.69%	29.88%	34.66%	38.99%	42.87%	46.34%	49.44%	52.22%	54.72%	56.98%
19%	20.35%	25.57%	30.53%	35.13%	39.31%	43.08%	46.48%	49.53%	52.28%	54.76%	57.00%
21%	21.50%	26.51%	31.26%	35.67%	39.71%	43.37%	46.68%	49.67%	52.38%	54.83%	57.05%
23%	22.67%	27.48%	32.05%	36.28%	40.18%	43.72%	46.95%	49.87%	52.52%	54.93%	57.12%
25%	23.84%	28.49%	32.88%	36.96%	40.71%	44.14%	47.27%	50.12%	52.72%	55.08%	57.24%
27%	25.02%	29.52%	33.75%	37.68%	41.30%	44.62%	47.66%	50.43%	52.96%	55.27%	57.39%
29%	26.21%	30.56%	34.65%	38.44%	41.94%	45.15%	48.09%	50.78%	53.25%	55.51%	57.58%
31%	27.40%	31.62%	35.57%	39.23%	42.61%	45.72%	48.57%	51.19%	53.59%	55.79%	57.82%
33%	28.59%	32.68%	36.51%	40.05%	43.32%	46.33%	49.09%	51.63%	53.97%	56.11%	58.09%
35%	29.78%	33.76%	37.46%	40.89%	44.06%	46.97%	49.65%	52.12%	54.38%	56.48%	58.41%
37%	30.96%	34.84%	38.43%	41.75%	44.82%	47.64%	50.24%	52.63%	54.84%	56.87%	58.75%
39%	32.15%	35.92%	39.41%	42.63%	45.60%	48.34%	50.85%	53.18%	55.32%	57.30%	59.13%
41%	33.33%	37.00%	40.39%	43.52%	46.40%	49.05%	51.49%	53.75%	55.83%	57.75%	59.54%
43%	34.50%	38.08%	41.38%	44.41%	47.21%	49.78%	52.15%	54.34%	56.36%	58.24%	59.97%
45%	35.67%	39.16%	42.37%	45.32%	48.03%	50.53%	52.83%	54.96%	56.92%	58.74%	60.43%
47%	36.83%	40.23%	43.36%	46.22%	48.86%	51.29%	53.52%	55.59%	57.50%	59.26%	60.90%
49%	37.99%	41.31%	44.35%	47.14%	49.70%	52.05%	54.23%	56.23%	58.09%	59.81%	61.40%
51%	39.14%	42.38%	45.34%	48.05%	50.54%	52.83%	54.94%	56.89%	58.69%	60.36%	61.92%
53%	40.28%	43.44%	46.33%	48.97%	51.39%	53.61%	55.66%	57.56%	59.31%	60.93%	62.44%
55%	41.42%	44.50%	47.31%	49.88%	52.24%	54.40%	56.39%	58.23%	59.94%	61.52%	62.99%
57%	42.55%	45.55%	48.29%	50.79%	53.08%	55.19%	57.13%	58.92%	60.57%	62.11%	63.54%
59%	43.66%	46.60%	49.27%	51.70%	53.93%	55.98%	57.87%	59.61%	61.22%	62.71%	64.10%
61%	44.77%	47.64%	50.24%	52.61%	54.78%	56.77%	58.61%	60.30%	61.86%	63.32%	64.67%
63%	45.87%	48.67%	51.21%	53.52%	55.63%	57.57%	59.35%	60.99%	62.52%	63.93%	65.25%
65%	46.96%	49.69%	52.17%	54.42%	56.47%	58.36%	60.09%	61.69%	63.17%	64.55%	65.83%
67%	48.04%	50.71%	53.12%	55.31%	57.31%	59.15%	60.84%	62.39%	63.83%	65.17%	66.41%
69%	49.11%	51.71%	54.06%	56.20%	58.15%	59.94%	61.58%	63.09%	64.49%	65.79%	67.00%
71%	50.17%	52.71%	55.00%	57.08%	58.98%	60.72%	62.32%	63.79%	65.15%	66.42%	67.60%
73%	51.22%	53.70%	55.93%	57.96%	59.81%	61.50%	63.06%	64.49%	65.82%	67.05%	68.19%
75%	52.25%	54.67%	56.85%	58.83%	60.63%	62.28%	63.79%	65.18%	66.47%	67.67%	68.79%
77%	53.28%	55.64%	57.77%	59.69%	61.45%	63.05%	64.52%	65.88%	67.13%	68.30%	69.38%
79%	54.29%	56.60%	58.67%	60.55%	62.25%	63.81%	65.25%	66.57%	67.79%	68.92%	69.97%
81%	55.30%	57.54%	59.57%	61.39%	63.06%	64.57%	65.97%	67.25%	68.44%	69.54%	70.57%
83%	56.29%	58.48%	60.45%	62.23%	63.85%	65.33%	66.68%	67.93%	69.09%	70.16%	71.16%
85%	57.27%	59.41%	61.33%	63.06%	64.64%	66.07%	67.39%	68.61%	69.73%	70.78%	71.75%
87%	58.23%	60.32%	62.19%	63.88%	65.41%	66.81%	68.10%	69.28%	70.37%	71.39%	72.33%
89%	59.19%	61.22%	63.05%	64.69%	66.18%	67.55%	68.80%	69.95%	71.01%	72.00%	72.91%
91%	60.13%	62.11%	63.89%	65.49%	66.95%	68.27%	69.49%	70.61%	71.64%	72.60%	73.49%
93%	61.06%	62.99%	64.72%	66.28%	67.70%	68.99%	70.17%	71.26%	72.27%	73.20%	74.06%
95%	61.97%	63.86%	65.55%	67.07%	68.44%	69.70%	70.85%	71.91%	72.88%	73.79%	74.63%
97%	62.88%	64.72%	66.36%	67.84%	69.18%	70.40%	71.52%	72.55%	73.50%	74.38%	75.20%
99%	63.77%	65.56%	67.16%	68.60%	69.90%	71.09%	72.18%	73.18%	74.10%	74.96%	75.76%
101%	64.65%	66.39%	67.95%	69.35%	70.62%	71.77%	72.83%	73.81%	74.70%	75.54%	76.31%

Real Options Analysis Value (5-year maturity at 5% risk-free rate)

	Profitability Ratio (% in-the-money)									
Volatility	-99%	-90%	-80%	-70%	-60%	-50%	-40%	-30%	-20%	-10%
1%	0.00%	0.00%	0.00%	0.00%	0.00%	0.00%	0.00%	0.00%	2.77%	13.47%
3%	0.00%	0.00%	0.00%	0.00%	0.00%	0.00%	0.00%	0.17%	4.17%	13.50%
5%	0.00%	0.00%	0.00%	0.00%	0.00%	0.00%	0.04%	1.07%	5.85%	13.95%
7%	0.00%	0.00%	0.00%	0.00%	0.00%	0.01%	0.35%	2.43%	7.57%	14.86%
9%	0.00%	0.00%	0.00%	0.00%	0.00%	0.12%	1.05%	3.99%	9.30%	16.05%
11%	0.00%	0.00%	0.00%	0.00%	0.04%	0.43%	2.07%	5.66%	11.04%	17.39%
13%	0.00%	0.00%	0.00%	0.01%	0.15%	1.00%	3.32%	7.38%	12.78%	18.81%
15%	0.00%	0.00%	0.00%	0.03%	0.41%	1.80%	4.74%	9.14%	14.51%	20.28%
17%	0.00%	0.00%	0.00%	0.12%	0.84%	2.82%	6.27%	10.91%	16.24%	21.78%
19%	0.00%	0.00%	0.02%	0.29%	1.46%	4.01%	7.88%	12.69%	17.96%	23.31%
21%	0.00%	0.00%	0.05%	0.58%	2.26%	5.34%	9.56%	14.47%	19.67%	24.84%
23%	0.00%	0.00%	0.13%	1.00%	3.22%	6.78%	11.27%	16.26%	21.38%	26.39%
25%	0.00%	0.00%	0.26%	1.57%	4.33%	8.30%	13.01%	18.04%	23.07%	27.93%
27%	0.00%	0.01%	0.48%	2.29%	5.57%	9.90%	14.77%	19.81%	24.76%	29.47%
29%	0.00%	0.04%	0.80%	3.15%	6.92%	11.55%	16.55%	21.58%	26.43%	31.01%
31%	0.00%	0.08%	1.23%	4.14%	8.35%	13.24%	18.33%	23.33%	28.10%	32.54%
33%	0.00%	0.16%	1.77%	5.24%	9.87%	14.96%	20.11%	25.08%	29.75%	34.07%
35%	0.00%	0.28%	2.43%	6.46%	11.44%	16.71%	21.90%	26.81%	31.38%	35.59%
37%	0.00%	0.46%	3.21%	7.77%	13.07%	18.48%	23.67%	28.53%	33.00%	37.09%
39%	0.00%	0.70%	4.11%	9.17%	14.74%	20.25%	25.45%	30.24%	34.61%	38.59%
41%	0.00%	1.03%	5.11%	10.64%	16.45%	22.03%	27.21%	31.93%	36.20%	40.07%
43%	0.00%	1.44%	6.22%	12.18%	18.18%	23.82%	28.96%	33.60%	37.78%	41.54%
45%	0.00%	1.94%	7.42%	13.77%	19.94%	25.60%	30.70%	35.26%	39.34%	42.99%
47%	0.00%	2.53%	8.71%	15.41%	21.71%	27.38%	32.42%	36.90%	40.88%	44.43%
49%	0.01%	3.23%	10.07%	17.09%	23.48%	29.15%	34.13%	38.52%	42.40%	45.86%
51%	0.01%	4.02%	11.51%	18.79%	25.27%	30.91%	35.82%	40.12%	43.91%	47.26%
53%	0.03%	4.90%	13.01%	20.53%	27.05%	32.66%	37.50%	41.71%	45.40%	48.65%
55%	0.05%	5.88%	14.57%	22.28%	28.83%	34.39%	39.15%	43.27%	46.86%	50.03%
57%	0.08%	6.95%	16.17%	24.05%	30.61%	36.11%	40.79%	44.81%	48.31%	51.38%
59%	0.12%	8.10%	17.82%	25.83%	32.38%	37.81%	42.40%	46.33%	49.74%	52.72%
61%	0.19%	9.33%	19.50%	27.61%	34.13%	39.50%	43.99%	47.83%	51.14%	54.04%
63%	0.28%	10.64%	21.21%	29.39%	35.88%	41.16%	45.56%	49.30%	52.52%	55.33%
65%	0.39%	12.02%	22.95%	31.17%	37.61%	42.80%	47.11%	50.76%	53.89%	56.61%
67%	0.55%	13.46%	24.70%	32.95%	39.32%	44.42%	48.64%	52.19%	55.23%	57.87%
69%	0.74%	14.96%	26.47%	34.72%	41.01%	46.02%	50.14%	53.59%	56.55%	59.11%
71%	0.99%	16.51%	28.25%	36.48%	42.69%	47.60%	51.61%	54.97%	57.84%	60.32%
73%	1.28%	18.11%	30.03%	38.22%	44.34%	49.15%	53.06%	56.33%	59.11%	61.52%
75%	1.63%	19.75%	31.81%	39.95%	45.97%	50.67%	54.49%	57.67%	60.36%	62.69%
77%	2.04%	21.42%	33.60%	41.66%	47.58%	52.17%	55.89%	58.97%	61.59%	63.85%
79%	2.52%	23.12%	35.37%	43.35%	49.16%	53.65%	57.26%	60.26%	62.79%	64.98%
81%	3.06%	24.85%	37.14%	45.03%	50.71%	55.10%	58.61%	61.52%	63.97%	66.09%
83%	3.68%	26.60%	38.90%	46.67%	52.25%	56.52%	59.93%	62.75%	65.13%	67.17%
85%	4.37%	28.36%	40.64%	48.30%	53.75%	57.91%	61.23%	63.96%	66.26%	68.24%
87%	5.13%	30.13%	42.37%	49.90%	55.23%	59.27%	62.50%	65.14%	67.37%	69.28%
89%	5.97%	31.92%	44.08%	51.48%	56.68%	60.61%	63.74%	66.30%	68.46%	70.30%
91%	6.88%	33.70%	45.77%	53.02%	58.10%	61.92%	64.95%	67.44%	69.52%	71.30%
93%	7.87%	35.48%	47.43%	54.55%	59.49%	63.20%	66.14%	68.54%	70.55%	72.27%
95%	8.93%	37.26%	49.08%	56.04%	60.85%	64.46%	67.30%	69.62%	71.57%	73.23%
97%	10.06%	39.03%	50.70%	57.50%	62.18%	65.68%	68.44%	70.68%	72.56%	74.16%
99%	11.26%	40.79%	52.29%	58.94%	63.49%	66.88%	69.54%	71.71%	73.52%	75.07%
101%	12.52%	42.54%	53.86%	60.34%	64.76%	68.05%	70.62%	72.72%	74.47%	75.95%

Profitability Ratio (% in-the-money)

olatility	0%	10%	20%	30%	40%	50%	60%	70%	80%	90%	100%
1%	22.12%	29.20%	35.10%	40.09%	44.37%	48.08%	51.32%	54.19%	56.73%	59.01%	61.06%
3%	22.12%	29.20%	35.10%	40.09%	44.37%	48.08%	51.32%	54.19%	56.73%	59.01%	61.06%
5%	22.16%	29.20%	35.10%	40.09%	44.37%	48.08%	51.32%	54.19%	56.73%	59.01%	61.06%
7%	22.44%	29.26%	35.11%	40.09%	44.37%	48.08%	51.32%	54.19%	56.73%	59.01%	61.06%
9%	23.03%	29.50%	35.19%	40.12%	44.38%	48.08%	51.33%	54.19%	56.73%	59.01%	61.06%
11%	23.86%	29.95%	35.41%	40.22%	44.42%	48.10%	51.33%	54.19%	56.73%	59.01%	61.06%
13%	24.87%	30.60%	35.80%	40.44%	44.55%	48.17%	51.37%	54.21%	56.74%	59.02%	61.06%
15%	26.00%	31.40%	36.35%	40.80%	44.77%	48.31%	51.46%	54.26%	56.78%	59.04%	61.08%
17%	27.21%	32.33%	37.03%	41.29%	45.11%	48.55%	51.62%	54.37%	56.85%	59.09%	61.11%
19%	28.49%	33.35%	37.82%	41.89%	45.57%	48.88%	51.86%	54.56%	56.98%	59.18%	61.18%
21%	29.80%	34.43%	38.70%	42.59%	46.11%	49.31%	52.20%	54.81%	57.18%	59.34%	61.30%
23%	31.14%	35.57%	39.64%	43.36%	46.75%	49.82%	52.61%	55.14%	57.45%	59.55%	61.47%
25%	32.50%	36.75%	40.64%	44.21%	47.45%	50.41%	53.10%	55.55%	57.78%	59.83%	61.70%
27%	33.88%	37.95%	41.69%	45.10%	48.22%	51.06%	53.65%	56.02%	58.18%	60.16%	61.99%
29%	35.26%	39.18%	42.77%	46.05%	49.04%	51.77%	54.26%	56.55%	58.64%	60.56%	62.33%
31%	36.65%	40.42%	43.87%	47.02%	49.89%	52.52%	54.92%	57.13%	59.15%	61.01%	62.72%
33%	38.04%	41.68%	44.99%	48.02%	50.79%	53.31%	55.63%	57.75%	59.70%	61.50%	63.16%
35%	39.43%	42.94%	46.13%	49.05%	51.71%	54.14%	56.37%	58.41%	60.30%	62.03%	63.64%
37%	40.81%	44.20%	47.28%	50.09%	52.65%	54.99%	57.14%	59.11%	60.93%	62.60%	64.15%
39%	42.19%	45.46%	48.43%	51.14%	53.60%	55.86%	57.93%	59.83%	61.58%	63.20%	64.70%
41%	43.56%	46.72%	49.59%	52.20%	54.58%	56.75%	58.75%	60.58%	62.27%	63.83%	65.28%
43%	44.92%	47.98%	50.75%	53.26%	55.56%	57.65%	59.58%	61.34%	62.98%	64.48%	65.88%
45%	46.27%	49.23%	51.90%	54.33%	56.54%	58.57%	60.42%	62.13%	63.70%	65.15%	66.50%
47%	47.61%	50.47%	53.06%	55.40%	57.53%	59.48%	61.27%	62.92%	64.44%	65.84%	67.14%
49%	48.94%	51.71%	54.20%	56.47%	58.53%	60.41%	62.13%	63.72%	65.19%	66.54%	67.80%
51%	50.25%	52.93%	55.34%	57.53%	59.52%	61.33%	63.00%	64.53%	65.94%	67.25%	68.47%
53%	51.55%	54.14%	56.48%	58.59%	60.51%	62.26%	63.87%	65.34%	66.71%	67.97%	69.14%
55%	52.84%	55.34%	57.60%	59.64%	61.49%	63.18%	64.73%	66.16%	67.48%	68.70%	69.83%
57%	54.10%	56.53%	58.71%	60.68%	62.47%	64.11%	65.60%	66.98%	68.25%	69.42%	70.52%
59%	55.36%	57.71%	59.82%	61.72%	63.45%	65.02%	66.47%	67.79%	69.02%	70.15%	71.21%
61%	56.59%	58.87%	60.90%	62.74%	64.41%	65.93%	67.33%	68.61%	69.79%	70.89%	71.90%
63%	57.81%	60.01%	61.98%	63.76%	65.37%	66.84%	68.18%	69.42%	70.56%	71.62%	72.60%
65%	59.01%	61.14%	63.04%	64.76%	66.32%	67.73%	69.03%	70.22%	71.32%	72.34%	73.29%
67%	60.19%	62.25%	64.09%	65.75%	67.25%	68.62%	69.87%	71.02%	72.09%	73.07%	73.98%
69%	61.36%	63.35%	65.13%	66.73%	68.18%	69.50%	70.71%	71.82%	72.84%	73.79%	74.67%
71%	62.50%	64.43%	66.15%	67.69%	69.09%	70.37%	71.53%	72.60%	73.59%	74.50%	75.35%
73%	63.63%	65.49%	67.15%	68.64%	69.99%	71.22%	72.35%	73.38%	74.33%	75.21%	76.03%
75%	64.73%	66.53%	68.13%	69.58%	70.88%	72.07%	73.15%	74.15%	75.06%	75.91%	76.70%
77%	65.82%	67.56%	69.10%	70.50%	71.75%	72.90%	73.94%	74.90%	75.79%	76.61%	77.37%
79%	66.88%	68.56%	70.06%	71.40%	72.61%	73.72%	74.72%	75.65%	76.50%	77.29%	78.03%
81%	67.93%	69.55%	70.99%	72.29%	73.46%	74.52%	75.49%	76.39%	77.21%	77.97%	78.68%
83%	68.95%	70.52%	71.91%	73.16%	74.29%	75.31%	76.25%	77.11%	77.90%	78.64%	79.32%
85%	69.96%	71.47%	72.81%	74.02%	75.10%	76.09%	76.99%	77.82%	78.59%	79.29%	79.95%
87%	70.94%	72.40%	73.69%	74.86%	75.90%	76.86%	77.73%	78.52%	79.26%	79.94%	80.57%
89%	71.90%	73.31%	74.56%	75.68%	76.69%	77.61%	78.44%	79.21%	79.92%	80.57%	81.18%
91%	72.84%	74.20%	75.41%	76.48%	77.46%	78.34%	79.15%	79.89%	80.57%	81.20%	81.78%
93%	73.76%	75.07%	76.23%	77.27%	78.21%	79.06%	79.84%	80.55%	81.20%	81.81%	82.37%
95%	74.66%	75.93%	77.04%	78.05%	78.95%	79.77%	80.51%	81.20%	81.83%	82.41%	82.95%
97%	75.54%	76.76%	77.84%	78.80%	79.67%	80.46%	81.17%	81.83%	82.44%	83.00%	83.52%
99%	76.40%	77.57%	78.61%	79.54%	80.37%	81.13%	81.82%	82.45%	83.04%	83.58%	84.08%
101%	77.24%	78.37%	79.36%	80.26%	81.06%	81.79%	82.45%	83.06%	83.62%	84.14%	84.62%

Real Options Analysis Value (7-Year Maturity at 5% Risk-free Rate)

	Profitability Ratio (% in-the-money)									
Volatility	-99%	-90%	-80%	-70%	-60%	-50%	-40%	-30%	-20%	-10%
1%	0.00%	0.00%	0.00%	0.00%	0.00%	0.00%	0.00%	0.76%	11.91%	21.70%
3%	0.00%	0.00%	0.00%	0.00%	0.00%	0.00%	0.07%	2.85%	12.09%	21.70%
5%	0.00%	0.00%	0.00%	0.00%	0.00%	0.02%	0.78%	4.96%	13.03%	21.85%
7%	0.00%	0.00%	0.00%	0.00%	0.01%	0.27%	2.13%	7.07%	14.46%	22.41%
9%	0.00%	0.00%	0.00%	0.00%	0.09%	0.94%	3.83%	9.18%	16.10%	23.36%
11%	0.00%	0.00%	0.00%	0.02%	0.38%	2.01%	5.71%	11.28%	17.85%	24.56%
13%	0.00%	0.00%	0.00%	0.11%	0.94%	3.39%	7.70%	13.37%	19.65%	25.93%
15%	0.00%	0.00%	0.01%	0.34%	1.79%	4.99%	9.74%	15.45%	21.49%	27.41%
17%	0.00%	0.00%	0.06%	0.75%	2.91%	6.75%	11.82%	17.52%	23.34%	28.95%
19%	0.00%	0.00%	0.18%	1.38%	4.25%	8.63%	13.92%	19.58%	25.20%	30.54%
21%	0.00%	0.01%	0.41%	2.23%	5.78%	10.59%	16.03%	21.62%	27.06%	32.16%
23%	0.00%	0.03%	0.77%	3.29%	7.45%	12.61%	18.14%	23.65%	28.91%	33.80%
25%	0.00%	0.08%	1.30%	4.53%	9.24%	14.66%	20.25%	25.67%	30.76%	35.45%
27%	0.00%	0.17%	2.00%	5.94%	11.12%	16.75%	22.35%	27.66%	32.59%	37.10%
29%	0.00%	0.33%	2.87%	7.49%	13.07%	18.85%	24.43%	29.64%	34.42%	38.75%
31%	0.00%	0.59%	3.91%	9.17%	15.08%	20.96%	26.50%	31.60%	36.22%	40.40%
33%	0.00%	0.94%	5.11%	10.95%	17.13%	23.07%	28.56%	33.54%	38.02%	42.04%
35%	0.00%	1.43%	6.45%	12.81%	19.20%	25.18%	30.59%	35.45%	39.79%	43.67%
37%	0.00%	2.04%	7.93%	14.74%	21.30%	27.27%	32.61%	37.34%	41.54%	45.28%
39%	0.00%	2.79%	9.52%	16.73%	23.41%	29.36%	34.60%	39.21%	43.27%	46.88%
41%	0.01%	3.68%	11.22%	18.76%	25.52%	31.42%	36.56%	41.05%	44.98%	48.46%
43%	0.02%	4.70%	13.00%	20.82%	27.63%	33.47%	38.50%	42.86%	46.67%	50.02%
45%	0.04%	5.86%	14.87%	22.91%	29.73%	35.50%	40.42%	44.65%	48.33%	51.56%
47%	0.07%	7.14%	16.79%	25.01%	31.82%	37.50%	42.30%	46.41%	49.97%	53.08%
49%	0.12%	8.55%	18.77%	27.12%	33.89%	39.47%	44.16%	48.14%	51.58%	54.58%
51%	0.20%	10.06%	20.80%	29.23%	35.95%	41.42%	45.98%	49.84%	53.17%	56.06%
53%	0.32%	11.68%	22.85%	31.34%	37.98%	43.34%	47.77%	51.52%	54.72%	57.51%
55%	0.48%	13.38%	24.94%	33.43%	39.98%	45.22%	49.53%	53.16%	56.25%	58.94%
57%	0.70%	15.17%	27.03%	35.52%	41.96%	47.08%	51.26%	54.77%	57.75%	60.34%
59%	0.99%	17.03%	29.14%	37.58%	43.91%	48.90%	52.96%	56.34%	59.22%	61.71%
61%	1.34%	18.95%	31.25%	39.62%	45.83%	50.69%	54.62%	57.89%	60.67%	63.06%
63%	1.78%	20.92%	33.36%	41.64%	47.72%	52.44%	56.25%	59.40%	62.08%	64.38%
65%	2.31%	22.93%	35.46%	43.63%	49.57%	54.15%	57.84%	60.88%	63.46%	65.67%
67%	2.93%	24.98%	37.55%	45.59%	51.38%	55.83%	59.39%	62.33%	64.81%	66.93%
69%	3.65%	27.06%	39.62%	47.52%	53.16%	57.47%	60.91%	63.74%	66.13%	68.17%
71%	4.47%	29.15%	41.66%	49.42%	54.91%	59.08%	62.40%	65.12%	67.41%	69.37%
73%	5.40%	31.25%	43.69%	51.28%	56.61%	60.65%	63.85%	66.47%	68.67%	70.55%
75%	6.44%	33.36%	45.68%	53.10%	58.27%	62.17%	65.26%	67.78%	69.89%	71.70%
77%	7.58%	35.47%	47.65%	54.88%	59.90%	63.66%	66.63%	69.06%	71.09%	72.82%
79%	8.82%	37.58%	49.58%	56.62%	61.48%	65.12%	67.97%	70.30%	72.25%	73.91%
81%	10.16%	39.67%	51.47%	58.33%	63.03%	66.53%	69.28%	71.51%	73.38%	74.97%
83%	11.60%	41.74%	53.33%	59.99%	64.53%	67.90%	70.54%	72.69%	74.48%	76.00%
85%	13.13%	43.80%	55.15%	61.61%	65.99%	69.24%	71.77%	73.83%	75.54%	77.00%
87%	14.74%	45.83%	56.93%	63.19%	67.42%	70.54%	72.97%	74.94%	76.58%	77.97%
89%	16.43%	47.83%	58.67%	64.73%	68.80%	71.79%	74.13%	76.01%	77.58%	78.91%
91%	18.20%	49.80%	60.37%	66.22%	70.14%	73.02%	75.25%	77.06%	78.56%	79.83%
93%	20.03%	51.74%	62.02%	67.67%	71.44%	74.20%	76.34%	78.07%	79.50%	80.71%
95%	21.93%	53.64%	63.63%	69.08%	72.70%	75.34%	77.39%	79.05%	80.41%	81.57%
97%	23.87%	55.50%	65.19%	70.44%	73.92%	76.45%	78.41%	79.99%	81.30%	82.40%
99%	25.86%	57.32%	66.71%	71.77%	75.10%	77.52%	79.40%	80.90%	82.15%	83.20%
101%	27.88%	59.10%	68.19%	73.05%	76.24%	78.56%	80.35%	81.79%	82.98%	83.98%

	Profitability Ratio (% in-the-money)										
Volatility	0%	10%	20%	30%	40%	50%	60%	70%	80%	90%	100%
1%	29.53%	35.94%	41.28%	45.79%	49.67%	53.02%	55.96%	58.55%	60.85%	62.91%	64.77%
3%	29.53%	35.94%	41.28%	45.79%	49.67%	53.02%	55.96%	58.55%	60.85%	62.91%	64.77%
5%	29.55%	35.94%	41.28%	45.79%	49.67%	53.02%	55.96%	58.55%	60.85%	62.91%	64.77%
7%	29.71%	35.98%	41.28%	45.79%	49.67%	53.02%	55.96%	58.55%	60.85%	62.91%	64.77%
9%	30.16%	36.16%	41.36%	45.82%	49.67%	53.02%	55.96%	58.55%	60.85%	62.91%	64.77%
11%	30.88%	36.57%	41.57%	45.93%	49.73%	53.05%	55.97%	58.55%	60.85%	62.91%	64.77%
13%	31.84%	37.19%	41.96%	46.17%	49.87%	53.14%	56.02%	58.58%	60.87%	62.92%	64.77%
15%	32.95%	38.00%	42.53%	46.56%	50.14%	53.31%	56.14%	58.66%	60.92%	62.96%	64.80%
17%	34.18%	38.95%	43.24%	47.09%	50.53%	53.60%	56.35%	58.82%	61.04%	63.04%	64.86%
19%	35.49%	40.01%	44.08%	47.75%	51.04%	54.00%	56.66%	59.06%	61.22%	63.18%	64.97%
21%	36.87%	41.15%	45.02%	48.52%	51.67%	54.51%	57.07%	59.38%	61.49%	63.40%	65.14%
23%	38.28%	42.36%	46.04%	49.37%	52.38%	55.10%	57.56%	59.80%	61.83%	63.69%	65.38%
25%	39.73%	43.61%	47.13%	50.30%	53.18%	55.78%	58.14%	60.29%	62.25%	64.05%	65.69%
27%	41.20%	44.90%	48.26%	51.29%	54.03%	56.53%	58.79%	60.86%	62.75%	64.48%	66.06%
29%	42.68%	46.22%	49.42%	52.32%	54.94%	57.33%	59.50%	61.48%	63.30%	64.96%	66.50%
31%	44.16%	47.55%	50.62%	53.38%	55.90%	58.18%	60.26%	62.16%	63.91%	65.51%	66.99%
33%	45.65%	48.90%	51.83%	54.48%	56.88%	59.07%	61.06%	62.88%	64.56%	66.10%	67.52%
35%	47.14%	50.25%	53.06%	55.59%	57.89%	59.98%	61.90%	63.65%	65.25%	66.73%	68.10%
37%	48.61%	51.60%	54.29%	56.72%	58.92%	60.93%	62.76%	64.44%	65.98%	67.40%	68.71%
39%	50.08%	52.95%	55.53%	57.86%	59.97%	61.89%	63.64%	65.25%	66.73%	68.10%	69.36%
41%	51.54%	54.30%	56.77%	59.00%	61.02%	62.86%	64.55%	66.09%	67.51%	68.82%	70.03%
43%	52.99%	55.63%	58.01%	60.15%	62.08%	63.85%	65.46%	66.94%	68.30%	69.56%	70.72%
45%	54.42%	56.96%	59.24%	61.29%	63.15%	64.84%	66.38%	67.80%	69.11%	70.31%	71.43%
47%	55.83%	58.27%	60.46%	62.43%	64.21%	65.83%	67.31%	68.67%	69.92%	71.08%	72.15%
49%	57.22%	59.57%	61.67%	63.56%	65.27%	66.82%	68.24%	69.54%	70.74%	71.85%	72.88%
51%	58.60%	60.85%	62.87%	64.68%	66.32%	67.81%	69.17%	70.42%	71.57%	72.63%	73.62%
53%	59.95%	62.12%	64.05%	65.79%	67.36%	68.79%	70.09%	71.29%	72.39%	73.41%	74.36%
55%	61.29%	63.37%	65.22%	66.89%	68.39%	69.76%	71.01%	72.16%	73.22%	74.20%	75.10%
57%	62.60%	64.59%	66.37%	67.97%	69.42%	70.73%	71.93%	73.03%	74.04%	74.98%	75.85%
59%	63.88%	65.80%	67.51%	69.04%	70.43%	71.68%	72.83%	73.89%	74.86%	75.75%	76.59%
61%	65.14%	66.99%	68.62%	70.09%	71.42%	72.63%	73.73%	74.74%	75.67%	76.53%	77.32%
63%	66.38%	68.15%	69.72%	71.13%	72.40%	73.56%	74.61%	75.58%	76.47%	77.29%	78.05%
65%	67.59%	69.29%	70.80%	72.15%	73.37%	74.47%	75.48%	76.41%	77.26%	78.05%	78.78%
67%	68.78%	70.41%	71.85%	73.15%	74.31%	75.37%	76.34%	77.22%	78.04%	78.80%	79.50%
69%	69.94%	71.50%	72.88%	74.12%	75.24%	76.26%	77.18%	78.03%	78.81%	79.53%	80.20%
71%	71.07%	72.57%	73.90%	75.08%	76.15%	77.12%	78.01%	78.82%	79.57%	80.26%	80.90%
73%	72.18%	73.61%	74.88%	76.02%	77.04%	77.97%	78.82%	79.60%	80.31%	80.97%	81.58%
75%	73.26%	74.63%	75.85%	76.94%	77.92%	78.80%	79.61%	80.36%	81.04%	81.67%	82.26%
77%	74.31%	75.63%	76.79%	77.83%	78.77%	79.62%	80.39%	81.10%	81.75%	82.36%	82.92%
79%	75.34%	76.60%	77.71%	78.71%	79.60%	80.41%	81.15%	81.83%	82.45%	83.03%	83.57%
81%	76.34%	77.54%	78.61%	79.56%	80.41%	81.19%	81.89%	82.54%	83.14%	83.69%	84.20%
83%	77.31%	78.46%	79.48%	80.39%	81.20%	81.94%	82.62%	83.24%	83.81%	84.33%	84.82%
85%	78.25%	79.35%	80.33%	81.19%	81.97%	82.68%	83.32%	83.91%	84.46%	84.96%	85.42%
87%	79.17%	80.22%	81.15%	81.98%	82.72%	83.40%	84.01%	84.58%	85.09%	85.57%	86.01%
89%	80.06%	81.06%	81.95%	82.74%	83.45%	84.09%	84.68%	85.22%	85.71%	86.17%	86.59%
91%	80.92%	81.88%	82.73%	83.48%	84.16%	84.77%	85.33%	85.84%	86.31%	86.75%	87.15%
93%	81.76%	82.67%	83.48%	84.20%	84.84%	85.43%	85.96%	86.45%	86.90%	87.31%	87.70%
95%	82.57%	83.44%	84.21%	84.89%	85.51%	86.07%	86.57%	87.04%	87.47%	87.86%	88.23%
97%	83.35%	84.18%	84.92%	85.57%	86.15%	86.69%	87.17%	87.61%	88.02%	88.39%	88.74%
99%	84.11%	84.90%	85.60%	86.22%	86.78%	87.28%	87.74%	88.16%	88.55%	88.91%	89.24%
101%	84.84%	85.60%	86.26%	86.85%	87.38%	87.86%	88.30%	88.70%	89.07%	89.41%	89.72%

Real Options Analysis Value (10-year maturity at 5% risk-free rate)

Volatility	Profitability Ratio (% in-the-money)									
	-99%	-90%	-80%	-70%	-60%	-50%	-40%	-30%	-20%	-10%
1%	0.00%	0.00%	0.00%	0.00%	0.00%	0.00%	0.80%	13.35%	24.18%	32.61%
3%	0.00%	0.00%	0.00%	0.00%	0.00%	0.08%	3.28%	13.61%	24.19%	32.61%
5%	0.00%	0.00%	0.00%	0.00%	0.03%	0.93%	5.81%	14.81%	24.41%	32.63%
7%	0.00%	0.00%	0.00%	0.01%	0.32%	2.56%	8.33%	16.56%	25.15%	32.88%
9%	0.00%	0.00%	0.00%	0.09%	1.11%	4.62%	10.84%	18.54%	26.34%	33.48%
11%	0.00%	0.00%	0.01%	0.39%	2.39%	6.89%	13.35%	20.63%	27.82%	34.42%
13%	0.00%	0.00%	0.07%	1.02%	4.06%	9.29%	15.84%	22.77%	29.47%	35.60%
15%	0.00%	0.00%	0.26%	2.01%	6.01%	11.75%	18.31%	24.95%	31.23%	36.96%
17%	0.00%	0.01%	0.65%	3.33%	8.15%	14.25%	20.77%	27.13%	33.06%	38.44%
19%	0.00%	0.05%	1.28%	4.93%	10.43%	16.77%	23.20%	29.32%	34.94%	40.00%
21%	0.00%	0.16%	2.18%	6.76%	12.81%	19.29%	25.61%	31.50%	36.83%	41.62%
23%	0.00%	0.36%	3.34%	8.78%	15.25%	21.81%	28.00%	33.66%	38.74%	43.28%
25%	0.00%	0.71%	4.74%	10.95%	17.74%	24.31%	30.36%	35.81%	40.66%	44.96%
27%	0.00%	1.23%	6.37%	13.24%	20.25%	26.80%	32.69%	37.93%	42.56%	46.66%
29%	0.00%	1.94%	8.18%	15.61%	22.77%	29.26%	34.99%	40.03%	44.46%	48.36%
31%	0.00%	2.85%	10.16%	18.04%	25.30%	31.69%	37.26%	42.11%	46.34%	50.06%
33%	0.01%	3.97%	12.28%	20.52%	27.81%	34.09%	39.49%	44.15%	48.20%	51.74%
35%	0.02%	5.29%	14.51%	23.03%	30.30%	36.46%	41.69%	46.17%	50.04%	53.42%
37%	0.04%	6.79%	16.84%	25.54%	32.77%	38.79%	43.84%	48.15%	51.86%	55.08%
39%	0.09%	8.48%	19.23%	28.07%	35.21%	41.08%	45.96%	50.10%	53.64%	56.72%
41%	0.18%	10.32%	21.68%	30.58%	37.62%	43.32%	48.04%	52.01%	55.40%	58.33%
43%	0.31%	12.30%	24.16%	33.08%	40.00%	45.53%	50.07%	53.88%	57.12%	59.92%
45%	0.51%	14.41%	26.67%	35.56%	42.33%	47.69%	52.07%	55.71%	58.81%	61.48%
47%	0.79%	16.62%	29.20%	38.01%	44.62%	49.81%	54.01%	57.51%	60.47%	63.02%
49%	1.17%	18.92%	31.72%	40.43%	46.86%	51.87%	55.91%	59.26%	62.09%	64.52%
51%	1.67%	21.30%	34.23%	42.80%	49.06%	53.89%	57.77%	60.97%	63.67%	65.99%
53%	2.29%	23.73%	36.73%	45.14%	51.20%	55.86%	59.58%	62.64%	65.22%	67.42%
55%	3.05%	26.20%	39.20%	47.43%	53.30%	57.78%	61.34%	64.27%	66.72%	68.82%
57%	3.95%	28.70%	41.64%	49.67%	55.34%	59.64%	63.06%	65.85%	68.19%	70.19%
59%	5.01%	31.22%	44.04%	51.85%	57.33%	61.46%	64.72%	67.39%	69.62%	71.52%
61%	6.21%	33.74%	46.40%	53.99%	59.26%	63.22%	66.34%	68.88%	71.00%	72.81%
63%	7.57%	36.26%	48.72%	56.07%	61.14%	64.93%	67.91%	70.33%	72.35%	74.06%
65%	9.07%	38.76%	50.98%	58.09%	62.96%	66.59%	69.43%	71.73%	73.65%	75.28%
67%	10.72%	41.24%	53.19%	60.06%	64.73%	68.19%	70.90%	73.09%	74.91%	76.46%
69%	12.50%	43.70%	55.35%	61.97%	66.44%	69.75%	72.32%	74.41%	76.14%	77.61%
71%	14.41%	46.11%	57.45%	63.82%	68.10%	71.25%	73.70%	75.68%	77.32%	78.71%
73%	16.43%	48.49%	59.49%	65.60%	69.69%	72.70%	75.02%	76.90%	78.46%	79.78%
75%	18.56%	50.82%	61.47%	67.33%	71.24%	74.09%	76.30%	78.09%	79.56%	80.81%
77%	20.78%	53.10%	63.39%	69.00%	72.72%	75.44%	77.54%	79.22%	80.62%	81.80%
79%	23.08%	55.32%	65.25%	70.61%	74.16%	76.73%	78.72%	80.32%	81.64%	82.76%
81%	25.44%	57.49%	67.04%	72.16%	75.53%	77.98%	79.86%	81.37%	82.62%	83.68%
83%	27.86%	59.59%	68.77%	73.66%	76.86%	79.17%	80.96%	82.39%	83.56%	84.56%
85%	30.33%	61.64%	70.44%	75.09%	78.13%	80.32%	82.01%	83.36%	84.47%	85.41%
87%	32.82%	63.61%	72.04%	76.47%	79.35%	81.42%	83.01%	84.29%	85.34%	86.22%
89%	35.34%	65.53%	73.58%	77.79%	80.51%	82.47%	83.98%	85.18%	86.17%	87.00%
91%	37.86%	67.38%	75.06%	79.05%	81.63%	83.48%	84.90%	86.03%	86.96%	87.74%
93%	40.38%	69.16%	76.48%	80.26%	82.70%	84.44%	85.78%	86.84%	87.72%	88.46%
95%	42.89%	70.87%	77.84%	81.42%	83.72%	85.36%	86.62%	87.62%	88.45%	89.14%
97%	45.38%	72.52%	79.14%	82.52%	84.69%	86.24%	87.42%	88.36%	89.14%	89.79%
99%	47.84%	74.10%	80.38%	83.57%	85.62%	87.07%	88.19%	89.07%	89.80%	90.40%
101%	50.26%	75.61%	81.56%	84.58%	86.50%	87.87%	88.91%	89.74%	90.42%	90.99%

	Profitability Ratio (% in-the-money)										
Volatility	0%	10%	20%	30%	40%	50%	60%	70%	80%	90%	100%
1%	39.35%	44.86%	49.46%	53.34%	56.68%	59.56%	62.09%	64.32%	66.30%	68.08%	69.67%
3%	39.35%	44.86%	49.46%	53.34%	56.68%	59.56%	62.09%	64.32%	66.30%	68.08%	69.67%
5%	39.35%	44.86%	49.46%	53.34%	56.68%	59.56%	62.09%	64.32%	66.30%	68.08%	69.67%
7%	39.42%	44.88%	49.46%	53.34%	56.68%	59.56%	62.09%	64.32%	66.30%	68.08%	69.67%
9%	39.70%	45.00%	49.51%	53.37%	56.69%	59.57%	62.09%	64.32%	66.30%	68.08%	69.67%
11%	40.25%	45.32%	49.69%	53.46%	56.74%	59.60%	62.11%	64.33%	66.31%	68.08%	69.67%
13%	41.06%	45.85%	50.04%	53.69%	56.88%	59.69%	62.17%	64.37%	66.33%	68.10%	69.69%
15%	42.07%	46.59%	50.57%	54.07%	57.15%	59.88%	62.31%	64.47%	66.40%	68.15%	69.72%
17%	43.24%	47.50%	51.27%	54.60%	57.56%	60.20%	62.55%	64.65%	66.55%	68.26%	69.81%
19%	44.52%	48.54%	52.11%	55.28%	58.11%	60.63%	62.90%	64.93%	66.77%	68.44%	69.96%
21%	45.89%	49.68%	53.06%	56.07%	58.76%	61.18%	63.35%	65.31%	67.09%	68.71%	70.18%
23%	47.31%	50.90%	54.10%	56.96%	59.52%	61.83%	63.90%	65.79%	67.50%	69.05%	70.48%
25%	48.78%	52.18%	55.22%	57.93%	60.36%	62.56%	64.54%	66.34%	67.98%	69.48%	70.85%
27%	50.28%	53.51%	56.38%	58.96%	61.27%	63.36%	65.25%	66.97%	68.54%	69.98%	71.30%
29%	51.80%	54.86%	57.59%	60.04%	62.24%	64.22%	66.03%	67.67%	69.17%	70.54%	71.81%
31%	53.33%	56.24%	58.83%	61.15%	63.24%	65.13%	66.85%	68.41%	69.85%	71.16%	72.37%
33%	54.86%	57.62%	60.09%	62.29%	64.28%	66.08%	67.71%	69.20%	70.57%	71.82%	72.98%
35%	56.39%	59.01%	61.35%	63.45%	65.34%	67.05%	68.61%	70.03%	71.33%	72.52%	73.63%
37%	57.90%	60.40%	62.63%	64.62%	66.42%	68.04%	69.52%	70.88%	72.12%	73.26%	74.31%
39%	59.41%	61.79%	63.90%	65.80%	67.51%	69.05%	70.46%	71.75%	72.93%	74.02%	75.02%
41%	60.90%	63.16%	65.17%	66.98%	68.60%	70.07%	71.41%	72.63%	73.76%	74.79%	75.75%
43%	62.37%	64.52%	66.43%	68.15%	69.69%	71.09%	72.36%	73.53%	74.60%	75.58%	76.49%
45%	63.81%	65.86%	67.68%	69.31%	70.78%	72.11%	73.32%	74.43%	75.44%	76.38%	77.25%
47%	65.23%	67.18%	68.92%	70.46%	71.86%	73.12%	74.27%	75.33%	76.29%	77.18%	78.01%
49%	66.63%	68.48%	70.13%	71.60%	72.93%	74.13%	75.22%	76.22%	77.14%	77.99%	78.77%
51%	68.00%	69.76%	71.33%	72.73%	73.99%	75.13%	76.16%	77.11%	77.99%	78.79%	79.54%
53%	69.33%	71.01%	72.50%	73.83%	75.03%	76.11%	77.10%	78.00%	78.83%	79.59%	80.30%
55%	70.64%	72.24%	73.65%	74.91%	76.05%	77.08%	78.01%	78.87%	79.66%	80.38%	81.06%
57%	71.92%	73.43%	74.78%	75.97%	77.05%	78.03%	78.92%	79.73%	80.48%	81.17%	81.80%
59%	73.16%	74.60%	75.88%	77.01%	78.04%	78.96%	79.80%	80.57%	81.28%	81.94%	82.54%
61%	74.37%	75.74%	76.95%	78.03%	79.00%	79.87%	80.67%	81.40%	82.08%	82.70%	83.27%
63%	75.55%	76.84%	77.99%	79.01%	79.93%	80.77%	81.52%	82.22%	82.85%	83.44%	83.98%
65%	76.69%	77.92%	79.01%	79.98%	80.85%	81.64%	82.35%	83.01%	83.61%	84.17%	84.68%
67%	77.80%	78.96%	79.99%	80.91%	81.74%	82.48%	83.16%	83.78%	84.35%	84.88%	85.37%
69%	78.87%	79.98%	80.95%	81.82%	82.60%	83.31%	83.95%	84.54%	85.08%	85.57%	86.04%
71%	79.91%	80.95%	81.88%	82.70%	83.44%	84.11%	84.71%	85.27%	85.78%	86.25%	86.69%
73%	80.91%	81.90%	82.77%	83.55%	84.25%	84.88%	85.46%	85.98%	86.46%	86.91%	87.32%
75%	81.88%	82.82%	83.64%	84.38%	85.04%	85.63%	86.18%	86.67%	87.13%	87.55%	87.94%
77%	82.81%	83.70%	84.48%	85.17%	85.80%	86.36%	86.87%	87.34%	87.77%	88.17%	88.53%
79%	83.71%	84.55%	85.29%	85.94%	86.53%	87.06%	87.54%	87.98%	88.39%	88.76%	89.11%
81%	84.58%	85.37%	86.06%	86.68%	87.24%	87.74%	88.19%	88.61%	88.99%	89.34%	89.67%
83%	85.41%	86.16%	86.81%	87.39%	87.92%	88.39%	88.82%	89.21%	89.57%	89.90%	90.21%
85%	86.21%	86.91%	87.53%	88.08%	88.57%	89.01%	89.42%	89.79%	90.13%	90.44%	90.73%
87%	86.98%	87.64%	88.22%	88.74%	89.20%	89.62%	90.00%	90.34%	90.66%	90.96%	91.23%
89%	87.71%	88.33%	88.88%	89.37%	89.80%	90.19%	90.55%	90.88%	91.18%	91.45%	91.71%
91%	88.42%	89.00%	89.51%	89.97%	90.38%	90.75%	91.08%	91.39%	91.67%	91.93%	92.17%
93%	89.09%	89.64%	90.12%	90.55%	90.93%	91.28%	91.59%	91.88%	92.15%	92.39%	92.62%
95%	89.73%	90.25%	90.70%	91.10%	91.46%	91.79%	92.08%	92.35%	92.60%	92.83%	93.04%
97%	90.34%	90.83%	91.25%	91.63%	91.97%	92.27%	92.55%	92.80%	93.03%	93.25%	93.45%
99%	90.93%	91.38%	91.78%	92.13%	92.45%	92.73%	92.99%	93.23%	93.45%	93.65%	93.84%
101%	91.48%	91.91%	92.28%	92.61%	92.91%	93.18%	93.42%	93.64%	93.85%	94.03%	94.21%

Real Options Analysis Value (15-year maturity at 5% risk-free rate)

Volatility	Profitability Ratio (% in-the-money)									
	-99%	-90%	-80%	-70%	-60%	-50%	-40%	-30%	-20%	-10%
1%	0.00%	0.00%	0.00%	0.00%	0.00%	5.65%	21.27%	32.52%	40.95%	47.51%
3%	0.00%	0.00%	0.00%	0.00%	0.43%	7.80%	21.35%	32.52%	40.95%	47.51%
5%	0.00%	0.00%	0.00%	0.08%	2.27%	10.58%	22.17%	32.64%	40.97%	47.52%
7%	0.00%	0.00%	0.01%	0.66%	4.84%	13.48%	23.75%	33.24%	41.16%	47.57%
9%	0.00%	0.00%	0.12%	1.96%	7.70%	16.39%	25.76%	34.36%	41.71%	47.83%
11%	0.00%	0.00%	0.52%	3.87%	10.71%	19.31%	27.98%	35.84%	42.63%	48.38%
13%	0.00%	0.03%	1.36%	6.20%	13.77%	22.21%	30.31%	37.56%	43.84%	49.21%
15%	0.00%	0.14%	2.66%	8.83%	16.86%	25.09%	32.71%	39.44%	45.27%	50.27%
17%	0.00%	0.42%	4.39%	11.66%	19.95%	27.94%	35.13%	41.42%	46.84%	51.51%
19%	0.00%	0.95%	6.47%	14.61%	23.02%	30.76%	37.57%	43.45%	48.52%	52.88%
21%	0.00%	1.79%	8.85%	17.63%	26.06%	33.54%	39.99%	45.52%	50.27%	54.35%
23%	0.00%	2.96%	11.46%	20.71%	29.07%	36.27%	42.40%	47.61%	52.06%	55.89%
25%	0.00%	4.45%	14.24%	23.79%	32.04%	38.96%	44.78%	49.69%	53.87%	57.47%
27%	0.02%	6.25%	17.14%	26.88%	34.95%	41.61%	47.13%	51.76%	55.70%	59.07%
29%	0.05%	8.33%	20.14%	29.95%	37.82%	44.19%	49.44%	53.81%	57.52%	60.69%
31%	0.13%	10.65%	23.19%	32.98%	40.63%	46.73%	51.70%	55.84%	59.33%	62.31%
33%	0.27%	13.18%	26.27%	35.97%	43.37%	49.21%	53.93%	57.83%	61.12%	63.93%
35%	0.50%	15.88%	29.36%	38.91%	46.06%	51.62%	56.10%	59.79%	62.88%	65.52%
37%	0.87%	18.71%	32.44%	41.80%	48.67%	53.97%	58.22%	61.70%	64.62%	67.10%
39%	1.39%	21.64%	35.49%	44.62%	51.22%	56.26%	60.28%	63.57%	66.31%	68.65%
41%	2.11%	24.65%	38.51%	47.37%	53.69%	58.49%	62.29%	65.39%	67.97%	70.17%
43%	3.03%	27.71%	41.47%	50.05%	56.09%	60.64%	64.24%	67.16%	69.59%	71.66%
45%	4.17%	30.80%	44.38%	52.65%	58.41%	62.73%	66.12%	68.88%	71.17%	73.11%
47%	5.54%	33.89%	47.22%	55.18%	60.66%	64.75%	67.95%	70.54%	72.70%	74.52%
49%	7.15%	36.96%	49.99%	57.62%	62.83%	66.70%	69.72%	72.15%	74.18%	75.89%
51%	8.98%	40.01%	52.69%	59.98%	64.93%	68.58%	71.42%	73.71%	75.61%	77.21%
53%	11.03%	43.01%	55.30%	62.26%	66.94%	70.39%	73.06%	75.21%	76.99%	78.50%
55%	13.28%	45.96%	57.82%	64.45%	68.88%	72.12%	74.64%	76.65%	78.32%	79.73%
57%	15.70%	48.85%	60.26%	66.56%	70.74%	73.79%	76.15%	78.04%	79.60%	80.92%
59%	18.30%	51.67%	62.61%	68.58%	72.52%	75.39%	77.60%	79.37%	80.83%	82.06%
61%	21.03%	54.40%	64.87%	70.52%	74.23%	76.92%	78.99%	80.65%	82.01%	83.16%
63%	23.87%	57.05%	67.04%	72.37%	75.86%	78.38%	80.32%	81.86%	83.14%	84.21%
65%	26.81%	59.61%	69.11%	74.14%	77.41%	79.77%	81.58%	83.03%	84.22%	85.22%
67%	29.82%	62.08%	71.09%	75.82%	78.89%	81.10%	82.79%	84.14%	85.24%	86.17%
69%	32.88%	64.45%	72.99%	77.43%	80.30%	82.36%	83.94%	85.19%	86.22%	87.09%
71%	35.96%	66.73%	74.79%	78.95%	81.64%	83.56%	85.03%	86.19%	87.15%	87.95%
73%	39.05%	68.90%	76.50%	80.40%	82.91%	84.70%	86.06%	87.14%	88.03%	88.78%
75%	42.12%	70.98%	78.13%	81.77%	84.11%	85.77%	87.04%	88.04%	88.87%	89.56%
77%	45.17%	72.96%	79.67%	83.07%	85.24%	86.79%	87.96%	88.90%	89.66%	90.30%
79%	48.18%	74.84%	81.13%	84.30%	86.31%	87.75%	88.84%	89.70%	90.41%	91.00%
81%	51.13%	76.62%	82.50%	85.45%	87.32%	88.65%	89.66%	90.46%	91.11%	91.66%
83%	54.01%	78.31%	83.80%	86.54%	88.28%	89.50%	90.44%	91.17%	91.78%	92.28%
85%	56.81%	79.91%	85.02%	87.56%	89.17%	90.30%	91.16%	91.85%	92.40%	92.87%
87%	59.53%	81.42%	86.17%	88.52%	90.01%	91.06%	91.85%	92.48%	92.99%	93.42%
89%	62.15%	82.83%	87.25%	89.42%	90.79%	91.76%	92.49%	93.07%	93.54%	93.93%
91%	64.67%	84.16%	88.26%	90.27%	91.53%	92.42%	93.09%	93.62%	94.05%	94.41%
93%	67.09%	85.41%	89.20%	91.05%	92.21%	93.03%	93.65%	94.13%	94.53%	94.86%
95%	69.41%	86.58%	90.08%	91.79%	92.85%	93.60%	94.17%	94.62%	94.98%	95.28%
97%	71.61%	87.68%	90.90%	92.47%	93.45%	94.14%	94.66%	95.06%	95.40%	95.68%
99%	73.70%	88.70%	91.67%	93.11%	94.00%	94.63%	95.11%	95.48%	95.79%	96.04%
101%	75.69%	89.65%	92.38%	93.70%	94.52%	95.09%	95.53%	95.87%	96.15%	96.38%

Volatility	Profitability Ratio (% in-the-money)										
	0%	10%	20%	30%	40%	50%	60%	70%	80%	90%	100%
1%	52.76%	57.06%	60.64%	63.66%	66.26%	68.51%	70.48%	72.21%	73.76%	75.14%	76.38%
3%	52.76%	57.06%	60.64%	63.66%	66.26%	68.51%	70.48%	72.21%	73.76%	75.14%	76.38%
5%	52.76%	57.06%	60.64%	63.66%	66.26%	68.51%	70.48%	72.21%	73.76%	75.14%	76.38%
7%	52.78%	57.06%	60.64%	63.66%	66.26%	68.51%	70.48%	72.21%	73.76%	75.14%	76.38%
9%	52.90%	57.11%	60.66%	63.68%	66.26%	68.51%	70.48%	72.21%	73.76%	75.14%	76.38%
11%	53.22%	57.30%	60.77%	63.74%	66.30%	68.53%	70.49%	72.22%	73.76%	75.14%	76.38%
13%	53.78%	57.68%	61.02%	63.91%	66.42%	68.61%	70.54%	72.26%	73.79%	75.16%	76.40%
15%	54.56%	58.26%	61.45%	64.22%	66.65%	68.78%	70.67%	72.36%	73.86%	75.22%	76.44%
17%	55.53%	59.02%	62.04%	64.69%	67.02%	69.08%	70.91%	72.54%	74.01%	75.33%	76.53%
19%	56.65%	59.93%	62.79%	65.30%	67.52%	69.49%	71.25%	72.82%	74.25%	75.53%	76.70%
21%	57.89%	60.96%	63.66%	66.03%	68.14%	70.02%	71.70%	73.21%	74.58%	75.82%	76.95%
23%	59.20%	62.09%	64.63%	66.87%	68.87%	70.65%	72.25%	73.69%	75.00%	76.19%	77.27%
25%	60.58%	63.29%	65.68%	67.80%	69.68%	71.37%	72.88%	74.26%	75.50%	76.64%	77.68%
27%	61.99%	64.55%	66.79%	68.79%	70.56%	72.16%	73.59%	74.89%	76.08%	77.16%	78.15%
29%	63.44%	65.84%	67.95%	69.83%	71.50%	73.00%	74.36%	75.59%	76.72%	77.74%	78.68%
31%	64.89%	67.15%	69.14%	70.90%	72.48%	73.90%	75.18%	76.34%	77.40%	78.38%	79.27%
33%	66.35%	68.47%	70.34%	72.00%	73.49%	74.82%	76.03%	77.13%	78.13%	79.05%	79.90%
35%	67.81%	69.80%	71.56%	73.12%	74.52%	75.77%	76.91%	77.95%	78.89%	79.76%	80.56%
37%	69.25%	71.12%	72.77%	74.24%	75.55%	76.74%	77.81%	78.79%	79.68%	80.50%	81.25%
39%	70.67%	72.43%	73.98%	75.36%	76.60%	77.71%	78.72%	79.64%	80.48%	81.25%	81.96%
41%	72.07%	73.72%	75.18%	76.48%	77.64%	78.68%	79.63%	80.49%	81.28%	82.01%	82.68%
43%	73.44%	74.99%	76.36%	77.58%	78.67%	79.65%	80.54%	81.35%	82.09%	82.78%	83.41%
45%	74.78%	76.24%	77.52%	78.66%	79.69%	80.61%	81.44%	82.21%	82.90%	83.55%	84.14%
47%	76.09%	77.46%	78.66%	79.73%	80.69%	81.55%	82.34%	83.05%	83.71%	84.31%	84.87%
49%	77.36%	78.64%	79.77%	80.77%	81.67%	82.48%	83.22%	83.89%	84.50%	85.06%	85.59%
51%	78.59%	79.79%	80.85%	81.79%	82.63%	83.39%	84.08%	84.70%	85.28%	85.81%	86.30%
53%	79.79%	80.91%	81.90%	82.78%	83.56%	84.27%	84.92%	85.51%	86.04%	86.54%	87.00%
55%	80.94%	81.99%	82.92%	83.74%	84.47%	85.14%	85.74%	86.29%	86.79%	87.25%	87.68%
57%	82.05%	83.03%	83.90%	84.66%	85.35%	85.97%	86.53%	87.05%	87.52%	87.95%	88.35%
59%	83.12%	84.04%	84.84%	85.56%	86.20%	86.78%	87.31%	87.78%	88.22%	88.63%	89.00%
61%	84.15%	85.00%	85.75%	86.42%	87.02%	87.56%	88.05%	88.50%	88.91%	89.28%	89.63%
63%	85.13%	85.93%	86.63%	87.25%	87.81%	88.31%	88.77%	89.18%	89.57%	89.92%	90.24%
65%	86.07%	86.81%	87.47%	88.05%	88.57%	89.03%	89.46%	89.85%	90.20%	90.53%	90.83%
67%	86.97%	87.66%	88.27%	88.81%	89.29%	89.73%	90.12%	90.48%	90.81%	91.11%	91.40%
69%	87.83%	88.47%	89.03%	89.53%	89.98%	90.39%	90.75%	91.09%	91.39%	91.68%	91.94%
71%	88.64%	89.24%	89.76%	90.23%	90.64%	91.02%	91.36%	91.67%	91.95%	92.22%	92.46%
73%	89.42%	89.97%	90.46%	90.89%	91.27%	91.62%	91.94%	92.22%	92.49%	92.73%	92.96%
75%	90.15%	90.67%	91.12%	91.51%	91.87%	92.19%	92.49%	92.75%	93.00%	93.22%	93.43%
77%	90.85%	91.32%	91.74%	92.11%	92.44%	92.74%	93.01%	93.25%	93.48%	93.69%	93.88%
79%	91.51%	91.95%	92.33%	92.67%	92.98%	93.25%	93.50%	93.73%	93.94%	94.13%	94.31%
81%	92.13%	92.53%	92.89%	93.20%	93.49%	93.74%	93.97%	94.18%	94.37%	94.55%	94.71%
83%	92.71%	93.09%	93.42%	93.71%	93.97%	94.20%	94.41%	94.61%	94.78%	94.95%	95.10%
85%	93.26%	93.61%	93.91%	94.18%	94.42%	94.63%	94.83%	95.01%	95.17%	95.32%	95.46%
87%	93.78%	94.10%	94.38%	94.62%	94.84%	95.04%	95.22%	95.39%	95.54%	95.67%	95.80%
89%	94.27%	94.56%	94.81%	95.04%	95.24%	95.42%	95.59%	95.74%	95.88%	96.01%	96.12%
91%	94.72%	94.99%	95.22%	95.43%	95.62%	95.78%	95.94%	96.07%	96.20%	96.32%	96.43%
93%	95.15%	95.39%	95.61%	95.80%	95.97%	96.12%	96.26%	96.39%	96.50%	96.61%	96.71%
95%	95.54%	95.77%	95.97%	96.14%	96.30%	96.44%	96.56%	96.68%	96.79%	96.88%	96.97%
97%	95.91%	96.12%	96.30%	96.46%	96.60%	96.73%	96.85%	96.95%	97.05%	97.14%	97.22%
99%	96.26%	96.45%	96.61%	96.76%	96.89%	97.00%	97.11%	97.21%	97.29%	97.38%	97.45%
101%	96.58%	96.75%	96.90%	97.03%	97.15%	97.26%	97.35%	97.44%	97.52%	97.60%	97.67%

Real Options Analysis Value (30-year maturity at 5% risk-free rate)

				Profitability Ratio (% in-the-money)						
Volatility	-99%	-90%	-80%	-70%	-60%	-50%	-40%	-30%	-20%	-10%
1%	0.00%	0.00%	0.05%	25.62%	44.22%	55.37%	62.81%	68.12%	72.11%	75.21%
3%	0.00%	0.00%	2.62%	25.82%	44.22%	55.37%	62.81%	68.12%	72.11%	75.21%
5%	0.00%	0.02%	6.64%	27.30%	44.34%	55.38%	62.81%	68.12%	72.11%	75.21%
7%	0.00%	0.37%	10.94%	29.75%	45.00%	55.54%	62.85%	68.13%	72.11%	75.21%
9%	0.00%	1.57%	15.31%	32.67%	46.31%	56.06%	63.06%	68.22%	72.15%	75.22%
11%	0.00%	3.71%	19.66%	35.80%	48.08%	57.01%	63.56%	68.49%	72.30%	75.31%
13%	0.00%	6.63%	23.98%	39.03%	50.16%	58.30%	64.37%	69.00%	72.63%	75.53%
15%	0.01%	10.13%	28.22%	42.28%	52.43%	59.86%	65.45%	69.76%	73.16%	75.91%
17%	0.04%	14.03%	32.38%	45.51%	54.80%	61.59%	66.72%	70.71%	73.89%	76.47%
19%	0.18%	18.17%	36.44%	48.70%	57.23%	63.44%	68.15%	71.83%	74.77%	77.18%
21%	0.50%	22.46%	40.40%	51.83%	59.66%	65.36%	69.67%	73.06%	75.78%	78.01%
23%	1.13%	26.82%	44.23%	54.88%	62.08%	67.30%	71.26%	74.37%	76.87%	78.94%
25%	2.15%	31.19%	47.94%	57.84%	64.47%	69.25%	72.88%	75.73%	78.03%	79.94%
27%	3.64%	35.51%	51.51%	60.70%	66.79%	71.18%	74.50%	77.11%	79.23%	80.98%
29%	5.62%	39.75%	54.94%	63.46%	69.06%	73.07%	76.11%	78.51%	80.45%	82.05%
31%	8.09%	43.88%	58.22%	66.10%	71.24%	74.92%	77.70%	79.89%	81.66%	83.13%
33%	11.01%	47.89%	61.36%	68.63%	73.35%	76.71%	79.25%	81.25%	82.87%	84.21%
35%	14.34%	51.74%	64.35%	71.04%	75.36%	78.43%	80.75%	82.57%	84.05%	85.28%
37%	18.02%	55.44%	67.18%	73.34%	77.28%	80.08%	82.19%	83.85%	85.20%	86.32%
39%	21.96%	58.96%	69.87%	75.51%	79.11%	81.66%	83.58%	85.09%	86.31%	87.33%
41%	26.11%	62.31%	72.40%	77.56%	80.84%	83.15%	84.90%	86.27%	87.38%	88.31%
43%	30.39%	65.48%	74.78%	79.49%	82.47%	84.57%	86.15%	87.39%	88.40%	89.24%
45%	34.74%	68.47%	77.01%	81.30%	84.00%	85.90%	87.34%	88.46%	89.37%	90.13%
47%	39.11%	71.28%	79.09%	82.99%	85.44%	87.16%	88.45%	89.47%	90.29%	90.98%
49%	43.44%	73.90%	81.04%	84.57%	86.78%	88.33%	89.50%	90.41%	91.16%	91.77%
51%	47.69%	76.35%	82.84%	86.04%	88.03%	89.43%	90.48%	91.30%	91.97%	92.52%
53%	51.82%	78.63%	84.52%	87.40%	89.19%	90.44%	91.39%	92.12%	92.72%	93.22%
55%	55.80%	80.74%	86.06%	88.65%	90.26%	91.39%	92.23%	92.89%	93.43%	93.87%
57%	59.62%	82.68%	87.49%	89.81%	91.25%	92.26%	93.01%	93.60%	94.08%	94.48%
59%	63.24%	84.47%	88.79%	90.87%	92.16%	93.06%	93.73%	94.26%	94.68%	95.04%
61%	66.67%	86.12%	89.99%	91.85%	92.99%	93.79%	94.39%	94.86%	95.24%	95.55%
63%	69.88%	87.62%	91.08%	92.73%	93.75%	94.46%	95.00%	95.41%	95.75%	96.03%
65%	72.88%	88.99%	92.07%	93.54%	94.45%	95.08%	95.55%	95.91%	96.21%	96.46%
67%	75.67%	90.23%	92.98%	94.28%	95.08%	95.63%	96.05%	96.37%	96.64%	96.86%
69%	78.25%	91.36%	93.79%	94.94%	95.65%	96.14%	96.50%	96.79%	97.02%	97.21%
71%	80.61%	92.38%	94.53%	95.54%	96.16%	96.59%	96.91%	97.16%	97.37%	97.54%
73%	82.78%	93.29%	95.19%	96.08%	96.62%	97.00%	97.28%	97.50%	97.68%	97.83%
75%	84.76%	94.11%	95.78%	96.56%	97.04%	97.37%	97.61%	97.81%	97.96%	98.09%
77%	86.55%	94.85%	96.31%	96.99%	97.41%	97.70%	97.91%	98.08%	98.22%	98.33%
79%	88.17%	95.50%	96.78%	97.37%	97.74%	97.99%	98.18%	98.32%	98.44%	98.54%
81%	89.63%	96.09%	97.20%	97.72%	98.03%	98.25%	98.41%	98.54%	98.64%	98.73%
83%	90.93%	96.60%	97.57%	98.02%	98.29%	98.48%	98.62%	98.73%	98.82%	98.90%
85%	92.10%	97.06%	97.90%	98.28%	98.52%	98.68%	98.81%	98.90%	98.98%	99.04%
87%	93.14%	97.46%	98.18%	98.52%	98.72%	98.86%	98.97%	99.05%	99.12%	99.17%
89%	94.06%	97.81%	98.44%	98.73%	98.90%	99.02%	99.11%	99.18%	99.24%	99.29%
91%	94.87%	98.12%	98.66%	98.91%	99.06%	99.16%	99.24%	99.30%	99.35%	99.39%
93%	95.58%	98.39%	98.85%	99.06%	99.19%	99.28%	99.35%	99.40%	99.44%	99.48%
95%	96.21%	98.63%	99.02%	99.20%	99.31%	99.39%	99.44%	99.49%	99.52%	99.55%
97%	96.76%	98.83%	99.17%	99.32%	99.41%	99.48%	99.53%	99.56%	99.59%	99.62%
99%	97.23%	99.01%	99.29%	99.42%	99.50%	99.56%	99.60%	99.63%	99.65%	99.68%
101%	97.65%	99.16%	99.40%	99.51%	99.58%	99.62%	99.66%	99.69%	99.71%	99.72%

Profitability Ratio (% in-the-money)

Volatility	0%	10%	20%	30%	40%	50%	60%	70%	80%	90%	100%
1%	77.69%	79.72%	81.41%	82.84%	84.06%	85.12%	86.05%	86.87%	87.60%	88.26%	88.84%
3%	77.69%	79.72%	81.41%	82.84%	84.06%	85.12%	86.05%	86.87%	87.60%	88.26%	88.84%
5%	77.69%	79.72%	81.41%	82.84%	84.06%	85.12%	86.05%	86.87%	87.60%	88.26%	88.84%
7%	77.69%	79.72%	81.41%	82.84%	84.06%	85.12%	86.05%	86.87%	87.60%	88.26%	88.84%
9%	77.69%	79.72%	81.41%	82.84%	84.06%	85.12%	86.05%	86.87%	87.60%	88.26%	88.84%
11%	77.74%	79.75%	81.43%	82.85%	84.07%	85.13%	86.06%	86.88%	87.61%	88.26%	88.84%
13%	77.89%	79.85%	81.49%	82.90%	84.10%	85.15%	86.08%	86.89%	87.62%	88.26%	88.85%
15%	78.17%	80.06%	81.65%	83.02%	84.20%	85.23%	86.13%	86.94%	87.65%	88.29%	88.87%
17%	78.61%	80.40%	81.92%	83.24%	84.37%	85.37%	86.25%	87.03%	87.73%	88.36%	88.93%
19%	79.18%	80.87%	82.31%	83.56%	84.65%	85.60%	86.45%	87.20%	87.88%	88.49%	89.04%
21%	79.88%	81.46%	82.81%	83.99%	85.01%	85.92%	86.73%	87.45%	88.09%	88.68%	89.21%
23%	80.67%	82.14%	83.40%	84.50%	85.47%	86.32%	87.08%	87.77%	88.38%	88.94%	89.44%
25%	81.53%	82.90%	84.07%	85.10%	86.00%	86.80%	87.51%	88.15%	88.73%	89.26%	89.74%
27%	82.45%	83.71%	84.80%	85.75%	86.59%	87.33%	88.00%	88.60%	89.14%	89.63%	90.08%
29%	83.41%	84.57%	85.57%	86.45%	87.22%	87.91%	88.53%	89.09%	89.59%	90.05%	90.47%
31%	84.38%	85.44%	86.36%	87.17%	87.89%	88.53%	89.10%	89.61%	90.08%	90.51%	90.90%
33%	85.35%	86.33%	87.17%	87.92%	88.57%	89.16%	89.69%	90.16%	90.60%	90.99%	91.35%
35%	86.32%	87.21%	87.99%	88.67%	89.27%	89.81%	90.29%	90.73%	91.13%	91.49%	91.83%
37%	87.27%	88.08%	88.79%	89.41%	89.96%	90.46%	90.90%	91.30%	91.67%	92.00%	92.31%
39%	88.19%	88.94%	89.58%	90.15%	90.65%	91.10%	91.51%	91.87%	92.21%	92.52%	92.80%
41%	89.09%	89.76%	90.35%	90.87%	91.33%	91.74%	92.11%	92.44%	92.75%	93.02%	93.28%
43%	89.95%	90.56%	91.10%	91.56%	91.98%	92.35%	92.69%	92.99%	93.27%	93.53%	93.76%
45%	90.77%	91.33%	91.81%	92.23%	92.61%	92.95%	93.25%	93.53%	93.78%	94.01%	94.23%
47%	91.56%	92.06%	92.49%	92.88%	93.22%	93.52%	93.80%	94.05%	94.28%	94.49%	94.68%
49%	92.30%	92.75%	93.14%	93.48%	93.79%	94.07%	94.32%	94.54%	94.75%	94.94%	95.11%
51%	92.99%	93.40%	93.75%	94.06%	94.34%	94.59%	94.81%	95.01%	95.20%	95.37%	95.53%
53%	93.64%	94.01%	94.32%	94.60%	94.85%	95.08%	95.28%	95.46%	95.63%	95.78%	95.92%
55%	94.25%	94.58%	94.86%	95.11%	95.33%	95.53%	95.71%	95.88%	96.03%	96.17%	96.29%
57%	94.82%	95.11%	95.36%	95.59%	95.78%	95.96%	96.12%	96.27%	96.40%	96.53%	96.64%
59%	95.34%	95.60%	95.83%	96.02%	96.20%	96.36%	96.51%	96.64%	96.76%	96.87%	96.97%
61%	95.82%	96.05%	96.25%	96.43%	96.59%	96.73%	96.86%	96.98%	97.08%	97.18%	97.27%
63%	96.27%	96.47%	96.65%	96.81%	96.95%	97.07%	97.19%	97.29%	97.38%	97.47%	97.55%
65%	96.67%	96.85%	97.01%	97.15%	97.27%	97.38%	97.49%	97.58%	97.66%	97.74%	97.81%
67%	97.04%	97.20%	97.34%	97.46%	97.57%	97.67%	97.76%	97.84%	97.91%	97.98%	98.05%
69%	97.38%	97.52%	97.64%	97.75%	97.85%	97.93%	98.01%	98.08%	98.15%	98.21%	98.26%
71%	97.68%	97.81%	97.91%	98.01%	98.09%	98.17%	98.24%	98.30%	98.36%	98.41%	98.46%
73%	97.96%	98.07%	98.16%	98.24%	98.32%	98.38%	98.44%	98.50%	98.55%	98.60%	98.64%
75%	98.20%	98.30%	98.38%	98.45%	98.52%	98.58%	98.63%	98.68%	98.72%	98.76%	98.80%
77%	98.43%	98.51%	98.58%	98.64%	98.70%	98.75%	98.80%	98.84%	98.88%	98.91%	98.95%
79%	98.62%	98.70%	98.76%	98.81%	98.86%	98.91%	98.95%	98.98%	99.02%	99.05%	99.08%
81%	98.80%	98.86%	98.92%	98.97%	99.01%	99.05%	99.08%	99.11%	99.14%	99.17%	99.19%
83%	98.96%	99.01%	99.06%	99.10%	99.14%	99.17%	99.20%	99.23%	99.25%	99.28%	99.30%
85%	99.10%	99.14%	99.18%	99.22%	99.25%	99.28%	99.31%	99.33%	99.35%	99.37%	99.39%
87%	99.22%	99.26%	99.29%	99.33%	99.35%	99.38%	99.40%	99.42%	99.44%	99.46%	99.47%
89%	99.33%	99.36%	99.39%	99.42%	99.44%	99.46%	99.48%	99.50%	99.52%	99.53%	99.54%
91%	99.42%	99.45%	99.48%	99.50%	99.52%	99.54%	99.55%	99.57%	99.58%	99.60%	99.61%
93%	99.50%	99.53%	99.55%	99.57%	99.59%	99.60%	99.62%	99.63%	99.64%	99.65%	99.66%
95%	99.58%	99.60%	99.62%	99.63%	99.65%	99.66%	99.67%	99.68%	99.69%	99.70%	99.71%
97%	99.64%	99.66%	99.67%	99.69%	99.70%	99.71%	99.72%	99.73%	99.74%	99.75%	99.75%
99%	99.69%	99.71%	99.72%	99.73%	99.74%	99.75%	99.76%	99.77%	99.78%	99.78%	99.79%
101%	99.74%	99.75%	99.76%	99.77%	99.78%	99.79%	99.80%	99.81%	99.81%	99.82%	99.82%

Answers to End of Chapter Questions and Exercises

Chapter 1   Beyond Uncertainty

1. Why is risk important in making decisions?
   Risk is important in decision making as it provides an added element of insight into the project being evaluated. Projects with higher returns usually carry with them higher risks, and neglecting the element of risk means that the decision maker may unnecessarily select the riskiest projects.

2. Describe the concept of bang for the buck.
   Bang for the buck implies selecting the best project or combination of projects that yields the highest returns subject to the minimum amount of risk. That is, given some set of risk, what is the best project or combination of projects that provide the best returns? Conversely, it also answers what the minimum level of risk is subject to some prespecified return. This concept is the Markowitz efficient frontier in portfolio optimization discussed later in the book.

3. Compare and contrast between risk and uncertainty.
   Uncertainty implies an event's outcome in which no one knows for sure what may occur. Uncertainties can range from the fluctuation in the stock market to the occurrences of sunspots. In contrast, uncertainties that affect the outcome of a project or asset's value directly or indirectly are termed risks.

Chapter 2   From Risk to Riches

1. What is the efficient frontier and when is it used?
   The efficient frontier was first introduced by Nobel laureate Harry Markowitz and it captures the concept of bang for the buck where projects or assets are first grouped into portfolios. Then, the combinations of projects or assets that provide the highest returns subject to the varying degrees of risk are calculated. The best and most efficient combinations of projects or assets are graphically represented and termed the efficient frontier.

2. What are inferential statistics and what steps are required in making inferences?

Inferential statistics refers to the branch of statistics that performs statistical analysis on smaller-size samples to infer the true nature of the population. The steps undertaken include designing the experiment, collecting the data, analyzing the data, estimating or predicting alternative conditions, testing of the hypothesis, testing of goodness-of-fit, and making decisions based on the results.

3. When is using standard deviation less desirable than using semi-standard deviation as a measure of risk?

Standard deviation measures the average deviation of each data point from the mean, which implies that both upside and downside deviations are captured in a standard deviation calculation. In contrast, only the downside deviations are captured in the semi-standard deviation measure. The semi-standard deviation when used as a measure of risk is more appropriate if only downside occurrences are deemed as risky.

4. If comparing three projects with similar first, second, and fourth moments, would you prefer a project that has no skew, a positive skew, or a negative skew?

Holding everything else constant, projects with negative skew are preferred as the higher probability of occurrences are weighted more on the higher returns.

5. If comparing three projects with similar first to third moments, would you prefer a project that is leptokurtic (high kurtosis), mesokurtic (average kurtosis), or platykurtic (low kurtosis)? Explain your reasoning with respect to a distribution's tail area. Under what conditions would your answer change?

The answer depends on the type of project. For instance, for financial assets such as stocks, clearly a lower kurtosis stock implies a lower probability of occurrence in the extreme areas, or that catastrophic losses are less likely to occur. However, the disadvantage is that the probability of an extreme upside is also lessened.

6. What are the differences and similarities between value-at-risk and worst-case scenario as a measure of risk?

Value-at-Risk (VaR) measures the worst-case outcome for a particular holding period with respect to a given probability. For instance, the worst-case 5 percent probability VaR of a particular project is $1 million for a 10-year economic life with a 90 percent statistical confidence. Compare that to a simplistic worst-case scenario, which in most cases are single-point estimates, for example, the worst-case scenario for the project is a $10,000 loss. Worst-case scenarios can be added to probabilistic results as in the VaR approach but are usually single-point estimates (usually just a management assumption or guesstimate).

Chapter 3   A Gentleman's Guide to Model Building

For the answers to Chapter 3's Exercises, refer to the enclosed CD-ROM. The files are located in the folder: *Answers to End of Chapter Questions and Exercises.*

Chapter 4   On the Shores of Monaco

1. Compare and contrast parametric and nonparametric simulation.
   Parametric simulation is an approach that requires distributional parameters to be first assigned before it can begin. For instance, a Monte Carlo simulation of 1,000 trials using input assumptions in a normal distribution with an average of 10 and standard deviation of 2 is a parametric simulation. In contrast, nonparametric simulation uses historical or comparable data to run the simulation, where specific distributional assumptions (i.e., size and shape of the distribution, type of distribution and its related inputs such as average or standard deviation, and so forth) are not required. Nonparametric simulation is used when the data is "left alone to tell the story."

2. What is a stochastic process (e.g., Brownian Motion)?
   The term "stochastic" means the opposite of "deterministic." Stochastic variables are characterized by their randomness, for example, a stock's price movement over time. A stochastic process is a mathematical relationship that captures this random characteristic over time. The most common stochastic process is the Brownian Motion used to simulate stock prices.

3. What does the *RAND()* function do in Excel?
   The *RAND()* function in Excel creates a random number from the uniform distribution between 0 and 1. Hitting F9 repeatedly on the keyboard will generate additional random numbers from the same distribution.

4. What does the *NORMSINV()* function do in Excel?
   The *NORMSINV()* function in Excel calculates the inverse of the standard cumulative normal distribution with a mean of zero and a standard deviation of one.

5. What happens when both functions are used together, that is, *NORMSINV(RAND())*?
   When used in conjunction, the function *NORMSINV(RAND())* simulates a standard normal distribution random variable.

6. For modeling each of the following, determine which distribution(s) is/are most applicable and explain why. (Refer to Appendix to Chapter 4 for the different distributions).
   a. Number of phone calls a minute or number of errors in a page.
      Poisson

b. Number of defective items in a batch of 100 items.
   Binomial
c. Real estate prices and stock prices.
   Lognormal
d. Measuring earthquakes and rainfall frequency.
   Extreme Value
e. Number of sales calls required to get to the 10th successful sale.
   Geometric
f. Height, weight, and IQ of individuals.
   Normal

Chapter 5   Peering into the Crystal Ball

1. What are the typical five steps required when running a Monte Carlo simulation model?
   First, an Excel model must be created. Then, the input assumptions and output forecasts have to be defined. The simulation's preferences must then be defined, followed by actually running the simulation. Finally, the results from the simulation are interpreted and decisions are then made.
2. Explain what each of the following does:
   a. Defining an assumption
      Defining an assumption means to assign an input variable under uncertainty to be simulated.
   b. Defining a forecast
      Defining a forecast means to assign a calculated output result as the variable of interest in a simulation.
3. What do cumulative charts and reverse cumulative charts represent?
   Cumulative charts represent the sum of the probabilities leading up to a particular point on the distribution. For instance, if a particular discrete distribution's probabilities are: $P(X = 1) = 10\%$, $P(X = 2) = 15\%$, and $P(X = 3) = 5\%$, then the cumulative chart will show a probability of $P(X \leq 3) = 30\%$. The reverse cumulative chart shows the probabilities opposite to the cumulative chart, that is, $P(X \geq 3) = 70\%$.

Chapter 6   Pandora's Tool Box

1. Why is tornado analysis used before a simulation is run while sensitivity analysis is used after a simulation is run?
   A tornado analysis is useful as a first step prior to simulation as it performs a perturbation analysis (changes in a result are captured after perturbing each precedent variable some prespecified value while holding all

other variables constant) to determine which precedent variables impact the resulting variable the most. These high-impact variables, which are also uncertain, are the prime candidates for simulation. While tornado analysis is a static analysis, sensitivity analysis is a dynamic analysis performed after a simulation is run where multiple input assumptions are perturbed simultaneously to see their combined interactive effects (these effects are more prevalent if certain variables are correlated).

2. Explain what would happen to the results if two simulated random variables that are negatively correlated in real life are not correlated in the model?

   A negative correlation between two variables will result in a smaller variance in the forecast distribution. Neglecting to correlate variables that are correlated in real life will yield results that are wider and more variable than are actually experienced in real life.

3. What is the Delphi method?

   The Delphi method is simply a form of qualitative forecasting where a panel of experts' opinions are obtained and tabulated to determine the most probable forecast of the future.

4. Provide an example where running a two-dimensional simulation is appropriate.

   A two-dimensional simulation runs an outer loop to simulate the uncertainty values, and then freezes the uncertainty values while it runs an inner loop of the whole model to simulate the variability. An example of uncertainty is the size of an oil reservoir while the variability is the number of small geological pockets that exist in the reservoir.

5. Compare and contrast the three typical goodness-of-fit tests, that is, when is each test appropriate under different circumstances?

Comparison of the Three Statistical Tests	Kolmogorov–Smirnov	Anderson–Darling	Chi-Square
Applicable to continuous distributions	yes	yes	yes
Applicable to discrete distributions	no	no	yes
Parametric statistical test	no	yes	no
Nonparametric statistical test	yes	no	no
Semi-parametric statistical test	no	no	yes
Two-tailed statistical test	yes	no	yes
One-tailed statistical test	no	yes	no
Validity depends on bin size	no	no	yes
Validity sensitive to center of distribution	yes	no	no
Validity sensitive to tails of distribution	no	yes	no
Validity sensitive to data size	no	no	yes

Chapter 8   Tomorrow's Forecast Today

1. Why are confidence intervals (e.g., 5th and 95th percentiles) required in forecasting?

   Instead of relying on single-point estimates of a future forecast value, confidence intervals are often used to enhance the forecast results. Confidence intervals provide a much better view of the probabilistic outcomes of the future rather than relying on a single-point estimate (which on a continuous basis has a zero probability of occurrence).

2. What is a time-series model and what types of data are typically used in a time-series model?

   As the name suggests, time-series models are only applicable for forecasting variables that are dependent on time or that change and can be measured over time. Examples of time-series variables include stock prices, inflation rates, interest rates, and so forth.

3. What are some examples of variables that exhibit seasonality versus cyclicality?

   Examples of seasonality effects are seen on variables such as sales or weather, which exhibit relatively stable seasonal cycles (e.g., 12 months in a year). In contrast, cyclical effects are seen on variables with no stable seasonal cycles but, on a macro view, exhibit unpredictable cycles (e.g., gross domestic product).

4. What are the similarities and differences between seasonality and cyclicality?

   Both exhibit cyclical behavior over time. However, seasonal variables tend to follow certain periodicities and are short and predictable (e.g., monthly, quarterly), while cyclical variables have longer cycles that are less predictable (e.g., stock price crashes, gross domestic product growth).

Chapter 9   Using the Past to Predict the Future

1. Explain what each of the following terms means:
   a. Time-series analysis

      The application of forecasting methodology on data that depends on time.

   b. Ordinary least squares

      A type of regression analysis that minimizes the sum of the square of errors.

   c. Regression analysis

      The estimation of the best-fitting line through a series of historical data used to predict a statistical relationship or to forecast the future based on this relationship.

   d. Heteroskedasticity

The variance of the errors of a regression analysis is unstable over time.
  e. Autocorrelation
    The historical data of a variable depends on or is correlated to itself over time.
  f. Multicollinearity
    The independent variables are highly correlated to each other or there exists an exact linear relationship between the independent variables.
  g. ARIMA
    Autoregressive Integrated Moving Average—a type of forecasting methodology.
2. What is the difference between the R-squared versus the adjusted R-squared measure in a regression analysis? When is each applicable and why?
  The R-squared or coefficient of determination is used on bivariate regressions, whereas the adjusted R-squared is used on multivariate regressions. The latter penalizes the excessive use of independent variables through a degree of freedom correction, making it a more conservative measure useful in multivariate regressions.
3. Explain why if each of the following is not detected properly or corrected for in the model, the estimated regression model will be flawed:
  a. Heteroskedasticity
    In the event of heteroskedasticity, the estimated R-squared is fairly low and the regression equation is both insufficient and incomplete, leading to potentially large estimation errors.
  b. Autocorrelation
    If autocorrelated dependent variable values exist, the estimates of the slope and intercept will be unbiased, but the estimates of their variances will not be reliable and hence the validity of certain statistical goodness-of-fit tests will be flawed.
  c. Multicollinearity
    In perfect multicollinearity, the regression equation cannot be estimated at all. In near-perfect collinearity, the estimated regression equation will be inefficient and inaccurate. The corresponding R-squared is inflated and the t-statistics are lower than actual.
4. Explain briefly how to fix the problem of nonlinearity in the data set.
  Nonlinear independent variables can be transformed into linear variables by taking the logarithm, square (or higher powers), square root, or multiplicative combinations of the independent variables. A new regression is then run based on these newly transformed variables.

For the answers to Exercise 9.1, refer to the enclosed CD-ROM. The files are located in the folder: *Answers to End of Chapter Questions and Exercises*.

Chapter 10   The Search for the Optimal Decision

1. What is the difference between deterministic optimization and optimization under uncertainty?

   Deterministic optimization means that the input variables are single-point deterministic values, whereas optimization under uncertainty means that the input variables are uncertain and simulated while the optimization process is occurring.

2. Define then compare and contrast each of the following:

   a. Objective

   An objective is the forecast output value that is to be maximized or minimized in an optimization (e.g., profits).

   b. Constraint

   A constraint is a restriction that is observed in an optimization (e.g., budget constraint).

   c. Decision variable

   The variables that can be changed based on management decisions such that the objective is achieved. These variables are usually subject to the constraints in the model.

   d. Requirement

   A restriction on a forecast statistic that requires the statistic to fall between specified lower and upper limits for a solution to be considered feasible. Requirements can be seen as a weak objective, a side variable, but not the final goal of the optimization.

3. Explain what some of the problems are in a graphical linear programming approach and if they can be easily solved.

   Some problems arising from a graphical linear programming approach include nonlinear constraints, unbounded solutions, no feasible solutions, multiple solutions, and too many constraints. These problems cannot be easily solved graphically.

4. What are some of the approaches to solve an optimization problem? List each approach as well as its corresponding pros and cons.

   The graphical approach is simple to implement but may sometimes be too tedious if too many constraints or nonlinear constraints exist. Optimization can also be solved mathematically by taking first and second derivatives but is more difficult to do. Excel's Solver add-in can be used to systematically search by brute force through a series of input combinations to find the optimal solution, but the results may be local minimums or local maximums, providing incorrect answers. OptQuest also can be used to solve an optimization problem under uncertainty when the input assumptions are unknown and simulated.

Chapter 11   Optimization under Certainty

1. Compare and contrast between a discrete versus continuous decision variable when used in an optimization under uncertainty.

   In an optimization under uncertainty, discrete decision variables can only take on discrete or specific steps within some specified range (e.g., 1, 2, 3, or 1.1, 1.2, 1.3, and so forth). An example includes the selection of projects, that is, 0 for a no-go decision and 1 for a go decision. In contrast, a continuous decision variable can take on any value within some specified range (e.g., 23.45 percent, 25.71 percent, and so forth). An example includes the allocation of assets within a portfolio of stocks.

   For the answers to Exercise 11.1, refer to the enclosed CD-ROM. The files are located in the folder: *Answers to End of Chapter Questions and Exercises*.

Chapter 12   What Is So Real About Real Options, and Why Are They Optional?

1. Create your own definition of real options analysis. That is, define real options analysis in a paragraph.

   Real options analysis is an analytical decision-making process involving the use of financial options theory, corporate finance, investments, statistics, and simulation. Its primary use is to quantitatively estimate the strategic value of certain projects that exhibit flexibility under uncertainty.

2. What are some of the possible approaches used to solve a real options analysis problem?

   The three mainstream approaches used to solve a real options problem are binomial or multinomial lattices, closed-form models, and Monte Carlo simulation.

3. In choosing the right methodology to be used in a real options analysis, what are some of the key requirements that should be considered?

   Ease of use, exposition ease, replicability, modeling flexibility, ease of view, integration with other techniques, and the availability of a process.

4. What are the necessary conditions that must exist before real options analysis can be applied on a project?

   A financial model must first be created; uncertainties must exist; these uncertainties must impact the value of the project or asset; management must have strategic flexibility to take advantage of uncertainty when it becomes resolved over time; and management must be credible enough to execute the relevant options when they become optimal to do so.

Chapter 15   The Warning Signs

1. Define what is meant by negligent entrustment.

   "Negligent entrustment" simply means that management takes the results from some fancy analytics generated by an analyst as is, without any due diligence performed on them. This situation usually occurs because management does not understand the approach used or the relevant questions to ask.

2. What are some of the general types of errors encountered by an analyst when creating a model?

   Some general types of errors encountered when creating a model include model errors, assumption and input errors, analytical errors, user errors, and interpretation errors.

3. Why is truncation in a model's assumption important? What would happen to the results if truncation is not applied when it should be?

   If truncation is not applied when it should be, then the resulting forecast distribution will be too wide and the errors of estimations too large. Therefore, truncation is important as it provides results that are more accurate with lower errors.

4. What is a critical success factor?

   A critical success factor is an input variable that has significant impact on the output result. By itself, the input variable is also highly uncertain and should be simulated.

5. What are some of the normal-looking statistics?

   A skewness of 0 and a kurtosis of 3 are considered normal-looking statistics. Be aware that some kurtosis measures are centered on 0 instead of 3.

6. What are structural breaks and specification errors, and why are they important?

   Structural breaks occur when the underlying variable undergoes certain economic, business or financial shifts (e.g., merger or divestiture). Specification errors occur when the underlying variable follows some non-linearities (e.g., growth curves, exponential, or cyclical curves) but the regression is estimated based on a strict linear model.

About the CD-ROM

INTRODUCTION

The enclosed CD-ROM contains an academic trial version of Crystal Ball Professional Monte Carlo simulation software; sample Excel worksheets on simulation, optimization, and forecasting; and answers to questions and exercises in the book. For obtaining a trial version of the Real Options Analysis Toolkit software (see Chapter 13), contact the author or visit www. crystalball.com for details.

MINIMUM SYSTEM REQUIREMENTS

Make sure that your computer meets the minimum system requirements listed in this section. If your computer does not match up to most of these requirements, you may have a problem using the contents of the CD.

- IBM PC or compatible computer with Pentium II or higher processor
- 64 MB RAM
- 75 MB hard-disk space
- CD-ROM drive
- SVGA monitor with 256 Color
- Excel 2000, XP, or later
- Windows 2000, NT, XP, or higher

USING THE CD

To run the setup program, do the following:

1. Insert the enclosed CD-ROM into the CD-ROM drive of your computer.
2. Open Windows Explorer and locate the folders on the CD-ROM drive.
3. Open the *Crystal Ball Student Trial Version* folder and double click on the *Setup.exe* file to install the Crystal Ball Monte Carlo software. Read

and follow the online instructions. Leave the registration number empty for the academic trial period.

The enclosed academic trial version of Crystal Ball software will expire 140 days from first use. If you have questions about obtaining the fully functional software or to obtain the trial version of *Real Options Analysis Toolkit* software that is referred to in Chapter 13, contact Dr. Johnathan Mun at JohnathanMun@cs.com or visit the Decisioneering Web site at www.crystalball.com or www.decisioneering.com.

TROUBLESHOOTING

If you have difficulty installing or using any of the materials on the companion CD, try the following solutions:

- **Turn off any antivirus software that you may have running.** Installers sometimes mimic virus activity and can make your computer incorrectly believe that it is being infected by a virus. (Be sure to turn the antivirus software back on later.)
- **Close all running programs.** The more programs you are running, the less memory is available to other programs. Installers also typically update files and programs; if you keep other programs running, installation may not work properly.
- **Reference the ReadMe:** Refer to the ReadMe file located at the root of the CD-ROM for the latest product information at the time of publication.

If you still have trouble with the CD-ROM, call the Wiley Product Technical Support phone number: (800) 762-2974. Outside the United States, call 1(317) 572-3994. You can also contact Wiley Product Technical Support at www.wiley.com/techsupport. Wiley Publishing will provide technical support only for installation and other general quality control items; for technical support on the applications themselves, consult the program's vendor or author.

To place additional orders or to request information about other Wiley products, call (800) 225-5945.

Index

Abandonment option, 270–271, 280–283, 288, 374
Actual cash flow, 18
Additive seasonality, 195–197, 199
Adjusted R-squared statistic, 206, 209. *See also* R-squared statistic
Advanced time-series forecasting, *see* ARIMA (Auto Regressive Integrated Moving Average) forecasting
Aesthetic models, 47–48
Alpha, time-series forecasts, 188–189, 191, 193, 195, 213, 224–225
American options
  abandonment, 279–283
  call, 326–328
  characteristics of, 298–304, 308–320
  put option, 328
Anderson–Darling (AD) test, 117, 129–131
ANOVA, 210
Applied business risk analysis, 12
Appraisals, real options analysis, 326–327, 329–332, 335
ARIMA (Auto Regressive Integrated Moving Average) forecasting, 225–226, 233, 368
Asset allocation, 258–261
Asset class, 261
Assumptions
  distributional fitting and, 113–114
  implications of, generally, 91, 98, 140
  Monte Carlo simulation, 62, 96, 122, 358–359
  optimization model, 242

regression analysis, 223–224
tornado charts, 106, 109–110
Autocorrelation, in regression analysis, 210, 225–226, 233–234
Automated models, 46–47
Autoregressive effects, 370–372
Auxiliary regression, 230
Average annual pharmaceutical price increases (APPIs), 140
Average value, 29

Bang for the buck, 15, 28
Banker's Trust
  risk and return analysis, 25
  Risk Management Advisory (RMA), 382–383
Barings Bank, 25–26
Basson, Gary, 127–128
Benchmarks, 27, 362
Best-case scenarios, 16, 114, 127, 359, 362
Best-fitting distribution, 117
Beta
  characteristics of, 34, 86–87
  optimization model, 250
  time-series forecasts, 193
Binomial distribution
  characteristics of, 81–82
  negative, 89–90
Binomial lattices
  characteristics of, 272–275
  employee stock option case illustration, 299–300, 303–304, 308, 312–320
  real estate development case illustration, 326–327, 337

449

BioAxia Incorporated, deal-making case illustration, 135–156

Biotechnology industry, deal-making case illustration, 135–156

Bivariate regression, 201, 203–204, 213

Black–Scholes model (BSM), 272–275, 295, 298–302, 304, 315, 319, 321

Boeing project analysis, real options case illustration, 275–276

Bootstrap simulation, 64, 121–122

Bottom-line profits, 13, 17

Break-even point, 119

Breusch–Godfrey autocorrelation test, 233

Brown, Jeff, 182

Brownian Motion, 65

Business-unit valuation, 342

Capital asset pricing model (CAPM), 28, 34

Case illustrations

change management, Banker's Trust Risk Management Advisory (RMA), 382–383

chemical risk assessment at Environment Canada, 384–386

corporate restructuring, credit risk evaluation using stochastic optimization and valuation models, 341–350

cost-effective business solutions at Sierra Systems Group Inc., 168–171

deal making in biotechnology and pharmaceutical industry, 135–156

deal making in oil and gas industry, 156–168

environmental impact statement (EPA), 36–37

flexibility and efficiency analysis at TRW Inc., 103–104

Monte Carlo simulation, Colorado School of Mines property valuation, 73–74

project analysis at Boeing, 275–276

real estate development using real options analysis, 325–340

shareholder value at Deloitte & Touche Consulting, 127–128

simulations, Hewlett-Packard marketing decisions, 75–76

unit cost estimates at 3M, 126–127

value-at-risk decision making at Farmland, 35–36

Cash-flow present value, 146–148, 154, 156

Cash flows, 127–128, 158–159

Causality, 371

CD-ROM, generally

minimum system requirements, 447

setup program, 447–448

troubleshooting, 448

Cell warnings, user-friendly models, 44–45

Center of distribution, 29

Central Limit Theorem, 122

Change management, 377–379

Chemical risk assessment, 384–386

Chi-square critical values, table, 412–413

Chi-square distribution, 87–88

Chi-square test, 117, 130–131

Citibank, 25

Closed-form real options models, 272–275

COCOMO (Constructive Cost Model), 182

Coefficient of determination, 207–208, 220, 213

Coefficient of variation (CV), 31, 34, 148, 154–156

Coincidences, time-series forecasting, 368

Colorado School of Mines property valuation, Monte Carlo simulation case illustration, 73–74

Comarketing, 137

Competing options, 373–374

Compulsory purchase order (CPO), 327–328

Confidence intervals, 79, 117, 119, 121, 180
Constable, Miles, 384–385
Constraints, optimization process, 240–242, 255–256, 260
Continuous distribution, 78, 129–130
Copromotion, 137
Corporate culture, change strategies
  acceptance of risk analysis, 377
  case illustration, 382–383
  change management, 377–379
  forecasts, 381–382
  paradigm shift, 378–381
Corporate restructuring credit risk evaluation, real options analysis case illustration
  background to, 341–342
  business case, 342–343
  business history, 343–350
Correlation(s)
  effects, generally, 62, 371
  input assumptions, 112–117
  sensitivity chart, 110–112
Correlation coefficient, 113, 210
Cost-effective business solutions, case illustration, 168–170
Cost minimization, 239
Credit risk, 12, 341–350
Critical values, 129
Cross-correlation, portfolio optimization, 258–259
Crystal Ball software
  applications, *see specific case illustrations*
  basics of, 91–94
  Correlation Matrix, 250
  Decision Table, 124–126
  Developer Kit, 127–128
  distributions, 113–117,
  getting started with, 94–95
  interpreting simulation results, 100–102
  Monte Carlo simulation, 65–76, 96–100, 117
  optimization tools, 239–241, 249–250
  OptQuest, 239–240, 250–251, 255, 259–260, 343–344, 353, 375
  precision control, 117–122
  Predictor, 175–181, 206, 210–211, 226, 353
  Professional, 249–251, 353
  Project Pro, 253
  Real Options Analysis Toolkit, 278–321, 353
  sensitivity analysis, 126–127
  sensitivity chart, 110–112
  Sharpe Portfolio, 258
  tornado chart, 106–110, 112
  two-dimensional simulation, 123
Cumulative density function (CDF), 386
Cumulative distribution, 129–130
Customized options, real options analysis, 288–292
Cyclical effects, 371

Daiwa Bank, 25
Data, generally
  analysis, inferential statistics, 29
  collection, inferential statistics, 29
  mining, 370
  points, regression analysis, 224–225
  validation, user-friendly models, 44–45
Davis, Dr. Graham, 73
Deal-making case illustrations
  biotechnology and pharmaceutical industry, 135–156
  deal types, 136–137
  deal valuations, 142–154. *See also* Deal valuations, case illustration
  financial models, 138
  financial terms of, 137–139
  historical deal background, 138, 140–142
  negotiated deal structure, 138, 140–142
  oil and gas industry, 156–168
  risk and return comparison, 154–156

Deal valuations, case illustration
  higher-value, higher-risk (HVHR),
     140, 150–154
  higher-value, lower-risk (HVLR),
     144–150
  historical, 142–145
  Monte Carlo assumptions and
     decision variable sensitivities,
     142–144, 149–150
Decision Lattice, real options analysis
     (ROA), 283
Decision-making processes, 13–14, 29,
     381
Decision tables, 124–126
Decision variables, optimization
     process, 240–242, 255, 259,
     374–375
Degrees of freedom, 131, 208, 227,
     230
Deloitte & Touche Consulting,
     127–128
Delphi method, 113
Dependent variable, regression analysis
  implications of, 203, 205, 207, 210,
     212, 218–219, 223
  lack of independence in, 224
  warning signs, 369–371
Derivatives, 262
Descriptive statistics, 28
Deterministic analysis, 19
Dietz, Paul, 262
Discounted cash flow (DCF), 18, 138,
     181, 268, 293, 343, 347
Discrete optimization under
     uncertainty, 253–258
Discrete probability distributions, 77–
     78
Distribution
  center of, 29
  correlations and, 112–117
  probability, see Probability
     distributions
  skew of, 31–32
  spread, 29–31
  tail events, 32–33

Distributional fitting, 113–117, 358,
     363, 365
Distributional truncation, 359–360
Dividends, American options, 300,
     303, 308, 310–311, 313–314, 316,
     321
Documentation, in model building
  document changes, 39, 41
  executive summary, 39, 41
  file properties, 39–41
  formula illustrations, 39, 41
  importance of, 38–39, 355
  model navigation, 40–41
  naming conventions, 39, 41
  reporting structure, 40–41
  results interpretation, 39–41
  strategizing, 39, 41
Double exponential smoothing (DES),
     191–195
Due diligence, 137, 156, 354, 357
DuPont Merck, 104
Durbin–Watson statistic, 206,
     210–211, 233–234
  critical values table, 405
Dynamic optimization, 272, 275

ECM (Error Correction Models), 233,
     368
Economic conditions, impact of,
     362–363, 367, 372
Economics theory, 87
Economies of scale, 109, 358
Efficient frontier, 260. See also
     Markowitz Efficient Frontier
Employee stock options, real options
     analysis case illustration
  analytical comparison, 303–320
  binomial lattices, 303
  Black–Scholes model (BSM),
     301–302
  conclusion and suggestions, 319, 321
  executive summary, 297–299
  introduction, 301
  key points and recommendations,
     300–301

Monte Carlo path simulation, 302–303
Endpoints, 361–362
Environmental Impact Analysis, Environmental Protection Agency (EPA), 36–37
Environment Canada, chemical risk assessment, 384–386
Erlang distribution, 87–88
Error alerts, user-friendly models, 44–45
Error-in-variables model, 224
Estimation, inferential statistics, 29
European options, 274, 305–307
Eve, Gerald, 325
Excel (Microsoft)
 applications, generally, 91, 177, 179, 359–360
 Data Analysis, 206
 simulations, 71–72, 91, 96
 Solver, 190–191, 193, 227–229, 243, 246–247, 375
 spreadsheets, 38, 48–57, 249, 292–295, 342–343
 Visual Basic Environment (VBE), 48–57
Executive summary
 in model building, 39, 41
 real options analysis case study, 287–300
Expected cash flow, 136
Expected frequency, 131
Expected net returns, 13
Expected rate of return, 29
Expected returns, 258
ExperCorp, 21–22
Experiment design, inferential statistics, 29
Explained variation (ESS), 208
Exponential distribution, 85
Extreme value distribution, 89, 361
Extrinsic value, 268

Fair market value, 297, 321
Farmland Industries, 35–36

F-distribution critical statistics, tables, 414–421
Financial Accounting Standard 123 (FAS 123), 297–322
Financial Accounting Standards Board (FASB), 297, 303, 319
Financial analysis, 19, 73
First moment, distribution, 29
Flaw of averages, 63–64
Flexibility option value, 374
Forecasting, generally
 autocorrelation, 233–234
 case illustrations, 182–183
 defined, 175–176
 heteroskedasticity, 220–223, 230–231, 372
 intervals, 226–227
 methodology, overview, 175
 multicollinearity, 231–233
 nature and view of, 176–181
 optimization and, 242
 pitfalls of, 215–223
 significance of, 18–19, 61–62
Foreign exchange market, 13
Foreign exchange risk, 364
Fourt, Robert, 5–6, 325
Fourth moment, 32–33
Free cash flow, 18
F-statistic, 206, 209, 230
Full-time equivalent (FTE), 142, 149–150
Future cash flow, 347

Gamma distribution, 87–88
Garbage in, garbage out (GIGO), 15, 355
GARCH (generalized autoregressive conditional heteroskedasticity), 388
Generalized Black–Scholes model (GBM), 298–302, 304, 308–309, 311, 313–321
Geometric distribution, 82–83
Glantz, Morton, 341
Goodness-of-fit, inferential statistics, 29

Goodness-of-fit tests
  Anderson–Darling (AD) test,
    129–130
  benefits of, 117, 128
  chi-square test, 130–131
  Kolmogorov–Smirnov (KS) test,
    128–129
Government bonds, 261
Gross development value (GDV), 381
Gumbel distribution, 89

Hardy, Dr. Charles, 135
Hart, Michael, 75–76
Hedging, 373
Help environment, real options analysis
  (ROA), 288
Heteroskedasticity, in regression
  analysis, 220–223, 230–231, 369,
  372
Hewlett-Packard case illustrations
  marketing decisions, 75–76
  production forecasts, 182–183
Higher-value, higher-risk (HVHR) deal,
  140, 148, 150–154
Higher-value, lower-risk (HVLR) deal,
  144–151
Histograms, 76–77
Historical data
  significance of, 19, 84, 114, 117,
    121, 175–177, 362–363, 365
  time-series forecasts and, 187, 191,
    193
Historical deal scenario, 142–145
Hoffman, Dr. F. Owen, 36–37
Holt–Winters' seasonality
  additive, 197, 199–201
  multiplicative, 197, 201–203
Hoye, Steve, 135, 156
Hypergeometric distribution, 83–84
Hypothesis testing, 29, 128–129,
  209–210

Income statements, 18, 262
Independent variable, regression
  analysis

implications of, 203, 205, 207, 210,
    212, 219, 223
  random, 224
  warning signs, 369–371
Industry applications, see Case
  illustrations
Inferential statistics, 28–29
Inflation, impact of, 140
Input messages, user-friendly models,
  44–45
Inputs, in model building, 42–43
Insurance risk theory, 87
Intellectual property, 137
Intercept, in regression analysis, 203,
  206, 219, 223–225, 228
Interpretation errors, real options
  analysis, 374–375
Intervals, in forecasts, 226–227,
  360–361. See also Confidence
  intervals
Intrinsic value, 268–269
Inventory control, 87
Investigational new drug (IND)
  applications, 138, 140, 142,
  149–150

Jamal, Iqbal, 169–170
Japanese yen, 26
Jump processes, 371–372

Kolmogorov–Smirnov (KS) test, 117,
  128–129, 131
Kurtosis, 32–33, 142, 366

Large-cap stocks, 114–115, 261
Latin Hypercube sampling, 78–79
Lattice viewer, real options analysis,
  284–287
Law of demand, 213
Law of Large Numbers, 122
Least squares regression, 204–205,
  217–218, 223
Leeson, Nicholas, 25–26
Leptokurtic project, 32
Licensing cash flow, 142

Linear programming, 245–248
Linear regression, 224, 368–369
Logistic distribution, 88
Lognormal distribution, 68–69, 84, 366–367
Lognormal parameter sets, 84–85
Long Term Capital Management, 25

McKinsey & Company, Inc., 342
Macros
  benefits of, generally, 127, 171
  Visual Basic Environment (VBE), 48–57
Management dashboard, 42
Marketing costs, 219–220
Markowitz, Harry, 27–28
Markowitz Efficient Frontier, 27–28
Mean, 29, 32, 85
Mean absolute deviation (MAD), 186, 188
Mean absolute percent error (MAPE), 186, 188
Mean-reversion, 65, 372
Mean-squared error (MSE), 186–188
Median, 29
Meriweather, John, 25
Merrill Lynch, 25
Metallgesellschaft, 25
Micro-cap stocks, 261
Middle management, 382
Minnesota Power, portfolio risk management illustration, 262–263
Minority investment alliance, 137
Mode, 29
Model building
  aesthetics, 47–48
  automation, 46–47
  documentation, 38–41
  inputs, 42–43
  model growth and modification, 43
  protection of, 43–44
  report and model printing, 43
  tracking, 46
  user-friendly, 44–45

Visual Basic Environment (VBE) case illustration, 48–57
worksheets, 41–42
Monte Carlo simulation
  assumptions, 112
  benefits of, generally, 21–22, 33
  bootstrap simulation distinguished from, 121
  case illustrations, 74–76
  change management, 379–380
  Crystal Ball software applications, 65–76, 91–92, 96–100, 117
  deal-making applications, 136, 142–144, 149–150
  deal valuation, 156
  defined, 61–62
  financial analysis, 73
  forecasting, 181–183
  oil and gas industry applications, 158–159, 161, 164–168
  optimization case illustration, 263
  precision control, 117–121
  real estate development case illustration, 331, 336, 339
  real options analysis, 272, 274, 292, 295–296, 299–303, 319, 321
  warning signs in, 358–387
Moody's KMV, 344, 346
Morgan, J. P., 34
Most-likely case scenarios, 114, 127
Motorola, 170–171
Moving average, time-series forecasts
  autoregressive integrated, 226
  double, 191
  single, 185–187
Muilenburg, Michael, 126
Multicollinearity, 211, 220–221, 231–233, 369–370
Multinomial lattices, 272–273
Multiple linear regression, 213–215, 231–232
Multiplicative seasonality, 197–198
Multivariate regressions, 209, 220, 354, 363, 369

Naming convention, 39
Negative binomial distribution, 89–90
Negative correlation, 113
Negligent entrustment, 353–354
Net present value (NPV)
    forecasting and, 181
    implications of, 74, 127–128, 138,
        169
    oil and gas industry, 159, 163–165,
        167
    project optimization, 253
    real options analysis, 275–276, 326,
        331, 335–336, 340
New drug application (NDA), 140
Nominal-case scenarios, 16, 359
Nonlinearity, in regression analysis,
    218–219, 223
Nonparametric bootstrap simulation,
    64–65, 72
Normal distribution, 62, 80, 117,
    365–366
    tables, 402, 403
Null hypothesis, 129–130, 209–210,
    225

Objectives, optimization process,
    240–242, 256
Oil and gas industry, production and
    exploration, 156–168
Olson, Dr. William L., 170–171
Omitted variables, 369
One-dimensional simulation, 123
Open market value (OMV), 327–328
Operating expenses, oil and gas
    industry, 162–163
Optimization model
    case illustrations, 248–252
    characteristics of, 237–238
    deterministic, 240
    dynamic, 272, 275
    graph solutions, 243–244
    linear programming, 245–248
    purpose of, 237–238
    traveling financial planner problem,
        238–240

terminology, 240–243
under uncertainty, see Optimization
    under uncertainty
Optimization under uncertainty
    components of, 253–263
    defined, 239
    warning signs in, 374–375
Option to wait, 269
OptQuest (Crystal Ball), 239–240,
    250–251, 255, 259–260, 343–344,
    353, 375
Ordinary least squares, 204, 227–229
Out-of-range forecasts, 367–368
Outliers, regression analysis, 217–219
Overinflation, 372–374

Pandora's tool box
    sensitivity analysis, 109–110
    sensitivity chart, 110–112
    tornado chart, 106–111
Paradigm shift, 378–381
Parametric simulation, 64–65
Pareto distribution, 88–89
Park's test, 231
Partial-differential equations, 272,
    274–275
Percentile analysis, 31, 74
Perturbation analysis, 109
Pharmaceutical industry, deal-making
    case illustration, 135–156
Point estimates, 66
Poisson distribution, 82
Population, precision control factor,
    119
Portfolio allocation model, 112–113
Portfolio management, case illustration,
    249–250
Portfolio optimization, using risk and
    return, 258–261
Portfolio risk, 259–260
Portfolio theory, 156
Positive correlation, 113
Power users, 353
Precision control, 117–121
Prediction, inferential statistics, 29

Predictor (Crystal Ball), 175–181, 206, 210–211, 226, 353
Present value, 347
Probability distributions
  beta distribution, 86–87
  binomial distribution, 81–82
  characteristics of, 76–77
  confidence intervals, 79
  exponential distribution, 85
  extreme value distribution, 89
  gamma distribution, 87–88
  geometric distribution, 82–83
  hypergeometric distribution, 83–84
  logistic distribution, 88
  lognormal distribution, 68–69, 84
  lognormal parameter sets, 84–85
  negative binomial distribution, 89–90
  normal distribution, 62, 80
  Pareto distribution, 88–89
  Poisson distribution, 82
  selection of, 78
  triangular distribution, 81, 98
  uniform distribution, 79–80
  Weibull distribution, 85–86
Probability of occurrences, 33
Product acquisition, 137
Product fostering, 137
Product improvement, case illustration, 170–171
Production
  forecasts, Hewlett-Packard case illustration, 182–183
  risk, oil and gas industry case illustration, 157, 160–161
Product licensing, 137–138, 140
Product mix model, 124–126
Pro forma cash flow, 262
Project selection model, 253–258
Property, plants, and equipment (PPE), 157
Protection, in model building, 43–44
ProVise Management Group, 249–250

Quadratic loss function, 188

Raddatz, William L., 249–250
Random numbers
  eight-digit, table, 408–409
  normal, table, 406–407
  uniform, table, 410–411
Random walks, 65, 371–372
Rayleigh distribution, 85–86
Real estate development, real options analysis case illustration
  background information, 325–328
  base-scoping approach, 327, 329–332
  development strategy matrix, 329
  explanation, 327, 336, 340
  mapping the problem, 327–329
  quantitative analysis, 327, 335–336
  uncertainty inputs, internal and external, 327, 332–335
Real estate value, 269–270
Real options, *see also* Real options analysis (ROA)
  characteristics of, 267–269
  in deal-making, 136, 156
  strategic, 269–270
Real Options Analysis (Mun), 325
Real options analysis (ROA)
  applications, generally, 268
  binomial lattices, 272–275, 299–300, 303–304, 308, 312–320
  case illustrations, *see* Real options analysis case illustrations
  closed-form models, 273–275
  dynamic optimization, 275
  implementation of, 271
  Monte Carlo path simulation, 274
  multinomial lattices, 273
  partial-differential equations, 274–275
  strategic options, 269–271
  Super Lattice, 281–282
  toolkit, *see* Real options analysis toolkit
  values, tables, 422–435
  variance reduction, 275
  warning signs, 372–374

Real options analysis case illustrations
  employee stock options expensing
    (FAS 123), 287–321
  real estate development, 325–340
  project analysis at Boeing, 275–276
Real Options Analysis Course (Mun),
  325
Real options analysis toolkit
  customized options, 288–282
  getting started with, 278–283
  Help environment, 288
  Lattice Viewer, 284–287
  selection criteria, 272–273
  simulations, 282–287
Redundant variables, 369, 372
Regression analysis
  applications, generally, 19, 176, 201,
    203–206
  assumptions, 211–215
  bivariate regression, 201, 203–204,
    213
  goodness-of-fit, 206–211
  least squares, 204–205, 217–218,
    223
  linear, 368–369
  multiple linear regression, 213–215,
    231–232
  multivariate regression, 209, 220,
    354, 363, 369
  nonlinear transformation, 218–219,
    223
  ordinary least squares, 204, 227–
    229
  pitfalls of, 215–223
  regression output, 206–207
  technical issues, 223–225
  warning signs in, 354, 369–372
Regressor, defined, 203
Reichmann, Paul, 25
Reliability measures, 106
Reports, in model building, 40, 43
Research and development (R&D), 27,
  140, 142–144, 148, 276, 362
Return on equity (ROE), 169
Returns-to-risk ratio, 241

Revenues, oil and gas industry,
  161–162
Risk, generally
  basics of, 26–27
  in decision-making process, 13–15
  deterministic analysis, 19
  historical perspective, 11–12
  measurements of, 33–34
  nature of, 27–28
  statistics, 28–33
  traditional approaches to, 15–18
  uncertainty versus, 12–13, 18–21
Risk-adjusted return on capital
    (RAROC), 34, 365
Risk-deterministic analysis, 18–19
Risk diversification
  optimal decision, 237–251
  optimization under uncertainty,
    253–263
Risk evaluation
  case illustrations, 35–37
  model building, 38–57
  risk measurement, 33–34
  risk and return analysis, generally,
    25–28
  statistics, 28–33
Risk-free rate, real options analysis,
  320
Risk identification
  case illustration, 21–22
  decision-making process, 13–15
  risk defined, 11–12
  strategies for, 15–18
  uncertainty, 12–13, 18–21
Risk management
  change management, 377–384
  warning signs, 353–375
Risk measurement
  beta, 34
  coefficient of variation, 34
  probability of occurrences, 33
  risk-adjusted return on capital
    (RAROC), 34
  semi-standard deviation, 33–34
  standard deviation, 33

value at risk, 34
variance, 33
volatility, 34
worst-case scenario and regret, 34
RiskMetrics, 34
Risk mitigation, *see* Real options
    analysis (ROA)
Risk prediction
    advanced forecasting, 225–226
    forecasting, generally, 175–183,
        226–227
    time-series forecasts, 184–203
    regression analysis, 201, 203–225,
        227–234
Risk quantification
    bootstrapping, 121–122
    case illustrations, 126–128
    correlated simulation, 112–117
    decision tables, 124–126
    goodness-of-fit tests, 128–131
    Monte Carlo simulation, 61–104
    precision control, 117–121
    probability distributions, 76–90
    sensitivity charts, 110–111
    tornado charts, 106–111
    two-dimensional simulation,
        122–123
Risk tolerance, 249
Rodney, Bill, 6, 325–326
Root mean-squared error (RMSE), 186,
    188, 228
Royalties, 138, 140, 142, 147–148
R-squared statistic, 206–207, 209–210,
    232. *See also* Adjusted R-squared
    statistic
Ruthrauff, Rick, 251

Sample, in descriptive statistics, 28
Sample size, precision control factor,
    119
Sawyer, Dennis, 103
Scatter plot, 211–214, 216–219,
    222–223
Scenario analysis, 15–18, 66–67

Seasonality, time-series forecasts, 191
    additive, 195–197, 199
    multiplicative, 197–198
    with trend, 197
Seasonality effects, 371
Secondary regression, 230
Second moment, distribution, 29–31
Self-selection bias, 370
Semi-standard deviation, 33–34
Senior management buy-in, real options
    analysis, 271
Sensitivity analysis
    benefits of, 16–18, 66, 74, 109–110
    corporate restructuring credit risk
        evaluation, 348
    oil and gas industry case illustration,
        166
    real estate development case
        illustration, 338
Sensitivity chart, 110–112, 153–154,
    358, 367
Serial correlation, 371
Shareholder value, 127–128, 142, 341
Sharpe, William, 28
Sharpe portfolio, 258–259
Sharpe ratio, 259–260
Sierra Systems Group Inc., 168–170
Simulations, *see also* Monte Carlo
    simulation
    case illustrations, 73–76
    in change management, 379, 381
    corporate restructuring credit risk
        evaluation, 344, 346–349
    Crystal Ball applications, 70–73,
        97–100
    Excel applications, 70–72
    importance of, 13, 17–18, 62–65
    probability distributions, 76–90
    sampling methods, 78–79
    traditional analyses compared with,
        65–69
Single exponential smoothing (SES),
    188–190
Single-point estimate, 15, 33, 365
Single-point forecasts, 178, 360, 379

Skew/skewness, 31–32, 142–143, 366
Slope, in regression analysis, 203,
    205–206, 209, 218–219, 223–225,
    231–232
Small-cap stocks, 113, 261
Smoothing
    double exponential (DES), 191–195
    real options analysis, 333
    single exponential (SES), 188–190
Solver (Excel), 190–191, 193, 227–229,
    243, 246–247, 375
Soros, George, 25
Spread, 29–31
Spreadsheet applications, 38, 249, 292,
    300, 342, 343
Spring model, 106–107
Spurious regression, 370, 372
Standard deviation, 31, 33, 85
Statistics
    defined, 28
    descriptive, 28
    inferential, 28–29
    sample, 28
Statistics of statistics, 122
Step-wise regression, 231, 363, 370
Stochastic optimization
    certainty of, 375
    continuous, 258–261
    corporate restructuring credit risk
        evaluation case illustration,
        341–350
    in deal-making, 136, 156
    implications of, 126
Stochastic processes, 372
Stock price fluctuations, 30–31
Strategic alliances, 136–137, 154
Strategic options, 269–270
Structural breaks, 362–363, 368
Sublicense, 138
Sumimoto Corporation, 25
Sums of squares of the errors (SSE),
    207–208
SunTrust Banks, Inc., forecasting
    illustration, 183
Superfund, 36

Super Lattice, real options analysis
    (ROA), 281–282
Survivorship bias, 370

Tail events, in distribution, 32–33, 128,
    366
Texaco, optimization case illustration,
    251
Theil's U statistic, 188
Third moment, distribution, 31–32
3M Company, 126–127
Time dependency, 370
Time horizon, 27
Time lag, 370–372
Time-series analysis, 19
Time-series forecasts
    advanced, see ARIMA (Auto
        Regressive Integrated Moving
        Average) forecasting
    applications, generally, 65, 175,
        178
    autocorrelation, 233–234
    error estimation, 186–188
    heteroskedasticity, 230–231, 369
    methodology, overview, 184–185
    multicollinearity, 211, 220–221,
        231–233, 369–370
    no trend and no seasonality,
        185–191
    no trend with seasonality, 195–201
    optimizing parameters, 190–191
    out-of-range, 367–368
    specification errors, 368–369
    with trend but no seasonality,
        191–195
    warning signs in, 367–379
Tornado analysis, 74–75
Tornado chart, 75, 103, 106–111,
    142–143, 145, 151–153, 358,
    366–367
Total sums of squares (TSS), 207–208
Toxic waste site model, 122–124
Traveling financial planner problem,
    238–240
Trend charts, 125–126

Trials
  importance of, 91
  number of, 62
  precision control factor, 119–120
  without replacement, 83
Triangular distribution, 81, 98,
    359–360
TRW Inc., flexibility and efficiency
    analysis, 103–104
t-distribution table, 404
t-statistic, 206, 209, 213, 215, 226
Two-dimensional simulation, 122–124

Uncertainty
  analysis, 363–364
  characteristics of, 18–22
  optimization under, 126, 239, 242,
    253–263
  in real estate development, 325–339
  risk distinguished from, 12–13
  volatility and, 18–20
Uniform distribution, 79–80
U.S. Treasuries, 319
Univariate regression, 203
User error, 361

Valuation, corporate restructuring
    credit risk evaluation case
    illustration, 341–350
Valuation Lattice, real options analysis
    (ROA), 283
Value at Risk (VaR), 34–36, 326,
    363–365
Value-based management, 127–128
Variability, 122–123
Variance
  impact of, 31, 33
  reduction, real options analysis, 272,
    275
Variance inflation factor (VIF), 232
Venture planning case illustration,
    21–22
Vesting, employee stock options,
    309–310, 316–317, 321

Visual Basic Environment (VBE), model
    building
  benefits of, 48–49
  custom equations, 49–51
  forms, 56–57
  icons, 56–57
  input boxes, 55–56
  macros, 52–57
  navigational codes, 54–55
Volatility
  cash-flow, 151
  corporate restructuring, real options
    analysis, 342, 347
  implications of, generally, 18–20,
    34
  real estate development, real options
    analysis, 333–334, 336, 339
  real options analysis, 281, 310,
    312–313, 318–319, 373–374

Warning signs
  analyst's sins, 354–358
  management's due diligence, 354,
    357
  in Monte Carlo simulation, 356–367
  negligent entrustment, 353–354
  in optimization under uncertainty,
    374–375
  in real options analysis, 372–374
  in regression analysis, 368–372
  in time-series forecasting, 367–379
Weibull distribution, 85–86, 131
Weighted average cost of capital
    (WACC), 138, 159, 163
Weighted least squares (WLS)
    regression, 230–231
What-if analysis, 16–17, 127
White's test statistic, 230
Worksheets, 39, 41–42, 254
Worst-case scenario, 16, 34, 114, 127,
    359

Z-score, 120
Z-value, 226

For information about the CD-ROM see the
About the CD-ROM section on page 447.

WILEY